Europeanization and Globalization

Volume 5

Series editors
Nada Bodiroga-Vukobrat
Rijeka, Croatia

Siniša Rodin
Luxembourg, Luxembourg

Gerald G. Sander
Ludwigsburg, Germany

More information about this series at http://www.springer.com/series/13467

Nada Bodiroga-Vukobrat • Daniel Rukavina •
Krešimir Pavelić • Gerald G. Sander
Editors

Personalized Medicine in Healthcare Systems

Legal, Medical and Economic Implications

 Springer

Editors
Nada Bodiroga-Vukobrat
Faculty of Law
University of Rijeka
Rijeka, Croatia

Krešimir Pavelić
Juraj Dobrila University of Pula
Faculty of Medicine
Pula, Croatia

Department of Biotechnology
Centre for High-Throughput Technologies
University of Rijeka
Rijeka, Croatia

Daniel Rukavina
Croatian Academy of Sciences and Arts
Rijeka, Croatia

Gerald G. Sander
University of Applied Sciences
Ludwigsburg, Germany

ISSN 2366-0953   ISSN 2366-0961   (electronic)
Europeanization and Globalization
ISBN 978-3-030-16464-5   ISBN 978-3-030-16465-2   (eBook)
https://doi.org/10.1007/978-3-030-16465-2

This Springer imprint is published by the registered company Springer Nature Switzerland AG.
The registered company address is: Gewerbestrasse 11, 6330 Cham, Switzerland

Preface

This book comprehensively presents biomedical, technological and socio-humanistic aspects of personalized medicine. We decided to use the term "personalized medicine" even though today a number of terms are used for this concept including precision medicine, customized drug therapy, genomic medicine or genotype-based therapy, individualized or individual-based medicine, information-based medicine, integrated healthcare, precise medicine or *omics*-based medicine: pharmacogenomics/pharmacogenetics/pharmacoproteomics, predictive medicine, rational drug selection, systems medicine, tailored therapy, translational medicine and stratified medicine. We still think that the term personalized medicine encompasses in the most appropriate way the patient and human complexity as well as other factors of relevance in the medical environment.

The articles published in this book are contributions of invited speakers attending the symposium under the title "Personalized Medicine: Basic and Social Aspects (Challenges for Social Security Systems)". The symposium was held in Rijeka (November 20–21, 2017) in organization of the Department of Biomedical Sciences in Rijeka – Croatian Academy of Sciences and Arts, Jean Monnet Inter-University Center of Excellence in Opatija (Croatia) and University of Rijeka.

The whole concept of the book is thus built on the premise that the individual approach towards the patient might transform the quality of healthcare and effectiveness of medicine in the widest sense. Personalized medicine is gaining momentum and significance as it changes the historical paradigm of "medicine for all" and focuses on the person, on the human being. This shift has been facilitated, among other things, by the use of modern and advanced high-throughput technologies and molecular genetics as well as by system biology approaches that regaining importance daily. Such a change in medicine necessarily requires changes in the healthcare system, health economics and socio-legal aspects with all the implications coming along with that. For example, changes in relationship between a physician and patient are immanent, whereby healthcare professionals will have to make decisions based on complex biological and environmental information as well as on the patient's life style. An equally important aspect of personalized medicine is also in a proper development of innovative technological solutions for citizens and patients, already recognized as necessary means for advancements in the medical field by European policies. This means that each person will be in charge of own health, a concept that is still in its beginnings. A wide interdisciplinary initiative is required to educate such active participants in decision-making complex issues such as genomics, information and privacy promotion as well as novel technologies. Adequate levels of healthcare literacy should be therefore in the focus of citizen education. Consequently, this book has also been prepared with the intention of encompassing important scientific-medical and socio-humanistic aspects of personalized medicine for a wider professional audience. Expectations from implementation of personalized medicine in the daily healthcare are huge both from the perspectives of the patients and from the doctors. First of all, strengthening and full realization of important principles in the physician–patient relationship are required: the physician is obliged to act in the patient's best interest, patients need to be treated with respect, without discrimination during the whole process, even if the relationship seems to be coming to an end and maximal high-quality healthcare needs to be ensured. The unique relationship depends indeed on the trust between the patient and the physician.

As editors of this book, we believe that policy makers, health authorities and public bodies are encouraged to enter this cross-sectorial debate and enhance public dialogue on this relatively new medical concept and conditions for its success. We would like to thank our dear colleague and friend, one of the main initiators and inspirators of this project, Professor Nada Bodiroga-Vukobrat, who unfortunately passed away recently. With her innovativeness and energy, she has succeeded among a wide audience and scientific community in building the awareness on a comprehensive approach to the problem of personalized medicine in the healthcare system, considering legal, medical and economic implications as inherent aspects of this subject. Thank you, Nada, for the legacy that we now want to share with the readers of the book in a joint forward look towards the future medicine—personalized medicine.

Rijeka, Croatia   Daniel Rukavina
Pula, Croatia   Krešimir Pavelić
Ludwigsburg, Germany   Gerald G. Sander

Contents

Part IV Clinical Aspects of Personalised Medicine

Part I
Introduction

Options for Realising and Financing Innovation in the German Healthcare System

Bernd Baron von Maydell and Boris Baron von Maydell

Abstract Personalised healthcare is experiencing the same difficulties as other innovations when it is introduced to the different health systems of countries. However, the high treatment costs and the complicated evaluation of the added value compared to existing methods and procedures represent particularly great challenges for personalised medicine providers and healthcare systems. In the German health care system, a large number of mechanisms have been implemented, on the one hand, to enable the fundamental introduction of innovations and, on the other hand, to permit only those innovations for standard care that bring additional benefits to the respective patients.

The first part of this article discusses the question of the prerequisites and framework conditions that help an innovation to be included in the benefits catalogue of statutory health insurance in Germany. Once this question has been successfully addressed, providers and cost bearers are faced with the difficult task of financially evaluating the new service. This is the subject of the second part.

Ultimately, a new method can only improve care if it is recognised and financed by the health systems. Against the background of increasing costs for new treatment methods, it is the task of the processes described to prevent scaling in new medical procedures.

1 Introduction

The range of medical services offered worldwide continues to grow at an extreme pace. New forms of treatment are extending life expectancy significantly, even for illnesses for which there were no therapy options just a few years ago. Innovations are changing all

---

Bernd Baron von Maydell was deceased at the time of publication.

B. B. von Maydell (✉)
Department Ambulatory Care, Association of Substitute Health Funds (vdek head office),
Berlin, Germany
e-mail: boris.vonmaydell@vdek.com

© Springer Nature Switzerland AG 2019
N. Bodiroga-Vukobrat et al. (eds.), *Personalized Medicine in Healthcare Systems*,
Europeanization and Globalization 5, https://doi.org/10.1007/978-3-030-16465-2_1

areas of medical care to a significant degree, whether it is new methods for examination and treatment, pharmaceuticals, medical products or telematics in the healthcare sector. This rather positive trend is associated worldwide with starkly increasing costs for healthcare systems, with the successful implementation of an innovation in the healthcare sector promising significant returns. There is a large potential for care seen in areas related to Personalised Medicine in particular, which in turn brings with it costs for medicines as well as expenses for the required genetic diagnostics.

In addition to the large potential of some innovations, it is sometimes harder to obtain actual evidence in favour of the manufacturer's promises of a cure once the initial euphoria has dissipated, and not all new forms of treatment actually show better results than already long-established methods. Consequently, the welfare systems of countries around the world are faced with two large issues when implementing innovations:

1. Does the innovation really lead to an objective improvement in care?
2. Are the costs associated with the introduction of the innovation and its incorporation in the healthcare system's benefits catalogue truly justified?

It is probably not in the least possible to answer either question neutrally. Answers can, for example, be dependent on the financial strength of an economy, the affordability of a healthcare system, a society's ethical standards or many other factors. Accordingly, there are different standards for evaluation, and the mechanisms in the world's welfare systems that have been implemented by societies to account for healthcare innovations differ based on those standards. In practical terms, a healthcare system that is barely able to finance conventional radiation therapy for cancer patients would never bother considering whether it is a good idea to add a form of proton therapy to its benefits catalogue. In a healthcare system of this nature, a discussion about rationalisation would take strong precedence over a discussion about implementing innovations.

The healthcare system in Germany, which acts as the focus of this study, is completely different in this respect. In Germany, there is no significant innovation that has not been incorporated into care for cost reasons—in recent years at least. The German healthcare system's mechanisms for responding to the questions, described below, can therefore be transferred to other countries only partially. They have developed from the peculiarities of a self-regulatory, socialised[1] health insurance system and, on top of that, are subject to an ongoing evolution process instigated by numerous healthcare reforms, particularly over the last few years.

What is understood as an 'innovation' is open to a great deal of interpretation. For this article, the phrase 'innovation in the healthcare sector' assumes a broad approach that includes new products and processes along with services and innovations to the system itself. An innovation in the healthcare sector is therefore a

---

[1]Self-regulation is the overarching organisational principle for Statutory Health Insurance in Germany. It means that providers in the healthcare sector, insured persons and employers handle organisation themselves to direct and help shape the healthcare system (Verband der Ersatzkassen e. V. 2018).

significant change to its structures, products, processes or methods to prevent, treat or relieve health risks or illnesses (Bührlein 2007, p. 6).

This article deals with the point in time at which a healthcare system makes the decision to incorporate new innovations in the market into care and, by extension, the decision to finance these innovations for those insured. Section 2 analyses the various structures for financing innovations in the German healthcare system. Section 3 focuses on the pricing mechanisms developed from those structures. Special attention is also given to pharmaceuticals, as it is in this sector in particular that healthcare system cost increases are dominated by new medicines and expanding Personalised Medicine.

2 Options for Financing the Introduction of Innovations in the German Healthcare System

Innovations may enter the German healthcare system through highly varied means. Firstly, these means are dependent on the dual insurance system in Germany, where 72.4 million people (as of October 2017) have Statutory Health Insurance and 8.8 million people (as of May 2017) are covered by a Private Health Insurance fund. The two systems handle innovations differently and have come to differing regulations on how innovations are financed. Secondly, there are also regulations within the Statutory Health Insurance system that are mandatory for all funds as well as regulations that each fund is free to make a decision on with policyholders. This freedom of contract represents a significant aspect of the competition between Statutory Health Insurance funds in Germany. Also, within the Private Health Insurance system, there are different providers that each offer different insurance policies, with each being a result of the competition between the funds and thereby more or less also allowing policyholders to utilise innovations. Figure 1 illustrates the various options through which innovations can penetrate the German healthcare sector. A discussion of the processes developed specifically for the Statutory Health Insurance system then follows, as almost 90% of the German population are insured under this system and therefore can use only it to take advantage of innovations.

2.1 Benefit Assessment by the Federal Joint Committee[2] Upon Integration Into the Standard Care Offered by Statutory Health Insurance (Block I in Fig. 1)

The German healthcare system is characterised by a stark distinction between Out-of-Hospital and In-Hospital Care. This distinction is also reflected in the way

---

[2]The Federal Joint Committee (G-BA, *Gemeinsamer Bundesausschuss*) is the highest-level decision-making committee run by German doctors, dentists, psychotherapists, hospitals and health

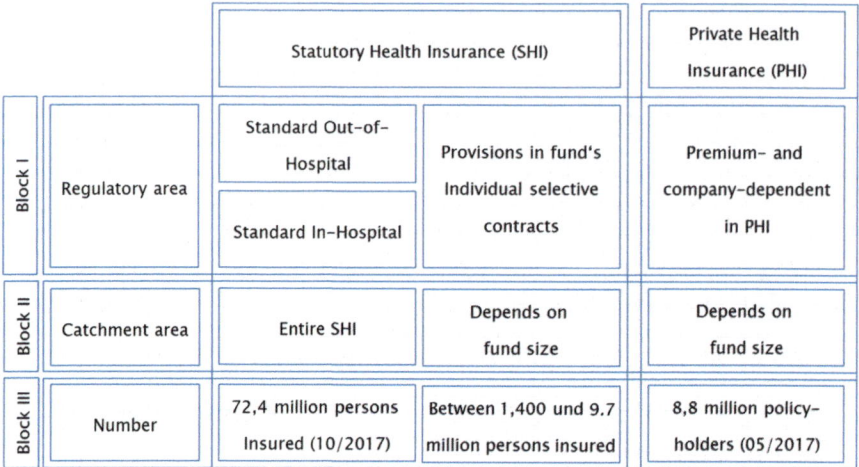

		Statutory Health Insurance (SHI)		Private Health Insurance (PHI)
Block I	Regulatory area	Standard Out-of-Hospital Standard In-Hospital	Provisions in fund's Individual selective contracts	Premium- and company-dependent in PHI
Block II	Catchment area	Entire SHI	Depends on fund size	Depends on fund size
Block III	Number	72,4 million persons Insured (10/2017)	Between 1,400 und 9.7 million persons insured	8,8 million policy-holders (05/2017)

Fig. 1 Options for financing innovations in the German healthcare system (own illustration)

innovations are treated in the respective areas. Based on SGB V (*Sozialgesetzbuch, Social Security Statute Book 5*) Section 135(1), Out-of-Hospital Care is subject to general '*prohibition before authorisation*'. This means that new methods of examination and treatment may only be provided if the Federal Joint Committee have explicitly approved of their therapeutic benefit, medical necessity and economic viability. For In-Hospital Care, on the other hand, SGB V Section 137c provides for general '*authorisation before prohibition*'. This means that a hospital may provide a new examination or treatment method as long as the Federal Joint Committee has not explicitly ruled out its use. Accordingly, there are no limits to the utilisation of innovations in In-Hospital Care resulting from the influence of legislators. However, it cannot be assumed that the use of innovations in hospitals is completely unregulated. Rather, the regulation for financing hospital treatment via DRG payments acts in itself as a natural limit to costly innovations. If innovations are not factored into the calculation of DRGs, hospital trusts are only able to finance their usage to a limited degree.

The Joint Federal Committee therefore acts as a hub for the approval of innovations when seeking authorisation in the Out-of-Hospital Care sector or when prohibition is sought in the In-Hospital Care sector. The committee is the highest-level decision-making committee run by doctors, dentists, psychotherapists, hospitals and health insurance funds working jointly. They regulate large parts of the healthcare system by issuing directives per SGB V Section 91 et seq. Examples of innovations

---

insurance funds working jointly. By issuing directives, they set the catalogue of benefits offered by the Statutory Health Insurance funds for more than 70 million insured persons and, in doing so, determine what benefits are eligible for payouts under the medical care offered by the Statutory Health Insurance system. Furthermore, the G-BA decides on actions for quality assurance in hospital and non-hospital areas of the healthcare sector (Federal Joint Commitee 2018b).

that are relevant in this respect are new methods of examination and treatment per SGB V Section 468 or the early benefit assessment of pharmaceuticals under SGB V Section 35a. The G-BA contract the Institute for Quality and Efficiency in Health Care (IQWiG) to prepare for their decisions. IQWiG conducts research and analyses academic material (studies) to formulate a recommendation that, after a plausibility review by the G-BA, leads to corresponding directives and, finally, a decision that is binding for health insurance funds (Federal Joint Committee 2018a).

2.2 Establishment of Innovations by Means of Regulations in Selective Contracts with Statutory Health Insurance Funds (Block II in Fig. 1)

Statutory Health Insurance funds are permitted to enter into 'selective', i.e. optional, contracts for any benefits that have not yet been rejected by the Federal Joint Committee. Consequently, individual funds can, by themselves or in cooperation with others, integrate additional innovations into their standard care that would otherwise not or not yet be included. SGB V offers an array of legal foundations that funds can use to substitute or add on to benefits included with standard care. Examples of these are:

- selective contracts per SGB V Section 140a (Special Care)
- pilot projects run by health funds per SGB V Section 63
- benefits described in a health fund's charter per SGB V Section 11(6)
- general practitioner contracts per SGB V Section 73a (Primary Care Practitioners)

To encourage the use of selective contracts, an innovation fund was established at the G-BA in 2015 through the Statutory Health Insurance Care Improvement Act. An annual budget of €300 million was provided to promote projects that improve care across sectors and have the potential to be incorporated into care on a permanent basis. For example, these could include telemedicine, care projects in structurally weak areas, pilot projects with delegation and substitution of benefits; and pilot projects focussing on safety in pharmaceuticals. An innovation committee at the G-BA defines concrete criteria for funding and decides on applications for funding (Leonhardt 2015, p. 33) (Fig. 2).

The innovation fund was introduced so as to fix deficits resulting from the parallel existence of collective and selective contracts. The original goal when implementing this fund-specific freedom through selective contracts was to try out innovations on a small scale before incorporating the agreed benefit into the standard catalogue offered by the Statutory Health Insurance system in the instance of its success. Because of a lack of evaluation of existing selective contracts, there are few past examples of such a transition of benefits from selective to collective contract being successful. The health funds responsible for the selective contracts only had a limited individual interest in financing a cost-intensive evaluation on top of the usually

Example 2 – Innovation fund of €1.2 billion

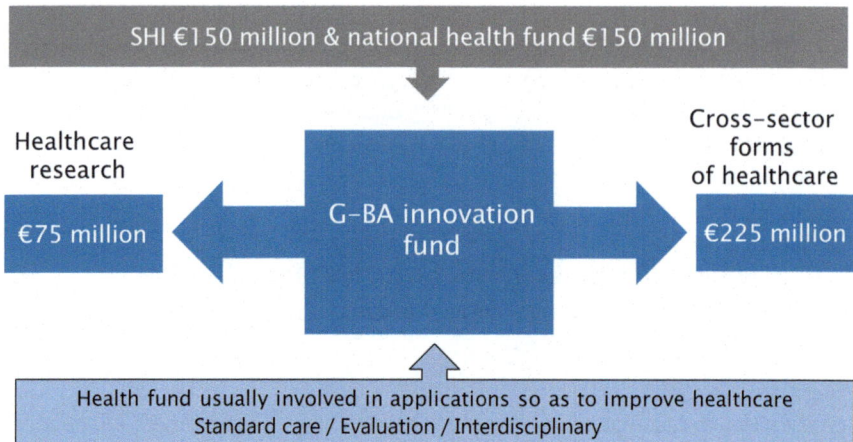

Fig. 2 Financing of the innovation fund in the Statutory Health Insurance system (own illustration)

already expensive benefits in the selective contract. The innovation fund addresses this deficit by making evaluation a requirement for funding and financing the innovative benefit in parallel.

2.3   Fast Entry Options for Innovations Via Private Insurance or Direct Financing (Block III in Fig. 1)

Approximately 10% of the German population are covered by Private Health Insurance. The principle of prohibition before explicit authorisation, as described above, does not normally apply when medical benefits are provided under a Private Health Insurance policy (depending on the policy). As a consequence, a doctor or dentist, for example, has the option of billing using the Fee Schedule for Doctors/Dentists (GOÄ/ GOZ) for services that are not included in the Statutory Health Insurance benefits catalogue. Professor Jürgen Wasem describes the parallel existence of Private and Statutory Health Insurance in relation to the implementation of innovations as follows: *'The competition between the two systems definitely has its positive sides. The minor barriers to market entry and the relatively flexible system for remuneration in the Private Health Insurance system promote the rapid introduction of innovations. That being said, emphasis is put on efficiency and evidence in the Statutory Health Insurance system and this leads to the necessary proof of quality and also process innovations. All patients benefit from this gain in quality.'* (Wasem 2017).

The early integration of innovations can lead to the advantages described above, yet, on the other hand, can also result in medical problems resulting from still insufficient evidence. The conflict between early implementation of an innovation and less than clear evidence can be illustrated using two practical examples:

Private Health Insurance covered the costs of antibody-coated, drug-eluting stents for coronary heart disease from an early stage. However, the final report by the IQWiG, dated 29 September 2015, concluded that there was no noticeable benefit provided by such stents over time. There was not one patient-relevant endpoint for which there was an indication of benefit or harm associated with treatment by implanting an antibody-coated, drug-eluting stent when compared with the control group, and in either case these were patients for whom a stent implant was indicated because of coronary heart disease (IQWiG 2015a, p. 12).

The second example concerns biomarker testing for breast cancer. In this respect too the IQWiG has concluded that there is no indication of benefit or harm for any of the currently offered biomarkers when it comes to a biomarker-based strategy for deciding for or against adjuvant chemotherapy in cases of primary mammary carcinoma (IQWiG 2015b). This example is all the more significant as patients have opted to forgo chemotherapy because of biomarker testing, although chemotherapy would have been beneficial at later stages of the disease.

Both examples show that early integration of innovations is not always in the patient's interests and, by extension, early financing of innovations does not generally lead to better care.

3 Pricing When Implementing Innovations in Care

Even if innovations improve the efficiency of a healthcare system over the short term and even increase efficiency reserves over the long term, they can sometimes cause considerable cost pressures at the time of implementation. On one hand, this can be attributed to the development of the innovation often incurring great costs and industry seeking to recoup the cost of these investments as soon as possible. On the other hand, an innovation may create an alternative treatment that in some circumstances may also for the first time enable a chance of recovery for patients with a specific and/or life-threatening illness. To deny such patients this new treatment method for financial reasons cannot be ethically justified in these individual cases. Healthcare systems must therefore respond to cases such as these, while at the same time the financing options described in Sect. 2 have utterly different mechanisms for enabling or denying provision of the service.

Examples of exceedingly expensive innovations in the healthcare system have grown in number over recent years. This in turn means that publicly financed healthcare systems in particular are faced with serious problems. If a decision is made in favour of rationalisation, insured persons will be excluded from a medical advance that is potentially relevant to their care. If a decision is made to cover such innovations, mechanisms must be found that influence the pricing or use of the innovation such that inclusion of the new benefits is enabled without affecting other sectors of the healthcare system. Universal healthcare systems are characterised by

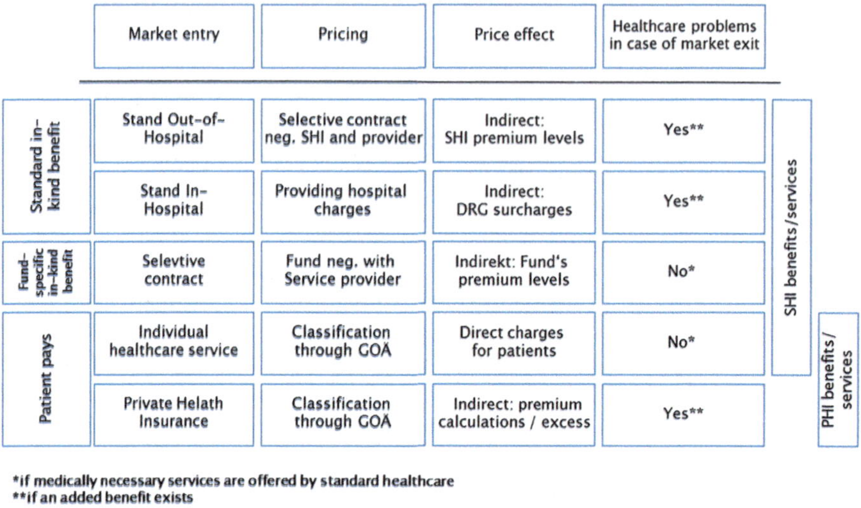

	Market entry	Pricing	Price effect	Healthcare problems in case of market exit	
Standard in-kind benefit	Stand Out-of-Hospital	Selective contract neg. SHI and provider	Indirect: SHI premium levels	Yes**	**SHI benefits/services**
	Stand In-Hospital	Providing hospital charges	Indirect: DRG surcharges	Yes**	
Fund-specific in-kind benefit	Selevtive contract	Fund neg. with Service provider	Indirekt: Fund's premium levels	No*	
Patient pays	Individual healthcare service	Classification through GOA	Direct charges for patients	No*	**PHI benefits/services**
	Private Helath Insurance	Classification through GOA	Indirect: premium calculations / excess	Yes**	

*if medically necessary services are offered by standard healthcare
**if an added benefit exists

Fig. 3 Pricing, price effects and healthcare problems in case of market exit depending on market entry (own illustration)

scarce financial resources which, in Germany for example, have led to the efficiency dictate specified in SGB V Section 12, which has had a decisive influence on case law in all aspects of that statute book.

Pricing in healthcare depends on the way in which a new service has entered the system. Impacts and the potential occurrence of healthcare issues because of a foreseeable exit of the service provider depend on the market entry. Figure 3 illustrates schematically the pricing, price effects and potential healthcare problems depending on the method of market entry.

3.1 Pricing Based on the Benefit-in-Kind Principle of Statutory Health Insurance

Different pricing mechanisms have emerged in the Out-of-Hospital and In-Hospital sectors because of the aforementioned difference between the principles of *'prohibition before authorisation'* and *'authorisation before prohibition'*. The basis for remuneration of standard In-Hospital care in Germany are the diagnosis-related groups (DRGs). They allow every hospital to make its own decisions based on the principle of authorisation before prohibition on what medical intervention is medically necessary for a patient and, by consequence, what intervention will be used during In-Hospital treatment. This free decision enables the use of medical innovations. However, there is a need to balance budgets resulting from the size of any given DRG, which of course limits the willingness of a hospital to subsidise the use of expensive investments over the longer term. SGB V provides for mechanisms to offset this financing problem via adjustments, supplements and deductions.

Pricing in standard Out-of-Hospital healthcare is based on a benefit assessment conducted by the Federal Joint Committee. If the assessment finds a positive benefit, prices are set in a manner that varies depending on the type of innovation. If it relates to services performed by doctors, for example, the Valuation Committee,[3] a joint committee made up by the National Association of Statutory Health Insurance Physicians[4] and National Confederation of Regional Statutory Health Insurance Associations,[5] determines an appropriate fee for the new service. If the innovation relates to new pharmaceutical products, negotiations are held directly between the manufacturer and the National Confederation of Regional Statutory Health Insurance Associations. SGB V provides escalation mechanisms for all pricing processes by way of arbitration offices or arbitrators. Because the pharmaceuticals sector in particular has been affected by costly innovations in the last few years, further analysis specific to the sector is provided later in this article, using the example of the Sofosbuvir drug for hepatitis C.

Statutory Health Insurance funds in Germany spent €202.05 billion in 2015. Of that, €34.84 billion went to pharmaceuticals (Federal Ministry of Health 2017). In 2015, the rates of increase in the pharmaceuticals sector were especially dominated by new treatment methods for patients with chronic hepatitis C. €1.265 billion alone was spent on medicines for treating hepatitis C, with expenditure for Sofosbuvir and Ledipasvir running up to €725.3 million (Schwabe and Paffrath 2016, pp. 9–10). Considering that the number of patients with an HCV antibody prevalence needing treatment is approximately 0.3% of the overall German population (Robert Koch Institute 2017, p. 280) and that total expenditure in the Statutory Health Insurance system was €202 billion for 71 million people, the extent of the financial burden on the healthcare system is noticeable.

On 17 July 2014, the Joint Federal Committee attested a substantial added benefit for the treatment of patients with chronic hepatitis C viral infection (HCV) for the

---

[3]The Valuation Committee is a committee of doctors and health funds acting jointly for organisational purposes. For this reason, it is also known as the Doctors' Valuation Committee. It is made up of six members, with three appointed by the National Association of Statutory Health Insurance Physicians and three by the National Confederation of Regional Statutory Health Insurance Associations. The Institute for the Valuation Committee manages the Valuation Committee (Institute for the Valuation Committee 2018).

[4]The National Association of Statutory Health Insurance Physicians is the umbrella association for the 17 regional Associations of Statutory Health Insurance Physicians. It organises extensive, locally-provided Out-of-Hospital healthcare and represents at national level the interests of doctors and psychotherapists working in the Statutory Health Insurance system (National Association of Statutory Health Insurance Physicians 2018).

[5]The National Confederation of Regional Statutory Health Insurance Associations (*GKV-Spitzenverband*) is the main representative of Statutory Health and Nursing Insurance funds in Germany and at European and international levels. It is responsible for the overall conditions necessary for healthy competition in quality and efficiency in healthcare and nursing care (National Confederation of Regional Statutory Health Insurance Associations 2018).

drug Sofosbuvir in their benefit assessment of pharmaceuticals with new agents (Federal Joint Committee 2014). The process for including new medicines in the benefits catalogue is regulated by the Act on the Reform of the Market for Medicinal Products and came into effect on 1 January 2011. The purpose of the legislation is to stem the strongly increasing expenses incurred by Statutory Health Insurance funds on medicine in recent years. The process for assessing benefit and calculating the amount coverable is depicted in Fig. 4.

After the decision of the Federal Joint Committee on the added benefit of Sofosbuvir, the provider Gilead's pharmacy retail price (including manufacturer discount) was set at €18,860.00 for a packet of 28 tablets (i.e. around €700 per tablet). In the subsequent negotiations between the manufacturer and the National Confederation of Regional Statutory Health Insurance Associations (see Fig. 5), the manufacturer's selling price and therefore also the pharmacy retail price was reduced to €16,840.00 (Arznei Telegramm 2015). Nobody can objectively evaluate whether the above pricing is appropriate for an incidence rate of 300,000 patients in Germany alone. What is obvious, however, is that only few healthcare systems worldwide can finance such pricing given the incidence rate described above. As illustrated in Fig. 5, prices are set through negotiations between the provider and the National Confederation of Regional Statutory Health Insurance Associations when the product's market entry is through standard Out-of-Hospital care. Because of the financial volume, the Sofosbuvir example truly has a direct impact on the premiums charged for Statutory Health Insurance. Many innovations do not result in this level of direct impact because of smaller financial volume, however the cumulative effect of various innovations can be similar. If an agreement had not been reached when setting the price of Sofosbuvir and an arbitration office not found an appropriate price for both parties either, the manufacturer would most probably have taken its product off the market. This would have had considerable consequences on the options for treating hepatitis C patients in Germany. In hindsight, the purpose of this exercise was not to question whether Sofosbuvir needed to be incorporated into standard care, but whether its negotiated price was justified.

3.1.1 Pharmaceuticals Focus 1: What Price Is Appropriate for a Medicinal Product in Germany?

It is difficult to find neutral factors that can be used to calculate a suitable price for a medicinal product. An initial benchmark would be the economic strength of the country in which a medicinal product is offered. The OECD compared average per-capita expenditure on medicinal products in 31 industrial nations for the year 2015. At US$766, Germany comes in at fourth place behind the US, Switzerland and Japan. Average per-capita expenses were US$553 per year (OECD 2017). Germany therefore ranks in the upper quartile of OECD nations. That may be appropriate given the country's economic strength, although, when compared to the average, the question arises as to why this difference exists.

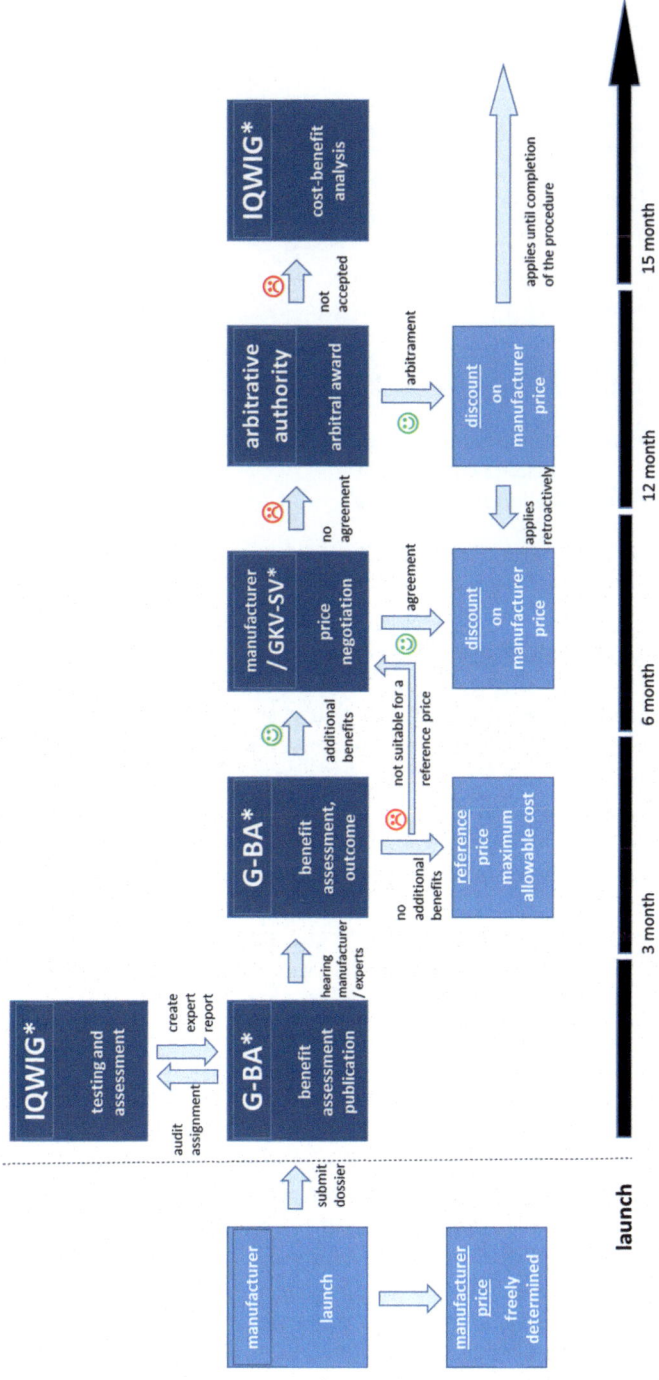

Fig. 4 Infographics on the Act on the Reform of the Market for Medicinal Products (own illustration based on Federal Ministry of Health 2010, p. 18)

* IQWIG: Institut für Qualität und Wirtschaftlichkeit im Gesundheitswesen - Institute for Quality and Economic Efficiency in Health Care
G-BA: Gemeinsamer Bundesausschuss - Federal Joint Committee
GKV-SV: GKV-Spitzenverband - National Association of Statutory Health Insurance Funds

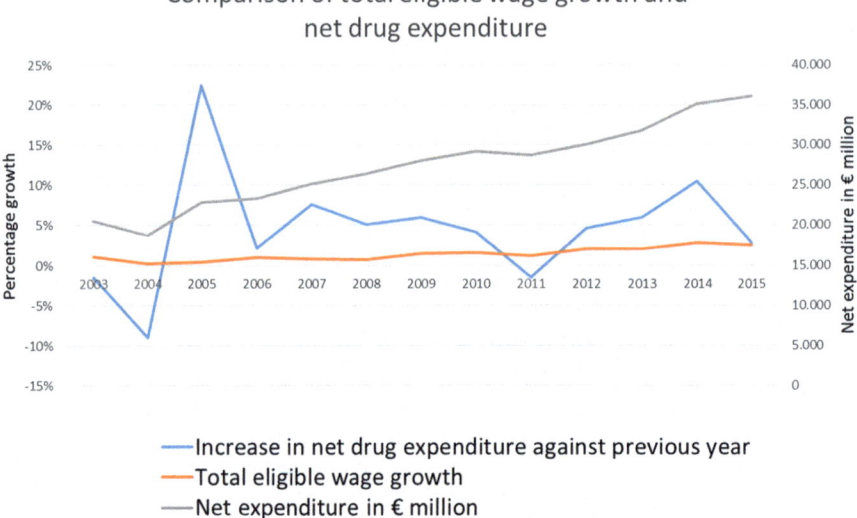

Fig. 5 Rate of increase in pharmaceutical expenditure relative to eligible wage growth (own illustration based on von Maydell and Carstensen 2016, p. 197)

A look at the increase of pharmaceuticals in Germany over the last few years (see Fig. 5) explains the high figure produced by the international comparison. In Germany, pharmaceutical expenses in the last 10 years continually increased more than the sum of basic wages did, i.e. the sum of wages and salaries from which health insurance premiums are drawn.

Generic drugs are not relevant for this rate of increase, as the Statutory Health Insurance funds' tenders for discount contracts result in below-average prices in international terms, with the result that patented drugs are instead causing it.

A comparison of EU prices by the AOK Research Institute shows that Germany remains frontrunner amongst the 250 most frequently sold patented drugs. In all countries studied, prices are between 18% (UK) and 35% (Sweden) lower than the public German catalogue prices after being adjusted for GDP. Even when considering all known discounts, the prices in the comparison countries are still 4% (UK) and 24% (Sweden) lower than the reduced German catalogue prices (Busse et al. 2017, p. 201f). One reason for this significant difference could be the rapid entry of pharmaceuticals into the German market. Germany generally has the largest share of medicinal products entering the market for the first time. The time between approval and sales launch is also shorter than in all other European countries. In 2015, the average time between approval and the date of first sale in Germany was 3.1 months. In the United Kingdom, for example, it was 4.5 months, in the Netherlands 13 months and in Greece even 25 months (QuintilesIMS 2017, p. 12).

Summarised briefly, there is a sophisticated benefit assessment performed when introducing innovations in Germany. A negotiation process regulated in detail by relevant legislation then follows this and includes predetermined escalation mechanisms. All steps in this process lead to a quick implementation of innovations for positive healthcare, although not to a price that is suitable for the process, that is at least on average when compared internationally or that in any way considers the enormous potential sales for manufacturers in the German healthcare market. So what must be changed to, firstly, achieve pricing that is average when compared internationally and, secondly, prevent an increasing burden on the social security system because of a rate of increase that exceeds eligible wage growth?

3.1.2 Pharmaceuticals Focus 2: Lack of Pricing Regulation for Pharmaceutical Innovations in Germany

One important reason for the relatively low price reduction for Sofosbuvir was the disparity at the negotiating table between the pharmaceutical industry and the National Confederation of Regional Statutory Health Insurance Associations. The disparity is primarily the result of the manufacturer's monopoly position when it owns a drug with added benefits. This monopoly situation means that payers face a classic dilemma, because the potential threat of a manufacturer not to offer the corresponding medicine on the German market could result in deficient care. According to von Maydell and Carstensen (2016), manufacturers and payers currently apply the criteria described in Fig. 6 during negotiations on drug prices.

To shift the disparity in negotiations between the manufacturer and the payer in favour of the latter and add more weight to the argument for lower pricing, there are currently various additions being discussed in Germany. These include expansion of the benefit assessment used by the Federal Joint Committee for medicines into a cost-benefit analysis as normally used by the NHS in the United Kingdom. Furthermore, manufacturer research and development costs should only be factored in if they are the result of the manufacturer's own research (and not of research that is already government-funded) and divided proportionate to the share of the global market held. It is incomprehensible why research and development costs consistently receive new funding from every country in which a drug is approved. A third line of reasoning currently being discussed is the limited ability to prescribe innovations for subpopulations for which the benefit assessment has said there is a

Manufacturer criteria	Payer criteria
• Extent and probability of added benefit relative to appropriate, comparable treatment • Proportion of patients enjoying added benefit relative to the overall population for which the drug is approved • Comparable drugs • Comparable European prices	• potential savings on future illness costs • investment, research and development costs (depending on need and relevance) • threat potential of a market withdrawal

Fig. 6 Criteria when negotiating drug prices

tangible added benefit and, based on that, offer different pricing for such subpopulations (von Maydell and Carstensen 2016, p. 209ff).

3.2   Price Setting by Health Insurance Funds and Service Providers Through Selective Contracts

The selective contracts entered into by health funds vary dramatically in terms of content. Insured persons participate in the model of care offered by the selective contract and utilise the associated new benefits on a voluntary basis. Figure 4 shows that significant care issues should not arise when a selective contract is terminated because otherwise the selective contract's content would have to be transferred to standard insurance coverage. As the benefit assessment requires a long period of time in the Joint Federal Committee, selective contracts are ideal for temporarily covering new services with added benefit for patients.

In addition to content, the costs incurred by the benefits offered in a selective contract vary considerably. The Organisation of Professional Paediatricians, for example, offers a selective contract in telemedicine that has already been taken up by several funds. PädExpert networks paediatricians working in a general physician capacity with paediatricians who are qualified as or work as specialists. The aim of the network is to treat children and youths with chronic or rare diseases. Using PädExpert, the 'general practitioner' for the child or youth can consult a highly qualified paediatrician online and ask for support—from diagnosis through to potential options for treatment (Association of Professional Paediatricians (BVKJ) 2018). The model on offer improves care when compared to consultation with a single paediatrician, and at relatively low cost too. An evaluation would be needed to confirm whether it is also of benefit when compared to personal contact with a specialist paediatrician or whether there are increased benefits for overall care by consulting specialist paediatricians more frequently. Such an evaluation would be required before the model could be incorporated into standard healthcare, with the current selective contract acting as a useful complement to the system.

A model of care in another league entirely is proton therapy, which previously has only been covered in Germany through selective contracts. In Essen, for example, an ion beam therapy centre opened in 2015 for radiotherapy of cancer cells. Launching the centre cost approximately €140 million. The higher accuracy of this form of particle therapy seems to enable better treatment results than with traditional forms of radiation for certain types of cancer, e.g. hepatocellular, lung, pancreatic and oesophageal carcinomas and head and throat tumours. The cost of treatment is triple that for conventional cancer therapy and comes in at round €18,000.

Although both of the aforementioned selective contracts are completely different and cover entirely different areas of medicine, pricing is based solely on negotiations between the service provider and the fund offering the benefit. Standard insurance coverage offers alternatives for both forms of treatment that are sufficient, suitable and efficient for the efficiency dictate for Statutory Health Insurance funds per SGB V Section 12. The differing level of severity amongst the patients who need treatment and have access to one of the two selective contracts then, however, leads to a difference in the benefits offered if a fund has not entered into these selective contracts. Where proton therapy is indicated, the mechanisms for cost reimbursement described in Sect. 3.2 will probably come into effect, whereas such mechanisms will not be available for patients who wish to make use of the telemedicine services offered by PädExpert.

3.3   Pricing Based on the Reimbursement Principle of Private Health Insurance and for Services Paid Directly

Individual doctors may offer services that exceed the scope of the Statutory Health Insurance benefits catalogue. As these services are not covered under the benefit-in-kind principle, patients must themselves pay the doctor directly for these services. In the German healthcare system, these services have come to be known as 'individual healthcare services', with the services on offer being many and diverse. For any individual healthcare service to have gained such status, either the Federal Joint Committee must have not (yet) found added benefit at the current point in time—as these services would otherwise be incorporated into standard coverage—or the service must have received a negative assessment. Individual healthcare services are offered by doctors on a private basis and may be billed using the Fee Schedule for Doctors (GOÄ) if the specific service is listed on it. As the rate used by the doctor to multiply the fee listed on the schedule varies based on time and effort for the service, so too does the price paid by the patient, which means that supply and demand determine the cost for a patient when they go to the doctor's practice. Should the service in question not be listed on the schedule, the doctor has the option of billing for a service of similar value in terms of nature, expense and time required. This mechanism strengthens the options a doctor has to set individual prices. Treating individual healthcare services and innovations in the same manner is difficult because a service rejected by the Joint Federal Committee can surely no longer be seen as an innovation. The same service delivery and pricing conditions apply to individual healthcare services as with other innovations that are covered by Private Health Insurance. Setting prices based on the services of comparable value results in there only being hurdles when introducing services that are extremely expensive or contain something highly unusual. Market entry is therefore easier than under the Statutory Health Insurance system.

While individual healthcare services mean that persons with Statutory Health Insurance have a direct financial burden, innovations have a more indirect effect on Private Health Insurance policyholders via premium and excess adjustments.

Services rendered outside of the standard insurance system gain particular importance if a patient is suffering from a life-threatening illness, all approved treatment methods have been tried and there is still a method for which the Federal Joint Committee has not yet issued a final statement. As scientific evidence of the added benefit of an innovation may sometimes take years to collect, situations such as the preceding one may also arise in the interim period when the medical benefit of an innovation is still being scientifically evaluated. In the German Out-of-Hospital Care sector prior to 2006, there was a problem whereby patients with serious illnesses wanted to utilise services for which the Federal Joint Committee had not yet taken a decision or for which there were not yet any sufficient studies that could be used as a basis for a final decision. The Federal Constitutional Court issued the so-called 'Santa Claus judgement' on 6 December 2005 (case no.: 1 BvR 347/98) for this situation. Under this judgement, persons with Statutory Health Insurance and a life-threatening illness for which the standard system does not offer a method of treatment can apply for non-standard services that offer a not-entirely-remote prospect of recovery or improvement in the disease's progression. This judgement by the Federal Constitutional Court was a milestone in the German healthcare system's handling of medical innovations. It is now the responsibility of Statutory Health Insurance funds to assess the described situation in each individual case and cover the costs for the insured person if a positive decision is made. On 1 January 2012, the Federal Government's *Act on the Improvement of Healthcare Structures in the Statutory Health Insurance System* integrated the contents of the 'Santa Claus judgement' into the new Section 2(1a) of SGB V and, in doing so, filled a difficult hole in healthcare coverage with new methods of treatment. Thanks to the balanced wording of Section 2(1a), legislators have succeeded in, firstly, maintaining the important limitations on market entry provided by evidence-based benefit assessments by the Federal Joint Committee and, secondly, addressing the individual interests in treatment alternatives for patients with life-threatening illnesses.

4   Final Observation

Medical progress in the form of innovations must be provided to all insured persons even if the system of health insurance is publicly financed. At the same time, innovations should not be allowed to destabilise a public health insurance system because of high costs. If it is assumed that innovations at least make treatments more expensive over the short term, then the design of a healthcare system will inevitably involve a conflict between the promotion of medical progress and the necessity of having a realistic model for funding it.

Benefit exclusions are not available as instruments for rationalisation in the German healthcare system, which means that the question arises of whether the described instruments are enough to allow innovations without endangering the system's financial viability. The arguments concerning the introduction and financing of innovations that have been presented in this article can be summarised with the following theses:

- The German healthcare system offers various options for introducing innovations.
- There is a successful system for assessing the benefit of innovations presided over by the Federal Joint Committee.
- The demand for evidence-based medicine means that time is required for evaluation. Selective contracts and one-off, situation-dependent decisions on reimbursement can be used to provide innovations in the mean time while innovations are evaluated.
- Pharmaceutical innovations in particular are integrated into care very rapidly.
- The payer (i.e. health fund) and the service provider frequently negotiate prices for innovations based on their added benefit.
- The German healthcare system pays very highly for innovations in comparison to other countries.

The German social security system received sufficient funding in 2017 thanks to a high employment rate. Consequently, the high prices for implemented innovations have not yet led a discussion on rationalisation. Changes to the age pyramid in Germany and an associated reduction in the number of employees paying into the social security system will mean that the finances of the Statutory Health Insurance system will take a noticeable turn for the worse over the coming years. For this reason, the disparity between payers and manufacturers during price negotiations should be counteracted in the future and the payer's position in price negotiations bolstered by means of legislation. This process can be supported even further by more strongly establishing cost-benefit analyses during the evaluation of innovations.

References

Arznei Telegramm (2015) Weiterhin Mondpreise für Hepatitis-C-Mittel. https://www.arznei-telegramm.de/html/sonder/1502017_01.html. 1 Jan 2016

Association of Professional Paediatricians (BVKJ) (2018) PädExpert© - Telemedizinisches Konsil für die ambulante Pädiatrie. https://www.paedexpert.de/paedexpert/. 1 Jan 2018

Bührlein B (2007) Innovationssystem Gesundheit: Ziele und Nutzen von Gesundheitsinnovationen. In: Bührlein B, Kickbusch I (eds) http://www.isi.fraunhofer.de/isi-wAssets/docs/t/de/publikationen/Innovationssystem-Gesundheit_1_.pdf. 17 Jan 2018

Busse R, Panteli D, Schröder H, Schröder M, Telschow C, Weiss J (2017) Europäischer Preisvergleich für patentgeschützte Arzneimittel. In: Schwabe U, Paffrath D (eds) Arzneiverordnungsreport 2017, Berlin, pp 195–208

Federal Joint Committee (2014) Frühe Nutzenbewertung: Beträchtlicher Zusatznutzen für Wirkstoff gegen chronische Hepatitis C. https://www.g-ba.de/institution/presse/pressemitteilungen/546/. 17 July 2017

Federal Joint Committee (2018a) Institute for Quality and Efficiency in Health Care (IQWiG). https://www.g-ba.de/institution/aufgabe/arbeitsweise/sachverstaendige/. 4 Jan 2016

Federal Joint Committee (2018b) Institution. https://www.g-ba.de/. 1 Jan 2018

Federal Ministry of Health (2010) Die Spreu vom Weizen trennen - Das Arzneimittelmarktneuordnungsgesetz (AMNOG). https://www.bundesgesundheitsministerium.

de/fileadmin/Dateien/5_Publikationen/Gesundheit/Broschueren/Broschuere_Die_Spreu_vom_ Weizen_trennen_-_Das_Arzneimittelmarktneuordnungsgesetz.pdf. 1 Jan 2018

Federal Ministry of Health (2017) Gesetzliche Krankenversicherung - Kennzahlen und Faustformeln. https://www.bundesgesundheitsministerium.de/fileadmin/Dateien/3_Down loads/Statistiken/GKV/Kennzahlen_Daten/KF2018Bund_Januar_2018.pdf. 1 Jan 2018

Institute for the Valuation Committee (2018) Bewertungsausschuss Ärzte. https://institut-ba.de/ba. html. 1 Jan 2018

IQWiG (2015a) IQWiG-Berichte – Nr. 326 - Antikörperbeschichtete, medikamentenfreisetzende Stents zur Behandlung von Koronargefäßstenosen (Antibody-coated drug-eluting stents for treatment of coronary artery stenosis). https://www.iqwig.de/download/N13-01_ Abschlussbericht_Antikoerperbeschichtete-medikamentenfreisetzende%20Stents.pdf. 24 Sept 2015

IQWiG (2015b) Biomarker tests in breast cancer: decision on chemotherapy remains difficult. https://www.iqwig.de/en/press/press-releases/biomarker-tests-in-breast-cancer-decision-on-che motherapy-remains-difficult.7700.html. 5 Dec 2016

Leonhardt U (2015) Innovationsfonds - Qualitative Weiterentwicklung. In: vdek (eds) ersatzkasse magazin 1./2.2015. Berlin, 33

National Association of Statutory Health Insurance Physicians (2018) Die KBV. http://www.kbv. de/html/die_kbv.php. 1 Jan 2018

National Confederation of Regional Statutory Health Insurance Associations (2018) Der Verband. https://www.gkv-spitzenverband.de/gkv_spitzenverband/der_verband/wir_ueber_uns.jsp. 1 Jan 2018

OECD (2017) Pharmaceutical expenditure. In: OECD (eds) Health at a Glance 2017 – OECD Indicators. Paris

QuintilesIMS (2017) Pricing and Market Access Outlook – 2017 Edition. https://www.iqvia.com/-/ media/quintilesims/pdfs/pricing-and-market-access-outlook-magazine-web.pdf. 1 Jan 2018

Robert Koch Institute (2017) Epidemiologisches Bulletin – Zur Situation bei wichtigen Infektionskrankheiten in Deutschland – Hepatitis C im Jahr 2016. https://www.rki.de/DE/ Content/Infekt/EpidBull/Archiv/2017/Ausgaben/30_17.pdf?__blob=publicationFile. 27 July 2017

Schwabe U, Paffrath D (2016) Arzneiverordnungen 2015 im Überblick. In: Schwabe U, Paffrath D (eds) Arzneiverordnungsreport 2016. Berlin, pp 9–10

Verband der Ersatzkassen e. V (2018) Selbstverwaltung. https://www.vdek.com/presse/glossar_ gesundheitswesen/selbstverwaltung.html. 1 Jan 2018

Von Maydell B, Carstensen K (2016) Wie viel darf therapeutischer Fortschritt kosten? Arzneimittelpreise zwischen Innovation und Ausgabenkontrolle. In: Repschläger U, Schulte C, Osterkamp N (eds) BARMER GEK Gesundheitswesen aktuell 2016. Cologne, pp 196–217

Wasem J (2017) Innovationen im GKV- / PKV-System. http://veranstaltungen.handelsblatt.com/ health/innovationen-im-gkv-pkv-system/. 1 Jan 2018

Clinical Evaluation of Medical Devices in Europe

Hans P. Zenner and Mijo Božić

Abstract The new EU Regulation (EU) 2017/745 on medical devices, which took effect on May 26, 2017, is crucially important for medical device manufacturers and CE certification, as well as the recertification of their products. On clinical evaluation, the present contribution discusses the main differences between EU Directive 93/42/EEC and EU Regulation 2017/745 in the following six areas: (i) Stronger requirements for clinical safety and evidence of clinical efficacy, (ii) Classification, (iii) Clinical evaluation, possibly including clinical trials, (iv) Post-market clinical surveillance, (v) Clinical documentation and reporting, and (vi) Introduction of the European Commission's scrutiny procedure.

1 Introduction

The new EU Medical Device Regulation (MDR)[1] is of crucial importance for manufacturers of medical devices when it comes to certification and recertification of their products, with the exception of in vitro diagnostic medical devices. In addition to comprehensive extensions, the MDR combines provisions of the Directive 93/42/EEC concerning medical devices (MDD) and Active Implantable Medical Devices Directive 90/385/EEC (AIMDD), which it supplemented. The older MDD and AIMDD remaining in force until 2020 contain provisions for putting a medical device into service based on clinical evaluation.

---

[1]For the main reasons behind the adoption of the new Regulation on medical devices see for example Gemke (2017) p. 15 or Handorn (2018) p. 95.

H. P. Zenner (✉)
HP Zenner Clinical Evaluation, Tübingen, Germany

The University of Tübingen, Tübingen, Germany
e-mail: office@hpzenner.de

M. Božić
The University of Tübingen, Tübingen, Germany
e-mail: Mijo.Bozic@med.uni-tuebingen.de

© Springer Nature Switzerland AG 2019
N. Bodiroga-Vukobrat et al. (eds.), *Personalized Medicine in Healthcare Systems*,
Europeanization and Globalization 5, https://doi.org/10.1007/978-3-030-16465-2_2

Unlike the directives, the new EU regulation is directly applicable in all EU states. An additional adaptation of national laws on medical devices like the Mediziniproduktgesetz (MPG) in Germany remains possible.

A separate EU regulation applies to in vitro diagnostics—the Regulation (EU) 2017/746 on in vitro diagnostic medical devices (IVDR) from April 5, 2017, replacing the hitherto valid Directive 98/79/EC on in vitro diagnostic medical devices.

The new MDR and certification procedure resulting from this are much more complex than the procedures previously applied under MDD/AIMDD/MPG. Compared to the MDD, the MDR contains a hundred additional provisions. The number of annexes has increased, and there is a series of further legal documents, the preparation of which is still ongoing.

However, there are no significant differences in many areas. Despite more detailed wording, no entirely new requirements are foreseen.

2 Results and Discussion

2.1 Regulatory Sphere

The MDR will apply from May 26, 2020. The manufacturers will have to follow the MDR when placing medical devices on the market for the first time. Products already approved on the market must be adapted to MDR no later than 5 years after the date of application of MDR. For products approved under MDD/AIMDD/ MPG from the second quarter of 2020, this period will be shortened to 4 years. If there is no new EU declaration of conformity because, for example, the clinical evaluation in the technical documentation is incomplete, the EU certificate may be refused.

Each medical device is assigned to a particular class. This classification system is based on the potential hazard, type of application, and approval requirements. Classification was previously performed under rules set out in MDD/AIMDD.

In the case of a first-time CE certification under the MDR, the medical device (if applicable, also some products intended for non-medical use) is assigned to a class according to 22 classification criteria set out in Annex VIII "Classification rules". Annex VIII to EU MDR also provides for a different classification. In the course of MDR, the previous assignment of some medical devices to a particular class will be changed compared to the procedure applied under MDD/AIMDD, which is expiring in 2020.

Two new MDR classification rules for active medical devices are particularly notable. Under Rule 11, stand-alone software is hardly assigned to class I any longer, as most software falls at least in class IIa or higher, especially if the software can cause death or persistent adverse health effects. From class IIa on a notified body involvement is required. Under Rule 22, a number of systems (e.g., closed-loop feed-back systems: invasive control systems, such as active therapeutic devices with integrated or embedded diagnostic function) and implants (e.g., orthopedic joint and spinal implants) previously assigned to class IIb are now supposed to meet the more stringent requirements of class III. All products that contain or consist of non-material are also affected (Rule 19). The same holds for invasive devices with respect to body orifices, which are intended to administer medicinal products by inhalation (except surgically invasive devices; Rule 20), as well as devices composed of substances or combinations of substances that are intended to be introduced into the human body via a body orifice or applied to the skin and that are absorbed by or locally dispersed in the human body (Rule 21). Devices manufactured utilizing animal or human tissue or drugs (e.g., insulin) are subject to more stringent requirements.

Under the MDR, manufacturers of products that have been put into service under MDD/AIMDD must timely review the new classification rules and update their technical documentation, including clinical evaluation and possibly including a clinical trial. Class IIa, IIb, and III medical devices may require a systematic clinical reassessment. In doing so, they must consider the new provision on the equivalence of the products, as well as the options under which a clinical trial can legitimately be dispensed. If such a review is omitted, the CE certificate may be invalid.

Under the new EU MDR, this evidence of the clinical efficacy of a medical device and patient safety is generally provided by a clinical evaluator who is a specialist in the relevant medical specialty possessing personal clinical experiences in the application of the specific or similar medical devices and/or in the diagnosis and management of the conditions intended to be diagnosed or managed by the device.[2]

More often than before, a clinical trial will be required. The MDR sets out in detail how clinical evaluations and clinical trials should be performed. Clinical evaluation of medical devices is part of the technical documentation relating to a medical device. At the same time, the manufacturer must submit a clinical development plan, including a plan for post-market clinical follow-up.

An explicit rule relating to non-critical products, which would allow a waiver of clinical evaluation, does not exist. A waiver of clinical data for a clinical evaluation, however, is basically permitted for absolutely non-critical products, such as screws, wedges, plates, and instruments.

In addition to the EU MDR, there are other regulations and standards that require a clinical evaluation of medical devices. These include the established MEDDEV guidelines[3] to ensure compliance with the old guidelines.

---

[2]MEDDEV 2.7/1 rev 4, p. 15: "With respect to the particular device under evaluation, the evaluator should in addition have knowledge of: - the device technology and its application; - diagnosis and management of the conditions intended to be diagnosed or managed by the device, knowledge of medical alternatives, treatment standards and technology (e.g. specialist clinical expertise in the relevant medical specialty)".

[3]European Commission's guidance documents to assist stakeholders in implementing directives related to medical devices. List of Guidance MEDDEVs available on: https://ec.europa.eu/growth/sectors/medical-devices/guidance_en, accessed on July 28th 2018.

Furthermore, not only the manufacturers, but also the suppliers, importers, distributors, and sales organizations (economic operators) can be affected. Exceptions in this regard are economic operators of component parts, such as screws, wedges, plates, and instruments.

If comparable devices are used for clinical evaluation, then these reference products must be technically, biologically, and clinically equivalent to investigated products being subject to evaluation. As with the MEDDEV 2.7/1 rev 4 there should be no clinically relevant differences. Manufacturers must demonstrate an equivalence by providing the data for the reference product. Class III and implantable devices can only refer to data of comparable validity if the manufacturer has the reference devices in its possession and able to generate the necessary data. As a rule, they (manufacturers) need contractually regulated access to all data and test results relating to the reference product.

In addition to the new MDR clinical trials of medical products must be planned and performed under EN ISO 14155[4] "Clinical investigations of medical devices for human subjects - Good clinical practice" and other relevant regulations.[5]

The reporting system includes the results of the clinical evaluation, possibly including (if applicable) the clinical trial protocol documents, investigator's brochure, patient information, and informed consent, as well as additional reports and plans, such as the Clinical Development Plan and the Summary of Safety and Clinical Performance. The MEDDEV 2.7/1 rev. 4 also sets out requirements to be met. The clinical evaluation combined with risk management can be tested as well.[6] Furthermore, documents on clinical post-market surveillance are required.

Post-market Surveillance is a continuous process that updates the clinical evaluation (Annex XIV Part B). This applies in particular to class III medical products and implantable devices that are subject to more stringent clinical requirements as set out in EU MDR. Clinical post-market surveillance includes:

- Post-market Clinical Follow-up (PMCF)
- Other studies
- Vigilance system/reporting of incidents to responsible national authorities—in Germany, the Federal institute for Drugs and Medical Devices
- Customer contacts
- Screening of scientific literature and other sources of clinical data
- Identifying possible systematic misuse or off-label use of the device
- Continuous review and update of clinical evaluation.

---

[4]ISO 14155 is now a single standard that consolidates the previous 14155-1 and ISO 14155-2. ISO 14155 does not apply to in vitro diagnostic medical devices.

[5]These include national regulations, such as the German Regulation on Clinical Trials with Medical Devices and the German Medical Devices Safety Plan Regulation. On the other hand, the following provisions will no longer apply: Medical Devices Act sec. 20 ff., and the Ordinance on Clinical Trials with Medical Devices.

[6]Such a test is meant to show if the results of clinical evaluation are consistent with the statements in the risk management file.

Additional reports and plans under the MDR include the Post-market Surveillance Report, Periodic Safety Update Report (PSUR), and Summary of Safety and Clinical Performance. As part of the PMCF for class III and implantable devices, the safety/clinical evaluation/performance summary reports must be updated at least once annually.

An important issue in this context is the reporting of serious incidents.[7] They should be reported without delay within the framework of the vigilance procedure. 'Incident' means any malfunction or deterioration in the characteristics or performance of a device made available on the market, including use-error because of ergonomic features, as well as any inadequacy in the information supplied by the manufacturer and any undesirable side effect (MDR Art. 2 no. 64).

'Serious incident' within the meaning of MDR Art. 2 no. 65 means any incident that directly or indirectly led, might have led, or might lead to any of the following:

(a) The death of a patient, user, or other person
(b) The temporary or permanent serious deterioration of a patient's, user's, or other person's state of health
(c) A serious public health threat.

Responsible national authorities (in Germany, the Federal institute for Drugs and Medical Devices, BfArM) evaluate the risk resulting from the incident. At the same time, the manufacturer undertakes corrective measures in cooperation with the national authorities to eliminate existing risk.

Manufacturers are also required to report any significant increase in the frequency or severity of incidents that are not serious or are expected to have undesirable side effects that could have a significant impact on the benefit-risk analysis (Art. 88 (1) MDR). Furthermore, serious adverse events (SAEs) must be reported in the course of a clinical trial or performance evaluation (Medical Devices Safety Plan Ordinance, sec. 3 (5)).

2.2 Classification of a Medical Device

Classification has a significant impact on the necessity and extent of a potentially required clinical evaluation, including clinical trials and clinical post-market surveillance.

The MDD contains 18 rules, which are divided into rules relating to non-invasive, invasive, and active products, as well as special rules. Each MDD/AIMDD medical device is assigned to one of four classes based on the hazard potential, type of application, and licensing requirements.

In the case of a first time CE certification and recertification according to MDR the classification of a medical device—and some products not intended for medical

---

[7]See more on these issues in Lippert (2018), pp. 299–303.

use[8]—will be conducted according to 22 classification criteria set out in Annex VIII "Classification criteria".

In the case of CE certification (2020 at the latest) or recertification according to MDR (no later than 2024), the assignment of some medical devices to a particular class will change compared to the currently applicable MDD/AIMDD expiring in 2020. Two new classification rules relating to active medical devices should be mentioned.

Software intended to provide information that is used to make diagnostic or therapeutic decisions—especially if such decisions have an effect that may cause death or an irreversible deterioration of a person's state of health—is classified as class IIa and higher.

A number of systems (e.g., closed-loop feedback systems: invasive control systems, such as active therapeutic devices with integrated or embedded diagnostic function) and implants (e.g., orthopedic joint and spinal implants[9]) previously assigned to class IIb, are now expected to meet the more stringent requirements of class III. Active therapeutic devices with an integrated or incorporated diagnostic function, which significantly determines patient management by the device, such as closed loop systems or automated external defibrillators, are classified as class III.

All devices incorporating or consisting of nanomaterial (Rule 19); all invasive devices with respect to body orifices, with the exception for invasive devices, which are intended to administer medicinal products by inhalation (Rule 20); and devices that are composed of substances or of combinations of substances that are intended to be introduced into the human body via a body orifice or applied to the skin and that are absorbed by or locally dispersed in the human body (Rule 21), are affected as well.

All devices manufactured utilizing tissues or cells of human or animal origin, or their derivatives (e.g., insulin) will have to meet more stringent requirements.

Not only the manufacturers, but also suppliers, importers, distributors, and sales organizations (economic operators) included in a supply chain, can be affected.

---

[8]Under the MDR, a total of six product groups can be optionally marked with "CE". They are listed in Annex XVI "Products without an intended medical purpose". A prerequisite is that they meet requirements relating to medical devices provided for in the EU MDR.

[9]Prostheses for all joints and many, if not all, joint prostheses in the body are currently assumed to fall in future into the class III. It is not clear if this (rebuttable) presumption applies to all joints equally. The MDR significantly expands the range of joint implants that were already classified higher by Directive 2005/50/EC. Under Rule 8, partial joint replacements and other joint implants also fall into class III. For manufacturers, it may be helpful to think in advance of whether their products affect joints as defined by the MDR, e.g., the hand or tarsal bones or temporomandibular/jaw joint. Spinal disc replacement implants and implantable devices that come into contact with the spinal column are assigned to class III. However, the phrase "implantable devices that come into contact with the spinal column" raises questions. Strictly speaking, it could also include bone cements for vertebral body erection. An exception applies to (ancillary) components, such as screws, wedges, plates, and instruments. It is not yet clear how a rod or screw system should be classified and what is meant by a wedge in spinal column surgery. Therefore, further publications are needed to make the content, meaning, and scope of this rule more precise.

Their activities can be subjected to auditing by notified bodies and, thus, be part of a clinical evaluation. The exception in this regard applies to manufacturers' economic operators dealing with minor components, such as screws, wedges, plates, and instruments.

The MDR is a novelty, as it provides for manufacturers to submit a clinical development plan, including a plan for clinical follow-up. Consequently, in addition to the normative and technical requirements relating to a new product, the specification will have to include evidence of clinical safety, minimal possible stress, and effective benefits.

The planning and execution of an essential part of preclinical tests relating to a new medical device will of course be influenced by the subsequent clinical use of the product in question. Therefore, in the course of examining the technical documentation, the notified body will also consider the clinical interpretation of the preclinical tests relating to medical devices.

2.3   Clinical Evaluation of the Medical Device

The new EU regulation significantly increases the requirements regarding the burden of proof for safety and efficacy by means of a clinical evaluation and, if applicable, the manufacturer's own clinical examination. Under the MDR, this proof of the clinical efficacy of a medical device and patient safety is generally performed by a clinical evaluator by means of a specialist clinical evaluation of medical devices. The clinical evaluation of medical devices is a substantial part of the technical documentation for each medical device. For some medical devices, clinical evaluation will also require a complex clinical trial. Clinical trials will tend to be the exception rather than the rule. In a large number of cases in the future, clinical evaluation will also be performed without clinical trials.

The evaluation includes evidence of the clinical function being claimed, including the effect size and related efficacy in patients. Notified bodies may also consider further claims of the manufacturer in their examination, which may then also be clinically proven. Further, risk-benefit analysis will be required.

Further clinical aspects may include, for example hygiene requirements up to the sterilizability, biocompatibility, impermeability, stability, or measuring the accuracy of a product. Issues such as compatibility with other products, including third-party products, safety, and operating instructions, and training programs for healthcare professionals may be tested as well.

The evaluation is completed by assessment of the acceptability of the benefit/risk ratio. In this final consideration of risk, burden, and benefit, the benefits must clearly outweigh the risks.

Procedure Without Clinical Trial A benefit-risk analysis and the related assessment are based on the collection and review of the data and literature. The clinical evaluation is based mostly on clinical data,[10] which must already exist. Necessary data and literature selection are determined by whether the medical device is novel or comparable to an already existing technology. For existing data, clinical evaluation will be based primarily on data from literature databases recognized by the US Federal Drugs Agency (FDA) and/or BfArM notifications, or data from competing companies.

As required by MEDDEV 2.7/1 rev. 4, the reference product must be technically, biologically, and clinically equivalent to a product in question to such an extent that there are no clinically relevant differences. Moreover, the manufacturers must demonstrate an equivalence by providing the data for the reference product. In the case of class III and implantable devices, the manufacturer can only refer to data of comparable validity if it has the reference devices in its possession and is able to generate the necessary data. As a rule, they need contractually regulated access to all data and test results relating to the reference product. Otherwise, the company will have to submit its own clinical results.

In contrast to the integrated software of a medical device, which is clinically evaluated together with the medical device, stand-alone software[11] is characterized by having only two essential interfaces:

1. Graphical user-product interface (GUI)
2. Product (data) interface.[12]

Unlike pharmaceutical law, medical device law protects not only the patient, but also users and third parties. The scope of protection is broader, which usually requires more effort related to the clinical risk assessment of medical devices.

The results of the clinical evaluation significantly influence risk management. Only the clinical evaluation can support the assumptions of benefit and, thus, the acceptance of the benefit-risk ratio as presented in the risk management file. The clinical evaluation must also support the assumptions in the risk management file related to risk. The results of the post-market clinical follow-up should also be considered in clinical evaluation and risk management.

A clinical evaluation without clinical data may apply to some non-critical products only. The exception shall be justified by a clinical evaluation demonstrating compliance with the essential requirements by means of a technical performance assessment, product testing, and preclinical assessment, considering the features of the body-product interaction, the intended clinical performance, and the manufacturer's information.

---

[10]Regarding the clinical evaluation requirements for medical devices, the MDR is a novelty as it provides that manufacturers must produce a clinical development plan, including a post-market clinical follow-up plan.

[11]See more on medical device software in Lücker (2018), p. 282 ff.

[12]See more on clinical evaluation of stand-alone software in Terhechte (2018), p. 324 ff.

Clinical Trials of Medical Products If sufficient clinical evidence is not available to demonstrate the required clinical safety and performance of a product, clinical trials must be performed. Novel products, implantable medical devices, and class III devices must always undergo a clinical trial. In particular cases, this can be waived if existing clinical data are sufficient. A clinical trial is to be performed without exception on:

- New indication
- New anatomical region of the human body
- Modifications to a product being placed on the market/put into service when these might have a significant effect on safety or efficacy
- Significant extension of application time
- Insufficient literature on effectiveness/efficacy and risks.

Clinical trials on medical products must be planned and performed under EN ISO 14155 "Clinical investigations of medical devices for human subjects - Good clinical practice" and other relevant regulations.[13]

The requirements of EN ISO 14155 are comparable to those of the International Conference on Harmonization of technical requirements for registration of pharmaceuticals for human use—Guideline for Good Clinical Practice (ICH-GCP) for clinical trials with medicinal products. Further provisions to be followed can be found in the German Regulation on Clinical Trials with Medical Devices ("Verordnung über klinische Prüfung von Medizinprodukten", MPKPV) and in the German Medical Devices Safety Plan Regulation ("Medizinproduktesicherheitsplanverordnung", MPSV).

The conduct of clinical trials with medical products and IVD requires approval by the responsible national authorities. Thus, In Germany this requires under MPG sec. 20 (1), approval by the responsible higher federal authorities, such as the Federal Institute for Drugs and Medical Devices (BfArM), or the Federal Institute for Vaccines and Biomedicines (PEI, Paul Ehrlich Institute), and a favorable opinion by a legally approved ethics committee, such as of a public law Chamber of Medicine (Landesärztekammer) or of a university hospital (Universitätsklinikum). Applications must be submitted via the German Institute of Medical Documentation and Information (DIMDI).

2.4   Documentation and Scrutiny Procedures

In addition to the medical or clinical quality of the clinical evaluation, documentation and traceability form part of the complex and demanding reports and plans.

The reporting system includes the results of the clinical evaluation, including any applicable clinical trial protocol documents, investigator's brochure, patient

---

[13]See footnote number 6.

information, and informed consent, as well as additional reports and plans, such as the Clinical Development Plan and the Summary of Safety and Clinical Performance. The MEDDEV 2.7/1 rev. 4 also sets out requirements to be met. By the notified body accordance of the risk management with the clinical evaluation may be checked as well.[14] Furthermore, documents on clinical post-market surveillance are required.

As far as notified bodies are concerned, the supervision of their activities by the competent authorities will be intensified, which may result in increased documentation burden and the growing pressure of self-justification on their side.

This includes the new scrutiny procedure, which focuses on reviewing the submitted clinical evaluation. To meet this task, the notified body will create a CEAR for implantable class III products and active class IIb products intended to administer drugs/medicinal products in the human body based on the clinical evaluation, with exceptions for cases in which recertification or mere modification is being carried out. The CEAR will be submitted to the Medical Device Coordination Group (MDCG), an expert committee of the European Commission, which must decide within 21 days whether it will present a scientific opinion on the CEAR.

If applicable, the panel must provide the scientific opinion on the CEAR within 60 days. The notified body must consider the scientific opinion by making its decision and, if necessary, grant the certificate with restrictions or conditions. If the opinion is not completed by the deadline, the notified body may proceed with the certification with no amendment.

2.5   Post-Market Clinical Follow-Up (PMCF)

Following the placement of a medical device on the market, the EU MDR requires a manufacturer to carry out PMCF continuously to assess the benefits and risks related to the device. The main purpose of PMCF is to identify potential long-term risks that could not be detected within the pre-market clinical evaluation. The results of the follow-up should be considered within the continuous update of the clinical evaluation and risk management. Clinical evaluation is therefore an ongoing process that must be repeatedly documented through regularly reviewed plans and reports by the notified body.

To assess potential safety risks, manufacturers need to gather clinical data continuously. The manufacturer is supposed to create a structured system of long-term follow-up including clinical trial results, registers, controls, or spot checks.

The documentation should comprise essential updates, including but not restricted to additional reports and plans such as a post-market surveillance report, PMCF report, Periodic Safety Update Report (PSUR), and Summary of Safety and Clinical Performance. For specific product groups, manufacturers must submit

---

[14]See footnote number 7.

safety/clinical evaluation/performance summary reports relating to the safety and performance of their products on an annual basis. This applies in particular to class III medical devices and implantable products, which are subject to more stringent clinical requirements for PMCF.

Certain incidents during post-market surveillance and during clinical trials are to be reported to the National Authorities i.e. in Germany the Federal Institute for Drugs and Medical Devices (BfArM) or the Paul Ehrlich Institute (PEI) via the electronic system for vigilance and post-market surveillance (currently DIMDI). 'Incident' means any malfunction or deterioration in the characteristics or performance of a device made available on the market, including use-error because of ergonomic features, as well as any inadequacy in the information supplied by the manufacturer and any undesirable side effect (MDR Art. 2 no. 64).

The EU MDR extends the notified body's powers regarding post-market clinical surveillance. Unannounced audits, spot checks, and product tests strengthen the role of the EU in implementing procedures and help reduce risks resulting from unsafe medical devices.

2.6 Recertification

After first-time certification, the notified body carries out annual reaudits. Moreover, medical devices must be recertified by notified bodies no later than 5 years after the CE mark is awarded. Upon successful completion of the (re)audit, a product is awarded with a renewed Certificate of Conformity. Exceptions are currently being negotiated.

Under the still applicable MDD/AIMDD rules, recertifications by the notified bodies are only possible until the end of the transitional period ending on May 26, 2020. From that date forward, manufacturers must be able to produce an EC certificate under the new MDR for the recertification of medical devices. Thus, manufacturers have the option to apply for an extension of their existing certificates immediately prior to May 26, 2020. These would be valid then until the middle of 2024 at the latest.

Under the MDR, proof of the clinical effectiveness of a medical device and its safety in the course of recertification should be provided by means of a specialist clinical evaluation only in exceptional cases. A waiver of clinical data for clinical evaluation is basically permitted only for non-critical products, such as screws, wedges, plates, and instruments.

The evaluation is completed by assessing the reasonableness of the benefit/risk ratio. In this final balance of risk, burden, and benefit, the benefits must clearly outweigh.

The benefit-risk analysis and assessment is based on the collection and review of data and the literature. The clinical evaluation is based on clinical data from recognized literature databases, FDA and BfArM notifications,[15] personal data from PMS, or data from competing companies.

References

Gemke G (2017) Die neue Medizinprodukteverordnung EU. Ästhetische Dermatologie Kosmetologie 3:15–17

Handorn B (2018) Die Reform des Medizinprodukterechts in Deutschland und der EU. In: Spickhoff A, Kossak V, Kvit N (eds) Aktuelle Fragen des Medizinrechts. MedR Schriftenreihe Medizinrecht. Springer, Berlin, pp 93–101

Lippert H-D (2018) Vorkommnisse und unerwünschte Ereignisse im Recht der Medizinprodukte und der In-vitro-Diagnostika. MedR 36:299–303

Lücker V (2018) Medizinprodukterechtliche Rahmenbedingungenfür E-Health-Produkte im europäischen Wirtschaftsraum. Bundesgesundheitsblatt-Gesundheitsforschung-Gesundheitsschutz 3:278–284

Terhechte A (2018) Medizinische Software/Medical Apps Aufgaben, Anforderungen und Erfahrungen aus Sicht einer Überwachungsbehörde. Bundesgesundheitsblatt – Gesundheitsforschung – Gesundheitsschutz 61:321–327

---

[15]BfArM notifications, FDA reports on problems (Manufacturer and User Facility Device Experience, MAUDE database), clinical trial results being published, e.g., in PubMed (only clinical data from "peer-reviewed" publications can be considered), feedback from the field.

Personalized Medicine: Cutting Edge Developments

Hans P. Zenner and Mijo Božić

Abstract A fundamental problem of classical medicine is that preexisting therapies, such as medications or medical devices are not effective in all affected indviduals. For suitable patients, personalized (or individualized) medicine is thought to remedy this. Classic personalized medicine is based on the molecular dimension using so-called "omics" methods such as genomics, proteomics, metabolomics, or bacteriomics. While these methods involve stratification of the patients with respect to a pre-existing therapy procedure, tailored medicine means that the therapy is tailored specifically for the patient. Both, molecular dimension and tailored medicine paved the way for incorporation of cutting edge medical device technology into personalized medicine. One result of the omics procedures may be the identification of biomarkers. These may allow the use of additional dimensions such as the functional-anatomical dimension. This may play a role in biomarker-specific imaging procedures or in the biomarker-based stratification of medical devices such as pacemakers or cochlear implants. The last but not least dimension to addressed in this paper is the big data dimension which is expected to contribute to further breakthroughs in personalized medicine

1   Introduction

A fundamental problem of classical medicine is that preexisting therapies, such as medications or medical devices are not effective in all affected individuals. For example, efficacy is limited to 38% for antidepressants, 50% for arthritis, 70% for

H. P. Zenner (✉)
HP Zenner Clinical Evaluation, Tübingen, Germany

The University of Tübingen, Tübingen, Germany
e-mail: office@hpzenner.de

M. Božić
The University of Tübingen, Tübingen, Germany
e-mail: Mijo.Bozic@med.uni-tuebingen.de

Alzheimer's disease and only 74% for chemotherapy.[1] For suitable patients, personalized (or individualized) medicine should remedy this.

Modern personalized medicine can be described in several dimensions. These include the molecular dimension using so-called "omics" methods such as genomics, proteomics, metabolomics or bacterioomics. One result of the omics procedures may be the identification of biomarkers. These may allow the use of additional dimensions such as the functional-anatomical dimension. This may play a role in biomarker-specific imaging procedures or in the biomarker-based stratification of medical devices such as pacemakers or cochlear implants.

While the above methods involve stratification of the patients with respect to a pre-existing therapy procedure, tailored medicine means that the therapy is tailored specifically for the patient. The last dimension to address in this paper is the big data dimension.

2 Molecular Dimension

Using high throughput methods like NGS the "omex" methods of the molecular dimension of personalized medicine perform a broad search for a **biomarker as a target.** This should allow a predictive test for the efficacy or toxicity of a preexisting treatment, usually of a drug or a medical device.

An important clinical application is the avoidance of adverse reactions. The drug Vemurafenib is used in malignant melanoma, where it acts as a BRAF inhibitor. However, it can produce spinaliomas as a side effect. With the help of genomics-based identification of RAS mutations prediction of the individual risk for skin carcinomas may be possible.[2]

In the prediction of the therapeutic efficacy, gene variants may play a role in determining changes in drug metabolism, drug delivery, or excretion. Statins serve to reduce the level of cholesterol. However, they are effective only after uptake into the liver. This requires transport proteins. Gene variants of these transport proteins may reduce the transport of statins.[3] Tamoxifen may be used after the surgery of estrogen receptor positive breast carcinomas for the prevention of recurrences and metastases. However, the efficacy of tamoxifen requires enzymatic conversion. Thus, in cases of defects of the genes responsible for the production of these enzymes (10% of European women are affected), the medication may be less effective.[4]

An important target of oncological drugs is tyrosine kinase (TK). The TK antibody trastuzumab (Herceptin) can be used for breast tumors if there is an

---

[1]LEOPOLDINA statement (2014).

[2]Suh et al. (2013).

[3]Canestaro et al. (2012), pp. 158–174.

[4]Goetz (2018), pp. 102–105.

HER2 gene expression disorder.[5] Vemurafenib is used for malignant melanoma (MM) when it is a BRAF-V600E-mutated or BRAF-V600K-mutated MM.

Another important target is the hedgehog pathway, which plays a role in skin cancer basal cell carcinoma. Different proteins and their genes like the hedgehog protein (PCTH1 gene) and smoothened protein (SMO gene) may play a role. Therapeutic approach is a hedgehog protein inhibition e.g. by small molecules.

In particular, the genomics approach partly together with genom editing methods[6] has made a significant contribution to finding an entry into clinical care of **gene therapy.** This includes application to the eye for the retina in Weber amaurosis and the vestibular organ. Phase I/II studies on the treatment of monogenetic hereditary eye diseases by gene therapy are e.g. for x-linked Chronic Granulomatosis, for ADA-SCID ("Adenosine Deaminase Deficient Severe Combined Immunodeficiency") and for Wiskott-Aldrich Syndrome.[7] Cochlea, heart muscle, spinal cord, kidney, cartilage and lung are also expected as target organs.

Molecular personalized medicine my not only play a role for drug application but also for the **indication for medical devices.** Technologically this is also based on targeted gene capture and high-throughput sequencing. An example is the stratification of a few months old totally deafened newborns for early pediatric cochlear implantation (CI). Instead of the usual single-gene diagnostics, high-throughput sequencing can sequence all known genes for deafness (currently about 110, in the future probably around 200) in parallel. If genetic deafness is suspected, the molecular cause can be elucidated in more than 50% of cases.[8] Frequently found of gene disorders may be linked to connexin, KCNQ4 or OTOF. Depending on the affected gene and its functional significance the chances of success for cochlear implantation may also be limited (e.g., for the gene TMPRSS3). Conversely, for a purely sensory and non-neuronal genetic cause, the functional prognosis for cochlear implantation is favorable (e.g., for the GJB2 or MYO7A genes). If it is an early childhood auditory neuropathy, the molecular genetic analysis of the gene OTOF, which encodes the protein otoferlin, can be helpful. Otoferlin is important for the control of an ion channel of hair cells, which in turn plays a role in frequency coding.[9] The mutational analysis of connexin 26 in bilateral high-grade deafness and deafness plays a widespread role.[10] Missing or inadequate expression leads to disruptions in gap junctions of the inner ear.[11] The human genetic analysis of the gene encoding connexin 26 is therefore often used for the indication of early childhood cochlear implantation.[12] In addition, the routine analysis of the DFNA2 gene, which codes for

---

[5]Slamon et al. (1989), pp. 707–712; Slamon et al. (2001), pp. 783–792.

[6]Karimian et al. (2019).

[7]Anliker et al. (2015), pp. 11–12.

[8]Friese et al. (2015), pp. 428–433.

[9]Friese et al. (2015), pp. 428–433.

[10]Brown and Rehm (2012).

[11]Qu et al. (2012), pp. 245–250.

[12]Black et al. (2011), pp. 67–93.

the ion channel KCNQ4 in hair cells, is emerging. KCNQ4 is an important ion channel that plays an indispensable role at the end of the transduction cycle.[13] Its absence can lead to deafness and may thus contribute to the early childhood indication of a cochlear implant.[14] Further, in the future, all known Usher genes can be examined early for changes in to early identify the Usher syndrome at the onset of deafness or early onset of vision problems, especially in childhood.[15] In this way, the indication for a cochlear implant can be made in good time so that a communication ability is maintained despite deafness and blindness.[16]

In the area of inherited heart disease, namely dilated cardiomyopathy, there is evidence for the installation of an ICD (Implantable Cardioverter Defibrillator) in the presence of a mutation in the LMNA gene. Patients with long QT syndrome and mutations in the genes KCNH2 or SCN5A can also receive an ICD early on.[17]

3   Functional-Anatomical Dimension of Individualization

Modern imaging techniques contribute to the anatomical dimension of personalized medicine. Positron emission tomography (PET) and single-photon emission computed tomography (SPECT) provide the ability to display the distribution of a radiolabeled biomarker (tracer) on an individual molecular target in a patient's body three-dimensionally (3D).[18] This applies, for example, to receptors. Using these approaches individualized biomarker-based image localization, for example of tumors, is possible, which may play an important role in individualized radiotherapy.

Equally based on imaging techniques an important patient stratification for medical devices consists in the consideration and use of the individual anatomy. A typical example is cochlear implantology. The consideration of the individual anatomy is technologically based on the high-resolution digital imaging combined with the functional topodiagnostics of modern audiometry allowing mapping the individual frequency card of the patient on the measured total length of the cochlea. Depending on the extent of the functional SNHL the individually distorted area along the cochlea can be calculated. This results in the selection of an electrode length matched to the individual residual hearing function.

---

[13]Gitter et al. (1986), pp. 68–75.

[14]Walter et al. (2011).

[15]Yang et al. (2012), pp. 1165–1183.

[16]Loundon et al. (2003), pp. 216–221.

[17]van Rijsingen et al. (2012), pp. 493–500; Priori et al. (2003), pp. 1866–1874; Priori et al. (2015), pp. 2793–2867.

[18]Schober and Heindel (2010), Bailey et al. (2015), pp. 595–608. Hicks and Hofman (2012), pp. 712–720; Weber (2006), pp. 3282–3292. Mankoff et al. (2014), pp. 525–528; Mankoff et al. (2016), pp. 47–56; Haberkorn et al. (2016), pp. 9–15.

4 Tailored Medicine

Tailored medicine has been available in a conventional manner for many years, when prostheses and implants for skull reconstruction, orthopedic implants or even dental implants and cardio-vascular stents are made individualized. Today, however, tailored medicine has reached new horizons and uses approaches derived from cellular and molecular medicine. In oncology by introducing a so-called chimeric antigen receptor (CAR) into T cells, CAR- expressing T cells are able to specifically bind to and destroy cancer cells in the patient.[19] In addition to the clinical success, however, these therapies sometimes also show severe side effects. This includes e.g. the so-called cytokine release syndrome, in which patients show excessive inflammatory response with high fever, pulmonary edema and organ failure.

T cells can also be obtained as directed virus-specific T cells from donors by leukapheresis and subsequently purified after incubation with the corresponding virus peptides. Furthermore, genomic analyzes may identify neo-antigens and the associated DNA and RNA, which together with an X-point blockade should allow the production of neo-antigenic vaccines. Moreover, patients with severe viral infections, in whom conventional therapies are exhausted and no longer effective, can benefit from the transfer of virus-specific T cells as individualized medicine.[20]

A further approach of tailored medicine includes regenerative medicine that serves to restore the structure and function of destroyed cells, tissues and organs. As a rule, regenerative medicine targets certain cells, be they somatic or stem cells— natural or artificial—on which the restoration of tissues, organs and functions depends. On the one hand, the regenerative therapy is carried out directly in the patient's organism, e.g. genes, cell cycle inhibitors or activators, cell products or components or growth factors can be introduced either systemically or locally. The goal is cell and subsequent tissue regeneration by cell division or by cellular transformation.

Regeneration may include tissue engineering. Clearly individualized tissue engineering is not new. Ex vivo applications may include scaffold cell/tissue hybrids using, for example, a patient's own skin cells, brain cells, peripheral nerve cells, bone cells, cartilage cells, islet cells, sensory cells, heart cells, connective tissue or even tendons[21] to produce e.g. skin, heart valves or even stents. The underlying cell

---

[19]Maus et al. (2014), pp. 2625–2635.

[20]Feucht et al. (2015), pp. 1986–1994. Tischer et al. (2014), p. 336.

[21]Frick et al. (2017), pp. 105–114; Tudorache et al. (2016a), pp. 89–97; Tudorache et al. (2016b), pp. 1228–1238; Flanagan et al. (2007), pp. 3388–3397; Koch et al. (2010), pp. 4731–4739; Weinandy et al. (2012), pp. 1818–1826; Moreira et al. (2014), pp. 741–748; Hess et al. (2010), pp. 3043–3053; Wiegmann et al. (2014), pp. 8123–8133; Dietrich et al. (2015), Fuehner et al. (2012), pp. 763–768; Schmitz and Grabow (2015), pp. 143–162; Soares and Moore (2015), Haude et al. (2016), pp. 2701–2709; Piazza and Cribier (2012).

culture processes may be highly specialized and should enable rapid and qualitatively reproducible production of cells or tissues in large numbers.[22]

The possibility of reprogramming specialized differentiated body cells in personalized iPS cells has led to a significant paradigm shift.[23] On a therapeutic level, there are future opportunities for obtaining patient-derived stem cells for cell therapies and for use in somatic gene therapy. On the other hand, it should also be pointed out that iPS cells are usually derived from adult cells, thus kind of old cells are obtained, which may already be afflicted with mutations, which are then also contained in the iPS cells. It is also unclear to what extent an epigenetic "memory" of the initial cells in iPS cells has an effect on the differentiation of iPS cells.[24] From the ethical and regulatory point of view iPS cells are not subject e.g. to the German Embryo Protection Act (Embryonenschutzgesetz—EschG). They also do not fall under the regulations of the German Stem Cell Act (Stammzellgesetz—StZG). The handling of iPS cells is therefore not regulated by law; although they are pluripotent, as determined in par. 3 no. 1 StZG for stem cells. However, to be covered by the provisions of the StZG, they would have to have been obtained from embryos (par. 3 no. 2 StZG) and would have been pluripotent at the time they were obtained from the embryos (par. 3 no. 1 in conjunction with no. 2 StZG). In fact, the latter requirement is lacking because iPS cells become pluripotent only through reprogramming. They are not taken from embryos in their capacity as pluripotent cells.

5 Big Data

Final dimension is the big data dimension produced by digitized medicine. Increasingly digitized data from an individual patient is available through, for example, imaging, laboratory analysis, or functional examinations. Merging and processing of huge amounts of data enables individualized organ modeling such as mathematical cardiac models. Such a personalized model may be based on a patient's myocardial cell and their ion channels and the interaction of the cells in the heart tissue. Then the whole organ may be considered and finally the organ may be embedded in the circulation and the body.[25]

Such a model may allow determining the individual impact of individual ionic channel variant and relevant drugs on heart electrophysiology, pumping function and the entire cardiovascular system.[26] Other examples are organ models of the ear

---

[22]Lee et al. (2015), pp. 2379–2387; Egami et al. (2014), pp. 96–106; Fraunhofer (2016): http://www.ipa.fraunhofer.de/automatisierte_zellkultur.html.

[23]Hou et al. (2014), pp. 179–188.

[24]acatech POSITION (2017).

[25]acatech POSITION (2017).

[26]acatech POSITION (2017).

which allow subtraction of the middle ear physiology to thereby capture parameters of the inner ear from the eardrum.

Further modeling may include models of tumor growth and influence of tumor growth by cytostatics and ionizing radiation, models of human circulation for anesthesia, models of bones and joints for orthopedics and surgery, models of respiration and gas exchange in the lung, models of sugar metabolism for diabetes patients, and models of electrolyte balance for dialysis patients.[27]

References

acatech (Hrsg.) (2017) Individualisierte Medizin durch Medizintechnik (acatech POSITION). Herbert Utz Verlag, München, 100 p. https://www.acatech.de/wp-content/uploads/2018/03/acatech_POSITION_Indiv-Medizintechnik_WEB.pdf

Anliker B, Renner M, Schweizer M (2015) Therapeutic approaches using genetically modified cells. Bundesgesundheitsblatt Gesundheitsforschung Gesundheitsschutz. 58 (11–12):1274–1280. https://doi.org/10.1007/s00103-015-2245-z

Bailey DL, Pichler BJ, Gückel B, Barthel H, Beer AJ, Bremerich J, Czernin J, Drzezga A, Francius C, Goh V, Hartenbach M, Iida H, Kjaer A, la Fougère C, Ladefoged CN, Law I, Nikolaou K, Quick HH, Sabri O, Schäfer J, Schäfers M, Wehrl HF, Beyer T (2015) Combined PET/MRI: multi-modality multiparametric imaging is here. Mol Imaging Biol 17:595–608. https://doi.org/10.1007/s11307-015-0886-9

Black J, Hickson L, Black B, Perry C (2011) Prognostic indicators in paediatric cochlear implant surgery: a systematic literature review. Cochlear Implants Int 12(2):67–93

Brown KK, Rehm HL (2012) Molecular diagnosis of hearing loss. Curr Protoc Hum Genet Chapter 9:Unit 9.16. https://doi.org/10.1002/0471142905.hg0916s72

Canestaro WJ, Brooks DG, Chaplin D, Choudhry NK, Lawler E, Martell L, Brennan T, Wassman ER (2012) Statin pharmacogenomics: opportunities to improve patient outcomes and healthcare costs with genetic testing. J Pers Med 2:158–174

Dietrich M, Finocchiaro N, Olszweski S, Arens J, Schmitz-Rode T, Sachweh J, Jockenhoevel S, Cornelissen CG (2015) ENDOXY - development of a biomimetic oxygenator-test-device. PLoS One 10(12):e0142961

Egami M, Haraguchi Y, Shimizu T, Yamato M, Okano T (2014) Latest status of the clinical and industrial applications of cell sheet engineering and regenerative medicine. Arch Pharm Res 37 (1):96–106

Feucht J, Opherk K, Lang P, Kayser S, Hartl L, Bethge W, Matthes-Martin S, Bader P, Albert MH, Maecker-Kolhoff B, Greil J, Einsele H, Schlegel PG, Schuster FR, Kremens B, Rossig C, Gruhn B, Handgretinger R, Feuchtinger T (2015) Adoptive T-cell therapy with hexon-specific Th1 cells as a treatment of refractory adenovirus infection after HSCT. Blood 125 (12):1986–1994

Flanagan TC, Cornelissen C, Koch S, Tschoeke B, Sachweh JS, Schmitz-Rode T, Jockenhoevel S (2007) The in vitro development of autologous fibrin-based tissue-engineered heart valves through optimised dynamic conditioning. Biomaterials 28(23):3388–3397

Fraunhofer (2016). http://www.ipa.fraunhofer.de/automatisierte_zellkultur.html

Frick C, Müller M, Wank U, Tropitzsch A, Kramer B, Senn P, Rask-Andersen H, Wiesmüller KH, Löwenheim H (2017) Biofunctionalized peptide-based hydrogels provide permissive scaffolds to attract neurite outgrowth from spiral ganglion neurons. Colloids Surf B Biointerfaces 149:105–114

---

[27]acatech POSITION (2017).

Friese N, Braun K, Müller M, Tropitzsch A (2015) Personalized medicine in otology. The role of genetic diagnostics in patients with hearing impairment. HNO 63(6):428–433

Fuehner T, Kuehn C, Hadem J, Wiesner O, Gottlieb J, Tudorache I, Olsson KM, Greer M, Sommer W, Welte T, Haverich A, Hoeper MM, Warnecke G (2012) Extracorporeal membrane oxygenation in awake patients as bridge to lung transplantation. Am J Respir Crit Care Med 185 (7):763–768

German National Academy of Sciences Leopoldina, Acatech – National Academy of Science and Engineering and Union of the German Academies of Sciences and Humanities (2014) Individualised Medicine – Prerequisites and Consequences Halle (Saale), 104 p. https://www. leopoldina.org/uploads/tx_leopublication/2014_Stellungnahme_IndividualisierteMedizin_EN. pdf

Gitter AH, Zenner HP, Frömter E (1986) Membrane potential and ion channels in isolated outer hair cells of guinea pig cochlea. ORL J Otorhinolaryngol Relat Spec 48(2):68–75

Goetz MP (2018) The development of endoxifen for breast cancer. Clin Adv Hematol Oncol. 16 (2):102–105

Haberkorn U, Eder M, Kopka K, Babich JW, Eisenhut M (2016) New strategies in prostate cancer: Prostate-Specific Membrane Antigen (PSMA) ligands for diagnosis and therapy. Clin Cancer Res 22(1):9–15

Haude M, Ince H, Abizaid A, Toelg R, Lemos PA, von Birgelen C, Christiansen EH, Wijns W, Neumann FJ, Kaiser C, Eeckhout E, Lim ST, Escaned J, Garcia-Garcia HM, Waksman R (2016) Safety and performance of the second-generation drug-eluting absorbable metal scaffold in patients with de-novo coronary artery lesions (BIOSOLVE-II): 6 month results of a prospective, multicentre, non-randomised, first-in-man trial. Eur Heart J 37(35):2701–2709

Hess C, Wiegmann B, Maurer AN, Fischer P, Möller L, Martin U, Hilfiker A, Haverich A, Fischer S (2010) Reduced thrombocyte adhesion to endothelialized poly 4-methyl-1-pentene gas exchange membranes—a first step toward bioartificial lung development. Tissue Eng Part A 16(10):3043–3053

Hicks RJ, Hofman MS (2012) Is there still a role for SPECT-CT in oncology in the PET-CT Era? Nat Rev Clin Oncol 9(12):712–720

Hou J, Yang S, Yang H, Liu Y, Liu Y, Hai Y, Chen Z, Guo Y, Gong Y, Gao WQ, Li Z, He Z (2014) Generation of male differentiated germ cells from various types of stem cells. Reproduction 147 (6):R179–R188

Karimian A, Azizian K, Parsian H, Rafieian S, Shafiei-Irannejad V, Kheyrollah M, Yousefi M, Majidinia M, Yousefi B (2019) CRISPR/Cas9 technology as a potent molecular tool for gene therapy. J Cell Physiol. https://doi.org/10.1002/jcp.27972

Koch S, Flanagan TC, Sachweh JS, Tanios F, Schnoering H, Deichmann T, Ellä V, Kellomäki M, Gronloh N, Gries T, Tolba R, Schmitz-Rode T, Jockenhoevel S (2010) Fibrin-polylactide-based tissue-engineered vascular graft in the arterial circulation. Biomaterials 31(17):4731–4739

Lee DH, Bae CY, Kwon S, Park JK (2015) User-friendly 3D bioassays with cell-containing hydrogel modules: narrowing the gap between microfluidic bioassays and clinical end-users' needs. Lab Chip 15(11):2379–2387

Loundon N, Marlin S, Busquet D, Denoyelle F, Roger G, Renaud F, Garabedian EN (2003) Usher syndrome and cochlear implantation. Otol Neurotol 24(2):216–221

Mankoff DA, Pryma DA, Clark AS (2014) Molecular imaging biomarkers for oncology clinical trials. J Nucl Med 55(4):525–528

Mankoff DA, Edmonds CE, Farwell MD, Pryma DA (2016) Development of companion diagnostics. Semin Nucl Med 46(1):47–56

Maus MV, Grupp SA, Porter DL, June CH (2014) Antibody-modified T cells: CARs take the front seat for hematologic malignancies. Blood 123(17):2625–2635

Moreira R, Gesche VN, Hurtado-Aguilar LG, Schmitz-Rode T, Frese J, Jockenhoevel S, Mela P (2014) TexMi: development of tissue-engineered textile-reinforced mitral valve prosthesis. Tissue Eng Part C Methods 20(9):741–748

Piazza N, Cribier A (2012) Transcatheter aortic valve implantation. Percutaneous Interventional Cardiovascular Medicine. The PCR-EAPCI Textbook

Priori SG, Schwartz PJ, Napolitano C, Bloise R, Ronchetti E, Grillo M, Vicentini A, Spazzolini C, Nastoli J, Bottelli G, Folli R, Cappelletti D (2003) Risk stratification in the long-QT syndrome. N Engl J Med. 348(19):1866–1874

Priori SG, Blomström-Lundqvist C, Mazzanti A, Blom N, Borggrefe M, Camm J, Elliott PM, Fitzsimons D, Hatala R, Hindricks G, Kirchhof P, Kjeldsen K, Kuck KH, Hernandez-Madrid A, Nikolaou N, Norekvål TM, Spaulding C, Van Veldhuisen DJ, ESC Scientific Document Group (2015) ESC Guidelines for the management of patients with ventricular arrhythmias and the prevention of sudden cardiac death: The Task Force for the Management of Patients with Ventricular Arrhythmias and the Prevention of Sudden Cardiac Death of the European Society of Cardiology (ESC). Endorsed by: Association for European Paediatric and Congenital Cardiology (AEPC). Eur Heart J 36(41):2793–2867

Qu Y, Tang W, Zhou B, Ahmad S, Chang Q, Li X, Lin X (2012) Early developmental expression of connexin26 in the cochlea contributes to its dominate functional role in the cochlear gap junctions. Biochem Biophys Res Commun 417(1):245–250

Schmitz KP, Grabow N (2015) Kardiovaskuläre Implantate – trends in der Stenttechnologie. Nova Acta Leopoldina (N.F.) 122(410):S.143–S.162

Schober O, Heindel W (2010) PET-CT hybrid imaging. Thieme, New York, p 296

Slamon DJ, Godolphin W, Jones LA, Holt JA, Wong SG, Keith DE, Levin WJ, Stuart SG, Udove J, Ullrich A et al (1989) Studies of the HER-2/neu proto-oncogene in human breast and ovarian cancer. Science 244(4905):707–712

Slamon DJ, Leyland-Jones B, Shak S, Fuchs H, Paton V, Bajamonde A, Fleming T, Eiermann W, Wolter J, Pegram M, Baselga J, Norton L (2001) Use of chemotherapy plus a monoclonal antibody against HER2 for metastatic breast cancer that overexpresses HER2. N Engl J Med 344 (11):783–792

Soares JS, Moore JE (2015) Biomechanical challenges to polymeric biodegradable stents. Ann Biomed Eng. https://doi.org/10.1007/s10439-015-1477-2

Suh KS, Sarojini S, Youssif M, Nalley K, Milinovikj N, Elloumi F, Russell S, Pecora A, Schecter E, Goy A (2013) Tissue banking bioinformatics electronic medical records: the front-end requirements for personalized medicine. J Oncol 2013:368751. https://doi.org/10.1155/2013/368751

Tischer S, Priesner C, Heuft HG, Goudeva L, Mende W, Barthold M, Klöß S, Arseniev L, Aleksandrova K, Maecker-Kolhoff B, Blasczyk R, Koehl U, Eiz-Vesper B (2014) Rapid generation of clinical-grade antiviral T cells: Selection of suitable T-cell donors and GMP-compliant manufacturing of antiviral T cells. J Transl Med 12:336

Tudorache I, Horke A, Cebotari S, Sarikouch S, Boethig D, Breymann T, Beerbaum P, Bertram H, Westhoff-Bleck M, Theodoridis K, Bobylev D, Cheptanaru E, Ciubotaru A, Haverich A (2016a) Decellularized aortic homografts for aortic valve and aorta ascendens replacement. Eur J Cardiothorac Surg 50(1):89–97

Tudorache I, Theodoridis K, Baraki H, Sarikouch S, Bara C, Meyer T, Höffler K, Hartung D, Hilfiker A, Haverich A, Cebotari S (2016b) Decellularized aortic allografts versus pulmonary autografts for aortic valve replacement in the growing sheep model: haemodynamic and morphological results at 20 months after implantation. Eur J Cardiothorac Surg 49 (4):1228–1238

van Rijsingen IA, Arbustini E, Elliott PM, Mogensen J, Hermans-van Ast JF, Van der Kooi AJ, Van Tintelen JP, van den Berg MP, Pilotto A, Pasotti M, Jenkins S, Rowland C, Aslam U, Wild AA, Perrot A, Pankuweit S, Zwinderman AH, Charron P, Pinto YM (2012) Risk factors for malignant ventricular arrhythmias in lamin a / c mutation carriers a European cohort study. J Am Coll Cardiol 59:493–500

Walter S, Atzmon G, Demerath EW, Garcia ME, Kaplan RC, Kumari M, Lunetta KL, Milaneschi Y, Tanaka T, Tranah GJ, Völker U, Yu L, Arnold A, Benjamin EJ, Biffar R, Buchman AS, Boerwinkle E, Couper D, De Jager PL, Evans DA, Harris TB, Hoffmann W, Hofman A, Karasik D, Kiel DP, Kocher T, Kuningas M, Launer LJ, Lohman KK, Lutsey PL,

Mackenbach J, Marciante K, Psaty BM, Reiman EM, Rotter JI, Seshadri S, Shardell MD, Smith AV, van Duijn C, Walston J, Zillikens MC, Bandinelli S, Baumeister SE, Bennett DA, Ferrucci L, Gudnason V, Kivimaki M, Liu Y, Murabito JM, Newman AB, Tiemeier H, Franceschini N (2011) A genome-wide association study of aging. Neurobiol Aging 32 (11):2109.e15–2109.e28

Weber WA (2006) Positron emission tomography as an imaging biomarker. J Clin Oncol 24 (20):3282–3292

Weinandy S, Rongen L, Schreiber F, Cornelissen C, Flanagan TC, Mahnken A, Gries T, Schmitz-Rode T, Jockenhoevel S (2012) The BioStent: novel concept for a viable stent structure. Tissue Eng Part A 18(17–18):1818–1826

Wiegmann B, Figueiredo C, Gras C, Pflaum M, Schmeckebier S, Korossis S, Haverich A, Blasczyk R (2014) Prevention of rejection of allogeneic endothelial cells in a biohybrid lung by silencing HLA-class I expression. Biomaterials 35(28):8123–8133

Yang J, Wang L, Song H, Sokolov M (2012) Current understanding of usher syndrome type II. Front Biosci (Landmark Ed) 17:1165–1183

Part II
Methodological and Technological Aspects Important for Personalised Medicine

Nanotechnology Approaches for Autologous Stem Cell Manipulation in Personalized Regenerative Medicine

Jelena Ban and Miranda Mladinić Pejatović

Abstract Personalized medicine is a new interdisciplinary approach, focused on the development of patient-specific therapies, which considers the fact that every person has unique genetic and physiological characteristics. Modern bionanotechnological procedures are used in personalized medicine mostly to allow the identification of a person's genetic profile, but also to develop new diagnostic and therapeutic tools and procedures.

Stem cells are a promising source of donor cells in regenerative medicine. In particular, induced pluripotent stem cells (iPSCs) represent a unique opportunity for self-therapies in a personalized approach. They can be derived from the patient's somatic cells, such as fibroblasts, by the reprogramming process and successively differentiated *in vitro* into a required cell type, to be finally transplanted back into the patient. This autologous therapy eliminates the possibility of rejection and is ethically acceptable because it does not require manipulation of human embryos. Several disease-specific human iPSCs have been produced since their discovery, but also some serious problems have emerged. In this chapter we will describe how nanotechnological approaches, such as the use of nanoparticles (NPs) and nanostructured materials, can contribute in overcoming these obstacles to allow clinical applications of iPSCs.

1 Introduction

Personalized medicine is a new trend in medicine: it tries to overcome the traditional approach of giving the same standard therapy to every patient suffering from a particular disease. The effort is made to optimize for each patient the specific, personalized therapy, based on its unique genetic and physiological characteristics. This approach is dependent on interdisciplinary modern biotechnological procedures that allow the identification of a person's genetic profile, the integration of which

J. Ban (✉) · M. Mladinić Pejatović
Department of Biotechnology, Centre for High-Throughput Technologies, University of Rijeka, Rijeka, Croatia
e-mail: jelena.ban@biotech.uniri.hr

© Springer Nature Switzerland AG 2019
N. Bodiroga-Vukobrat et al. (eds.), *Personalized Medicine in Healthcare Systems*, Europeanization and Globalization 5, https://doi.org/10.1007/978-3-030-16465-2_4

with clinical symptoms and biomarker changes, leads to the prediction of disease susceptibility, diagnosis and response to specific therapies. Many of the novel biotechnological approaches are based on the use of nanoparticles (NPs), that contribute to the development of new diagnostic tools and procedures that are rapid, less invasive, more reliable and informative. Also, NPs can contribute to the development of these new, more reliable, drug delivery systems that are targeted to particular body cells, with simple administration, increased safety and efficacy. In this chapter we will describe the new nanotechnology-based approaches for autologous stem cell manipulation in personalized regenerative medicine.

2   Discovery of the Induced Pluripotent Stem Cells (iPSCs)

Stem cells represent a promising source of donor cells in regenerative medicine. By definition, "stem cells" are cells that can proliferate almost indefinitely while their differentiation is suppressed (so-called *self-renewal*), although not permanently. Actually, the main property that distinguishes different stem cell types is their differentiation potential, or *potency*.

Embryonic stem cells (ESCs), isolated from the preimplantation embryos, are "naïve" pluripotent cells (Nichols and Smith 2009). They are capable of differentiating into all somatic cell lines, except for the extraembryonic tissues, and this property makes them an ideal source for cell therapy. On the other hand, adult or somatic stem cells have limited source and restricted differentiation potential. They are multipotent, thus capable to differentiate into the cell lines related or specific to the tissue from which they are derived. For instance, neural stem cells (NSCs) in the neurogenic subventricular zone (SVZ) of the brain, generate the three major lineages of the nervous system: neurons, astrocytes, and oligodendrocytes.

Induced pluripotent stem cells (iPSCs) are the specific stem cells which represent an excellent opportunity in personalized medicine. iPSCs are derived from the adult somatic cells such as fibroblasts, by the *in vitro* reprogramming process that returns them to a pluripotent state. Subsequently, the reprogrammed cells are differentiated *in vitro* into the specific cell type and ultimately transplanted back to the patient, at the site of interest (lesioned or degenerated tissue). The possibility to repair or replace lost or degenerated cells from the patient-derived cell source eliminates the possibility of transplant rejection. This approach is also ethically acceptable because it does not require the use of human embryonic tissues or cells, one of the major concerns in ESC applications.

The properties and differences between the stem cell types mentioned above are summarized in Fig. 1.

In 2006, Takahashi and Yamanaka discovered that by forcing the expression of four genes responsible for the pluripotency, namely Oct3/4, Sox2, c-Myc, and Klf4 (thereafter named *Yamanaka factors*), it is possible to revert terminally differentiated mouse fibroblasts into pluripotent stem cells, capable of differentiating *ex-novo* into cell types of all three germ layers including neural tissues, cartilage, and columnar

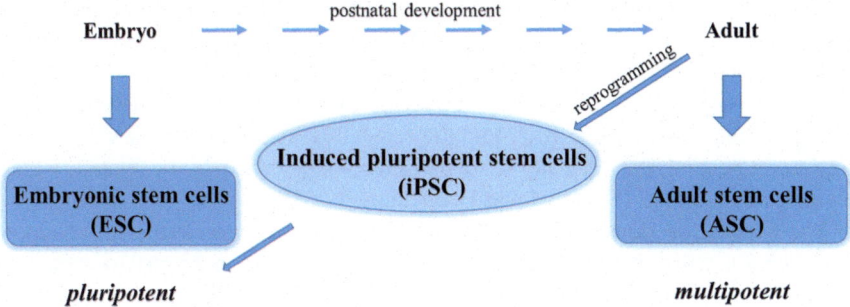

Fig. 1 Scheme explaining the unique properties of iPSCs: pluripotent as ESCs, but derived from somatic cells by reprogramming

epithelium (Takahashi and Yamanaka 2006). Based on the same approach, human iPSCs were generated already one year later (Takahashi et al. 2007; Yu et al. 2007). Those discoveries opened the possibility to develop iPSCs-based procedures to treat the damage of the tissues with limited or reduced regenerative potential, central nervous system (CNS) in particular.

Several patient-specific human iPSCs have been produced since then and have been shown to be useful to alleviate the symptoms in the animal disease models. For instance, patient-specific human iPSCs have been shown to alleviate the symptoms of Parkinson's disease in the rat models (Wernig et al. 2008). As the animal models cannot reproduce all pathophysiological characteristics of human diseases, the direct application of the iPSCs in clinical trials is still remote. However, the iPSCs are intensively used in the basic research studies to facilitate drug discovery (Liu et al. 2015; Stadtfeld and Hochedlinger 2010). These basic studies discovered the difficulties in the iPSCs production and potential risks of their use in clinics.

3   Problems in iPSCs Production and Risks in Their Clinical Application

Patient-specific iPSCs retain mutations of the gene(s) of interest, but also the epigenetic features of that specific individual (Jang et al. 2014). This very important aspect that should be exhaustively studied in the future and should be considered in clinical applications of iPSCs. Several other difficulties have emerged in the iPSCs research. One is related to the iPSCs production method based on the retro- or lentiviral vectors that integrate into the host genome and thus can cause insertion mutations and genomic aberrance (Liu et al. 2015). Moreover, residual activity or reactivation of the viral transgenes, because of their incomplete silencing, interferes with the developmental potential of the iPSC-derived somatic cells and frequently leads to tumorigenesis (Stadtfeld and Hochedlinger 2010). Therefore, because of the safety risks, the use of the retro- or lentiviral vectors is unacceptable in clinical applications. Nevertheless, the alternative nonviral-based methods to produce iPSCs have been developed. For example, the DNA or RNA electroporation or polymer/lipid-based nanoparticles (NPs) are used to deliver *Yamanaka factors* into somatic cells. Although those procedures are safer than virus-based methods, their reprogramming efficiency is 1000-fold lower: ~0.001% against 0.1–1% of retroviral vectors. In general, the difficulty to reprogram somatic cells may be related to their "epigenetic memory" (Stadtfeld and Hochedlinger 2010).

The over-expression of *Yamanaka factors* is not, however, sufficient to reprogram somatic cells into the pluripotent stem cells. It is also necessary to overcome several transcriptional and epigenetic barriers that normally block the pluripotency induction in somatic cells. Thus, upon the exogenous introduction of Yamanaka factors, the spontaneous down-regulation of somatic markers should occur, followed by the activation of early pluripotency markers such as SSEA-1, alkaline phosphatase, and Fbxo15. Also, the endogenous expression by DNA demethylation of pluripotency genes Nanog and Oct4 must become independent from the *Yamanaka factors*. This process may continue for several cell-division cycles accompanied by chromatin modifications, such as DNA and histone methylation, hopefully leading to the ESC-like state (Stadtfeld and Hochedlinger 2010).

During the reprograming procedure, only a subset of fibroblasts (or other somatic cells used to derive iPSCs) succeed in becoming pluripotent. This explains the slow kinetics of reprogramming that displays a broad distribution spanning from 2 to 18 weeks necessary for iPSCs generation (Hanna et al. 2010).

In recent years efforts have been made to enhance both the efficiency and the kinetics of the iPSCs reprogramming process. The expression of Nanog gene has been shown to be a better pluripotency marker for the selection of reprogrammed cells, than initially used Fbxo15 (Okita et al. 2007). Thus, the over-expression of Nanog, as well as other pluripotency associated transcriptional regulators such as Tbx3 and Sall4, has been shown to accelerate reprogramming (Hanna et al. 2010). The gene expression analysis demonstrated that even after prolonged culture, iPSCs retain their specific expression signature, irrespective of their origin or method of derivation. Therefore, iPSCs represent a very special subtype of pluripotent cells, and should not be considered identical to ESC. It has been often wrongly stated that iPSCs are "nearly identical" to their embryonic-derived counterparts (Chin et al. 2009). But iPSCs show lower levels of expression of several pluripotency genes and differences in DNA methylation, when compared to ESCs. For instance, the incomplete demethylation of the Oct4 promoter has been observed in iPSCs, suggesting their incomplete reprogramming. Indeed, upon the injection into blastocyst, iPSCs failed to produce postnatal chimeras (Takahashi and Yamanaka 2006). In contrast, ESCs form a chimeric mouse (i.e. composed of both host and injected cells) when injected into a mouse blastocyst, and this is one of the assays performed to demonstrate cell pluripotency.

Another critical point in iPSCs application is their difficult differentiation into functional cell types of different tissues. Current differentiation protocols allow iPSCs differentiation into the limited number of somatic cell types. In particular, neural differentiation of human iPSCs is much less efficient and shows increased variability if compared to human ESCs. The heterogeneity in differentiation potential has been observed for a number of human iPSCs lines, independently of the reprogramming protocol used and regardless of the presence or absence of reprogramming transgenes in their genome (Hu et al. 2010). Therefore, in addition to the removal of reprogramming transgenes, techniques that increase iPSCs differentiation efficiency and potency are required.

The integration of nanotechnology could provide significant improvements to iPSC reprogramming protocols and allow overcoming the problems related to differentiation.

4 Nanotechnology in iPSCs Reprogramming

In recent years nanotechnology approaches have been extensively studied and successfully applied in different biomedical fields, mostly used as vehicle for targeted drug delivery and bioimaging (Jang et al. 2014; Liu et al. 2015). The implementations of NPs in stem cell protocols are still rare (Jang et al. 2014), although they could be important in developing new methods and protocols for iPSCs reprogramming and clinical applications.

NPs are small particles (with a diameter between 10 and 200 nm), characterized by a high surface area and inert nature, which makes them ideal carriers for different drugs or molecules. NPs are small enough to enter the cell by endocytosis and thus could be employed to deliver reprogramming genes into patient-specific iPSCs. The polymer-based gene carriers do not integrate into the host cell genome, like viral vectors, so the approach is clinically acceptable.

For instance, iPSCs have been derived from human umbilical cord mesenchymal stem cells by (co)delivering Yamanaka factors through plasmid-encapsulated calcium phosphate NPs (Cao et al. 2013).

Different NPs (polymeric, lipidic, metal) can have additional beneficial activity in iPSCs reprograming protocols. Thus, poly (D,L-lactide-co-glycolide) (PLGA), poly (lactic acid) (PLA), poly (ε-caprolactone), gelatin and chitosan not only can bring DNA or RNA into the cell, but can also protect it from nucleases (Liu et al. 2015).

Positively charged mesoporous silica nanoparticles (MSNs) coupled with plasmids carrying hepatocyte nuclear factor 3β (HNF3β) gene have been shown to improve and accelerate differentiation of treated iPSCs into hepatocyte-like cells (Chen et al. 2013). Moreover, fluorescein isothiocynate (FITC)-conjugated MSNs have been efficiently internalized by iPSCs without causing cytotoxicity, providing additional advantage for cell labeling and tracking of transplanted cells.

Liposomal magnetofection is another virus-free method that could be used for iPSCs reprogramming. When incubated with liposomes, DNA plasmids encoding for reprogramming factors self-assemble into DNA lipoplexes that are further combined with CombiMag NPs (Park et al. 2012). Such complexes are added to the cultured fibroblasts and a magnetic field is applied to transfect the cells. Compared to the other virus-free methods, the magnetofection is more rapid and efficient, with reprogramming efficiency comparable to retroviral vector systems. This method has been used for the transient expression of reprogramming genes employing biodegradable cationic polyethylenimine (PEI)-coated superparamagnetic NPs (Lee et al. 2011).

In addition to plasmid-based gene delivery, several different approaches—including RNA and protein delivery—have been established to prevent genomic integration. Recent studies have revealed the role of certain microRNAs (miRNAs) as essential supporters of genes that regulate pluripotency, being highly expressed in ESCs and required for iPSCs generation. ESC-specific miRNAs encapsulated in the acid sensitive polyketal (PK3-miRNAs) NPs have been used to generate iPSC-like cells from bone marrow-derived hematopoietic cells in just 8 days (Sohn et al. 2013).

Next, delivery of recombinant cell-penetrating reprogramming proteins has been developed to avoid genetic modification of the host cells (Zhou et al. 2009). Cationic amphiphiles have been used for the protein delivery-based reprogramming (Khan et al. 2013). Chitosan NPs have been recently used for encapsulation of OCT4 protein, strongly stabilizing its DNA-binding activity (Tammam et al. 2016). Although protein-based reprogramming is safer and faster, it remains mostly inefficient.

Finally, the idea of creating iPSCs solely with chemicals, without the need of reprogramming transcription factors, emerged (Stadtfeld and Hochedlinger 2010). Screenings for chemical compounds that induce pluripotency have been performed and certain number of molecules that significantly increase reprogramming efficiency were identified. Indeed, mouse iPSC have been generated by the treatment containing a combination of seven small-molecule compounds, completely replacing Yamanaka factors (Hou et al. 2013). The generation of human chemically induced PSCs represents the next challenge in chemical reprogramming (De Los Angeles and Daley 2013).

Further investigations are required to understand the role of small molecules and verify if they could be sufficient to substitute reprogramming factors.

5 Large Scale Amplification of Stem Cells Using Nanosubstrates

Nanomaterials have been implemented in stem cell research with two main purposes: for large scale amplification of stem cells and for improved differentiation efficiency. Efforts have been mainly directed toward the production of neuronal cells, important for the development of therapies to treat neurodegenerative diseases.

The fundamentally important prerequisite for cell transplantation procedures is a large number of cells that should be efficiently maintained in their stem, i.e. undifferentiated state during amplification process (Kingham and Oreffo 2013). Therefore, proliferation-promoting nanosubstrates for large-scale expansion of stem cells have been investigated. For instance, 3D nanofibrillar and nanoporous matrix made by electrospinning of polyamide fibers enhance proliferation of mouse ESCs by upregulating self-renewal marker Nanog through phosphoinositide 3-kinase (PI3K) signaling pathway (Nur-E-Kamal et al. 2006).

Several different materials have been developed and tested for their positive effect on stem cell proliferation and self-renewal, including carbon-based materials (carbon nanotubes, graphene and its derivatives) (Chen et al. 2012a), synthetic/ organic polymeric nanofibers, and others (for review, please see Chueng et al. 2016; Wei and Ma 2008).

In the current protocols for the maintenance and amplification of both murine and human ESCs and iPSCs, murine embryonic fibroblasts (MEFs) are used as feeder cell layer (Jozefczuk et al. 2012). Their presence carries a risk of contamination and immune reaction after transplantation. Therefore, nanostructured materials have been investigated to obtain feeder-free culture systems. Recently it has been shown that ESCs can be successfully maintained in the absence of feeder cells on polyacrylamide substrates that mimic the topography and stiffness of MEFs (López-Fagundo et al. 2016).

6 Directing iPSCs Differentiation Using Nanosubstrates

The efficient differentiation of stem cells remains a crucial requisite for their therapeutic applications, as the presence of residual undifferentiated cells is related to the possibility of teratoma formation.

As effective neuronal differentiation of iPSCs is one of the most challenging issues in regenerative medicine, biocompatible nanomaterials are extensively studied to allow neural differentiation of iPSCs (Riehemann et al. 2009). Beside their chemical sensitivity, cells perceive the physical and topographical features of their environment, fact that is often neglected (Kingham and Oreffo 2013). Therefore, the combination of both chemical and mechanical cues should be employed for the efficient *in vitro* iPSCs differentiation.

Nanomaterials to be tested as modulators of stem cell fate can be coated to the surfaces on which the iPSCs grow, in the form of nanofibers or nanowires. This nanostructuring can be performed using different physical or chemical procedures or by self-assembly. The designed nanomaterials can be of different stiffness, charge, conductivity, roughness, chemical reactivity and biocompatibility (Riehemann et al. 2009). All these characteristics can substantially influence the cell viability, growth and differentiation. The main idea is to mimic as much as possible the natural extracellular matrix (ECM) of the tissue of interest, for instance brain tissue. Collagen-like nanofibers can enhance cell-matrix interactions (Wei and Ma 2008) and soft substrates can promote ESCs self-renewal (Chowdhury et al. 2010), showing the substrate-induced specific cell response.

Electrically conductive materials such as carbon nanotubes in combination with electrospun poly L-lactic acid (PLLA) nanofibers (Kabiri et al. 2012) or silk (Chen et al. 2012b) have been shown to increase neuronal differentiation, expressing neural markers such as nestin and β-tubulin III (Chen et al. 2012b). In addition to enhanced cell adhesion and differentiation, nanomaterials can electrically activate neuronal cells or stimulate and direct the growth of their neurites. Thus, graphene substrates have been able to electrically stimulate human NSCs (Chueng et al. 2016; Park et al. 2011), while electrospun biodegradable poly(ε-caprolactone) (PCL) nanofibers have enhanced the neuronal differentiation of mouse ESCs, and have also promoted and guided neurite outgrowth (Xie et al. 2009).

Nanomaterials have been shown also to be useful for the directed differentiation of iPSCs not only toward neuronal, but also toward specific glial cell lines. Thus, PCL–graphene oxide (GO) hybrid scaffold, composed of nanofibers that mimic oligodendrocyte ECM, have shown tenfold increase in oligodendrocyte differentiation (Chueng et al. 2016). Indeed, oligodendrocytes are important for the re-myelination process in CNS regeneration studies.

7 Conclusion

The application of nanomaterials has influenced modern biomedicine, especially toward the development of personalized treatments. Induced pluripotent stem cells (iPSCs) could be considered a revolutionary discovery for personalized medicine: they offer a unique possibility for autologous stem cell transplantation. Despite the unresolved limitations and problems regarding their clinical application, iPSCs represent a valid tool for understanding molecular mechanisms underlying a disease and for patient-specific drug screening. They remain a promising instrument for the development of future personalized autologous cell treatments. For those treatments to become possible, it is of fundamental importance to resolve technical problems related to the controlled production and differentiation of iPSCs. Nanotechnology holds a great potential for improving iPSCs technology, and many studies, described in this chapter, represent an important progress in safer and more efficient approaches for autologous stem cell-based therapeutics. Nanostructured materials, able to mimic the extracellular environment in its fundamental physical characteristics, represent a valuable tool for controlled manipulation of stem cells, less risky than genetic or chemical biotechnology tools.

Although further progress is required, the concept of drug-encapsulated NPs and iPSCs nanotechnology is, and will be even more in the future, an important contribution to personalized medicine.

References

Cao X, Deng W, Qu R, Yu Q, Li J, Yang Y, Cao Y, Gao X, Xu X, Yu J (2013) Non-viral co-delivery of the four Yamanaka factors for generation of human induced pluripotent stem cells via calcium phosphate nanocomposite particles. Adv Funct Mater 23:5403–5411. https://doi.org/10.1002/adfm.201203646

Chen G-Y, Pang DW-P, Hwang S-M, Tuan H-Y, Hu Y-C (2012a) A graphene-based platform for induced pluripotent stem cells culture and differentiation. Biomaterials 33:418–427. https://doi.org/10.1016/j.biomaterials.2011.09.071

Chen C-S, Soni S, Le C, Biasca M, Farr E, Chen EY-T, Chin W-C (2012b) Human stem cell neuronal differentiation on silk-carbon nanotube composite. Nanoscale Res Lett 7:126. https://doi.org/10.1186/1556-276X-7-126

Chen W, Tsai P-H, Hung Y, Chiou S-H, Mou C-Y (2013) Nonviral cell labeling and differentiation agent for induced pluripotent stem cells based on mesoporous silica nanoparticles. ACS Nano 7:8423–8440. https://doi.org/10.1021/nn401418n

Chin MH, Mason MJ, Xie W, Volinia S, Singer M, Peterson C, Ambartsumyan G, Aimiuwu O, Richter L, Zhang J, Khvorostov I, Ott V, Grunstein M, Lavon N, Benvenisty N, Croce CM, Clark AT, Baxter T, Pyle AD, Teitell MA, Pelegrini M, Plath K, Lowry WE (2009) Induced pluripotent stem cells and embryonic stem cells are distinguished by gene expression signatures. Cell Stem Cell 5:111–123. https://doi.org/10.1016/j.stem.2009.06.008

Chowdhury F, Li Y, Poh Y-C, Yokohama-Tamaki T, Wang N, Tanaka TS (2010) Soft substrates promote homogeneous self-renewal of embryonic stem cells via downregulating cell-matrix tractions. PLoS One 5:e15655. https://doi.org/10.1371/journal.pone.0015655

Chueng S-TD, Yang L, Zhang Y, Lee K-B (2016) Multidimensional nanomaterials for the control of stem cell fate. Nano Converg 3:23. https://doi.org/10.1186/s40580-016-0083-9

De Los Angeles A, Daley GQ (2013) A chemical logic for reprogramming to pluripotency. Cell Res 23:1337–1338. https://doi.org/10.1038/cr.2013.119

Hanna JH, Saha K, Jaenisch R (2010) Somatic cell reprogramming and transitions between pluripotent states: facts, hypotheses, unresolved issues. Cell 143:508–525. https://doi.org/10.1016/j.cell.2010.10.008

Hou P, Li Y, Zhang X, Liu C, Guan J, Li H, Zhao T, Ye J, Yang W, Liu K, Ge J, Xu J, Zhang Q, Zhao Y, Deng H (2013) Pluripotent stem cells induced from mouse somatic cells by small-molecule compounds. Science 341:651–654. https://doi.org/10.1126/science.1239278

Hu B-Y, Weick JP, Yu J, Ma L-X, Zhang X-Q, Thomson JA, Zhang S-C (2010) Neural differentiation of human induced pluripotent stem cells follows developmental principles but with variable potency. Proc Natl Acad Sci USA 107:4335–4340. https://doi.org/10.1073/pnas.0910012107

Jang S-F, Liu W-H, Song W-S, Chiang K-L, Ma H-I, Kao C-L, Chen M-T (2014) Nanomedicine-based neuroprotective strategies in patient specific-iPSC and personalized medicine. Int J Mol Sci 15:3904–3925. https://doi.org/10.3390/ijms15033904

Jozefczuk J, Drews K, Adjaye J (2012) Preparation of mouse embryonic fibroblast cells suitable for culturing human embryonic and induced pluripotent stem cells. J Vis Exp JoVE. https://doi.org/10.3791/3854

Kabiri M, Soleimani M, Shabani I, Futrega K, Ghaemi N, Ahvaz HH, Elahi E, Doran MR (2012) Neural differentiation of mouse embryonic stem cells on conductive nanofiber scaffolds. Biotechnol Lett 34:1357–1365. https://doi.org/10.1007/s10529-012-0889-4

Khan M, Narayanan K, Lu H, Choo Y, Du C, Wiradharma N, Yang Y-Y, Wan ACA (2013) Delivery of reprogramming factors into fibroblasts for generation of non-genetic induced pluripotent stem cells using a cationic bolaamphiphile as a non-viral vector. Biomaterials 34:5336–5343. https://doi.org/10.1016/j.biomaterials.2013.03.072

Kingham E, Oreffo ROC (2013) Embryonic and induced pluripotent stem cells: understanding, creating, and exploiting the nano-niche for regenerative medicine. ACS Nano 7:1867–1881. https://doi.org/10.1021/nn3037094

Lee CH, Kim J-H, Lee HJ, Jeon K, Lim H, Choi H y, Lee E-R, Park SH, Park J-Y, Hong S, Kim S, Cho S-G (2011) The generation of iPS cells using non-viral magnetic nanoparticle based transfection. Biomaterials 32:6683–6691. https://doi.org/10.1016/j.biomaterials.2011.05.070

Liu W-H, Chang Y-L, Lo W-L, Li H-Y, Hsiao C-W, Peng C-H, Chiou S-H, Ma H-I, Chen S-J (2015) Human induced pluripotent stem cell and nanotechnology-based therapeutics. Cell Transplant 24:2185–2195. https://doi.org/10.3727/096368914X685113

López-Fagundo C, Livi LL, Ramchal T, Darling EM, Hoffman-Kim D (2016) A biomimetic synthetic feeder layer supports the proliferation and self-renewal of mouse embryonic stem cells. Acta Biomater 39:55–64. https://doi.org/10.1016/j.actbio.2016.04.047

Nichols J, Smith A (2009) Naive and primed pluripotent states. Cell Stem Cell 4:487–492. https://doi.org/10.1016/j.stem.2009.05.015

Nur-E-Kamal A, Ahmed I, Kamal J, Schindler M, Meiners S (2006) Three-dimensional nanofibrillar surfaces promote self-renewal in mouse embryonic stem cells. Stem Cells Dayt Ohio 24:426–433. https://doi.org/10.1634/stemcells.2005-0170

Okita K, Ichisaka T, Yamanaka S (2007) Generation of germline-competent induced pluripotent stem cells. Nature 448:313–317. https://doi.org/10.1038/nature05934

Park SY, Park J, Sim SH, Sung MG, Kim KS, Hong BH, Hong S (2011) Enhanced differentiation of human neural stem cells into neurons on graphene. Adv Mater 23:H263–H267. https://doi.org/10.1002/adma.201101503

Park HY, Noh EH, Chung H-M, Kang M-J, Kim EY, Park SP (2012) Efficient generation of virus-free iPS cells using liposomal magnetofection. PLoS One 7:e45812. https://doi.org/10.1371/journal.pone.0045812

Riehemann K, Schneider SW, Luger TA, Godin B, Ferrari M, Fuchs H (2009) Nanomedicine – challenge and perspectives. Angew Chem Int Ed Engl 48:872–897. https://doi.org/10.1002/anie.200802585

Sohn Y-D, Somasuntharam I, Che P-L, Jayswal R, Murthy N, Davis ME, Yoon Y (2013) Induction of pluripotency in bone marrow mononuclear cells via polyketal nanoparticle-mediated delivery of mature microRNAs. Biomaterials 34:4235–4241. https://doi.org/10.1016/j.biomaterials.2013.02.005

Stadtfeld M, Hochedlinger K (2010) Induced pluripotency: history, mechanisms, and applications. Genes Dev 24:2239–2263. https://doi.org/10.1101/gad.1963910

Takahashi K, Yamanaka S (2006) Induction of pluripotent stem cells from mouse embryonic and adult fibroblast cultures by defined factors. Cell 126:663–676. https://doi.org/10.1016/j.cell.2006.07.024

Takahashi K, Tanabe K, Ohnuki M, Narita M, Ichisaka T, Tomoda K, Yamanaka S (2007) Induction of pluripotent stem cells from adult human fibroblasts by defined factors. Cell 131:861–872. https://doi.org/10.1016/j.cell.2007.11.019

Tammam S, Malak P, Correa D, Rothfuss O, Azzazy HME, Lamprecht A, Schulze-Osthoff K (2016) Nuclear delivery of recombinant OCT4 by chitosan nanoparticles for transgene-free generation of protein-induced pluripotent stem cells. Oncotarget 7:37728–37739. https://doi.org/10.18632/oncotarget.9276

Wei G, Ma PX (2008) Nanostructured biomaterials for regeneration. Adv Funct Mater 18:3566–3582. https://doi.org/10.1002/adfm.200800662

Wernig M, Zhao J-P, Pruszak J, Hedlund E, Fu D, Soldner F, Broccoli V, Constantine-Paton M, Isacson O, Jaenisch R (2008) Neurons derived from reprogrammed fibroblasts functionally integrate into the fetal brain and improve symptoms of rats with Parkinson's disease. Proc Natl Acad Sci 105:5856–5861. https://doi.org/10.1073/pnas.0801677105

Xie J, Willerth SM, Li X, Macewan MR, Rader A, Sakiyama-Elbert SE, Xia Y (2009) The differentiation of embryonic stem cells seeded on electrospun nanofibers into neural lineages. Biomaterials 30:354–362. https://doi.org/10.1016/j.biomaterials.2008.09.046

Yu J, Vodyanik MA, Smuga-Otto K, Antosiewicz-Bourget J, Frane JL, Tian S, Nie J, Jonsdottir GA, Ruotti V, Stewart R, Slukvin II, Thomson JA (2007) Induced pluripotent stem cell lines derived from human somatic cells. Science 318:1917–1920. https://doi.org/10.1126/science.1151526

Zhou H, Wu S, Joo JY, Zhu S, Han DW, Lin T, Trauger S, Bien G, Yao S, Zhu Y, Siuzdak G, Schöler HR, Duan L, Ding S (2009) Generation of induced pluripotent stem cells using recombinant proteins. Cell Stem Cell 4:381–384. https://doi.org/10.1016/j.stem.2009.04.005

Patient–Doctor Relationship: Data Protection in the Context of Personalised Medicine

Nada Bodiroga Vukobrat and Hana Horak

> *In order to be able to offer each of our patients a course of treatment perfectly adapted to his illness and to himself, we try to obtain a complete, objective idea of his case; we gather together in a file of his own all the information we have about him.*
>
> *(Sournia 1962)*

Abstract This chapter provides an overview of the most important issues surrounding the data protection in the context of personalised medicine. It analyses the existing regulatory framework at EU level and interpretations provided in the relevant judgments of the Court of Justice of the EU. It proceeds with identifying the potential gaps and challenges, especially concerning the application of eHealth system.

1 Introduction

Health and healthcare issues in patient-doctor relations currently represent one of the most challenging issues in the economy of knowledge, where highly sophisticated services like health care services play an important role in the society based on digital economy.

Author "**Nada Bodiroga Vukobrat**" is deceased at the time of publication.

H. Horak (✉)
Department of Law, University of Zagreb, Faculty of Economics and Business, Zagreb, Croatia
e-mail: hhorak@efzg.hr

© Springer Nature Switzerland AG 2019
N. Bodiroga-Vukobrat et al. (eds.), *Personalized Medicine in Healthcare Systems*, Europeanization and Globalization 5, https://doi.org/10.1007/978-3-030-16465-2_5

55

Data protection in the digital world and processing on a daily basis a number of information is one of the most important achievements that must be taken into account when considering regulatory framework in micro and macro surrounding. Data and data protection are crucial and the most important issues in the process of connecting and consolidating information. Data protection reform is one of the cornerstones of the Digital Single Market. The third Pillar of the Digital Market Strategy "Maximising the Growth and Potential of the Digital Economy" is dedicated, among other, to emerging legal issues and obstacles in establishing European Data Economy. Today at the European Union level we are facing numerous obstacles and "grey zones" which enable disclosure of data. The idea on supranational and national level is to remove all existing obstacles and establish an interoperable system within the EU Member States until 2020. Special focus among others must be in bringing down the legal barriers and protecting the most vulnerable groups, for example patients.

In-depth analyses and studies have shown that the main discrepancies are between different regulatory frameworks of the Member States and within the different stages of implementation of EU legal actions on national level. It is important to recognise that today without interdisciplinary approach in personalised medicine we cannot reach all benefits that new technologies can provide.

One of the most important issues within the eHealth, besides data protection, is the standardisation of the Electronic Health Record systems and laws.

The advancement of new technologies in medical, biomedical and technical sciences, especially nanotechnology; coupled with an ever-growing development of science in general faces various legal obstacles. Legislation is by its very nature rigid, and development of specific relations and occurrences precedes any legislative activity. Legislation reacts to these developments, often restrictively. The personal data protection in the patient-doctor relationship is a perfect example, which has stirred a lot of doctrinal debates. The scientific discoveries of modern, highly technicised medicine bring many advantages. However, they also elevate the risk of experimentation and manipulation in relation to personality rights. Patients represent a particularly vulnerable group when this data is used and processed as "Big Data". Patient-doctor relationship is faced with new challenges. Informatisation of health care systems is not always accompanied by sufficient education of doctors and other medical staff, especially in post-socialist European countries. The systems are interconnected, and the sensitive information that should, by its nature, be available only to doctors involved in the treatment is accessible to broader categories of persons.

The main question is whether legal actions are fast enough to ensure the flow of personal data in real time and whether protection of personal data in a digital economy will become a reality that ensures safety.

2 Patient–Doctor Relationship: Personal Data Protection in the Context of Personalised Medicine

The nature of the patient-doctor relationship has always been a topic of discussions. Siegler identifies three stages in the development of this relationship as "the age of paternalism", "the age of autonomy" and "the age of responsiveness" (Siegler 1985). Balint's famous claim: "the doctor is the drug" (Balint 1957) is often invoked in daily communication.

Some of the earlier research of this topic (Robin DiMatteo 1979; Robin DiMatteo et al. 1980; Bensing 1991) detected and concentrated on the three possible dimensions of the patient-doctor relationship:

1. a traditional technical dimension which involves technical knowledge, skill, etc.;
2. a non-traditional dimension which involves concern for psychosocial aspect of care;
3. an "art" dimension which involves the interpersonal behaviour of the physician, his or her personal qualities and in general how the care is delivered.

As the Kerr White Report (1988) rightly questions, faced with existing evidence, why has medicine been "so slow in acting to implement and increase this knowledge" and keeps behaving as if it did not exist? However, they also elevate the risk of experimentation and manipulation in relation to personality rights. Patients represent a particularly vulnerable group when this data is used and processed as "Big Data" (Bodiroga-Vukobrat and Horak 2016).

3 Personal Data Protection in the Decisions of the Court of Justice of the EU

Under Article 8(1) of the Charter of fundamental rights of the EU, everyone has the right to the protection of personal data concerning him or her. This fundamental right is, however, not absolute.[1] In its judgment of 8 April 2014 in the case *Digital Rights Ireland*,[2] the Court of Justice of the EU (hereinafter: CJEU) reminds that the personal data protection arising out of explicit obligation prescribed in Article 8 (1) of the Charter is pertinent for the protection of private life stipulated in Article 7 thereof.

Patient-doctor relationship is faced with new challenges. The question here is about the protection of sensitive personal data. Informatisation of health care

---

[1]Joined cases C-92/09 (Volker und Markus Schecke GbR) and C-93/09 (Hartmut Eifert) v Land Hessen, EU:C:2010:662.

[2]Joined cases C-293/12 and C-594/12, Digital Rights Ireland Ltd v Minister for Communications, Marine and Natural Resources and Others and Kärntner Landesregierung and Others, EU: C:2014:238.

systems poses new problems, especially in connection with appropriate education of doctors and other medical staff. Post-socialist European countries seem to experience similar problems here. The systems are interconnected, and the sensitive information that should, by its nature, be available only to doctors involved in the treatment is accessible to broader categories of persons. This is the source of numerous issues. Medical data which is subject to professional secrecy shall not be revealed to any third person, but only to the patient, persons who take care of him or her and who need such information to provide the care of adequate quality, unless otherwise provided in special regulations, laws or statutes. To quote Giovanni Buttarelli, the European Data Protection Supervisor, "Data protection is a democratic value and it can reinforce democracy in a digital age. We should value our privacy because the control of our own personal information is essential to our sense of self." (Buttarelli 2015, 2016).

The CJEU, as the highest authority for interpretation of EU law, which is binding for national courts in the Member States is also dealing in its judgments with personal data protection (especially health data) and they are enormously important for national courts.

The CJEU judgement in case *Schrems*[3] of 6 October 2015 re-establishes the importance of the fundamental right to personal data protection, as provided in the Charter of fundamental rights of the EU, including in cases where such data is exported outside the EU (European Commission 2015).

Under the settled case law, the protection of the fundamental right to private life guaranteed under Article 7 of the Charter of fundamental rights of the EU requires that derogations and limitation in relation to personal data protection must apply only in so far as is strictly necessary. In its judgement of 11 December 2014 in the case *Ryneš*[4] the CJEU reiterates that "since the provisions of Directive 95/46, in so far as they govern the processing of personal data liable to infringe fundamental freedoms, in particular the right to privacy, must necessarily be interpreted in the light of the fundamental rights set out in the Charter, the exception provided for in the second indent of Article 3(2) of that directive must be narrowly construed".[5]

In the General Court's judgment of 3 December 2015 regarding the application for compensation of damages allegedly suffered by the applicant following the dissemination on the Parliament's website of certain personal (health) data relating to the applicant, it is concluded that 'data concerning health' must be given a wide interpretation so as to include information concerning all aspects, both physical and mental, of the health of an individual.[6]

In the coming years, information technologies will continue to develop. In the close future, huge amount of stored data will be momentarily accessible. In fact, any

---

[3]Case C-362/14, Maximillian Schrems v Data Protection Commissioner, EU:C:2015:650.
[4]Case C-212/13, František Ryneš v Úřad pro ochranu osobních údajů, EU:C:2014:2428.
[5]Case C-212/13, Ryneš, para. 29.
[6]Case T-343/13, CN v European Parliament, T-343/13, EU:C:2015:926.

document or media content will be retrievable, from any device at current convenience (personal computer, mobile phone, TV, etc.).

On the one hand, the technology which is becoming all the more accessible will spread social and economic advantages, but it will also create big databases, especially involving sensible data.

One of the main assumptions regarding the acceptance of IT technologies in the field of health protection is the question of trust placed by the patients in the security of personal data, but also the patient-doctor confidentiality; i.e. how are the sensitive data concerning health protected as personal data.

The complexity of this question is obvious, so is the need for legal and technical adjustments of national legislations to the EU *acquis* by Member States, as well as candidate countries.

Apart from the classical patient-doctor relation, the protection of personal data in personalised medicine is one of the main issues (especially when it comes to genome sequencing, diagnosis which concerns not only the patient, but also his or her family members and predictive tests).

4 Regulatory Framework

Notwithstanding the regulatory framework of the European Union, the fundamental rights in relation with the data protection are contained in a number of acts, primarily the European Convention on Human Rights (Article 8; restrictions laid down in Article 8.2), Council of Europe Convention for the Protection of Individuals with Regard to Automatic Processing of Personal Data (Article 10); as well as Convention for the Protection of Human Rights and Dignity of Human Being with Regard to the Application of Biology and Medicine. Numerous cases of the European Court of Human Rights likewise point to the need for a clearer definition of the right of a person to seek deletion of his personal data from public registers.[7]

On the EU level, provisions are contained in TFEU, Article 16 and the provisions of the Charter of Fundamental Rights,[8] which is applicable when Member States implement EU law.

Guarantees regarding the right to the integrity of the person are provided in Article 3 of the Charter of Fundamental Rights of the EU. The right to respect for physical and mental integrity is especially elaborated for the fields of medicine and biology. The following principles that must be respected:

---

[7]S. and Marper v. the United Kingdom, ECHR App. No. 30562/04 and 30566/04, Judgment of 4.12.2008; see more in Horak and Bodiroga-Vukobrat (2017).

[8]Treaty of Lisbon amending the Treaty on the European Union and the Treaty Establishing the European Community, OJ C 306 of 17 December 2007, for the latest consolidated version thereof see Consolidated versions of the Treaty on European Union and the Treaty on the Functioning of the European Union, OJ C 202, 7.6.2016; Charter of Fundamental Rights of the European Union, OJ C 202, 7.6.2016.

- free and informed consent of the person concerned,
- the prohibition of eugenic practices,
- the prohibition of making the human body and its parts a source of financial gain,
- the prohibition of the reproductive cloning of human beings.

These principles reflect the determination of Member States to supervise and limit potential bio-medical manipulations and understanding of the growing number of questions which are yet to arise with further development of medical sciences and biotechnologies.

Article 35 of the Charter guarantees the right of access to preventive health care and the right to benefit from medical treatment under the conditions established by national laws and practices. The principle enshrined in this provision has its origins in Article 168 of the Treaty on the Functioning of the European Union (TFEU), Article 11 of the European Social Charter and Article 13 of the Revised European Social Charter. Accessibility and non-discrimination are crucial for realisation of the right to health.

Secondary EU legislation regarding processing of health-related personal data is of great importance in connection with the protection of fundamental rights and freedoms of natural persons. In the EU Member States, the regulation on data protection was based on Data Protection Directive 95/46 and Directive on privacy and electronic communications 2002/58.[9]

Administrative barriers, as well as different approach in application of implementing instruments by national authorities represented the main obstacles and "grey zones", which hindered the efficiency of these instruments. It seems that to achieve the goals of the EU Digital Single Market, directive was not the right legal instrument for the harmonisation. So, a regulation with its direct applicability is probably a better instrument for harmonisation of national rules. Adoption of a directly applicable data protection regulation was necessary to resolve the practical issues regarding diverse interpretation and transposition of certain provisions of the Directive in national legislations.

Regulation (EU) 2016/679 of the European Parliament and of the Council of 27 April 2016 on the protection of natural persons with regard to the processing of personal data and on the free movement of such data, and repealing Directive 95/46/EC (General Data Protection Regulation, GDPR)[10] took effect on 24 May 2016, it shall apply from 25 May 2018. Regulation reinforces the subject's right to access

---

[9]Directive 95/46/EC of the European Parliament and of the Council of 24 October 1995 on the protection of individuals with regard to the processing of personal data and on the free movement of such data, OJ L 281, 23.11.1995, p. 31 and Directive 2002/58/EC of the European Parliament and of the Council of 12 July 2002 concerning the processing of personal data and the protection of privacy in the electronic communications sector (Directive on privacy and electronic communications), OJ L 201, 31.7.2002, p. 37.

[10]Regulation (EU) 2016/679 of the European Parliament and of the Council of 27 April 2016 on the protection of natural persons with regard to the processing of personal data and on the free movement of such data, and repealing Directive 95/46/EC (General Data Protection Regulation), OJ L 119, 4.5.2016.

personal data, change and delete them, including the "right to be forgotten". The principles of data protection should apply to any information concerning an identified or identifiable natural person. Personal data that have undergone pseudonymisation, which could be attributed to a natural person by the use of additional information, should be considered to be information on an identifiable natural person.

Consent is the cornerstone for data protection and especially health data. It should be given by a clear affirmative act establishing a freely given, specific, informed and unambiguous indication of the data subject's agreement to the processing of personal data relating to him or her, such as by a written statement, including by electronic means, or an oral statement. This could include ticking a box when visiting an internet website, choosing technical settings for information society services or another statement or conduct which clearly indicates in this context the data subject's acceptance of the proposed processing of his or her personal data. Silence, pre-ticked boxes or inactivity should not therefore constitute consent. Consent should cover all processing activities carried out for the same purpose or purposes. When the processing has multiple purposes, consent should be given for all of them. If the data subject's consent is to be given following a request by electronic means, the request must be clear, concise and not unnecessarily disruptive to the use of the service for which it is provided.

In the GDPR, health data are considered as sensitive data. They include, for example, a hospital processing its patients' genetic and health data (within hospital information system). Also health data are defined as concerning vulnerable data subjects and there is need for Data Protection Impact Assessment (DPIA). DPIA process is used for building and demonstrating compliance. Or, as explained in the guidelines: "DPIA is required when a processing operation is likely to result in a high risk to the rights and freedoms of natural person" (Article 35(1) GDPR, see III. B.a of DPIA Guidelines).[11] As an example, the processing of health data on a large scale is considered as likely to result in a high risk, and requires a DPIA; then, it is the responsibility of the data controller to assess the risks to the rights and freedoms of data subjects and to identify the measures envisaged to reduce those risks to an acceptable level and to demonstrate compliance with the GDPR (Article 35 (7) GDPR, see III.C.c of DPIA Guidelines).

An example could be the storage of personal data on laptop computers with appropriate technical and organisational security measures (effective full disk encryption, robust key management, appropriate access control, secured backups, etc.) in addition to existing policies (notice, consent, right of access, right to object, etc.).[12]

---

[11] Article 29 Data Protection Working Party (2017) Guidelines on Data Protection Impact Assessment (DPIA) and determining whether processing is "likely to result in a high risk" for the purposes of Regulation 2016/679 (wp248rev.01) (hereinafter: DPIA Guidelines), adopted on 4 April 2017, http://ec.europa.eu/newsroom/article29/item-detail.cfm?item_id=611236, pp. 10–18.

[12] DPIA Guidelines (2017), pp. 10–18.

Non-compliance with DPIA requirements can lead to fines imposed by the competent authority in Member State

5 Interconnection of Health Systems

Health systems and health policies across the EU are becoming more interconnected than ever in the past. There are several key factors:

1. Movement of patients and professionals facilitated by rulings of the CJEU, for example in cases *Kohll, Decker, Vanbraekel, Smits and Peerbooms, Müller-Fauré and Van Riet, Watts, Elchinov*,[13] and a number of other.
2. Common public expectations across Europe and dissemination of new medical technologies and techniques through information technology.

When developing the regulatory framework in this field, it is important to define the term eHealth. Under the definitions from the eHealth Action plan (European Commission 2012), eHealth is the use of ICT in health products, services and processes combined with organisational change in healthcare systems and new skills. eHealth covers the interaction between patients and health-service providers, institution to institution transmission of data, or peer to peer communication between patients and/or health professionals.

It can be concluded that on the European level data protection is one of the main features regarding patients' rights and for the interoperability and cooperation between eHealth systems.

It should be borne in mind that eHealth is among other elements consisted mainly of cross-border eHealth services. This brings along a number of legal and ethical issues and not only in terms of the data sharing, but also in terms of identity certification, professional accreditation, liability for shared care and other issues yet to be identified. The legal and regulatory issues include also administrative regulations such as those of reimbursement, and—in the context of cross border care—the mutual recognition of professional qualifications and the complex issue of entitlement to care.

---

[13]Cases C-158/96, Raymond Kohll v Union des caisses de maladie, EU:C:1998:171; C-120/95, Nicolas Decker v Caisse de maladie des employés privés, EU:C:1998:167; C-368/98, Abdon Vanbraekel and Others v Alliance nationale des mutualités chrétiennes (ANMC), EU:C:2001:400; C-157/99, B.S.M. Geraets-Smits v Stichting Ziekenfonds VGZ and H.T.M. Peerbooms v Stichting CZ Groep Zorgverzekeringen, EU:C:2001:404; C-385/99, V.G. Müller-Fauré v Onderlinge Waarborgmaatschappij OZ Zorgverzekeringen UA and E.E.M. van Riet v Onderlinge Waarborgmaatschappij ZAO Zorgverzekeringen, EU:C:2003:270; C-372/04, The Queen, on the application of Yvonne Watts v Bedford Primary Care Trust and Secretary of State for Health, EU:C:2006:325; C-173/09, Georgi Ivanov Elchinov v Natsionalna zdravnoosiguritelna kasa, EU:C:2010:581.

The idea on supranational and national level is to remove all existing obstacles and establish interoperable system within EU Member States until 2020. Special focus among others must be in bringing down the legal barriers. In-depth analyses and studies[14] have shown that the main discrepancies are between different regulatory frameworks of the Member States and within the different stages of implementation of EU legal actions on national level.[15]

Within the eHealth Network one of the most important issues, besides data protection, is the standardisation of the European Health Record systems and laws. Of course, this action should be taken in line with other, mainly non-legal aspects of the Electronic Health Record (EHR) (European Commission 2008).

6 European Health Record and Data Protection Issues

European Health Record[16] (EHR) has been recognised as a one of the cornerstones of the Health revolution (Rynning 2007).

Like every revolutionary achievement it has its positive and negative sides. EHR *in favorem* of patients facilitates sharing of information, cross-border, between all interested stakeholders.[17] On the other hand data protection issues have been

---

[14]Mileu Ltd. – Time.lex (2014) Overview of the national laws on electronic health records in the EU Member States and their interaction with the provision of cross-border eHealth services. Final report and recommendations, http://ec.europa.eu/health/ehealth/docs/laws_report_recommendations_en. pdf.

[15]Commission Implementing Decision of 22 December 2011 providing the rules for the establishment, the management and the functioning of the network of national responsible authorities on eHealth (2011/890/EU), OJ L 344, 28.12.2011.

[16]The 2008 Commission recommendation on cross-border interoperability of electronic health record systems defines the terms 'electronic health record' as "a comprehensive medical record or similar documentation of the past and present physical and mental state of health of an individual in electronic form, and providing for ready availability of these data for medical treatment and other closely related purposes";

'electronic health record system' as a system for recording, retrieving and manipulating information in electronic health records; and

'patient's summary, emergency data set, medication record' as subsets of electronic health records that contain information for a particular application and particular purpose of use, such as an unscheduled care event or ePrescription. See European Commission (2008).

[17]Under the 2008 Commission recommendation on cross-border interoperability of electronic health record systems stakeholders include patients, defined as any natural person who receives or wishes to receive health care in a Member State; and

health professionals, a term which includes a doctor of medicine or a nurse responsible for general care or a dental practitioner or a midwife or a pharmacist within the meaning of Directive 2005/36/EC of the European Parliament and of the Council of 7 September 2005 on the recognition of professional qualifications or another professional exercising activities in the healthcare sector which are restricted to a regulated profession as defined in Article 3(1)(a) of Directive 2005/36/EC; and medical service too. See more about stakeholders in Hartlev (2007, p. 167).

recognised as one of the major challenges in the implementation process of eHealth (European Commission 2012, p. 8).

Personal data concerning health should include all data pertaining to the health status of a data subject which reveal information relating to the past, current or future physical or mental health status of the data subject. This includes information about the natural person collected in the course of the registration for, or the provision of, health care services as referred to in Directive 2011/24/EU to that natural person; a number, symbol or particular assigned to a natural person to uniquely identify the natural person for health purposes. Also information derived from the testing or examination of a body part or bodily substance, including from genetic data and biological samples. Furthermore, any information on, for example, a disease, disability, disease risk, medical history, clinical treatment or the physiological or biomedical state of the data subject independent of its source, for example from a physician or other health professional, a hospital, a medical device or an *in vitro* diagnostic test.

Despite the opportunities and benefits, major barriers hamper the wider uptake of eHealth. Some of detected barriers are lack of awareness and confidence in eHealth solutions among patients, citizens and healthcare professionals, lack of interoperability between eHealth solutions. Limited large-scale evidence of the cost-effectiveness of eHealth tools and services. Partial legal clarity for health and wellbeing mobile applications and the lack of transparency regarding the utilisation of data collected by such applications. Inadequate or fragmented legal frameworks including the lack of reimbursement schemes for eHealth services. From the economic aspects high start-up costs involved in setting up eHealth systems. Regional differences in accessing ICT services, limited access in deprived areas.

7   Conclusion

Sensitive data permeate all aspects of health care. Finding and applying the appropriate regulatory framework for their processing and storage is an on-going task for regulators at the EU and national levels. However, the technology of data processing and storage has been evolving faster than the accompanying regulation. This issue becomes even more pronounced with the development of personalised medicine and its implementation in the clinical practice. Personalised medicine approach relies heavily on the personal data processing and predictive genetic testing. This implies a constant search for new regulatory solutions, which will allow for a balancing of conflicting interests involved. It remains to be seen how the EU regulator and courts will respond to these new challenges *in favorem* patients—EU citizens.

References

Balint M (1957) The doctor, his patient and the illness. Pitman Medical, London

Bensing J (1991) Doctor-patient communication and the quality of care. Soc Sci Med 32 (11):1301–1310

Bodiroga-Vukobrat N, Horak H (2016) Challenges of personalised medicine: socio-legal disputes and possible solutions. In: Bodiroga-Vukobrat N, Rukavina D, Pavelić K, Sander GG (eds) Personalized medicine: a new medical and social challenge. Springer, pp 31–53

Buttarelli G (2015) Data protection as a bulwark for digital democracy. Keynote speech at the 6th International e-Democracy 2015 Conference on Citizen rights in the world of the new computing paradigms, Athens, December 10, 2015. https://edps.europa.eu/sites/edp/files/publication/15-12-10_edemocracy_en.pdf

Buttarelli G (2016) A New Year, a new chapter, New Europe, January 4, 2016. https://www.neweurope.eu/article/a-new-year-a-new-chapter/

European Commission (2008) Commission recommendation on cross-border interoperability of electronic health record systems (C(2008) 3282), OJ L 190, 18.7.2008

European Commission (2012) eHealth Action Plan 2012–2020: innovative care for the 21st century. https://ec.europa.eu/digital-single-market/en/news/ehealth-action-plan-2012-2020-innovative-healthcare-21st-century

European Commission (2015) Communication from the Commission to the European Parliament and the Council on the Transfer of Personal Data from the EU to the United States of America under Directive 95/46/EC following the Judgment by the Court of Justice in Case C-362/14 (Schrems), COM(2015) 566 final, Bruxelles, 6.11.2015

Hartlev M (2007) Striking the right balance: patient's rights and opposing interests with regard to health information. Eur J Health Law 14(2):165–176

Horak H, Bodiroga-Vukobrat N (2017) Can we protect data in digital economy: reality or myth? 4th International Multidisciplinary Scientific Conference on Social Sciences and Arts SGEM 2017, Conference Proceedings, pp 381–386

Robin DiMatteo M (1979) A social-psychological analysis of physician-patient rapport: toward a science of the art of medicine. J Soc Issues 35(1):12–33

Robin DiMatteo M, Taranta A, Friedman HS, Prince LM (1980) Predicting patient satisfaction from physicians' nonverbal communication skills. Med Care 18(4):376–387

Rynning E (2007) Public trust and privacy in shared electronic health record. Eur J Health Law 14(2):105–112

Siegler M (1985) The progression of medicine: from physician paternalism to patient autonomy to bureaucratic parsimony. Arch Intern Med 145(4):713–715

Sournia J-C (1962) Logique et morale du diagnostic. Gallimard, Paris

White Kerr L (1988) The task of medicine. Dialogue at Wickenburg, The Henry J. Kaiser Family Foundation, Menlo Park

High-Throughput Analytics in the Function of Personalized Medicine

Djuro Josić, Tamara Martinović, Urh Černigoj, Jana Vidič, and Krešimir Pavelić

Abstract Rapid and highly reliable analysis of patient sample is the first premise and simultaneously the first step in the direction of right diagnosis and personalized treatment. However, this fact is frequently neglected. Despite this situation, almost unnoticed activities in this field started 55 years ago with the concept of a biosensor for fast monitoring of blood glucose and diabetes control, and blood glucose determination is still the driving force for optimization of these kinds of high-throughput analytical devices. The development of devices for high-throughput analytical methods for fast and accurate analysis started with the separation of molecules based on different size, charge and hydrophobicity and with the introduction of chromatographic and electrophoretic methods into clinical laboratories. The next step was their optimization towards the strategy for a fast analysis and miniaturization. One of the main tools for such kinds of analyses are different optimized supports and instruments for signal amplification that are used in such devices. The discovery and use of miniaturized chromatographic and electrophoretic systems based on monolithic supports was briefly discussed here. Their development in the direction of further miniaturization towards biosensors and nanobiosensors was also presented.

D. Josić (✉)
Department of Biotechnology, Centre for High-Throughput Technologies, University of Rijeka, Rijeka, Croatia

Department of Medicine, Warren Alpert Medical School, Brown University, Providence, RI, USA

Juraj Dobrila University of Pula, Faculty of Medicine, Pula, Croatia
e-mail: djosic@biotech.uniri.hr

T. Martinović
Department of Biotechnology, Centre for High-Throughput Technologies, University of Rijeka, Rijeka, Croatia

U. Černigoj · J. Vidič
BIA Separations d.o.o., Ajdovščina, Slovenia

K. Pavelić
Juraj Dobrila University of Pula, Faculty of Medicine, Pula, Croatia

Department of Biotechnology, Centre for High-Throughput Technologies, University of Rijeka, Rijeka, Croatia

1   Introduction

One of the most important problems in life sciences, especially in medicine, is to understand how to prevent illness and to provide the answer to the question why people get sick. Scientists are intensively working on discovering which of the existing technologies and new knowledge should be used to achieve optimal healthcare. One of these technologies is the all-embracing -omics technology or high-tech analytical technology, which provides insight into the global profile of each individual. We are certainly entering a period of a new medical paradigm in which we will be obtaining increasingly relevant biomarkers, be it genetic, protein, glycoprotein, but also other biopolymers or even small molecules. This will enable an insight into all or most of the relevant "players" important for a particular process. Such technologies, especially those related to the new generation of imaging methods (such as the mass spectrometry imaging), will allow personalized access to patients. On the one hand, technology and, on the other, the development of personalized medicine, allow for an answer to the question why different diseases develop and behave differently in different people.

Individual treatment today represents a new attitude that replaces the *one-treat-ment-fits-all* approach. This is a new trend in medicine because there are more and more scientific discoveries suggesting that some people need different treatment because their illness is different, although it belongs to the same group of disease. Such new treatments are adapted to the patient's genetic makeup, epigenetics, life history, lifestyle, age, gender, and all other factors that may affect the development of the disease.

In 2007, the European Science Foundation[1] documented five main directions of future medicine development. These are high-tech technologies (-omics) in biomedicine, personalized medicine, regenerative medicine, stem cell therapy, and nanomedicine. The latter, just as the -omics methods, is essential for the development of personalized medicine. There are also challenges facing medicine such as globalization of society, new or changed infectious diseases, climate change, and demographic changes with aging populations. On the other hand, technological prerequisites for personalized medicine are based on the fact that biological systems are complex and that the current reductionist paradigm is not sufficient for new challenges in medicine. Biological functions, namely, are generated by a combined activity of multiple molecular and cellular functions. Live organisms behave non-linearly, meaning that one input can produce several outputs. There is a need for a new paradigm in medicine based on the development of personalized medicine and the application of high-throughput analytical methods, as well as the fact that there are still serious "holes" in our knowledge about disease causes, the presence of (relevant) markers or stages and factors influencing the effectiveness of possible medicines. There is also a need to increase the cost of health care and to minimize the

---

[1]ESF Forward Look (2012).

disproportion between a larger amount of money being spent on health care and the lack of positive results that citizens receive in return.

In one of the scenarios, we can imagine that the patient's sample (blood, urine, tissue, and other body fluids) will be "attacked" with all available high-throughput analyses, namely proteomic, genomic, transcriptional, metabolic, glycomic, lipidomic etc. A huge number of data will be aligned with the existing database of clinically relevant facts. From this information, it is possible to obtain the patient's prognostic index and an individual molecular profile, but also the knowledge of biochemical pathways, early stage detection, and prediction of disease outcomes. This approach can be used to overcome the current neglect of the concept of continuity. Namely, the concept of continuity implies a whole range of conditions—from total health through hidden malaise to dysfunction and serious illness. Today's medicine mainly deals with illnesses and neglects the so-called grey zone in which it is much easier to intervene and prevent the disease.[2]

Perhaps high-throughput technologies have gone far beyond genomics. The amount of data that these methods produce today is measured with a tera- and petabyte scale. Meaningful interpretation of such data poses a great challenge. It depends on the interpretation of clinical, genomic, and experimental information using prior knowledge of genotype-phenotype relationships accumulated in numerous databases available to the public. The task of translational medicine is to apply sophisticated approaches that coordinate various analytical steps involved in extracting useful knowledge, *i.e.* clinical and experimental data. Numerous challenges are: management of high-throughput data, their transfer, storage, and access control, computer infrastructure, as well as analysis of large scale multidimensional data for extraction for clinical purposes.

We can say that modern high-throughput analytical methods have helped to develop systems biology and a holistic approach to precision modeling of complex diseases. Such technologies require expensive and sophisticated equipment and are only available to certain, rich, and well-equipped environments and states. Therefore, some people may find that personalized medicine creates an even greater gap between wealthy and poorer countries when it comes to health care. This is also evident from the increased discrepancy in our ability to generate and analyze the so-called massive data. The reason for the complicated transition from conventional to personalized medicine was elaborated in our book.[3] There are some other important reasons: generating cost-effective high-speed data, interdisciplinary education and teams, storing huge amounts of data and processing them, integrating and interpreting data, and individual and global relevance.

---

[2]Bošnjak et al. (2008).
[3]Pavelić et al. (2016).

2   Development and Introduction of High-Throughput Methods in Analytical Biotechnology and Clinical Chemistry

Separation of molecules based on different size and charge is the fundament of all biochemical analyses. This ability was first described in 1912 by J.J. Thompson, and further developed in the next years by his followers in Great Britain and Northern America. In the early years of development, mass spectrometry (MS) was mainly a method for the analysis of small molecules. Despite years of intense development, this method was for over 70 years elusive for large macromolecules as proteins, polysaccharides and nucleic acids. A breakthrough was achieved at the end of the last century, and about 10 years later, according to The Royal Swedish Academy of Sciences, "The Nobel Prize" in Chemistry in 2002 was to be shared between scientists working on two very important methods of chemical analysis applied to biological macromolecules: mass spectrometry and nuclear magnetic resonance (NMR). Laureates John B. Fenn, Koichi Tanaka (MS) and Kurt Wüthrich (NMR) have pioneered the successful application of their techniques to biological macro-molecules.[4] Both MS and NMR are now column-bearing methods in clinical chemistry and diagnostics, and they were the basis for further development of all -omics methods.[5] About 40 years after J.J. Thompson, in 1948, the Swedish Chemist Arne Tiselius was awarded with the Nobel Prize for his work on electrophoretic and chromatographic separation of molecules.[6] By use of these methods separation of large biomolecules was possible, but very complicated and time consuming. His work was continued by his followers, mostly by Porath[7] and Hjertén.[8] The impor-tance of these investigations was early recognized, yielding first commercial prod-ucts for separation of large molecules based on cross-linked polysaccharides (so-called "Sephadex" and "Sepharose"). It was an important, but compared to MS and NMR, not a very spectacular development of these two methods, and no one of the followers, not even Porath, was awarded with the Nobel Prize, at least, not until now. However, no biochemical or clinical laboratory can function without the application of these basic methods (or their modifications). Their further develop-ment in both scaling up and scaling down directions, as well as in the direction of reaching very short analysis time and high-throughput analysis of a thousand of samples, is still not completed. It took a lot of time and optimization before the application of liquid chromatography and electrophoresis could be performed in a high-throughput manner. Problems such as instrumentation, unspecific interactions and insufficient diffusion of biomolecules that could lead to their denaturation and

---

[4]The Royal Swedish Academy of Sciences (2002).
[5]Josić and Andjelković (2016).
[6]Nobel Lectures Chemistry (1964).
[7]Axén and Porath (1966).
[8]Johansson et al. (1975).

irreversible adsorption to the separation medium had to first be solved,[9] before further development towards a high-throughput analysis strategy could be pursued. A huge challenge was the miniaturization of the separation device, especially if chromatographic separation was performed. One of the main problems was sample distribution at the inlet and the low stability of miniaturized columns packed with bulk supports that tend to build channels during in-flow chromatographic separation. We tried to overcome it by use of cellulose membranes that were modified with different ligands, however, with limited success. The main reason was low mechanical stability of such devices.[10] At the end of the 1980s, Švec and Tennikova and Hjertén's group developed polymer based monolithic supports, firstly called "macroporous membranes"[11] or "continuous polymer beds".[12] They are porous structures that contain channels and that bear chemically active groups on their surface. In the next step, these groups can be chemically modified with different ligands. Both groups demonstrated their successful use for chromatographic separations of standard proteins. During following years, glycidyl-polymethacrylate monoliths have been accepted as a more practical solution,[13] and they are now in broad use for separation of biopolymers[14] immobilization of enzymes and fast, in-flow enzymatic conversions.[15] Early experiments also demonstrated that both scaling down and scaling up of these separation units was possible almost without limitations, however, only if a proper distribution of the mobile phase at the inlet of the separation unit was provided. This problem was early recognized and solved at both small and large scale,[16,17] and first attempts towards miniaturization and construction of chips based on monoliths were performed already in the late 1990s of the last century[18] (see Fig. 1). It was also demonstrated that miniaturized monolithic columns with immobilized antibodies could be applied for fast detection of potential (glyco)protein biomarkers, such as some membrane proteins as markers for malignant transformation or inter-alpha trypsin inhibitor as a marker for sepsis and septic shock in trauma patients.[19] Low pressure drop during the separation process on monoliths and their compact structure enabled so-called "conjoint chromatography" by combining columns with different ligands. Such miniaturized units enabled multidimensional separations, such as a combination of affinity chromatography (that enabled removal of some proteins with high abundance, *e.g.* serum albumin)

---

[9]Unger (1979) and Chang et al. (1976).

[10]Josić et al. (1989).

[11]Tennikova et al. (1990).

[12]Hjertén et al. (1989).

[13]Josić et al. (1992).

[14]Josić et al. (1992) and Svec and Huber (2006).

[15]Svec and Huber (2006) and Josić and Buchacher (2001).

[16]Štrancar et al. (1996).

[17]Podgornik et al. (2000).

[18]Wu et al. (2001) and Švec and Lv (2015).

[19]Ručević et al. (2006) and Opal et al. (2007).

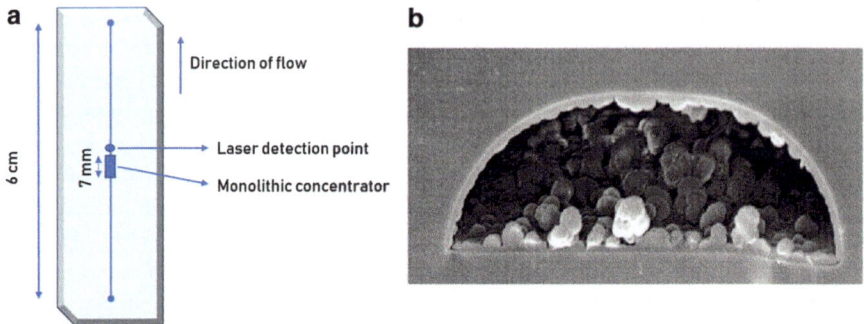

Fig. 1 Construction and composition of a microfluidic chip for sample concentration based on monolithic support. (**a**) Layout; (**b**) scanning electron microscopy of the support. Adapted from Wu et al. (2001) with permission

with adsorption chromatography (*e.g.* ion-exchange), that yielded further sample fractionation. On-line combination of reactors with immobilized enzymes such as proteases or glycosydases and further fractionation of reaction products by use of fast ion-exchange, reversed-phase or hydrophobic interaction chromatography was also demonstrated.[20] However, in this early time, technical development in the direction of automation and high-throughput sample processing (*e.g.* by use of robotics and follow-up data management) were still in an early phase of development, and a few years were necessary for these results to become topics for follow-up investigations, especially these ones with inter-alpha trypsin inhibitor. This group of related glycoproteins is predicted to have a potential therapeutic and diagnostic value.[21] Further strategy was targeted in the direction of building miniaturized monolithic columns for chromatographic and affinity-based separation of biopolymers that are mounted into ELISA plates and their application for high- throughput analysis of biological molecules by use of laboratory robotics (see Fig. 2). In early experiments, we developed different schemes for high-throughput fractionation of proteins from human plasma by use of laboratory robotics, and performed LC-MS/MS analysis.[22] About 2000 samples of human serum were analyzed in less than 1 month.[23]

The search after new, alternative solution for high-throughput isolation of biopolymers was also the reason that one mode of displacement chromatography, namely sample displacement chromatography (SDC), gained on actuality. SDC is based on the same principle as DC, but, under overloading conditions, sample molecules that have a higher affinity for binding sites on the chromatographic support compete with sample components of lower affinity. Because of

[20] Josić and Buchacher (2001).

[21] Opal et al. (2007) and Chaaban et al. (2015).

[22] Breen et al. (2012).

[23] Pučić et al. (2011).

Fig. 2 The 96-well plates containing small (50 μL) monolithic columns for high-throughput sample preparation. Reprinted from Šrajer Gajdošik et al. (2012) with permission

displacement, the components with lower affinity are concentrated, and replaced by components with higher affinity.[24] Already in 1988, Hodge's and Mant's group described SDC as "a novel approach to preparative liquid chromatography which takes advantage of the differential relative hydrophobicities of components of a sample mixture, so that the column is optimally ("over-" added by these authors) loaded with an aqueous solution of the sample mixture, there is competition among the sample components for the adsorption sites on the hydrophobic stationary phase. The more hydrophobic components compete more successfully for these sites than more hydrophilic components, which are displaced and immediately eluted from the column".[25] If extended to every ligand such as ion-exchange, affinity and corresponding, additional modes of interactions, it is still the best definition of SDC.[26] Only two years later, the same group developed a multi column system for preparative purification of peptides that was optimized about ten years later.[27]

In parallel investigations, Veeraragavan et al. applied ion-exchange chromatography in SDC mode for separation of proteins and removal of impurities from crude ovalbumin and trypsin inhibitor preparations.[28] This group also introduced a multi column system for protein fractionation in SDC ion-exchange mode. Manseth et al. used immobilized heparin for the isolation of enzymatically active thrombin from plasma of Atlantic Salmon.[29] A low-pressure multicolumn affinity system was used for SDC separation. Recently, it was also demonstrated that hydrophobic-interaction chromatography can be used for further fractionation and preparative isolation of low-abundance proteins from human plasma, and the role of different salts in mobile phase was investigated.[30] In the last years, Schlüter's group uses ion-exchange and

---

[24]Brgles et al. (2011).

[25]Burke et al. (1988).

[26]Veeraragavan et al. (1991) and Manseth et al. (2004).

[27]Husband et al. (2000).

[28]Veeraragavan et al. (1991).

[29]Manseth et al. (2004).

[30]Brgles et al. (2011) and Šrajer Gajdošik et al. (2012).

reversed-phase SDC for sample preparation in proteomic investigations, and has successfully demonstrated use of this technique for micro-scale separations.[31]

Shu et al. documented displacement of components on a chromatographic bead by confocal laser scanning microscopy.[32] If a complex biological mixture like human plasma diluted with buffer with low ionic strength is continuously loaded onto a system that contains three anion-exchange columns that are successively ordered, the sample displacement effect occurs, and different plasma proteins are enriched. Human serum albumin that binds weakly to the support has been pushed and concentrated at the column's end, and can be eluted as a highly concentrated preparation. Strongly binding plasma proteins like ceruloplasmin are concentrated at the last column in the row.[33] This phenomenon was observed years ago, and in plasma fractionation, a so-called a batch solid phase extraction step by use of inexpensive anion-exchange supports was introduced before further fractionation and isolation of therapeutic proteins, such as serum albumin and immunoglobulin G.[34] After washing and elution with concentrated NaCl solution, the eluate was used as starting material for the isolation of prothrombin complex (PCC) or clotting factor IX concentrate.[35] For years, but without further systematic analysis, sample displacement was routinely noted, and also used for chromatography (especially affinity chromatography[36]) and for biological assays, such as reverse displacement immunoassay.[37] Recently, Černigoj et al. also demonstrated the use of monolithic disks for separation of nanoparticles, such as protein aggregates, and successful fractionation of plasmid DNA isoforms.[38]

The (practical) lack of diffusion and component binding on the surface that is driven mainly by convection during chromatographic separation makes monolithic supports almost ideal media for SDC. As demonstrated by Brown et al., for the polishing step for the purification of monoclonal antibodies (mAbs) produced by CHO cells, under overloading conditions, the residual low-abundance impurities, such as host cell proteins, bind preferentially to the ion-exchange membrane and displace mAbs as a product of interest.[39] However, the authors discuss the overloading of the ion-exchange membranes, and do not mention sample displacement effects explicitly. Anion- and cation-exchange CIM monoliths were used for fractionation of proteins from human plasma by use of SDC. Again, under overloading conditions, weakly binding proteins of high abundance, such as human serum albumin in anion-exchange as well as immunoglobulin G in cation-

[31]Ahrends et al. (2010), Kotasinska et al. (2012) and Trusch et al. (2012).

[32]Shu et al. (2012).

[33]Šrajer Gajdošik et al. (2014).

[34]Burnouf (2007).

[35]Burnouf (2007) and Josić et al. (2000).

[36]Cho (2015).

[37]Schiel et al. (2011).

[38]Černigoj et al. (2015).

[39]Brown et al. (2010).

exchange mode, are displaced by stronger binding proteins of lower abundance.[40] This phenomenon is not dependent on column size, and SDC can be used for both large and micro scale preparations.

Sample displacement chromatography (SDC) is a simple, inexpensive and very effective method for the fractionation of complex, multicomponent mixtures containing protein aggregates, proteins and also other macromolecules and nanoparticles. Except for the size-exclusion chromatography, this method can be performed in practically every chromatographic mode, namely in reversed phase, hydrophobic and hydrophilic interaction and in affinity mode on a very small, or on large scale.

Application of SDC for the separation of complex protein and peptide mixtures on an analytical and microanalytical scale enables broad perspectives for high-throughput sample preparation in proteomics and peptidomics.[41]

3 Recent Progress in the Application of Newly Developed Materials for High-Throughput Detection

As mentioned above, the advantage of monolithic materials for both very fast separation and enzymatic conversion of biopolymers was recognized short time after their discovery.[42] However, a relatively long time was necessary for the development of corresponding hardware for separation devices, and for the construction of miniaturized monolithic devices that has led to a further development of monolith-based biosensors both for high-throughput analysis and sample preparation.[43] Experiments with conversions of different substrates as sugars, polysaccharides and proteins confirmed that such supports carrying immobilized enzymes can also be used for conversions of large and complex molecules.[44] Systematic investigation of sample displacement effects on the surface of monoliths demonstrated their ability for simple and fast concentration of low abundant components[45] and possible use for high-throughput sample preparation.[46] First ideas for use of these supports in proteomic technology were summarized already 10 years ago.[47] Optimization of immobilization of different ligands yielded in very effective monolithic columns carrying recombinant protein A and protein G. For the

---

[40]Brgles et al. (2011).

[41]Brgles et al. (2011), Šrajer Gajdošik et al. (2012), Ahrends et al. (2010), Kotasinska et al. (2012), Trusch et al. (2012) and Josić and Clifton (2007).

[42]Josić et al. (1992) and Abou-Rebyeh et al. (1991).

[43]Štrancar et al. (1996).

[44]Svec and Fréchet (1996).

[45]Brgles et al. (2011), Ahrends et al. (2010) and Šrajer Gajdošik et al. (2014).

[46]Ahrends et al. (2010).

[47]Josić and Clifton (2007).

development of immunoaffinity columns, different strategies for immobilization of monoclonal and polyclonal antibodies were investigated. Finally, ligand antibody immobilization to a hydrazide column was chosen.[48] By use of this chemistry, both the oriented immobilization via an oligosaccharide chain in the constant region of immunoglobulin G, as well as full activity of the immobilized antibody, were achieved (see Fig. 1). Following investigations in the direction of isolation of further blood plasma and plasma membrane proteins are ongoing. A high-throughput enzymatic reactor based on monolithic supports for online tryptic digestion of proteins before their LC-MS/MS analysis (so-called tryp-IMERs) was recently developed and its efficacy was demonstrated. The optimized IMER-based analytical platform allowed the on-line digestion of proteins, following chromatographic separation and the acquisition of the MS/MS spectra in an automated manner, and finally protein identification by a search in the protein data bank.[49] Recently developed ELISA plates with mounted columns with different ion-exchange, affinity and pseudo-affinity ligands, as well as immobilized enzymes, confirmed the suitability of these miniaturized columns for high-throughput sample preparation and enzymatic digestion by use of laboratory robotics[50] and directed their use for the development of monolith-based biosensors.[51]

4   Biosensors: Development, Use and Strategies

Biosensors are ideal tools for fast determination of disease biomarkers. Ideal samples that enable invasive or minimally invasive sampling are body fluids, such as blood plasma (or serum) and urine, and nowadays, saliva, tears or even sweat.[52] Biosensors are indispensible tools in point-of care diagnostics.[53] The initial concept of a glucose enzyme was proposed by Clark and Lyons already in 1962, and it was the starting point for the development of biosensors for real time measurement of blood glucose and diabetes control, but in addition to this, such devices can also be applied for bioprocess monitoring and food analysis. However, determination of blood glucose is the main driving force for the development of glucose sensors, and "the management of diabetes represents the first example of individualized (personalized) medicine".[54] Miniaturized devices for very fast determination of glucose in blood account for nearly 85% of the world's market of biosensors, and this enormous commercial potential is a driving force for their further optimization.[55] The

---

[48]Trbojević-Akmačić et al. (2016).

[49]Naldi et al. (2017).

[50]Breen et al. (2012), Pučić et al. (2011), Naldi et al. (2017) and Breen et al. (2016).

[51]Peterson et al. (2002).

[52]Makaram et al. (2014).

[53]Nayak et al. (2017).

[54]Wang (2008).

[55]Nayak et al. (2017), Wang (2008) and Witkowska Nery et al. (2016).

enormous success and every-day use of glucose biosensors has also stimulated the development of similar devices for monitoring of other physiologically important compounds, such as uric acid,[56] creatinine,[57] ascorbic acid and dopamine.[58] Both lactate[59] and succinate[60] have been recently established as markers of systemic hypoxia and potential predictors of mortality in patients with severe trauma. Metabolites of glucose, glutamine and other main carbon sources, have also been considered as biomarker candidates for deregulated immunity,[61] inflammation[62] and cancer.[63] This documents the very high actuality and practical importance of this technique, especially for high-throughput measurements for fast diagnostic purposes and biomarker investigation in personalized medicine, but also in analytical biotechnology, and in-process control in biotech industry.[64] The above shortly discussed blood glucose-measuring device[65] clearly demonstrates the advantages of biosensors over other methods, especially for "every day", routine use. Firstly, it is the possibility of miniaturization (down to the development of nano-devices) and secondly, high-throughput analysis. However, proper sample preparation can still be time consuming.[66] According to Alves et al., "…although the analytical measurement is immediate (and the sensor is considered as a "high-throughput device", Authors' comment), the time spent in the preparation of the sample is often not considered".[67] If biosensors are used for measurements of small molecules (as presented in above listed applications), these problems are less acute and appropriate high-throughput techniques, such as fast extraction or chromatographic separation, can be used.[68]

Generally, biosensor is a device that contains a biological recognition component and a signal transduction (and signal amplification) element that is connected to a miniaturized instrument for both data acquisition and processing. The reaction between the target and sensing molecule can be further sensed and amplified by use of different methods.[69] Regarding electrochemical immunosensors, reference can be made to recent comprehensive reviews by Wen et al.[70] (with more than 230 References!), and Yang et al.,[71] where the most frequently used detection techniques were listed,

---

[56]Zang et al. (2004).

[57]Chen et al. (2013).

[58]Sheng et al. (2012).

[59]Odom et al. (2013).

[60]Lusczek et al. (2017).

[61]Champagne et al. (2016).

[62]Cavally et al. (2017).

[63]Vander Heiden et al. (2009).

[64]Nayak et al. (2017), Du and Dong (2017) and Liu et al. (2010).

[65]Wang (2008) and Witkowska Nery et al. (2016).

[66]Clark et al. (2016).

[67]Alves et al. (2016).

[68]Zamperi et al. (2017) and Švec and Lv (2015).

[69]Fu et al. (2017), Du and Dong (2017) and Ashley et al. (2017).

[70]Wen et al. (2017).

[71]Yang et al. (2017).

based on: (i) voltammetry and amperometry; (ii) electrochemiluminescence; (iii) photoelectrochemistry; and (iv) impedance. The mostly used amplification methods are nanomaterial-enhanced amplification, enzyme-based amplification and DNA-based amplification. Regarding additional detection techniques that are used for nucleic acid-based biosensors, Du and Dong listed the following ones: (i) fluorescent; (ii) electrochemiluminiscent; (iii) chemiluminiscent; (iv) colorimetric; (v) surface plasmon resonance; (vi) surface-enhanced Raman scattering; and (vi) gravimetric detection.[72] During the last years, surface plasmon resonance (SPR) has been repeatedly optimized in the direction of high-throughput detection and quantification of allergens by implementation of multiplex analyses automation, and use of robotics.[73] Important progress was also achieved in lowering the limit of detection, especially for large molecules that can be used as disease biomarkers.[74]

In the last few years, nanomaterial-based amplification is a rapidly growing application in this field. Because both their large surfaces and electron-transfer abilities, nanomaterials also have a very high catalytic activity, they are biocompatible, and can be used as biolabels with significant signal amplification.[75] The use of optical nanoprobes in immunoassays lead to an enormous increase in sensitivity and selectivity for the detection of analytes, such as trace amounts of molecules that must be detected as biomarkers for potential patient's disease or physiological status.[76] According to Fu et al., nanomaterials are used (i) as supports for the loading of numerous indicators (*e.g.* biomolecules or fluorescent dyes) to amplify recognition through their high surface-to-volume ratio (see above) and/or (ii) as an indicator that is generated with the aid of biochemical reactions to achieve multiple signal amplifications.[77]

4.1 Current Perspectives in Biosensor Development

Again, new directions and strategies for blood glucose monitoring can be considered as pilot investigations for the development of control devices for observation and correct treatment of other chronic diseases.[78] Almost ten years ago, Wang stressed that new, innovative approaches for non-invasive monitoring and the development of chronically implanted devices, should be one of the main tools for improving control and management of diabetes.[79] A recent review by Witkowska Nery et al. presents recent developments in this direction (see also Fig. 3), but also the

---

[72]Du and Dong (2017).

[73]Ashley et al. (2017).

[74]Ručević et al. (2006).

[75]Švec and Lv (2015) and Malik et al. (2013).

[76]Huang et al. (2016a).

[77]Fu et al. (2017).

[78]Nayak et al. (2017), Wang (2008) and Witkowska Nery et al. (2016).

[79]Wang (2008).

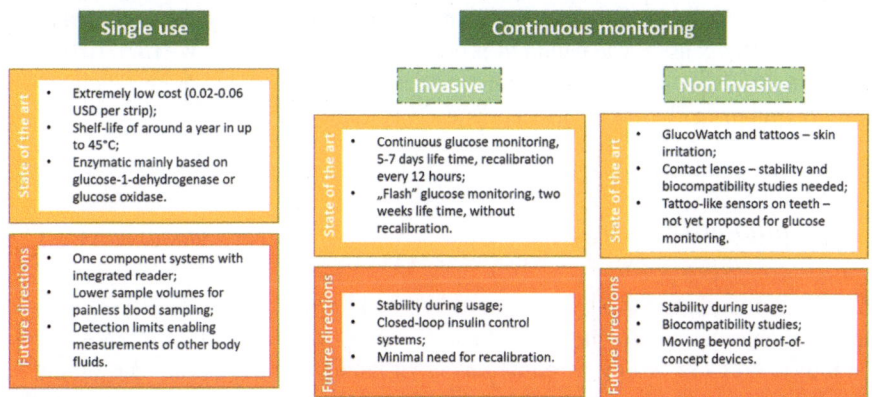

Fig. 3 State of the art and future directions of different types of glucose sensors. Adapted from Witkowska Nery et al. (2016) with permission

shortcomings in their use—limitations of current enzymatic and non-enzymatic approaches for glucose reactions (and different small molecules for monitoring of other diseases mentioned above), and the necessity for the development of a better, more stable catalyst for the reaction of the biomarker in the direction of fast and effective measurement of the reaction product (see Fig. 3).[80]

The use of biosensors for the detection and quantitative determination of large molecules, mostly proteins, was recently successfully applied for a fast and efficient determination of allergens,[81] and this development can be considered as a kind of guide for further developments of this strategy for the discovery of biomarkers for other mostly studied diseases, such as cancer, neurodegenerative diseases and cardiovascular diseases. For a long time neglected, microarray technology for the determination of biomarkers (mostly proteins and peptides) for the sake of both disease diagnosis and monitoring had recently presented a remarkable development. A group of scientists participating in the allergy EU Framework Research Program that introduced an optimized allergen chip for monitoring of IgE and IgG reactivity again 170 allergen molecules and sera (so-called MeDALL allergen chip that was initially designed in 2002).[82] Huang et al. present a recent development of membrane-based lateral flow immunochromatographic strips (LFICS) that can be used for fast and inexpensive multiplex detection of molecules, and optimization of this method towards quantitative analysis.[83] Some interesting approaches for the integration of sample preparation into devices for biomarker detection and quanti-fication can be also emphasized.[84] Zhong et al. developed mass-barcoded

---

[80]Witkowska Nery et al. (2016).

[81]Lupinek et al. (2014).

[82]Lupinek et al. (2014).

[83]Huang et al. (2016a).

[84]Huang et al. (2016b).

nanoparticles with immobilized antihuman IgE antibodies for immunomagnetic capture of allergens.[85] The captured proteins were identified by MALDI ToF mass spectrometry. Comprehensive reviews about the development of this field were recently published by Fu et al.,[86] Du and Dong[87] and Wen et al.[88]

4.2   Nanobiosensors

The term sensor refers to a device that detects and responds to a certain type of input from its physical environment. This specific input can be light, heat, movement, humidity, pressure or any of numerous environmental phenomena. The output is usually a signal that has been converted into a record either at the location of the sensor or is transmitted over a certain network for reading and processing. Sensors designed for medical purposes can detect nucleic acids, proteins, ions, and other small molecules important for diagnosis and follow up of the healing process. They can operate in gas or liquid phase, thereby opening up an enormous potential of downstream applications. In this way, biosensors help in our understanding of the living systems, but they also serve for practical purposes, especially in medicine, drug design, process control, food safety, as well as in personal safety, toxicology, and environmental monitoring. Together with the advancement of telecommunication technology, expert systems and their prompt diagnostic function, they open up new horizons in the health care process.

The smaller the sensor, the more efficient and the better it usually is. Therefore, nanosensors are particularly interesting for the future. Direct DNA and protein detection can significantly facilitate the speed, precision, and susceptibility of biosensors compared to conventional sensors. In principle, nanobiosensors are portable and cheap to manufacture. It is even possible to develop implantable detection and monitoring nanobiosensors. Some of the systems are listed in Table 1. Nanostructures obtained through nanotechnology have revolutionized molecular biology because they have enabled manipulation of atoms and molecules, and monitoring of biological phenomena at the physiological level with far greater precision. These sensors are made of nanomaterials such as nanotubes, nanoporous structures or nanoparticles. Nanotechnology has largely favored the development of a new generation of biosensors and has contributed significantly to the creation of more sensible and efficient biosensors. There are also portable biosensors that can analyze multiple components. Such constructions are usually used for self-assembly techniques (SAM). The use of SAM has also contributed to the development of new

[85]Zhong et al. (2016).

[86]Fu et al. (2017).

[87]Du and Dong (2017).

[88]Wen et al. (2017).

Table 1 Some specific nanobiosensors and technology (modified to Jain 2008)

Cantilever biosensors for molecular diagnostic

Antibody-coated nanocantilevers for detection of microorganisms
   Nanocantilevers for molecular diagnostics
   Nanocantilevers for direct detection of active genes
   Portable nanocantilever system for diagnosis

Carbon nanotubes biosensors
Carbon nanotube sensors coated with ssDNA and electronic readout   Carbon nanotube sensors wrapped with DNA and optical detection
FRET-*Fluorescence Resonance Energy Transfer* based DNA nanosensors
Ion channel switch biosensor technology
Electronic nanobiosensors
Quartz nanobalance biosensors
Viral nanosensors
PEBBLE—Probes Encapsulated by Biologically Localized Embedding nanosensors
Microneedle-mounted biosensors
Optical biosensors
Nanowire biosensors
Nanoscale erasable biodetectors

types of transmission mechanisms in biosensors with significantly greater sensitivity and selectivity.[89]

Nanobiosensor design has undergone significant changes in recent years. Nanomaterials have a relatively high surface area to volume ratios, which allows this surface to be used in a better and significantly different functional sense. The dimensions of these materials make them very special because most of their constituents—atoms are located near their surface and they have vital physical-chemical properties that are significantly different from the resulting bulk materials. Conversely, the smaller the material, the more its properties change.

There is great variability in use of nanobiosensors that are made of nanoparticles or nanostructures: amperometric devices for enzymatic detection of glucose, quantum dots as fluorescence detecting agents for the detection of biding, and the use of bioconjugated nanomaterials for specific biomolecular detection. This includes colloidal nanoparticles which may be used for conjugation with antibody immunoassays and immuno-markers. These materials can be used to improve and enhance electron microscopic detection. Furthermore, nanoparticles based on metallic particles can be excellent for electronic and optical applications and can be effectively used for detecting nucleic acid sequences by exploiting their optoelectronic properties.[90]

An important factor to be considered when using nanomaterials as sensors is monitoring and optimizing their optical properties. Phenomena such as surface

---

[89] Jianrong et al. (2004).
[90] MacKenzie et al. (2009) and Zeng et al. (2011).

plasmon resonances (SPR) are very interesting. SPR refers to the excitation of particle surface with ionic species and charged particles that create ions and result in the excitation of the charged particle fluid. This property is extremely suitable because of their unique optical properties that give them photonic character and excellent ability to be used as fluorophores.[91]

Nanobiosensor classification is a very divergent area. The reason for this is that this classification is based on the nature of nanomaterials incorporated in the biosenzing operation. Biosensors are classified according to two criteria: the type of material to be analyzed and the signal transfer mechanism.[92]

The future of nanobiosensors is very probable. It is highly likely that the systemic blood protein analysis will prevail. Blood reflects the state of health and illness of most organs. Therefore, detection of a molecular blood sample can give a very sensitive insight into the state of health. It is certain that nanobiosensors will significantly shorten the waiting time for test results. Future diagnostic trends will continue with the miniaturization of biochip technology on a nanoscale and will be based on the development and implementation of miniaturized biochips with nanoscale technologies. The trend is likely to be the development of a device by using bottom-up procedure starting from the smallest building elements. The trend is also going towards the miniaturization of fluorescence markers, with significant results obtained with fluorescent nanoparticles. Molecular electronics and chemical nanosensors already allow the construction of nanosensors capable of detecting patterns of chemical behavior in the fluid. Yet, despite progress, we are still missing robust and suitable sensors for body chemistry monitoring.[93]

5 Conclusions

High-tech analytical -omics technology opens the way to the insight into the global profile of each individual.

The first step is the analysis of the patient's sample by application of minimally invasive methods, by use of body fluids, such as blood serum or plasma, urine and other less frequently used ones, such as tears and saliva. Proper sampling is the first, crucial step by application of this strategy, followed by high-throughput analyses by use of proteomic, genomic, transcriptomic and metabolomic methods. Getting this information enables the further setting of an individual's prognostic index and patient's molecular profile.

Nowadays, no modern clinical laboratory can function without the application of basic separation methods, such as chromatography and electrophoresis. High-

---

[91]Malik et al. (2013) and Jianrong et al. (2004).

[92]MacKenzie et al. (2009) and Zeng et al. (2011).

[93]Tiwari and Turner (2014).

throughput analysis strategy requires their further development towards miniaturization and in the direction of nanotechnology.

Chromatographic and electrophoretic supports, as well as supports for enzyme immobilizations, based on monoliths that are presented here are frequently used tools for the construction of such integrated analytical devices. These supports have a great perspective for the development in the direction of biosensors and nanobiosensors.

Acknowledgement This research was supported by the European Union (Marie Currie Programme, HTP-Glycomet "Methods for high-throughput glycoproteomic analysis") and University of Rijeka (Project No. 13.11.1.3.03).

References

Abou-Rebyeh H, Körber F, Schubert-Rehberg K, Reusch J, Josić D (1991) Carrier membrane as a stationary phase for affinity chromatography and kinetic studies of membrane bound enzymes. J Chromatogr B 566:341–350

Ahrends R, Lichtner B, Bertsch A, Kohlbacher O, Hildebrand D, Trusch M, Schlüter H (2010) Application of displacement chromatography for the proteome analysis of a human plasma protein fraction. J Chromatogr A 1217:3321–3329

Alves RC, Barroso MF, González-García MB, Oliveira MB, Delerue-Matos C (2016) New trends in food allergens detection: toward biosensing strategies. Crit Rev Food Sci Nutr 56:2304–2319

Ashley J, Piekarska M, Segers C, Trinth L, Rodgers T, Willey R, Tothill IE (2017) An SPR based sensor for allergens detection. Biosens Bioelectron 88:109–113

Axén R, Porath J (1966) Chemical coupling of enzymes to cross-linked dextran ("Sephadex"). Nature 210:367–369

Bošnjak H, Pavelić K, Kraljević Pavelić S (2008) Towards preventive medicine. High-throughput methods from molecular biology are about to change daily clinical practice. EMBO Rep 9:1056–1060

Breen L, Cao L, Eom L, Šrajer Gajdošik M, Camara L, Giacometti J, Dupuy D, Josić D (2012) High-throughput fractionation of human plasma for fast enrichment of low- and high-abundance proteins. Blood Trans 10(Suppl 2):S89–S100

Breen L, Pučić-Baković M, Vučković F, Reiding K, Trbojević-Akmačić I, Šrajer Gajdošik M, Cook MI, Lopez M, Wuhrer M, Camara LM, Andjelković U, Dupuy DE, Josić D (2016) IgG and IgM glycosylation patterns in patients undergoing image-guided tumor ablation. Biochim Biophys Acta Gen Subj 1860:1786–1794

Brgles M, Clifton J, Walsh R, Huang F, Ručević M, Cao L, Hixson D, Müller E, Josić D (2011) Selectivity of monolithic supports under overloading conditions and their use for separation of human plasma and isolation of low abundance proteins. J Chromatogr A 1218:2389–2395

Brown A, Bill J, Tully T, Radhamohan A, Dowd C (2010) Overloading ion-exchange membranes as a purification step for monoclonal antibodies. Biotechnol Appl Biochem 56:59–70

Burke LTW, Mant CT, Hodges RS (1988) A novel approach to reversed-phase preparative high-performance liquid chromatography of peptides. J Liq Chromat 11:1229–1247

Burnouf T (2007) Modern plasma fractionation. Transfusion Med Rev 21:101–117

Cavally G, Justice JN, Boyle KE, D'Alessandro A, Eisenmesser EZ, Herrera JJ (2017) Interleukin 37 reverses the metabolic cost of inflammation, increases oxidative respiration, and improves exercise tolerance. Proc Natl Acad Sci USA 114:2313–2318

Černigoj U, Martinuč U, Cardoso S, Sekirnik R, Lendero Kranjc N, Štrancar A (2015) Sample displacement chromatography of plasmid DNA forms. J Chromatogr A 1414:103–109

Chaaban H, Keshari RS, Silasi-Mansat R, Popescu NI, Mehta-D'Souza P, Lim Y-P, Lupu F (2015) Inter-α-inhibitor protein and its associated glycosaminolglycans protect against histone-induced injury. Blood 125:2286–2296

Champagne DP, Hatle KM, Fortner KA, D'Alessandro A, Thornton TM, Yang R, Torraba D, Tomás-Cortázar J, Jun YW, Ahn KH, Hansen KC, Haynes L, Anguita J, Rincon M (2016) Fine tuning of CD8 (+) T cell mitochondrial metabolism by the respiratory chain repressor MCJ dictates protection to influenza virus. Immunity 44:1299–1311

Chang S-H, Noel R, Regnier FE (1976) High speed ion exchange chromatography of proteins. Anal Chem 48:1839–1845

Chen P, Peng Y, He M, Yan X-C, Zhang Y, Liu X-N (2013) Sensitive electrochemical detection of creatinine at disposable screnn-printed carbon electrode mixed with ferrocenemethanol. Int J Electrochem Sci 8:8931–8939

Cho W (2015) Displacement phenomena in lectin affinity chromatography. Anal Chem 87:9612–9620

Clark KD, Zhang C, Anderson JL (2016) Sample preparation for bioanalytical and pharmaceutical analysis. Anal Chem 88:11262–11270

Du Y, Dong S (2017) Nucleic acid biosensors: recent advances and perspectives. Anal Chem 89:189–215

ESF Forward Look (2012) Personalised medicine for the European citizen. Towards more precise medicine for the diagnosis, treatment and prevention of disease (iPM). European Science Foundation, Strasbourg

Fu X, Chen L, Choo J (2017) Optical probes for ultrasensitive immunoassay. Anal Chem 89:124–137

Hjertén S, Liao JL, Zhang R (1989) High-performance liquid chromatography on continuous polymer beds. J Chromatogr A 473:273–275

Huang X, Aguilar ZP, Xu H, Li W, Xiong Y (2016a) Membrane-based lateral flow immunochromatograhic strip with nanoparticles as reporters for detection: a review. Biosens Bioelctron 75:166–180

Huang H, Jiang D, Zhu P, Pi F, Ji J, Sun C, Sun J, Sun X (2016b) A novel mast cell co-culture microfluidic chip for the electrochemical evaluation of food allergen. Biosens Bioelctron 83:126–133

Husband DL, Mant CT, Hodges RS (2000) Development of simultaneous purification methodology for multiple synthetic peptides by reversed-phase sample displacement chromatography. J Chromatogr A 893:81–94

Jain KK (2008) The handbook of nanomedicine. Humana Press, Basel, pp 91–116

Jianrong C, Yuging M, Nongyne H, Xiaohua W, Sijiao L (2004) Nanotechnology and biosensors. Biotech Adv 22:505–518

Johansson KE, Blomqvist J, Hjertén S (1975) Purification of membrane proteins from Acholeplasma laidlawii by agarose suspension electrophoresis in Tween 20 and polyacrylamide and dextran gel electrophoresis in detergent-free media. J Biol Chem 250:2463–2469

Josić D, Andjelković U (2016) The role of proteomics in personalized medicine. In: Bodiroga-Vukobrat N, Pavelić K, Rukavina D, Sander GG (eds) Personalised medicine: a new medical and social challenge (Europeanization and globalization). Springer International Publishing, Switzerland, pp 179–218

Josić D, Buchacher A (2001) Application of monoliths as supports for affinity chromatography and fast enzymatic conversion. J Biochem Biophys Methods 49:153–174

Josić D, Clifton JG (2007) Use of monolithic supports in proteomics technology. J Chromatogr A 1144:2–13

Josić D, Zeilinger K, Lim Y-P, Raps M, Hofmann W, Reutter W (1989) Preparative isolation of glycoproteins from plasma membranes of different rat organs. J Chromatogr A 484:327–335

Josić D, Reusch J, Löster K, Baum O, Reutter W (1992) High performance membrane chromatography of serum and plasma membrane proteins. J Chromatogr A 590:59–76

Josić D, Hoffer L, Buchacher A, Schwill F, Biesert L, Klöcking H-P, Hellstern P, Rokicka-Milewska R, Klukowska A (2000) Manufacturing of prothrombin complex concentrate aiming a low thrombinicity. Thromb Res 100:433–441

Kotasinska M, Richter W, Thiemann J, Schlüter H (2012) Cation exchange displacement batch chromatography of proteins guided by screening of protein purification parameters. Electrophoresis 35:3170–3176

Liu J, Chen C-F, Chang C-W, DeVoe DL (2010) Flow-through immunosensors using antibody-immobilized polymer monoliths. Biosens Bioelectron 26:182–188

Lupinek C, Wollmann E, Baar A, Banerjee S, Breiteneder H, Broecker BM et al (2014) Advances in allergen-microarray technology for diagnosis and monitoring of allergy: the MeDALL allergen-chip. Methods 66:106–119

Lusczek ER, Muratore SL, Dubick MA, Beilman J (2017) Assessment of key plasma metabolites in combat causalities. J Trauma Acute Care Surg 82:309–316

MacKenzie R, Auzelyte V, Olliges S et al (2009) Nanowire development and characterization for applications in biosensing. In: Micheli G, Leblebici Y, Gijs M, Vörös J (eds) Nanosyst design & technology. Springer, pp 143–173

Makaram P, Owens D, Aceros J (2014) Trends in nanomaterial-based non-invasive diabetes sensing technologies. Diagnostica (Basel) 4:27–46

Malik P, Katyal V, Malik V, Asatkar A, Inwati G, Mukherjee TK (2013) ISRN nanobiosensors: concepts and variations nanomaterials. Article ID 327435

Manseth E, Skjervold PO, Flengsrud R (2004) Sample displacement chromatography of Atlantic Salmon (Salmo salar) thrombin. J Biochem Biophys Methods 60:39–47

Naldi M, Černogoj U, Štrancar A, Bartolini M (2017) Towards automation in protein digestion: development of monolithic trypsin immobilized reactor for highly efficient on-line digestion and analysis. Talanta 167:143–157

Nayak S, Blumenfeld NR, Laksanasopin T, Sia SK (2017) Point-of-care diagnostic: recent developments in connected age. Anal Chem 89:102–123

Nobel Lectures Chemistry 1942–1962 (1964) Elsevier, Amsterdam

Odom SR, Howell MD, Silva GS, Nielsen VM, Grupta A, Shapiro NI, Talmor D (2013) Lactate clearance as a predictor of mortality in trauma patients. J Trauma Acute Care Surg 74:999–1004

Opal SM, Lim Y-P, Siryaporn E, Moldawer LL, Pribble JP, Palardy JE, Souza S (2007) Longitudinal studies of inter-alpha inhibitor proteins in severely septic patients: a potential clinical marker and mediator of severe sepsis. Crit Care Med 35:387–392

Pavelić K, Sedić M, Pavelić Kraljević S (2016) Introduction to personalized medicine. In: Bodiroga-Vukobrat N, Pavelić K, Rukavina D, Sander GG (eds) Personalised medicine: a new medical and social challenge (Europeanization and globalization). Springer International Publishing, Switzerland, pp 300–320

Peterson DS, Rohr T, Svec F, Fréchet MJ (2002) Enzymatic microreactor-on-a-chip: protein mapping using trypsin immobilized on porous polymer monoliths moulded in channels of microfluidic devices. Anal Chem 74:4081–4088

Podgornik A, Barut M, Štrancar A, Josić D, Koloini T (2000) Construction of large-volume monolithic columns. Anal Chem 72:5693–5699

Pučić M, Knežević A, Vidič J, Adamczyk B, Novoknet M, Polašek O (2011) High throughput isolation and glycosylation analysis of IgG-variability and heritability of the IgG glycome in three isolated human populations. Mol Cell Proteomics 10:M111.010090

Ručević M, Clifton JG, Huang F, Li X, Callanan H, Hixson DC, Josić D (2006) Use of short monolithic columns for isolation of low abundance membrane proteins. J Chromatogr A 1123:199–204

Schiel JE, Tong Z, Sakulthaew C, Hage DS (2011) Development of a flow-based ultafast immunoextraction and reverse displacement immunoassay: analysis of free drug fractions. Anal Chem 83:9387–9390

Sheng Z-H, Zheng X-Q, Xu J-Y, Bao W-J, Wang F-B, Xia X-H (2012) Electrochemical sensor based on nitrogen doped graphene: simultaneous determination of ascorbic acid, dopamine and uric acid. Biosens Biolectron 34:125–131

Shu Q-H, Shi Z-C, Sun Y (2012) Dynamic behavior of binary component ion-exchange displacement chromatography of proteins visualized by confocal laser scanning microscopy. J Chromatogr A 1257:48–57

Šrajer Gajdošik M, Clifton J, Josić D (2012) Sample displacement chromatography as a method for purification of proteins and peptides from complex mixtures. J Chromatogr A 1239:1–9

Šrajer Gajdošik M, Kovač S, Malatesti N, Müller E, Josić D (2014) Ion-exchange sample displacement chromatography as a method for fast and simple isolation of low- and high-abundance proteins from complex biological mixtures. Food Technol Biotechnol 52:58–63

Štrancar A, Koselj P, Schwinn H, Josić D (1996) Application of compact, porous disks for fast separation of biopolymers and in-process control in biotechnology. Anal Chem 68:3483–3488

Svec F, Fréchet JM (1996) New designs of macroporous polymers and supports: from separation to biocatalysis. Science 273:205–211

Svec F, Huber F (2006) Monolithic materials: promises, challenges, achievements. Anal Chem 78:2101–2107

Švec F, Lv Y (2015) Advances and recent trends in the field of monolithic columns for chromatography. Anal Chem 87:250–273

Tennikova TB, Svec F, Belenkii BG (1990) High performance membrane chromatography. A novel method for protein separation. J Liquid Chromatogr 13:63–70

The Royal Swedish Academy of Sciences (2002) Advanced Information on the Nobel Prize in Chemistry 2002. www.nobel.se/chemistry/laureates/2002/chemady.pdf

Tiwari A, Turner PF (eds) (2014) Biosensors nanotehnology. Wiley, Scrivene Publishing, USA

Trbojević-Akmačić I, Nemec B, Vidič U, Malić S, Miklić K, Černogoj U, Vidič J, Lendero Kranjc N, Štrancar A, Lauc G, Lenac Roviš T, Pučić-Baković M (2016) Chromatographic monoliths for high-throughput immunoaffinity isolation of transferrin from human plasma. Croat Chem Acta 89:203–211

Trusch M, Tillack K, Kwiatkowski M, Bertsch A, Ahrends R, Kohlbacher O, Martin R, Sospedra M, Schlüter H (2012) Displacement chromatography as a first separating step in online two-dimensional chromatography coupled to mass spectrometry analysis of complex protein sample – the proteome of neutrophils. J Chromatogr A 1232:288–294

Unger KK (1979) Porous silica: its properties and use in column liquid chromatography. J Chromatogr Library, Elsevier

Vander Heiden MG, Cantley LC, Thompson B (2009) Understanding the Warburg effect: the metabolic requirements of cell proliferation. Science 324:1029–1033

Veeraragavan K, Bernier A, Braendli E (1991) Sample displacement mode chromatography: purification of proteins by use of a high-performance anion-exchange column. J Chromatogr A 541:207–220

Wang J (2008) Electrochemical glucose biosensors. Chem Rev 108:814–825

Wen W, Yan X, Zhu C, Du D, Lin Y (2017) Recent advances in electrochemical immunoassays. Anal Chem 89:138–156

Witkowska Nery E, Kundys M, Jeleń PS, Jönsson-Niedziółka M (2016) Electrochemical glucose sensing: is there still room for improvement. Anal Chem 88:11271–11282

Wu C, Davey MH, Svec F, Fréchet MJ (2001) Monolithic porous polymer for on-chip solid phase extraction and preconcentration prepared by photoinitiated in situ polymerization within a microfluidic device. Anal Chem 71:5088–5096

Yang Y, Noviana E, Nguyen MP, Geiss BJ, Dandy DS, Henry CS (2017) Paper-based microfluidic devices: emerging themes and applications. Anal Chem 89:71–91

Zamperi M, Sekar K, Zamboni N, Sauer U (2017) Frontiers of high-throughput metabolomics. Curr Opin Chem Biol 36:15–23

Zang F, Wang X, Ai S, Sun Z, Wan Q, Zhu Z, Xian Y, Jin L, Yamamoto K (2004) Immobilization of uricase on ZnO nanorods for a reagentless uric acid biosensor. Anal Chim Acta 519:155–160

Zeng S, Yong K-T, Roy I, Dinh X-Q, Yu X, Luan F (2011) A review on functionalized gold nanoparticles for biosensing applications. Plasmonics 6:491–506

Zhong X, Qiao L, Gasilova N, Liu B, Girault HH (2016) Mass barcode signal amplification for multiplex allergy diagnosis by MALDI-MS. Anal Chem 88:6184–6189

Bacteria—Human Interactions: Leads for Personalized Medicine

Željka Maglica and Marina Ožbolt

Abstract Bacteria are an integral part of the human body. Together with other microorganisms they form a community in and on the human body known as human microbiome. The microbiome has been found to be crucial for immunologic, hormonal and metabolic homeostasis of its human host. The composition of the microbiome varies considerably among humans and we present the main factors that influence this variability. In addition, the composition of the microbiome has been associated with changes in the central nervous system through the so called "gut-brain axes". The latest research from this new and exciting field is presented. We then switch our focus from beneficial to pathogenic bacteria. We present the main techniques and methods used to identify pathogenic bacteria and test their sensitivity to antibacterial drugs. Bacteria, like humans, demonstrate individuality in their behavior. This individuality is also present in their drug response, leading to long antibacterial therapy and the possibility of recurrent infections with the same pathogen. Finally, we present data that suggests bacteria are associated with Modic Type 1 changes, pathological changes in the vertebrae. These changes are closely correlated with lower back pain, the most frequent cause of disability for people younger than 45 years of age.

1 Introduction to the Human Microbiome

Numerous studies have emphasized the microbiome to be a very important part of human health. Much has been learned about the diversity and distribution of the human-associated microbiome, but we still know little about its biology and function during healthy state or disease.[1] It is a known fact that this complex

---

[1]Integrative HMP (iHMP) Research Network Consortium (2014).

Ž. Maglica (✉) · M. Ožbolt
Department of Biotechnology, Centre for High-Throughput Technologies, University of Rijeka, Rijeka, Croatia
e-mail: zeljka.maglica@uniri.hr

© Springer Nature Switzerland AG 2019
N. Bodiroga-Vukobrat et al. (eds.), *Personalized Medicine in Healthcare Systems*,
Europeanization and Globalization 5, https://doi.org/10.1007/978-3-030-16465-2_7

symbiosis between a host and their microbiome can influence host metabolism, physiology and gene expression.[2]

These many symbiotic physiological functions include defense against pathogens and stimulation of immunity, mediated through a number of microbial metabolites, as well as fermentation of substrates otherwise indigestible by the host, resulting in recovery of metabolic energy for the host.[3] The microbiome utilizes indigestible dietary fibers and produces short chain fatty acids, which are an important energy source and crucial for modulating immune response and tumorogenesis in the gut.[4] Moreover, the gut microbiome is also capable of performing a range of bio-transformations on drugs and their metabolites, in ways that can affect absorption and bioavailability.[5]

Both healthy and ill individuals vary remarkably in the composition of microbiome in their skin, gut and genitals.[6] Although this diversity is not entirely explained, environmental and host factors, such as early microbial exposure, host genetics, geographic origin, drugs, diet and age, have been implicated as the factors that contribute most to the individuality of the microbiome.[7]

The human microbiome undergoes considerable changes from birth to old age. The human gastrointestinal tract is sterile before birth. The microbial colonization of the newborn infant starts at the minute of birth and it is primarily affected by the mode of delivery.[8] Vaginally delivered infants possess bacteria resembling their mothers' vaginal microbiome, as opposed to infants delivered by C-section in which intestinal colonization by *Lactobacillus*, *Bifidobacterium* and *Bacteroides* is delayed. Moreover, it is observed that infants delivered by C-section are more susceptible to allergies and asthma. This rate can be reduced by the administration of probiotics.[9] At around 18 to 24 months of age, the gut microbiome stabilizes and reaches its "adult-like" form. However, the mechanism of this homeostasis for now remains unknown.[10]

Healthy adults typically harbor more than 1000 species of bacteria, mostly belonging to *Bacteroidetes* and *Firmicutes*, followed by *Proteobacteria* and *Actinobacteria*. Although the human microbiome consists of many species that can be cultivated, it also includes ones that have not been characterized by cultivation yet. Body site–specific communities of bacteria differ greatly among individuals and the biggest diversity is noticed in gut.[11]

---

[2]Kinross et al. (2008).

[3]Nicholson et al. (2005) and Wilson and Nicholson (2009).

[4]Shreiner et al. (2015).

[5]Shreiner et al. (2015).

[6]Huttenhower et al. (2012).

[7]Huttenhower et al. (2012) and Turpin et al. (2016).

[8]Benson et al. (2010) and ElRakaiby et al. (2014).

[9]Benson et al. (2010) and ElRakaiby et al. (2014).

[10]Claesson et al. (2011).

[11]Pflughoeft and Versalovic (2012), Shreiner et al. (2015) and Zoetendal et al. (2008).

The composition of gut microbiome of older people (>65 years of age) differs from the core microbiome and diversity levels of younger adults because of alterations caused by physiological changes that affect food digestion and absorption, as well as the immune system.[12] These insights suggest that adjustments in diet and administration of probiotic supplements could promote healthier ageing by regulating the gut microbiome.[13]

The human microbiome is mostly in a state of homeostasis by adult age. Disruption of normal microflora (dysbiosis) has been linked with changes in diet and lifestyle, along with allergies, diabetes, obesity, coronary heart disease, inflammatory bowel disease and even cancer.[14] These are all multifactorial states/diseases, caused both by environmental and genetic factors, where the composition of the gut microbiome is considered as an environmental component.[15]

In general, dysbiosis of the human-associated microbiome can be difficult to define, but could be considered as a perturbation that differs from an otherwise balanced system. Finding traits that distinguish healthy from unhealthy microbiome will be of great importance in the diagnosis of microbiome-related diseases. These traits could provide a new approach in personalized medicine, not only through diagnosis of different diseases and states, but also in the prediction and prevention or improvement of present prognosis.[16]

2 The Gut-Brain Axis: The Microbiome Is Important for Healthy Brain Function

In addition to the mechanisms of action described above including immune and metabolic pathways, the gut microbiome can also interact directly with the central nervous system of the host through the neuroendocrine and neural pathways, which are part of the so called gut-brain axis.[17] New studies emphasize a specific role of the gut microbiome in the regulation of mood and behavior, involving bidirectional communication along the gut-brain axis.[18] This bidirectional communication can influence homeostasis and may contribute to the risk of disease through changes in the gastrointestinal, nervous and immune systems.[19] Surprisingly, the composition of the microbiome in individuals was suggested to be associated with anxiety and

---

[12]Claesson et al. (2011) and Claesson et al. (2016).

[13]Claesson et al. (2011) and Claesson et al. (2016).

[14]Benson et al. (2010), Claesson et al. (2016), ElRakaiby et al. (2014) and Lloyd-Price et al. (2016).

[15]Benson et al. (2010) and ElRakaiby et al. (2014).

[16]Lloyd-Price et al. (2016).

[17]Dinan and Cryan (2017).

[18]Clarke et al. (2013).

[19]Foster and McVey Neufeld (2013).

depression, as well as with autism spectrum disorder, where patients present specific microbiome alterations according to the severity of the disease.[20]

Preliminary studies have shown differences in the composition of the microbiome in patients with depression compared with healthy individuals.[21] In individuals with depression, the microbiome had alterations in species belonging to three bacterial phyla: *Firmicutes, Actinobacteria* and *Bacteroidetes*. Studies have also shown that transplantation of the microbiome from patients with depression to germ-free mice and rats induced behavioral and physiological features characteristic of depression in the recipients (anhedonia, anxiety-like behaviors and alterations in tryptophan metabolism), while transplantation from healthy patients had no behavioral effect.[22] Evidence in animals suggests that brain function and behavior are influenced by different microbial metabolites, such as short-chain fatty acids (e.g. butyrate, propionate and acetate). It has been shown in mice that increased production of acetate by an altered gut microbiome leads to activation of the parasympathetic nervous system, which promotes an increase in glucose-stimulated insulin secretion, increased ghrelin secretion, hyperphagia and obesity.[23] Although experiments on animals are promising, currently no real direct evidence exists that those metabolites travel through the circulatory system to the brain in humans.[24]

The fact that stress-related psychiatric symptoms such as anxiety are more common in individuals with gastrointestinal disorders, including irritable bowel disorder and inflammatory bowel disorder, than in individuals with no gastro-intestinal disorders emphasizes the importance and role of the gut-brain axis.[25] A growing body of evidence suggests that changes in the gut microbiome could influence stress response, but whether these changes are central to the pathophysi-ology of at least some psychiatric disorders in humans (e.g. depression and autism spectrum disorder) has yet to be confirmed. Interestingly, many of the effects listed above appear to be strain-specific.[26]

Most of the existing findings regarding the gut-brain axis have been obtained from preclinical animal experiments, but further studies are needed to confirm if they are valid for humans. More detailed knowledge of the gut microbiome composition and related mechanisms could help in development of novel types of therapy using specific bacterial strains.

---

[20]Carabottia et al. (2015).

[21]Jiang et al. (2015).

[22]Kelly et al. (2016) and Zheng et al. (2016).

[23]Perry et al. (2016).

[24]Dinan and Cryan (2017).

[25]Cryan and O'Mahony (2011).

[26]Dinan and Cryan (2017) and Carabottia et al. (2015).

3 Clinical Microbiology

One of the main reasons to study the microbiome, and microorganisms in general, is to understand the causes and mechanisms of different diseases and to find a way to control or cure them. To get an answer to these questions, clinical (medical) microbiology came into existence, a branch of medical science that includes prevention, diagnosis and treatment of infectious diseases. It also studies various clinical applications of microorganisms for the improvement of human health.

The ability of a clinical microbiology laboratory to perform its tasks depends greatly on the quality of sample collected from the patient, on the conditions of transportation of these samples to the laboratory (to ensure viability of microbes) and on the methods used for cultivation and identification of potential microorganisms.[27] The most common specimens include blood samples, biopsy material, cerebrospinal fluid, stool and urine samples, gastric washings, and various swabs (throat, nose, wound, vaginal etc.).

Clinical microbiology techniques include microbial culture, microscopy, genotyping and serological tests. Microbial culture is used for testing tissue and/or fluid samples for the presence of a specific pathogen, which is determined by growth in a selective or differential medium. Culturing is usually followed by a microscopic examination to help in the identification of microbes. Characteristic morphological properties are used as a preliminary identifier for most microorganisms. This classic microscopic examination is often paired with variety of sample staining methods (e.g. differential, acid-fast, fluorescent staining) and biochemical analysis.[28] Furthermore, nucleic acids and proteins can be used in pathogen identification, by using techniques such as DNA sequencing, polymerase chain reaction (PCR) and mass spectrometry.[29] Different immunological methods (e.g. ELISA, Western blot) are also used to detect, identify and quantify antigen in clinical samples.[30]

Clinical microbiology not only identifies but also tests bacterial susceptibility to different concentrations and classes of antimicrobials in order to determine the best antimicrobial therapy. This is most often done by the disk diffusion method.[31] As resistance traits are genetically encoded, we can sometimes test for the specific genes that confer antibiotic resistance by using PCR and DNA hybridization methods.[32]

---

[27]Tille (2013).

[28]Tille (2013).

[29]Caliendo (2011) and Kothari et al. (2014).

[30]de Matos et al. (2010).

[31]Balouiri et al. (2016).

[32]Fluit et al. (2001).

4 Individuality of Bacterial Responses to Antibacterials

So far this overview has covered topics related to differences between humans in their bacterial composition and how different microorganisms affect human health. However, it is very often overlooked that there is individuality among bacteria from the same bacterial isolate. Even genetically identical cells can behave differently. This non-genetic, cell-to-cell, phenotypic variation was observed in many cellular functions including growth rate, gene expression, stress resistance and, importantly, drug response.[33] The exact mechanisms that govern these variations are not fully understood. Some of these behavioral differences were shown to be because of noise in gene regulation, asymmetric division, differences in protein synthesis and folding efficiency.[34]

The main reason why this phenotypic variability is often overlooked is because the majority of bacteriological assays are based on measuring a mean value of some quantifiable cell parameter in a large bacterial population. Such averaged value can be misleading because the existence of small bacterial populations exhibiting different behavior can easily go unnoticed.[35] Generally, small populations of cells can only be identified by assays performed at the single-cell level, such as flow cytometry and high-resolution microscopy.[36]

Recent development of microfluidic devices, fluorescent probes, and automated microscopes have made it possible to follow multiple live cells in real-time. This technique has been used to investigate cell-to-cell variability in gene expression, cell division, metabolite concentration, and antimicrobial effects and to gain extraordinary insight into single cell function.[37] A study using ATP reporters showed that different classes of antibacterial drugs affect cells with different kinetics, and that there is a large variability in drug response even within a clonal population growing in a homogeneous environment.[38] This cell-to-cell variability in response to antimicrobial treatment is suspected to be the cause of recurrent chronic bacterial infections common among certain pathogenic bacteria.[39] In addition, these surviving bacterial cells can serve as a pool for development of mutants resistant to antibacterial therapy, thereby limiting the selection of effective antibiotics. As the development of new antibiotics has dramatically slowed down in recent decades while the number of antibiotic resistant bacterial strains increased, many researches believe we are facing a great public health crisis unless we can better manage available antibacterial

---

[33]Ackermann (2015).

[34]Ackermann (2015).

[35]Dhar and McKinney (2007).

[36]Davis and Isberg (2016).

[37]Bhaskar et al. (2014), Bhat et al. (2016), Locke and Elowitz (2009), Locke et al. (2011), Mekterovic et al. (2014), Santi et al. (2013) and Wakamoto et al. (2013).

[38]Maglica et al. (2015).

[39]Bhaskar et al. (2014), Bhat et al. (2016), Mouton et al. (2016).

drugs.[40] New studies are urgently needed to explain how drug-susceptible bacteria survive antibiotic treatment and exactly what mechanisms govern variability in drug response.

5 Antibacterials as a Possible Treatment for Modic Changes Type 1 and Lower Back Pain

Antibiotics have traditionally been used to treat acute bacterial diseases like respiratory and urinary tract infections. However, recent studies suggest that antibiotics might be useful even for patients that have other type of symptoms, like lower back pain. Modic changes (MC) type 1 are bone edema in vertebrae, only visible on magnetic resonance images (MRI). They are observed in 6% of the general population, as well as in 35–40% of people with chronic lower back pain.[41] There are both degenerative/mechanical pathways and recently discovered infectious pathways shown to cause MC type 1. When an intervertebral disc is herniated, it forces nuclear material into the spinal canal where neocapillarization occurs, followed by inflammation with an increased presence of macrophages.

Different bacterial species have been isolated from the disc and herniated discal tissue. The most commonly found bacteria are different subtypes of *Proprionibacterium acnes*, followed by *Corynebacterium propinquum* and *Staphylococcus*.[42] One of the metabolites of these bacteria is propionic acid, which is able to dissolve fatty bone marrow and bone. It is assumed that diffusion of propionic acid from the disc into the vertebrae causes MC type 1. *P. acnes* are commensal anaerobic bacteria which can be found in the oral cavity and in hair follicles in the skin. During tooth brushing, they can easily enter the circulatory system, but they do not present an immediate health risk because of the aerobic environment in the blood stream.[43] However, the spinal canal provides an ideal anaerobic environment for *P. acnes* proliferation. *P. acnes* is frequently neglected as a possible cause of medical conditions, as it is a member of the normal skin and oral microbiome. Nevertheless, it has been shown that they have pathogenic role in inflammatory skin conditions such as acne vulgaris, and it is assumed that they have an important role in a number of other infections and clinical conditions.[44]

For these reasons, Modic antibiotic spine therapy (MAST) is proposed as a potentially efficient therapy. A decrease in volume of the lesions (MRI Modic grading) in treated patients has been demonstrated, along with decreased back and

---

[40]Lewis (2013).

[41]Albert et al. (2013a, b).

[42]Albert et al. (2013a) and Manniche and Jordan (2016).

[43]Albert et al. (2013b) and Rollason et al. (2013).

[44]Rollason et al. (2013).

leg pain intensity and general improvement.[45] To avoid excessive antibiotic use, further research is needed, along with determination of criteria for patients who are suitable for this kind of therapy.

6 Conclusion

This overview has attempted to present the importance of bacteria in health and disease. This topic is not new but there is a lot of new data that offer novel insight in the role bacteria play in human lives. Bacterial composition in the human gut is highly variable and this variability has been linked not only with gastrointestinal and metabolic diseases but also with autoimmune and neurological disorders. This is currently a hot topic and many studies are underway that will, hopefully, shed more light into the mechanisms behind these bacteria-human interactions and how they can be translated into personalized therapy. In addition, more personalized antimicrobial therapy is necessary in order to limit the spread of drug-resistant bacteria and prolong the usefulness of currently available antimicrobial agents.

References

Ackermann M (2015) A functional perspective on phenotypic heterogeneity in microorganisms. Nat Rev Microbiol 13:497–508

Albert HB, Sorensen JS, Christensen BS, Manniche C (2013a) Antibiotic treatment in patients with chronic low back pain and vertebral bone edema (Modic type 1 changes): a double-blind randomized clinical controlled trial of efficacy. Eur Spine J 22:697–707

Albert HB, Lambert P, Rollason J, Sorensen JS, Worthington T, Pedersen MB, Nørgaard HS, Vernallis A, Busch F, Manniche C et al (2013b) Does nuclear tissue infected with bacteria following disc herniations lead to Modic changes in the adjacent vertebrae? Eur Spine J 22:690–696

Balouiri M, Sadiki M, Ibnsouda SK (2016) Methods for in vitro evaluating antimicrobial activity: a review. J Pharm Anal 6:71–79

Benson AK, Kelly SA, Legge R, Ma F, Low SJ, Kim J, Zhang M, Oh PL, Nehrenberg D, Hua K et al (2010) Individuality in gut microbiota composition is a complex polygenic trait shaped by multiple environmental and host genetic factors. Proc Natl Acad Sci 107:18933–18938

Bhaskar A, Chawla M, Mehta M, Parikh P, Chandra P, Bhave D, Kumar D, Carroll KS, Singh A (2014) Reengineering redox sensitive GFP to measure mycothiol redox potential of *Mycobacterium tuberculosis* during infection. PLoS Pathog 10:e1003902

Bhat SA, Iqbal IK, Kumar A (2016) Imaging the NADH:NAD(+) homeostasis for understanding the metabolic response of mycobacterium to physiologically relevant stresses. Front Cell Infect Microbiol 6:145

Caliendo AM (2011) Multiplex PCR and emerging technologies for the detection of respiratory pathogens. Clin Infect Dis 52:S326–S330

---

[45] Albert et al. (2013a, b).

Carabottia M, Sciroccoa A, Masellib MA, Severia C (2015) The gut-brain axis: interactions between enteric microbiota, central and enteric nervous systems. Ann Gastroenterol 28:1–7

Claesson MJ, Cusack S, O'Sullivan O, Greene-Diniz R, de Weerd H, Flannery E, Marchesi JR, Falush D, Dinan T, Fitzgerald G et al (2011) Composition, variability, and temporal stability of the intestinal microbiota of the elderly. Proc Natl Acad Sci 108:4586–4591

Claesson MJ, Jeffery IB, Conde S, Power SE, O'Connor EM, Cusack S, Harris HMB, Coakley M, Lakshminarayanan B, O'Sullivan O et al (2016) Gut microbiota composition correlates with diet and health in the elderly. Nature 488:178–184

Clarke G, Grenham S, Scully P, Fitzgerald P, Moloney RD, Shanahan F, Dinan TG, Cryan JF (2013) The microbiome-gut-brain axis during early life regulates the hippocampal serotonergic system in a sex-dependent manner. Mol Psychiatry 18:666–673

Cryan JF, O'Mahony SM (2011) The microbiome-gut-brain axis: from bowel to behavior: from bowel to behavior. Neurogastroenterol Motil 23:187–192

Davis KM, Isberg RR (2016) Defining heterogeneity within bacterial populations via single cell approaches. BioEssays 38:782–790

de Matos LL, Trufelli DC, de Matos MGL, da Silva Pinhal MA (2010) Immunohistochemistry as an important tool in biomarkers detection and clinical practice. Biomark Insights 5:9–20

Dhar N, McKinney JD (2007) Microbial phenotypic heterogeneity and antibiotic tolerance. Curr Opin Microbiol 10:30–38

Dinan TG, Cryan JF (2017) Gut-brain axis in 2016: brain-gut-microbiota axis - mood, metabolism and behaviour. Nat Rev Gastroenterol Hepatol 14(2):69–70

ElRakaiby M, Dutilh BE, Rizkallah MR, Boleij A, Cole JN, Aziz RK (2014) Pharmaco-microbiomics: the impact of human microbiome variations on systems pharmacology and personalized therapeutics. OMICS J Integr Biol 18:402–414

Fluit AC, Visser MR, Schmitz F-J (2001) Molecular detection of antimicrobial resistance. Clin Microbiol Rev 14:836–871

Foster JA, McVey Neufeld K-A (2013) Gut–brain axis: how the microbiome influences anxiety and depression. Trends Neurosci 36:305–312

Huttenhower C, Gevers D, Knight R, Abubucker S, Badger JH, Chinwalla AT, Creasy HH, Earl AM, FitzGerald MG, Fulton RS et al (2012) Structure, function and diversity of the healthy human microbiome. Nature 486:207–214

Integrative HMP (iHMP) Research Network Consortium (2014) The integrative human microbiome project: dynamic analysis of microbiome-host omics profiles during periods of human health and disease. Cell Host Microbe 16:276–289

Jiang H, Ling Z, Zhang Y, Mao H, Ma Z, Yin Y, Wang W, Tang W, Tan Z, Shi J et al (2015) Altered fecal microbiota composition in patients with major depressive disorder. Brain Behav Immun 48:186–194

Kelly JR, Borre Y, O' Brien C, Patterson E, El Aidy S, Deane J, Kennedy PJ, Beers S, Scott K, Moloney G et al (2016) Transferring the blues: depression-associated gut microbiota induces neurobehavioural changes in the rat. J Psychiatr Res 82:109–118

Kinross JM, von Roon AC, Holmes E, Darzi A, Nicholson JK (2008) The human gut microbiome: implications for future health care. Curr Gastroenterol Rep 10:396–403

Kothari A, Morgan M, Haake DA (2014) Emerging technologies for rapid identification of bloodstream pathogens. Clin Infect Dis 59:272–278

Lewis K (2013) Platforms for antibiotic discovery. Nat Rev Drug Discov 12:371–387

Lloyd-Price J, Abu-Ali G, Huttenhower C (2016) The healthy human microbiome. Genome Med 8

Locke JC, Elowitz MB (2009) Using movies to analyse gene circuit dynamics in single cells. Nat Rev Microbiol 7:383–392

Locke JC, Young JW, Fontes M, Hernandez Jimenez MJ, Elowitz MB (2011) Stochastic pulse regulation in bacterial stress response. Science 334:366–369

Maglica Ž, Özdemir E, McKinney JD (2015) Single-cell tracking reveals antibiotic-induced changes in mycobacterial energy metabolism. MBio 6:e02236–e02214

Manniche C, Jordan A (2016) 10 years of research: from ignoring Modic changes to considerations regarding treatment and prevention of low-grade disc infections. Future Sci OA 2

Mekterovic I, Mekterovic D, Maglica Z (2014) BactImAS: a platform for processing and analysis of bacterial time-lapse microscopy movies. BMC Bioinforma 15:251

Mouton JM, Helaine S, Holden DW, Sampson SL (2016) Elucidating population-wide mycobacterial replication dynamics at the single-cell level. Microbiol Read Engl 162:966–978

Nicholson JK, Holmes E, Wilson ID (2005) Opinion: gut microorganisms, mammalian metabolism and personalized health care. Nat Rev Microbiol 3:431–438

Perry RJ, Peng L, Barry NA, Cline GW, Zhang D, Cardone RL, Petersen KF, Kibbey RG, Goodman AL, Shulman GI (2016) Acetate mediates a microbiome-brain-β-cell axis to promote metabolic syndrome. Nature 534:213–217

Pflughoeft KJ, Versalovic J (2012) Human microbiome in health and disease. Annu Rev Pathol Mech Dis 7:99–122

Rollason J, McDowell A, Albert HB, Barnard E, Worthington T, Hilton AC, Vernallis A, Patrick S, Elliott T, Lambert P (2013) Genotypic and antimicrobial characterisation of *Propionibacterium acnes* isolates from surgically excised lumbar disc herniations. Biomed Res Int 2013:1–7

Santi I, Dhar N, Bousbaine D, Wakamoto Y, McKinney JD (2013) Single-cell dynamics of the chromosome replication and cell division cycles in mycobacteria. Nat Commun 4:2470

Shreiner AB, Kao JY, Young VB (2015) The gut microbiome in health and in disease. Curr Opin Gastroenterol 31:69–75

Tille P (2013) Bailey & Scott's diagnostic microbiology, 13th edn. Mosby, St. Louis

Turpin W, Espin-Garcia O, Xu W, Silverberg MS, Kevans D, Smith MI, Guttman DS, Griffiths A, Panaccione R, Otley A et al (2016) Association of host genome with intestinal microbial composition in a large healthy cohort. Nat Genet 48:1413–1417

Wakamoto Y, Dhar N, Chait R, Schneider K, Signorino-Gelo F, Leibler S, McKinney JD (2013) Dynamic persistence of antibiotic-stressed mycobacteria. Science 339:91–95

Wilson ID, Nicholson JK (2009) The role of gut microbiota in drug response. Curr Pharm Des 15:1519–1523

Zheng P, Zeng B, Zhou C, Liu M, Fang Z, Xu X, Zeng L, Chen J, Fan S, Du X et al (2016) Gut microbiome remodeling induces depressive-like behaviors through a pathway mediated by the host's metabolism. Mol Psychiatry 21:786–796

Zoetendal EG, Rajilic-Stojanovic M, de Vos WM (2008) High-throughput diversity and functionality analysis of the gastrointestinal tract microbiota. Gut 57:1605–1615

Present and Future in Personalized Clinical and Laboratory Approaches to In Vitro Fertilization Procedures

Anđelka Radojčić Badovinac, Neda Smiljan Severinski, and Sanja Dević Pavlić

Abstract Personalized approach to a patient engaged into an infertility treatment has been present since the early beginnings of the assisted reproductive technologies, and is constantly developing because of the progress of therapy, medication and laboratory methods. Personalization of the infertility treatment can be discussed on three different levels: approach to the patient, selection of gametes and assessment of embryos. Personalization of the approach to the patient includes adjustment of controlled ovarian stimulation strategy as well as usage of the biomarkers for the ovarian response to the hormone stimulation. Regarding gametes and embryo assessment, personalization includes application of novel OMICS and other high-throughput methods for selection of the oocytes and/or embryos with the highest developmental potential. Personalization of the treatment approaches and ovarian stimulation protocols along with improved laboratory techniques would lead to better treatment efficiency with improved safety for the patient, higher percentage of babies born per cycle and higher cumulative live birth rate for couple in shorter period of time.

1 Introduction

Questions regarding human reproduction are rather sensitive. Personalized approach to a patient has been present since early beginnings, and is constantly developing because of the progress of therapy, medication and laboratory methods. Personalization can be discussed on three levels: approach to a patient, precisely infertile couple, selection of gametes and assessment of embryo for its implantation potential. The main goal of infertility treatment (in vitro fertilization; IVF) using assisted reproductive technologies (ART) is single healthy baby born at term. For all kinds

A. Radojčić Badovinac (✉) · S. Dević Pavlić
Department of Biotechnology, Centre for High-Throughput Technologies, University of Rijeka, Rijeka, Croatia
e-mail: andjelka@biotech.uniri.hr

N. Smiljan Severinski
Department of Obstetrics and Gynaecology, Clinical Hospital Centre Rijeka, Rijeka, Croatia

© Springer Nature Switzerland AG 2019
N. Bodiroga-Vukobrat et al. (eds.), *Personalized Medicine in Healthcare Systems*, Europeanization and Globalization 5, https://doi.org/10.1007/978-3-030-16465-2_8

of infertility treatments this is the only true measure of success. Millions of infertile couples achieve parenthood because of IVF treatment, but many of them give up for various reasons. Major concerns of infertility treatment are the time which patients spend in treatment and uncertain outcome. In treatment approach clinicians need to focus on reducing the time of treatment and increasing the take-home baby rate. There are many difficulties that couple faces when they decide to enter treatment, some of them resulting even with withdrawal. Some of these issues are postponed beginning of the treatment, physical or psychological difficulties, personal and/or relationship issues, treatment rejection, psychological disorders and clinical or organizational problems.[1] The patients have their own perspective about the treatment and expect individual approach, high quality treatment with minimal side-effects, as well as quick end of the treatment with successful outcome. Therefore, the question is: what is today approach in infertility treatment and how can we personalize the treatment even more?

2 The Strategies of the Controlled Ovarian Stimulation (COS) and Treatment Approach Using Biomarkers

Basic and clinical research combined with new technologies led to a series of innovations, especially in the field of controlled ovarian stimulation. Follicle stimulating hormone (FSH), urinary or recombinant, can be applied alone or together with luteinizing hormone (LH) derived from human menopausal gonadotrophin (HMG), human chorionic gonadotrophin or as human recombinant LH. Treatment protocols which beside FSH include agonist or antagonist gonadotrophin analogues (GnRH) and occasional use of steroid hormones, such as progesterone, estrogen, testosterone, dehydroepiandrosterone (DHEA) or growth hormone (hGH) ensures versatility, thus enabling personalized approach for each couple, although this sometimes tends to be confusing.

Ovarian reserve tests help in prediction of individual response on COS, and therefore, in choosing the best treatment options for patients undergoing IVF. Presently, the scientific research on ovarian reserve markers represent one of the most interesting areas of reproductive medicine with wide clinical use. Anti-Müllerian hormone (AMH), a marker of ovarian reserve status, and antral follicle count (AFC) help in prediction of ovarian response to COS. Prediction of ovarian response is crucial for individualization of the treatments, improving efficacy and safety for the patients.[2] Improved technologies and automated AMH determination assays together with advanced ultrasound technologies (3D, 4D) in AFC estimation significantly contribute to standardization, accuracy and prediction of ovarian response to hormone stimulation.

---

[1]Gameiro et al. (2012).
[2]Broer et al. (2011, 2013).

Poor ovarian response (POR) is a symptom of decreased ovarian reserve and ovarian inability to respond to ovarian hormone stimulation. A poor responder patients show decreased follicular response, resulting in a reduced number of oocytes being retrieved and consequently low number of embryos being transferred. The definition of POR patients is still missing because of heterogeneity of investigated groups of patients. The lack of uniform definition on POR makes it impossible to compare studies or even to create assessment protocols to improve the treatment outcome. Many studies on poor response to treatment showed very low live birth rates, irrespective of patients' age, used treatment protocol, or POR criteria considered.[3] Using this approach the definition of poor ($\leq$3 oocytes) and high ($>$15 oocytes) ovarian response to hormone stimulation is well defined, but normal (10–15 oocytes) and suboptimal (4–9 oocytes) ovarian response remains unclear. Nevertheless, the fact remains that larger number of oocytes retrieved after ovarian stimulation result with higher number of born babies, upon all (fresh and cryopreserved) embryos and oocytes being used.[4]

Besides ovarian reserve, the response to ovarian hormone stimulation depends upon ovarian sensitivity too. It has been shown that there is an association between single nucleotide polymorphisms (SNP's) of the FSH receptor (FSHR) and the ovarian activity.[5] Some FSHR gene polymorphisms can be associated with positive ovarian response on gonadotrophins. Therefore, the pharmacogenetics approach should also be applied for individualization of gonadotrophin doses and prediction of ovarian response during COS. There is no association between FSHR gene polymorphism and the markers of ovarian reserve, AMH and AFC.[6]

A second level of the personalized approach to the human reproductive capacity are analyses of the each oocyte or embryo meant to be transferred to uterus in IVF procedure. Quality of MII oocite is investigated in context of its maturation in cumulus-oocyte complex (COC) and follicular fluid (FF) content.

3 Embryo Quality Assessment Based on OMICS Methods and Research of the Oocyte Microenvironment

Current embryo assessment methodologies that are used in ART are mainly based on embryo morphology. Although standardization and combination of different morphology assessment approaches led to improvement of pregnancy rates, their precision and objectivity are still unsatisfactory.[7] Therefore there is constant pursuit for

---

[3]Ferraretti et al. (2011), La Marca et al. (2015), and Polyzos et al. (2014).

[4]Drakopoulos et al. (2016).

[5]Simoni and Casarini (2014).

[6]Mohiyiddeen et al. (2012).

[7]Benkhalifa et al. (2015), Bromer and Seli (2008), and Uyar et al. (2013).

the development of an objective, reliable and accurate test for assessment of oocyte and embryo quality as well as clinical outcome of ART procedure.

In an attempt to discover a novel techniques and/or biomarkers for embryo quality assessment many of new methods have been applied, such as: gene expression and transcriptome analysis, as well as proteomics and metabolomics analysis.

One of the key factors that influence the success rate of the medically assisted reproduction is the quality of the oocyte. Adequately conducted, parallel and synchronized folliculogenesis, oogenesis and meiosis are necessary for oocyte development. All of these events take place in the microenvironment that surrounds the oocyte which includes the cumulus cells (CCs) and the follicular fluid.[8] Cumulus cells are in close contact with the oocyte, together forming the cumulus-oocyte complex (COC), while follicular fluid is secreted by granulosa and theca cells and is also a part of the microenvironment surrounding the developing oocyte.[9] One of the advantages of the analysis conducted on FF and CC is their accessibility and non-invasiveness of the procedures of their collection. Understanding the nature and the diversity of all the substances that transmit around them is still insufficient.

Methods that are used for the transcriptome analysis include qualitative and quantitative characterization of gene expression in CCs, oocytes or embryos. Quantitative polymerase chain reaction (qRT-PCR) is used for the analysis of individual genes of interest, while microarray analysis or high throughput deep sequencing are conducted for the analysis of the whole genome transcriptome. Although the latter mentioned methods are more precise and provide more detailed results, their price and complexity are still restrictive for the clinical use. It is more likely that the particular genes identified by those methods would be recognized as predictors of oocyte and/or embryo quality and then subsequently assessed by qRT-PCR. Recently, a number of studies investigated oocyte and cumulus cells transcriptome trying to identify a potential predictor of embryo quality, but no accurate exclusive biomarker was yet distinguished. The discrepancies of the obtained results may be because of differences in used technologies, study populations (age, diagnosis, treatment etc.), in vitro laboratory procedures or study outcomes.[10] Nevertheless, constant development of new technologies will hopefully soon lead to definition of group of transcripts that will successfully predict embryo quality.

In the past decade there is the emergence of the so called OMICS methods that include proteomics (investigation of the proteins expression) and metabolomics (investigation of the protein secretion in the intracellular space).[11] Most of those methods aim to discover specific biomarkers of oocyte or embryo quality. Recent advances in proteomic technology are mostly related to mass spectrometry (MS) instrumentation. Current major downsides of proteomic and metabolomic

---

[8]Rienzi et al. (2012).

[9]Revelli et al. (2009).

[10]Dumesic et al. (2015).

[11]Egea et al. (2014).

profiling methods are their price and duration of analysis.[12] Hopefully, constant development of given technologies would lead to facilitation of their clinical application.

Possibilities for the single embryo transfer in assisted reproduction methods will significantly lover a risk to both mother and babies. Selection of the most viable embryo in routine IVF laboratory today lies on morphology assignment. In everyday clinical practice in ART looking good is still important. Main morphological parameters are size and symmetry of the blastomeres, nucleation and time of division. Nevertheless, none of the parameters can be considered as an absolute indicator of embryo viability or euploidy, although the assessment of human embryo can be plausible by the combination of the time-lapse microscopy and OMICS algorithms. Grading system for the embryo selection/deselection is often not associated with embryo physiology. Key biomarkers for the most viable embryos analyzed through non-invasive methods are measurements of glucose uptake and oxygen consumption combined with analyses of key amino acids and generation of lactate in cultivating media.[13]

Time-laps incubation provides kinetics pattern and helps to quantify embryo viability. There is neither agreement about normal or abnormal intervals of division nor single morphokinetic parameter which could predict embryo implantation potential.[14] Considering non-invasive analyses of embryo physiology, no highly sufficient method of embryo selection is still available.

4 Screening of Biopsied Embryo

Invasive methods of embryo selection are based on blastomere or trophoectoderm biopsies. Preimplantation genetic diagnosis (PGD) did not give exclusive results and reliability as expected. Future trends toward array comparative genomic hybridization (aCGH) or next generation sequencing as a rapid and most reliable means of analysis and selection of genetically and chromosomally normal embryos could be suitable for each IVF clinic in the future. Not every euploid embryo has the potential to result with pregnancy. Another independent biomarker for the prediction of euploid blastocyst implantation potential can be mitochondrial DNA (mtDNA) quantity in screened embryo. Underlying biological cause of elevated mtDNA in preimplantation embryo is not known, but its negative predictive value is very high.[15]

---

[12]Chronowska (2014).

[13]Gardner et al. (2001), and Gardner (2015).

[14]Kaser and Racowsky (2014).

[15]Ravichandran et al. (2017).

5 Conclusion

To ensure identification of biomarkers that could reliably and objectively predict embryo quality in the IVF laboratory, basic science should continue with the research that will provide better insight in the oocyte physiology and biochemical processes involved in the oocyte maturation. It is expected that the best way to improve efficiency of the embryo assessment would be combining conventional morphology assessment with some of the new high-throughput techniques.

Accuracy, prediction and personalization of the infertility treatment significantly reduces the time between beginning of the treatment and parenthood achievement, thus making it integral part of preparation and treatment strategy. Various treatment approaches and ovarian stimulation protocols along with improved laboratory techniques contribute to better treatment efficiency with improved safety for the patient, higher percentage of babies born per cycle and higher cumulative live birth rate for couple in shorter period of time.

References

Benkhalifa M, Madkour A et al (2015) From global proteome profiling to single targeted molecules of follicular fluid and oocyte: contribution to embryo development and IVF outcome. Expert Rev Proteomics 12(4):407–423. https://doi.org/10.1586/14789450.2015.1056782

Broer SL, Dólleman M et al (2011) AMH and AFC as predictors of excessive response in controlled ovarian hyperstimulation: a meta-analysis. Hum Reprod Update 17(1):46–54. https://doi.org/10.1093/humupd/dmq034

Broer SL, Dólleman M et al (2013) Prediction of an excessive response in in vitro fertilization from patient characteristics and ovarian reserve tests and comparison in subgroups: an individual patient data meta-analysis. Fertil Steril 100(2):420–429. https://doi.org/10.1016/j.fertnstert.2013.04.024

Bromer JG, Seli E (2008) Assessment of embryo viability in assisted reproductive technology: shortcomings of current approaches and the emerging role of metabolomics. Curr Opin Obstet Gynecol 20(3):234–241. https://doi.org/10.1097/GCO.0b013e3282fe723d

Chronowska E (2014) High-throughput analysis of ovarian granulosa cell transcriptome. Biomed Res Int 2014:213570. https://doi.org/10.1155/2014/213570

Drakopoulos P, Blockeel C et al (2016) Conventional ovarian stimulation and single embryo transfer for IVF/ICSI. How many oocytes do we need to maximize cumulative live birth rates after utilization of all fresh and frozen embryos? Hum Reprod 31(2):370–376. https://doi.org/10.1093/humrep/dev316

Dumesic DA, Meldrum DR et al (2015) Oocyte environment: follicular fluid and cumulus cells are critical for oocyte health. Fertil Steril 103(2):303–316. https://doi.org/10.1016/j.fertnstert.2014.11.015

Egea RR, Puchalt NG et al (2014) OMICS: current and future perspectives in reproductive medicine and technology. J Hum Reprod Sci 7(2):73–92. https://doi.org/10.4103/0974-1208.138857

Ferraretti AP, La Marca A et al (2011) ESHRE consensus on the definition of 'poor response' to ovarian stimulation for in vitro fertilization: the Bologna criteria. Hum Reprod 26(7):1616–1624. https://doi.org/10.1093/humrep/der092

Gameiro S, Boivin J et al (2012) Why do patients discontinue fertility treatment? A systematic review of reasons and predictors of discontinuation in fertility treatment. Hum Reprod Update 18(6):652–669. https://doi.org/10.1093/humupd/dms031

Gardner DK (2015) Lactate production by the mammalian blastocyst: manipulating the microenvironment for uterine implantation and invasion? BioEssays 37(4):364–371. https://doi.org/10.1002/bies.201400155

Gardner DK, Lane M et al (2001) Noninvasive assessment of human embryo nutrient consumption as a measure of developmental potential. Fertil Steril 76(6):1175–1180

Kaser DJ, Racowsky C (2014) Clinical outcomes following selection of human preimplantation embryos with time-lapse monitoring: a systematic review. Hum Reprod Update 20(5):617–631. https://doi.org/10.1093/humupd/dmu023

La Marca A, Grisendi V et al (2015) Live birth rates in the different combinations of the Bologna criteria poor ovarian responders: a validation study. J Assist Reprod Genet 32(6):931–937. https://doi.org/10.1007/s10815-015-0476-4

Mohiyiddeen L, Newman WG et al (2012) Follicle-stimulating hormone receptor gene polymorphisms are not associated with ovarian reserve markers. Fertil Steril 97(3):677–681. https://doi.org/10.1016/j.fertnstert.2011.12.040

Polyzos NP, Nwoye M et al (2014) Live birth rates in Bologna poor responders treated with ovarian stimulation for IVF/ICSI. Reprod Biomed Online 28(4):469–474. https://doi.org/10.1016/j.rbmo.2013.11.010

Ravichandran K, McCaffrey C et al (2017) Mitochondrial DNA quantification as a tool for embryo viability assessment: retrospective analysis of data from single euploid blastocyst transfers. Hum Reprod 6:1–11. https://doi.org/10.1093/humrep/dex070

Revelli A, Delle Piane L et al (2009) Follicular fluid content and oocyte quality: from single biochemical markers to metabolomics. Reprod Biol Endocrinol 7:40. https://doi.org/10.1186/1477-7827-7-40

Rienzi L, Balaban B et al (2012) The oocyte. Hum Reprod 1:i2–i121. https://doi.org/10.1093/humrep/des200

Simoni M, Casarini L (2014) Mechanisms in endocrinology: genetics of FSH action: a 2014-and-beyond view. Eur J Endocrinol 170(3):R91–R107. https://doi.org/10.1530/EJE-13-0624

Uyar A, Torrealday S et al (2013) Cumulus and granulosa cell markers of oocyte and embryo quality. Fertil Steril 99(4):979–997. https://doi.org/10.1016/j.fertnstert.2013.01.129

Microbiota: Novel Gateway Towards Personalised Medicine

Jurica Zucko, Antonio Starcevic, Janko Diminic, and Damir Oros

Abstract Microbes living in and on us have been recognized in the last decade as important part of ourselves and have been assigned a status of an organ with a wide range of functions—from metabolizing food to training our immune system. The intraindividual and interindividual variation of normal microbiota is vast and its composition is influenced by various external factors—most notable being diet, antibiotics and medication. External factors can cause a disturbance in microbiota frequently termed as dysbiosis which is often associated with a range of diseases—from inflammatory bowel disease and diabetes to obesity and cancer. Pioneering works in manipulating the microbiota for preventing and treating disease shows huge promise but also open a number of questions—from standardization and safety to personalization and reproducibility.

1 Introduction

Personal medicine has long been searching for markers and targets to optimize treatment for each patient with focus on proteins, genes and small molecules. Now a new player has come in sight with an ever increasingly important role—microbes living in and on us. We call those microbes living side by side with us microbiota and it is believed their number roughly matches that of our cells.[1] Besides sheer number, their strength also lies in the genetic potential they possess—and it is a huge one, with an estimated number of genes more than 100 times larger than human gene complement.[2] From this plethora of genes each might be crucial to adding a function for host's wellbeing. They are an inseparable part of ourselves influencing metabolism, modulating drug interactions, modulating onset of disease and affecting our

---

[1] Sender et al. (2016).
[2] Qin et al. (2010).

J. Zucko (✉) · A. Starcevic · J. Diminic · D. Oros
Faculty of Food Technology and Biotechnology, University of Zagreb, Zagreb, Croatia
e-mail: jzucko@pbf.hr

© Springer Nature Switzerland AG 2019
N. Bodiroga-Vukobrat et al. (eds.), *Personalized Medicine in Healthcare Systems*,
Europeanization and Globalization 5, https://doi.org/10.1007/978-3-030-16465-2_9

immune system.[3] With the notion of microbiota's importance for host's health and enabled by advances in sequencing technologies several projects started with the aim of cataloguing our microbes. Most notable were the Human Microbiome Project (HMP) and Metagenomics of Human Intestinal Tract (MetaHit) Consortium. The aim of the Human Microbiome Project was to catalogue all microbes from several body sites of American adults using both 16S rRNA gene sequencing and metagenome sequencing.[4] MetaHIT was oriented only on faecal samples and succeeded in identifying minimal gut bacterial genome and gut metagenome based on functions present in all individuals and most bacteria (see footnote 3). This work resulted in the definition of three enterotypes based on the abundance of specific phyla[5]—a concept that was later disputed.[6] As microbes can also be correlated to diseased states of the host, a concept of dysbiosis has been formed defined as a disturbance of microbiota homeostasis caused by imbalance in the microbiota, its distribution or changes in its functional composition and metabolic activities.[7] In both animal and human models dysbiosis has been implicated in the development of a wide range of diseases—among them inflammatory bowel disease, obesity, colorectal cancer, allergic disorders and autism spectrum disorders.[8]

2   Normal Microbiota and Factors Affecting It

To be able to diagnose dysbiosis and potentially start treating it we have to understand how normal microbiota looks like across populations of different geography, age and cultural (e.g. culinary) backgrounds. A lot of research has been carried out in recent years trying to define normal dynamics of microbiota and genetic and environmental factors affecting it. It is believed we acquire microbiota at the moment of birth, although infants are exposed to microbes earlier on, while in the placenta.[9] Depending on the delivery method newborn's microbiota in all body sites resembles microbial composition of mother's skin for babies delivered by caesarian section or microbial composition of mother's vagina for babies delivered vaginally. Newborns delivered by cesarean section have microbiota dominant by *Staphylococcus, Corynebacterium* and *Propionibacterium* while newborns delivered vaginally have microbiota dominated by *Lactobacillus, Prevotella* or *Sneathia* spp.[10] For the first 3 years of child's life gut microbiota is characterized by low

---

[3]Grice and Segre (2012).

[4]Turnbaugh et al. (2007).

[5]Arumugam et al. (2011).

[6]Knights et al. (2014).

[7]Bien et al. (2013), and Knights et al. (2013).

[8]DeGruttola et al. (2016).

[9]Aagaard et al. (2014).

[10]Dominguez-Bello et al. (2010).

species diversity and high instability and within time it is gradually transformed to resemble adult community dominated by *Firmicutes* and *Bacteroidetes*.[11] This change happens in a series of discrete steps punctuated by life events.[12] Major life events in early life affecting microbiota are considered to be breast or formula—feeding, starting rice cereals and table foods, antibiotic treatments and ending of breast milk and formula feeding. A study comparing Italian and African children's gut microbiota showed that breastfed children had similar microbial populations dominated by *Bifidobacterium* species regardless of their geographic origin. When starting solid foods of their respective Western or African diets children clustered into distinct geographic groupings reflecting the importance of food in shaping long-term gut microbial profiles.[13] Typical western adult gut microbiome is comprised of half a dozen bacterial phyla dominated by *Bacteroidetes* and *Firmicutes*.[14] Expanded data estimates total western genus richness at 784 ± 40 and the size of the core western microbiota (genera shared by 95% of sampled individuals) to be composed of 17 genera. When extending data to studies covering non-western populations estimated size of human core microbiome is reduced to 14 genera.[15] Although composition of microbiota in an individual remains fairly consistent over time it is possible to alter human gut microbiome by introducing diets composed entirely of animal or plant products which rapidly and transiently change the composition.[16] Besides transient changes more important are long term effects of diet on our microbiota. Several studies have shown distinct microbiota in individuals from Malawi, Venezuela and United States,[17] children from Italy and Burkina Faso (see footnote 14), children from Bangladesh and United States,[18] and between rural Africans and African Americans[19] which is partially caused by diet. The difference in microbiota composition is also reflected in enrichment of certain enzymes/pathways. In United States populations enzymes involved in protein degradation and bile salt metabolism were enriched due to the diet rich in proteins and fat while in Amerindian and Malawian populations starch degrading enzymes were enriched due to diets poor in protein and rich in starch. Similar observation was found in Hadza tribe from Tanzania where microbes able to ferment fibrous plant foods were enriched. The study also identified differences in microbiota composition between sexes which is believed to be caused by division of labour with regard to foraging and higher levels of microbial richness and biodiversity when compared to

---

[11]Lozupone et al. (2012).

[12]Koenig et al. (2011).

[13]De Filippo et al. (2010).

[14]Eckburg et al. (2005).

[15]Falony et al. (2016).

[16]David et al. (2014).

[17]Yatsunenko et al. (2012).

[18]Lin et al. (2013).

[19]Ou et al. (2013).

populations following the western diet.[20] Besides diet, several external factors can affect microbiota such as antibiotics, prebiotics, probiotics and sanitation. Antibiotics are compounds causing significant disturbances in gut microbiota and by suppression of both beneficial and pathogenic ones can produce emergence of multidrug-resistant pathogens.[21] The effects of antibiotics on bacterial flora can be long lasting—from several months up to 2 years after treatment in which microbiota can have low diversity and significant disturbances in bacterial community.[22] Special care should be taken when prescribing antibiotics to children in the first year of life due to an increased risk of developing childhood asthma and allergies.[23] Probiotics are defined as live microorganisms which, when administered in adequate amounts, confer a health benefit to the host. Most of these probiotic microorganisms are members of the *Lactobacillus* and *Bifidobacterium* genus. Results of studies on humans are varied, most likely due to methodological differences and differences in host cohorts. But what was clearly shown in humans and animal models is that efficacy in promoting health is strain dependent and not species or genus specific.[24] Prebiotics, on the other hand, are non-digestible food ingredients which selectively stimulate growth of *Lactobacillus* and *Bifidobacterium* species in the large intestine and consequently translate health benefits to the host.[25] Besides intentional introduction of microbes, accidental exposure to various organisms can change the composition of microbiota. One such example is the specific change of microbiome composition and diversity correlated with *Entamoeba* parasite presence in rural Cameroon populations.[26] It is believed that sanitation, drinking water treatment and other hygienic practices are the cause behind reduced biodiversity in westernized microbiomes.[27] A plethora of factors can be correlated with the composition of microbiota in humans. A recent study on Flemish and Dutch cohorts from 503 metadata variables identified 69 factors that correlate significantly with overall microbiome community variation. Medication having the largest explanatory power on microbiome composition and stool consistency, defined by Bristol stool scale, being the top single nonredundant microbiome covariate in metadata (see footnote 16). Other than environmental factors it is believed that host genetics can affect the composition of the gut microbiome. Knowledge of before mentioned environmental factors influencing microbiota is essential for removing "noise" and focusing only on host genetic effects driving the variation in the microbiota.[28] Although early research on twins failed to find a significant difference in microbiota

---

[20]Schnorr et al. (2014).

[21]Becattini et al. (2016).

[22]Jernberg et al. (2010).

[23]Risnes et al. (2011).

[24]Conlon and Bird (2015).

[25]Voreades et al. (2014).

[26]Morton et al. (2015).

[27]Martinez et al. (2015).

[28]Spor et al. (2011).

composition, newer research on using host reads from Human Microbiome Project (HMP) identified significant association between host genetic variation and microbiome composition in 10 of the 15 body sites sampled. It is believed host genetic variation in immunity-related pathways, especially in the genes previously associated with microbiome-related complex diseases such as inflammatory bowel disease and obesity-related disorders are drivers of microbiota variability among individuals.[29] From small number of studies several taxa were found to be related to host genotype. *Bifidobacterium* levels and lactase encoding LCT gene region linked to lactase persistence and lactose tolerance in adults were strongly associated in HMP and TwinsUK data sets. Taxa *Turicibacter,* which directly contacts host cells and is implicated in inflammation and cancer, is associated with genetic variation for susceptibility to hepatocellular carcinomas in murine models. Levels of genus *Akkermansia*, which is enriched in lean individuals and is linked to improved glucose metabolism, were associated with variations in genes responsible for tri-glyceride levels and gonadal fat, genes associated with obesity and sialic acid binding lectin. It is believed that environmental factors outweigh host genetics in shaping the composition of the gut microbiome. However, since field elucidating interactions of host genetics to microbiota is still in infancy recent developments in sample acquisition, data generation and analysis will shed more light on the interplay between host genetic variants and microbiota composition.[30]

3   Microbiota and Disease

Changes in the gut microbiota have been observed in number of diseases, including metabolic diseases such as obesity and type 2 diabetes, irritable bowel syndrome, autism spectrum disorders and cancer. Underlying mechanisms how microbiota modulates disease are still largely unknown and only a few studies have validated causality in animal models and humans. What is known is that in a number of diseased states we can observe a change in microbial composition causing an imbalance between beneficial and potentially pathogenic bacteria. This deviation from healthy microbiota was termed dysbiosis and 'was defined as a disturbance of gut microbiota homeostasis due to the imbalance in the flora itself, changes in their functional composition and metabolic activities or changes in their local distribution (see footnote 8). Three events can be characteristic of dysbiosis: loss of beneficial microbes, excessive growth of potentially pathogenic microbes and loss of overall microbial diversity. These events are not mutually exclusive and occur simulta-neously in most cases. In the last decade genomic and metabolomic technologies enabled association of microbiota with various disease states, some of which are mentioned here. It is also important to note that diagnosing dysbiosis requires taking

---

[29]Blekhman et al. (2015).
[30]Goodrich et al. (2016).

into account all changes in microbiota occurring in the population e.g. related to different diets, medication, lifestyle or age group.

Diseases related to gastrointestinal tract were first to be associated with microbiota imbalance. Inflammatory Bowel Disease (IBD)—a group of inflammatory conditions of the colon and small intestine was one of the first where the search for single pathogen cause was started more than a decade ago. In this time many microbes were associated with IBD: *Mycobacterium avium* subsp *paratuberculosis*, adherent-invasive *Escherichia coli*, number of *Proteobacteria* and non-jejuni and -coli *Campylobacter* (see footnote 9). Due to a number of inconsistent results current focus has shifted towards the idea that IBD is caused by the imbalance of commensal microbes and is associated with more complex interactions between the host and the whole of intestinal microbiota.[31] Characteristic signature of microbiota change has been observed in IBD. For Chron's disease (CD) this signature is characterized by a reduction in *Firmicutes* and change in the level of *Bacteroidetes*.[32] *Faecalibacterium prausnitzii* was the most significantly reduced member of *Firmicutes* in patients with Chron's disease and this is believed to play a key role in developing CD.[33] Change in the abundance of phyla *Firmicutes* and *Bacteroidetes* is linked to an increase in abundance of microbes from phylum *Proteobacteria*, which are believed to play "aggressor" role in the initiation of chronic inflammation in patients with IBD.[34]

Obesity is a metabolic disease believed to be caused by higher energy intake and low energy expenditure. However, newer findings show a potential relationship between the gut microbiota and development of obese phenotype and shift the focus to microbes.[35] Mouse models showed an increased level of *Firmicutes* and decrease of *Bacteroidetes* species in obese mice[36] but results in human studies remain controversial.[37] Although debate whether microbiota causes obesity in humans is still not resolved experiments on germ-free mice support the idea.[38] Support also came from the recent finding that human obese phenotype can be transferred to germ-free mice by transplanting "obese" microbiota. Alternately, cohousing them with mice containing lean microbiota prevented the development of obesity.[39] Recent studies have stopped treating obesity as single phenotype and started correlating microbial signatures to features associated with metabolic syndromes, such as diabetes type II. Genome-wide association studies on Chinese[40] and

---

[31]Shanahan and Bernstein (2009).

[32]Marchesi et al. (2015).

[33]Hansen et al. (2012).

[34]Lupp et al. (2007).

[35]Turnbaugh et al. (2006).

[36]Ley et al. (2005).

[37]Ley et al. (2006), and Duncan et al. (2008).

[38]Turnbaugh et al. (2008).

[39]Ridaura et al. (2013).

[40]Qin et al. (2012).

European[41] populations identified several markers associated with diabetic patients at the gene functional level but failed to find consensus on the species level, indicating biomarkers could be population specific.

Although microbiota has also been associated with diseases such as autism spectrum disorders and some chronic liver diseases in this short review we will focus on the disease with which microbiota has the most intimate connection— colorectal cancer (CRC). Evidence that colonic microbiota plays important role in onset of sporadic CRC is increasing (see footnote 20). Patients with CRC show specific pattern involving a decrease of butyrate producing bacteria and an increase in the proportion of opportunistic pathogens. The biggest decrease was noted in *Proteobacteria, Bifidobacteria* and *Prevotella* while increase was noted in *Firmicutes, Bacteroidetes, Enterobacteriaceae* and *Fusobacteria*.[42] There are several hypotheses on how microbiota is related to the onset of CRC. One states that certain low abundance microbiota members possess specific virulence traits which remodel the remaining microbiota in a way to promote mucosal immune response and changes in colonic epithelial cells.[43] Other states a two-step process is behind the onset of CRC- initiated by DNA damage caused by specific proteins or metabolites produced by indigenous intestinal bacteria leading to tumorigenesis, followed by changes that favour the proliferation of opportunistic pathogens.[44] Opportunistic pathogens have been found at higher abundance in CRC but it is still unclear whether they are involved in the onset of the disease or just benefit from changes in the environment.[45] From human studies few pathobionts have been linked to CRC including *Streptococcus gallolyticus, Enterococcus faecalis* and *Bacteroides fragilis*. Diet is also believed to play important role in development of CRC, with fiber-rich diets believed to have a protective effect while high fat and high protein diets increasing the risk.[46]

4 Microbiota as Cure

Altered intestinal microbiota has been linked with more than 25 disease states— ranging from gastrointestinal diseases and metabolic diseases to diseases like Alzheimer's disease, autistic spectrum disorders and autoimmune diseases. Although alterations in the microbiota were correlated to a number of diseases it is still unclear whether they are the cause or the effect of the disease and whether

---

[41]Karlsson et al. (2013).

[42]Schulz et al. (2014).

[43]Sears and Pardoll (2011).

[44]Tjalsma et al. (2012).

[45]Warren et al. (2013).

[46]O'Keefe et al. (2015).

manipulation of the microbiota could help to prevent or treat the disease.[47] There have been examples of manipulating microbiota to improve human health using probiotics, prebiotics and faecal transfers.

Using prebiotics to manipulate gut microbiota is an indirect method in which prebiotics act as a growth substrate boosting the growth of beneficial microbes in the colon, thus potentially correcting dysbiosis associated with the disease. Work on pure cultures showed varying selectivity for different prebiotics—with fructooligosaccharides being less selective than galactooligosaccharides for tested obligate gut anaerobes, and a smaller number of tested bacteria able to utilize starch and long-chain inulin for growth.[48] Since these results came from research performed on pure cultures and *in vitro* models caution should be exercised when applying them to mixed cultures and *in vivo* conditions of the human colon. To successfully apply prebiotic treatment we should be able to assess the importance of specific microbe to development of the disease, its response to specific prebiotic and finally net effect its abundance plays in the patient's diseased state. Currently, only a handful of bacterial species which show potential to respond to prebiotics have been associated with diseases. *Faecalibacterium prausnitzii*, a bacterium shown to have an anti-inflammatory effect[49] and its low abundance is correlated with Chron's disease,[50] is currently best candidate for prebiotic manipulation since it was shown to respond to mixed chain length fructan supplementation.[51]

Probiotics were developed based on the concept that certain bacteria can provide a health benefit for the host and were first consumed through fermented foods. Nowadays available probiotic supplements contain one or more strains from *Lactobacillus* species, *Bifidobacterium* species, *Streptococcus* species, *Escherichia coli* and *Enterococcus* species.[52] European Food Safety Authority has recognized health benefits of different probiotics with the only accepted claim being benefit on lactose digestion. Probiotics express their action either by direct interaction with the host or indirect one, by modulation of present commensal microbiota. There is a growing body of evidence that specific probiotic strains or combinations of strains can be beneficial in different diseases. For ulcerative colitis *Escherichia coli* Nissle 1917 strain has been shown to be equally successful compared with standard treatment in regards to relapse.[53] With the establishment of the gut-brain axis many of the commensal bacteria and their metabolic products have been associated with changes of behaviour.[54] Probiotics have also been shown to have a protective effect when given in parallel with antibiotics, preventing or at least meliorating disruption of gut

---

[47]Scott et al. (2015).

[48]Scott et al. (2014).

[49]Sokol et al. (2008).

[50]Sokol et al. (2009).

[51]Ramirez-Farias et al. (2009).

[52]Andrews and Tan (2012).

[53]Kruis et al. (2004).

[54]Hsiao et al. (2013).

microbiota.[55] Probiotics were also shown to reduce body weight and BMI with greater effect when multiple species of probiotics were consumed.[56] Testing of probiotics supplementation for weight loss also showed that specific strains of probiotics do not have the same generic effect. Research indicates that *Lactobacillus rhamnosus* CGMCC1.3724 given for weight loss is effective in women and not in men.[57]

The most extreme method of manipulating gut microbiota is the faecal microbiota transplant (FMT)—a concept that has been with us for centuries. Early records going back to fourth century China where the use of human faecal suspension by mouth was used for treating food poisoning and severe diarrhoea.[58] Later practice was expanded to various forms of faecal preparations, additional symptoms and to veterinary medicine.[59] In the last two decades FMT has been promoted from sidelines and obscurity into the spotlight after increasing evidence for its success in treating recurrent *Clostridium difficile* infections.[60] FMT can be performed in various ways—using nasogastric or nasoduodenal tube, colonoscope, enema or capsule,[61] using faecal transplant form single or multiple donors. Two most common conditions for which FMT is used are antibiotic-associated diarrhoea and *Clostridium difficile*-associated diarrhoea where obtained evidence indicate superior or equal to best results obtained by antibiotic therapy.[62] FMT has been tested for treating various other diseases—including metabolic and cardiovascular diseases, autoimmune and allergic diseases. Although some studies show promising results, more randomized control trials with larger cohorts are needed to confirm the efficacy of FMT for those diseases. Previous studies stated no health concern regarding FMT[63] although recently development of new-onset obesity after receiving stool from a healthy but overweight donor[64] has been reported. Defining and standardizing screening procedures and protocols as well as donor and sample management is of utmost importance to prevent any possible transfer of possibly pathogenic microbes.[65] The onset of public stool banks also allows the selection of optimal donors that will have greater colonization success and optimal donor-recipient compatibility.[66]

---

[55]Engelbrektson et al. (2009).

[56]Zhang et al. (2015).

[57]Sanchez et al. (2014).

[58]Zhang et al. (2012).

[59]Borody et al. (2004).

[60]Drekonja et al. (2015).

[61]Choi and Cho (2016).

[62]Bakken et al. (2011), and Surawicz et al. (2013).

[63]Brandt and Aroniadis (2013).

[64]Alang and Kelly (2015).

[65]Kazerouni et al. (2015).

[66]Li et al. (2016b).

Besides being treated as a possible cure, the microbiota of the individual should also be taken into account as an important factor when prescribing medication. Numerous drugs must be metabolized to become active and metabolic activation by the host has been well studied, unlike metabolism by the intestinal microbiota.[67] Currently there are dozens of clinical drugs that have been demonstrated to be co-metabolized by the host and gut microbiota with mechanisms underlying gut microbial modulation on drug metabolism still largely unknown. Knowledge of gut microbial effect on drug metabolism will provide new insight for personalized medicine to influence therapeutic outcomes by influencing gut microbiota.[68]

Although the field is at its infancy and still none of the questions regarding microbiota's effect on the host have been fully studied, just the glimpse of promises microbiota holds for a normal and healthy life are astounding.

References

Aagaard K, Ma J, Antony KM, Ganu R, Petrosino J, Versalovic J (2014) The placenta harbors a unique microbiome. Sci Transl Med 6(237):237ra65. https://doi.org/10.1126/scitranslmed. 3008599

Alang N, Kelly CR (2015) Weight gain after fecal microbiota transplantation. Open Forum Infect Dis 2(1):ofv004. https://doi.org/10.1093/ofid/ofv004

Andrews JM, Tan M (2012) Probiotics in luminal gastroenterology: the current state of play. Intern Med J 42(12):1287–1291. https://doi.org/10.1111/imj.12015

Arumugam M, Raes J, Pelletier E, Le Paslier D, Yamada T, Mende DR et al (2011) Enterotypes of the human gut microbiome. Nature 473(7346):174–180. https://doi.org/10.1038/nature09944

Bakken JS, Borody T, Brandt LJ, Brill JV, Demarco DC, Franzos MA et al (2011) Treating Clostridium difficile infection with fecal microbiota transplantation. Clin Gastroenterol Hepatol 9(12):1044–1049. https://doi.org/10.1016/j.cgh.2011.08.014

Becattini S, Taur Y, Pamer EG (2016) Antibiotic-induced changes in the intestinal microbiota and disease. Trends Mol Med 22(6):458–478. https://doi.org/10.1016/j.molmed.2016.04.003

Bien J, Palagani V, Bozko P (2013) The intestinal microbiota dysbiosis and Clostridium difficile infection: is there a relationship with inflammatory bowel disease? Ther Adv Gastroenterol 6 (1):53–68. https://doi.org/10.1177/1756283X12454590

Blekhman R, Goodrich JK, Huang K, Sun Q, Bukowski R, Bell JT et al (2015) Host genetic variation impacts microbiome composition across human body sites. Genome Biol 16(1):191. https://doi.org/10.1186/s13059-015-0759-1

Borody TJ, Warren EF, Leis SM, Surace R, Ashman O, Siarakas S (2004) Bacteriotherapy using fecal flora: toying with human motions. J Clin Gastroenterol 38(6):475–483

Brandt LJ, Aroniadis OC (2013) An overview of fecal microbiota transplantation: techniques, indications, and outcomes. Gastrointest Endosc 78(2):240–249. https://doi.org/10.1016/j.gie. 2013.03.1329

Choi HH, Cho Y-S (2016) Fecal microbiota transplantation: current applications, effectiveness, and future perspectives. Clin Endosc 49(3):257–265. https://doi.org/10.5946/ce.2015.117

Conlon MA, Bird AR (2015) The impact of diet and lifestyle on gut microbiota and human health. Nutrients 7(1):17–44. https://doi.org/10.3390/nu7010017

---

[67]Kang et al. (2013).

[68]Li et al. (2016a).

David LA, Maurice CF, Carmody RN, Gootenberg DB, Button JE, Wolfe BE et al (2014) Diet rapidly and reproducibly alters the human gut microbiome. Nature 505(7484):559–563. https://doi.org/10.1038/nature12820

De Filippo C, Cavalieri D, Di Paola M, Ramazzotti M, Poullet JB, Massart S et al (2010) Impact of diet in shaping gut microbiota revealed by a comparative study in children from Europe and rural Africa. Proc Natl Acad Sci U S A 107(33):14691–14696. https://doi.org/10.1073/pnas.1005963107

DeGruttola AK, Low D, Mizoguchi A, Mizoguchi E (2016) Current understanding of dysbiosis in disease in human and animal models. Inflamm Bowel Dis 22(5):1137–1150. https://doi.org/10.1097/MIB.0000000000000750

Dominguez-Bello MG, Costello EK, Contreras M, Magris M, Hidalgo G, Fierer N, Knight R (2010) Delivery mode shapes the acquisition and structure of the initial microbiota across multiple body habitats in newborns. Proc Natl Acad Sci U S A 107(26):11971–11975. https://doi.org/10.1073/pnas.1002601107

Drekonja D, Reich J, Gezahegn S, Greer N, Shaukat A, MacDonald R, Rutks I, Wilt TJ (2015) Fecal Microbiota Transplantation for Clostridium difficile Infection: A Systematic Review. Ann Intern Med 162(9):630–638. https://doi.org/10.7326/M14-2693

Duncan SH, Lobley GE, Holtrop G, Ince J, Johnstone AM, Louis P, Flint HJ (2008) Human colonic microbiota associated with diet, obesity and weight loss. Int J Obes (Lond) 32(11):1720–1724. https://doi.org/10.1038/ijo.2008.155

Eckburg PB, Bik EM, Bernstein CN, Purdom E, Dethlefsen L, Sargent M et al (2005) Diversity of the human intestinal microbial flora. Science (New York, NY) 308(5728):1635–1638. https://doi.org/10.1126/science.1110591

Engelbrektson A, Korzenik JR, Pittler A, Sanders ME, Klaenhammer TR, Leyer G, Kitts CL (2009) Probiotics to minimize the disruption of faecal microbiota in healthy subjects undergoing antibiotic therapy. J Med Microbiol 58(Pt 5):663–670. https://doi.org/10.1099/jmm.0.47615-0

Falony G, Joossens M, Vieira-Silva S, Wang J, Darzi Y, Faust K et al (2016) Population-level analysis of gut microbiome variation. Science (New York, NY) 352(6285):560–564. https://doi.org/10.1126/science.aad3503

Goodrich JK, Davenport ER, Waters JL, Clark AG, Ley RE (2016) Cross-species comparisons of host genetic associations with the microbiome. Science (New York, NY) 352(6285):532–535. https://doi.org/10.1126/science.aad9379

Grice EA, Segre JA (2012) The human microbiome: our second genome. Annu Rev Genomics Hum Genet 13:151–170. https://doi.org/10.1146/annurev-genom-090711-163814

Hansen R, Russell RK, Reiff C, Louis P, McIntosh F, Berry SH et al (2012) Microbiota of de-novo pediatric IBD: increased Faecalibacterium prausnitzii and reduced bacterial diversity in Crohn's but not in ulcerative colitis. Am J Gastroenterol 107(12):1913–1922. https://doi.org/10.1038/ajg.2012.335

Hsiao EY, McBride SW, Hsien S, Sharon G, Hyde ER, McCue T et al (2013) Microbiota modulate behavioral and physiological abnormalities associated with neurodevelopmental disorders. Cell 155(7):1451–1463. https://doi.org/10.1016/j.cell.2013.11.024

Jernberg C, Lofmark S, Edlund C, Jansson JK (2010) Long-term impacts of antibiotic exposure on the human intestinal microbiota. Microbiology (Reading, England) 156(Pt 11):3216–3223. https://doi.org/10.1099/mic.0.040618-0

Kang MJ, Kim HG, Kim JS, Oh DG, Um YJ, Seo CS et al (2013) The effect of gut microbiota on drug metabolism. Expert Opin Drug Metab Toxicol 9(10):1295–1308. https://doi.org/10.1517/17425255.2013.807798

Karlsson FH, Tremaroli V, Nookaew I, Bergstrom G, Behre CJ, Fagerberg B et al (2013) Gut metagenome in European women with normal, impaired and diabetic glucose control. Nature 498(7452):99–103. https://doi.org/10.1038/nature12198

Kazerouni A, Burgess J, Burns LJ, Wein LM (2015) Optimal screening and donor management in a public stool bank. Microbiome 3:75. https://doi.org/10.1186/s40168-015-0140-3

Knights D, Lassen KG, Xavier RJ (2013) Advances in inflammatory bowel disease pathogenesis: linking host genetics and the microbiome. Gut 62(10):1505–1510. https://doi.org/10.1136/gutjnl-2012-303954

Knights D, Ward TL, McKinlay CE, Miller H, Gonzalez A, McDonald D, Knight R (2014) Rethinking "enterotypes". Cell Host Microbe 16(4):433–437. https://doi.org/10.1016/j.chom.2014.09.013

Koenig JE, Spor A, Scalfone N, Fricker AD, Stombaugh J, Knight R et al (2011) Succession of microbial consortia in the developing infant gut microbiome. Proc Natl Acad Sci U S A 108 (Suppl 1):4578–4585. https://doi.org/10.1073/pnas.1000081107

Kruis W, Fric P, Pokrotnieks J, Lukas M, Fixa B, Kascak M et al (2004) Maintaining remission of ulcerative colitis with the probiotic Escherichia coli Nissle 1917 is as effective as with standard mesalazine. Gut 53(11):1617–1623. https://doi.org/10.1136/gut.2003.037747

Ley RE, Backhed F, Turnbaugh P, Lozupone CA, Knight RD, Gordon JI (2005) Obesity alters gut microbial ecology. Proc Natl Acad Sci U S A 102(31):11070–11075. https://doi.org/10.1073/pnas.0504978102

Ley RE, Turnbaugh PJ, Klein S, Gordon JI (2006) Microbial ecology: human gut microbes associated with obesity. Nature 444(7122):1022–1023. https://doi.org/10.1038/4441022a

Li H, He J, Jia W (2016a) The influence of gut microbiota on drug metabolism and toxicity. Expert Opin Drug Metab Toxicol 12(1):31–40. https://doi.org/10.1517/17425255.2016.1121234

Li SS, Zhu A, Benes V, Costea PI, Hercog R, Hildebrand F et al (2016b) Durable coexistence of donor and recipient strains after fecal microbiota transplantation. Science (New York, NY) 352 (6285):586–589. https://doi.org/10.1126/science.aad8852

Lin A, Bik EM, Costello EK, Dethlefsen L, Haque R, Relman DA, Singh U (2013) Distinct distal gut microbiome diversity and composition in healthy children from Bangladesh and the United States. PLoS One 8(1):e53838. https://doi.org/10.1371/journal.pone.0053838

Lozupone CA, Stombaugh JI, Gordon JI, Jansson JK, Knight R (2012) Diversity, stability and resilience of the human gut microbiota. Nature 489(7415):220–230. https://doi.org/10.1038/nature11550

Lupp C, Robertson ML, Wickham ME, Sekirov I, Champion OL, Gaynor EC, Finlay BB (2007) Host-mediated inflammation disrupts the intestinal microbiota and promotes the overgrowth of Enterobacteriaceae. Cell Host Microbe 2(3):204

Marchesi JR, Adams DH, Fava F, Hermes GDA, Hirschfield GM, Hold G et al (2015) The gut microbiota and host health: a new clinical frontier. Gut 65(2):330–339. https://doi.org/10.1136/gutjnl-2015-309990

Martinez I, Stegen JC, Maldonado-Gomez MX, Eren AM, Siba PM, Greenhill AR, Walter J (2015) The gut microbiota of rural papua new guineans: composition, diversity patterns, and ecological processes. Cell Rep 11(4):527–538. https://doi.org/10.1016/j.celrep.2015.03.049

Morton ER, Lynch J, Froment A, Lafosse S, Heyer E, Przeworski M et al (2015) Variation in Rural African Gut microbiota is strongly correlated with colonization by Entamoeba and subsistence. PLoS Genet 11(11):e1005658. https://doi.org/10.1371/journal.pgen.1005658

O'Keefe SJ, Li JV, Lahti L, Ou J, Carbonero F, Mohammed K, Posma JM, Kinross J, Wahl E, Ruder E, Vipperla K, Naidoo V, Mtshali L, Tims S, Puylaert PG, DeLany J, Krasinskas A, Benefiel AC, Kaseb HO, Newton K, Nicholson JK, de Vos WM, Gaskins HR, Zoetendal EG (2015) Fat, fibre and cancer risk in African Americans and rural Africans. Nat Commun 6:6342. https://doi.org/10.1038/ncomms7342

Ou J, Carbonero F, Zoetendal EG, DeLany JP, Wang M, Newton K et al (2013) Diet, microbiota, and microbial metabolites in colon cancer risk in rural Africans and African Americans. Am J Clin Nutr 98(1):111–120. https://doi.org/10.3945/ajcn.112.056689

Qin J, Li R, Raes J, Arumugam M, Burgdorf KS, Manichanh C et al (2010) A human gut microbial gene catalogue established by metagenomic sequencing. Nature 464(7285):59–65. https://doi.org/10.1038/nature08821

Qin J, Li Y, Cai Z, Li S, Zhu J, Zhang F et al (2012) A metagenome-wide association study of gut microbiota in type 2 diabetes. Nature 490(7418):55–60. https://doi.org/10.1038/nature11450

Ramirez-Farias C, Slezak K, Fuller Z, Duncan A, Holtrop G, Louis P (2009) Effect of inulin on the human gut microbiota: stimulation of Bifidobacterium adolescentis and Faecalibacterium prausnitzii. Br J Nutr 101(4):541–550. https://doi.org/10.1017/S0007114508019880

Ridaura VK, Faith JJ, Rey FE, Cheng J, Duncan AE, Kau AL et al (2013) Gut microbiota from twins discordant for obesity modulate metabolism in mice. Science 341(6150):1241214. https://doi.org/10.1126/science.1241214

Risnes KR, Belanger K, Murk W, Bracken MB (2011) Antibiotic exposure by 6 months and asthma and allergy at 6 years: Findings in a cohort of 1,401 US children. Am J Epidemiol 173 (3):310–318. https://doi.org/10.1093/aje/kwq400

Sanchez M, Darimont C, Drapeau V, Emady-Azar S, Lepage M, Rezzonico E et al (2014) Effect of Lactobacillus rhamnosus CGMCC1.3724 supplementation on weight loss and maintenance in obese men and women. Br J Nutr 111(8):1507–1519. https://doi.org/10.1017/S0007114513003875

Schnorr SL, Candela M, Rampelli S, Centanni M, Consolandi C, Basaglia G et al (2014) Gut microbiome of the Hadza hunter-gatherers. Nat Commun 5:3654. https://doi.org/10.1038/ncomms4654

Schulz MD, Atay C, Heringer J, Romrig FK, Schwitalla S, Aydin B et al (2014) High-fat-diet-mediated dysbiosis promotes intestinal carcinogenesis independently of obesity. Nature 514 (7523):508–512. https://doi.org/10.1038/nature13398

Scott KP, Martin JC, Duncan SH, Flint HJ (2014) Prebiotic stimulation of human colonic butyrate-producing bacteria and bifidobacteria, in vitro. FEMS Microbiol Ecol 87(1):30–40. https://doi.org/10.1111/1574-6941.12186

Scott KP, Antoine J-M, Midtvedt T, van Hemert S (2015) Manipulating the gut microbiota to maintain health and treat disease. Microb Ecol Health Dis 26:25877

Sears CL, Pardoll DM (2011) Perspective: alpha-bugs, their microbial partners, and the link to colon cancer. J Infect Dis 203(3):306–311. https://doi.org/10.1093/jinfdis/jiq061

Sender R, Fuchs S, Milo R (2016) Revised estimates for the number of human and bacteria cells in the body. PLoS Biol 14(8):e1002533. https://doi.org/10.1371/journal.pbio.1002533

Shanahan F, Bernstein CN (2009) The evolving epidemiology of inflammatory bowel disease. Curr Opin Gastroenterol 25(4):301–305. https://doi.org/10.1097/MOG.0b013e32832b12ef

Sokol H, Pigneur B, Watterlot L, Lakhdari O, Bermudez-Humaran LG, Gratadoux J-J et al (2008) Faecalibacterium prausnitzii is an anti-inflammatory commensal bacterium identified by gut microbiota analysis of Crohn disease patients. Proc Natl Acad Sci U S A 105(43):16731–16736. https://doi.org/10.1073/pnas.0804812105

Sokol H, Seksik P, Furet JP, Firmesse O, Nion-Larmurier I, Beaugerie L et al (2009) Low counts of Faecalibacterium prausnitzii in colitis microbiota. Inflamm Bowel Dis 15(8):1183–1189. https://doi.org/10.1002/ibd.20903

Spor A, Koren O, Ley R (2011) Unravelling the effects of the environment and host genotype on the gut microbiome. Nat Rev Microbiol 9(4):279–290. https://doi.org/10.1038/nrmicro2540

Surawicz CM, Brandt LJ, Binion DG, Ananthakrishnan AN, Curry SR, Gilligan PH et al (2013) Guidelines for diagnosis, treatment, and prevention of clostridium difficile infections. Am J Gastroenterol 108(4):478–498; quiz 499. https://doi.org/10.1038/ajg.2013.4

Tjalsma H, Boleij A, Marchesi JR, Dutilh BE (2012) A bacterial driver-passenger model for colorectal cancer: beyond the usual suspects. Nat Rev Microbiol. https://doi.org/10.1038/nrmicro2819

Turnbaugh PJ, Ley RE, Mahowald MA, Magrini V, Mardis ER, Gordon JI (2006) An obesity-associated gut microbiome with increased capacity for energy harvest. Nature 444 (7122):1027–1031. https://doi.org/10.1038/nature05414

Turnbaugh PJ, Ley RE, Hamady M, Fraser-Liggett CM, Knight R, Gordon JI (2007) The human microbiome project. Nature 449(7164):804–810. https://doi.org/10.1038/nature06244

Turnbaugh PJ, Backhed F, Fulton L, Gordon JI (2008) Diet-induced obesity is linked to marked but reversible alterations in the mouse distal gut microbiome. Cell Host Microbe 3(4):213–223. https://doi.org/10.1016/j.chom.2008.02.015

Voreades N, Kozil A, Weir TL (2014) Diet and the development of the human intestinal microbiome. Front Microbiol 5:494. https://doi.org/10.3389/fmicb.2014.00494

Warren RL, Freeman DJ, Pleasance S, Watson P, Moore RA, Cochrane K et al (2013) Co-occurrence of anaerobic bacteria in colorectal carcinomas. Microbiome 1(1):16. https://doi.org/10.1186/2049-2618-1-16

Yatsunenko T, Rey FE, Manary MJ, Trehan I, Dominguez-Bello MG, Contreras M et al (2012) Human gut microbiome viewed across age and geography. Nature 486(7402):222–227. https://doi.org/10.1038/nature11053

Zhang F, Luo W, Shi Y, Fan Z, Ji G (2012) Should we standardize the 1,700-year-old fecal microbiota transplantation? Am J Gastroenterol. https://doi.org/10.1038/ajg.2012.251

Zhang Q, Wu Y, Fei X (2015) Effect of probiotics on body weight and body-mass index: a systematic review and meta-analysis of randomized, controlled trials. Int J Food Sci Nutr 67 (5):571–580. https://doi.org/10.1080/09637486.2016.1181156

The Right Not to Know in the Context of Genetic Testing

Gerald G. Sander and Mijo Božić

Abstract The use of new analytical techniques in genetic testing makes it difficult to provide the test person with useful information on all relevant outcomes of the examination at issue. In cases of incurable diseases, the affected person frequently does not want to be informed about test results. Against this background, it is essential to inform him—before commencing the testing—about his right not to know. This right is now broadly recognised. However, it is not absolute, although exceptions to the rule are limited to a very few situations.

This paper examines the difficulties inherent in the right not to know from the point of view of the now broadly applied diagnostic methods based on analyses of the test person's genetic constitution.

1 Introduction

Genetic testing is becoming increasingly common in medical diagnostics. This method helps to identify the genetic basis that can cause a disease or health disorder. Because of steady progress in the field of genomics, it has meanwhile become possible to identify a significant number of changes in chromosomes, genes, or proteins.

Knowing about the risk of disease or a health disorder can distress the affected person enormously.[1] Situations that can particularly lead to despair can be summarised as follows[2]: a genetic test predicts a diagnosis or prognosis, but

---

The authors wish to thank Professor Hans-Peter Zenner, University of Tübingen and Clinical Evaluation Services Tübingen for reviewing this chapter.

[1]Leopoldina (2014), p. 15.

[2]Based on Council of Europe (2012), accessed March 7th 2017.

G. G. Sander (✉) · M. Božić
University of Applied Sciences Ludwigsburg, Ludwigsburg, Germany
e-mail: gerald.sander@hs-ludwigsburg.de; mijo.bozic@hs-ludwigsburg.de

© Springer Nature Switzerland AG 2019
N. Bodiroga-Vukobrat et al. (eds.), *Personalized Medicine in Healthcare Systems*,
Europeanization and Globalization 5, https://doi.org/10.1007/978-3-030-16465-2_10

intervention or treatment is impossible or unavailable[3]; a meaningful genetic explanation for a specific condition is impossible (for instance, a test is not available because the genetic basis for the condition has not been identified); while a genetic basis has been identified as causing the ailment, it is not possible to predict how severely the test person[4] will be affected (especially problematic, in this context, are test results which reveal risks affecting genetic relatives, who may not want to know about them); and finally, a test result reveals a family secret, such as paternity or adoption.

For these and other reasons (not stipulated here), each individual is or should nowadays (be) granted the right not to be informed, which is also called the right not to know.[5]

2   The Right to Informational Self-Determination

Genetic testing under the German Genetic Diagnostics Act (GenDG)[6] is permissible only if the test person has consented to it after being informed about the purpose, scope, level of expression, and consequences of the intended examination—GenDG Sec. 8 (1) in conjunction with 9 (1). This process for obtaining permission from the affected individual before conducting a test or, in general, a medical intervention is known as 'informed consent.' The very idea of informed consent correlates closely with the right to informational self-determination.[7] The concept of informed consent is the result of a long struggle to enforce the right to informational self-determination in the field of health care.[8] Accordingly, a modern doctor-patient relationship is intended to be based on equality and no longer on paternalism, as used to be the case.[9] Meanwhile, this concept of informational self-determination has been made

---

[3]The prediction of an incurable monogenetic disease is especially distressing, considering that the underlying mutation will lead, with virtual certainty, to the onset of the disease (e.g. Huntington's chorea). The patient is here put in the situation of being a 'healthy sick' individual. See Leopoldina (2014), p. 61.

[4]In the context of this paper, the expression 'test person' is used as an umbrella term to cover patients, clients, and clinical trial study participants.

[5]For more on this issue see Leopoldina (2014), p. 61, and Chiapperino (2016), p. 78 ff.

[6]*Gesetz über genetische Untersuchungen bei Menschen*, hereinafter abbreviated to GenDG. The act took effect on February 1st, 2010. GenDG aims at defining the prerequisites for conducting genetic studies and analyses and for using samples and data obtained through genetic testing. The scope of application of the GenDG is laid down in Sec. 2 (1). Accordingly, the act applies to genetic studies and to genetic analysis carried out as part of genetic studies on those already born as well as on embryos and fetuses during pregnancy. It also applies to the treatment of genetic samples and genetic data obtained in the course of genetic testing for medical purposes and for research on descent. In addition, GenDG applies to genetic studies in the insurance industry and in employment.

[7]Okada (1998), accessed March 7th 2017.

[8]*Ibid.*

[9]*Ibid.*

part of international and national legislation. For example, the European Convention on Human Rights and Biomedicine (1997) stipulates in Article 10.2 (1) that "everyone is entitled to know any information collected about his or her health". The common expression to refer to this entitlement is the right to be informed or the right to know. It is also now accepted that the individual's right to be informed entails a correlative right: the right not to be informed or right not to know (sometimes also called the right to ignorance). The European Convention on Human Rights and Biomedicine (1997) makes it explicit in Article 10.2 (2): "the wishes of individuals not to be informed about their medical condition shall be observed too".

3 A Short History of the Right Not to Know

The concept of informed consent has evolved over the last decades. In the mid 1980s, it was argued "that there can be no such 'right' to refuse relevant information, and that the claims for such a right are inconsistent with both deontological and utilitarian ethics. [. . .] The right to be informed is shown to be a mandatory right [. . .]; persons are thus seen to have both a right and a duty to be informed".[10] This idea prevailed up until the turn of the century, when the debate erupted again[11] in response to the swift development of new analytical techniques. More and more scholars started to advocate the necessity of acknowledging the right not to know. In particular, the increased use of predictive genetic tests in clinical practice contributed to the paradigm shift.[12]

4 Legal Sources of the Right Not to Know

Academic lobbying of legislative bodies at the turn of the millennium to recognise the right not to know were fruitful. Even if the scope of its application and the conditions under which it applies are still not sufficiently clear, the right to ignorance is nowadays widely recognised.

4.1 International Documents

The most important international sources of the right not to know—regardless of their binding or non-binding nature—are as follows:

---

[10]Ost (1984), accessed March 7th 2017.

[11]See the overview of the most relevant papers on these issues in English: Nijsingh (2016), p. 1. The most relevant paper in German from this era is Taupitz (1998), pp. 583–602.

[12]Andorno (2004), pp. 435–439; accessed March 7th 2017.

- Declaration on the Rights of the Patient adopted by the World Medical Association in 1981 and amended in 1995. Under Article 7d, "the patient has the right not to be informed on his explicit request, unless required for the protection of another person's life".
- The WHO Guidelines on Ethical Issues in Medical Genetics and the Provision of Genetic Services (1997) stipulate in Table No. 7 that "the wish of individuals and families not to know genetic information, including test results, should be respected, except in testing of newborn babies or children for treatable conditions".
- As previously mentioned, the European Convention on Human Rights and Biomedicine [1997] Article 10.2 states: "Everyone is entitled to know any information collected about his or her health. However, the wishes of individuals not to be so informed shall be observed."
- The UNESCO Universal Declaration on the Human Genome and Human Rights [1997] lists in Article 5 (c) "the right of each individual to decide whether or not to be informed of the results of genetic examination and the resulting consequences should be respected".

4.2   German Domestic Sources

Apart from its sources in international law, the right not to know is derived in German national law from the right to informational self-determination, which is one of the manifestations of the general right to personality, as laid down in the German constitution (Grundgesetz) Article 2 (1) in conjunction with 1 (1) and clarified and developed over the years through the case law of the German Constitutional Court.[13] In academic literature, the right not to know is usually described as a negative variant of the right to informational self-determination, especially relevant in the context of genome analysis.[14]

As for the area of genetic diagnostics, the right not to know is set out *expressis verbis* in GenDG Sec. 9 (2) No. 5. Notwithstanding that the right not to know is

---

[13]The right to informational self-determination was first affirmed in the ruling of the German Federal Constitutional Court [Bundesverfassungsgericht, BVerfG] relating to personal information collected during the 1983 census; judgement of the German Federal Constitutional Court from December 15th 1983 - 1 BvR 209/83 et al. - BVerfGE 65, 1 (in German). The BVerfG ruled that: "[. . .] in the context of modern data processing, the protections of the individual against unlimited collection, storage, use and disclosure of his personal data is encompassed by the general personal rights of the German constitution. This basic right warrants in this respect the capacity of the individual to determine in principle the disclosure and use of his/her personal data."

[14]See, for example, Di Fabio, in: Maunz/Dürig, Grundgesetz, 78th suppl, September 2016, GG Art. 2 para. 192.

statutorily regulated, there is still a great deal of uncertainty as to the scope of its application and conditions under which it applies.[15] However, the German Federal Court has made its first ruling on the right not to know.[16] The ruling made clear that the right not to know's *ratione personae* are only the test person himself and his genetic relatives. A mother of a child whose father has been diagnosed with Huntington's chorea is thus not protected by the right not to know.[17] This ruling is a small but important step towards clarifying the right's scope of application and its limits. The Court did not rule on other important questions concerning the right, such as whether—and if so under what circumstances and conditions—a medical doctor might be entitled or even bound under GenDG to breach medical confidentiality and share his findings.[18] In the absence of relevant court rulings, the recommendations of the BMBF project group[19] can serve as (rough) guidelines. They can be seen as groundbreaking methods for implementing the right not to know.

5   Genetic Testing, Personalised Medicine and the Right Not to Know

Awareness of an incurable disease or of a predisposition to such an ailment has always had significant potential for affecting the quality of life of the patient and his relatives. The possibility to make a diagnosis through genetic testing has just exacerbated the situation in this regard. The new diagnostic methods use analytical techniques that are essentially based on an increased use of biomathematics, which helps us to understand the molecular basis of disease. They are key tools of personalised molecular medicine, a new approach to medicine and healthcare.[20]

Implementing the right not to know is associated with significant conflicts within the realm of personalised medicine.[21] Some techniques, such as large-scale genetic sequencing, generate a large amount of genetic data and excess information. Some

---

[15]BMBF-Projektgruppe (2016), p. 399.

[16]See the judgment of the German Federal Court [Bundesgerichtshof, BGH] from May 20th 2014— BGH VI ZR 381/13; available on http://juris.bundesgerichtshof.de/cgi-bin/rechtsprechung/docu ment.py?Gericht=bgh&Art=en&az=VI%20ZR%20381/13&nr=67940; accessed June 30th 2017.

[17]Schneider (2014), p. 3133.

[18]*Ibid.*, p. 3134.

[19]BMBF-Projektgruppe (2016), p. 399.

[20]The German National Academy of Sciences "Leopoldina" in its position paper on Individualised Medicine [one of the synonyms for Personalised Medicine] explains the goals of this new model in a very clear manner: "Individualised Medicine aims to improve the efficacy and quality of treatment through targeted prevention, systematic diagnostics and tailored therapeutic procedures that are oriented to the needs of individual patients or patient groups; at the same time, Individualised Medicine aims to reduce side effects and increase the cost-effectiveness of treatment over the long term." Leopoldina (2014), p. 15.

[21]Leopoldina (2014), p. 61 ff.

excess information might include important so-called incidental (and secondary) findings. Other excess information may not be meaningfully interpreted, so that their expressiveness regarding a potential disease risk is still quite insignificant.[22] This notwithstanding, a significant proportion of genetic testing has been out-sourced from the traditional clinical setting to private vendors (Direct-to-consumer tests, usually abbreviated to DTC).

These issues will be discussed in more detail in the further course of the paper. Beforehand, however, it is imperative to briefly delineate medical duties regarding information, consent and genetic counselling under GenDG.

5.1 Information, Consent and Genetic Counselling

Under GenDG Sections 8 and 9 (see also Sec. 10), the physician has a duty to provide the test person with all the information relating to genetic characteristics that is obtainable through the examination at issue. Subsequently, the test person ought to decide whether he wants to undergo genetic testing for medical purposes and define the scope of the examination. In addition, he must make a decision as to what extent the test results should be notified to him and how much information should be destroyed.[23]

To ensure the implementation of the right not to know, it is necessary before commencing the examination to inform the test person as thoroughly as possible about the existing disease(s), predispositions to that disease(s) or health disorder (s) and other risk scenarios that could be identified by the investigation. This should enable him to imagine the consequences with which he might be confronted with. All the information that might be relevant to subsequent treatment or counselling should be included in this explanation as well. In case of doubt, the request for testing should be restricted as far as possible.[24] After he has been examined and before the test results are disclosed to him, the test person ought to be asked once again whether he wants to be informed about the test results in accordance with the previous agreement. If yes, suspicious findings, whether relating to existing ailments or risk scenarios which could occur in the future, must be discussed in detail and addressed to the specific life situation of the affected individual. If necessary, further medical, psychological and social therapeutic consultations and aid should be offered.[25]

---

[22]See more on this issue in Na et al. (2015), p. 4; accessed March 7th 2017. See also Duttge (2016), p. 668.

[23]See German Ethics Council (2013), p. 74.

[24]BMBF-Projektgruppe (2016), pp. 401 ff.

[25]BMBF-Projektgruppe (2016), p. 402.

5.2 Interpretation of Genetic Data

The sheer volume of genetic data and excess information generated by the new diagnostic methods has direct implications for information, consent, and genetic counselling. Considering the quantity of information, it is often impossible to provide the test person with an explanation of every piece of information that may be revealed, especially when it comes to methods of complete exome or genome sequencing.[26]

Bearing in mind that implementing informed consent and consequently the right not to know under such circumstances is hard to achieve, experts propose its redefinition and transformation into the concept of "informed ignorance" (*informiertes Nichtwissen* in German). This new concept is based on the acknowledgement, primarily by the treating physician, that existing knowledge is limited. Accordingly, the doctor should disclose to the test person what fraction of the knowledge is available and what part of it is missing in a particular case: i.e. the test person should be unambiguously informed of gaps in knowledge if the specific genetic testing situation results in a sort of "fishing in murky waters."[27] After these issues are resolved, the test person must make an *informed decision*.

Before that, however, and to support a patient's informed decision physician and test person may make a joint decision that seems reasonable and feasible in the particular case, considering all the existing limitations of knowledge. This concept is known as "shared decision making."[28] Based on the concept of "shared decision making," it is necessary that the physician indicates the problematic nature of genetic testing, disclosing everything to the test person that he can and cannot explain. The medical doctor should not suggest explicitly to the test person to make use of his right not to know, no matter how vague genetic testing in a particular case could be. It is then up to the test person to decide, based on this clarification, whether he wants to make use of his right not to know.

5.3 Incidental Findings

The currently applied methods for DNA sequencing make it possible to sequence cost-effectively nearly the entire genome or exome.[29]

Since the completion of the Human Genome Project, the cost to generate a human genome sequence has declined tremendously, from $10–50 million to $3–5000. Currently it takes only 1 to 2 days to complete this task, as distinguished from the

---

[26]German Ethics Council (2013), pp. 74 ff.

[27]Eckhardt et al. (2014), pp. 98 ff. (referring to an interview with Max Baumann).

[28]*Ibid*. See also on these issues Manyonga et al. (2014), pp. 561–562; accessed July 16th 2018.

[29]See more on this issue in Na et al. (2015), p. 4; accessed March 7th 2017.

3 to 4 months that it took at the time of the Human Genome Project.[30] This development may enable medical doctors to make better treatment choices.[31]

This use of modern diagnostic methods generates a large amount of genetic data. Only a fraction of these data, however, may be of clinical relevance. Essentially, a significant proportion of them may be of unknown or uncertain medical value.[32] However, it can easily be overlooked that findings of unknown significance at the time of testing might, because of the progress of medical science, later become associated with important diseases or conditions.[33] Information about the test results is always restricted to the genetic characteristic to be clarified, as agreed between the treating doctor and the test person in the particular case and defined by the test person's request for testing (mandate). In cases where the method is capable of providing information on genetic characteristics that are not subject to the examination—i.e. where the examination might result in incidental findings—the test person must be informed of this possibility as well as the fact that all excess information will be destroyed as provided for under GenDG Sec. 8 (1) sentence 2,[34] unless the test person has given explicit consent to their disclosure. The test person ought to be informed about possible incidental findings before commencing the testing and asked whether, and if so to what extent, these findings should be notified to him.[35] Principles of shared decision making should apply, *mutatis mutandis*, to incidental findings.

From the general public's point of view, the concept of incidental findings is simple and clear. Accordingly, incidental findings are those not sought by the diagnostician, regardless of whether they could have been anticipated—or even intentionally sought—or not. This conception is however inadequate, as not every diagnostic test is likely to give rise to incidental and secondary findings. Tests for pregnancy or HIV, for instance, are unlikely to result in such findings. By way of contrast, analytical techniques such as large-scale genetic sequencing have significant potential to produce not only the results sought but also other findings.[36]

---

[30]Personalized Medicine Coalition (2014) Figure 1, p. 5; accessed March 7th 2017.

[31]See https://www.genome.gov/10001177/, accessed March 7th 2017.

[32]Presidential Commission for the Study of Bioethical Issues (2013), p. 33; accessed March 7th 2017.

[33]*Ibid.*

[34]German Ethics Council (2013), p. 75 fn. 146.

[35]BMBF-Projektgruppe (2016), p. 402, Recommendation #5.

[36]Presidential Commission for the Study of Bioethical Issues (2013), p. 34. For the sake of completeness, it is necessary to point out that imaging is also capable of resulting in incidental and secondary findings. However, here the potential for such findings is inherent in the test. Imaging usually captures the surrounding organs or areas outside the focus of the test itself. However, this technique is irrelevant in the context of the present paper, as imaging is not a specific characteristic of genetic testing.

To bring conceptual clarity to the variety of findings that can arise, it is necessary to adopt a more differentiated definitional framework. Based on the Presidential Commissions'[37] paper *Ethical Management of Incidental and Secondary Findings in the Clinical, Research, and Direct-to-Consumer Contexts,* all individual results of medical tests can be classified into five categories:

1. primary findings,
2. anticipated incidental findings (known to be associated with the test or procedure),
3. unanticipated incidental findings (findings that cannot be anticipated based on the current state of knowledge),
4. secondary findings (actively sought parallel to the primary target) and
5. discovery findings (from a wide-ranging test intended to discover anything of interest).[38]

All these categories should be addressed adequately through the provision of information before commencing the testing. Special attention should, however, be given to incidental unanticipated findings, because the surprising effects that they can cause are generally more significant than the outcomes of the others.

Here, it must be emphasised that the ordinary test person will usually be overwhelmed by the huge quantity of data and potential findings.[39] This stresses once again the importance of shifting the prevailing paradigm of informed consent towards an additional shared decision making. Positive law, however, still implicitly assumes that "informed consent" subsequent to the provision of information about the examination can be achieved, no matter how complex the examination and regardless of the possibility that testing might reveal incidental findings (see GenDG Sec. 8 (1)).[40]

5.3.1 Genetic Relatives

Examination findings do not only affect the test person. His genetic relatives may also be affected by test results. This is most evident in identical twins, but it may also affect other blood relatives. Nowadays it is uncontested that the genetic relatives of an affected person enjoy an unlimited right not to know. However, it may be hard to implement this principle in a specific practical situation.

---

[37]The Presidential Commission for the Study of Bioethical Issues (Bioethics Commission) was an advisory panel of the nation's leaders in medicine, science, ethics, religion, law, and engineering. The Bioethics Commission advised the US President Barack Obama [2009–2017] on bioethical issues arising from advances in biomedicine and related areas of science and technology.

[38]Presidential Commission for the Study of Bioethical Issues (2013), p. 27.

[39]Eckhardt et al. (2014), p. 98.

[40]The same is true for Switzerland under the Gesetz über genetische Untersuchungen beim Menschen (GUMG) Sec. 18 (1); see Eckhardt et al. (2014), p. 98.

GenDG Sec. 10 (3) 4 provides *expressis verbis* that the genetic counselling should also encompass the recommendation to the test person to advise his genetic relatives to undergo genetic counselling whenever it may be assumed that they might be affected by a curable or preventable disease or health disorder. This provision applies *mutatis mutandis* to tests on embryos and foetuses, GenDG Sec. 10 (3) 5. Accordingly, it behooves the test person to inform his genetic relative (s) about test results and recommend genetic counselling and, where relevant, genetic testing.

The situation in which the test person shows a cooperative attitude is the ideal constellation for the treating medical doctor, and does not require discussion.

The practical question of how to proceed in cases in which the test person is uncooperative is difficult to answer. The general view on this dilemma is that—as a general rule—the test person's right not to know should be respected.[41] However, the right not to know in such situations is not absolute.[42] In the BMBF project group's view, there are three different situations that should entitle the treating doctor to inform genetic relatives of potential risks, thereby ignoring the test person's wishes in this regard. Under this view, the doctor should inform genetic relatives of existing risks whenever a disease is treatable and a timely therapeutic intervention can prevent severe suffering for the affected relative. The same holds true for cases with a high risk of serious genetic disease for unborn children where the affected relatives are of reproductive age. Finally, the physician should ignore the test person's decision if the disease is treatable and the test person has a duty of care to the affected genetic relative (e.g. a minor child).[43] Based on the BGH judgement, the doctor might, in such a case, inform the affected relative's legal representative of the risk[44] without fear of violating positive law.

5.3.2 Making Test Results Public

Some test persons release their test results (which, in the case of celebrities, make them instantly subject to intensive media coverage). Such statements make implementing the right not to know of genetic relatives practically impossible. There is a view in the literature that public statements on test results should be legally prohibited, if genetic relatives have not given their consent.[45] However, such revelations can hardly be sanctioned by legal means, so that a legal prohibition would not be an effective way to protect the position of genetic relatives. Not only

---

[41]Leopoldina (2014), p. 62.

[42]Leopoldina (2014), p. 62; BMBF-Projektgruppe (2016), p. 402.

[43]BMBF-Projektgruppe (2016), p. 403, Recommendation #13; see also BGH VI ZR 381/13, judgement from May 20th 2014. The Leopoldina takes an obviously different view, based on Heyers (2009), pp. 507–512; Leopoldina (2014), p. 62.

[44]If the latter himself is not a genetic relative of the test person, of course.

[45]Eckhardt et al. (2014), p. 99.

close genetic relatives may be affected by the revelation, but also distant ones, so that the group of affected persons becomes too wide and impossible to demarcate. Thus it would be practically impossible for the test person to obtain the consent of all those who might be affected, even if he decided to do so. In addition, it would also be ethically problematic to ban revelations of test results if the test person wishes to raise awareness of a particular threat to large parts of the population—which was A. Jolie's (2013)[46] apparent motivation for revealing the results of her test for breast cancer risk.

Accordingly, the treating physician may point out to the test person during the genetic counselling that public revelations of medical findings might cause serious harm to his genetic relatives and that therefore he would be well-advised not to make them public. However, it is the responsibility of the test person to decide whether to follow such a recommendation.

5.3.3 Direct-to-Consumer Tests

One of the characteristics of contemporary medicine is that clinical services are no longer offered only in the traditional clinical setting. Private companies are ever more active in the market and compete for business with hospitals, especially in the field of diagnostics. Nowadays the general public has almost unlimited access to medical tests and procedures outside the traditional clinical setting.[47] Direct-to-consumer genetic tests have become a convenient method to help people discover their genetic constitution.[48] Access to the internet and a credit card are all that an interested individual needs to purchase such a service.[49] The sellers are private companies situated somewhere between medicine and business.[50] They offer the general public additional mechanisms for obtaining health-related information in exchange for money.[51] Usually the consumer orders the genetic test from the company by sending a DNA sample (usually saliva) to its laboratory. Subsequently, the company makes the analysis and informs the consumer on the completion of the test. As a rule, he can download the test results digitally using a code previously sent to him by the company by electronic means (i.e. via email).[52]

As a general rule, the right not to know is applicable to DTC as well. However, it is difficult to achieve its implementation in practice. From the point of view of

---

[46]See, for example, the actor's Angelina Jolie revelation in the online edition of *The New York Times*, published on May 14th 2013, available on http://www.nytimes.com/2013/05/14/opinion/my-medical-choice.html; accessed March 7th 2017.

[47]Presidential Commission for the Study of Bioethical Issues (2013), p. 17.

[48]Laestadius et al. (2016); accessed March 7th 2017.

[49]Prainsack (2013), p. 26; accessed July 16th 2018.

[50]Presidential Commission for the Study of Bioethical Issues (2013), p. 17.

[51]*Ibid.*

[52]German Ethics Council (2013), p. 84.

German law, direct-to-consumer tests are not capable of complying with the require-ments of the GenDG.[53] The GenDG requires, *inter alia*, the involvement of a medical doctor in all stages of genetic testing for medical purposes—i.e. from clarification via taking the genetic sample through to informing on the test result and the subsequent counselling of the test person—and this is clearly not the case here. Clarification in DTC tests is usually made in the form of a reference to particular internet pages. Even if there were a possibility to inform the test person in an adequate manner, it would still be impossible to identify whether he is capable of consenting.[54] Under such circumstances it is impossible to inform the test person of the scope and consequences of the testing as required by law.[55] Consequently, it is not possible to make him aware of his right not to know.

For all the reasons stated above, the Leopoldina has come to the conclusion that direct-to-consumer tests are not permitted in Germany.[56]

6 Non-Observance of the Test Person's Right Not to Know

Exceptions to the general rule of the almost unlimited protection of the test person's right not to know are limited to very few constellations. The BMBF project group takes the view that the treating medical doctor is entitled to ignore the right not to know as invoked by the test person in only two cases.

The physician may inform the test person of the test results when the diagnosed disease is curable and a timely therapeutic intervention can protect him from a serious health-related harm, such as (e.g.) premature death, loss of reproductive capacity or of an important limb, sight or hearing, aphasia, considerable and permanent disfigurement, lingering illness, paralysis, mental illness or disability. This enumeration is in line with the German Criminal Code section [abbr. to StGB] 226 (1) on causing grievous bodily harm.[57]

The same rule applies in cases where the diagnosed illness might pose a consid-erable risk to others or to the general public (especially in the context of professions such as airline pilot, bus driver, engine driver, etc.). The notification of findings and

---

[53] *Ibid.*

[54] *Ibid.*

[55] German Ethics Council (2013), p. 84. The German Ethics Council points to one more problematic aspect of DTC testing, namely the difficulty of determining whether the genetic sample comes from the person ordering the genetic diagnosis. However, this aspect is less crucial in the context of the discussion of the right not to know.

[56] Leopoldina (2010) Recommendation #19, p. X. Leopoldina's paper is concerned exclusively with predictive genetic tests. However, the relevant provisions of GenDG on information, consent and genetic counselling apply equally to predictive and diagnostic genetic tests. Consequently, based on this view, the prohibition should apply to all categories of genetic tests. See on this issue also Borry et al. (2012), pp. 715–721; accessed July 5th 2017.

[57] BMBF-Projektgruppe, p. 402 fn. 31.

subsequent treatment in such cases is imperative,[58] because protecting the health of others is a legitimate reason for restricting the right not to know which is basically the manifestation of the human right to self-determination.

7 Conclusion

The patient's right to informational self-determination has evolved over the last few decades. The duty to take note of findings has been supplemented by the right not to know.

As the knowledge of an incurable disease or disorder might cause enormous mental stress, as a general rule the right not to know must be followed. However, this right is not absolute. The physician is entitled to disregard the test person's right not to know whenever the disease is curable and the interests of third parties are at stake.

References

Position Papers, Statements, Documents

Council of Europe (2012) Genetic Tests for Health Purposes. Available on: http://www.coe.int/t/dg3/healthbioethic/Source/en_geneticTests_hd.pdf

German Ethics Council (2013) The future of genetic diagnosis – from research to clinical practice – Opinion. Available under http://www.ethikrat.org/files/opinion-the-future-of-genetic-diagnosis.pdf

German National Academy of Sciences Leopoldina, acatech – National Academy of Science and Engineering and Union of the German Academies of Sciences and Humanities (2014) Individualised Medicine – Prerequisites and Consequences Halle (Saale), 104 p. Available on: http://www.leopoldina.org/uploads/tx_leopublication/2014_Stellungnahme_IndividualisierteMedizin_EN.pdf

German National Academy of Sciences Leopoldina, acatech – National Academy of Science and Engineering, Berlin Brandenburg Academy of Sciences and Humanities and Union of the German Academies of Sciences and Humanities (2010) Statement on Predictive Genetic Diagnostics as an Instrument of Disease Prevention, November 2010. Available on: https://www.leopoldina.org/uploads/tx_leopublication/201011_natEmpf_praedikative-EN_01.pdf

Personalized Medicine Coalition (2014) The case for personalized medicine, 4th edn. Available on: http://www.personalizedmedicinecoalition.org/Userfiles/PMC-Corporate/file/pmc_case_for_personalized_medicine.pdf

Presidential Commission for the Study of Bioethical Issues, Anticipate and Communicate – Ethical Management of Incidental and Secondary Findings in the Clinical, Research, and Direct-to-Consumer Contexts (2013) Available on: https://upload.wikimedia.org/wikipedia/commons/6/6e/Anticipate_and_Communicate_-_Ethical_Management_of_Incidental_and_Secondary_Findings.pdf

---

[58] *Ibid.*

Select Bibliography

Andorno R (2004) The right not to know: an autonomy based approach. J Med Ethics 30:435–439

Borry P, van Hellemondt RE, Sprumont D, Fittipaldi Darte Jales C, Rial-Sebbag E, Spranger TM, Curren L, Kaye J, Nys H, Howard H (2012) Legislation on direct-to-consumer genetic testing in seven European countries. Eur J Hum Genet 20(7):715–721

BMBF-Projektgruppe (2016) "Recht auf Nichtwissen", Empfehlungen zum Umgang mit dem "Recht auf Nichtwissen". Medizinrecht 34:399–405

Chiapperino L (2016) The "Right-not-to-Know". Ethical counselling and medical decision-making in the era of personalised medicine. Springer, pp 77–88

Di Fabio U (2016) In: Maunz T, Dürig G (eds) Grundgesetz, Loseblatt-Kommentar. C. H. Beck, München

Duttge G (2016) Das Recht auf Nichtwissen in einer informationell vernetzten Gesundheitsversorgung. Medizinrecht 34:664–669

Eckhardt A, Navarini AA, Recher A, Rippe KP, Rütsche B, Telser H, Marti M (2014) Personalisierte Medizin. vdf Hochschulverlag, Zürich

Heyers J (2009) Prädiktive Gesundheitsinformationen – Persönlichkeitsrechte und Drittinteressen – insbesondere am Beispiel der Gendiagnostik bei Abschluß von Privatversicherungen. Medizinrecht 27:507–512

Laestadius LI, Rich JR, Auer PL (2016) All your data (effectively) belong to us: data practices among direct-to-consumer genetic testing firms. Genet Med. https://doi.org/10.1038/gim.2016.136; Available on: https://www.ncbi.nlm.nih.gov/pubmed/27657678

Manyonga H, Howarth G, Dinwoodie M, Nisselle P, Whitehouse S (2014) From informed consent to shared decision-making. S Afr Med J 104(8):561–562. https://doi.org/10.7196/samj.8287. Available on: https://www.researchgate.net/publication/265610789_From_informed_consent_to_shared_decision-making

Na YJ, Sohn KA, Kim JH (2015) Interpretation of personal genome sequencing data in terms of disease ranks based on mutual information. BMC Med Genomics, 8(suppl 2):4. Available on: https://www.researchgate.net/publication/277778826_Interpretation_of_personal_genome_sequencing_data_in_terms_of_disease_ranks_based_on_mutual_information

Nijsingh N (2016) Consent to epistemic interventions: a contribution to the debate on the right (not) to know. Med Health Care Philos 19(1):103–110

Okada M (1998) Informed consent - on the right of self-determination [Article in Japanese]. Hokkaido Igaku Zasshi 73(1):35–36. Abstract [in English]; Available on: https://www.ncbi.nlm.nih.gov/pubmed/9546144

Ost DE (1984) The 'right' not to know. Abstract [in English]. J Med Philos 9(3):301–312. Available on: https://www.ncbi.nlm.nih.gov/pubmed/6491557

Prainsack B (2013) Personalisierte Medizin aus Sicht des Patienten – Nutzen oder Überforderung? In: German Ethics Council (ed) Personalisierte Medizin – der Patient als Nutznießer oder Opfer?, pp 23–32. Available on: http://www.ethikrat.org/dateien/pdf/tagungsdokumentation-personalisierte-medizin.pdf

Schneider A (2014) Umfang und Grenzen des Rechts auf Nichtwissen der eigenen genetischen Veranlagung. NJW, pp 3133–3135

Taupitz J (1998) Das Recht auf Nichtwissen. Festschrift für Günther Wiese zum 70. Geburtstag, Neuwied, pp 583–602

Part III
Social and Humanistic Aspects of Personal Medicine

Personalized Medicine, Justice and Equality

Elvio Baccarini

Abstract Like some other texts, this paper embraces the idea that, because of the scarcity of resources on the one hand, and extended requests on the other, we need to set limits in health care. Likewise, the paper endorses the thesis that such limits must be fair. Further, it accepts and further develops the idea that limits must be set fairly through proper deliberative procedures. In addition, it defends and applies Rawls's idea of public reason. This is the idea that, even in a fair procedure, proposals and decisions must be justified through public reasons, i.e. reasons that each agent can accept as reasonable to be legitimate. Mere majoritarian vote is not sufficient for legitimacy. Contrary to other proposals in health care justice that are immediately concerned with real world deliberation and do not attribute a proper function to the personal perspective, this paper endorses two levels of deliberation. The idealized level is needed to establish which are the strongest rights, which can be limited only if they conflict with each other, but not if they conflict with less important rights and values. Here, a set of eligible decisions is established for real life deliberation. Using the example of the methodology of justification, which considers the importance of the personal meaning of health care decisions, as well as of public reasons in ideal and in real life contexts, the thesis is defended that life prolonging therapies have a strong priority as rights.

Many thanks to my colleagues and students Ivan Cerovac, Antonio Dijak, Helena Drmić, Marko Jurjako, Kristina Lekić, Luca Malatesti, Tomislav Miletić, Leonard Pektor, Aleksandar Šušnjar and Nebojša Zelič, to the audience of my talk organized by Igor Pribac and held at the University of Lubiana in April 2017, as well as to the participants of the course "The Diversity of Human Rights", at the Interuniversity Center in Dubrovnik in September 2017. Many thank, also, to Sarah Czerny for language editing.

E. Baccarini (✉)
Faculty of Humanities and Social Science, University of Rijeka, Rijeka, Croatia
e-mail: ebaccarini@ffri.hr

© Springer Nature Switzerland AG 2019
N. Bodiroga-Vukobrat et al. (eds.), *Personalized Medicine in Healthcare Systems*, Europeanization and Globalization 5, https://doi.org/10.1007/978-3-030-16465-2_11

1 Introduction

This paper discusses issues of justice related to personalized medicine (PM). The salient feature of PM for this paper is that the use of drugs affects different individual subjects of administration in different ways because of specific differences between them. This is why, for example, drug administration must be personalized and adapted to the characteristics of each single patient.[1]

PM could be the new frontier of medicine. It promises several advantages. To mention just one of them, it offers the perspective of overcoming adverse drug reaction (ADR). ADR is one of the leading causes of death, and the percentage of patients who respond adequately to treatment with traditional drugs is unsatisfactorily low.[2]

PM also has a worrisome side to it. There is the danger of increased costs, thereby making the health care system unsustainable. Consequent problems of justice appear. The problem discussed here concerns the allocation of expensive therapies in conditions of limited resources. If we orient a sensible amount of money to curing a patient, or category of patients, we deny such money to other persons or to other possibly valuable goals. The basic question, thus, as in the title of Daniels's and Sabin's book, is setting limits fairly.[3] How can we do this?

Some authors, correctly, remark that we cannot resolve issues of justice by merely appealing to those principles of justice that we think are the true principles. The proper strategy is represented by the employment of fair procedures to make decisions.[4]

I agree that we cannot resolve the issue with a direct appeal to principles not procedurally confirmed. Fair deliberation is needed. However, I think that real life deliberation must be supplemented and constrained by principles established in an idealized deliberation. Further, among limits and constraints to deliberation that I remark, there is a stronger consideration of the personal perspective than in the authors that I discuss. In considering such a perspective, I remark upon the need to respect the personal meaning that a decision has for an agent.

I do not only describe the methodology of public deliberation. Also, I suggest what I think should be the responses to the procedures of public deliberation that I recommend. This is for two reasons. First, I think that this is valuable in itself. Namely, establishing procedures is only a part of the job. After this, the job is to deliberate with the intention of arriving at the most reasonable result. I offer my contribution to such deliberation. Second, by exemplifying public reasoning, I hope to better clarify it.

My final idea for real world justice is a strong, although not absolute, priority in giving allocation to life prolonging therapies, as well as to subsidiary therapies

---

[1]Lewis et al. (2014), pp. 137–146; Olivier et al. (2008), p. 110.

[2]Olivier et al. (2008), pp. 108–109.

[3]Daniels Sabin (2008).

[4]Daniels Sabin (2008) and Fleck (2013).

directed at postponing the progression of the illness for these patients. Cost effectiveness considerations enter into play and this is why I am speaking of a strong, but not absolute, priority of these therapies. However, in the paper I speak only about life prolonging therapies, and not about other therapies that might be given to these patients.

2   Sustainability of Health Care Systems and Questions of Justice

In a possibly optimistic view, PM has the effect of decreasing the overall costs of a health care system.[5] But there are reasons for pessimism, as well. It is doubtful that PM will enhance the conditions for economic sustainability of the pharmaceutical industry, and, even if this is the case, it might manifest itself in the form of long term economic sustainability, and not with immediate financial return. The laboratory tests needed for PM might be initially quite expensive.[6] PM, which focuses on therapies that offer benefits to smaller populations, fragments markets, and, thus, reduces the potential for sales. An increase of burdens in health care systems may appear.[7] A further economic problem related to PM might derive from it being efficacious. Namely, some traditional medicines are for long term use by patients, while personalized medicines may not need to be taken for a life-long, or, in any case, comparatively extended period of time.[8] In general, it is remarked that part of the increased costs in medicine derives from its success, which creates new requirements. Enhanced possibilities of medicine improve its application, and, thus, requirements for it, which, in turn, causes increased expenses and conflicts concerning issues of allocation. This is why we need to put limits to the right to access to health care. "Limits are the price of medical success, not medical failure".[9]

My paper discusses ethical issues in the context of the possible bad scenario, with increased costs and heavier issues of social justice. Such possible increased costs would put pressure on the public health system, and favor the commercialization and privatization of health care, undermining the solidaristic conception of health care.[10] But then, it could be that PM strategies are too expensive for parts of the population, and, thus social disparities, in particular in the health care field, might be exacerbated.

Even if a public health care system survives, difficult questions appear. From the standpoint of institutions allocating resources, a hard choice might be between

---

[5]Brother Rothstein (2015), p. 47.
[6]Brother Rothstein (2015), p. 46; Arnason (2012), p. 115.
[7]Olivier et al. (2008), pp. 109–112.
[8]Fleck (2013), p. 128.
[9]Daniels Sabin (2008), p. 2.
[10]Arnason (2012), p. 116.

supporting a small subpopulation in contrast to increasing services offered to vast amounts of people.[11] Groups with less common genotypes risk being neglected.[12]

Because of possible worrisome scenario when thinking about PM, we must seriously consider Daniels's and Sabin's "central question about justice and health care: how can a society or health plan meet population health care needs fairly under resource limitation? Because resources are limited, all societies must set limits to care and establish priorities about how resources will be used".[13] This is true in general, but it might be exacerbated by PM if the pessimistic scenario proves to be warranted. How can we deal with this question?

3   Fair Public Deliberation

One of the traditional approaches by philosophers is to look for general principles that, then, serve as foundations of conclusions regarding policies. This approach is defined as problematic by other philosophers. The basic problem is that these principles are controversial. In conditions of pluralism there is no agreement about these principles. Even if there is agreement about the principles, there is disagreement about their interpretation and application.[14] This is problematic because public policies are legitimate only if they are justifiable to the involved parts.[15] In cases of the indicated pluralism, some philosophers say, the principlist approach is not able to respond to this task.

Several authors think the proper strategy is that of looking for answers in a fair procedure, and not by relying on some non-procedurally supposedly warranted rules.[16]

I accept the idea that the outcomes of fair procedures are legitimate answers for public decisions in the absence of uncontroversial principles of justice. But it is important to establish further details of the fair procedures that generate the legitimacy of public decisions. There are various characterizations and I focus on one of them. According to this view, a public decision is not legitimate if it is only the result of a mere majoritarian vote, even in a fair procedure. It is important that when people vote for the decision, they must care about whether other people can reasonably endorse reasons that justify the decision. Thus, even when one defends and, then, votes for a decision, she must not be ready to merely outvote other parts. Instead, she must address her justification to the other parts. Conversely, she must care about whether the other parts can have reasons that justify the decision.

---

[11]Lewis et al. (2014), p. 140; Arnason (2012), p. 107.

[12]Arnason (2012), p. 111.

[13]Daniels Sabin (2008), p. vii.

[14]Wolff (2011), Fleck (2013), pp. 131–133; Daniels Sabin (2008), pp. 2–4, pp. 30–34.

[15]Gaus (2011).

[16]Daniels Sabin (2008), Arnason (2012), and Fleck (2013).

Justification to agents, i.e. justification based on reasons that agents can reasonably endorse, is crucially important, because in its absence public decisions are not legitimate. I do not justify, here, this claim and I rely for the justification on the great tradition that finds in Rawls and Gaus its prominent contemporary representatives.[17] Daniels and Sabin have offered a convincing explanation of this kind of justification in health care justice.[18]

I only mention a sketch of the rationale for this view of legitimacy in the health care domain. Here, people are particularly threatened and worried, frequently even scared, by their life situation. Their social and political influence frequently decreases. This is one of the reasons why this is a context where we must pay special attention to the protection of the interests of agents. Justification to agents, and not impersonal justification with reasons that are possibly alien to the agents, is a resource for this end.

The specific protection through justification addressed to agents is also needed because "limit setting is often greeted with distrust and with challenges to the moral authority, or legitimacy, of those who sets limits".[19]

The crucial reason for the importance of special protection in health care is that health is special. There are various reasons to justify this claim that converge to it, but I do not elaborate on this. I suppose the claim is sufficiently shared.

Thus, persons in health care contexts deserve special protection. A condition for achieving this is to constrain the decision procedure with the requirement to deliberate based on reasons apt to represent reasonable justification to the involved persons, and not justifications alien to them.

The leading political philosopher John Rawls writes that the proper way to respect this condition is represented by the employment of reasons that we can reasonably expect agents will accept as reasonable.[20] Such reasons are called public reasons, because they are all shared by reasonable persons and are appropriate for public justification. They are not impersonal, because their criterion of validity is that reasonable agents are able to endorse them.

This is not to radically personalize justification to each individual's specific perspective. The intention is to base justification on reasons endorsed by the agent, but that she, also, can share with other reasonable agents. Importantly, these reasons are not personalized in the sense that they apply specifically to single persons. Instead, they have a universal form, i.e. they apply to all relevantly similar cases.

An endorsement of the Rawlsian approach is already present in the debate. Daniels and Sabin endorse a version of it that constitutes one of the aspects of the fairness of deliberation. In their view, "the grounds for decisions must be ones that fair-minded people can agree are relevant to meeting health care needs fairly under reasonable resource constraints. [...] Some kinds of reasons are easier to get

---

[17]Rawls (1993/2005), and Gaus (2011).

[18]Daniels Sabin (2008).

[19]Daniels Sabin (2008), p. vi.

[20]Rawls (1993/2005).

agreement on than others: safety and efficacy, for example, will be less problematic, by themselves, than cost-effectiveness".[21]

In my view, the Rawlsian model appears at two levels of public justification. First, in the basic justificatory process, the public reason model appears in the reasoning of idealized agents, who reason in somehow idealized conditions. Second, it also appears in real life deliberation, as a requirement for real life agents who deliberate about questions of justice. This is because there will still be indeterminacies, for example, about how to mutually accommodate the priorities in real life contexts of conditions of scarcity. At this level, the strong priorities established at the idealized level appear as public reasons that serve like reasons to provide justification in the deliberative process and set limits to legitimate decisions. The final decisions are limited to eligible conclusions justified by the priorities established in the ideal procedure. In real life deliberation, we must choose between these eligible conclusions. Here, my view is strongly influenced by the public reason view of John Rawls and Gerald Gaus.[22]

Real life decisions, thus, have legitimacy. They will be made in a democratic procedure where every reasonable citizen has an equal say, and where choices are made from proposals that are eligible. This is because they are justified by reasons not alien to agents, but accessible to them in the proper employment of their capacities.

4   The Strong Priority of Life Prolonging Therapies

Now I relate this model of decision making to questions of PM and I show what I think is the most reasonable outcome of it.

The authors that I discuss attribute legitimacy to decisions in real life deliberation. The context of deliberation includes the high costs of therapies and the impossibility to give therapy to all those in need. Thus, they assume the need to set fair limits to the provision of therapies.

The flaw in their reasoning is that they do not attribute a sufficiently strong role to the personal perspective, in the sense that they do not properly consider the meaning that a decision has for an agent. Further, refinements are required when they assume the necessity to set limits to the provision of life prolonging therapies for the sake of other therapies, as well as for other needs. Daniels and Sabin, for example, say that "however important, health care [. . .] is not the only important social good".[23] But strong constraints are needed to avoid the risk of legitimizing, in the real life deliberative process, wrong policies, i.e. to reduce the provision of support for the most urgent needs, for the sake of weaker needs.

---

[21]Daniels Sabin (2008), p. 12.

[22]Gaus (2011). Rawls (1993/2005).

[23]Daniels Sabin (2008), p. 2.

The flaw of this approach is it doesn't remark upon the importance and strength of some basic rights. Daniels and Sabin speak about health care distributive justice in general,[24] while Fleck speaks mainly about PM,[25] but from the standpoint of the focus of my present paper, their approaches overlap.

Fleck illustrates the specific context of justice and legitimacy in personalized medicine with the case of expensive cancer therapies. The basic worrisome aspect is represented by resistance to cancer therapy. In some cases, such resistance manifests itself in relation to first-line chemotherapies. In other cases, resistance develops in relation to the applied therapies. In response to such resistance, several drugs might be used in sequence, or contemporarily in combination with one another. This is not without its risks and problems. One of them is greater toxicity. Another problem is represented by the vast number of theoretical combinations.[26]

Because of all the complexities, says Fleck, we cannot hope for more than that sensible efforts will result in a sensible prolongation of a reasonable quality of life in patients with metastases. By keeping these benefits in mind, unfortunately, we cannot neglect the great costs in conditions of scarcity.[27] A constraint that, in Fleck's view, we cannot reasonably neglect is that of cost-effectiveness. Thus, the question is: "would a just and caring society with limited resources to meet virtually unlimited health care needs be morally obligated to provide social funding for all these target therapies for these cancer patients?".[28]

Fleck's punch line is to remind us about the costs and unsustainability of offering a full coverage of health care to all patients in need of life prolonging therapies. As he says, imagine that it would be judged as reasonable to pay USD 100,000 for a patient who needs life prolonging therapy. First, there is the uncertainty about whether it will be successful. It might be that the need to change combinatorial therapies in sequence appears. This would mean an enormous cost. Fleck says there are 600,000 patients dying of cancer in USA each year, which implies a cost of USD 60 billion. If therapies are successful in prolonging life for a further year, this would raise the annual cost to USD 120 billion. Obviously, costs increase in proportion to how successful the therapy is. He elaborates the point further, but I stop with this initial sketch.[29]

Fleck reminds us that, in virtue of the scarcity and competition of requirements we must be aware that offering an opportunity to one patient means denying the opportunity to others.[30] Together with thinking about the interests of all patients, we must think, amongst other things, about the expenses of research, which means caring about future patients. Thus, actual patients must consider that they are now the

---

[24]Daniels Sabin (2008).

[25]Fleck (2013).

[26]Fleck (2013), pp. 125–127.

[27]Fleck (2013), p. 129.

[28]Fleck (2013), p. 131.

[29]Fleck (2013), p. 130.

[30]Fleck (2013), p. 140.

beneficiaries of the endorsement of this rationing strategy from the past, in the same way as future patients will be in relation to actual rationing.

His recommendation is to take cost effectiveness calculus as an important criterion. This is reasonable. However, I think the model of justification must be completed. Unconstrained real life deliberation risks neglecting higher priority needs in comparison to needs with weaker normative strength. In addition, as the public reason model suggests, in the justification we must not forget the perspective of the agent. This is because we must reasonably expect that the agent can reasonably endorse the rule. We must ask ourselves whether the agent can endorse the justification, or whether we are imposing a justification alien to the agent.

I show, now, an exemplification of the two levels of thinking about the question. In the relevant idealization, I presuppose relatively favorable conditions. In such favorable conditions, rights do not need to be limited because of conflicts in the implementation of the same right in various instances, but only because of conflicts with other rights. The test for strong rights is whether we would be reasonably ready to accept, and whether we can reasonably expect that others can reasonably accept, to limit this right for the sake of another right.

Now, think about a case where, let's say, prolonging life for 5 months would cost USD 200,000. As I have said, when we justify a decision to an agent, we must consider the meaning of this decision for the agent. For the person involved, and for her dear ones, these 5 months are their whole life, all that they have. We cannot expect any agent to reasonably accept the rule that life prolonging therapies must be denied when they are expensive, because money must be invested for the totally efficacious treatment of, let's say, a migraine. To confirm this, let us think whether we would rather renounce the treatment of a migraine, or to chemotherapy (if in the latter case we evaluate our life as worth it). How can it be possibly said that one can reasonably endorse a rule that for her means renouncing what remains of life to her, i.e. to everything that she has of life (the supposition is that the quality of life is such that for her such a life is better than no life)? The 5 months, thus, have an overriding value from the standpoint of reasons that agents can reasonably endorse.

My point, here, is that we cannot embrace considerations of cost-effectiveness without considering meanings for the agents, if we seriously consider the duty to justify decisions through reasons that agents can endorse. If we consider their meaning for the agent, these 5 months have a strong value and a strong priority.

Importantly, this does not represent a mere personal reason. Because the view is generally shared by people, or hypothetically in the relevant situation, supporters of the reason can put it forward as a public reason. Here we have a public reason, and not a mere personal perspective, in the sense that we cannot reasonably expect that an agent will reasonably accept a rule that deprives her of what, for her, is the whole life.

Does it follow that life-prolonging therapy is due at any moment, unconditionally? No. We have to consider other needs, as well. For this end, I introduce a thought experiment that extends the previous one. Imagine that there is clash between the satisfaction of needs. We are ready to limit the satisfaction of each need for the satisfaction of some other needs. Let's say, we are ready to reduce the satisfaction of life-prolonging therapies for the sake of removing incapacities that fundamentally and comprehensively limit our agency. We are, also, ready to limit health care provision for the sake of good public education.

Imagine, however, that we are, as reasonable agents, ready to limit the satisfaction of each of these needs only for the satisfaction of the other two that I have mentioned, but not for other needs. We have established, then, a hierarchy of needs. The hierarchy is not strict in that it puts every single need into an order of strict priority. It establishes the priority of a set of needs. As we cannot fully satisfy the most urgent needs, we must not orient public resources towards the less urgent needs. Thus, the requirement for life prolonging therapies has a strong priority.

My insistence is on rules that agents can reasonably endorse. But agents do not deliberate reasonably if they reason by focusing only on their present need, nor if they reason egocentrically. A rule of reciprocity is crucial. No agent is allowed to require for herself what she cannot concede to others. In conditions of scarcity, one must be aware that she cannot require for herself, without special justification, the full satisfaction of a need, if this means that the same need of another person in a relevantly similar condition is neglected. This is true for life prolonging therapies, as well. Considerations about the unsustainability of full coverage, here, are important, because of the conflicts of demands that they create. In such a condition, the question is whether to approve a rule that implements a health care right by not equally favoring all the equivalent parts. We cannot approve such a rule because it is unreasonable.

This is part of the truth in Daniels's and Sabin's, as well as in Fleck's proposal. But there is a difference between their proposal and mine. I explicitly remark upon the priority of the set of some rights. Other needs or requirements are fully excluded prior to real life deliberation when the strong rights in this set cannot be fully satisfied because of scarcity. Such an approach helps us to see what is a possible and just outcome of real life deliberation, and what is no longer just. Real life deliberation must not be such that it makes a strong right fade away. This reduction is not something one can reasonably accept.

So, how does the previous debate help in relation to distributive issues? We are cautioned to not renounce the satisfaction of a strong need in the favor of weaker demands. Priorities must be set as a matter of justice and be constraints even over real life democratic deliberation.

To be sure, health care is not the only domain that can claim strong priority. There are other very important needs, as well, like the protection of basic liberties that requires public resources, security, education, etc.[31] A further problem is represented by the fact that health is importantly affected by social and economic inequalities.[32] Health is influenced by life-style in general, and this might depend on the socio-financial situation of the person.[33] For example, genomic tests might indicate that a

---

[31]Farrelly (2007), Daniels Sabin (2008), and Wolff (2011).

[32]Daniels Sabin (2008), p. 18.

[33]Brother Rothstein (2015), p. 48.

person has to change her behavior, but this can be difficult for her because of her social or financial status. This is where a serious problem and potential conflict for equity appears. A situation might appear as a challenge to justice where resources can be directed to high-tech health care innovations, while the societal determinants of health are neglected for this reason.[34]

Although there are persistent dilemmas, the concept of strong priority has not become meaningless. It is true that in society, we have various needs, and they are competing. But not all of them remain at the same level of importance. We can and we must rank them, and we do this in the idealized procedure.

An important deliberative constraint is indicated by Rawls, who, again, sets an enlightening criterion. He says that there are fields reasonably not unanimously judged as of priority value, i.e. they are matters of reasonable disagreement. People may reasonably disagree about the value of operas, contemporary visual arts, the importance of studying the origin of the universe, some parts of philosophical analyses, etc.[35] Thus, such activities can receive public financial support based on democratic deliberation only after primary matters of justice are satisfied, because they are not sufficiently supported by public reason, in particular in comparison to other requirements that are strongly supported by public reason. Such are, importantly for the present paper, life prolonging therapies.

How to manage the persistent impossibility to fully satisfy various competing needs in health care, as well as other needs of primary importance, like basic liberties, equality, etc., even after their priority as a set has been established?

Probably we cannot even fully satisfy those requirements strongly supported by public reason and, thus, we cannot avoid conclusively setting limits in a real life fair procedure for the provision of even strong rights. The reason is represented by conflicts between strong rights. The reasonable outcomes of such procedures, as it is already visible, must be respectful of the general priority of some strong basic rights, and, among them, the right to life prolonging therapies. This means that, although, in real life, we cannot establish an absolute priority of each single need, we can try to establish their priority as a set over other kinds of needs. Here, we see the persistent influence of the outcomes of idealized deliberation.

What if, even after we have established such a priority, we cannot respond satisfactorily to these needs? This might still be too expensive, and high priority needs may be in competition with each other, like, as we have already seen, Fleck represents with a calculus.

This may create pressure to leave the solution to private financial possibilities. But, then, even if such pressure is justified for the sake of the sustainability of the public system, there is legitimacy, based on the strong right to health care, for some policies oriented to reducing inequalities, or supporting the worst-off. Such policies would render the concession to full justice reasonable. For example, we can reduce the problem of unsustainability by rendering expensive therapies available only with

---

[34]Arnason (2012), pp. 114–115.
[35]Rawls (2001), pp. 151–152.

payment for those people who have a high level of income, while providing them without payment to others. A possibility is also to render payment proportional to the incomes of persons, like progressive taxation. A further possibility is that of leaving individual persons to pay for those therapies that are the least advantageous from the standpoint of cost-effectiveness, but to put high taxes on such payments, and, then, invest the money into benefits for the worst-off from the standpoint of health care, as well as of financial and social status.

5 Conclusion

In conclusion, life prolonging therapies are not absolute rights that must be provided no matter what other needs there are. However, they remain very strong rights that put very strong constraints on real life deliberation. Thus, they have a strong priority as part of the set of strong priorities over other instances of health care, as well as over other possible social investments, in particular, as Rawls says, over those that are disputed matters of reasonable disagreement. Even if there are difficulties in pursuing policies of strong priority, justice has not become ephemeral. The conception of justice still has implications for policies and it orients contextually appropriate decisions.

References

Arnason V (2012) The personal is political. Ethics and personalized medicine. Ethical Perspect 19(1):103–122

Brother KB, Rothstein MA (2015) Ethical, legal and social implications of incorporating personalized medicine into healthcare. Pers Med 12(1):43–51

Daniels N, Sabin JE (2008) Setting limits fairly: learning to share resources for health. Oxford University Press, Oxford

Farrelly C (2007) Justice, democracy and reasonable agreement. Palgrave MacMillan, Basingstoke

Fleck LM (2013) "Just Caring". Can we afford the ethical and economic costs of circumventing cancer drug resistance? J Pers Med 3(3):124–143

Gaus G (2011) The order of public reason. Cambridge University Press, Cambridge

Lewis J, Lipworth W, Kerridge I (2014) Ethics, evidence and economics in the pursuit of "personalized medicine". J Pers Med 2(4):137–146

Olivier C et al (2008) Personalized medicine, bioethics and social responsibilities. Re-thinking the pharmaceutical industry to remedy inequities in patient care and international health. Curr Pharmacogenomics Pers Med 6(2):108–120

Rawls J (1993/2005) Political liberalism. Columbia University Press, New York

Rawls J (2001) Justice as fairness: a restatement. Harvard University Press, Cambridge

Wolff J (2011) Ethics and public policy. Routledge, London

Evolution Paths of Business Models in Personalized Medicine

Marija Kastelan Mrak and Danijela Sokolic

Abstract As a new personalized health care system is emerging, old roles, rules, and positions gradually decrease in influence and a new constellation of power emerges. To provide a better understanding of possible sources of social and economic value and distribution of surpluses, we find it necessary to map this emerging system. The purpose of this paper is to detect technology development paths and help regulators in the process of designing instruments that will guide the institutionalization of personalized medicine into a socially beneficent, as well as economically sustainable health care model.

Models are conceptual representatives of complex ideas or systems. As such, they carry more or less explanatory power. The same holds true for business models. Essentially, our design of a business model represents a description of (dynamic) power relations that may evolve in the personalized medicine sector. Actors considered in our design are the medical and the pharmaceutical sector, the insurance industry, the IT industry, educators, regulatory institutions, agencies and bodies, NGO-s, etc.

The paper starts by identifying the meaning, dynamics, and economic implications of personalized medicine. Further on, the authors provide a list of relevant stakeholders, analyze their roles and changing power positions.

1 Introduction

The main idea behind personalized medicine (PM) is to provide the right medical treatment to the right person. This "new paradigm"[1] in medical science prefers personally tailored rather than broad-scope solutions. Such an orientation changes patient treatment trajectory, i.e. it requires a different type of clinical trial that focuses

---

[1] Juengst et al. (2012).

M. K. Mrak (✉) · D. Sokolic
University of Rijeka, Faculty of Economics and Business, Department for Organization and Management, Rijeka, Croatia
e-mail: kastelan@efri.hr; dsokolic@efri.hr

© Springer Nature Switzerland AG 2019
N. Bodiroga-Vukobrat et al. (eds.), *Personalized Medicine in Healthcare Systems*,
Europeanization and Globalization 5, https://doi.org/10.1007/978-3-030-16465-2_12

on individual, not average, responses to therapy.[2] Conceptually, the basic idea of the "the right drug" is related to tailor-made medicaments produced upon detecting changes and pathogenic processes measured on specific individual and his/her specific biomarker.[3] Progress in medical science and supporting fields has made it possible to scan and analyze human genomes and detect and isolate pathogenic processes and mutations developed at the individual level, thus facilitating the idea of tailor-made drugs. The value of tailor-made targeted therapeutic interventions can be seen both in social and economic implications for the health care system and for the patient: improving patient dignity, safety and quality of life, preventing undesirable yet avoidable side-effects, raising the effectiveness of the medical treatments and lowering total cost to the patient.

The EC Health Research Directorate in 2010 defines personalized medicine as a medical model using molecular profiling technologies for tailoring **right therapeutic strategy** for the right person at the right time, and determine **predisposition to disease** at the population level, and to deliver timely and **stratified** solutions.[4] At a first glance, the economic consequences implied by this definition are ambiguous: a stratification of the population suggests an excessive number of differentiated products. It also implies value creation on narrow, niche markets that economic theory relates to higher overall costs because of the lack of scale economies. On the other hand, determination of the population's predisposition to disease and intervention in a timely manner, implies lower costs for the health care system in the end.

Although simple in concept, personalized medicine has proven difficult to implement. The challenges are both conventional and operational.[5] At this moment, due primarily to economic reasons (inefficiencies), cases of tailor-made drugs produced for a specific individual are relatively rare. However, there are more and more cases of producing medicine for smaller groups of patients designed upon isolating changes on their biomaterial. Because of high rate of R&D in those products, their price tends to be high. The higher number of specific indication treatments (drugs) present on the market for small scale target groups (patients who fall within the scope of narrow stratification), the more difficult for national economies to adjust their inclusion into public health care budgets. This fact represents a threat to European health care systems because their financing depends heavily (and leans on) public money.[6] Financing of health care system is also specifically delicate issue in the United States, where the cost of health care is on an unsustainable upward climb. On

---

[2]Schork (2015).

[3]A biomarker is a naturally occurring molecule, gene, or characteristic biological property that can be detected and measured in parts of the body (blood, tissue, etc.) and by which a particular pathological or psychological process, including disease, can be identified. It is a characteristic that is objectively measured and evaluated as an indicator of normal biological processes, pathogenic processes, or pharmacological responses to a therapeutic intervention (National Institute of Health Biomarkers 1998).

[4]EC Health Research Directorate (2010).

[5]Schork (2015).

[6]WHO (2017).

the other hand, early data shows indications that personalized medical care has the potential to reduce health care costs worldwide. In addition, smart incorporation of personalized medicine into the health care system can help resolve many embedded system inefficiencies.

2 A Multidirectional Approach to Personalized Medicine and Economic Implications

Challenges to the advancement and adoption of personalized medicine can be classified as scientific, medical, technological, social, ethical, legal, psychological, and economic. **Scientific and medical** challenges are related to the understanding of molecular mechanisms and learning how biomarkers in their environments cause different diseases, interpreting complex tests results, etc. **Technological** issues are related to development and utilization of new technologies, including property rights. Personal medicine raises also all sorts of **social, legal, and ethical concerns**, as well as concerns related to **regulation**. Among many other factors, issues to be discussed include safety of direct-to-consumer PM product and services, data storing, transparency, privacy, availability of PM for broad spectra of patients, possible notion of elitism based on high costs of PM products and services, procedures for ensuring the utility of new genetic tests before they are introduced, issues of genetic discrimination in employment, etc. and all the way towards human rights and scientific integrity.[7] **Psychological** issues are related to human emotions and safety concerns, fears, etc. All these concerns should be appropriately addressed to insure stable health care system and sound **policymaking** based on accurate information.

This research is mainly concerned with the **economic challenges** of PM development and tries to foresee the implications of implementing PM into existing health care systems. We will consider two levels in approaching the issue of **value creation** in personalized medicine: (a) System level (Macro level) and (b) Operational level (Micro level).

Economic issues at the macro level are often related to value creation and appropriation, incentives structure, stakeholders' relationships, etc. Economic issues should be considered also at a level of individual business entities and at the level of single persons. Compared to the broader, society level, these lower range (analysis) platforms may well be treated as **operational challenges.** However, **business-modeling** itself is complex, involving decisions on business entity establishment, investments in capacity building, as well as planing for capacity utilizing, budget allocation, recruiting and developing human resources, etc.

Berwick argues that in contemporary settings, in order to understand the process of disseminating innovations in health care, we need to consider an ever more complex combinations of factors including the reasoning of discrete individuals

---

[7]Juengst et al. (2012).

who may consider adopting the change.[8] Reasons for technology diffusion can also prove incidental; for example, a successful physician is the one with the most positive outcomes and the success is more probable[9] if more tests/analyses are done, and if more money is invested in innovations and education.

Here, we are more concerned with the possibility of a model rendering some insight in the **value creation process**. Value assessment tools often used on micro level include various cost-benefit analyses, such as cost-effectiveness analysis, cost-utility analysis, well-being valuation analysis, etc. The boundaries of the system are yet to be precisely defined and so are the roles and bargaining positions of traditional players, considering that positions are changing as new technologies emerge. New technologies allow early entrants (developers) to create temporary monopolies, control information, make alliances, develop new knowledge and expertise, and thus affect existent flows/channels/paths of value creation and appropriation.

Along with new value creation and prospective benefits to patients, new technologies are likely to raise the overall costs of the health care system, both for reasons of seeking technological leadership (early entrants' benefits), and those of costs readjustments, as players in the health care system must revise their roles and positions. One group of costs is related to necessary regulatory (institutional) adjustments. As health care system is very bureaucratic in its nature, it is expected that changes will happen very slowly. In a global survey conducted in 2014, 100 CEO of pharmaceutical companies find "lack of regulatory guidelines" most important obstacle to PM implementation.[10] Professional surveys also claim that regulation is by far the biggest challenge inhibiting further advances in personalized medicine. The pharma markets have been in intensive R&D expansion for over a decade, heavily relying on medical R&D but also on the development of data analytics (i.e. big data).[11]

3 Mapping the System

We use a model approach to present a system structure (Fig. 1). Four main groups of stakeholders influencing PM development are distinguished and identified by their major role in the system:

1. Policy makers (regulators)
2. Payers
3. Health care service providers
4. Technology providers (pharma and equipment industry, research facilities)

---

[8]Berwick (2003).
[9]Fleming et al. (2015).
[10]Reed Smith LLP Report (2016).
[11]Reed Smith LLP Report (2016).

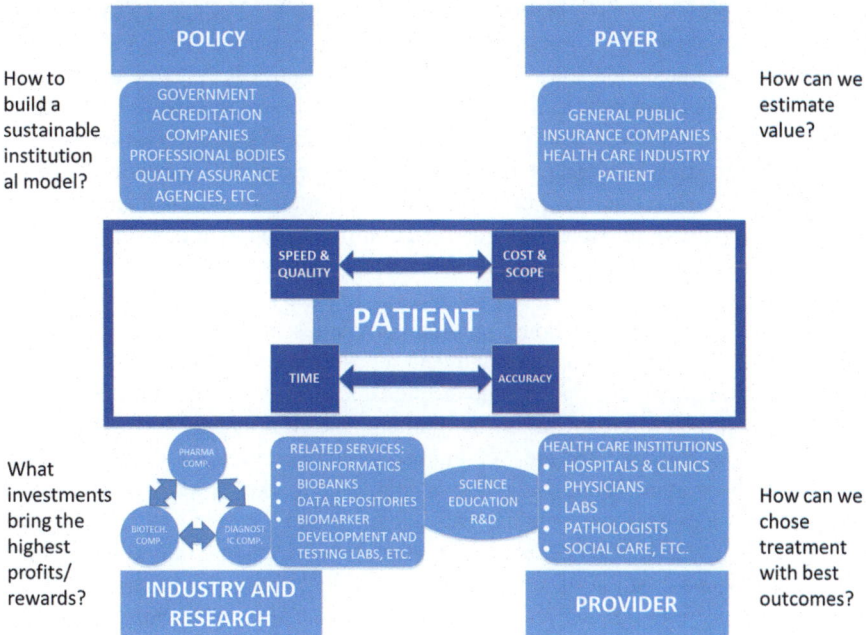

Fig. 1 Stakeholders in the health care system. Source: Authors

The term **Regulator** refers both to public and private entities responsible and/or authorized for (contributing to) policymaking; such as governments and their agencies (approval agencies, quality assurance agencies, etc.), accreditation companies, professional associations, and other professional bodies. The regulators' main concern is maintaining an effective, efficient, and sustainable health care system. Thus, the policy maker mediates in the players' relationships by facilitating access, requiring transparency, enacting and controlling standards, providing or facilitating financial coverage (reimbursement and pricing), etc.

Payers include various actors: the population paying taxes and contributions, insurance companies, patients, and health care industry in cases of costs spillovers (i.e. when insurance does not cover drug prescription or costs of testing). Payer not only seeks for medical, but also for economic value. In social states, health care is mostly financed through tax contributions; in liberalized markets health product and services are more or less covered through insurance schemes. Willingness to pay is, among other factors, also related to ability of calculation of long-term savings for short-term investments, evidence of the successfulness of treatments, and possibilities of health risk measurement (health hazard).

Medical service providers include hospitals and clinics, physicians, labs, pathologists, social care providers, and other professionals and institutions involved in treating patients. Their concerns are focused on choosing treatments with the highest positive outcomes for patients, controlling their own sustainability and rewards. The fact that the providers have highest awareness of treatment efficiency makes their role crucial in supporting innovation and diffusion of new treatments. PM development and implementation may result in spending significant part of a hospital's budget on single treatment, thus deprivating the treatment of other patients. Providers worldwide operate under very different institutional settings (market based or publicly financed), which makes the prediction of developmental paths for PM even more complex. Nevertheless, hospitals tend to compete based on their treatment success; competitive relations serve as selection mechanisms in competing/negotiating on markets or bidding for public resources.

Technology providers include, but are not limited to, all kinds of public and private life science organizations: pharma companies, biotechnology companies, bioinformatics, big data companies and data repositories, diagnostic test producers, bio banks, biomarker development and testing labs, institutes, universities, centers of excellence, etc. they create need (biomarkers, bio-informatics, bio banks, data repositories—some services are yet on the beginning of their developed). An important observation about this group is that their market is *global*, while other stakeholders dominantly maintain localized influence. To some extent, they are protected by intellectual property rights (patents) and licensing, thus enabling high entry barriers and creation of temporary monopolies.[12] Factors best describing the PM industry are high R&D investments and time struggle (need for market speed— short time to approval/market, trial sizes and times related issues), high hidden costs, difficulties to enforce standard protocols, payers' price scrutiny and sensitivity (rate of payer adoption), scientific and commercial potential and constraints, etc. Their incentives are mostly profit driven, and before taking actions, they analyze most beneficial investments. Because of a highly competitive and dynamic market, the potential to generate greater value after marketing is sometimes more important for the economics of the pharmaceutical and biotechnology companies than making development more productive, putting profits and market shares before health and ethics. On the other hand, they represent the most powerful and most creative element of the whole system in the sense of promoting new developments. Thus, if the model is not adequately designed, and their rewards are insufficient to motivate entering the market and constant R&D investments, the development and/or implementation, along with value creation, would be slowed down. Therefore, the model should prevent monopoly creation and monopolistic protection, and ensure entering and existing dynamics based on market principles: efficiency based competitive advantage and level of rewards allowing additional investments in development.

---

[12]Staton (2014).

4 Shifting Power Position Through Regulation and Incentives

Value creation and appropriation occurs in a loop (Fig. 2). If the policy makers can predict individuals' decisions, they can employ incentives to induce involved parties into the adoption of a specific behavioral path; in our case, policy can direct innovations and technology dissemination.

At this moment, we can observe *circumstantial evidence* supported by some indicative facts. A continuous increase of patent filling for world-wide protection (the so-called Madrid System) suggests many technology providers are counting on future profits from present investments in R&D.

An important indicator of trend in medicine comes from the percentage of new drug approvals. While in 2005 FDA's Center for Drug Evaluation and Research approved only one personalized medicine, in 2014 20% of new medicines approved by FDA were personalized medicines. In 2015, FDA approved 13 targeted therapeutic treatments accounting for 28% of the year's total approvals.[13] Data demonstrates that pharmaceutical industry has embraced personalized medicine, despite the absence of a tried and tested business model that ensures success.

Although technology development proved a 'one-size-fits-all' approach to drug prescription to be inadequate, pharmaceutical companies still manage their product portfolios mostly on broad-spectra drugs. In many cases, this is because of the predictable regulatory path making the development of broad indication drugs more reliable and effective. There is also a substantial commercial market for

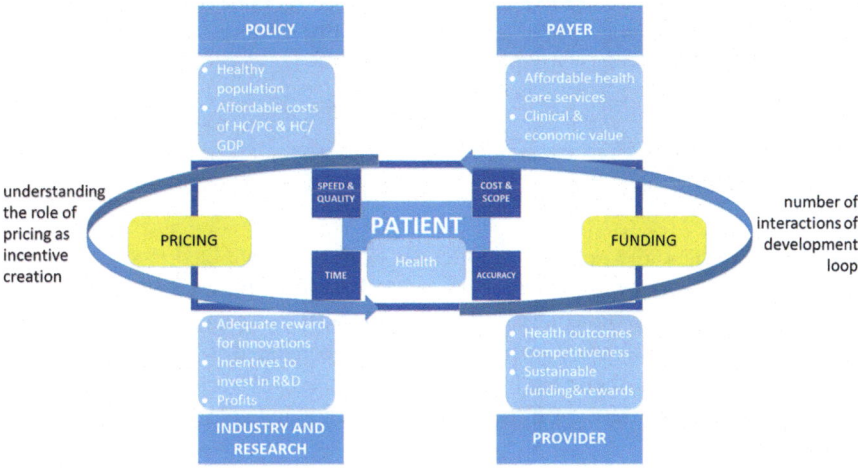

Fig. 2 Value creation and appropriation. Source: Authors

---

[13] Abrahams and Eck (2016).

these drugs, with almost half of life sciences companies seeing this as an incentive for developing further treatments. The conclusion is that although personalized medicine is undoubtedly an area with huge potential, it will continue to operate alongside traditional broad-spectra products in the near future.[14]

Aspinall and Hamermesh identified four main barriers to PM implementation: current profits in the pharmaceutical industry, maladjusted regulatory environment, dysfunctional payment systems, and physician behavior rooted in trial-and-error medicine.[15] While their emphases were on pharmaceutical industry's devotion to its historically successful blockbusters acting as the single major obstacle for hindering the transition from trial-and-error medicine to personalized medicine, more recent research highlights regulatory and payment systems as the major reason for relatively slow adoption of PM. Regulation and reimbursement systems do not keep pace with the implications of the new discoveries regarding individual variation and the development of new technologies that facilitate more precise diagnoses. Abrahams and Eck find that regulatory and payment factors are more influential for PM development than inherent biological complexity of targeting treatments or reluctance on the part of industry.[16]

The main balance that must be fine-tuned is the one between the pricing and the funding system, because pricing is incentive for value creation, but funding is the way to control the cycle and make it constantly rolling. Even countries with liberal market regulation tradition, like the USA, that base their health care systems on private paying for health care services, have considerable government health care budgets (for example, WHO data[17] indicates general government health expenditure to be 21% of total general government expenditures for USA, in 2014, which is 7pp higher than the EU average ratio 14%).

To conclude, although personalized medicine is undoubtedly an area of huge potential, it will continue to operate alongside traditional broad-spectra health care products, at least in the near future.

5   Conclusion

To fully understand the economic challenges of personalized medicine, it is necessary to briefly describe the concept. Personalized medicine (also known as precision medicine, individualized medicine) optimizes medical treatment for the patient, but requires a different trajectory in patient treatment compared to traditional medical approaches. Targeted therapeutic interventions that use precise diagnostics and pharmaceutical drugs rely on biomarkers to identify mutation and so personalize

---

[14]Reed Smith LLP Report (2016).

[15]Aspinall and Hamermesh (2007).

[16]Abrahams and Eck (2016).

[17]WHO data (2017).

optimal therapeutic interventions. Drugs are usually prescribed based on accompanying testing results made with specific, again narrow in scope, companion diagnostic tools and adjusted to specific patient or group of patients. Thus, patient populations are stratified into subpopulations of different drug responses based on their individual characteristics.

Adjustments in the whole health care system have become eminent, and so are readjustments in the value chain. Because of advancements in science and technology, change in medicament and pharmaceutical industry has already began, carrying along related industries, insurance, IT, education; as well as regulatory institutions, agencies and bodies, NGO-s, etc. A more personalized health care system is emerging, and old roles, rules, and positions are changing, while new players are taking places. To understand new the sources of power and the evolving value creation chains, it is necessary to map the essential elements of this emerging system.

Health care systems may be able to benefit from the shift of resources towards individuals to whom an personalized intervention can provide a better outcome, leaving out those with lower odds for improvement, thus resulting in an economic advantage when medical resources are scarce or expensive. It can be expected that some of the existing stakeholders will support the change and try to reinforce their market position, while others will strongly resist and try to impose barriers to new rules and new entries to maintain their current position on the market. Subsequently, the new dynamics on the health care market pose a new burden on national governments in providing equal access to health care services for every group of citizens, and thus maintaining social and economic welfare.

Further research will be needed to determine more precisely how can new achievements and innovations be supported and successfully implemented into the health care system for the system to be both affordable for the patient, and sustainable for society. The evidence on economic sustainability of personalized medicine as the dominant health care model is still scarce. There are some statistics on personalized treatments effectiveness in medical terms, but there is lack of evidence (i.e. economic analysis) of PM contribution to disease prevention at the broader population level, along with related health care efficiencies, and calculations of direct impact on local/national budgets.

References

Abrahams E, Eck S (2016) Towards targeted therapeutics: the pharmaceutical industry and personalized medicine, The journal of precision medicine, Cognoscienti, pp 31–37

Aspinall M, Hamermesh R (2007) Realizing the promise of personalized medicine. Harv Bus Rev 85:108. October 2017

Berwick DM (2003) Disseminating innovation in health care, JAMA, Online article on June 3, 2009, Available at https://www.researchgate.net/profile/Donald_Berwick/publication/10802283_Disseminating_Innovations_in_Health_Care/links/0c96051ffa429cb1f6000000/Disseminating-Innovations-in-Health-Care.pdf

EC Health Research Directorate (2010) Omics in personalized medicine, Report

Fleming C et al (2015) Measuring changes in the economics of medical practice, available at: https://www.ncbi.nlm.nih.gov/pmc/articles/PMC4512969/

Juengst ET et al (2012) After the revolution? Ethical and social challenges in 'Personalized Genomic Medicine,'. Pers Med 9:429–441. at 431

National Institute of Health Biomarkers (1998)

Frenier D, Yam P (2016) LLP report, deal dimensions, life lines: life sciences M&A and the rise of personalised medicine, Reed Smith. http://dealdimensions.reedsmith.com/life-sciences (November 12, 2017)

Schork NJ (2015) Personalized medicine: time for one-person trials. Nature 520:609–611. http://www.mpmi.manchester.ac.uk/aboutprecisionmedicine/ (March 25, 2017)

Staton T (2014) Who are the stars of personalized medicine? Roche, Novartis and J&J, http://www.fiercepharma.com/sales-and-marketing/who-are-stars-of-personalized-medicine-roche-novartis-and-j-j (April 5, 2017)

World Health Organization (WHO) data (2017) Accessed 17 Feb 2017

Socio-Humanistic and Political Context of Personalized Medicine

Drago Kraljević

Abstract The topic of personalized medicine is discussed in the socio-political context. Particularly, the following questions are critically elaborated: how will confrontation with different types of society and culture be evidenced in the future?; what kind of relationship will be established between personalized medicine and education?; how will the complex ethical and legal issues of the modern society be addressed?; how will the relationship between physician and patient be develop when the patient will be approached as an integral human being?; what role will be played and what responsibilities will be taken by the politics as substantial political changes occurred in the twenty-first century? Expected socio-political aspect and consequences because of the introduction of personalized medicine in everyday clinical practice, will probably be positive especially in the area of creating improved, high-quality legal and ethical regulation measures. In addition, introduction of new methods and contents in medicine along with adequate and intensified patient education are expected to allow patients to actively and responsibly participate in the implementation of newly adopted social standards and regulations in this area. In the process of achieving expected goals within the field of personalized medicine, two aspects may be particularly highlighted. One aspect is focused on how to live better and longer, while the second is focused on how to maximize personal patients' data protection because data, including personal data, is highly relevant for this important humanistic project of extraordinary interest to humanity.

D. Kraljević (✉)
Coordination of Croatian Friendship Associations, Zagreb, Croatia

VerbumlandiArt - cenacolo internazionale per la creatività espressiva e il dialogo, Galatone, Puglia, Italy

Accademia Europeista del F.V.G., Gorizia, Italy

© Springer Nature Switzerland AG 2019
N. Bodiroga-Vukobrat et al. (eds.), *Personalized Medicine in Healthcare Systems*, Europeanization and Globalization 5, https://doi.org/10.1007/978-3-030-16465-2_13

1 Expectations, Challenges

Man is a unique and unrepeatable being with needs, a life story, personal goals, and feelings. It should thereby be born in mind that "our humanity is most evident precisely in our feelings."[1] Modern research shows that people by nature are not merely egoistic, materialistic, and utilitarian, and that not everything is subject to self-interest. People are also empathetic.[2] Thus, personalized medicine, which represents a new horizon of medicine in the twenty-first century that will provide a step forward to man's needs for health because of, among other things, modern technologies and acquired knowledge. Advances in genetics, pharmaceuticals, new technologies, computer science, and medicine in general have led to a real scientific revolution that is also reflected in the design of personalized medicine. Expectations related to this project for the time being are many. Among the expected outcomes are optimized treatment, reduction of side effects of the treatment, economic benefits, development of new technologies and science. From personalized medicine, it is not only expected to provide quality improvements in the treatment of people, but it should also significantly affect people's lives and thus change the society as a whole.

Some experts say that "personalized medicine is simultaneously a complete concept of medicine and a health care system of the future".[3] Great expectations from this project are justified, because it offers a treatment of a patient in an individualized way, considering his genetic and other characteristics, which includes his lifestyle, diet, environment, and living conditions. Conversely, personalized medicine provides a detailed profile of the patient, which in itself includes various aspects of his social life. Therefore, we can conclude that personalized medicine is an introduction of a new project of health policies on a global scale.[4] This project includes scientists, physicians, health institutions, politics, economics, education, production activities, patients' associations, and many others. As they all gather around a common goal, which is to improve the diagnosis, prevention, and treatment of people, the project of personalized medicine may well be called a twenty-first century social project. This also includes many ethical, political, legal, and social aspects, which personalized medicine should face. This also includes genetic information about the patient and the question of privacy protection, the need for additional training of the medical staff and ethics committees, and a number of people who work in the health system, as well as citizens and patients themselves. Given that this is a global project in its implementation, it will be inevitably encountered on different continents, in countries and regions, with different ethical approaches to man and the patient, with different policies in the field of public health, different cultures, religions, and traditions. This will especially come to the fore when certain research, new objectives, and methods of personalized medicine

---

[1] Goleman (2012).
[2] Rifkin (2010).
[3] Meier-Abt (2012).
[4] Brand (2012a, b).

are carried out, and potential risks about which the participants of this process should be informed are determined, and the like. In short, it will not always be easy to achieve the desired consensus on these questions.

2 Dealing with Different Types of Society and Culture

Personalized medicine is expected to significantly affect the development of the pharmaceutical industry and the production of new-targeted products. All this will consequently affect the large financial investment in new technologies, employment, and other fields in this sector. When it comes to the doctor-patient relationship, it is realistic to expect that a clear improvement over the existing situation should be achieved even in this segment. At some point, during the pursuit of the goals of personalized medicine, project holders will inevitably must deal with societies dominated by utilitarianism, or the principle of utility. These are countries headed usually by conservatives and neoliberals. What effect this will have on the doctor-patient relationship, the adoption of appropriate legislation that should regulate the number of ethical, legal, and other questions, the fact that the gap between rich and poor patients is widening, remains to be seen. In other areas, the project of personalized medicine must deal with the prevailing ethics of egalitarianism, where the so-called "good intentions" are important, and where there is a different approach to understanding the principle of utility. These are in most cases less-developed countries, where representatives of center-left or authoritarian political parties are in power. So far, there are only first experiences in some developed Western countries how the predominant type of ethics is reflected on the project of personalized medicine.

3 Personalized Medicine and Education

For example, in the Strategic Plan of Research of the University of Montreal (Plan stratégique de recherche 2011–2016), which was presented to the University Assembly on 17 October 2011, personalized medicine occupies a prominent place. This University is committed to the establishment of the Institute of public health, which will consolidate international health, occupational health, and administrative activities in the field of public health, social sciences, bioethics, and education. The aim is to create a wide synergy in the field of public health and education of citizens. Interest in the patient through the medical model is apparently spreading to many areas of the society, including the production. As this process is closely linked to the education system, the work of national and alternative schools must be supported with more determination and vigor, but also by introducing the subject of personalized medicine in the curriculum of medical schools. In Switzerland, for example, a program has been introduced to grammar school, which should contribute to strengthening the professional knowledge in the field of personalized medicine.[5] In this way, the society can release a new major resource of knowledge and alternatives that will ultimately positively affect the process of spreading awareness among people, finding effective solutions for this crisis, and will help people to better understand and accept themselves for what they really are. Precisely the human approach to man in personalized medicine and beyond—in education, can contribute to a person coping with one of the biggest problems of our time, and that is the lack of meaning of life, which consequently has a devastating effect on health. Further, the EU Council in its conclusions from 2015 calls on Member States to provide education, training, and continuing professional development of health professionals to acquire the necessary additional knowledge, skills, and competences for optimum utilization of the benefits, which personalized medicine offers to patients and health care systems.[6] Discussions and dialogue between doctors and patients, which is often practiced for instance in the field of homeopathy and Chinese medicine, offers a convenient way of treating each patient.

4 Ethical and Legal Questions

Many ethical and legal questions inevitably emerge while implementing the project of personalized medicine. For example, how to handle the collection, storage, and use of personal samples (human tissue, blood, etc.)? When it comes to the privacy of data that will simply impress people with its size and content, quality discussion is necessary on ethical questions in which patient associations and the public should certainly participate. In this connection Article 14 of the Universal Declaration on Bioethics and Human Rights (2005) should be recalled, which contains the "principle of social and political responsibility for human health."[7] Under the provisions of the Universal Declaration, UNESCO has established an international ethics committee. At the same time, ethics committees are established at the national level. Under Article 83 of this Declaration, national ethics committees should be independent bodies, pluridisciplinary in composition, whose responsibilities are not only in the field of medicine, but are also related to natural and social sciences and technology. Their primary task is to prepare quality proposals for discussion and education, and to sensitize the public when it comes to bioethical questions. It will probably be neither easy nor simple to achieve consensus on new rules and methods; however, this is the inevitable approach. Will public debates within the existing democratic procedures be used in this endeavor when, for example, it comes to the adoption of regulations and codes of ethics of "biobanks"? Bartha Maria Knoppers, a Canadian lawyer specializing in the area of genomics, genetics, and biotechnology, tackles

---

[5]Conféderation Suisse, Secrétariat d'Etat à la formation (2016).
[6]Conclusions of the EU Council on personalized medicine for patients (2015b).
[7]UNESCO, Déclaration universelle sur la bioéthique et les droits de l'homme (2005).

many sensitive issues of personalized medicine. She supports a project of public interest for population genomics, in the context of international non-profit organizations, whereby she encourages collaboration between researchers. Bartha is also the founder of the project "CARTaGENE," which is of great importance to Canada, and which, apart from personalized medicine, includes the biobank for the area of Québec.

These are some examples that demonstrate the role of non-profit organizations in promoting the goals of personalized medicine.[8] A sensitive and acute question of education of those who need to educate others is thereby opened. For example, UNESCO promotes programs for the education of a new generation of ethics teachers. Personalized medicine obviously raises new demands and requires integration into international standards. It is therefore legitimate to ask the question whether patients are sufficiently protected under existing legal regulations of possible discrimination in the results of personalized medicine. What are the consequences of the application of current regulations in the area of research and innovation? What are the requirements in the area of data use in personalized medicine, such as for research and commercial purposes?

5 Personalized Medicine and the Complexity of the Modern Society

It is expected that personalized medicine will encourage transnational research, which will have a positive effect on the development of science, education, production, and employment of young professionals. One should not ignore that the talk about personalized medicine also means indicating and encouraging certain essential aspects of civilized society, as some societies still lack many (civilization) values that respect the dignity of man as an individual and the freedom he needs to strengthen his own abilities and opportunities. In developed societies, there are many more opportunities for the acquisition of knowledge, creative and empathic reasoning,[9] awakening one's feelings, and the like. However, material interests, the interests of the powerful and the rich, dominate in today's modern society, which consequently has a stressful and depressing effect on many people. The project of personalized medicine must face such a state of the modern world. In the society where we live, our future is mostly defined as something that will be more or less determined, and with innovation in the field of new technologies and financial investments. This, on the one hand, is only natural to be expected, but the question is whether this will be a future made according to man's liking—the kind in which man's needs to not only be financially taken care of and rich, but in which he is also satisfied with life? Can we think of our future only in terms of leaving it to the

---

[8]Maria (2009).
[9]Goleman (2012).

development of modern technology, techniques, material interest, and profit, while ignoring human needs that fall within the scope of their intimate life, emotion, and compassion? These are all questions that will be in one way or another answered through the design of personalized medicine. Man in the living environment, which is dominated by money and profit, is over the course of life constantly exposed to significant risks and uncertainties, he is subject to many diseases, many of which are caused by today's way and pace of life. "Stress caused by life pressure is perhaps the emotion with the greatest weight of scientific evidence that is associated with early disease and the process of recovery," said D. Goldman.[10] A particular challenge for personalized medicine will be the Chinese society, which is characterized by its dynamism and unprecedented rapid development in human history. However, China is now confronted with major dilemmas. "After 30 years of rapid development, economic growth has been slowing down. In addition, the efficiency of the political system has not been accompanied by economic development. At the same time the development of the economy and society is finding it difficult to tolerate the gap between the rich and the poor, and the conflict between environmental protection and economic development is growing. All this points to the discrepancy between expectations and actual results, and it negatively affects the stability of the Chinese society."[11] This is a country where many citizens are faced with extremely stressful and complex situations, because the priorities of the country are oriented towards global relationships and achieving competitiveness at the global level, solving very complex economic and social problems in the country; in short, towards financial, technological, industrial, consumer, and other priorities of material nature. All this affects the major changes in the life as well as the rhythm and mode of people in this most populated country in the world. Here, personalized medicine will face the problem of providing treatment in an appropriate way, considering that this is a different culture and tradition, the huge differences in the financial situation among the population, specific public health, and the like.

6 Relationship Doctor: Patient as a Complete Human Being

Given that we live in a world where life is often a means of achieving goals which are outside of man, such as money, power, manufacturing, trade, instead of knowledge, health, compassion, education, culture, etc., it will without any doubt be a big challenge for personalized medicine in actual practice. Will the physician-patient relationship be decisive/prevailing in dealing with patients or will the relationship computer-patient dominate? It should be expected that physicians, scientists, and others who genuinely want this project maximally adjusted to man's needs, thereby appreciating the real circumstances in the societies where they live, will be able to

---

[10]Goleman (2012).
[11]Zhe (2016).

help people to primarily help themselves. This project should be an incentive for the society as a whole to further strengthen the process of individuation of man in general through their programs. We live at a time when the foundations of human values are dangerously eroded, which in people causes mental disorientation. That is one of the challenges that the project of personalized medicine must consider.[12] Every awareness of causes in general, including the causes of disease, changes in man his worldview, helps him to better understand and accept broader interests and needs of the community in which he lives. "From a historical perspective, medicine has in the modern society defined its mission as treatment of disease, thereby ignoring the disease - the patient's experience of the disease. Now already with scientific arguments it can be argued that there is progress in medical effectiveness, both in the field of prevention, as well as in the area of treatment, which can be achieved by treating the patient's emotional state along with his medical condition," said Dan Goleman.[13] In developed countries like Switzerland programs are pre-pared, such as "Pour une nouvelle politique des Generations" (for a new generation of policies). This is preceded with the discussion involving representatives from politics, administration, science, and the civil society. Further, there is a need to elaborate one global generation of policies, which would include: education, family, fiscal, publications, and social policies. The European Alliance for Personalized Medicine (EAPM) is a non-profit organization based in Brussels, which connects experts in the field of health, and its main goal is to improve health care and the application of personalized medicine and diagnostics.[14] The emergence of person-alized medicine should also be welcomed for the reason that it assumes that man is biologically and spiritually complete/unique, regardless of racial, national or other affiliations. Every person is unique and should be treated as such, not only in medicine but also in the society in general. The path to man's individuation is much easier if one is not alone, but has the support and help of friends, physicians, scientists, priests; it allows him to have a more meaningful life. Just as personalized medicine should integrate all the possibilities which the official and alternative medicine have at their disposals, the process of education in the society should act parallel to this to strengthen the conscious knowledge and integration of all its opportunities, in a way that would enable everyone to more easily identify their own direction and personal mission in life. Individuation, which should go hand in hand with personalized medicine, gives impetus to man to seek "real" primordial Self in it. Thus, one could, with the help of modern science and technology, more

---

[12]Within the European alliance, "European Alliance for Personalized Medicine," in Italy there is the "Alleanza Italiana per la medicine personalizzata" (IAPMO). Here is an interesting assessment of the Italian branch: "Despite the achieved results in recent years in the field of personalized medicine, a lot more should be achieved in Europe. There are great challenges that are facing us with patients, health systems, and health care institutions, which have to be adapted to appropriate standards, and there are also the problems that occur with patients when they need to cross the border..." ("Raccomandazioni per la medicina parsonalizzata," 2014).

[13]Goleman (2012).

[14]Académie Suisse des Sciences Médicales, Conti (2009).

easily and more responsibly contemplate about his future. In today's world, the process of individuation is unfortunately developing at a quite slow pace, because people are still strongly influenced by various idol groups, ideologies, leaders, sects, etc. The problem probably lies in the fact that people are afraid of the future. Alternatively, maybe the problem is in part hidden in the fact that many people are under strongly influenced by the past, which brings numerous failed futures and unfulfilled expectations?

7 Humanistic Context

One of the key questions that arises when it comes to the humanistic context of personalized medicine is the protection of the patient's genetic data, particularly the protection of its possible misuse to prevent possible discrimination. The key issue is that the protection of the patient's sensitive types of data be treated as a national issue. Thus, public institutions must provide a guarantee for the preservation of the dignity and freedom of the patient. When a patient undergoes genetic testing, he is placed in a specific psychological situation that can have serious consequences, e.g. for the family, especially if there is no adequate specialist support. It is also a challenge for physicians: how to change the approach to work?[15]

8 The Role and Responsibility of Politics

Using new methods in personalized medicine raises many questions, including the one how to involve politics in all of this? This means that new strategies in medicine will increasingly become the scene of a battle of political parties. The public debate about personalized medicine has already detected one important question: is it perhaps not reserved for the rich and famous? The media have already pointed out the high cost of individual drugs and individual therapy. In addition, they warn of the danger of possible speculative activities of individual companies.[16] It is the responsibility of politics and politicians not to allow personalized medicine to become the privilege of only the rich. Further, the EU Council in its conclusions noted with concern that "not all patients have access to innovative methods of targeted prevention, diagnosis, and treatment, and that Member States are faced with a significant challenge in promoting the appropriate level of acceptance within health care systems to ensure the integration into clinical practice, which is in accordance with the principles of solidarity and universal and equal access to high-quality care with

---

[15]Médicine personalisée en France, Les grandes défis a relever- Dossier de presse, 8 Dec Tambourine (2015) (Grand auditorium de la Bibliotheque nationale de France).

[16]Fronte (2014).

full respect of the competence of Member States and ensuring the sustainability of their national health systems."[17]

A large number of innovations in the field of biology in Europe, the US, and China is currently primarily being used by rich families and richer societies. This means that many people in the world are from the very beginning placed in a subordinate position. The reply of competent ministers for health in national governments should be clear and unambiguous: "We must all ensure access/treatment regardless of one's financial status."[18] There are many things associated with the health system of nation-states, their organization, resources allocated to health care, the strategy defined by the government, etc. At present, the United States is the leader in promoting the goals of personalized medicine, primarily because they are investing large amounts of financial resources into the development of technology centers and are encouraging leading enterprises in the field of biotechnology and pharmaceuticals.[19] The French Government is of the opinion that the development of personalized medicine will significantly contribute to the development of new technologies, patents, and research. On 3 June 2016, Lydia Mutsch, the Luxembourg Minister of Health, stated that "personalized medicine in her Duchy is the priority of public healthcare."[20] As personalized medicine, on the one hand, requires significant investment, "it is the task of politics, not just the profession, to explain to the citizens the real reasons why it is necessary to invest in personalized medicine, given that it will result in multiple returns on investment, in particular by improving the quality of health," said Prof. G. Martinelli of the University of Bologna.[21] The task of politics is to encourage work, especially the kinds that make the key decisions in this sector to set the foundations of a long-term strategy of personalized medicine. For example, the French Ministry of Labor, Employment, and Health, in its guidelines for the period from 2011 to 2025, is committed to promoting equality in health care, solidarity, and reducing inequalities. The German Government has also incorporated personalized medicine into its priorities and has entrusted the key role to research centers in Heidelberg and Munich. Likewise, the EU has also included personalized medicine into their priorities. However, in practice, many problems will appear that require appropriate and realistic solutions. In recent years, the cost of public health in the countries of the Organization for Cooperation and Economic Development

---

[17]Conclusions of the EU Council on personalized medicine for patients (2015/C 421/03), Official Journal of the European Union, 17 Dec 2015a, Pt. 15. The Council also calls on Member States to support, based on the need and in accordance with national regulations, access to clinically effective and financially sustainable personalized medicine by creating policies aimed at the needs of the patient, which, where applicable, include the empowerment of patients and inclusion of the patients' perspective in the creation of regulatory procedures, in collaboration with patient organizations and other relevant stakeholders.

[18]Ross (2016).

[19]"1Dossier de presservivre l'inovation"- Medecine personalisée en France les grands défis, Grand auditorium de la Bibliotheque nationale de France, 8 Dec 2015.

[20]Mutsch (2015).

[21]Martinelli (2014).

(OCSE) has been constantly surpassing economic growth by 2% on average. At the same time, the welfare state is in crisis. The question then justly posed what would the health paradigm of the twenty-first century be? Will personalized medicine be able to affect the "personalized welfare," which will ask of its users a much greater responsibility: from the evolution of his needs to the responsible behavior in life, which Alessandro Venturi, a professor at the University of Bologna, discusses. Finally, it is the role of politics to make personalized medicine a gradual priority in the national health care policy.

9 Instead of a Conclusion

The development of personalized medicine will probably require more complex and more powerful computers, which will encourage the development of new technologies, production, and employment. Faster and more powerful computers will significantly influence decision diagnosis, therapy, and the like. Regardless that it is a necessity, in personalized medicine it should never be allowed that a machine completely replaces man/physician, because only he (the physician) can determine a diagnosis that comprises particularly the psychological aspect of the patient. Not only when it comes to disease, but also many other things in life that happen to man. Everything that has its own physical expression also has a spiritual background, which all participants in the process of personalized medicine should never forget and ignore. Without such an approach, it is impossible to consider certain diseases and problems in the life of the patient/person. Affirmation of personalized medicine in some countries will require the use of similar or identical standards. This is desirable, because so that a larger numbers of patients could provide high quality standards of treatment. The only question is the extent to which it will be able to accomplish this. When it comes to the social aspect and consequences of the implementation of personalized medicine, we should also expect a positive development in the field of high-quality legal and ethical regulations, the application of new methods and content in medicine, and education of patients who should also in a responsible manner apply the adopted community standards and regulations in this area, especially when using personal data. At the end, it should once again be highlighted that in the context of achieving the goals of personalized medicine, two factors play a very important role. One is how to lead a better and longer life, while the second is how to achieve maximum protection of personal data, so as not to become subject to trafficking and exploitation. The project of personalized medicine is above all a human project in the interest of man.

References

Brand A (2012a) Académie Suisse des Sciences Médicales (ASSM), Bulletin ASSM 3/12, Bâle
Brand A (2012b) La médecine personnalisée: de la vision a la réalité - Académie Suisse des Sciences Médicales (ASSM) Bulletin ASSM 2/12, Bern

Conti C (2009) Les DRG: l'éthique contre l'économie - L'introduction de SwissDRG, Bulletin ASSM 1/09, Editeur: Académie Suisse des Sciences Médicales CH-Bâle

Déclaration universelle sur la bioéthique et les droits de l'homme, UNESCO, Paris, 19 Oct 2005; Article 11 of the Declaration applies to ethical issues in the field of medicine and technology, taking into account the social, political, legal, and environmental aspects

Enseignement dans la formation gymnasiale // Renforcement de la formation professionnelle supérieure // Initiative d'encouragement pour la médecine personnalisée, News SEFRI, Conféderation Suisse, Editeur; Secrétariat d'Etat à la formation, Bern (CH), May 2016

"European Alliance for Personalized Medicine," Italian branch "Alleanza Italiana per la medicina personalizzata" (IAPMO) - Raccomandazioni per la medicina parsonalizzata, 2014

Fronte M (12 March 2014) Italian journalist focused on medicine, science, and environment, "Focus it,"

Goleman D (2012) Emocionalna inteligencija (Emotional intelligence). Tisak, Zagreb

Maria B (30 June 2009) Knoppers-Centre de génomique et politiques, Genome Québec, Montreal

Martinelli G (2014) "Raccomandazioni dell'Alleanza italiana per la medicina personalizzata," EAPM

Meier-Abt P (2012) Académie Suisse des Sciences Médicales (ASSM), Bulletin ASSM 3/12, Bâle

Mutsch L (2–3 June 2015) 3e Conférence annuelle de l'Alliance européenne pour une médecine personnalisée (EAPM), Gouvernement du Luxembourg, Bruxelles

Official Journal of the European Union, Conclusions of the EU Council on personalized medicine for patients (2015/C 421/03), Bruxelles, 17 Dec 2015a, Pt. 19

Official Journal of the European Union, Conclusions of the EU Council on personalized medicine for patients (2015/C 421/03), Bruxelles, 17 Dec 2015b

Rifkin J (2010) La civilta' dell'empatia (The Age of Empathy). Mondadori, Torino

Ross A (2016) The industries of the future – Il nostro futuro. Feltrinelli Editore, Milano

Tambourine P (2015) Médicine personalisée en France, Les grandes défis a relever - Dossier de presse, 8 dec 2015, Genopole-Amgen, Évry

Zhe W (June 2016) La via cinese alle riforme neoliberiste, Rivista Aspenia n. 73, Rome

Personalized Medicine and Personalized Pricing: Degrees of Price Discrimination

Davor Mance, Diana Mance, and Dinko Vitezić

Abstract Economics developed a set of three degrees of price discrimination dependent on whether the seller targets individuals or groups, and whether buyers wish to use quantity rebates. The seller's reason to price discriminate is to capture as much of the buyers utility surplus. Price discrimination is deemed unfair and immoral, and this is especially so in the market for pharmaceutical therapies. However, sometimes it can indeed be socially useful to price discriminate as the practice, under circumstances, enhances efficiency and social welfare.

The market for pharmaceuticals is a non-typical market as irreversible costs of research and development form the brunt of the cost structure. As pharmaceutical companies are driven by profit and bounded by patent expiration dates, discriminatory pricing schemes are necessary to recover investment costs of research and development as quickly as possible. The first degree of price discrimination consists of perfect, individually targeted, price/quality combinations that fully extract consumers' surplus. The second-degree price discrimination consists of quantity rebates. The third degree of price discrimination is based on group targeting according to the group average willingness to pay.

We introduce a fourth degree of price discrimination based on qualitative features of pharmaceuticals on a market for antiviral drugs. We use the SVR as an example of quality differentials causing market price differentials. The fourth type of discrimination would be of particular interest to the pharmaceutical industry and health management organisations as it introduces non-linear price-quality combinations.

D. Mance (✉)
Faculty of Economics, University of Rijeka, Rijeka, Croatia
e-mail: davor.mance@efri.hr

D. Mance
Department of Physics, University of Rijeka, Rijeka, Croatia
e-mail: diana.mance@uniri.hr

D. Vitezić
Faculty of Medicine, University of Rijeka, Rijeka, Croatia
e-mail: dinko.vitezic@medri.uniri.hr

© Springer Nature Switzerland AG 2019
N. Bodiroga-Vukobrat et al. (eds.), *Personalized Medicine in Healthcare Systems,*
Europeanization and Globalization 5, https://doi.org/10.1007/978-3-030-16465-2_14

Table 1 Opportunity costs based classification of goods and markets

		Opportunity costs of production (prospective sunk costs of research and development)	
		Significant	Insignificant
Opportunity costs of consumption (marginal costs of production)	Significant	Pure private goods	Common goods
	Insignificant	Club goods	Pure public goods

1   Introduction

A product's market structure is defined by the opportunity costs of its production and the opportunity costs in consumption (Table 1).[1]

The simplest case scenario of pharmaceutical production may be represented by the following total cost (TC) function:

$$TC(q) = MC \cdot q + SC \tag{1}$$

where MC is the marginal cost of production, SC the sunk cost of research and development (R&D), and q the production quantity.

The pharmaceutical industry is a typical club-good-providing industry with significant opportunity costs of production in form of SC of R&D, insignificant opportunity costs of consumption in terms of production MCs, and bounded by patent expiration dates. During this limited time, a drug needs to repay for its own R&D costs, as well as R&D costs of every other drug that failed to be approved. Discriminatory pricing schemes are necessary to recover initial SC of R&D investment. Pharmaceutical companies price their products as high as possible, capturing as much of the consumer surplus represented by the willingness to pay of the Health Management Organisation (HMO).[2] The personalized medicine approach requires access to unique combinations of proprietary patient information and disease aetiology, providing the pharmaceutical industry with the possibility of product differentiation and price discrimination. Adequate usage of patient information in combination of disease aetiology should primarily result in better cost/effectiveness ratios of medical therapies, and cost advantages per final result.

Our aim is to give an overview of price discrimination methods used by pharma industry, their necessity, and to put them into the context of personalized medicine. To achieve this goal, we shall firstly make ourselves familiar with different approaches to medicine going from symptomatic, with neither the patient nor the

---

[1]An opportunity cost is the cost of the next best alternative. For more on opportunity costs see Mance et al. (2015a).

[2]For a survey on European pricing schemes, see: Garattini et al. (2016).

Table 2 Medical approaches according to proprietary information usage

		Usage of proprietary patient information (genotype, phenotype and medication history)	
		Comprehensive usage	Limited usage
Usage of disease aetiology and pharmaco-dynamics	Comprehensive usage	Personalized medicine	Disease centered medicine (one type of medicine fits all patients)
	Limited usage	Patient centered symptomatic medicine without resort to disease aetiology	Symptomatic medicine (analgesics, antitussive, anti-inflammatory, antihistaminic)

disease aetiology being in focus, to the ones focused on either the patient or the disease, and finally ending with personalised medicine with drugs and therapies aimed at specific disease aetiology considering pharmacodynamics, pharmacokinetics and patient's genotype.

After having described the different approaches to medicine, we shall say something about the specificities of the pharmacological markets and pricing necessities leading to techniques of price discrimination.

2   From Personalized Medicine to Personalized Pricing

Personalized medicine or precision medicine, stratified medicine, targeted medicine and P4 medicine (personalized, predictive, preventive and participatory), as it is also called, is a form of medical procedure combining patient's individual information on his genome, epigenome, proteome and other phenome such as patient's characteristics, physiology and pathophysiology with drug pharmaco-dynamics and pharmacokinetics.[3] Personalized medicine thus infers personal benefits to the patient in form of his better individual treatment and/or reduces costs to the health care provider. In contrast to traditional symptomatic, patient centered or disease centered medicine, personalized medicine consists of the usage of both proprietary information on patient and disease in a comprehensive way as shown in Table 2.

The benefit personalized medicine approach might ultimately confer is the reduction of harmful iatrogenic effects (side effects, negative drug interactions, medication errors in hospitals, and other medical errors in hospitals), reduction of unnecessary surgeries, reduction of nosocomial infections in hospitals, reduction of costs through more economic use of resources, enabling the health care provider either to increase the number of patients it could ultimately treat and/or to increase the quality of treatment of present patients. This is an increase in efficiency resulting from better use of aetiological data, focusing the medical procedure on disease causes and not solely on its symptoms.

---

[3]U.S. Food and Drug Administration (2013), Pavelić et al. (2016), Bodiroga-Vukobrat and Horak (2016) and Vitezić et al. (2016a).

Table 3 Standard of care for naïve HCV GT1 non-CC patients in Croatia

Fibrosis status	Specificity	Therapy
F1, F2	IL28B CC genotype	pegIFN + RBV
F1, F2	IL28B CT/TT genotype	pegIFN + RBV Optionally + SMV/SOF
F3		SMV + pegIFN + RBV SOF + pegIFN + RBV
F4 (compensated cirrhosis)		OBV/PTV/r/DSV ± RBV SOF + LED ± RBV SOF + SMV ± RBV
Independent of fibrosis status	Contraindications for pegIFN HIV coinfection Extrahepatic manifestations organ transplant patients	OBV/PTV/r/DSV ± RBV SOF + LED ± RBV SOF + SMV ± RBV

Data Source: Poropat et al. (2016). *pegIFN* pegylated interferon, *RBV* ribavirin, *SMV* simeprevir, *SOF* sofosbuvir, *OBV/PTV/r/DSV* ombitasvir, paritaprevir, ritonavir and dasabuvir, *LED* ledipasvir

We give an example of a comprehensive personalised medicine approach on a hepatitis C virus (HCV) infection. The patients' IL28B gene is involved in the immune response to HCV genotype 1 (GT 1) infection. There are three IL28B genotypes: CC, CT, and TT. People with CC genotype are two to three times more likely to be cured with pegylated interferon (pegIFN) and ribavirin (RBV) dual therapy, than non-CC genotype patients.[4] For IL28B non-CC genotype patients, as well as patients who either developed contraindications for pegIFN, have previously not been successfully treated with pegIFN, have some extrahepatic manifestations or are organ transplant patients, currently the most effective therapy comes from the new DAA (direct acting antiviral) combination therapies.[5] Although new generation DAA therapies are more expensive in absolute terms compared to older therapies, they are for some patient subgroups, more cost effective in terms of price per achieved sustained virological response (SVR).[6] Example of a standard of care (SoC) for HCV GT 1 patients, combining their group disease aetiology, patient genotype specificities and therapy effectiveness is given in Table 3.

By knowing probabilities and time lapses of natural disease progression between various hepatitis C fibrosis states (Fig. 1), as well as knowing the price and probabilities of individual SVRs, a health care provider is able to make rational decisions on behalf of its patients maximizing their health state under total budget constraint.

Personalized medicine may realize significant cost savings as it can discriminate against cost ineffective drugs/therapies. Thus, for example in the case of those HCV genotypes that can successfully be treated with a dual therapy, there is no need of

---

[4]Ge et al. (2009).
[5]Mance et al. (2015b).
[6]Mance et al. (2016a).

Fig. 1 Hepatitis C genotype 1 natural progression. *F0–F4 METAVIR* fibrosis scores, *CC* compensated cirrhosis, *SVR* sustained virological response, *HCC* hepatocellular carcinoma

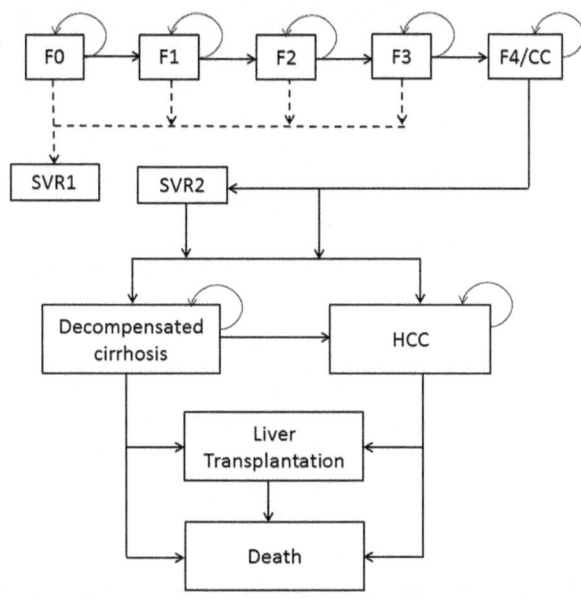

using new and very expensive DAA combination therapies.[7] Moreover, one of the new combination therapies goes even further into the HCV genotype classification, recognizing the necessity for twice as long treatment times for HCV GT 1a subtype than the GT 1b subtype, doubling the treatment costs.[8]

With expansion of modern medicine, complex therapies, such as the HCV example shown here, are expected to become even more numerous in the future. More specific the disease aetiology, more differentiated is the final product and its market, and subsequently also the price differentiation called price discrimination.

3 Degrees of Price Discrimination

In economics, there are three recognized degrees of price discrimination dependent on two classification criteria: the seller's targeting of individuals or groups, and buyers wishing to use quantity or quality rebates.[9] Price discrimination is often deemed unfair and immoral, but sometimes it is socially useful to price discriminate as the practice, enhances social welfare.

In the following chapters, we summarize the three degrees of price discrimination and introduce the fourth one respecting the above-mentioned classification criteria.

---

[7]Hrstić and Ostojić (2013) and Vitezić et al. (2016b).

[8]Mance et al. (2016a).

[9]Carlton and Perloff (2000).

3.1 Price Discrimination of the First Degree

Perfect or price discrimination of the first degree is a form of price discrimination whereby consumers are individually targeted and left without any consumer surplus. The price an individual consumer pays is equal to his maximal willingness to pay. Price discrimination of the first degree truly consists of personalized pricing as it presumes selling to each patient the therapy/intervention perfectly tailored to his own needs and his ability and willingness to pay.

The classic example of first degree price discrimination consists for example of airlines charging different prices for same flights and supply them under different categories. In medicine, examples could be found in the fields of ophthalmology, dermatology, and aesthetic surgery, as well as in dentistry just to mention a few.

To engage in first-degree price discrimination, a pharmaceutical company needs to know the ability-to-pay of its customers and needs to be able to prevent resale. Personalized medicine consists of treatment personalization according to personally specific characteristics (e.g. genotype and phenotype combinations) between patients and disease with the goal to improve outcomes and/or decrease costs of medical treatment and care. Most often, producers are not able to negotiate prices directly with the patient. In a third-party payer system, HMO as a health care provider and intermediary between patients and producers is not willing to allow for large differences in prices for similar medical services, as it is bounded by law to explicit menu costs. We may conclude that because of the aforementioned reasons, there is a limited applicability of the first degree price discrimination to standardized medical services provided by the HMO.

3.2 Price Discrimination of the Second Degree

Price discrimination of second degree consists of quantity-based rebates that are given to individual customers, so they are not widely applicable in health services as therapies are usually not divisible, i.e. there is a fixed amount of health services necessary to achieve a desired health state. Exceptions are chronic diseases that necessitate a prolonged supply of medications. Any such prolonged producer-patient or producer-buyer relationship gives the producer the possibility to tie-in the consumer via long-term agreements. Long-term tie-in agreements are beneficial for both sides: the consumer gets a quantity rebate, and the producer ends up with a lower market risk, i.e. a secure market. Thus, time dependent quantity rebates are a form of forward agreements. In theory, quantity dependent discrimination, extracts the consumer surplus from the consumer by charging the reservation price for the first and every subsequent unit, by letting the consumer choose rebates or differentiated product lines positioned along the downwardly sloped marginal utility curve. The existence of second degree price discrimination is problematic from the incentives perspective: the drug producers have an incentive to prolong the seller-consumer relationship as long as possible. The sellers might thus be inclined to tie patients with long-term contracts by giving them quantity rebates.

3.3 Price Discrimination of the Third Degree

Price discrimination of third degree or price discrimination by direct segmentation uses group membership (country, nationality, age, and similar characteristics) to charge differential prices according to the average group ability to pay. The seller needs to know the common group characteristics. The group might consist of people of same genotype having the same disease.

A firm price discriminates to increase its profits. Nevertheless, profits are increased only after all costs have been recovered. As the pharmaceutical industry is characterized by very high SC of R&D, as well as low probabilities of research success, price discrimination of some sort is not only welcome, but also indispensable to recover costs.

Pricing policies are formulated based on dominant markets' ability to pay. The dominant market is the market with the highest sales volume. It consists of: USA, Japan, and the EU five countries (Germany, UK, France, Italy, and Spain). The profits are maximized when, the pharma company charges the monopoly price on every market separately. The price is set according to the group average ability to pay, i.e. the group average unitary elasticity of demand. The subsequent result is efficient and Pareto optimal as the discriminating monopoly produces more and sells more in terms of quantity than the non-discriminating monopoly.

There have been some contradictory approaches to the issue of pharmaceutical pricing policies from the EU regulators in the past.[10] The prohibition of price discrimination on the EU market may result in lower pharmaceutical prices in higher-income countries but unfortunately leads to higher prices in lower-income countries.[11] To mitigate the prohibition of differential pricing across EU, member states developed new types of contracts: cost-sharing, risk-sharing, pay-by-result, hidden discounts, free stock, and similar agreements.[12]

---

[10]For a comprehensive survey on the application of EU competition law in the pharmaceutical sector, see Hull and Clancy (2016).

[11]Elek et al. (2017).

[12]For a comprehensive survey of price agreements in the EU pharmaceutical sector, see Van de Vooren et al. (2015).

Table 4 Four degrees of price discrimination

		The seller targets	
		Quality	Quantity
The seller targets	Individuals	First degree price discrimination: individually tailored price-quality combinations are perceived as different qualities	Second degree price discrimination: rebates are given on incremental sales and follow the slope of the demand curve
	Groups	Fourth degree price discrimination: group-tailored price-quality differentials	Third degree price discrimination: prices are equal to the group mean unitary elasticity of demand

3.4 Price Discrimination of the Fourth Degree

The quality/quantity and the individual/group price discrimination framework is based on present differentiation of discrimination policies according to two basic differentiating criteria: producers' ability to target individual clients by recognizing their individual abilities or willingness's to pay, or producers ability to target quality differences. We introduce a fourth degree of price discrimination based on the criteria used in the previous three degrees and we call it *qualitative disutility discounts* (Table 4).

To be able to define the additional, fourth type of consumer discrimination, one needs to acquire a special functional definition of goods and markets instead of the substantive one. Thus, the good is not defined by its substance and form (chemical and physical properties) but by its ability to produce utility in form of desired health state, i.e. its biochemical effects.

Quality is an important component of value in health care, and it is usually defined as adherence to evidence-based guidelines. We agree with Porter (2010), there is no substitute for measuring actual outcomes as a measure of quality in health care. The example of a fourth degree discrimination based on qualitative disutility discounts is shown on the example of the market for HCV pharmaceuticals (Fig. 2).

In a third-party payer system, value is determined by the customer acting indirectly via the HMO, and the HMO's ability and willingness to pay for the medical service. The market effectively recognizes the difference in qualities between health care technologies and values technologies with higher qualities (in our example the SVR rates) disproportionately more. There is a qualitative disutility discount because the price of a therapy should not be higher than the equivalent price per SVR considering the risk of non-cure, side-effects, and other disutility discounts.[13] The disutility discount measures the non-linear degree of cumulative subjective loss of utility as a function of decreasing certainty of a possible positive outcome. Observe the non-linearity between price/quality (price/SVR) ratios. The value of the utility of the expected value is thus always smaller than the expected value.

---

[13]Mance et al. (2016b).

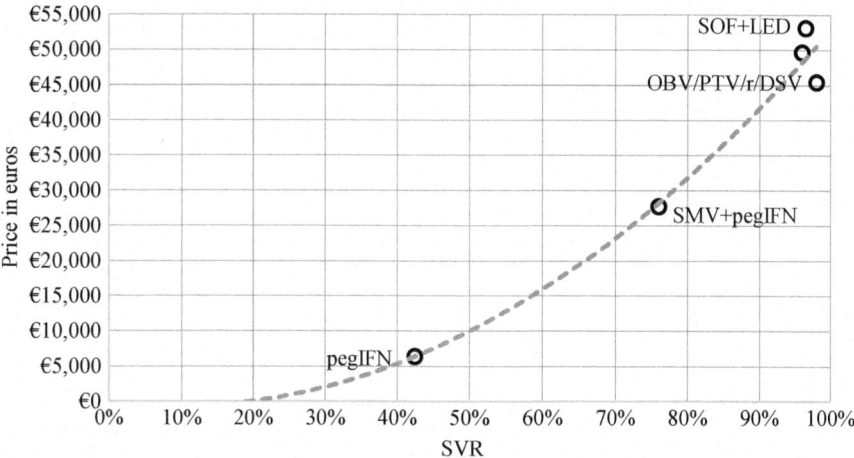

Fig. 2 Non-linear price/quality (price/SVR) relationship (Price data from the Croatian Health Insurance Fund (2016)). *pegIFN* pegylated interferon, *SMV* simeprevir, *SOF* sofosbuvir, *OBV/PTV/r/DSV* ombitasvir, paritaprevir, ritonavir and dasabuvir, *LED* ledipasvir, *SVR* sustained virological response

4 Conclusion

Personalized medical treatments that consider patient's characteristics in combination with the specific disease aetiology information (disease genotype and drug pharmaco-dynamics and pharmacokinetics) can be made more cost effective brought by more efficient use of information. Personalized medicine enables the producers of medical technologies, besides using the exclusive protection of patent rights, to also use other barriers to entry in the form of absolute cost advantages because of proprietary knowledge, cost advantages because of economies of scale and scope, large sunk costs as disincentives of entry for potential competitors, but principally advantages from ultimate product differentiation possibilities of tailor made products. The producers of medical therapies are thus able to recoup the sunk costs of R&D of successful therapies but also of unsuccessful or discontinued therapies. The price of a good is ultimately determined by consumers' willingness and ability to pay considering its opportunity costs, aggregate preferences and trade-offs between prices and risks of side-effects and insufficient SVRs.

Based on traditional quantity/quality and individual/group targeting distinction from economic literature, a fourth degree of price discrimination might be added. The fourth degree of price discrimination consists of lower quality therapies given at much lower prices to provide lower ability-to-pay patients with health care. The fourth type of price discrimination enables large savings and is thus cost-efficient and Pareto optimal.

References

Bodiroga-Vukobrat N, Horak H (2016) Challenges of personalized medicine: socio-legal disputes and possible solutions. In: Bodiroga-Vukobrat N, Rukavina D, Pavelić K, Sander GG (eds) Personalized medicine: a new medical and social challenge. Springer, Basel, pp 31–51. ISBN 978-3-319-39347-6

Carlton DW, Perloff JM (2000) Modern industrial organization, 3rd edn. Addison Wesley Longman, Boston

Croatian Health Insurance Fund. Medication lists (June 2016). Available from: http://www.hzzo.hr/zdravstveni-sustav-rh/trazilica-za-lijekove-s-vazecih-lista/arhiva-liste-lijekova/

Elek P, Takács E, Merész G, Kaló Z (2017) Implication of external price referencing and parallel trade on pharmaceutical expenditure: indirect evidence from lower-income European countries. Health Policy Plan 32(3):349–358

Garattini L, Curto A, Freemantle N (2016) Pharmaceutical price schemes in Europe: time for a 'continental' one? PharmacoEconomics 34:423–426

Ge D, Fellay J, Thompson AJ, Simon JS, Shianna KV, Urban TJ, Heinzen EL, Qiu P, Bertelsen AH, Muir AJ, Sulkowski M, McHutchison JG, Goldstein DB (2009) Genetic variation in IL28B predicts hepatitis C treatment-induced viral clearance. Nature 461(7262):399–401

Hrstić I, Ostojić R (2013) Treatment of non-1 genotype chronic hepatitis C patients. Acta Med Croatica 67:339–343

Hull DW, Clancy MJ (2016) The application of EU competition law in the pharmaceutical sector. J Eur Compet Law Practice 7(2):150–161

Mance D, Vretenar N, Katunar J (2015a) Opportunity cost classification of goods and markets. Int Public Adm Rev XIII(1):119–134

Mance D, Mance D, Vitezić D (2015b) Introduction of new combination therapy for treatment of experienced HCV GT1 patients: budget impact analysis, the Croatian perspective. Value Health 18(7):A623–A623

Mance D, Mance D, Vitezić D (2016a) Incremental cost-effectiveness pharmacoeconomic assessment of hepatitis C virus therapy: an approach for less wealthy members of the common market. Croat Med J 57(6):582–590

Mance D, Mance D, Vitezić D (2016b) Pharmaceutical pricing: how much for the risk of non-cure? Clin Ther 38(10):17–18

Pavelić K, Kraljević Pavelić S, Sedić M (2016) Personalized medicine: the path to new medicine. In: Bodiroga-Vukobrat N, Rukavina D, Pavelić K, Sander GG (eds) Personalized medicine: a new medical and social challenge. Springer, Basel, pp 1–21

Poropat G, Milić D, Štimac D (2016) Contemporary approach to chronic hepatitis C. Medicina Fluminensis 1:4–13. [in Croatian]

Porter ME (2010) What is value in health care? N Engl J Med 363(26):2477–2481

U.S. Food and Drug Administration (2013) Paving the way for personalized medicine: FDA's role in a new era of medical product development

Van de Vooren K, Curto A, Freemantle N, Garattini L (2015) Market-access agreements for anti-cancer drugs. J R Soc Med 108(5):166–170

Vitezić D, Božina D, Mršić-Pelčić J, Erdeljić Turk V, Francetić I (2016a) Personalized medicine in clinical pharmacology. In: Bodiroga-Vukobrat N, Rukavina D, Pavelić K, Sander GG (eds) Personalized medicine: a new medical and social challenge. Springer, Basel, pp 265–278. ISBN 978-3-319-39347-6

Vitezić D, Mance D, Mance D, Vitezić M, Mršić Pelčić J (2016b) Treatment of chronic hepatitis C virus genotype 1 infection: comparison of health-economic outcomes for Naïve patients. Value Health 19(3):A314–A314

Personalised Medicine in Health Care Systems and EU Law: The Role of Solidarity?

Adrijana Martinović

Abstract This contribution addresses the role of EU law in the field of health care and the promotion of personalised medicine paradigm. While respecting the competence of the Member States for the definition of their health policy and for the organisation and delivery of the health services and medical care, the European Union is increasingly getting involved in the promotion of the personalised medicine concept through various initiatives. Among other topics, the question of access of patients to innovative forms of diagnostic, treatment and pharmaceuticals raises particular concern. The implementation of the personalised medicine approach in various Member States may put a strain on one of the fundamental features of all health care systems: the principle of solidarity. The reconstruction of the health care systems to accommodate the new paradigm is inevitable. The question is, how will it affect the core values and principles that lie at the foundations of health care? The focal point of this chapter will therefore revolve around the main challenges and possible directions for integration of personalised medicine models in clinical practice, notably through health technology assessment.

1 Introduction

The advances in medicine and medical technology are overwhelming. From human genome and human microbiome projects to stem cell research, targeted cancer therapies, and even medical 3D printing, we are witnessing an era of astounding discoveries that gradually translate into clinical practice. These developments are challenging traditional patterns in healthcare and require novel approaches to healthcare delivery models. One concept that appears particularly appealing and promising is the personalised medicine, a health care model focused on delivering personalised or individual prevention, diagnosis and treatment strategies based on individual patient's genomic, epigenomic and proteomic profile, including the

A. Martinović (✉)
Department of EU Public Law, University of Rijeka Faculty of Law, Rijeka, Croatia
e-mail: adrijana@pravri.hr

© Springer Nature Switzerland AG 2019   181
N. Bodiroga-Vukobrat et al. (eds.), *Personalized Medicine in Healthcare Systems*,
Europeanization and Globalization 5, https://doi.org/10.1007/978-3-030-16465-2_15

patient's personal situation.[1] The aim of personalised medicine is "to match the right drug to the right patient",[2] avoiding the one-size-fits-all approach based on trial and error. The European Union seems to have embraced this concept, promoting it through various initiatives despite the limited influence of EU law in this field and the diversity of national healthcare systems in EU Member States. This contribution will first explore the role and influence of EU law in the field of public health and promotion of personalised medicine paradigm (Sects. 2 and 3). The main point of concern is how to improve patient's access to the outputs and advantages of personalised medicine. One of the tools that could help in this process is health technology assessment. The role of health technology assessment in personalised medicine and its impact on convergence of national healthcare systems will therefore be investigated, with particular emphasis on the Croatian regulatory regime for health technology assessment (Sects. 4 and 5). It is submitted that health technology assessment has a great potential to encourage the proliferation of the personalised medicine paradigm in EU Member States, without affecting the core values of all healthcare systems, most notably the principle of solidarity (Sects. 6 and 7).

2 EU Competences in the Field of Public Health

The promotion of the personalised medicine paradigm has been steadily advancing in the recent years in the European Union. The approach, objectives and modalities of the Union's actions in the field of personalised medicine and its integration in the national health care systems are evident in a number of policy papers and soft steering instruments, such as guidelines and conclusions. For example, some of the most influential documents include the 2015 Council Conclusions on personalised medicine for the patients,[3] the 2014 Council Conclusions on innovations for the benefit of the patients[4] or the Commission Staff Working Document on the use of 'omics' technologies from 2013.[5]

Before attempting to unravel the potential of the EU approach to personalised medicine, there should be a clear understanding of the correlation between EU law and national health care systems. What is the role of the EU law, and what are the Union's competences in the field of healthcare? Is the Union equipped with powers to interfere in the national health care systems? The answer to those questions would be very short and simple if one would concentrate solely on Article 168(7) of the Treaty on the Functioning of the European Union: "Union action shall respect the responsibilities of the Member States for the definition of their health policy and for

---

[1]Mathur and Sutton (2017), pp. 3–5.

[2]Jain (2015), p. 1.

[3]Council (2015).

[4]Council (2014).

[5]European Commission (2013).

the organisation and delivery of health services and medical care. The responsibilities of the Member States shall include the management of health services and medical care and the allocation of the resources assigned to them."[6] Therefore, all issues in connection with the organisation of national health systems remain under the exclusive competence of the Member States. However, things are not as simple as they appear at first glance.

The EU has supplementary or coordinating competences in the field of public health, meaning that the EU has the power to complement national policies with the aim of improving public health, to encourage cooperation among Member States and, if necessary, to support their actions. A high level of human health protection shall be ensured in the definition and implementation of all Union policies and activities.[7] This is a so-called horizontal clause that also exists, for example, in the field of environment or consumer protection.[8]

It is in this sphere of supplementary competences that the Union's action in promoting personalised medicine paradigm is manifested. Generally, the Union may adopt incentive measures designed to protect and improve human health, including measures concerning monitoring, early warning of and combating serious cross-border health threats, as well as measures directed at the protection of public health regarding tobacco and the abuse of alcohol.[9] The objectives of the Union's action in this field are construed broad enough ('protect' and 'improve' human health, 'combat' health threats) to allow the Union's involvement in various policy setting initiatives and financing of research and innovation in health care.[10] However, the adopted measures exclude any harmonisation of the laws and regulations of the Member States.[11]

For example, Regulation (EU) No. 282/2014 of the European Parliament and of the Council of 11 March 2014 on the establishment of a third Programme for the Union's action in the field of health (2014–2020)[12] was adopted on this legal basis. This instrument serves as the legal basis for financing Member States' actions in the field of health, which aim at achieving its defined general and specific objectives, such as supporting public health capacity-building, and contributing to innovative, efficient and sustainable health care systems. All priorities within this programme

---

[6]Article 168(7) Treaty on the Functioning of the European Union (consolidated version) OJ C 202, 7.6.2016 (hereinafter: TFEU).

[7]Article 168(1) TFEU.

[8]E.g. Articles 11 and 12 TFEU.

[9]Article 168(5) TFEU.

[10]Although the EU's competence in the area of public health is still very limited, it nevertheless "[. . .] provides the basis for governing at a distance". See Flear (2015), p. 40.

[11]Measures are adopted in accordance with the ordinary legislative procedure, upon consultation with the Economic and Social Committee and the Committee of the Regions (Article 168 (5) TFEU).

[12]Regulation (EU) No 282/2014 of the European Parliament and of the Council of 11 March 2014 on the establishment of a third Programme for the Union's action in the field of health (2014–2020) and repealing Decision No 1350/2007/EC, OJ L 86, 21.3.2014.

potentially include various projects involving implementation of personalised medicine paradigm in the clinical practice. In addition, a substantial financial envelope is dedicated for financing research and innovation in the field of personalised medicine under the Horizon 2020 programme.[13] The "steering through funding"[14] approach is proved to be a reliable tool in supporting the development of new health technologies and personalised medicine.[15]

3 EU Approach to Personalised Medicine

Personalised medicine has therefore grown into a focal point of interest of the Union's actions.[16] A working definition of personalised medicine found in the EU documents is that it refers to a medical model using characterisation of individuals' phenotypes and genotypes (e.g. molecular profiling, medical imaging, lifestyle data) for tailoring the right therapeutic strategy for the right person at the right time, and/or to determine the predisposition to disease and/or to deliver timely and targeted prevention.[17] A prevailing understanding of personalised medicine in literature is therefore that it presents "a model of health care that customizes individual differences of patients in all phases – from prevention, diagnosis and treatment up to post-treatment monitoring".[18] This "model" works on the premise that we can retrieve, collect, analyse and put to use personal medical information, based on biomarkers and other biological information, either for prevention or for treatment.[19]

Some claim that personalised medicine is a dramatical revolution in health care, comparable to the antibiotics revolution in the twentieth century.[20] Others call it a

---

[13]Regulation (EU) No 1291/2013 of the European Parliament and of the Council of 11 December 2013 establishing Horizon 2020—the Framework Programme for Research and Innovation (2014–2020) and repealing Decision No 1982/2006/EC, OJ 347/104, 20.12.2013.

[14]Flear (2015), p. 72.

[15]For a thorough account of the EU approach in supporting research and new health technologies, see Brosset and Mahalatchimy (2017), pp. 197–221.

[16]In German literature, the term 'individualised medicine' ('individualisierte Medizin') is preferred over the term 'personalised medicine'. For the detailed conceptual analyses of both terms see Keil (2015), pp. 18–21. Although conceptually not entirely identical, these two terms are often used interchangeably in legal and medical academic literature, see Becker (2016), p. 23; Wienke et al. (2014), Grech and Grossman (2015), and Jain (2015), pp. 1–5.

[17]See, e.g. Council (2015). Personalised medicine allows stratification of patients into groups based on their biomarkers to tailor medical intervention to a particular group of patients, which is more efficacious than the dominant 'one size fits all' approach. See European Commission (2013), pp. 5–6.

[18]Pavelić et al. (2016), p. 3.

[19]See more Mićović et al. (2016), pp. 81–93; Becker (2016), pp. 21–29.

[20]Guglielmi Gaetano, presentation at the Personalised medicine conference 2016 Brussels, Challenge 5 Shaping sustainable healthcare, available at https://ec.europa.eu/info/events/personalised-medicine-conference-2016-2016-jun-01_en.

"disruptive innovation" in medicine, which will ultimately and unexpectedly overtake the existing market.[21] Undeniably, there exists a wide consensus on the promotion of this paradigm. However, this paradigm must be implemented and accomplished in a given reality of national health care systems, which all struggle to balance limited resources with growing expenses, under the imperative of ensuring equal access of the population to health care. One of the most commonly highlighted challenges of personalised medicine is that it may put additional pressure on public health care budgets.[22] In addition, it may also require more responsibility from the patients themselves,[23] and even lead to higher costs of health coverage for patients with specific health risks.[24]

A decade ago, a study from 2008 showed that the potential impact of personalised medicine in the context of German health care system was still relatively limited.[25] However, the costs of genetic testing, for example, have decreased significantly since then.[26] The relatively high(er) costs of applying the personalised medicine approach on the side of prevention and diagnosis could be offset by savings on the side of treatment of the disease. Indubitably, the cost of the targeted treatment and innovative health procedures and medicines represents an additional burden to the already high and growing expenses in public health care. For example, the costs of production of the so-called orphan medicines for rare diseases are enormous and cannot be compensated by the proceeds from their sale, as the production of these medicines is not profitable for pharmaceutical industries under normal market conditions because they are aimed at a very small part of population; or expensive diagnostic tests that enable the adaptation of therapy to suit the health needs of a specific person at a specific time, but also increase the overall costs of treatment.[27] The development of necessary IT instruments and solutions, as well as accompanying training of medical staff to use such sophisticated tools represents an additional cost factor to be calculated in the overall expense of the treatment.

Cost is precisely one of the factors that has a great influence on the implementation of the personalised medicine paradigm: how much can a society spend on health care in general, and would it be more cost efficient to adopt a personalised medicine approach?

---

[21]Ricciardi Walter, presentation at the Personalised medicine conference 2016 Brussels, A framework on impact of PM in national health systems, available at: https://ec.europa.eu/info/events/personalised-medicine-conference-2016-2016-jun-01_en.

[22]Council (2015).

[23]Hüsing et al. (2008), p. 282.

[24]Hüsing et al. (2008), p. 283.

[25]See Hüsing et al. (2008), p. 291.

[26]See, for example, Genetics Home Reference, What is the cost of genetic testing, and how long does it take to get the results?, https://ghr.nlm.nih.gov/primer/testing/costresults; Breastcancer.org, Genetic testing facilities and cost, http://www.breastcancer.org/symptoms/testing/genetic/facility_cost.

[27]European Commission (2013), pp. 24–25.

There are great expectations from benefits of personalised medicine for patients, especially through expected increase of efficiency of treatments and abandoning the old 'blockbuster', 'one-size-fits-all' strategy.[28] But so far, there is very little evidence that personalised medicine approach is efficient not only concerning benefits for the patients, but also concerning its cost.[29]

The reception of the personalised medicine approach in national health care systems depends on whether such approach will be acceptable to those who pay for medical services and products: public health care systems and private health insurers. The question of market authorisation for innovative medical products or diagnostic tests is a separate issue. Despite the fact that there are available treatments and products with market authorisation, they may not be accessible for patients if they are not covered by the health care system available in their country. Generally, there must exist a strong evidence to support their coverage: their cost and clinical efficiency will be meticulously compared with other therapies available for the treatment of the same disease.

4   The Importance of Health Technology Assessment in Personalised Medicine

One of the methods to evaluate efficiency and benefits of introducing personalised medicine approach is through the already existing system of health technology assessment, or 'HTA'. This system of evaluation is increasingly being used in all EU Member States, and its main objective is to provide unbiased, expert, objective and transparent recommendation for rendering a decision justifying the implementation of the new technology or replacement of the previously applicable health technology. The term 'health technology' is used to refer to a medicine, medical product or health procedure applicable with the aim of prevention, diagnosis, treatment or rehabilitation, without limitation to 'new' or 'innovative' technologies.[30] The Patients' Rights Directive, for example, defines 'health technology' as "a

---

[28]Pavelić et al. (2015), p. 134.

[29]See, e.g. Joyner and Paneth (2015), Brittain et al. (2017), p. 551; Maughan (2017), p. 17; Haycox et al. (2014), p. 1058.

[30]The World Health Organisation (WHO) defines health technology as "the application of organized knowledge and skills in the form of devices, medicines, vaccines, procedures and systems developed to solve a health problem and improve quality of lives", see WHO Resolution (2007) WHA60.29. The UK National Institute for Health and Clinical Excellence (NICE), one of the leading health technology assessment organisations in the world, defines health technology as "[A] ny method used by those working in health services to promote health, prevent and treat disease, and improve rehabilitation and long-term care. Technologies in this context are not confined to new drugs or medical technologies." See NICE Guide to the methods of technology appraisal 2013, Glossary, available at https://www.nice.org.uk/process/pmg9/chapter/glossary#health-technology; see also the definition of health technology in the EUnetHTA Strategy 2012 and beyond, available at: http://www.eunethta.eu/sites/default/files/sites/5026.fedimbo.belgium.be/files/EUnetHTA%

medicinal product, a medical device or medical and surgical procedures as well as measures for disease prevention, diagnosis or treatment used in healthcare".[31] The new proposal for a Regulation of the European Parliament and of the Council on health technology assessment and amending Directive 2011/24[32] refers to the same definition of health technology, but aims to replace the existing provision of Article 15 from the Directive 2011/24 on the assessment of health technologies with a completely new set of common EU rules. The proposal also includes a common definition of the health technology assessment as a "multidisciplinary comparative assessment process, based on clinical and non-clinical assessment domains, which compiles and evaluates the available evidence about the clinical and non-clinical issues related to the use of a health technology".[33]

Health technology assessment, in essence, analyses the cost-effectiveness and budget impact of a certain health technology, considering (or so it should) patient outcome, safety, organisational, legal, ethical and societal aspects.[34] HTA is used as a tool to inform coverage and reimbursement decisions in national healthcare systems.[35] Given that it involves assessment of various circumstances associated with the use of a health technology, HTA is better suited to personalised medicine approach than, for example, reference based pricing.[36]

20Strategy%202012%20and%20beyond.pdf. One of the earliest definitions was applied by the U.S. Office of Technology Assessment, which describes medical technology (later referred to in broader term as 'health' technology) as "drugs, devices, and medical and surgical procedures used in medical care, and the organisational and supportive systems within which such care is provided", see Office of Technology Assessment, Assessing the efficacy and safety of medical technologies, Washington DC: U.S. Government Printing Office, 1978. Health technologies, as noted by some authors, are not defined as a single regulatory category by the EU, as evident in the definition of health technologies for Patients' Rights Directive, in comparison with the EU marketing legislation, such as Directive 2001/83, Directive 93/42 or Regulation 726/2004. See Bache et al. (2013), p. 9.

[31] Article 3(1)(l) Directive 2011/24/EU of the European Parliament and of the Council of 9 March 2011 on the application of patients' rights in cross-border healthcare, OJ L 88, 4.4.2011 (hereinafter: the Patients' Rights Directive).

[32] European Commission (2018).

[33] Article 2(1)(d) of the Proposal for a Regulation of the European Parliament and of the Council on health technology assessment and amending Directive 2011/24/EU COM(2018) 51 final.

[34] European Commission (2013), p. 26.

[35] Although HTA reports may and have been used by a range of decision makers, they are increasingly being commissioned to inform particular resource allocation decisions. In comparison to other concepts which enable evidence-based decision making, such as evidence-based medicine (EBM) or comparative effectiveness research (CSR), HTA "explores of elements of value of a technology [...]" with the underlying question "[...] "Is the technology worth it?" [...]". See Drummond et al. (2008), pp. 244–258.

[36] Both reference pricing and health technology assessment can be viewed as policies designed to obtain "more value for money from pharmaceuticals". Reference pricing is based on clustering of similar drugs and setting a single level of reimbursement for the cluster, "usually based on the price of the cheapest drug in the group or some average of existing prices." Drummond et al. (2011), pp. 263–264.

In addition to HTA, there are other methods or activities that could be used to inform evidence-based health care decision making, for example evidence-based medicine (EBM) or comparative effectiveness research (CER), and their roles are often misunderstood or confused. Of the three concepts, only EBM is a decision process used to assist individual patients' and/or physicians' decisions, whereas CER and HTA are applied specifically to feed into reimbursement/coverage decision making.[37] However, HTA is primarily oriented on "Is it worth it?" question: "for a health care intervention to be "worth it", the value of the clinical and economic benefits needs to be greater than the clinical harms and economic costs",[38] with due account of social, ethical and legal issues.

It is therefore not surprising that the Union is inviting Member States to develop or adjust their procedures aimed at assessing the effects of personalised medicine, especially HTA procedures, in relation to the specific nature of personalised medicine, considering, among other, added value from the patients' perspective, as well as enforced cooperation and exchange of best practices, with full respect of Member States' competences.[39]

While the health technology assessment in general has the potential to develop standardised, EU-wide methodologies and secure that the personalised medicine benefits reach the patients across borders of EU Member States, there are also factors that limit the applicability of HTA methodologies to personalised medicine. These may include inflexible procedures, inconsistent methodologies used in assessing companion diagnostics and associated treatments, inappropriate validation of patient evidence and experience, excessive bureaucracy and high costs.[40] This shows how important it is to formulate a framework for HTA with social and ethical considerations in mind: an effective HTA does not necessarily imply more effective and efficient health care.[41] The current Proposal for a Union Regulation on HTA aims to address some of these weaknesses. It aims to improve the availability of innovative health technologies for patients, ensure efficient use of resources and strengthen the quality of HTA across the EU, improve business predictability, as well to improve convergence of HTA processes and tools across EU Member States.[42]

---

[37]Luce et al. point out the outputs of CER activities are useful for developing clinical guidelines, whereas HTA output consist primarily in informing reimbursement and coverage decisions. See Luce et al. (2010), pp. 271–272.

[38]Luce et al. (2010), pp. 265–266.

[39]Council (2015), para. 22.

[40]European Alliance for Personalised Medicine, Innovation and Patient Access to Personalised Medicine, Report from Irish Presidency conference March 20th/21st 2013, https://www.euapm.eu/pdf/EAPM_REPORT_on_Innovation_and_Patient_Access_to_Personalised_Medicine.pdf, p. 22. See also Di Paolo et al. (2017), p. 289.

[41]O'Donnell et al. (2009), p. 4.

[42]European Commission (2018), p. 2.

5 HTA System in Croatia

HTA may be implemented differently in different countries.[43] Cultural, historical, political, and societal differences all account for heterogeneity of the HTA systems in various countries.[44] HTA is part of the health system, and health systems are rooted in country's history, culture, values and preferences.[45] Consequently, the situation in the EU Member States concerning health technology assessment differs.[46] In the Republic of Croatia for example, the Agency for quality and accreditation in health care and social welfare (hereinafter: the Agency) was established under the Act on Quality of Health Care and Social Welfare.[47] It is a public entity competent, inter alia, to conduct the procedures of health technology assessment, to keep a database of assessed health technologies, to establish a system for assessment of new or existing health technologies, etc. The Agency's Department for development, research and health technologies started its operations in 2009.[48]

Health technology assessment is defined in the Act on Quality of Health Care and Social Welfare as a multidisciplinary, professional, unbiased, objective, grounded on the principles of evidence-based medicine, transparent process of assessment of clinical efficiency and safety, with the economic analysis of new or already existing health technologies (medicines, medical products, surgical procedures, diagnostic procedures as well as other technologies in the area of prevention, diagnosis, treatment and rehabilitation), considering ethical, social, legal and organisational principles.[49]

However, the importance of this process in Croatia in the context of personalised medicine is still limited. There are many reasons for it.

First, the assessment itself is not obligatory, neither in connection with the placing of medicines to the list of medicines covered by the Croatian Health Insurance Fund, nor concerning decisions on medical products or procedures or any other technology at national level. Moreover, neither the recommendation rendered by the Agency concerning the use of assessed health technology is obligatory. The Act on Quality of Health Care and Social Welfare prescribes that the ultimate objective of the health technology assessment is "to provide unbiased, expert, objective and transparent *recommendation* on the justifiability of application

---

[43]Banta (1997), p. 133.

[44]As pointed by O'Donnell et al. "The refrain, *if you have seen one HTA system, you have seen them all*, simply does not apply." See O'Donnell et al. (2009), p. 3.

[45]Banta (2003), p. 122.

[46]For an overview of HTA agencies and HTA system in the EU Member States, see Löblová (2016), pp. 253–273.

[47]Act on Quality of Health Care and Social Welfare (*Zakon o kvaliteti zdravstvene zaštite i socijalne skrbi*), Official Gazette *Narodne novine* No. 124/11.

[48]Mittermayer et al. (2010), p. 430.

[49]Article 2 Act on Quality of Health Care and Social Welfare (*Zakon o kvaliteti zdravstvene zaštite i socijalne skrbi*), Official Gazette *Narodne novine* No. 124/11.

of new technology or replacement of the existing health technology with the aim of facilitating the adoption of a final objective health policy decision" (emphasis added).[50] Thus, recommendations depend on and may be overturned by political choices.

Another problem is the insufficient legal framework. Under Article 36, Agency shall propose to the competent Minister the adoption of the Ordinance on assessment of health technologies. The Minister should have adopted all required ordinances under the Act on Quality of Health Care and Social Welfare within the period of 6 months after the Act took effect. The Act is in force since 12 November 2011; almost 7 years after the Ordinance on assessment of health technology is still not adopted.[51] The inexistence of the implementing ordinance did not completely hinder HTA process. Health technology assessment is conducted in line with the Croatian guidelines for health technology assessment (hereinafter: Guidelines), prepared in 2011 by the Agency in cooperation with the multidisciplinary Workgroup for health technology assessment.[52]

The third problem concerns full economic analyses, as part of the HTA process. Their goal is to optimise cost efficiency, i.e. accomplish the greatest health benefit per unit of invested money. Under the Guidelines, CEA cost-effectiveness analysis and CUA cost-utility analysis should be used. In Croatia, however, there is no legal obligation to elaborate full economic analyses, only the obligation to elaborate the impact for the budget of the Croatian Health Insurance Institute. Quite often, there are no preconditions for economic evaluation—detailed description of costs and benefits arising from a certain medical technology. For example, the majority of assessment reports, if not all recommendations published in the HTA database on the website of the Agency point out that economic analyses have not been conducted because of the non-existence of appropriate experts, lack of regulatory framework, and that because of the lack of financial resources, it was not possible to engage international experts, so that recommendation is based on available foreign literature and conducted HTAs. For example, in a Report no. 05/2013 on assessment of particle beam radiation therapies for cancer it was determined, based on available data from literature,[53] that the construction of centres for radiotherapy of tumours with particles would not be cost efficient because of a relatively small number of

---

[50]Article 2 Act on Quality of Health Care and Social Welfare.

[51]Draft Ordinance was open for public consultations before its adoption in the period from 11 October to 10 November 2016, during the operation of a technical government. On 19 October, the 14th Government of the Republic of Croatia took office, and it seems that the competent Ministry of Health indefinitely postponed all further activities concerning the adoption of the Ordinance. For the text of the draft Ordinance from 2016 see https://zdravstvo.gov.hr/pristup-informacijama/savjetovanje-sa-zainteresiranom-javnoscu-1475/otvorena-savjetovanja/nacrt-prijedloga-pravilnika-o-procjeni-zdravstvenih-tehnologija/2784.

[52]The Croatian Guideline for Health Technology Assessment Process and Reporting (2011), http://aaz.hr/sites/default/files/hrvatske_smjernice_za_procjenu_zdravstvenih_tehnologija.pdf.

[53]HTA 5/2013, http://www.aaz.hr/sites/default/files/hta_05_2013.pdf.

patients with indications for such treatment and extremely high costs of constructing such centres and necessary equipment for its operation.

Another problem is that the process itself does not envisage the obligation of the Agency to contact and consult institutions or experts in Croatia who already have or use specific technology that is undergoing assessment, which could certainly affect the content and quality of assessment, if not even modify the decision on cost efficiency.

6 The Role of Solidarity in Health Technology Assessment

Now we arrive at a question, how to incorporate the principle of solidarity, as one of the fundamental principles of social security?

The principle of solidarity is associated with the financing of the system and ensuring equal access under equal conditions to equal benefits. It entails income redistribution. It implies not only help for an individual who is a member of a community of solidarity, but also equity in terms of social justice between members of a community and all other social groups.[54] The obligation to belong to a certain group enables financial redistribution, as a prerequisite for exclusion of risk assessment and coverage of otherwise barely insurable risks. In the social insurance system, equity in the community is accomplished especially through horizontal reciprocity: between young and old, healthy and sick, etc. Benefits are not determined according to the risk of the insured, but according to income. Every member of community contributes in accordance with his economic power, and in return receives benefits according to his needs. The amount of contributions has no impact on the amount of benefits. Equitable redistribution among different groups in society is accomplished also through support of the state. Therefore, those who are better off take some of the burden from those who earn less or nothing at all. In the systems organised based on national health services, the principle of solidarity is expressed through tax financing and equal benefits.

Solidarity is a fundamental value and principle of all health care systems in the EU Member States, along with universality, access to quality health care and equality.[55] And the entire story on costs as a significant part of health technology assessment and potential implementation of personalised medicine boils down to the question how does it affect the principle of solidarity, which at its core presupposes redistribution of income within the system.

Moving on from a wider picture of how personalised medicine might affect the principle of solidarity as a core principle of health care systems, we will now focus on the processes of health technology assessment and their impact on implementing the personalised medicine approach on the one hand, and on the other hand on their

---

[54]See Martinović (2015), pp. 335–352.
[55]Council (2006).

impact on the potential transformation of the principle of solidarity during that process.

Personalised medicine treatments are innovative and often expensive. Nevertheless, HTA processes help decide whether they would be cost-effective. How does solidarity fit in?

The principle of solidarity should not be understood here as a variable, to be adapted and changed in line with the situation in the society and available financial resources for financing of the health care system. So that there will be less solidarity and less benefits or higher contributions to be paid through direct payments or otherwise if there is less money in the system because of, for example, economic crisis, or if the costs of running the health care system rise, among other, because of the introduction of the new expensive technologies. Solidarity is a prerequisite for the functioning of the social state and the provision of social security.[56] The principle of solidarity must be incorporated in the assessment of new technologies, but not as a limiting factor.

There are three elements at the core of solidarity: universal coverage and access to health protection of all citizens; redistribution, including cross-subsidising from rich, healthier, younger to poorer, ill and older population; and equality in getting health protection and health services of standardised quality and equal content, which are provided based on a medical necessity.[57] That core cannot be altered, but the practical application of these aspects of solidarity may vary. If a decision whether to introduce some new technology is based solely on cost efficiency, precisely that could bring about erosion of solidarity, because most new expensive technologies are not accessible to most national health systems, so that only the richest would be able to acquire such treatment with their own resources. If we are to avoid such unwanted consequences from occurring, redistribution in the context of new technologies must be understood as a *redistribution from present to future and* vice versa, because the cost of introducing new technologies may be understood as an investment in future better health of the population. Ter Meulen suggests that the guiding principle for decision making as to what kind of health services are needed in a society should be the principle of "humanitarian solidarity".[58] This implies reinforced commitment to protect and support persons in need, even despite the limited financial resources. Similarly, Praynsack and Buyx believe that the public healthcare systems are best 'enablers' of personalised medicine and that the best way to implement personalised medicine is by increasing, not decreasing solidarity in healthcare institutions and practices.[59]

---

[56]Without the respect for the "[. . .] general duty of solidarity, from which no one is absolved [. . .], the state would be deprived of the resources that allows for the provision of social security". See Supiot (2015), pp. 114–115.

[57]Saltman (2015), p. 5; Brown and Chinitz (2015), p. 27. See also Kingreen (2003).

[58]Ter Meulen (2017), p. 185.

[59]Prainsack and Buyx (2017), p. 137.

From the current practice of the Croatian Agency concerning health technology assessment, one may conclude that solidarity is *intuitively* underlying the process of assessment and final recommendations.

We should take a look at the previously mentioned example of particle beam radiation therapy. As it was determined that the costs of introducing this technology would be disproportionate given the very low number of patients with indications for such treatment, it was recommended to refer patients with clear indications for this procedure to be treated abroad. Therefore, all of the elements of solidarity, at least in this example, are safeguarded, as patients in need for such treatment can get it at the expense of the Croatian Health Insurance Fund, but not in Croatia.

The problem is that the principle of solidarity is far too important to be left solely to intuition.

It is therefore extremely important to elaborate and improve the regulatory framework for health technology assessment in Croatia to clearly define parameters and legal framework for decision-making, and especially to enable conducting full economic analyses and to include interested stakeholders in the assessment procedure.

7 Concluding Remarks

Personalised medicine is about stratification; solidarity is about uniformity and redistribution. However, these concepts are not mutually exclusive, but complementary. As Prainsack and Buyx succinctly conclude, "[...] we *all* are different in our health risks, and that is exactly what unites us all and makes us similar".[60] There is great potential of HTA in the implementation of personalised medicine in clinical practice, especially given the fact that EU Member States have public health care systems, which are rooted in the principle of solidarity. Neither personalised medicine nor the HTA compromise this tradition. However, HTA, as one of the 'gateways' for personalised medicine into public health care systems, should be carefully designed to reinforce solidarity. HTA in public health care systems may be understood as a tool to reach informed decisions, not only on the economic cost of a certain health technology, but also on its societal impact. There is no denying that financial resources for health care funding are scarce and limited and that health policy choices must be based in economic evaluations. Nevertheless, objective, transparent and unbiased economic evaluations must also be complimented by solidarity considerations.

---

[60]Prainsack and Buyx (2017), p. 137.

References

Bache G, Flear ML, Hervey TK (2013) The defining features of the European Union's approach to regulating new health technologies. In: Flear ML et al (eds) European law and new health technologies. Oxford University Press, Oxford

Banta D (2003) The development of health technology assessment. Health Policy 63:121–132

Banta HD (1997) Introduction to the EUR-ASSESS report. Int J Technol Assess Health Care 13 (2):133–143

Becker U (2016) Legal aspects of personalised medicine. In: Bodiroga-Vukobrat N et al (eds) Personalized medicine. A new medical and social challenge. Springer, Switzerland, pp 21–30

Brittain HK, Scott R, Thomas E (2017) The rise of the genome and personalised medicine. Clin Med 17(6):545–551

Brosset E, Mahalatchimy A (2017) EU law and policy on new health technologies. In: Hervey TK, Young CA, Bishop LE (eds) Research handbook on EU health law and policy. Edward Elgar Publishing, Cheltenham, pp 197–221

Brown LD, Chinitz DP (2015) Saltman on solidarity. Israel J Health Policy Res 4:27

Council (2006) Council Conclusions on common values and principles in European Union health systems, 2006/C 146/01, OJ C 146/1, 22.6.2006

Council (2014) Council Conclusions on innovations for the benefit of the patients 2014/C 438/06, OJ C 438/12, 6.12.2014

Council (2015) Council Conclusions on personalised medicine for the patients 2015/C 421/03, OJ C 421/2, 17.12.2015

Di Paolo A, Sarkozy F, Ryll B et al (2017) Personalised medicine in Europe: not yet personal enough? BMC Health Serv Res 17(1):289

Drummond MF, Sanford Schwartz J, Jönsson B et al (2008) Key principles for the improved conduct of health technology assessments for resource allocation decisions. Int J Technol Assess Health Care 24(3):244–258

Drummond MF, Jönsson B, Rutten F et al (2011) Reimbursement of pharmaceuticals: reference pricing versus health technology assessment. Eur J Health Econ 12(3):263–271

European Commission (2013) Commission Staff Working Document "Use of 'omics' technologies in the development of personalised medicine", SWD(2013) 436 final, Brussels, 25.10.2013

European Commission (2018) Proposal for a Regulation of the European Parliament and of the Council on health technology assessment and amending Directive 2011/24/EU, COM(2018) 51 final

Flear ML (2015) Governing Public Health. EU law, regulation and biopolitics. Hart, Oxford

Grech G, Grossman I (eds) (2015) Preventive and predictive genetics: towards personalised medicine. Springer, Heidelberg

Haycox A, Pirmohamed M, McLeod C et al (2014) Through a glass darkly: economics and personalised medicine. Pharmacoeconomics 32(11):1055–1061. https://doi.org/10.1007/s40273-014-0190-6

Hüsing B, Hartig J, Bührlen B et al (2008) Individualiserte Medizin und Gesundheitssystem. Zukunftsreport. Büro für Technikfolgenabschätzung beim deutschen Bundestag, Arbeitsbericht Nr. 126

Jain K (2015) Textbook of personalised medicine, 2nd edn. Humana Press, Springer Science + Business Media, New York

Joyner MJ, Paneth N (2015) Seven questions for personalized medicine. JAMA 314(10):999–1000. https://doi.org/10.1001/jama.2015.7725

Keil M (2015) Rechtsfragen der individualisierten Medizin. Springer, Heidelberg

Kingreen T (2003) Das Sozialstaatsprinzip im europäischen Verfassungsverbund. Mohr Siebeck, Tübingen

Löblová O (2016) Three worlds of health technology assessment: explaining patterns of diffusion of HTA agencies in Europe. Health Econ Policy Law 11:253–273

Luce BR et al (2010) EBM, HTA and CER: clearing the confusion. Milbank Q 88(2):256–276

Martinović A (2015) Solidarity as key determinant of social security systems in the EU. Rev Soc Polit 22(3):335–352

Mathur S, Sutton J (2017) Personalized medicine could transform healthcare (review). Biomed Rep 7:3–5

Maughan T (2017) The promise and the hype of 'personalised medicine'. New Bioeth 23(1):13–20. https://doi.org/10.1080/20502877.2017.1314886

Mićović V, Sorta-Bilajac Turina I, Malatestinić Đ (2016) Personalised medicine and public health. In: Bodiroga-Vukobrat N et al (eds) Personalized medicine. A new medical and social challenge. Springer, Switzerland, pp 81–93

Mittermayer R, Huić M, Meštrović J (2010) Kvaliteta zdravstvene zaštite, akreditacija nositelja zdravstvene djelatnosti i procjena zdravstvenih tehnologija u Hrvatskoj: uloga Agencije za kvalitetu i akreditaciju u zdravstvu. Acta Med Croatica 64:425–434

O'Donnell JC, Pham SV, Pashos CL et al (2009) Health technology assessment: lessons learned from around the world – an overview. Value Health 12:1–5

Pavelić K, Martinović T, Kraljević Pavelić S (2015) Do we understand the personalized medicine paradigm? EMBO Rep 16(2):133–136

Pavelić K, Kraljević Pavelić S, Sedić M (2016) Personalized medicine: the path to new medicine. In: Bodiroga-Vukobrat N et al (eds) Personalized medicine. A new medical and social challenge. Springer, Switzerland, pp 1–20

Prainsack B, Buyx A (2017) Solidarity in biomedicine and beyond. Cambridge University Press, Cambridge

Saltman RB (2015) Health sector solidarity: a core European value but with broadly varying content. Israel J Health Policy Res 4:5

Supiot A (2015) Judicial enforcement of social solidarity. In: van der Walt J, Ellsworth J (eds) Constitutional sovereignty and social solidarity in Europe. Nomos, Baden-Baden, pp 109–138

Ter Meulen R (2017) Solidarity and justice in health and social care. Cambridge University Press, Cambridge

Wienke A, Dierks C, Janke K (eds) (2014) Rechtsfragen der Personalisierten Medizin. Springer, Heidelberg

Personalizing Privacy? Examining the Shifting Boundaries of a Fundamental Right in Preimplantation Genetic Testing of Embryos

Matija Miloš

Abstract This paper provides a comparative overview of the relationship between privacy and preimplantation genetic testing in the United States and select European jurisdictions. It aims to describe the legal means used to mediate the technological developments in question and the requirements of privacy as a core fundamental right. Other than the substantive aspects of this mediation, the paper deals with institutions that structure the process.

1 Introduction

It is said that personalized medicine blurs boundaries. Patients are no longer just patients, but are also consumers tasked with proactively taking care of their health.[1] The boundary of "taking care of one's health" is similarly being blurred by its interaction with the idea of self-improvement. Some means of personalized treatment do not tackle medical conditions alone, but are technically able to be extended into means of enhancing one's life.

Here I want to examine the boundary between treatment and life-enhancing technology regarding preimplantation genetic testing. The procedure is a component of *in vitro fertilization* (IVF) treatments. It is used to test genes of embryos created in the procedure. Preimplantation genetic testing allows for detection of genes that make pregnancies less viable, carry inheritable conditions or make one more predisposed towards them. In this manner, it allows medical professionals to select those embryos that do not carry the genetic disorder and implant these into the uterus.[2] As the primary purpose of the procedure is to tailor the IVF treatment to the needs of a particular pregnancy, it is fair to include it into the broad family of

---

[1] See, for instance, Swan (2009), pp. 492–525.

[2] It is currently possible to identify over 170 disorders. (Hershberger et al. 2011, str. 38.)

M. Miloš (✉)
Faculty of Law, University of Rijeka, Rijeka, Croatia
e-mail: mmilos@pravri.hr

© Springer Nature Switzerland AG 2019

N. Bodiroga-Vukobrat et al. (eds.), *Personalized Medicine in Healthcare Systems*, Europeanization and Globalization 5, https://doi.org/10.1007/978-3-030-16465-2_16

"personalized medicine" procedures.[3] Nonetheless, while currently used in such cases in a variety of European jurisdictions, preimplantation genetic testing could conceivably be used for a selection of embryos on other criteria or could eventually help in changing the genes of an offspring.[4]

Rather than attempting to discuss such broad implications, here I want to engage the ongoing debate on the expanded use of this technology in terms of privacy as a fundamental right. In this paper, I provide a comparative snapshot of the interaction between preimplantation genetic testing and privacy in the United States and in Europe. I examine the contents of privacy on both sides of the Atlantic and then look at the challenges that prompt a change in its shifting boundaries and the efforts to maintain the core of the privacy in the face of these trials. I then conclude with a brief note on the state of affairs in Croatia.

In the first part of the paper, (1) I expand more on the procedures that are involved in preimplantation genetic testing and outline the main challenges that face the law in regulating the call for their expanded use. (2) Then I look at the US case, characterized by a fragmented regulation of the technology and a concomitant delegation of authority in preimplantation testing procedures to experts. On the other hand, examples from Europe involve the existence of a regulatory authority that oversees the procedures and serves as a mediator between expert knowledge and the democratic public. (3) In Croatia, the procedure is regulated in law, but does not seem to be practiced within the country. Lessons from a comparative study in these matters, however, may be useful for a future democratic debate and may also be used within a broader discussion on the relationship between law, technology, and society.

2 Preimplantation Genetic Testing as a Challenge to the Boundaries of Bodily Privacy

As is the case with any other human right, privacy is not absolute. Its application flows from resolving conflicts it engages in with other interests. When analyzing the ways in which privacy should be balanced against competing interests, Daniel Solove argued that due regard should be had to societal interests. In his pragmatic approach, "privacy should win when it produces the best outcomes for society".[5] His argument requires us to ascertain why privacy is valuable and to then examine the best way to balance these interests with conflicting ones.

---

[3]See the criteria for determining the meaning of "personalized medicine" in Schleidgen et al. (2015), p. 19.

[4]As far as the Council of Europe is concerned, any such intervention on the human genome is currently prohibited by Article 12 of the Convention of the Protection of Human Rights and Dignity of the Human Being with regard to the Application of Biology and Medicine: Convention on Human Rights and Biomedicine (Oviedo Convention), ETS No. 164.

[5]Solove (2008), p. 87.

One need not accept Solove's argument to understand that the idea of constructing a "best outcome for society" and using it to regulate privacy remains difficult and contentious. While judicial reasoning punctuates the ongoing conflict over what is in "society's best interest", leaving legal standards in its wake, political activity continues and threatens to disturb seemingly neat balancing acts and established understandings. The law may then be seen as maintaining the "interpretation and application of intersubjective norms or standards".[6] These arguably serve to maintain the ongoing exchange within constructive bounds.

This paper deals with the societal challenges that preimplantation genetic testing places before privacy as a fundamental right. Preimplantation genetic testing is a broader category that includes preimplantation genetic screening and preimplantation genetic diagnostic procedures. While genetic screening is primarily used to increase the viability of pregnancies, especially in older women, genetic diagnostic techniques allow medical professionals to detect inheritable conditions. Both either enable pregnancy where it is harder or impossible to achieve or they ensure that an embryo containing specific genetic qualities is chosen for gestation. Both procedures can thus be technological extensions of one's ability to procreate.

Preimplantation genetic testing as a procedure applied in the context of assisted reproduction is a challenging technology because it is not a simple form of treatment, as is the case with a cough syrup or a brain surgery. Specifically, with procedures that are meant to alleviate a medical condition the harm can be readily identified in a patient who needs to be treated. The development of assisted reproductive technologies has loosened this tight bond between the patient and her condition. Instead of an individual, the medical professional treats an "infertile couple" and her actions are a service powerfully regulated by the state.[7] Moreover, these technologies allowed for the outcome of fertilization, an embryo, to be extracted from individual bodies and away from the act of copulation, making conception an act of "piecing together" in a laboratory setting.[8] Its results have in turn become subject to the law, with a variety of issues in its wake.[9] Treatable harm has thus become a contentious matter, the content and role of which is not naturally given.

Preimplantation genetic testing complicates matters further. In cases where it is used to determine which embryos would not be viable, it is possible to argue that preimplantation genetic testing is a part of the infertility treatment arsenal. However, as far as the technology is used to choose embryos that do not carry inheritable conditions or, on the contrary, carry particular qualities, the harm required can no longer be in an infertile aspiring parent. One is instead choosing between embryos based on their genetic makeup and the harm it may produce to their future existence. Thus, the embryo that is affected by a condition is not actually cured but is merely

---

[6]Post (2010), p. 1333.

[7]Sándor (2002), p. 117.

[8]Franklin (1996), p. 327.

[9]Sándor (2012), p. 1151.

not selected for gestation. One may argue that what is being treated is not actually the health of the embryo or the parents, but rather the "quality" of a future child's life and, by extension, the quality of the parents' existence.

Here, then, lies the blurry boundary between treatment and enhancement of one's existence that characterizes preimplantation genetic testing. As the procedure does not necessarily involve an actual treatment to an existing or potential individual, some have argued that its ability to improve an individual's existence should not be restricted to children that are born with its help or, indeed, that it should not be preconditioned by a genetic disorder at all. These suggestions commonly understand preimplantation genetic testing as a way to improve the range and/or quality of an individual's reproductive choice. The procedure would then be used beyond those cases where one's reproductive capacities are either frustrated or would lead to the child inheriting a debilitating inheritable condition.

The extended use of preimplantation genetic testing procedures is suggested in several variations. One is that it should be possible to avoid implanting embryos containing genes that may make the child susceptible to a disease, such as cancer, or carry a disease that may manifest later in the child's life.[10] Furthermore, there is the possibility of choosing an embryo based on its genetic compatibility with an already living child. This would make the new-born a "saviour sibling" as she would be able to donate tissue to treat her already living and ill sibling.[11] On the next level of the controversy scale stands the idea that preimplantation genetic testing should be allowed to choose embryos based solely on the future child's sex.[12] Here the choice of the parents would carry the day and family planning reasons would suffice to employ preimplantation genetic testing. Finally, it has been suggested that parents should not only have the possibility to choose an embryo without a genetic defect, but that they should be able to select one that carries the gene for a disability, such as deafness.[13]

These extended uses of preimplantation genetic testing are different, but they are all controversial. On the most basic level, the very idea that the procedure should be applied for "serious" conditions requires us to understand what "serious" means. The argument that parents should be able to choose their child on account of sex does not merely ensure that the child is genetically related to a parent, but allows parents to treat sex as a personal preference.[14] The argument for preimplantation genetic testing

---

[10]Robertson (2003), pp. 467–468; Ethics Committee of the American Society for Reproductive Medicine (2013), pp. 54–57.

[11]For a more extensive discussion on the topic, see Smith (2015).

[12]Pennings (2004), p. 268. Normally the choice of the child's sex is allowed only if the embryos carry a gene with an inheritable condition more likely to affect one sex than the other.

[13]Lee (2016), pp. 1–7. Implanting an embryo that would develop into a child with a disability also raises the matter of the so-called wrongful births. Cf. King (2008), pp. 377–395.

[14]It is for this reason questionable to claim that social sex selection is merely an extension of the right to have a genetically related child. (Fovargue and Bennett 2016, p. 12) Sex of the embryo can normally be selected only if there is a threat that the child might inherit.

that leads one to choose an embryo with a gene carrying a disability allows parents to potentially reshape the life of their future offspring.

Preimplantation genetic testing raises several social implications. As it is normally contained within IVF procedures, it forms a part of a process that is arduous and expensive. This means that the possibilities it offers are not likely to be accessible to everyone on an equal basis but also that it is not a particularly attractive way to reproduce. Secondly, the ability to choose embryos based on particular characteristics may be controversial as it may involve a particular interpretation of these. For instance, choosing against a particular disability may imply "a judgment as to what lives are worth living" or may extend to include characteristics that in themselves do not cause a significant loss in the quality of one's life, such as Down syndrome.[15]

In all this, it is necessary to investigate how constitutional law mediates between a promising present and an uncertain future. As Sándor points out, there is a need to timely regulate technology while maintaining sufficient space for different technologies to develop without being hampered by hasty legal solutions. At the same time, in this enterprise the law cannot simply abandon its normative criteria in favor of scientific ones, but must ensure a space for translating technological achievements in a way that will maintain constitutional essentials, such as privacy, in the new environment.[16] In what follows, I briefly examine how this is done in terms of privacy in the United States and in Europe.

3 Porous Constitutional Boundaries of Preimplantation Genetic Testing in the United States

The "right to be let alone" has its roots in an essay penned by Warren and Brandeis, The Right to Privacy. As one of the most famous treatises on privacy, it was motivated by the cramped living conditions of nineteenth century urban America. In an age characterized by life in close quarters and combined with the booming role of mass press, the public was saturated with all kinds of gossip or, as Warren and Brandeis called them, "trivialities".[17] In the circumstances, it made sense to claim that there is a right to be free of such interferences.

The right to privacy thus understood is entwined with a negative understanding of freedom. Privacy serves to exclude governmental interference in matters it encompasses. Reproductive freedom was recognized as one of these matters in *Skinner v. Oklahoma*.[18] In this case, the United States Supreme Court found unconstitutional

---

[15]Knoppers et al. (2006), p. 209.

[16]Sándor (2012), p. 1160.

[17]Warren (1890), p. 196.

[18]Skinner v. Oklahoma ex rel. Williamson, 316 US 535 (1942).

Oklahoma's legislation providing for forced sterilization of those convicted three or more times of crimes that may be understood as a form of "moral turpitude". Specifically, the legislation was found contrary to the Equal Protection Clause of the Fourteenth Amendment.

As is evident from *Skinner*, the US Constitution does not expressly enshrine privacy. Instead, this right has been recognized by drawing from its various provisions. Most famously and controversially, the Supreme Court found that the right of privacy inhabits the so-called "penumbras" projected by different constitutional provisions. These penumbras were first "discovered" in *Griswold v. Connecticut*[19] and have provided another foundation for a right to privacy. They would later be detected in a variety of cases unrelated to procreation, sovereignty included.[20] In terms of reproduction, penumbras have encompassed an array of reproduction-related matters, such as abortion. As Paonessa demonstrates, while there is no case law that explicitly places preimplantation genetic testing within these, the technology can arguably be associated with reproductive freedom. In such a case, any law regulating the procedure would be subject to strict scrutiny.[21] This would mean that there must be a necessity to achieve a compelling government purpose for a statute to survive judicial review.

It should be noted that the federal constitution does not empower the federation to regulate preimplantation genetic testing, but leaves this to the states. However, state legislation has been scarce, leading some to conclude that preimplantation genetic testing is a "laissez faire" matter, which is in part explained by an ongoing struggle over abortion, making everything related to reproduction a sensitive political matter.[22] Much has thus been relegated to professionals and their standards, with a fragmented oversight by regulatory authorities.[23] While different agencies are empowered to regulate specific aspects of preimplantation genetic testing procedures, such as the standards for handling embryos, there is no single agency dedicated to preimplantation genetic testing.

It is reported that preimplantation genetic testing procedure in the United States is practiced predominantly to treat infertility, although there has been demand for more controversial uses of the procedure, including requests to implant an embryo with a gene carrying a disability.[24] However, information on the way the procedure is deployed appears to be as fragmented as the regulatory framework that is applied to it. Damiano argues that this results in a lack of quality data that could help in better regulating the procedure.[25]

---

[19]Griswold v. Connecticut, 381 U.S. 479 (1965).
[20]Hershkoff (2011), p. 480.
[21]Paonessa (2007), pp. 353–355.
[22]Storrow (2015), p. 340.
[23]Ibid., p. 343.
[24]Baruch (2008), p. 257.
[25]Damiano (2011), p. 854.

If, as Solove argued, protecting privacy should hinge on the societal benefits it provides, the debate on preimplantation genetic testing demonstrates the layered and complex role of such interests and their role in articulating privacy. Indeed, in the US, there is little consensus on the legitimate scope of preimplantation genetic testing procedures.[26] Previous cases that have given substance to privacy do not provide a guiding principle that could be of much use. To begin with, the jurisprudence on reproductive freedom has been focused on abortion. This body of case law accounts poorly for preimplantation genetic testing which, by definition, involves embryos outside the womb.[27] At the most fundamental level, the issue at stake is the choice between possible pregnancies, rather than a decision over an ongoing pregnancy.

Moreover, the right to privacy in the United States has been strongly influenced by the "right to be let alone" which arguably does not account for a variety of issues that are involved in a preimplantation genetic test. It has already been noted that, in relation to abortion, such a notion of privacy fails to consider "woman's right to health, life, control of her own body, and social and legal equality".[28] Similarly, it can be argued that preimplantation genetic testing requires more than a right to be let alone. The technology employed is not a simple extension of one's bodily functions, but is embedded in social relationships that condition its use. The procedure cannot be used without expert knowledge and its acceptability does not hinge solely on an abstract relationship between an individual and the society she inhabits.

Reflecting on a reported three percent of American cases in which prospective parents want a child with a disability, Karpin insightfully examines the foundation of arguments against using preimplantation genetic testing for implanting an embryo carrying a disability gene. Discussing the cases of deaf parents who want to use preimplantation genetic testing to have deaf children, she argues for an understanding of disability that considers the way disability is socially constructed rather than being a clear boundary to permissible preimplantation genetic testing.[29] Deafness, rather than being a disability, could then be a characteristic whose meaning cannot be set in stone by a clear rule. The key challenge then is in finding institutional mechanisms that allow for creation of rules that remain flexible enough to accommodate the complexity of social relations in which preimplantation genetic testing procedures ought to apply. While much is left to individual practitioners in the United States, observing the European case reveals a different picture.

---

[26]Loc. cit.

[27]Robertson (2008), p. 1496.

[28]Sándor (2002), p. 123.

[29]Karpin (2007), available at http://ssrn.com/abstract=112014, pp. 89–102.

4   National and Supranational Mediation Between Privacy and Preimplantation Genetic Testing in Europe

As a matter of law, preimplantation genetic testing in Europe can normally be employed only as a means of treatment.[30] This is echoed in several national pieces of legislation that provide for the procedure. For instance, the Croatian law regulating the matter provides that preimplantation genetic testing may only be requested within the limits of IVF treatments. As with all other medically assisted reproduction treatments, preimplantation genetic testing may be conducted only if "previous fertility treatments were not successful or are without hope of success and in order to avoid" that the child inherits a "serious condition by way of natural conception".[31] Whether the previous treatment was unsuccessful or "hopeless" is determined by a gynecologist with an appropriate specialization, whilst the risk of a serious inheritable condition is ascertained by a geneticist.[32] Finally, the Law prohibits any treatment that involves the choice of the child's sex, unless such a choice is necessary to avoid a "serious inheritable condition related to sex".[33] Any exception in this sense requires authorization from the National council for medically assisted reproduction.[34]

The Croatian legal framework reflects some features of other European jurisdictions. Most importantly, a prerequisite for preimplantation genetic testing is a degree of harm that can be avoided by using the procedure. For instance, Spanish law allows preimplantation genetic testing only if it "has chances of success", does not cause harm to the "physical or mental" health of the woman receiving the treatment or her offspring and is not performed without a "free and conscious" informed consent. The Spanish statute also authorizes preimplantation genetic testing only in cases involving serious health conditions, which must have an early onset and must not be treatable "with postnatal means, in accordance with the state of medicine at the time the decision on the procedure is to be reached.[35] It is thus essentially provided that

---

[30]Grounds for providing for the procedure solely for reasons of health can be found in the Oviedo Convention. Other than prohibiting the procedure for sex-based embryo selection only in cases that involve a "serious hereditary sex-related disease" (Article 14), the Convention also provides for predictive genetic testing solely for health-related reasons. However, this prohibition arguably leaves some leeway for member states to determine whether preimplantation genetic testing is to be considered a form of "predictive genetic testing". (Duggan and Quinn 2014, p. 46).

[31]Article 4(1) of the Law on Medically Assisted Reproduction, Official Gazette Nr. 86/12 (hereinafter: Law on Medically Assisted Reproduction).

[32]Article 4(2) and (3) of the Law on Medically Assisted Reproduction.

[33]Article 27(2) of the Law on Medically Assisted Reproduction.

[34]Article 27(3) of the Law on Medically Assisted Reproduction.

[35]In Article 3(1), the Spanish *Ley 14/2006, de 26 de mayo, sobre técnicas de reproducción humana asistida* (BOE núm. 126 de 27 de Mayo de 2006). For a broader overview of various European jurisdictions, see the report on the legal state of the art in Council of Europe Member States. (*Background document on preimplantation and prenatal genetic testing*, DH-BIO/INF (2015) 6, pp. 17–20.

preimplantation genetic diagnosis is available solely as a treatment, i.e. to ensure that the child born does not carry a particularly serious condition or to make possible a pregnancy that would otherwise not be viable.

It should be noted at this point that "harm" here does not appear in the role provided for it by the so-called "harm principle". Articulated most famously by J. S. Mill in his classic, *On Liberty*, the harm principle, at least in its well-known liberal guise, allows the government to restrict another's behavior only when such behavior does harm. Harmless behavior is the stuff of liberty. Regulation of preimplantation genetic diagnosis deploys harm in a different role, as the state authorizes the exercise of one's autonomy only as far as it is required to *avoid* harm.

This does not mean that preimplantation genetic testing in Europe has nothing to do with privacy. Indeed, European jurisdictions which have adopted the European Convention on Human Rights and Fundamental Freedoms have also adopted an evolving notion of privacy. It can nowadays be described as a "mother-right".[36] The European Court of Human Rights repeatedly found that "private and family life" may not be exhaustively defined, but includes several daughter-rights and concepts, such as the right of everyone to realize themselves in relation to others, to be "autonomous" in their own life,[37] with respect to their own "physical and psychological identity".[38]

In this sense, privacy also includes those cases where one may make decisions concerning one's own body. This category of cases, which I have chosen to term "bodily privacy", encompasses a variety of situations. Looking at those that involve medicine, we may discern several subcategories. All of these involve privacy, but may also be read to include other rights and values, such as dignity.[39] These problematize the right to dispose with one's bodily characteristics and capacities, such as cases involving sex change,[40] euthanasia,[41] abortion[42] and reproductive capacities generally.[43] Some of them do not deal with the body as such, but information about it, which may involve information on one's DNA.[44] There are also cases where the ability to decide on matters related to one's body requires

---

[36]Barak (2015), p. 157.

[37]Cepeda Espinosa (2012), p. 969. See also Schoeman (1992), p. 13.

[38]*Pretty v. United Kingdom* (Application number 2346/02), para 61.

[39]Foster (2011), p. 124.

[40]*Hämäläinen v. Finland* (Application no. 37359/09).

[41]*Pretty v. United Kingdom* (Application no. 2346/02); *Y. Y. v. Turkey* (Application no. 14793/08).

[42]*Tysiąc v. Poland* (Application no. 5410/03); *R.R. v. Poland* (Application no. 27617/04).

[43]*S. H. and Others v. Austria* (Application no. 57813/00); *Evans v. the United Kingdom* (Application no. 6339/05). This category also includes cases where privacy is violated by an authorised presence of third persons in the delivery room. Konovalova v. Russia (Application no. 37873/04).

[44]See, for example, *L.H. v. Latvia* (Application no. 52019/07); *S. and Marper v. the United Kingdom* (Application nos. 30562/04 and 30566/04); *M.K. v. France* (Application no. 19522/09); *Dagregorio and Mosconi v. France* (Application no. 65714/11); *Aycaguer v. France* (Application No. 8806/12). The last two cases are currently pending before the ECtHR.

additional information and the failure in providing this information may result in violation of one's privacy.[45]

Bodily privacy extends to one's genetic heritage.[46] More importantly, it also encompasses one's "desire" to have that genetic heritage reflected in a child born free from a genetic disorder. This, as others have already argues, results from the decision of the European Court of Human Rights in *Costa and Pavan v. Italy*.[47] In this case, the Italian law barred applicants from using preimplantation genetic testing to prevent having a second child suffer from cystic fibrosis. Their only alternative was thus to abort each pregnancy after a prenatal test came out positive for cystic fibrosis. The European Court of Human Rights found that such an inconsistent regulation of the technology, which does not allow preimplantation genetic testing but allows a more arduous abortion, violates privacy. In the process, the Court recognized that the "desire to have a genetically healthy" child falls under the scope of privacy. The Court, however, only found that the right recognized here must not be arbitrarily regulated but did not yet decide any controversial cases on its application, such as the matter of savior siblings.

Thus, fleshing out the contents of privacy in preimplantation genetic testing still predominantly occurs within national legal spheres. In contrast to the regulatory fragmentation in the United States, some jurisdictions in Europe have established dedicated institutions empowered with oversight and regulatory powers. For example, the United Kingdom and Spain have established independent regulators, Human Fertilisation and Embryology Authority and Comisión Nacional de Reproducción Humana Asistida, respectively. These regulators authorize individual preimplantation genetic testing procedures. They normally must determine whether the harm that may occur in individual cases is serious enough to allow the preimplantation genetic testing procedure. Take for instance Spanish law which, in addition to introducing the standard of a "serious disease", provides that it must have an "early onset" and not be treatable by existing treatments after birth.[48] Obviously, this draws a tighter definition of "harm" but, again, still leaves open the question of determining what is harmful enough. Most importantly, it also introduces important socio-economic considerations, as treatments may be well available to a child of affluent parents but may be out of reach for a less well-off family.[49] What may be incurable is thus shown to be a category that goes well beyond the lack of ability to match the right disease with the right treatment.

---

[45]*Vilnes and Others v. Norway* (Application no. 52806/09).

[46]See *Parillo v. Italy* (Application no. 46470/11) (finding that decisions on one's genetic material represent "an intimate aspect of one's "personal life"").

[47]Application no. 54270/10. See Puppinck (2013), pp. 152–177.

[48]Article 12(1)(a) of the Ley 14/2006, de 26 de mayo, sobre técnicas de reproducción humana asistida, provides that the condition must be one of an "early onset" and that it must not be treatable "in line with medical achievements of the day".

[49]Knoppers, B. M., Rosario, I. M., op. cit., p. 2697.

These regulators are important not only because they supervise fertility treatments across the countries they operate in. As they authorize individual treatments, they gradually build up a body of practice that supplements national legislation and gives shape to bodily privacy in the field of medically assisted reproduction.[50] They also provide an informed basis for future amendments to the legislative framework. Moreover, they are an enduring point of contact between medical professionals and the public. HFEA, established in 1991 as the first body of its kind in the world, provides an example.[51] Among the key aspects of its activity are the continuous consultations with the public, reports and papers on new technological developments and a transparent approach to criteria used when deciding on individual cases of preimplantation genetic testing.

5 Conclusion

This brief overview of the relationship between privacy and preimplantation genetic testing suggests that, while preimplantation genetic testing can be associated with privacy in different legal systems, the procedure is not a simple extension of one's reproductive autonomy. Its use depends on a broader array of social relations in which one moves. To mediate these relationships, the individual and the technology involved, there is a need to generate institutions that will direct and shape knowledge, rather than governmental power. This is possibly the most pertinent lesson for Croatia, where preimplantation genetic testing is not widely practiced. Although current laws authorize the procedure in a way that avoids the problem faced by Italian law in *Costa and Pavan*, preimplantation genetic testing has not attracted significant attention at the time of writing. The independent commission in charge of supervising the procedure has yet to become an instigator of a broad democratic debate and research on the matter.

In conclusion, other than its complex relationship with privacy at present, preimplantation genetic testing also holds a troubled relationship with the future, which is perhaps its most challenging feature. The procedure stimulates a constant concern with how the future life of the child will unfold and, in a broader perspective, how future generations will be affected by allowing embryo selection in certain cases. This displacement of the procedure into the future further complicates the idea that we may easily construct the "harm" on which the procedure is authorized.

---

[50]It could thus be argued that they participate in "knowledge production" that gravitates around preimplantation genetic testing. On knowledge politics, see Demény (2010), pp. 19–37.

[51]The Warnock Report, which recommended that a regulator be introduced, similarly points out the importance of expert regulation that is not ignorant of the context in which it operates. (Department of Health and Social Security, Report of the Committee of Inquiry into Human Fertilisation and Embryology, July 1984, para 13.2.).

References

Aycaguer v. France (Application No. 8806/12)

Barak A (2015) Human dignity: the constitutional value and the constitutional right. Cambridge University Press, Cambridge

Baruch S (2008) Preimplantation genetic diagnosis and parental preferences: beyond deadly diseases. Houston J Health Law Policy 8:245–270

Cepeda Espinosa MJ (2012) Privacy, published in the Oxford handbook of comparative constitutional law. Oxford University Press, Oxford, pp 966–981

Convention of the Protection of Human Rights and Dignity of the Human Being with regard to the Application of Biology and Medicine: Convention on Human Rights and Biomedicine (Oviedo Convention), ETS No. 164

Costa and Pavan v. Italy (Application no. 54270/10)

Council of Europe, Background document on preimplantation and prenatal genetic testing, DH-BIO/INF (2015) 6, Available at http://bit.ly/2ogSIto. Last accessed on 9 Apr 2017

Dagregorio and Mosconi v. France (Application no. 65714/11)

Damiano L (2011) When parents can choose to have the "perfect" child: why fertility clinics should be required to report preimplantation genetic diagnosis dana? Family Court Rev 49:846–855

Demény E (2010) Universal values contextualization and bioethics: knowledge production in the age of genetics. Ann Dep Soc Sci Med Humanit 1(1):19–37

Department of Health and Social Security, Report of the Committee of Inquiry into Human Fertilisation and Embryology, July 1984., Available at: http://bit.ly/1F7a0L6. Last accessed on 9 Apr 2017

Duggan M, Quinn E (2014) Creating a legal framework for pre-implantation in genetic diagnosis in Ireland – regulation, recommendations and some potential tort law scenarios. Medico-Legal J Ireland 20(1):40–51

Ethics Committee of the American Society for Reproductive Medicine (2013) Use of preimplantation genetic diagnosis for serious adult onset conditions: a committee opinion. Fertil Steril 100 (1):54–57

Evans v. the United Kingdom (Application no. 6339/05)

Foster C (2011) Human dignity in bioethics and law. Hart Publishing, Portland

Fovargue S, Bennett R (2016) What role should public opinion play in ethico-legal decision making? The example of selecting sex for non-medical reasons using preimplantation genetic diagnosis. Med Law Rev:34–58

Franklin S (1996) Postmodern procreation: a cultural account of assisted reproduction. In: Ginsburg FD, Rapp R (eds) Conceiving the New World Order: The Global Politics of Reproduction. University of California Press, London

Griswold v. Connecticut, 381 U.S. 479 (1965)

Hämäläinen v. Finland (Application no. 37359/09)

Hershberger PE, Schoenfeld C, Tur-Kaspa I (2011) Unraveling preimplantation genetic diagnosis for high-risk couples: implications for nurses at the front line of care. Nurs Womens Health 15:36–45

Hershkoff H (2011) Horizontality and the "spooky" doctrines of American law. Buffalo Law Rev 59:455–506

Karpin I (2007) Choosing disability: Preimplantation genetic diagnosis and negative enhancement, The University of Sydney Law School, Legal Studies Research Paper No. 08/33, available at http://ssrn.com/abstract=1120142, pp 89–102

King J (2008) Duty to the unborn: a response to Smolensky. Hastings Law J 60:377–395

Knoppers BM, Bordet S, Isasi RM (2006) Preimplantation genetic diagnosis: an overview of socio-ethical and legal considerations. Ann Rev Genomics Hum Genet 7:201–221

Konovalova v. Russia (Application no. 37873/04)

L.H. v. Latvia (Application no. 52019/07)

Law on Medically Assisted Reproduction (Croatia), Official Gazette Nr. 86/12

Lee MJH, Chan B, Clark PA (2016) Deafness and prenatal testing: a study analysis. Internet J Fam Pract 14(1):1–7

Ley 14/2006, de 26 de mayo, sobre técnicas de reproducción humana asistida (Spain) (BOE núm. 126 de 27 de Mayo de 2006)

M.K. v. France (Application no. 19522/09)

Paonessa L (2007) Straightening your heir: On the constitutionality of regulating the sue of preimplantation technologies to select preembryos or modify the genetic profile thereof based on expected sexual orientation. Rutgers Comput Technol Law J 33:331–366

Parillo v. Italy (Application no. 46470/11)

Pennings G (2004) Sex selection, public policy and the HFEA's role in political decision making – response to Edgar Dahl's "The presumption in favour of liberty". Reprod BioMed Online 8 (3):268–269

Post R (2010) Theorizing disagreement: reconceiving the relationship between law and politics. Calif Law Rev 98(4):1319–1350

Pretty v. United Kingdom (Application no. 2346/02)

Puppinck G (2013) Costa and Pavan v. Italy and the convergence between human rights and biotechnologies. Commentary on the ECHR decision Costa and Pavan v. Italy, No. 54270/10, 28 August 2012. Quaderni di diritto mercato tecnologia 3(3):152–177

R.R. v. Poland (Application no. 27617/04)

Robertson JA (2003) Extending preimplantation genetic diagnosis: the ethical debate. Ethical issues in new uses of preimplantation genetic diagnosis. Hum Reprod 18(3):465–471

Robertson JA (2008) Assisting reproduction, choosing genes, and the scope of reproductive freedom. George Washington Law Rev 76:1490–1512

S. and Marper v. the United Kingdom (Application nos. 30562/04 and 30566/04)

S. H. and Others v. Austria (Application no. 57813/00)

Sándor J (2002) Reproduction, self, and state. Soc Res 69(1):115–141

Sándor J (2012) Bioethics and basic rights: persons, humans, and boundaries of life. In: Oxford Handbook of Comparative Constitutional Law (Rosenfeld, M., Sajó, A., ur.), pp 1142–1161

Schleidgen S, Klingler C, Bertram T, Rogowski WH, Marckmann G (2015) What is personalized medicine – medicine for the person? Concepts and contextual aspects, published in The Ethics of Personalized Medicine: Critical Perspectives (Vollman, Jochen; Sandow, Verena; Wäscher Sebastian and Schildmann, Jan, ur.). Ashgate, Farnham, pp 9–24

Schoeman FD (1992) Privacy and social freedom. Cambridge University Press, Cambridge

Skinner v. Oklahoma ex rel. Williamson, 316 US 535 (1942)

Smith MK (2015) Saviour siblings and the regulation of assisted reproductivetechnology. Harm, ethics and law. Routledge, New York

Solove DJ (2008) Understanding privacy. Harvard University Press, Cambridge

Storrow RF (2015) Regulatory aspects of embryo testing: am American view. In: Sills ES (ed) Screening the single Euploid Embryo: molecular genetics in reproductive medicine. Springer International Publishing, New York, pp 339–349

Swan M (2009) Examination of health social networks, consumer personalized medicine and quantified self-tracking. Int J Environ Res Public Health 6(2):492–525

Tysiąc v. Poland (Application no. 5410/03)

Vilnes and Others v. Norway (Application no. 52806/09)

Warren SD, Brandeis LD (1890) The right to privacy. Harv Law Rev 4(5):193–220

Y. Y. v. Turkey (Application no. 14793/08)

(Bio)ethical Aspects of Personalised Medicine: Revealing an "Inconvenient Truth"?

Amir Muzur and Iva Rinčić

Abstract Traditionally known as the individually tailored "one size fits all" health care helping individual patients, personalised medicine over the last few decades has slowly been transforming to "genetically-based" health care and pharmacogenetics, thereby luring the light of bioethics.

Although personalised medicine triggers different ethical levels and provokes main bioethical principles, the authors in the article examine two principles: the one of justice, and the other of autonomy, concluding with remarks on trembling equity and limitation in personal autonomy.

1 Introduction

"The failure to recognize the depth of the moral diversity that characterizes our context is understandable", says Tristram Engelhardt at the beginning of his book The Foundations of Bioethics, first time published in 1986 (Engelhardt 1996). More than two decades later, with a much longer history of trying to provide moral considerations and ethical responses to the challenges of modern civilisation, this statement is valid. The same claim resists especially in relation to the modern science, medicine and healthcare; bioethics, in the same time, trying to provide a solid answer to it, faces numerous obstacles and expectations, challenging its own mission and aim.

If we have to *pin up* modern science segment compressing the number and diversity of moral dilemmas, personalised medicine probably is the first choice. Beyond the fact that the personalised medicine in the last few decades has raised to a popular topic, even named the "term of art" (Lewis et al. 2014) widely present in

A. Muzur · I. Rinčić (✉)
Department of Social Sciences and Medical Humanities, Faculty of Medicine, University of Rijeka, Rijeka, Croatia

Department of Public Health, Faculty of Health Studies, University of Rijeka, Rijeka, Croatia
e-mail: iva.rincic@medri.uniri.hr

© Springer Nature Switzerland AG 2019
N. Bodiroga-Vukobrat et al. (eds.), *Personalized Medicine in Healthcare Systems*,
Europeanization and Globalization 5, https://doi.org/10.1007/978-3-030-16465-2_17

everyday use,[1] we are still far from a complete understanding of its development and application in everyday clinical routine. After all, the "depth of the moral diversity" particularly refers to personalised medicine, resulting in broad and complex interest of bioethicists. Why is that so and can we do anything about it?

2 Personalised Medicine: A Short Historical Insight

From the position of a neutral observer, personalised medicine represents one of the recent scientific-technological advancements, deeply rooted in human genome research, biotechnology, genetics, genomics, and pharmaceutical research, sharing a great interest of publicity[2] and is hard to be followed because of quantitative and qualitative differences. Traditionally known as the individually tailored "one size fits all" health care helping individual patients (Annas 2014), slowly transformed to "genetically-based" health care and pharmacogenetics. However, looking back in history, we could realise that the concept of personalised medicine shares a long history; according to some authors it started several hundred years ago (Food and Drug Administration 2013) or even earlier (1500 BC). Hippocrates, the father of Western medicine, was known for advocating personalised medicine (combining an estimation of the four humours—blood, phlegm, yellow bile and black bile (Personalised Medicine Coalition 2011, p. 2) and evaluating personal traits in prescribing drugs). Traditional systems of Indian, Chinese, and Korean medicine also used the practice of prescribing drugs by considering the differences and similarities of personal characteristics (Chatterjee and Pancholi 2011). Still, it was the nineteenth century development in chemistry, biology and microscopy that set the ground for the later development of the personalised medicine, while the twentieth century pharmaceutical industry has provided the full context for it. Some of the early examples of modern concepts of personalised medicine include the 1907 Reuben Ottenberg report of the "first known blood compatibility test for transfusion using blood typing techniques and cross-matching between donors and patients to prevent hemolytic transfusion reactions," and the discoveries of the genetic basis for the selective toxicity of bean ("favism"), of the antimalarial drug primaquine (Food and Drug Administration 2013).

As it is often the case, the development of a new biomedical focus such as personalised medicine has encouraged other discipline scientists including bioethicists to take a more active role in tackling a long list of new questions, covering topics from resource allocation, theoretical and principles dilemma, data use and storage, privacy, equity of access, consent, reimbursement etc. This new form of

---

[1]The first modern use of the term goes back to 1971, becoming more present during 1990s, and by 2009 "most papers no longer define the term", indicating general understanding in scientific community (Schleidgen et al. 2013).

[2]See the cover of the TIME magazine of the January 15, 2001 issue (Hedgecoe 2004).

investigation, often called "ELSI",[3] in the last few years is taking a new step further, from more theoretical and research level to considerations related to clinical application and patients care, and finally to problems of direct-to-consumers approach.

3 At the Crossroad of Medical Ethics and Bioethics

However, if we want to be open-minded, we should start with one legitimate question: Is the personalisation of medicine primarily a medical-ethical or a bioethical issue? There is a lot of cultural biasing involved in answering this question. If you would ask a representative of the Anglo-American "mainstream bioethics" (namely, the Georgetown principlistic doctrine), you would be probably faced with the counter-question: What is the difference between medical ethics and bioethics? And indeed, the pivotal work by Beauchamp and Childress, promoting the four principles, discusses "biomedical ethics" identifying it explicitly with bioethics. Similarly applies to some European countries, such as United Kingdom, Netherland, Denmark and other Scandinavian countries.

Van Rensselaer Potter, who, in 1970, had first used the term later adopted by the Kennedy Institute, coined "bioethics" out of "biological sciences" and "ethics," but interpreted the new discipline in a much broader way and related it to all forms of life and to environmental issues. Fritz Jahr, who coined the same term about as early as 1926, in Germany, used the Greek word *bios*, instead, but was actually suggesting quite similar directions to the Potterian ones (Rinčić and Muzur 2012). With all that in mind, we are offered the possibility of a much more subtle and diversified approach to the evaluation of the personalisation of medicine. If we accept the distinction between medical ethics as a particular professional ethics problematising the physician-patient relation, accessibility of health care, and other typical issues, as opposed to bioethics dealing with substantial life issues (but not only human life issues), then we shall come closer to the argument that the personalisation of medicine (or personalised medicine?) has much more to do with medical ethics, but has at least one aspect reducible to bioethics: the alterations of because of the intervention into human genetical basis.

A review of bioethical inputs to the discussion on personalised medicine brings us back to V. R. Potter, the American "inventor" of bioethics. Before venturing into bioethics, Potter used to be a very successful biochemist-oncologist and, as early as 1958, at the Philadelphia meeting of the Association of American Societies for Experimental Biology, stressed the impossibility of a unique cure for cancer (as neither the cause of cancer is unique), but anticipated the individualisation of chemotherapy. Even today, among the most important achievements of the Madison McArdle Laboratory, considered has been Potter's discovery that, in cancer therapy,

---

[3]Ethical, legal and social implication.

frequently a combination of drugs helps, defined according to the part of the cell onto which drugs individually work upon (Muzur and Rinčić 2015).

However, modern huge scientific endeavours, like the Human Genome Project and other more recent ones, have revealed new possibilities of decoding and manipulating human personal data and thus highly jeopardising privacy. The second problem emerging from those discoveries has been the attack on the individual free choice of not-knowing data containing potentially disturbing facts or presumptions. In a more dramatic view, one might anticipate the disappearance of one of the most important features of human life: its uncertainty. These and many other questions and fears must pop up in any discussion, scientific or not. Here, nevertheless, we would like to address one more particularly complex issue: the one of justice.

Justice has traditionally been considered one of the four basic principles of the "Georgetown Mantra", that is, of the Anglo-American *biomedical ethics* set: "(1) advances patient autonomy and agency; (2) promotes wellbeing; (3) prevents or minimizes harm; and (4) enables fairness and equity" (Lewis et al. 2014).

The last one, also known under the term of justice refers to the justful distribution of opportunities and goods. When we talk about healthcare, it basically refers to access to care and cure. Such demands are hard to be achieved within "traditional one-size-fit-all medicine", but the real challenge is: What is supposed to be a justful distribution of personalised medicine? No matter what aspect of it we call for— predictive medicine or individually-tailored therapy, or else—we certainly expect it to be very precise and therefore expensive, at least for a long time from now. Expensive has never been meant for masses: personalised medicine thus will never be meant for huge populations of Africa, Asia, Latin America, maybe even not for Eastern Europeans like some of us. Should we stand against personalised medicine only because we are not going to be a part of it? Well, we can hope that, some day, the manufacturing of personalised-medicine products and procedures will become cheap enough to be offered to us, too. Actually, something alike already happened: in the beginning of 1980, the then new Cephalosporin drug was used in Ljubljana to keep alive the Yugoslav president Josip Broz Tito, who was not only provided with a drug non-available to common mortals, but was also administered the dose related to individual pharmacokinetic measurements. Today, we all have Cephalosporins at our disposal: the pharmacokinetics, however, being somehow averaged. . .

In this perspective, pharmaceutical industry may find personalised medicine profitable enough to reduce or even stop researching and developing further drugs for mass use (to be more precise, all kinds of "non-personalised therapies"). One positive aspect of such a scenario would be that, most probably, the same industry would also stop deceiving the public by exaggerating health risks and dangers and manipulating with the health "safety limits."

One might consider the possibility that personalised medicine may even, paradoxically, additionally depersonalise medicine because of its high technical sophistication (Pavelić et al. 2014). The precision and objectivity, fostered and achieved by personalised medicine, may result in neglecting communication between doctor and patient. "Personalisation" of personalised medicine is mainly oriented to personalised diagnosis, cure or therapy, not to personalised approach.

This "objectivity" may also bring into jeopardy one more of the fundamental principles of the Anglo-American "biomedical ethics": the autonomy. Namely, if one is faced with such a certainty of diagnosis and a specifically-tailored treatment, one reduces the choice manoeuvre significantly. In this way, the very major value of the Anglo-American "biomedical-ethical" (and more general) tradition, has been questioned, especially under the pressure of the new mantra "Use it or lose it!" (Evans 2009).

The American glorifying of autonomy, according to the pioneer of bioethics, Daniel Callahan of the New York Hastings Center, should be viewed as opposed to the European ideal of solidarity: this opposition not only explains basic differences between the traditions of healthcare and insurance systems in the USA and Europe, but may also be the root of the divergences between Anglo-American and European approaches to bioethics. As Callahan puts it, "bioethics American style seems a bit too enamored of John Stuart Mill's 'harm principle' that we may act as we please as well as we do no harm to others [. . .] seems to leave little room for determining what we owe to others to advance their good and that of the society." Sometimes very explicit stands against the notions and practices of solidarity or communitarianism (cf., for instance, Margaret Thatcher's view that "there is no such thing as society"), represent a very good base for the development of personalised medicine, but only within the Anglo-American culture (Callahan and Symons 2015).

4 Conclusion

Before concluding, we believe another possible consequence should not be ignored as well: that is the lack of personalisation in personalised medicine. Namely, the term personalised is burdened by high expectations, but in the real life it is more the "matter of degree." Here, "personalized medication" can logically, but not realistically, be interpreted as medication developed to suit the single individual. The realistic interpretation is that personalised medication is "relatively individualized" in the sense of drugs having a more limited group specificity than the earlier "one size fits all" drugs (Evans 2009, pp. 427–434). It is more buying S, M or L size of the same T-shirt, than going to a tailor to make new clothing just for us.

In conclusion: it is not possible to slow down or stop developing personalised medicine. It should not be advisable to slow down or stop this development. However, like in any other field of medicine or human activity in general, one must expect new problems typically following new discoveries. Those problems will certainly include further deepening of the gap between the poor and the wealthy, as well as the gap between the inquisitive science and the overprotective ethics: but this is only a reflex of the eternal gap between the IS and the OUGHT.

References

Annas G (2014) Personalized medicine or public health? Bioethics, human rights, and choice. Rev Port Saude Publica 32(2):158–163

Callahan D (2015) Daniel Callahan on communitarian bioethics. BioEdge October 28. http://www.bioedge.org/bioethics/interview-with-daniel-callahan/11626. Accessed 30 Sep 2016 (interview by Xavier Symons)

Chatterjee B, Pancholi J (2011) *Prakriti*-based medicine: a step toward personalized medicine. Int Q J Res Ayurveda AYU 32(2):141–146

Engelhardt TH (1996) The foundations of bioethics. Oxford University Press, New York/Oxford, p 3

Evans K (2009) Personalized medicine in psychiatry: ethical challenges and opportunities. Dialogues Clin Neurosci 11(4):429

Food and Drug Administration (2013) Paving the way for personalized medicine: FDA's role in a new era of medical product development. http://www.fda.gov/. Accessed 26 June 2016

Hedgecoe A (2004) The politics of personalised medicine: pharmacogenetics in the clinic. Cambridge University Press, Oxford. (publisher book excerpt)

Lewis J, Lipworth W, Kerridge I (2014) Ethics, evidence and economics in the pursuit of personalized medicine. J Pers Med 4(2):137–146

Muzur A, Rinčić I (2015) Između znanja i mudrosti: Van Rensselaer Potter i njegovo mjesto u povijesti bioetike (Between knowledge and wisdom: Van Rensselaer Potter and his place in the history of bioethics). Pergamena, Zagreb

Pavelić K et al (2014) Do we understand the personalized medicine paradigm? EMBO Rep (16):133–136. https://doi.org/10.15252/embr.201439609

Personalised Medicine Coalition (2011) The case for personalised medicine, 3rd edn

Rinčić I, Muzur A (2012) Fritz Jahr i rađanje europske bioetike (Fritz Jahr and the emerging of European bioethics). Pergamena, Zagreb

Schleidgen S et al (2013) What is personalised medicine: sharpening a vague term based on a systematic literature review. BMC Biomed Ethics (14):55

Patient-Physician Relationship in Personalized Medicine

Krešimir Pavelić, Sandra Kraljević Pavelić, Tamara Martinović, Eugen Teklić, and Jelka Reberšek-Gorišek

Abstract Present paper comprehensively covers the patient-physician relationship, widely considered as a key factor in social care and essential for the realization of high quality health care. As the visit to the physician and the patient-physician relationship will experience significant changes in the near future, which is because of the implementation of personalized medicine into the health care system, we discuss current issues in development of this relationship. Health care professionals will indeed, make decisions based on complex biological and environmental information, as well as on the patient's life style in the near future. Therefore, development of technological solutions for citizens and patients (*e.g.* so-called *omics* technology) will be needed to help in decision making and their implementation will demand a close collaboration of technologists, health care professionals, communication experts, and citizens. A proper development of such possibilities would eventually lead to the transfer of individual health into the domain of the individual person who would then be in charge of their own health. With the intention to educate citizens as active participants in the process of decision-making on complex questions such as genomics, information, and privacy, promotion of adequate levels of health care literacy should be pursued by a wide interdisciplinary initiative.

K. Pavelić (✉)
Juraj Dobrila University of Pula, Faculty of Medicine, Pula, Croatia

Department of Biotechnology, Centre for High-Throughput Technologies, University of Rijeka, Rijeka, Croatia
e-mail: pavelic@unipu.hr

S. Kraljević Pavelić · T. Martinović
Department of Biotechnology, Centre for High-Throughput Technologies, University of Rijeka, Rijeka, Croatia
e-mail: sandrakp@uniri.hr

E. Teklić
Faculty of Medicine, Juraj Dobrila University of Pula, Pula, Croatia

J. Reberšek-Gorišek
University of Maribor, Maribor, Slovenia

© Springer Nature Switzerland AG 2019
N. Bodiroga-Vukobrat et al. (eds.), *Personalized Medicine in Healthcare Systems*, Europeanization and Globalization 5, https://doi.org/10.1007/978-3-030-16465-2_18

1   Introduction

Patient-doctor relationship is considered an important factor of the social care system. Undoubtedly, this relationship is essential for the realization of high quality health care and represents the very foundation of universal medicinal ethics.[1] Medicine students are lacking instructions on how to form and maintain a professional relationship towards the patient, how to keep the patient's dignity on a high level, and finally, how to respect the patient's privacy. Moreover, personalized medicine, as a relatively new medical discipline, opens new perspectives onto the patient-physician relationship.[2] In a broad sense, personalized medicine represents customization of health care system and welfare which is accommodating to the individual and its personality as much as possible and in all stages of the medical process—from prevention, over diagnosis and treatment, to monitoring of disease outcome upon treatment. Personalized medicine is usually described as a deflection from the *one-size-fits-all* approach to the one in which health care is based on distinct biological traits of each individual and in the frame of the specific sociocultural and ecological context.[3] Expectations from personalized medicine are high. Patients who are fully willing to participate are hoping that they will receive individually tailored therapy if the disease develops, as well as an individual approach to the strategy of prevention based on the continuous following of the biological profile. In general, there are too many faulty interpretations of personalized medicine, thus reading a recent review on this topic is recommended.[4] Patient-physician relationship is based on three important principles: (i) the physician is obliged to act in the patient's best interest, (ii) patients need to be treated with respect, without discrimination during the whole process, even if the relationship seems to be coming to an end (Policy Statement #3-08, 2013),[5] (iii) maximal high quality health care needs to be ensured. It is a unique relationship that depends on the trust between the patient and the physician. By accepting the patient, the physician is automatically obliged to ensure the best possible service quality. If the physician cannot comply, he should leave the relationship, for otherwise it could significantly influence the quality of the health care outcome.[6]

---

[1]Trnog (2012).

[2]Simpson et al. (1991).

[3]Pavelić et al. (2016).

[4]Pavelić et al. (2015).

[5]Policy Statement #3-08, College of physicians and Surgeons of Ontario. 1-4, 2013.

[6]Suchman and Matthews (1988) and Suchman et al. (1997).

2 Alternations in the Nature of the Relationship

During the last few years, the patient-physician relationship has been significantly changing.[7] More than 20 years ago, the patient was the one to ask a physician for help, who then brought an autonomous decision and the patient, in principle, agreed with the physician's decision. In the paternalistic relationship model, the physician used his skills to the best of his capabilities to choose interventions and procedures essential for solving the patient's hardships. In doing so, all the information was selected to help the patient to embrace the doctor's chosen approach, making the patient-physician interaction asymmetrical or unbalanced. During the last 20 years, that relationship has changed into a more active, autonomous and patient oriented one. It is characterized by a significantly higher control from the patient, reduced physician domination and a meaningfully more expressed mutual participation.[8] This trend continues and further potentiates in the era of personalized medicine, where the patient becomes responsible for the duration and the outcome of the health care process. In the 1950s and the 1960s, especially in the USA, patient-physician relationship came down to a patient-family doctor relationship. The family doctor, among other duties, supervised the hospital proceedings and took care of the cumulative health care. During the 1980s and the 1990s, the expenses of health care rose drastically and became a burden for the private sector and the state. On the one hand, the expenses rise because of the advancement of technologies, and on the other, the state attempts to reduce such expenses, but largely awards the advancement of medical technology, super-specialist training, and reduces its support to the family physicians. These processes are essentially worldwide ubiquitous. Family physicians are faced with reduced premiums, which force them to take on a larger number of patients (spending an average of ten minutes on a patient) with earnings that are half of the earnings of a specialist. This undoubtedly affects the negative patient-physician relationship.[9]

3 Factors That Influence Communication and the Relationship

When one discusses communication in a patient-physician relationship, several factors should be considered: different purposes and aims of medical communication, as well as communication analysis, specificity of communicative behavior, and the influence of communicative behavior on the patient's outcome (Table 1).

---

[7]Trnog (2012).

[8]Kaba and Sooriakumaren (2007).

[9]Hixon (2015).

Table 1 Factors that may influence the relationship	Education (both parties)
	Quality of medicine
	Number of patients
	Integrity of the doctor
	Access to reliable information
	Health care system
	Health care industry
	Degree of medicine personalization

Three goals of communication have been identified: creation of a respectable mutual relationship, information exchange, and treatment decision-making. Communication that takes place during the medical health care process can be analyzed using Interaction Analysis Systems (IAS). These systems differ on clinical relevance, observational strategy, reliability and value, as well as communicative behavior channels. At the same time, there are several communication codes of conduct that need to be considered; instrumental, mostly cure oriented *vs.* care oriented behavior, verbal *vs.* nonverbal communication, private behavior, behavior with good and bad control, and finally, medicinal *vs.* non medicinal everyday language vocabulary. Consequences and results of specific physician's behavior in relation to above-mentioned factors might be diverse for the patient: content, discontent, persistence, dedication to the treatment, understanding and accepting information.[10]

The quality of the patient-physician relationship may also be affected by factors such as race, ethnicity, and language. American studies show that minority population patients, especially those that are not fluent in English, have smaller chances of acquiring doctor's emphatic relationship and response, as well as getting doctor's adequate report and opinion. Consequently, such patients are somewhat discouraged, which does not contribute to the creation of a healthy relationship and accurate health care decisions.[11] System reforms also influence relationships. With the appearance of three models, especially in the USA, relationships are transforming rather quickly. Those three models are as follows: integrated health care model, direct primary health care model and retail care model. Pros and cons of these models have been elaborated in the literature,[12] and their impact on the patient-physician relationships might be drastic and variable, depending on the model's availability to the patient. Relationships are also affected by factors of changes in the society and challenges which medicine is facing. New challenges in medicine are the need for new breakthroughs because of the relative inefficacy of today's medicine, especially in the treatment of chronic diseases, the development of new generation global analytical technologies and methods which can be immediately implemented

---

[10]Ong and de Haes (1995).

[11]Ferguson and Candib (2002).

[12]Hixon (2015).

Table 2 Potential problems in the patient-physician relationship and the meaning of lacking time for patient

Less relating time and damage to care
Less-accurate and incomplete data
Difficulty in identifying the real problems
Less efficiency in test and treatment choices based on knowledge of the individual patient
Less trust
Less healing
More errors
More waste

into clinical practice,[13] fast society changes because of globalization, new, dangerous and fast spreading contagious diseases, modification of disease forms and therapy resistance, as well as demographic alterations with the aging of the population. The continuous increase of chronic illnesses whose roots partly lie in lifestyle habits should be considered as well. This amounts for more than 80% of medical care expenditures. Although an enormous progress in medicine has been noted, one starts to cope with the disease only when symptoms arise, and that does generally not help in solving the problem of chronic diseases. Therefore, the health care system faces new challenges and dictates structural changes of the system and the patient-physician relationship.[14]

4 What Can Challenge the Relationship?

The patient-physician relationship is highly important to both parties. The better the relationship is, considering mutual respect, trust, knowledge, shared values and available time, the better is the quantity and quality of information regarding patient's disease. This may directly affect a positive outcome in both directions, improve the exactness of the diagnosis, and perfect the patient's knowledge of the disease. In such cases where this relationship is poor, the doctor's ability to give a whole and quality judgment can negatively affect the results and perturb the patient's trust in diagnosis and suggested treatment, and cause patient's objections and complaints regarding the suggested medical actions. The relationship should not involve the difference in power and position between the patient and the doctor, although that is often not the case. There are numerous problems in the patient-physician relationship (Table 2). Hypothetical factors that can affect that relationship are, among others, the over- encumbrance of the doctor, as well as the burden of complexity of applying new high-throughput diagnostic procedures. The expeditious development of medicine and technology poses a problem for the physicians

---

[13]Pavelić et al. (2016).

[14]Hixon (2015).

Table 3 Control over medical data

A concern for personalized medicine is who retains control over data collected across the life course of the individual
One possible solution would be for individuals themselves to keep the information in the form of individual health records and other relevant datasets that are accessible through an appropriate technological interface
By shifting the locus of control away from the physician or health-care system, this may give citizens greater control of their own health and personal information

who have difficulties with following such dramatic changes next to everyday clinical practice.[15] There is also the danger of the uncritical use of sophisticated methods. The patient can become the subject of unnecessary follow-up tests, causing added morbidity. Finally, hypothetical factors encompass also the potential costs of personalized medicine that could substantially increase at the beginning, without an obvious benefit to the patient.[16]

From a legal point of view, the relationship is a fiduciary one,[17] as the physician is expected to treat the patient in his best interest, even when the patient's interest might be in contrast to the doctor's. Therefore, being a physician and practicing medical care is a moral act. Considering the efficacy (treatment result), the patient-physician relationship seems to have a small, but statistically significant, impact on the health care outcome. The outcome of the patient-physician relationship is also affected by evidence-based medicine. Practice standardization is typically used for care management to minimize the price or maximize quality care. Standardization essentially entails treating different individuals in the same way. The danger for the patient-physician relationship arises when an individual patient with individual needs and preferences gets only superficially appreciated, making it of great importance to follow previously adopted directives.

Technology which is becoming all the more accessible will spread social and economic advantages, but it will also create big databases, especially involving sensible data. One of the main assumptions regarding the acceptance of IT technologies in the field of health protection is the question of trust placed by the patients in the security of personal data, but also the patient-physician confidentiality; *i.e.* how are the sensitive data concerning health protected as personal data. The complexity of this question is obvious; so is the need for legal and technical adjustments of national legislations to the EU *acquis* by Member States, as well as candidate countries. Apart from the classical patient-physician relation, the protection of personal data in personalised medicine will be one of the main issues (especially when it comes to genome sequencing, diagnosis which concerns not only the patient, but also his or her family members and predictive tests) (Table 3).

---

[15]Weston and Hood (2004), Bošnjak et al. (2008).

[16]Hapgood (2003).

[17]Ludwig and Burke (2014).

5 The Relationship Participants' Education in the Context of Personalized Medicine

Patient's and physician's education are crucial factors in a patient-physician relationship. If citizens want to be active participants in the decision-making process related to questions on privacy (genomic and other personal information), there is a need to acknowledge and promote adequate levels of medical literacy for the benefit of the collaboration and participation of both parties. Information on health issues is, therefore, of great importance for the patient-physician relationship. Citizens equip themselves with skills that enable better control over their own health, as well as active participation in the personalized medicine system only through access to relevant information. Both sides will benefit from this approach—the individual and the society as a whole. Therefore, access to information is a key factor in the attempt to position the patient/citizen in the center of the health care process in personalized medicine. Participation does not mean a central positioning of the citizen only; it is actually a prerequisite for the realization of personal medicine. Personalized medicine is a highly data-driven approach and the development of an algorithm that will help with the choice of treatment, prognostic evaluation and monitoring will depend on the opportunity to access information by a large number of citizens with respect to regional, cultural, and socio-economical distribution. Many citizens already use a wide spectrum of technological tools (*e.g.* Smartphone applications) with the aim of generating and analyzing information. Some of those facts can be especially useful for research and clinical decision on adequate health care. Still, a too simplistic and technical approach to the informatics tools may be misleading and bring severe losses to the holistic concept of a human being. Currently, the citizens acquire information in the field of personalized medicine varyingly. Some will indeed need education and targeted information supply to augment their medical literacy. Others will need help in barrier removal and elevating quality standards. An important step towards wide social participation is to ensure that information is gathered and exchanged in an accessible way for each shareholders group. The principle is applicable at each level of participation. It is imperative to empower collaboration as opposed to hierarchical participation. Shareholder's participation is equally appropriate in relations between bio-scientists, technologists, and medical professionals. Primary care physicians and other specialist physicians will need to display complex data in a way that will ameliorate the speed of decision-making. To develop appropriate relationships, technologists will need to include the participation of medical professionals and listen to their desires and needs rather than to try and educate them in their own field. A positive impact on the patient-physician relationship is provided by an increased confidentiality in therapeutic decisions because of a combination between engrossed availability of diagnostic information and an improved system of decision support that ensures development in both communications and informatics technologies. The Internet nowadays plays a major role in patients' informing and, therefore, patients' activism is growing, which represents a notable challenge for physicians. Patients see the

Internet as an added source of support to the already established and useful relation with the doctor. A study has, for example, concluded that physicians should not feel threatened if patients bring information downloaded from the Internet, but should rather see it as an attempt of 'team work' and should adequately react in a positive manner.[18]

It is worth noting that personalized medicine implies collaboration and incorporation of multiple scientific disciplines but also social backgrounds related to culture and history, because each field that participates in such a social movement may contribute to realization of its goals. Patients' welfare is an important segment, making it a topic on which different social contexts in general terms may also give relevant judgments. Indeed, personal medicine is not only a medical, but a sociological movement as well.[19] Patient's welfare is, in everyday life, considered to be a general human quality, cherished as a civilization achievement. Technological achievements enable scientists to advance in genetics, cloning, stem cell research, regenerative medicine, personalized diagnosis etc. and such modern development enable a quality of life based on technological achievements. Still it should be noted that the value of life evaluated philosophically within different opinions or even religions makes an important contribution to individual's understanding of humanity or human beings, and in that context to the personalized medicine idea as well.[20,21] For example, the physical wellbeing of a patient through alleviation and elimination of disease symptoms is unquestionable. Still, ethical questions on the rights of a person to make decision by free will and to choose "not to know" or "not to be subjected to medical treatment" remain unanswered or differently explained. This is particularly important in the context of development of preventive medicine where technological advances may offer a deep insight into 'possibilities' to develop disease while not giving finite answers to whether these 'possibilities' will develop in time. As a concluding remark, society, institutions and even individuals have important means and tools to support a patient in different ways, not only by providing technical medical care but also to provide education that considers the individual societal context as well.

6 Relationship in the Context of "New Medicine"

In the beginning, the importance of the patient-physician relationship has been emphasized. A wholesome medical plan is based on that relationship—data gathering, planning of diagnostic procedures, treatment process, activity, and patient support. This relationship will likely dramatically change with the development of

---

[18]Stevenson et al. (2007).

[19]Pavelić et al. (2015).

[20]Clayton and Simpson (2006).

[21]Steiner (2004).

personalized medicine, although, in some aspects, it will stay alike. Personalized medicine offers a lifelong approach to health care through collecting and integrating information in an individual medical dossier throughout life. Such an approach provides abundant opportunities for prevention of individual risk of the development of specific diseases. Further, it enables significantly greater possibilities for an early intervention following the identification of the disease through exposing pathological changes, making it possible for an individual to generate his own personal physiology and, possibly, pathophysiology. The development of technological solutions for citizens and patients will demand a close collaboration of technologists, health care professionals, communication experts, and citizens. Such possibilities would lead to the transfer of the role for individual health into the domain of the individual who would then take care of his own health. The implementation of personalized medicine facilitates the participation of health care professionals and citizens, as well as others who could further spur the initiative. Now, the disciplines that keep personalized medicine informed are mostly not communicating. It is essential to promote mutual understanding and to develop the right tools for personalized medicine. A long-term future of personalized medicine lies in the training of interdisciplinary professionals who are adequately trained in biology, mathematics, and physics. It is important to further develop bioinformatics, imaging and -omics techniques needed for personalized medicine support. It is difficult to predict the future of a patient-physician relationship. It may be that a visit to the physician will radically change. One can assume that, in certain instances, the patient will talk to a certain software program through the screen.[22] Nano-sensors, built into the apartment and/or the organism, will be able to detect the disease in its pre-symptomatic phase and in that way enable intervention on time, still if the patient will opt for this approach in full consciousness and free will. Tissue engineering and stem cell therapy will enable reparation of already established organ damages.[23] The explosion of medicine is not sustained only by quantum theory but with the computer revolution as well. The patient-physician relationship will drastically change. Health care workers will be invited to make a decision based on a complex biological, ecological, and informational approach on lifestyle. Biologists and technologists will interact with each other while understanding the need for professional responsibility or patient's care. Citizens will have approach to unheard possibilities to take responsibility for their own health through active monitoring, preventive measures, and even through a direct choice of treatment. At the end, the decisions will be made on a synthesis and evaluation of very complex feedbacks where it seems that the human being will finally be in charge of decisions related to own health by a free, individual choice.[24]

---

[22]Kaku (2011).

[23]Martinović and Pavelić (2015).

[24]This paper is supported by the Croatian Science Foundation project no. IP-2013-11-5709 "Perspectives of maintaining the social state: towards the transformation of social security systems for individuals in personalized medicine" and University of Rijeka research grants 13.11.1.1.11 and

References

Bošnjak H, Pavelić K, Kraljević Pavelić S (2008) Towards preventive medicine. High-throughput methods from molecular biology are about to change daily clinical practice. EMBO Rep 9:1056–1060

Clayton PZ, Simpson Z (2006) The Oxford handbook of religion and science. Oxford University Press, New York

Ferguson WJ, Candib LMC (2002) Culture, language and the doctor-patient relationship. Fam Med 34:353–361

Hapgood R (2003) The potential and limitations of personalized medicine in the doctor-patient relationship. Pharmacogenomics 4:685–687

Hixon T (2015) The doctor/patient relationship is at a crossroads. Forbes:1–2

Kaba R, Sooriakumaren P (2007) The evolution of the doctor-patient relationship. Int J Surg 5:57–65

Kaku M (2011) Future of medicine. In: Physics of the future. Doubleday Inc., New York-Toronto, pp 68–96

Ludwig MJ, Burke W (2014) Physician-patient relationship. University of Washington School of Medicine

Martinović T, Pavelić K (2015) Stem cells and regenerative medicine: scientific, political and social aspects. Period Biol 117:5–10

Ong LM, de Haes JCJM (1995) Doctor-patient communication: a review of literature. Soc Sci Med 40:903–918

Pavelić K, Martinović T, Kraljević Pavelić S (2015) Do we understand the personalized medicine paradigm? Personalized medicine marks the beginning of a new attitude of medicine. EMBO Rep 16:133–136

Pavelić K, Sedić M, Kraljević Pavelić S (2016) Personalized medicine - the path to new medicine. In: Bodiroga-Vukobrat N, Rukavina D, Pavelić K, Sander GG (eds) Personalized medicine: a new medical and social challenge (Europeanization and globalization). Springer International Publishing, New York

Policy Statement #3-08: Ending the Physician-Patient Relationship. College of physicians and Surgeons of Ontario. 1–4, 2013

Simpson M, Buckman R, Stewart M, Maquire P, Lipkin M, Novack D, Till J (1991) Simpson-patient communication: the Toronto consensus statement. Br Med J 303:1385–1387

Steiner R (2004) Study of man: general education course (Kindle edition). Rudolf Steiner Press

Stevenson FA, Kerr C, Murray E, Nazareth I (2007) Information from the internet and the doctor-patient relationship: patient perspective – a quantitative study. BMC Fam Pract 8:47–54

Suchman AL, Matthews DA (1988) What makes the patient-physician relationship therapeutic? Exploring the connexional dimensions of medical care. Ann Intern Med 1008:125–130

Suchman AL, Markakis K, Beckman MB, Frankel R (1997) A model of emphatic communication in the medical interview. J Am Med Assoc 277:678–682

Trnog RD (2012) Patients and physicians- the evolution of a relationship. N Engl Med J 366:581–585

Weston AD, Hood L (2004) Systems biology, proteomics, and future of health care: toward predictive, preventative, and personalized medicine. J Proteom Res 3:179–196

13.11.1.2.01. We acknowledge University of Rijeka project "Research Infrastructure for Campus-based Laboratories at University of Rijeka", financed by European Regional Development Fund (ERDF).

Barriers Towards New Medicine: Personalized and Integrative Medicine Concepts

Krešimir Pavelić, Željko Perdija, and Sandra Kraljević Pavelić

Abstract Technological advancements and enormous achievements in the biomedical field are presented daily. Still, everyday clinical environment lacks major breakthroughs often because of individual set-up of patients making them unique when it comes to management and treatment. A truly individual approach might therefore, transform quality of health-care and effectiveness of medicine. Implementation of such individualized medicine requires new global technologies and methods as well as a holistic view to a patient. In this paper, we discuss and present the personalized and integrative medicine paradigms as major drivers of radical changes in the system of health care that may solve some major issues that medicine faces today, *i.e.* globalization, new and fast growing infectious diseases, changes in behavior patterns of disease and aging population. Policy makers, health-authorities and public bodies are encouraged to enter this cross-sectorial debate and facilitate the public dialogue on such medical concept value and conditions for its success.

1 Introduction

In modern society a scientist working in the field of life science, and in particular biomedicine, is being continuously supplied and confronted with enormous amounts of novel data, results, knowledge and technological advancements, all having common denominators 'promising' and 'exciting'. Controversially, growing

K. Pavelić (✉)
Juraj Dobrila University of Pula, Faculty of Medicine, Pula, Croatia

Department of Biotechnology, Centre for High-Throughput Technologies, University of Rijeka, Rijeka, Croatia
e-mail: pavelic@unipu.hr

Ž. Perdija
Medical Centre CIIM Plus, Maribor, Slovenia

S. Kraljević Pavelić
Department of Biotechnology, Centre for High-Throughput Technologies, University of Rijeka, Rijeka, Croatia
e-mail: sandrakp@uniri.hr

© Springer Nature Switzerland AG 2019
N. Bodiroga-Vukobrat et al. (eds.), *Personalized Medicine in Healthcare Systems*,
Europeanization and Globalization 5, https://doi.org/10.1007/978-3-030-16465-2_19

scientific evidence on elements of our material existence brings about fragmented points of view on a common, larger reality to which the study or scientific efforts have been addressed. In particular, in biomedical research enormous achievements are presented daily in the fields of gene manipulation, longevity, nanomedicine or regenerative medicine while in the everyday clinical environment major break-throughs are still lacking or are very slow. This is often because of individual set-up of every patient making her or him unique when it comes to management and treatment. For example, chronic diseases have been recognized among major societal challenges of developed countries and their outcome is rather individual. Indeed, for this group of disease, current medicine still lacks adequate solutions and no substantial progress in treatment regimens has been achieved so far. Moreover, medicine today faces rapid changes in society that are because of globalization, new and fast growing infectious diseases, changes in behavior patterns of some diseases, rapid and dramatic climate change and demographic changes—aging population.[1] Again, new and effective medicine based on personalized and integrative paradigms is far from clinical environments all over the world, in particular in developed countries. Therefore, an open cross-disciplinary discussion on factors hampering implementation of global technologies and methods (termed as –omics methods)[2,3] in clinical medicine should be openly promoted by wide scientific community.

Our opinion is that no rational counter-arguments about the need for implementation of new personalized medicine approach exist among general scientific community and elements of personalized medicine are already included in patient management in developed countries.[4,5] Personalized medicine might also well fit within the concept of integrative medicine and provide a solid base for its advancement. In spite of some controversies about the conditions and modalities of its implementation, a truly integrative approach in management of patients and adequate treatment may pave a way for the holistic medicine to come in the next years. Integrative medicine should be based on ever-growing biomedical innovation interconnected with traditional approaches with the aim to treat a certain patient's condition and at the same time reinforce the patient homeostasis/health and own mechanisms of regeneration and healing.[6] Although the benefits of integrative medicine are visible, we may witness some disputes over this term and the concept (for definition of integrative medicine please refer to the Academic Consortium for Integrative Medicine and Health).[7] Indeed, integrative medicine is perceived as just another term for holistic, complementary, or alternative medicine. This often brings to this discipline a bad image because of grey zones and uncertain outcomes for a

---

[1]Pavelić et al. (2016).
[2]Bošnjak et al. (2008).
[3]Kraljević et al. (2004).
[4]Pavelić et al. (2015).
[5]ESF (2012).
[6]Taw (2015).
[7]Snyderman and Weil (2002).

patient.[8,9] Moreover, this opposition towards integrative medicine is still routed in the traditional western understanding of science and medicine that is based on strong evidence and firm facts. Here, we think that incorporation of new knowledge and scientific achievements from one side with an integral view of life based on a wider understanding of the human being on the other side, may be possible also through personalized medicine approach which may be easily incorporated both within concepts of conventional medicine as well as complementary/alternative (CAM) medicine. One should note that medicine has always been personal but when we use the term 'personalized medicine' today, we emphasize a specific discipline that relies on more refined, sophisticated diagnostic set-up and technological platforms to identify the exact type of disease as well as outset to select the best treatment or determine the right dosage.[10] Doctor who uses personalized medicine tools and approaches considers a number of systemic factors, *i.e.* the patient's unique physiology and genetic background, the physiology of the virus or bacteria and the patient ability to metabolize particular drug (for more information on personalized medicine achievements and challenges please refer to FDA and Personalized medicine coalition).[11]

2 Holistic Medicine in a New Way

Two approaches to treat a patient have been generally recognized—the acknowledgment of the patient spiritual condition and/or acknowledgment of the patient physical state with the consecutive intervention. In our opinion, both the exclusive materialistic-based approach to patient treatment or a purely spiritual-based care may cause severe pitfalls in the healing process. A holistic approach may provide larger benefits to the patient. This approach is still opposed by many medical professionals and as a consequence, patients are increasingly seeking for combined conventional and CAM therapies. Conventional medicine and CAM therapies are then conceived as integrative medicine. The patients already opted for such approach. It seems indeed, that major barriers toward such holistic approach have been intuitively already understood by patients, are purely psychological among medical professionals and are a consequence of the conventional medicine way of teaching in the western countries. Indeed, medical schools and professional medical education is based on analytical dissection of parts (organ/tissue/functional systems) of the human bodies with an as much as possible detailed overview of the part anatomy and known function. However, a human body represents an incredibly complex system of interdependently connected known and unknown mental and physical

---

[8]McLachlan (2010).

[9]Rees and Weil (2001).

[10]Catchpoole et al. (2010).

[11]The Case for Personalized medicine (2014).

structures and functions. Any attempt to neglect any of these factors is conceptually wrong as there are so many examples of direct links between the spiritual and physical systems. For example, strong emotions (fear, anxiety, and excitement) cause release of adrenaline from adrenal glands. Also, in early childhood cortisol release and corresponding stress level is correlated with emotional security and child development.[12] Although spirituality is usually understood as something subjective that lacks much of the objective nature important for assessment by scientific methods, there is no doubt that spiritual state influences health in a great extent and that current science can neither affirm nor deny spirituality as an integral part of the human being.[13,14] Therefore, a designated treatment should be approached comprehensively and with the recognition of both components—spiritual and physical. The only question is how to choose the best treatment and how to harmonize physical and spiritual aspects.

Currently, CAM treatments in medicine are defined as "a group of diverse medical and health care systems, practices, and products that are not presently considered to be part of conventional medicine" (National Center for Complementary and Alternative Medicine (NCCAM). The Use of Complementary and Alternative Medicine in the United States Bethesda, Md: National Institutes of Health; December 2008 available at: https://nccih.nih.gov/research/statistics/2007/camsurvey_fs1.htm#about, accessed on December 2015) and are usually classified into (A) whole alternative medical systems, *i.e.* Chinese and Ayurvedic medicine, homeopathy, anthroposophy; (B) mind-body practice, *i.e.* meditation, prayer, artistic therapies; (C) biologically based practices (dietary supplements, herbal supplements, *i.e.* herbs, minerals, vitamins, or scientifically unproven therapies such as shark cartilage supplements (D) manipulative and body-based practices including chiropractic and massage and (E) energy therapies, *i.e.* qigong, reiki, and electromagnetic field therapies.[15] These approaches are inherently diverse as they rely on different traditions and knowledge and have not been studied extensively by standard scientific methods. For example, evidence has been provided for positive homeopathy effects in childhood diarrhoea, influenza, pain, side-effects of radio- or chemotherapy and upper respiratory tract infection.[16]

History of integrative medicine is relatively short and begins in 1990s when American doctors have become increasingly interested in integrating alternative approaches with their own medical practice. In 1999 the Consortium of Academic Health Centres for Integrative Medicine was established and up to now, almost all major hospitals in USA established centres for integrative medicine. Such centres are

---

[12]Badanes et al. (2012).

[13]Fisher (2011).

[14]Bell et al. (2012).

[15]Tabish (2008).

[16]Mathie (2003).

based in Johns Hopkins Clinic, Mayo Clinic, Duke University, and Georgetown University School of Medicine. American Board of Physician Specialties advertised in June 2013 that it will begin to accredit doctors from integrative medicine. These are important indicators for a change public reaction towards established conventional medicine. Also, a growing number of family physicians expressed interest in acupuncture, hypnotherapy and massage therapy training. Recent studies show that CAM is still increasing in the US and Europe. For example, treatment of pain is being more approached by these therapeutic options because of inefficiency of the standardly prescribed medications. More than half of these patients use dietary supplements or herbal remedies and almost two thirds of patients claim that CAM therapy helped. Between 30 and 70% of cancer patients are turning to CAM as well hoping that such treatment will help them in management of pain.[17]

Current medicine is nevertheless, 'evidence-based medicine' and requires established metric (scientific) methods to measure it's a treatment effectiveness. The currently accepted requirement for health care professionals is to rate quality of scientific evidence for effectiveness of the intervention under the established standards (discussed in 18).[18] Such approach may be considered among current pitfalls for development of integrative medicine. Also, medical research was usually not focused on systematic measurement of many CAM treatments' effectiveness in the manner required by conventional western medicine. At the same time it is often forgotten that many drugs used in conventional medicine originate from plants or natural products.

If the traditional idea of patient care in the focus and in the purpose of the medicine itself is to be considered, academic medicine should understand and "embrace" the research opportunities offered by CAM medicine, even those that do not fit easily within the established routes of western scientific philosophy. For example, the placebo effect has been recognized behind some CAM approaches, sometimes used by conventional medical practitioners as well.[19] Placebo has been recognized by CAM practitioners as a benefit for the patient that does not diminish the therapy validity, especially in reducing disease symptoms. A systemic study of CAM approaches and measurement of their effectiveness by conventional accepted tools and methods may be difficult as some of possible CAM outcomes may not be easily mapped and recorded by established scientific methods which add to discussions on how to evaluate these therapeutic approaches from a scientific point of view. One should note here that CAM approach towards health definition is different: conventional medicine defines it as absence of disease while in the CAM approach health is seen as a balance and homeostasis between the body and external factors. Also, a conventional medicine approach is focused on a particular body area

---

[17]Pan et al. (2000).

[18]Fontanarosa and Lundberg (1998).

[19]Kermen et al. (2010).

or symptoms while CAM works on restoring body homeostasis in general. How then to design a study that would be able to track and map all factors involved in CAM outcomes while so many diverse factors, philosophies and individual patients' traits should be encompassed? Personalized medicine may solve some of these challenges as it can scientifically map genetic factors and biomarkers of disease in the presimptomatic process or during therapy. Indeed, some important facts should be consensually accepted before introducing new, CAM treatments/drugs in medicine at our current scientific level of knowledge: (A) safety, (B) effectiveness and (C) efficiency based on objective evidence. This process is at its very beginning and scientific community and medicine is expected to develop improved evaluation approaches and tools in years to come to provide adequate scientific evidence.[20] Up to now, a number of scientific papers already proved efficacy of such approaches in a clinical environment. For example, acupuncture proved its effectiveness in chemotherapy-induced nausea and vomiting,[21] food supplements proved effective in prevention of high blood pressure and lowering of serum cholesterol,[22] management of heart failure patients[23] or in lowering lipid peroxidation in healthy, overweight, and smoker subjects.[24] Still, published literature on clinical evaluation of CAM provides a large amount of data that is often contradictory or scattered. Indeed, opponents of integrative medicine claim that CAM compromises the effectiveness of existing medicine by involving untested alternative approaches (see footnote 8) and many say that this is not evidence-based and scientific-based science.[25] In reconciling conventional and CAM medicine, an important role might be taken by psychology that is also based on scientific methods and proofs.[26] Psychologists are known to be prone to innovations but at the same time to seek for empirical support in their clinical practice.[27] For example, in conventional medicine, the major principle in healing the patient is based on acting against disease symptoms, which means acting contrary to disease. In psychology however, further to the standard approach, therapeutic stimuli known to produce symptoms like those of the very disorder being treated, are also used in some instances within the behavioural approach known as systematic desensitisation.[28] This interesting idea that a disease can be treated both by counteracting processes leading to symptoms as well as by use of processes and approaches similar to the very disease is very close to some CAM practices and may open up additional lines for integrated medicine research.

---

[20]Spear et al. (2001).

[21]Ezzo et al. (2005).

[22]Randall et al. (2001).

[23]Munkholm et al. (1999).

[24]Davinelli et al. (2015).

[25]Cassidy (2011).

[26]Laycock (1936).

[27]Goodheart et al. (2006).

[28]Dubord (2011).

3   Current Conventional Medicine Major Pitfalls

Current evidence-based medicine is built up around the concept of autonomous medical professional decision-maker who is the sole expert in charge to formulate and implement clinical practice guidelines.[29] Indeed, in current medical environment, valuable knowledge from other professionals or the patient opinion, are simply not usually considered within the patient management process. The reasons behind such system, although strong and historically justified, do not make it less rigid and difficult to evolve.

Moreover, a reductionist model of medicine at the moment lacks the so-called continuum concept of health, has still huge gaps in knowledge, functions on the trial-and-error approach, encounters inefficiency of some of the major drugs (one-drug-fits-all-concept) and in some developed countries declining of life expectancy and significantly more expensive health care system have been documented in the last decade (see footnote 1). The entire system of Western medical education based on the reductionist paradigm does not work for chronic diseases, since it tries to simplify one of the most complex systems—the human body. Further, the absence of continuum concept in contemporary Western medicine is witnessed by the clear-cut diagnostic approach (disease exists or not). By doing this, one may often ignore the whole range of states such as for example hidden health imbalances. If one neglects the continuum concept the possibility to intervene in all stages of the continuum are lost, even when disease symptoms are not present or are so mild that standard diagnostic procedures would not recognize them as such. The sooner we intervene, more chances for curing a patient exist. Accordingly, implementation of personalized medicine where –*omics* methods and approaches are used for mapping and discovering such pre-symptomatic health imbalances might be highly helpful (see footnotes 2, 4).

4   Personalized Medicine Within the Integrative Medicine Paradigm

The essential difference between personalized and integrative medicine is in a strictly conventional principle of personalized medicine where facts can be easily monitored and measured according to established scientific standards. Integrative medicine is less exact and less controllable according to currently available general scientific knowledge and established measurement tools. Although, these fields share common grounds: (A) patient and doctor are partners in the treatment process; (B) all factors that affect health and disease are considered; (C) both personalized and integrative medicines are inquiry driven and very open to new models of care;

---

[29]Timmermans and Mauck (2005).

(D) the concept of the treatment in both approaches goes broader and generally encompasses promotion of health and disease prevention as a vital pilasters of health ; (E) health care is individualized and aims to address the unique patient's condition, needs and circumstances. However, because of its strong scientific background personalized medicine is already implemented in a number of clinical niches. For example, 3D printed organ parts are made individually and are patient-tailored[30] or pharmacogenomics data is an essential requirement within clinical protocols in oncology.[31] This process of personalized medicine implementation in everyday clinical environments remains however slow because of number of reasons elaborated in details (see footnotes 1 and 4). Some of these reasons include historical blockbuster model (one-drug-fits-all-concept), problems in the regulatory environment (see footnote 3), dysfunctional payment system of health care that rewards doctors for activities (complete procedures and prescription drugs) rather than for diagnosis and prevention (see footnote 2) and doctors behavior that is deeply rooted in the trial-and-error medicine.[32] Besides these socially relevant factors, issues in the current validation set-up exist as well. For example, many discovered pharmacogenetics/pharmacogenomics biomarkers failed to be implemented in clinics because of inability to define clear genotype/phenotype associations that might be independently replicated. This might be partially both because of interpersonal variability among humans and variability in phenotype definition.[33] Personalized medicine in comparison to both conventional and integrative medicines wants to implement more refined, often technologically advanced diagnostic tools to identify disease and its outcome. To select the best possible treatment and determine the exact drug dose, doctors would consider the patient's unique physiology, and physiology of the virus or bacteria and the patient's ability to metabolize certain drugs. Here, no substantial differences are seen in comparison with integrative medicine that also reaffirms the importance of the physician-patient relationship by focusing on patient's unique evidence of disease and condition, while insisting on the most appropriate therapeutic approach (Consortium of Academic Health Centres for Integrative Medicine, https://www.imconsortium.org/, accessed on 30th December, 2015). Some university hospitals indeed, point out that a health care model of integrative medicine would take all the best from conventional medicine, available personalized approaches, CAM therapies and lifestyle guidelines emphasizing the healing process based on a firm relationship between the patient and the caregiver (Consortium of Academic Health Centres for Integrative Medicine, https://www.imconsortium.org/, accessed on 30th December, 2015). Personalized medicine can therefore fit perfectly into this paradigm as it may scientifically clarify some systemic features of the patient that is being treated. To effectively couple conventional approaches and personalized medicine procedures with CAM therapy,

---

[30]Ledford (2015).

[31]Reynolds et al. (2014).

[32]Aspinall and Hamermesh (2007).

[33]Carr et al. (2012).

students should however, learn about CAM as well. Students and medical professionals should therefore learn how to include patients in a dialogue on the principles already known within the CAM medicine and understand basics of such therapy. In the same way and *vice versa*, it is necessary to correctly interpret scientific research conducted on CAM therapies and to advise patients about the real, currently available evidence-based facts. This will lead to a more responsible use and application of CAM therapies. A platform for constructive mutual communication between professionals who deal with conventional medicine and those working in the field of CAM is requested by public. The European Science Foundation has already recognized this societal challenge and predicted that integrated and personalized medicine will completely change our current health care, improve population health and health economic model. This premise is based on a well-established fact that investing in scientific research in medicine brings enormous gain to society.[34] Already, the Academic Consortium for Integrative Medicine & Health has been established that brings together more than 60 top academic medical centers and affiliated institutions with the mission of improving the principles and implementation of integrative health care among medical centers. The Consortium provides institutional association with the community to support the academic mission and collective change of attitudes towards the integrative medicine through a wide support to professionals and scientists in the field as well as through advanced training of research and clinical care of integrative medicine.[35]

We see a new medical paradigm that might evolve further and deeper, creating a truly holistic and integrative model aimed to maintain a healthy state. Together doctors and patients might achieve health, providing the best medical treatment available or prevent disease before the symptoms arise. Because of this, some medical professionals feel the need to learn more about personalized and integrative medicine so that they can better screen the patient's condition or advise them which treatments might provide benefits. This is a critical issue as the importance to distinguish treatments that are meaningless still need more scientifically based data. Today, the necessity to create a state of health more than act against a disease *per se* is understood as an important individual achievement. Doctors are often too specialized so that their traditional role of a comprehensive care that focuses on healing and wellness has been gradually neglected. This is generally well-understood by physicians and especially primary care professionals. Some centers of integrative medicine in the United States, have therefore, established serious and comprehensive programs for integrative medicine and health care so far. Here it should be noted that integrative medicine is not synonymous with CAM medicine. Integrative medicine relies on an informative and reliable clinical practice in interactions with the patients; a patient-centered collaborative effort in many different clinical fields.[36] Integrative medicine programs include cooperation of clinical

---

[34]ESF (2007).

[35]Ring et al. (2014).

[36]Horrigan et al. (2012).

medicine, research, and education of students and the population in general. The purpose of such programs is to provide the basis of a widespread, multi-cultural, national model of integrated health care through clinical service, education, research, and consulting. Such programs are financed partly through competitive grants and partly by philanthropy, as the major issue remains a low-cost access to effective integrative therapies available to everyone. It is indeed, well known that some CAM therapies co-existed for centuries along with conventional medicine. Still, frauds drowned financial revenues, caused serious health complications, but still attracted people because of unavailable CAM therapies in the established medical centers. For example, one of three Americans used unconventional therapy and spent 13.7 million of USD on such treatments in the 1990s.[37] This number has been growing increasingly to 33.9 million of USD in 2009 (National Center for Complementary and Integrative Health (NCCIH) and the National Center for Health Statistics (NCHS), https://nccih.nih.gov/news/camstats/costs/costdatafs.htm, accessed on 30th December, 2015). A web platform 'Cohrane' has been created as a response to this trend, that is designed to catalogue scientific research data on CAM approaches in medical practice as a guideline for professionals for a choice of appropriate treatments (www.cochrane.org, accessed on 30th December, 2015). Some opponents of integrative medicine argue that this medicine should not be learned at medical colleagues, as they believe it is full of myths, superstitions, and pseudoscience. It is understandable therefore, why NIH established the Centre for Complementary and Alternative Medicine (NCCIH) to fund scientific basements within these treatments. After two decades of NCCIH existence, several of these treatments showed significantly better than placebo. The need for CAM curriculums within study programs, are meant both to educate the doctor might provide means to increase the dialogue patient-doctor as patients do not usually discuss CAM therapies they undergo with their doctors. Some CAM products may interact with conventional medical treatments and should be carefully monitored. Such lack of dialogue between patients and physicians might hamper the healing process and should be overcome.

5 Conclusions

Although the concept of personalized and integrative medicine is defined, we will need a radical change in the health care system organization and tools to make such a concept possible in a regular clinical practice. For that purpose, interdisciplinary and cross-disciplinary consensus will be required to address such a complex matter. Moreover, the success of personalized and integrative medicine will depend on both patients and doctors. Patients are seeking and will increasingly continue to seek for integrative medicine and this should be seriously considered by the medical

---

[37]Eisenberg et al. (1993).

community as to prevent possible fraudulence or misconducts. New paradigm of medicine will accordingly gradually convert the current, mainly reductionist oriented medicine in a really holistic and integrative medicine, which will focus on preservation of physical health. It has indeed, been recognized that such a focus on maintenance of good health is a basement to controlling healthcare costs. Further, some advancement in regulation of CAM professions is visible in recent years where professions such as chiropractor, osteopath and acupuncturist have been recognized even in many EU countries (Eurocam 2020: The contribution of Complementary and Alternative Medicine to sustainable healthcare in Europe, 2014, Belgium). Moreover, the official CAM curriculums (Bachelor of honors levels) have been introduced in some European Universities as well. This is so important as such holistic approach of the integrative medicine concept does not replace the standard, conventional medicine. It rather explores all possible parameters that lead to imbalances and health problems that a conventional medical doctor cannot usually afford within the limited period for patient management or within her or his regular training. Conventional medicine remains well postulated, helpful and its advancements in recent decades are clear and of great importance to the society. For example, in the case of acute problems, burst of symptoms or life-threatening or emergency situations, *i.e.* myocardial infarction, brain hemorrhage or ruptured appendix all require a fast and effective response. Moreover, a patient that has been successfully recovered from severe situations like that needs a follow-up for a true complete recovery that is currently not being practiced: doctors have a limited set of tools, time, or training possibilities at disposal, so they cannot offer a versatile and flexible approach to patients in the long-term healing process. It should not be forgotten that patient responsibility should be clearly postulated in further implementation platforms of the integrative concept in everyday medicine. Not all the responsibility might be left to health-care professionals. Patients should be aware indeed, that responsibility for their own healthcare is their personal obligation and choice. Here the role of professionals, especially educational and academic institutions is enormous in providing meaningful curriculums for students on one side, and information for citizens on the other side, to make them knowledgeable about broad health-related subjects. At last, the major challenge for development and implementation of integrative medicine, including personalized medicine in clinical practice will be on policy makers. The only way to move forward will be a large society debate of policy makers, health-authorities and other public bodies that should find the way to facilitate the public dialogue on the value of such medical concept and conditions for its success.[38]

[38]This paper is supported by the Croatian Science Foundation project "5709 - Perspectives of maintaining the social state: towards the transformation of social security systems for individuals in personalized medicine" and University of Rijeka research grants 13.11.1.1.11 and 13.11.1.2.01. We acknowledge the project "Research Infrastructure for Campus-based Laboratories at University of Rijeka", financed by European Regional Development Fund (ERDF).

References

Aspinall MG, Hamermesh RG (2007) Realizing the promise of personalised medicine. Harvard Business Review. www.hbrreprints.org. October, pp 1–9

Badanes LS, Dmitrieva J, Watamura SE (2012) Understanding cortisol reactivity across the day at child care: the potential buffering role of secure attachments to caregivers. Early Child Res Q 27 (1):156–165

Bell IR, Caspi O, Schwartz GE et al (2012) Integrative medicine and systemic outcomes research: issues in the emergence of a new model for primary health care. Arch Intern Med 162 (2):133–140

Bošnjak H, Pavelić K, Kraljević Pavelić S (2008) Towards preventive medicine. High-throughput methods from molecular biology are about to change daily clinical practice. EMBO Rep 9:1056–1060

Carr DF, Alfirevic A, Pirmohamed M (2012) Pharmacogenomics: current state-of-the-art. Genes 5:430–443

Cassidy J (2011) Lobby Watch: The College of Medicine. BMJ 342:d3712

Catchpoole DR, Kennedy P, Scillicorn DR et al (2010) The curse of dimensionality: a blessing to personalized medicine. J Clin Oncol 28:e723–e724

Davinelli S, Bertoglio JC, Zarrelli A et al (2015) A randomized clinical trial evaluating the efficacy of an Anthocyanin-Maqui Berry Extract (Delphinol®) on oxidative stress biomarkers. J Am Coll Nutr 34(Suppl 1):28–33

Dubord G (2011) Part 12: systematic desensitization. Can Fam Physician 57(11):1299–1299

Eisenberg DM, Kessler RC, Foster C et al (1993) Unconventional medicine in the United States. Prevalence, costs, and patterns of use. N Engl J Med 328:246–252

European Science Foundation (2007) EMRC White Paper. Present status and future strategy for medical research in Europe. The positive outcome of medical research 13–14

European Science Foundation (2012) Forward Look: personalised medicine for the European citizen. Towards more precise medicine for the diagnosis, treatment and prevention of disease (iPM)European Science Foundation, Strasbourg

Ezzo J, Vickers EA, Richardson MA et al (2005) Acupuncture-point stimulation for chemotherapy-induced nausea and vomiting. Jeanette J Clin Oncol 23(28):7188–7198

Fisher J (2011) The four domains model: connecting spirituality, health and well-being. Religions 2:17–28

Fontanarosa FB, Lundberg GD (1998) Alternative medicine meets science. JAMA 280 (18):1618–1619

Goodheart CD, Kazdin AE, Sternberg RJ (2006) Evidence-based psychotherapy: where practice and research meet. American Psychological Association, Washington, DC, p 296

Horrigan B, Lewis S, Abrams D, Pechura C (2012) Integrative medicine in America—how integrative medicine is being practiced in clinical centers across the United States. Glob Adv Health Med 1(3):18–94

Kermen R, Hickner J, Brody H, Hasham I (2010) Family physicians believe the placebo effect is therapeutic but often use real drugs as placebos. Fam Med 42(9):636–642

Kraljević S, Stambrook PJ, Pavelić K (2004) Accelerating drug discovery. EMBO Rep 5:837–842

Laycock SR (1936) The relation between physiology and medicine. Can Med Assoc J 35:434–438

Ledford H (2015) Printed body parts come alive. Nature 520:273–273

Mathie RT (2003) The research evidence base for homeopathy: a fresh assessment of the literature. Homeopathy 92(2):84–91

McLachlan JC (2010) Integrative medicine and the point of credulity. Br Med J (Feature) 341: c6979

Munkholm H, Hansen HH, Rasmussen K (1999) Coenzyme Q10 treatment in serious heart failure. Biofactors 9:285–289

Pan CX, Morrison RS, Ness J et al (2000) Complementary and alternative medicine in the management of pain, dyspnea, and nausea and vomiting near the end of life: a systematic review. J Pain Sympt Manag 20:374–387

Pavelić K, Martinović T, Kraljević Pavelić S (2015) Do we understand the personalized medicine paradigm? EMBO Rep 16:133–136

Pavelić K, Sedić M, Kraljević Pavelić S (2016) Personalised medicine - the path to new medicine. In: Bodiroga-Vukobrat N, Rukavina D, Pavelic K, Sander GG (eds) Personalized medicine: a new medical and social challenge (Europeanization and globalization). Springer International Publishing, New York, pp 300–320

Randall EM, Cynthia A et al (2001) A review of recent clinical trials of the nutritional supplement chlorella pyrenoidosa in the treatment of fibromyalgia, hypertension, and ulcerative colitis. Altern Ther Health Med 7(3):79–90

Rees L, Weil A (2001) Integrated medicine: imbues orthodox medicine with the values of complementary medicine. Br Med J 322:119–120

Reynolds K, Sarangi S, Bardia A, Dizon DS (2014) Precision medicine and personalized breast cancer: combination pertuzumab therapy. Pharmacogenomics Pers Med 7(1):95–105

Ring M, Brodsky M, Low Dog T, Sierpina V, Bailey M, Locke A, Kogan M, Rindfleisch JA, Saper R (2014) Supplemental digital content for: developing and implementing core competencies for integrative medicine fellowships. Acad Med 89(3):1–15

Snyderman R, Weil AT (2002) Integrative medicine: bringing medicine back to its roots. Arch Intern Med 162(4):395–397

Spear BB, Heath-Chiozzi M, Huff J (2001) Clinical application of pharmacogenetics. Trends Mol Med 7:201–204

Tabish SA (2008) Complementary and alternative healthcare: is it evidence-based? Int J Health Sci (Qassim) 2(1):5–9

Taw MB (2015) Integrative medicine, or not integrative medicine: that is the question. J Integr Med 13(6):350–352

The Case for Personalized medicine (2014) Personalized medicine coalition, 4th edn. Washington, DC

Timmermans S, Mauck A (2005) The promises and pitfalls of evidence-based medicine. Health Aff 24(1):18–28

The Reverse Payment Settlements in the European Pharmaceutical Market

Ana Pošćić

Abstract This chapter analyses the novelties in the EU competition law in pharmaceutical sector. Decisions in cases *Lundbeck*, *Servier* and *J&J/Novartis* reveal the Commission's approach to intellectual property and regulatory issues which delay the market entry of generic pharmaceuticals. This contribution exposes and analyses a recent practice applied by pharmaceutical undertakings as part of their strategy to keep the dominant position in the market. It involves settlements between producers of original and generic pharmaceuticals, under which the producers of original pharmaceuticals undertake the obligation to pay generic producers in exchange for delay of market entry of generic pharmaceuticals. Such settlements are called reverse patent settlements or so-called 'pay for delay' settlements.

1 Introductory Remarks

The pharmaceutical sector displays distinctive market features. It is a fluid and rapidly growing market characterised by high intensity research and development activities in search of new drugs. It occupies an important segment of the EU economy and a significant place in the industrial and health sector.[1] It is a global industry, scrutinised by media as well as regulators. In recent years, it has caught the attention of the European Commission, the most important 'watchman' in the field of competition law next to national regulators. However, a more systematic oversight of the application of competition rules in the pharmaceutical sector did not start

---

[1] See Desogus (2011), p. 28 and further.

A. Pošćić (✉)
Faculty of Law, University of Rijeka, Rijeka, Croatia
e-mail: aposcic@pravri.hr

© Springer Nature Switzerland AG 2019
N. Bodiroga-Vukobrat et al. (eds.), *Personalized Medicine in Healthcare Systems*, Europeanization and Globalization 5, https://doi.org/10.1007/978-3-030-16465-2_20

before 2008.[2] The initial doubt was whether it was appropriate to consider the application of competition rules in this sector at all.

The Commission's inquiry is focused on several different tracks.[3] The first area which causes significant disputes and ranks high on the Commission's list of priorities concerns agreements aimed at delaying the entry of generic companies in the market. A large number of settlements are concluded in this context, under which generic companies are paid to delay the market entry of a generic product which could jeopardise the existing patent of the originator company. Such agreements are called reverse patent settlements or 'pay-for-delay'. In addition to settlement agreements, co-promotion or joint marketing activities agreements are used for the same purpose: preventing generic entry. Although the Commission, as will be shown hereinafter, is mostly focused on reverse patent settlements, it always emphasises that every agreement aimed at postponing the generic entry is problematic from the competition aspect.

National regulators are also faced with the practice of originator companies who try to denigrate certain generic medicines. The European Commission has still not had the opportunity to take position on this issue, but the national regulators have already decided in such cases.[4]

Price setting practices are under scrutiny as well. Although it is known that the Commission does not readily intervene in price setting policies, it is attentive of the

---

[2]Communication from the Commission, Executive Summary of the Pharmaceutical Sector Inquiry Report, 8. July 2009, http://ec.europa.eu/competition/sectors/pharmaceuticals/inquiry/communication_en.pdf. Accessed 28 February 2017.

[3]See Hull and Clancy (2016).

[4]In this context, the judgment of the Paris Court of Appeal from 2014 is especially interesting. It was determined that Sanofi Aventis has abused its dominant position by denigrating generic versions of its blockbuster Plavix. The fine to be paid in this case was extremely high, EUR 40.6 million. The court has confirmed the decision of the French competition agency, which has determined that Sanofi Aventis was involved in a campaign aimed at systematic decrease of the use of the generic version of Plavix. Sanofi Aventis claimed that generic producers use different types of salts than the original medicine and that there are contraindications for the use of generic medicines in combination with aspirin. Sanofi Aventis has tried to defend this practice by arguing that they are required to reveal true information. However, the court emphasised that it is not about the content of information, but the way it was provided. The aim of their policy was to raise doubts in the use of generic products. They even required from doctors to write 'non replaceable' on their prescriptions and have instructed the pharmacists to provide their version of generic medicine, if generic medicine was prescribed. The court has highlighted that the abuse can take a wide variety of forms in practice, including denigration of potential or actual competitors. It emphasises that doctors are not keen on changing their established practice of prescribing verified medicines and they are always cautious about potential risks. Any dissemination of negative information or insinuation that generic medicines can represent a risk is capable of discouraging doctors and pharmacists from prescribing and issuing such medicines, if they have another option. It is especially problematic that Sanofi Aventis was distributing unverified and ambiguous information. In this case, advertising campaign was deemed abusive. It has caused enormous damages to the French social security system. Given the specificity of competition in this sector, it seems it is only a matter of time before another national agency receives similar complaint. Hull and Clancy (2016), p. 154.

certain pharmaceutical undertakings' discount policies, including possible overpricing.

Parallel trade is still controversial from the aspects of free movement of goods and competition. In the pharmaceutical sector, this issue remains unresolved. Different approaches are dictated by the fact that parallel trade has different impact on markets in specific states. Parallel distribution includes the transfer of original brand product approved under the EU legislation which is produced in one Member State, and marketed in another Member State. Such product competes with essentially similar product which is already present in a certain market based on the patent owner's licence. In its beginnings, parallel trade was considered negative and there were even attempts to completely prohibit it. The rationale for parallel trade lies in the possibility to profit from price differences in various Member States. In this context, Member States are responsible for maintaining a balance between assuring access to affordable, high-quality medicinal products and an incentive environment for future research and development, while at the same time preserving the stability of public spending.[5] The prices of medicines are not harmonised, which leaves room for parallel trade and resulting savings for public insurers and patients in importing countries.[6] Case law shows that restriction of parallel trade in principle represents infringement of competition, whether committed by collusion or unilateral behaviour. However, sometimes it can be justified by considering the specific features of the pharmaceutical sector. Consumer benefits are considered, backed up by economic indicators.[7] The pharmaceutical sector mostly agrees with this approach, but there is still lack of clarity and further development is uncertain.

---

[5]Mische et al. (2014), pp. 1910–1911.

[6]In the case of parallel trade, one must always consider the wider context of internal market, controls provided by Articles 101 and 102 TFEU (Treaty on the Functioning of the European Union, Consolidated version 2016, OJ C 202 7 June 2016), and also intellectual property rules. Pharmaceutical companies cannot prohibit parallel trade by invoking the breach of intellectual property. It is established that internal market is the core of the EU, and the Commission and EU courts have always criticised undertakings who tried to prevent parallel trade. Traditionally, the courts have always considered limitations of parallel trade as a restriction of competition by object under Article 101 of the TFEU. The exceptions from Article 101(3) TFEU apply rarely. This view still prevails. However, lately the courts' standpoints have started to change.

[7]The best illustration of the existing challenges is perhaps the case against Pfizer. The facts are the following: the procedure started in 2005, when a Spanish medicines wholesaler complained about Pfizer's policy aimed at restricting parallel trade. Pfizer has imposed lower prices for medicines destined for use in the Spanish health system and for medicines sold elsewhere, especially those destined for export. Commission has referred the matter to be decided by the Spanish competition authority, emphasising similarities with the case Glaxo which was decided by the Court of Justice of the EU. It concerned dual pricing and it was determined that it violates Article 101 TFEU.

However, despite the similarities in factual background, the Spanish competition authority has decided during 2009 that Pfizer did not violate Article 101 TFEU. According to that decision, Pfizer did not have two prices, but only one, more precisely, the higher one. Lower price was a necessary consequence of applying the Spanish medicines' price fixing regulations. The decision was surprising, especially because it departs from the opinion of the EU courts. This can be explained by different effects of parallel trade. Of course, the wholesaler appealed and the Spanish courts have

The practice of reverse payment or 'pay-for-delay' settlements will be analysed here. This concept covers the practice of paying the competitor to delay market entry of a generic product which brings competitive pressure to the existing patent.

2 Defining Reverse Payment Settlements

In competition law, one of the classic definitions of horizontal market power is that it provides the ability to control prices, thus preventing other competitors from entering the market. Any agreement which directly or indirectly fixes purchase or selling prices or any other trading conditions is prohibited in competition law. The U.S. competition law has been dealing with this question for years, but it only recently began to trouble the EU regulators: does the patent owner's payment to potential generic manufacturer represent a prohibited practice within the meaning of competition law? Doctrinal research and case law have lately started to devote more attention to this issue. The question is, what impact do these settlements have on competitiveness and innovation in the pharmaceutical sector? Opinions largely diverge.[8] The prevailing opinion is that preventing generic entry results in output decrease, and therefore, such settlements represent prohibited agreements. They extend the monopoly on original medicine and eventually decrease consumer welfare.[9] Others, backed up by certain indicators pointing to long-term consumer benefits, claim that such behaviour represents an independent competitive behaviour. This opens up a debate on whether consumers want to use benefits immediately in the form of some materialised interests, or have time to wait on long-term gains. This conflict is especially prominent when patients are involved.

Originator and generic companies often enter into settlements, whereby originator companies undertake to pay manufacturers of generic medicines in exchange for

---

accepted his arguments. They held that Pfizer's pricing and supply conditions fall under Article 101 TFEU and represent restriction of competition by object and effect. The Spanish Supreme court annulled the decision and referred the matter back to the Spanish competition authority to re-examine the issue. The Spanish competition authority has adopted a new decision on 19 January 2017. It has concluded that there was no breach of Competition Law (particularly Article 1 Spanish Competition Law) by the supply contracts signed by Pfizer. The 2015 decision is based on internal regulations on the Spanish medicines' price fixing regulations. It examines the different systems of fixing the prices of medicines in Spain (for example, in relation to which medicines does the State intervene; which prices may be freely fixed by companies; what is the wholesale price and the final price fixed by pharmacies?). The system regulation varies depending on who finances the product (in most cases the Spanish State through its agency). The conclusion is that Pfizer determines the product prices of medicines that are not subject to intervention by the Spanish State, but this price could vary considering different degree of rebates given to wholesalers. See Resolución (Expte. S/DC/0546/15 PFIZER/COFARES), 19.1.2017 as well as Mische et al. (2014), p. 1919.

[8]On different opinions see Drake et al. (2014).

[9]Hemphill (2006), p. 1572 and further. Generally on challenges in determination of consumer welfare see Pošćić (2014), p. 46 and further.

delay of generic entry. It is considered that such agreements result in anti-competitive market division. Parties defend such agreements as part of usual business practices intended to lower the costs and risks of long litigation proceedings.

Consumers pay extremely high prices for new original medicines protected by patent monopoly. Prices of those medicines fall when generic medicines enter the market. It is therefore possible to identify a short-term consumer interest in having generic medicines in the market as soon as possible. Nevertheless, there are also long-term benefits in promoting drug research, protected by patent exclusivity that must be considered.

It is important to highlight that settlements are not prohibited by themselves. They arise under problematic circumstances, because originator companies pay in exchange for agreed date of market entry. This reverse payment is aimed at compensating the competitor for delaying the marketing of a generic product. Therefore, the competitor's market entry is postponed, as is the adverse impact it might have on the existing patent. Reverse payments are usual in the context of intellectual property. Originator companies are paying to potential competitors to extend the period of exclusivity. These agreements are criticised as anti-competitive and contrary to public interests mostly because the patent owner pays potential competitors to delay generic entry. The consequence lies in higher consumer prices and less innovation.

The question with these types of agreements is how to strike a balance between innovation and consumer access to medication. The effect of such agreements is that they eliminate potential early competition and decrease the consumers' choices in finding cheaper medicines.

The pharmaceutical policy and the intellectual property policy are closely linked. The pharmaceutical sector relies heavily on the protection accorded by patents and intellectual property. Companies invest in innovation expecting profit, which is enabled by the patent industry. Companies enjoy patent protection for their products, so that they may return their investment in research and development.[10] The practices of certain pharmaceutical companies, however, may under some circumstances lead to infringments of competition. Competition forces the companies to invest in research and new products; settlements weaken these forces and accordingly, lower the motivation for further innovation.

European and American approach differ significantly. Unlike the United States, Europe does not have anything similar to the so-called Hatch-Waxman Act (the Drug Price Competition and Patent Term Restoration Act) from 1984,[11] which prescribes a procedure for dispute resolution between manufacturers of original medicines and manufacturers of generic products. In contrast to the United States, in the EU every Member State issues patents. Originator company which intends to prevent the generic entry must initiate judicial proceedings before courts in the Member States. Conversely, it is very hard and expensive for originator companies to protect their patents and prevent new market entry. If and when they manage to

---

[10]Hemphill (2006), pp. 1562–1563.

[11]See Connor (2015) and Drake et al. (2014), p. 3 and further.

enter the market in one Member State, generic medicines are liable of decreasing prices of medicines, thus creating spill-over effects in other states as well. Therefore, both the originator and the generic company are strongly motivated to close a deal. This deal benefits the generic company as well, because it receives a monetary compensation which is intended to replace the expected profit in case of market entry.[12]

It is important to highlight that under the U.S. case law, payment of a patent owner to potential competitor, which is intended to delay generic entry can be declared illegal, but only after weighing it against the rule of reason. In the EU, such payments are deemed as civil infractions.[13]

Before 2008, there was no guide in the EU on the lawfulness of such settlements. They formed a 'gray area', which eventually in 2004 led the Commission to declare that it intends to "initiate the analyses of such cases and attempt to adopt appropriate standards for examination of such settlements".[14] In 2009, the Commission has published the first report on competition in the pharmaceutical sector.[15] It was followed by seven additional inquiries, the last one being published at the end of 2016.[16] According to the Commission, it is possible to differentiate between agreements limiting the generic entry and those that do not. The first group can be subdivided into agreements that imply a certain value transfer, and those without such element. Settlements limiting the generic entry and having the value transfer element are the most problematic. Other settlements are not interesting from the aspect of competition law. The Commission interprets the concepts of "limitation of entry" and "value transfer" very broadly. Such agreements mostly contain a clause in which the generic company acknowledges the patent and sustains from market entry until the patent expires.[17] Even when such agreements include a provision under which the originator company provides the generic company with a licence, this can also be considered as limitation of entry. Conversely, generic company cannot enter the market unless it has concluded an agreement with the originator company. Value transfer can take different forms. It mostly involves monetary transfers, but it can also imply payment of legal costs to the generic company in a patent dispute. It can involve a distribution agreement, whereby the generic company becomes the distributor of the original medicines.

---

[12]Clancy et al. (2013), p. 9.

[13]See more: Connor (2015), p. 2.

[14]Clancy et al. (2013), p. 10.

[15]Communication from the Commission, Executive Summary of the Pharmaceutical Sector Inquiry Report, 8. July 2009, http://ec.europa.eu/competition/sectors/pharmaceuticals/inquiry/communica tion_en.pdf. Accessed 28 February 2017.

[16]Report on the Monitoring of Patent Settlements, (period: January–December 2015), http://ec. europa.eu/competition/sectors/pharmaceuticals/inquiry/patent_settlements_report7_en.pdf. Accessed 25 February 2017.

[17]See more on this subject: Schmid (2012), pp. 367–375.

2.1 Decisions of the European Commission

In recent years, the European Commission has dedicated more and more attention to settlements between manufacturers of original and generic medicines. Settlements containing the value transfer element as a consideration for delay of market entry are especially challenging from the aspect of competition law. The Commission has adopted only two decisions in this area, *Lundbeck* and *Servier*.

In the first *Lundbeck* decision,[18] the Commission has analysed six agreements in force during 2002 and 2003, among the Danish pharmaceutical originator company Lundbeck and four manufacturers of generic medicines. The Commission has established that these agreements have infringed competition law. The subject of infringement was an antidepressant medicine citalopram in the form of active pharmaceutical ingredient or medicine. The facts of the case are the following:

At the time of conclusion of those agreements, basic patents for the citalopram molecule and two original production processes have expired. Lundbeck still held a limited number of process patents, which gave Lundbeck exclusivity rights on certain (but not all) new ways of producing citalopram to the extent such patents would be found to be valid and infringed. But the general rule is that any undertaking using either the original production processes or any production process not covered by valid Lundbeck process patents could in principle freely market generic citalopram, provided the product and its production process met regulatory requirements applicable in individual Member States.[19]

Given the imminent market entry, it became really important for Lundbeck to delay as long as possible the entry of generic citalopram in European markets. Lundback has implemented various policies to delay the market entry of generic producers. It executed a complex strategy which included patenting citalopram manufacture processes, intervening in marketing authorisation procedures for generic citalopram and persuading generic suppliers to stop their efforts to enter the citalopram market.

It should be highlighted that the agreements were concluded to prevent potential patent related disputes between Lundbeck and generic manufacturers who intended to market citalopram, either in the form of active pharmaceutical compound or a medicine. The Commission has confirmed its standpoint that patent settlements in general represent acceptable and legitimate manner of resolving potential disagreements. They save time, and alleviate the pressure of courts and competent administrative bodies.[20]

Prior agreements were examined by the Danish competition agency and the Commission in 2003.[21] At the time the decision was published, the former Commissioner for competition Almunia declared it unacceptable for an undertaking to

---

[18]Case AT.39226—*Lundbeck*, Commission decision of 19.6.2013, C (2013) 3803 final.

[19]*Lundbeck*, para 3.

[20]*Lundbeck*, paras. 4–5.

[21]Clancy et al. (2013), p. 10.

pay off its competitors to keep off the market and delay the entry of cheaper generic medicines.[22] The decision was confirmed in the appelate procedure before the General Court.[23] It is the first CJEU judgment on reverse payment settlements. Although there were some ideas that the General Court might take a different approach, the decision has 'passed' the General Court's test. The confirmatory judgment of the General Court is not surprising, because even before it was adopted, it was possible to predict the direction the General Court would follow.

In *Centrafarm*,[24] the Court decided on the relation between competition law and intellectual property law by emphasising that the national intellectual property law itself is in no way affected by Article 101 TFEU, but the exercise of those rights may be affected by the prohibitions arising under Article 101 TFEU. This is especially so when the exercise of that right is the objective, method and consequence of the agreement. In case *Bayer*[25] the Court confirmed that the concept of agreement from Article 101 TFEU also includes settlements. There is no exception for settlements. It should be emphasised that the parties are always bound by competition rules, even when concluding settlements.[26]

A similar case *Servier*[27] was decided in July 2014. Servier and five generic manufacturers received one of the largest fines in the history of EU competition law: EUR 427,696,508.

The facts were the following: Servier has concluded several settlements with manufacturers of generic medicines, aiming to protect its medicine perindopril from generic competitors. In addition to concluding settlements, Servier has also bought technological processes, in an attempt to eliminate competition from the market and to prevent the market entry of a cheaper generic drug. The Commission considered these actions as contrary to public budgets and declared them contrary to the competition law.

As the competition Commissioner Almunia has stated, Servier's tactic was to buy all potential threats, so as to be sure that they will stay off the market. Such behaviour is anti-competitive and represents an abuse of dominant position. In addition to representing a harm to competition, such practice harms patients, national health systems and tax payers as well.[28]

Perindopril is a medicine which controls high blood pressure and it is Servier's best selling drug. Servier had a significant market power in the perindopril molecule

---

[22]European Commission, press release, Brussels, 19 June 2013, http://europa.eu/rapid/press-release_IP-13-563_en.htm. Accessed 2 March 2017.

[23]Case T-472/13, *H. Lundbeck A/S and Lundbeck Ltd v European Commission* [2016].

[24]Case 15/74, *Centrafarm BV and others/Sterling Drug* [1974] ECR 01147.

[25]Case 65/86, *Bayer/Süllhöfer* [1988] ECR 05249.

[26]Mische et al. (2014), pp. 1914–1915.

[27]Commission Decision of 9.7.2014, AT.39612 Perindopril (*Servier*), C (2014) 4955 final.

[28]European Commission, Antitrust: Commission fines Servier and five generic companies for curbing entry of cheaper versions of cardiovascular medicine, press release, Brussels, 9 July 2014, http://europa.eu/rapid/press-release_IP-14-799_en.htm. Accessed 3 January 2017.

market. Its position was potentially at risk from the generic entry. The molecule patent expired in 2003. There were some additional secondary patents for procedures and form of medicine, but they provided only a limited protection. The producers of cheaper generic medicines were ready to enter the market. Competitors have tried to access the technology protected by patent. However, during 2004, Servier has bought more advanced technology, thus forcing a great number of generic producers to give up the production. Servier has stated that such acquisition intends to strengthen the protection mechanism. Generic producers have tried to dispute Servier's patents before courts. In the period between 2005 and 2007, every time a generic producer tried to enter the market, Servier and that producer would conclude a settlement. However, this was no ordinary settlement. Generic producers have agreed with Servier that they will not compete with it, in exchange for a certain amount of money. This has happened five times at most in the previous period. Servier has paid tenths of millions of euros to generic undertakings. In one case, Servier has transferred a licence to an undertaking for seven markets. Thus, Servier made sure that generic producers will stay off the market and refrain from any legal proceedings for the duration of the settlement.

Each patent owner is entitled to protect its patent by any legal means. However, in this case Servier has abused legal instruments, among other, by buying a great number of competitors who have developed cheaper medicines.

From its analysis, the Commission has determined that Servier's actions constitute prohibited agreements from Article 101 TFEU, but also abuse of dominant position within the meaning of Article 102 TFEU. Therefore, Servier and four generic manufacturers were fined for entering into agreements aimed at preventing the market entry of a generic drug for high blood pressure. By itself, this would not be deemed as infringement, but it was the Servier's obligation to pay substantial amounts or provide other benefits to generic producers which turned it into a violation of competition law. Moreover, Servier has conducted other practices intending to prevent generic entry.

When examining the agreement's objective, it suffices that the agreement has a potential adverse impact on competition. Agreements are examined under Article 101 TFEU. This does not mean that settlements are prohibited, but only that they are susceptible to examination in the context of competition law. Servier has protected its medicine with additional patents (over 30 of them) protecting production processes and specific ingredients of the medicine. When two parties conclude a settlement, there is no value transfer. Article 101 TFEU protects not only direct interests of other competitors and consumers on the market, but also the market structure and competition itself. Such settlements have the potential of eliminating competition and thus diminishing the risk and usual insecurities in the market, which benefits the originator company.

According to the existing practice, further examination stops when it is determined that the objective of the agreement is to limit competition. An agreement may infringe competition by its object or effect: these conditions are prescribed alternatively. Nevertheless, the Commission has decided to proceed with the examination of the impact of limitations to the market structure. These circumstances are examined not only in the context of existing competition, but also in view of potential competition. When an agreement restricts competition by effect,[29] not only actual or potential infrigments of competition are considered, but also any possible restriction between existing and third parties. Restriction must be confirmed with a sufficient degree of certainty, and it depends on several elements. The Commission must first determine the actual effects of the settlement on potential competitors, i.e. establish the effect of removing generic producers as potential competitors from the market. The same applies when determining the effect of the agreement. In the second step of the examination, the Commission will turn to examining whether the elimination of one potential competitor has any impact on competitive market structure, and eventually, consumers. Facts existing at the time of conclusion of the settlement are considered, as well as circumstances surrounding the settlement's implementation.[30] The Commission always states that regardless of the fact that effective competition exists in the market, the fact that the new competitor is prevented from entering the market can represent significant restriction of competition.

According to the Commission, the agreements have not limited Servier's capability of starting potential infringement proceedings, the amount paid by Servier was based on the expected income the generic producer would receive in case of market entry and the generic producers' obligations were far bigger than what Servier would have received, if it had seek judicial protection. Agreements have significantly restricted competition and decreased actual possibility for competition among existing undertakings, but also the possibility for new competitors to enter the relevant market and compete with existing undertakings.

This is the first time that the Commission has examined the behaviour of a dominant undertaking. It has analysed whether the undertaking has abused its dominant position. It has examined the company's behaviour in connection with the acquisition of API (active pharmaceutical ingredient) technology and concluded that it supplemented the reverse payment settlement. It was established that agreements represent a single and continuous infringement of Article 102 TFEU.

If these two decisions are compared, it can be seen that the decision in *Servier* differs from the *Lundbeck* decision in two points: in *Lundbeck*, the Commission has examined only the agreement's objective, while in *Servier* it went on to examine the agreement's effects as well. This is surprising, given the existing practice. Further, in *Servier* the Commission has established that there was an abuse of dominant position from Article 102 TFEU in addition to infringement of Article 101 TFEU.

The co-promotion and joint marketing activities agreements may also prevent the market entry of generic medicines. One of the latest decisions is rendered in case

---

[29]See para. 27 of Communication from the Commission—Guidelines on the Application of Article 81(3) of the Treaty, OJ C 101 of 27.4.2004 and *Servier*, para. 1211 and further.

[30]Guidelines on the Application of Article 81(3) of the Treaty, para 29.

Fentanyl.[31] The Commission has examined the Co-promotion agreement between the Dutch subsidiaries of the pharmaceutical companies Johnson & Johnson and Novartis AG.

Under the terms of agreement, Johnson & Johnson was obliged to pay agreed monthly amounts, as long as its potential competitor Novartis refrains from entering the Dutch market with its generic fentanyl version. It is a strong pain killer, sold by Johnson & Johnson in various forms since 1960s. However, the patent protection for transdermal fentanyl patches produced by Johnson & Johnson expired in the Netherlands in 2005, and the company Sandoz, a subsidiary of Novartis, intended to market the generic version of the patch.

Instead of beginning with the sale of the patch, in July 2005 Sandoz has entered in Co-promotion agreement with Janssen-Cilag, a Dutch subsidiary of Johnson & Johnson. It is interesting that the monthly amounts paid to Sandoz have by far exceeded the potential earning from the sale of generic drug. Janssen-Cilag has paid to Sandoz approximately EUR five million in total, in monthly instalments. These monthly payments were made in exchange of undefined services of joint promotion. During the period covered by the initial agreement, Sandoz has conducted only limited promotion activities.

Instead of competition, Johnson & Johnson and Novartis have agreed to cooperate by preventing the marketing of generic transdermal patches and thus keeping the existing high price of the original medicine.

The Commission has concluded that the agreement represents the intentional restriction of Article 101 by object. Unlike Lundbeck and Servier, this decision bears no relation to the patent dispute, but the agreement has the same intent: exclusion of generic producers from the market.

3 Conclusion

The above mentioned agreements include complex issues and conflicting interests and rules of intellectual property law, competition law and health care. Research has shown that pharmaceutical companies are systematically using their exclusive intellectual property rights to eliminate competition and keep high medicine prices. It even seems as though they are investing more time and effort in developing different patent strategies than in research and development.

In principle, both intellectual property law and competition law strive to achieve the same objectives: innovation, mutual competition and eventually, benefits to consumers. Pharmaceutical industry and competition law are two sides of the same coin. Likewise, the Commission's viewpoints clearly confirm the interesting relationship between competition law and the intellectual property law.

---

[31] European Commission, Case AT:39685, *Fentanyl* of 10.12.2013, C (2013) 8870 final. See more in Westin and Healy (2014), pp. 402–412.

It seems that, as was the case in Servier, the effect on competition will have to be examined as well. So far, the General Court has confirmed the Commission's standpoint, and it remains to be seen what decision it will render in the case Servier. I believe that the General Court should in the future assume a firmer position and attempt to set the boundaries between disputing their efficiency and finding objective justifications for such settlements. It should not be forgotten that the pharmaceutical sector, in addition to having a significant impact on the health of individuals, also has a strong impact on public budgets of individual states.

Based on the above, it may be concluded that the Commission will keep its focus on settlements. It insists on the presentation of copies of all settlements concluded during 1 year, which are not prohibited, but may be problematic if they include a value transfer. Although the Commission collects statistical data, it does not reveal the real situation. The report does not provide any indicators pointing to settlements which are problematic from the competition aspect. After all these years of work, the Commission should be able to produce a report providing more detailed indicators for pharmaceutical companies.

Determining when the exercise of intellectual property rights has an adverse impact on consumer benefit represents a special challenge for competition law. It is clear that competition law should not be used to repair deficiencies of intellectual property law.

The companies who produce generic medicines traditionally highlight how important their presence on the market is for consumers, who have more choice at cheaper prices. However, at the same time they fail to mention how much they profit from their market presence. Pharmaceutical sector is one of the most profitable industry sectors, and it fits perfectly in the economic theory which highlights how higher risk implies greater return of investment. The question is why, if they bear such enormous loss as they claim, generic producers are still trying to be part of that industry?

The pharmaceutical sector is the main driver of research and development through a constant influx of innovative medicines which contribute to the overall health and well-being. However, few sectors are regulated as extensively as the pharmaceutical sector. Each step, from the initial concept to marketing authorisation, patent expiry and potential generic medicine market entry is regulated.

References

Clancy MJ, Geradin D, Lazerow A (2013) Reverse-Payment Patent Settlements in the Pharmaceutical Industry: An Analysis of US Antitrust Law and EU Competition Law. SSRN: https://ssrn.com/abstract=2345851 or https://doi.org/10.2139/ssrn.2345851
Connor JM (2015) Antitrust developments in food and pharma. Ann Rev Resour Econ 7:375–398
Desogus C (2011) Competition and innovation in the EU regulation of pharmaceuticals, the case of parallel trade. Intersentia, Cambridge

Drake KM, Starr MA, McGuire T (2014) Do "Reverse Payment" Settlements of Brand-generic Patent Disputes in the Pharmaceutical Industry Constitute an Anticompetitive Pay for Delay? NBER Working Paper No. 20292

Hemphill SC (2006) Paying for delay: pharmaceutical patent settlement as a regulatory design problem. NYU Law Rev 81:1553–1623

Hull DW, Clancy MJ (2016) The application of EU competition law in the pharmaceutical sector. J Eur Compet Law Pract 7(2):150–161

Mische H, Kamilarova E, Schnichels D (2014) Pharma. In: Faull J, Nikpay A (eds) The EU law of competition, 3rd edn. Oxford University Press, Oxford, pp 1869–1919

Pošćić A (2014) Europsko pravo tržišnog natjecanja i interesi potrošača. Narodne novine, Zagreb

Schmid M (2012) Pharmaceutical reverse payment settlements - a European perspective in the wake of the sector inquiry. Eur Compet Law Rev 33(8):367–375

Westin J, Healy M (2014) Pharmaceutical co-promotion, co-marketing and antitrust. Eur Compet Law Rev 35(8):402–412

Doping in Sports: Legal and Other Aspects

Vanja Smokvina

Abstract The issue of doping is always a very interesting topic in the modern sport. Doping is also interesting not just for medicine and biomedicine but for the law point of view. This paper firstly defines doping and gives a review of the legal framework (national and international). In the end, just to show how the issue of doping is complex, it discusses three cases decided before the Court of Arbitration for Sport (CAS): the *Strahija case*, the *Ademi case* and the *Dobud case*.

1 Introduction

The issue of doping is always a very interesting topic in the modern sport. Doping is very much connected to medicine and bio-medicine so we may not speak about doping or anti-doping fight without knowing its complexity and its intersection between science and law.[1]

Doping is contrary to ethical sports principles, contrary to fair-play and secondly doping may harm the athlete's health because of numerous involuntary reactions to drugs and methods that are known as doping.[2] The essence of a sporting contest is that it should be fairly conducted, with success or failure depending on competitors' natural talent and qualities, speed, strength (physical and mental), flexibility, sense and rhythm, endurance, tactical awareness, honed as they may be instruction, training and body maintenance. The use of drugs inserts an unwarranted factor into this equation, offers an unfair advantage to the user, and offends against notions of equality and the sporting concept of the level playing field.[3]

---

[1]See more Viret (2016).

[2]Boris Labar (2009), p. 255.

[3]Beloff et al. (2012), p. 251.

V. Smokvina (✉)
Faculty of Law, University of Rijeka, Rijeka, Croatia
e-mail: vsmokvina@pravri.hr

© Springer Nature Switzerland AG 2019
N. Bodiroga-Vukobrat et al. (eds.), *Personalized Medicine in Healthcare Systems*,
Europeanization and Globalization 5, https://doi.org/10.1007/978-3-030-16465-2_21

Regarding the legal framework, it should be highlighted that Croatia, as one of 183 States,[4] is a Member States of the UNESCO International Convention against Doping in Sport adopted in 2005.[5] Furthermore, Croatia is also one of 52 Member States of the Council of Europe Anti-Doping Convention[6] and the Copenhagen Declaration on Anti-Doping in Sport (Copenhagen Declaration),[7] just to mention some sources important in the fight against doping. Of course, we may not speak about doping and not mention the importance of World Anti-doping Agency (hereinafter: WADA) and World Anti-Doping Code (hereinafter: WADC) with its *sui generis* character of a semi private and semi public elements as a global norm setting model for the fight against doping.[8] The widespread acceptance of the WADC around the world has created an interlocking international network of agreements, which regulate doping maters, and establishes the necessary international disciplinary regime.[9] Anti-doping regulation is predicated on two important legal principles. Firstly, the relationship between sportspersons and their governing bodies is a contractual one, the terms of which include, *inter alia*, the doping regulations of that particular sport.[10]

In the Croatian Sports Act,[11] doping is defined in just one article, the Article 72 that defines doping very generally as 'prohibited substances". The National Olympic Committee of Croatia (hereinafter: NOC of Croatia) defines 'doping in sport" in Article 1(2) of the Rules on Fights against Doping[12] as occurrence of an anti-doping rule violation in line with Article 2(9) of the UNESCO International Convention against Doping in Sport.

The Croatian Institute for Toxicology and Anti-doping,[13] as the only authorised national body for the fight against doping, in its Regulations for the Fights Against

---

[4]UNESCO International Convention against Doping in Sport. http://www.unesco.org/eri/la/conven tion.asp?KO=31037&language=E. Accessed 27 July 2017.

[5]Act on Recognition of the International Convention Against Doping in Sport (*Zakon o potvrđivanju Međunarodne konvencije protiv dopinga u sportu*) Official Gazette of the Republic of Croatia—International Covenants No. 07/07.

[6]Council of Europe Anti-Doping Convention. http://www.coe.int/t/dg4/sport/Doping/convention_ en.asp. Accessed 27 July 2017.

[7]Copenhagen Declaration on Anti-Doping in Sport (Copenhagen Declaration). https://www.wada-ama.org/en/resources/world-anti-doping-program/copenhagen-declaration. Accessed 28 July 2017.

[8]Siekmann (2012), p. 331.

[9]David (2013), p. 122.

[10]Gardiner et al. (2012), p. 364.

[11]Sports Act (*Zakon o sportu*), Official Gazette of the Republic of Croatia, No. NN 71/06, 150/08, 124/10, 124/11, 86/12, 94/13, 85/15, 19/16.

[12]NOC of Croatia Rules on Fights against Doping (*Pravila za borbu protiv dopinga Hrvatskog odlimpijskog odbora*). http://www.hoo.hr/images/dokumenti/ostali-dokumenti/antidoping/Pravila_ za_borbu_protiv_dopinga-HOO-prosinac-2014.pdf. Accessed 30 July 2017.

[13]It is a specific body whose competence is the fight against doping. Firstly there was the Croatian Anti-Doping Agency (CroADA), which was established on February 22, 2007. The founder of CroADA was the Republic of Croatia and the founder's rights and obligations on behalf of the founder were assumed by the Ministry in charge of sports. With the amendments of the Sports Act

Doping in Sports[14] determines that doping consists of violating one or more anti-doping rules (ten in total) of the said Regulations. Those anti-doping rules are the same anti-doping rules as those defined in the WADC. The anti-doping rules are as follows:

(1) Presence of a prohibited substance or its metabolites or markers in an athlete's sample,
(2) Use or attempted use by an athlete of a prohibited substance or a prohibited method,
(3) Evading, refusing or failing to submit to sample collection,
(4) Whereabouts failures,
(5) Tampering or attempted tampering with any part of doping control,
(6) Possession of a prohibited substance or a prohibited method,
(7) Trafficking or attempted trafficking in any prohibited substance or prohibited method,
(8) Administration or attempted administration to any athlete in-competition of any prohibited substance or prohibited method, or administration or attempted administration to any athlete out-of-competition of any prohibited substance or any prohibited method that is prohibited out-of-competition,
(9) Complicity,
(10) Prohibited association.

The CITA in its Regulations for the Fights against Doping in Sports determines the general framework on the anti-doping. It is important that it includes the obligations to the NOC of Croatia and all national sports federations to include in its general act the application of the Regulations as sports rules obligatory for their members or participants. The NOC of Croatia adopted in 2014 its Rules on Fights against Doping and by its Article 7 recognises the competence of the CITA as national organisation in the fight against doping.

The anti-doping fight may be described as a three level fight. At the first level we find the Code, from the Code we obtain the standards (as a secondary level), which determine the list of prohibited substances, the exclusions from prohibitions, the

---

in 2010, with an agreement between Ministry in charge of sports and Ministry of Health, the Croatian Anti-doping Agency (CroADA) was adjoined to the Croatian Institute for Toxicology and a new institution got today's name: the Croatian Institute for Toxicology and Antidoping (CITA). The structure of CITA is regulated by a statute as an institution with four departments, three of them being toxicological departments and one a department designated to battling doping: Department for Risk Assessment, Department for Documentation and Registry, Department for Accident Prevention and Department for Anti-doping. The Institute continued its work on the anti-doping and continued the CROADA's work in conformity with international covenants and obligations. The CITA collaborate with the NOC of Croatia, the Para-Olympic Committee of Croatia, national sports federations and sports clubs. For its professional work it is subordinated to the Ministry in charge of sports.

[14]Croatian Institute for Toxicology Regulations for the fights against doping in sports (*Pravilnik za borbu protiv dopinga u sportu*). http://www.hoo.hr/images/dokumenti/ostali-dokumenti/antidoping/Pravilnik-za-borbu-protiv-dopinga-2015-HZTA.pdf. Accessed 30 July 2017.

process of testing and taking of samples with the laboratory analysis. The third level, determined by the rules, is performed by the national anti-doping organisations and internationals sports federations. Those rules, determines the guidelines and forms of performance of the anti-doping control.[15]

2 Sports Act and Anti-Doping

Doping and the fight against doping are defined, as seen *supra*, in just one article of the Sports Act, namely Article 72. Under this article, athletes must not take prohibited substances (doping) and they must not act against the rules of the NOC of Croatia, International Olympic Committee and the WADA. The coaches, authorised doctors and other persons in sports must not provide athletes with prohibited substances nor ask or incite athletes to take prohibited substances or apply procedures that are forbidden by the rules of WADA. If it is established that if an athlete or the coaches, authorised doctors and other persons in sports has acted against the previous provisions, the person and body which has established it shall act under the provisions of rules determined by NOC of Croatia, International Olympic Committee, WADA and Sports Act provisions. Finally, that article proscribe that athletes are obliged to allow the anti-doping control.

It is interesting to note that after the amendments of the Sports Act in 2012 there has been no criminal liability of athletes (for misdemeanour offences) for taking prohibited substances or does not allow the anti-doping control, which was prescribed by the Sports Act Article 87(4). Furthermore, there is also no longer criminal liability for the coach, the authorised doctor or other person in sport (for misdemeanour offences) under the Sports Act Article 87(5), but with the amendments of the Criminal Code, such behaviour could be defined as criminal offence, *see infra.*

In the Sports Act, before the amendments in 2012, there was also a criminal liability of legal persons and their responsible person, in Article 86(5) if it demanded or allowed an athlete to take prohibited substances or apply procedures prohibited by WADA rules. Such responsibility does not exist anymore.

3 Criminal Offences Interesting for the Sports Sector: Doping

Here it is important to note that there was firstly the intention that the doping offenders should be punished with the rules of the sports federations, but a more stronger intention to fight doping by the State resulted in situation that the State by its

---

[15]Labar (2009), p. 256.

laws regulated the fight against doping and defined it as a misdemeanour or a criminal offence.[16]

Regarding criminal offences in sports, it is interesting to note that the only criminal offence in which sport in general is mentioned actually deals with doping. It is the Article 191a of the Criminal Code,[17] named *Unauthorised manufacture of and trade in illicit substances banned in sports*. This criminal offence was introduced with the Amendments and supplement of the Criminal Code in 2012, which took effect in 2013.

In general, there is no criminal liability for an athlete who uses doping, or substances banned in sports. There is, however, the liability of those persons who may give an athlete such substances or influence the athlete to use such substances (coaches, doctors, clubs officials, other players). An athlete may be sanctioned for using doping or banned substances in sport only by competent sports bodies (NOC of Croatia, national federations, clubs), but there is no liability for a criminal offence or misdemeanour offence for the athlete.

The first paragraph of Article 191a states that whoever produces, processes, transports, imports or exports, procures or possesses substances banned in sports that are intended for unauthorised sale or putting into circulation in some other way, or offers them for sale without authorisation, or sells or transports them, or mediates in their sale or purchase, or markets them in some other way or incites another person to use them, or gives them to another person for his own use or for the use of some other person, shall be liable to imprisonment not exceeding 3 years.

The second paragraph of the same Article sets that whoever offers for sale, sells or mediates in the sale of substances referred to in the first paragraph to a child or a person with serious mental disorders, or incites him to use them, or gives them to him, or does this in school or at another place providing education to children or at which children engage in sporting or social activities, or in its immediate proximity, or in a penal institution, or whoever, to commit the offence referred to in the first paragraph, uses a child, or if a public official does this in relation to his/her function or public authority, shall be liable to imprisonment from 6 months to 5 years.

Whoever organises a network of resellers or dealers, to commit the offence defined in the first two paragraphs of the Article 191a, shall be liable to imprisonment from 1 to 8 years. Furthermore, whoever by the criminal offence previously referred causes the death of a person to whom he/she sold the substance referred to in the first paragraph of the Article 191a or to whom the substance was sold through his/her dealing shall be liable to imprisonment from 3 to 15 years.

Substances referred to in the first paragraph, substances that can be used for their production, the means of their production or processing, the means of transport adapted to conceal these substances and the paraphernalia for their use, shall be confiscated. Finally, if the perpetrator of the criminal offence referred to in the first

---

[16]Pajčić and Petković (2008), p. 552.

[17]Criminal Code (*Kazneni zakon*), Official Gazette of the Republic of Croatia No. 125/11, 144/12, 56/15, 61/15.

three paragraphs of Article 191a substantially contributes of his/her own free will to the discovery of the offence set out in Article 191a, the court may remit his/her punishment.

It is interesting to note, and the option chosen by the legislator is not a favourable one, that a criminal offence refers to an unauthorised manufacture of and trade in illicit substances banned in sports, but Article 191a does not specify that such substances may be given to an athlete (never mind if is he/she a professional or amateur athlete) for a criminal offense to be committed. Therefore, it follows that anyone could commit this criminal offense if they provide another person with an illicit substance, which is wrong. As alcohol is also a banned substance in sport, this would mean that anyone giving alcohol to some other person would be committing such a criminal offence. Obviously, this should be changed *de lege ferenda*.

To conclude, there is no directly prescribed criminal liability of an athlete for using doping, or substances banned in sports. There is liability under the Article 191a of the Criminal Code of those persons who may give an athlete such substances or influence the athlete to use such substances (coaches, doctors, clubs officials, other athletes). An athlete may be sanctioned for using doping or banned substances in sport only by sports bodies (NOC of Croatia, national sports federations, clubs), but there is no prescribed liability for criminal offences or misdemeanours offence for an athlete. However, we must also point out a very tricky question. Some authors indirectly conclude that the athlete who has taken doping may be prosecuted for committing the criminal offence of *Fraud (Article 236 of the Criminal Code)* towards other athletes, organisers of the competition in which the athlete who took the doping has taken part and sponsors. The athlete who competes in a sport competition obliged himself not to take doping and the athlete with such a behaviour misrepresented himself and kept all those persons involved in a competition in error.[18]

According to some authors, in case of doping there could also be some other criminal offences not strictly defined as offences in sport. Such criminal offence could be the criminal offence of *Aggravated Bodily Injury* (Article 118 of the Criminal Code), and potentially with the athlete's death also the criminal offence of *Murder* (Article 110 of the Criminal Code), *Aggravated Murder* (Article 111 of the Criminal Code) and *Negligent Homicide* (Article 113 of the Criminal Code,) with doctor, coach or other athlete as offenders; and also doctors may be prosecuted for committing the criminal offences of *Medical Malpractice* (Article 181 of the Criminal Code) and *Issuance and Use of False Medical or Veterinary Health Certificates* (Article 282 of the Criminal Code)[19] while the pharmacist could be liable for committing the criminal offences of *Carelessness in Preparation and Dispensing of Drugs* (Article 187 of the Criminal Code).[20]

---

[18]Pajčić and Petković (2008), pp. 573–575.

[19]Pajčić and Petković (2008), pp. 569–576.

[20]Pajčić and Sokanović (2010), pp. 402–403.

4 NOC of Croatia and Anti-Doping

The WADC, besides addressing all issues related to doping control, substances and methods, procedures to determine doping, procedures following a positive doping test and sanctions, also, of course, establishes the role and responsibilities of the NOCs from which the NOC of Croatia obligations arise as follows:

- to ensure that their anti-doping policies and rules conform to the Code,
- to require athletes who are not regular members of a National sports federation to be available for Sample collection and to provide accurate and up-to-date whereabouts information as part of the National Registered Testing Pool during the year before the Olympic Games as a condition of participation in the Olympic Games,
- to require as a condition of membership or recognition that National sports federations' anti-doping policies and rules are in compliance with the applicable provisions of the Code,
- to cooperate with their National Anti-Doping Organisation,
- to withhold some or all funding, during any period of his/her Ineligibility, to any athlete or athlete support personnel who has violated anti-doping rules,
- to withhold some or all funding to its members or recognised National Federations that do not comply with the Code.[21]

From the above cited, the NOC of Croatia Statutes in its Article 12(3) contain provisions whereby the NOC of Croatia shall 'combat doping and the use of substances and procedures prohibited by the IOC or international federations". The NOC of Croatia has adopted and applied the WADC and in such a way assure that the strategies and rules of the NOC of Croatia against doping, membership and financial demands together with management actions would be in line with the WADC, and respect all duties and responsibilities of a NOC regulated by the WADC (Article 13(8) of the NOC of Croatia Statutes). The NOC of Croatia also cooperates with CITA in combating doping in sports.

In the process of giving approval to the statutes of national sports federations, in harmonising the statutes of national sports federations with the NOC of Croatia Statute, the inclusion of the following provision is essential:

> participation in combating doping, the use of substances and prohibited procedures in federation member sports activities and competitions, pursuant to the WADC if this provision is not already included in the statute of a NOC of Croatia member national sports federation.[22]

The NOC of Croatia Council has also taken note of the acts of CITA: CITA Rules on Combating Doping, CITA Ordinance on the approval of therapeutic exceptions, Standing Rules of the CITA Disciplinary and Appeals Council, and the Opinion of the Health Commission of the Croatian Olympic Committee on the CITA Rules on

---

[21]Vrbek (2013), pp. 204–205.

[22]Vrbek (2013), p. 204.

Combating Doping and the notification of the WADA on the text of the Rules with the WADC. The NOC of Croatia Council has taken note of CITA's Rules on Combating Doping as an indispensable act in conducting anti-doping in sports and the act has been forwarded to NOC of Croatia member national sports federations for implementation such that they will become a part of sports rules and the rights and obligations of their members and participants.

5 The Croatian Sports Arbitration Council and Anti-Doping

The Croatian Sports Arbitration Council (hereinafter: CSAC)[23] as an important part of the system of sports justice in Croatia is in particular,[24] authorised to resolve disputes and issues pertaining to the execution of the tasks of the NOC of Croatia.

The CSAC is in particular authorised to resolve disputes and issues pertaining to the execution of the tasks of the NOC of Croatia. Particularly significant among these are decisions on disciplinary measures and decisions regarding doping, decisions on disciplinary and other procedures that involve or imply long-term bans or prohibition from participation in sports competitions, decisions that pertain to Olympic candidates or top athletes (category I to III), the principles and conditions of sports competitions and other issues regulated by the NOC of Croatia Statute. CSAC also have the general right of supervision upon the work of the Sports Arbitration Tribunal (hereinafter: CAS Croatia),[25] but has no competence to rule the cases before CAS Croatia,[26] and assure the conditions for its work.

6 Croatian Football Federation's Regulations

When it comes to private regulations about doping in sports, here will be analysed the rules and regulations of the Croatian Football Federation (hereinafter: CFF) mainly because, as for other issues of sports law, the regulations of the CFF may

---

[23]The Sports Arbitration Council (CSAC) decides on the requests for extraordinary reviews of decisions made by sports federations, sports communities, sports clubs and other sports associations where other means of legal protection have been used up or are non-existent, and where the sport or issue at hand is important for the fulfilment of tasks of the NOC of Croatia as determined by the Sports Act. Sports Act, Article 52(1)(2)(4).

[24]Smokvina (2017), pp. 109–114.

[25]The Sports Arbitration Tribunal (CAS Croatia) decides on the requests of such parties as have recognised the competence of this court to rule on disputes related to the performance of sporting activities, as well as the rights they can freely exercise, unless the law determines that decisions on certain kinds of disputes can only be made by the regular court of law.Sports Act, Article 52(1)(3).

[26]Momčinović (2009), p. 301.

give us a good general picture of the legal framework and CFF is actually the biggest national sports federation with most clubs and registered players in Croatia.

The CFF Statute[27] in Article 12 determines that the objectives of the CFF are to encourage and promote football in the Republic of Croatia, and to represent the Croatian football abroad. One of the activities through which the CFF accomplishes its objectives is promoting and enforcing anti-doping control and activities related to prevention of doping and substances abuse, and prohibited procedures in sports activities and competitions of the CFF, under the WADC.

In the CFF Disciplinary Code,[28] anti-doping rules are prescribed in Articles 75–78. Doping is forbidden and doping and offences defined as such by FIFA Anti-doping Regulations, Rules of Fight Against Doping of CITA or other state institutions competent to fight doping and list of forbidden substances made public by WADA. Such behaviour represents doping regardless if it happened or was discovered during or outside the competition.

The FIFA Anti-doping Regulations[29] provisions on the procedure and sanctions shall be applied directly for doping offences. The decisions in the procedure run in conformity with the Rules of fight against doping of CITA or other state institutions competent to fight doping have the same power, as it would be in case the decision would be made inside the football organisation.

Every player who takes part in a competition or happening organised by the CFF or the county football association or at the preparatory sessions before such a competition or a happening is willing to be tested by the CFF competent authorities. Furthermore, the player is willing to give samples in the procedure to be tested against presence of forbidden substances or the use of forbidden methods. All legally obligatory sanctions of other international sports federations or national doping organisations, which are in line with the basic legal principles, CFF would in general automatically recognise.

In the CFF formulary contracts,[30] i.e. the Contract of professional play, mostly used in Croatia, the Employment contract or the Scholarship contract, there is a specific provision on the anti-doping. In Article 8 of the Contract of professional play, Article 11 of the Employment contract and Article 7 of the Scholarship contract, the club and the player commit themselves to the anti-doping rules of FIFA, UEFA and CFF regulations. Doping is defined as the use of substances that are on the list of prohibited substances and the use of forbidden methods mentioned in the doping lists included with the regulations as well as in other relevant doping lists. The player commits himself not to use doping while the club takes the

---

[27]CFF Statute. http://hns-cff.hr/files/documents/2384/HNS%20Statutes%202016_eng.pdf. Accessed 1 Aug 2017.

[28]CFF Disciplinary Code. http://hns-cff.hr/files/documents/8316/Disciplinski%20pravilnik%202017.pdf. Accessed 1 Aug 2017.

[29]FIFA Anti-doping Regulations. http://resources.fifa.com/mm/document/affederation/administration/02/49/28/61/circularno.1458-fifaanti-dopingregulations_neutral.pdf. Accessed 1 Aug 2017.

[30]CFF formulary contracts. http://hns-cff.hr/hns/propisi-i-dokumenti/. Accessed 10 June 2017.

obligation that it will not order the player to use doping. Furthermore, the club takes the obligation to use all preventive measures in line to prevent the use of doping, together with the obligation of education of the player on the prevention of the use of doping.

7 Case-Law on Doping

Concentrating on the most straightforward doping infraction (Article 2.1. WADC), where blood samples collected from athlete have produced a positive test for the presence of a prohibited substance, the WADC adopts the rule of strict liability. This means that an athlete is strictly liable for the prohibited substance found in, and revealed by, the testing of their bodily specimen and that an-anti doping violation occurs whether the athlete intentionally or unintentionally used a prohibited substance or was negligent or otherwise at fault.[31] Nevertheless, as some examples show,[32] the operational definition of doping by WADA, which includes the principle of strict liability, regularly leads to conviction of athletes who had no intent to improve their performance by using forbidden substances or methods and in such a way sacrifice in principle innocent athletes.[33]

Although there are many cases before various courts and tribunals,[34] in this article there will be mentioned three cases before the Court of Arbitration for Sport (CAS) interesting not just for the Croatian case-law research, but also for a more general audience because of its specificities. The *Strahija case* and the *Ademi case* will show how sometimes innocent athletes may have their careers almost getting destroyed. The third case, the *Dobud case* shows how athletes may jeopardise their career because they avoided taking an anti-doping test, which is severely prohibited by WADC.

The *case of Marko Strahija* seems very interesting from the personalised medicine point of view. He was a backstroke swimmer from Croatia, who competed at three Summer Olympics between 1996 and 2008. In 2002 Strahija's urine sample, taken in an out-of-competition control, in two out of three samples tested positive for human chorionic gonadotropin (beta-hCG).[35] As hCG is a known tumor marker,

---

[31] Anderson (2010), p. 123.

[32] I.e. in tennis in the period 2003–2007 for the majority (68%) of the 40 doping cases the sanctioning bodies ruled that there was no intent to enhance performance or (no) fault or negligence, but nevertheless sanctions were applied, with significant negative impact for the players concerning their notoriety, income and career.

[33] Kayser (2011), pp. 85–86.

[34] See more in detail in Anderson (2013).

[35] Human chorionic gonadropin (hCG) in males helps to stimulate the production of male hormones such as testosterone and athletes may take hCG to increase the ability of their body to produce testosterone and prevent atrophy of the testicles that results from taking large doses of anabolic steroids. Halchin (2006), p. 28.

Strahija underwent medical tests that found nothing suspicious. He maintained his innocence and disputed scientific validity of testing for hCG. Nevertheless, in 2003 he received a 2-year suspension.[36] In October 2007, Strahija again tested positive for hCG, which caused him to miss the European Short Course Championships held in December that year. This time, subsequent medical tests found testicular cancer, and Strahija immediately underwent surgery. In February 2008, the International Swimming Federation exonerated Strahija, lifting his provisional suspension. In the end, he made a successful recovery, taking part in the 2008 Summer Olympics, but missed some of his best years of competition. Strahija's case opens a number of ethical questions such as inconclusive tests causing irreparable harm to athlete's reputation, inadequate medical care of professional athletes, etc.[37]

The second case is the *Arijan Ademi case*.[38] He is a Croatian-born football player who is registered with football club GNK Dinamo and a national team player of FYR Macedonia. On September 2015, the Player underwent a doping control test following the UEFA Champions League match between GNK Dinamo and Arsenal FC in Zagreb, Croatia. A few weeks later, in October 2015, the Player was notified by of an Adverse Analytical Finding for stanozolol metabolites in his sample. Stanozolol is a synthetic anabolic steroid derived from dihydrotestosterone that is a non-specified substance and is prohibited at all times, both in- and out-of-competition. The Player was certain he never intentionally doped and started his legal "fight". During the proceedings before the Control, Ethics and Disciplinary Body of UEFA (hereinafter: CEDB), the Player submitted that the stanozolol entered his body through the ingestion of a contaminated "over-the-counter dietary supplement called 'Megamin/ Megacomplex'" (hereinafter: product M), which he listed, among others, on his doping control form. The CEDB suspended the Player from participating in any football-related activity for a period of 4 years. In its decision, the CEDB found the Player merely presented various theories as to how the stanozolol could have entered his body without scientific foundation to support his claim that the product M was likely contaminated. In the proceedings before the UEFA Appeals body, the Player, among other things, repeated his claims and insisted on testing the products, which were, at this stage of the procedure, sent to the laboratory of the Institute of Biochemistry German Sport University Cologne. To prove that the product M was the contaminated source, the Player purchased more product M but could not find an equivalent bottle of product M to test because the original bottle's batch number was illegible and there was no new bottle with a similar expiration date to the one that was still partially existent on the original bottle. However, with the help of the Player's team doctor, the Player bought blister packs of product M (i.e. pills sealed in plastic as opposed to in a bottle) that were similar based on the expiration date. He subsequently sent the blister packs to two independent state-of-the-art accredited laboratories: RIKILT laboratory in the Netherlands and AEGIS laboratory in the

---

[36]CAS 2003/A/507, Marko Strahija v FINA, Award of 9 Feb 2004.
[37]Erceg and Fattorini (2011), p. 189.
[38]CAS 2016/A/4676, Arijan Ademi v UEFA, Award of 24 Mar 2017.

United States. While the results of the first Cologne laboratory test on a sealed container of product M were negative for stanozolol, the RIKILT and AEGIS laboratory tests were positive for stanozolol. Both RIKILT and AEGIS found the presence of stanozolol in the product M blister packs. On May 2016, the UEFA Appeals body dismissed the appeal lodged by the Player and affirmed the decision of the UEFA CEDB. The UEFA Appeals body stated that, on a balance of probabilities, the Player had failed to prove his contamination theory and that the "positive" results of the RIKILT and AEGIS laboratories should be disregarded because of breaches of the chain of custody (i.e. the testing of the opened and unsealed product). The Player than turned to CAS which finally reduced the Player's sanction from 4 years to 2 years (which is very rare in practice). The CAS Panel found in its decision that it did not need to establish the source of the prohibited substance to prove the absence of intent. Thus, although the Panel was not persuaded that the product M was the likely source of the banned substance stanozolol, the Panel found on the balance of probability (primarily through reliance on the Player's own testimony) that the anti-doping rule violation was not intentional. The Panel found that it could not impose a sanction of less than 2 years because it determined that the Player did not establish the likely source of the banned substance stanozolol, which would have qualified him for a reduction. For this reason, the Panel imposed the lowest sanction possible of 2 years while making it clear that the Player was not a cheat or someone who had used a prohibited substance intentionally.

In the end, the Player was satisfied with the outcome. His career was saved by the reduction from 4 to 2 years and the Panel explicitly found that he was not a cheater, thus saving his image and reputation. However, the Player will always believe that he should have had an even greater reduction because three independent laboratories found the presence of the banned substance stanozolol in the product M. In the Player's mind, what more could he have done to prove that this was a "*classic*" contamination case?[39]

The third case is the *case of Nikša Dobud*,[40] which is an example how an athlete may be suspended for doping because of evasion of a doping test. Dobud is an international water polo player from Croatia who has been suspended for 4 years for an attempt to evade a FINA drug test. He was a member of the Croatian national team, which won the Olympic Gold medal at the 2012 London Olympic Games, bronze medals in the FINA World Championships in Rome 2009, Shanghai 2011 and Barcelona 2013 and a gold medal at the 2010 European Water Polo Championships in Zagreb.

From the facts of the case, the evasion of the drug test occurred on the day after a preliminary match in the Water Polo World League in Montenegro. Following that preliminary match on Dobud submitted to an in-competition test. Dobud initially stated that the in-competition test forced him to miss the team bus for Croatia, at which point he stayed in Budva for the night. At the FINA hearing, however, the

---

[39]Greene and Kasalo (2017).
[40]CAS 2015/A/4163, Nikša Dobud v. FINA, Award of 15 Mar 2016.

athlete claimed he returned to his home after partying until around 5:00 in the morning with friends. The crux of the case centers on what happened the morning of March 21, 2015 at Dobud's home when a FINA agent reported to issue Dubod a drug test. Under the facts, the FINA report states that a doping control agent showed up at Dobud's house around 6:45 AM that morning and was met by Dobud's wife, who after answering the door went to wake up Dobud. According to the FINA agent, when Dobud came to the door and was told he was being drug tested, he shut the door and refused to let the doping agent come into his home. The agent says he proceeded to stand outside of Dobud's door until 9 AM, trying to communicate that if Dobud did not take the test it would count as an automatic failed test. However, Dobud claims that he never interacted with a FINA agent. Rather, in the hearing he states that his brother-in-law was staying at his house that night helping care for their young child while he was away competing. Dobud claims he never answered the door, but it was his brother-in-law who the FINA doping agent mistakenly identified. Furthermore, Dobud claims he was in a separate, adjoining apartment, as to not wake his family when he came home that morning. Dobud's version of the story was dismissed by FINA, who noted that he changed the details of the encounter between his initial letters (written April 8 and April 28) and the hearing. Additionally, the panel did not believe that Dubod's wife would be unaware of his whereabouts in the adjacent apartment. The CAS in the end has found that "*the Appellant (Nikša Dobud) twice sought to evade the consequences of his test evasion in a deceitful way by providing in sequence two inconsistent explanations and in his later version of events involving members of his family in the deceit. Having said this, the Panel is bound by the provisions of the WADC as embodied in the FINA regulations and there is no applicable provision for reducing a penalty for evasion of doping controls; the Panel is bound by to apply the code requirements if it finds that the standards for the violation have been met.*"[41]

8 Conclusion

Doping is a very interesting topic not just for law but also for medicine and biomedicine. The real fight for the "pure sport" needs the interdisciplinary approach. The personalised medicine could help in this regard. However, there is a need for a change in the legal framework of the WADC and other legal sources because it should never happen for an athlete, whose professional career lasts 8–10 years, to be suspended for a few years without fault or negligence, as shown in the *Strahija* and *Ademi* case. That may destroy his/her career and we may say also his/her human rights especially if they perform it professionally and do not have other means for living. Doping should be cancelled but the legal framework should consider such

---

[41]CAS 2015/A/4163, Nikša Dobud v. FINA (para. 97).

examples very seriously. That is when we may have the help of the personalised medicine.

References

Anderson J (2010) Modern sports law. Hart, Oxford

Anderson J (ed) (2013) Leading cases in sports law. Asser Press and Springer, The Hague

Beloff M, Kerr T, Demetriou M, Beloff R (2012) Sports law, 2nd edn. Hart, Oxford

David P (2013) A guide to the world anti-doping code, 2nd edn. Cambridge University Press, Cambridge

Erceg D, Fattorini I (2011) CROADA – our experience in fight against doping in sport. JAHR 2 (3):185–195

Gardiner S, O'Leary J, Welch R, Boyes S, Naidoo U (2012) Sports law, 4th edn. Routledge, Oxon

Greene PJ, Kasalo T (2017) Key challenges facing athletes in contaminated supplement cases: a review of the Arijan Ademi decision Available via LawInSport. https://www.lawinsport.com/articles/item/key-challenges-facing-athletes-in-contaminated-supplement-cases-a-review-of-the-arijan-ademi-decision. Accessed 10 July 2017

Halchin LE (2006) Anti-doping policies: the olympics and selected professional sports. In: Burns CN (ed) Doping in sports. Nova Science Publishers, New York, pp 1–36

Kayser B (2011) On the presumption of guilt without proof of intentionality and other consequences of current anti-doping policy. In: McNamee M, Møller V (eds) Doping and anti-doping policy in sport – ethical, legal and social perspectives. Routledge, Oxon, pp 84–98

Labar B (2009) Doping i sport. In: Crnić I et al. (Uvod u) športsko pravo. Inženjerski biro, Zagreb, pp 255–268

Momčinović H (2009) Športska arbitraža i rješavanje sporova u vezi sa športom. In: Crnić I et al. (Uvod u) športsko pravo. Inženjerski biro, Zagreb, pp 298–303

Pajčić M, Petković T (2008) Doping i kaznenopravna odgovornost. Zbornik radova Pravnog fakulteta u Splitu 45(3):551–582

Pajčić M, Sokanović L (2010) Anabolički steroidi kao predmet kaznenopravne regulacije. Zbornik radova Pravnog fakulteta u Splitu 47(2):387–409

Siekmann R (2012) Introduction to international and European sports law. Springer, Asser Press, The Hague

Smokvina V (2017) Sports law in Croatia. Wolters Kluwer, Aalphen aan den Rijn

Viret M (2016) Evidence in anti-doping at the intersection of science and law. Asser Press, Springer, The Hague

Vrbek B (2013) The role of the Croatian Olympic Committee in creating sports law. In: Siekmann R, Parrish R, Smokvina V, Bodiroga-Vukobrat N, Sander G (eds) Social dialogue in professional sports. Shaker Verlag, Aachen, pp 185–208

Personalised Medicine in Public Healthcare Systems

Maks Tajnikar and Petra Došenović Bonča

Abstract This chapter discusses the profound impact personalised medicine is expected to have on public healthcare systems. First, introducing personalised medicine will radically affect the healthcare value chain and stages in which the healthcare system plays the key role, namely in the form of lifelong care for a person's healthy life. Public healthcare networks will become increasingly international. Second, in the current situation, out-of-pocket payment is the most reasonable way of financing personalised medicine, but the future development of personalised medicine will depend on health insurance that resembles life insurance. Third, it is possible to ground collective financing only on solidarity and not on the differences between social and individual effects. Fourth, personalised medicine requires a great deal of state regulation. Fifth, personalised medicine is based on a large volume of information and only the individual should have the right to decide how this information is used.

This chapter addresses the relationship between personalised medicine and the public healthcare system. It is based on the hypothesis that the development of personalised medicine will call for a radical change in the foundations of public healthcare systems across the world.

1 Definition of Personalised Medicine

Despite the lack of one uniform definition, personalised medicine can be understood as a process of tailoring medicine to an individual person in terms of diagnoses, medical treatment and applied healthcare goods.[1] It is about the choice of the treatment that is most appropriate for a person, using state-of-the-art technologies. It is generally accepted that genomic medicine lies at the core of personalised

---

[1]Redekop and Mladsi (2013) and Jain (2015).

M. Tajnikar · P. Došenović Bonča (✉)
University of Ljubljana, School of Economics and Business, Ljubljana, Slovenia
e-mail: petra.d.bonca@ef.uni-lj.si

© Springer Nature Switzerland AG 2019
N. Bodiroga-Vukobrat et al. (eds.), *Personalized Medicine in Healthcare Systems*,
Europeanization and Globalization 5, https://doi.org/10.1007/978-3-030-16465-2_22

medicine. Genomic medicine is, however, not an adequate synonym for personalised medicine given that other factors must also be considered.[2] This is reflected also in the definition of personalised medicine used by EU Health Ministers in their Council conclusions on personalised medicine for patients.[3]

Although about 99.9% of our DNA sequence is identical, the small 0.1% difference is behind the hereditary susceptibility to virtually all diseases. For this very reason, molecular diagnostics and identification of DNA sequences, called sequencing, are important cores of personalised medicine. It is realistic to expect that, by the end of the second decade of the twenty-first century, the population will have access to genomic data generated from a blood sample by functional DNA sequencing and pinpointing genetic differences in functional genes.[4]

The ability to: (a) explore the human genome; (b) sequence, analyse and interpret the genome of an individual and identify possible consequences of specific features; and, especially (c) alter the human genome undoubtedly make up the fundamentals of personalised medicine. These form the bases for focussing on an individual and not only their health condition; hence, the name personalised medicine.

However, it is not simply genomic variation between individuals that personalised medicine considers. Namely, morbidity and susceptibility to certain diseases also result from the environment and lifestyle, with both varying from one person to another. Carlsten et al. even point out that "the prevailing focus on an individual's genes and biology insufficiently incorporates the important role of environmental factors in disease etiology and health".[5] Given each person's own genetic characteristics, these factors affect the choice of treatment strategy for a specific patient, determination of the right time to identify susceptibility to a disease as well as ensuring fast and targeted prevention. Clearly, today we can already assess how many cases of disease have occurred because of genetic factors and how many from environmental influences and a patient's lifestyle (genetic and non-genetic risk).

By looking at an individual's genome, environment and lifestyle, personalised medicine differs from traditional medicine in many respects. Developments in medicine are less a revolution and rather an evolution,[6] but separating personalised and traditional medicine helps us to identify those differences that must be considered when analysing the co-dependence of personalised medicine and public healthcare systems.

First, the mission of medicine is experiencing a sharp turnaround. Medicine thus no longer deals primarily with human illnesses but with an individual person, together with their characteristics and influential factors. It is an individual's genetic profile and the influence of the environment they live in, together with their lifestyle,

---

[2]Jain (2015).

[3]Official Journal of the European Union, 2015/C 421/03.

[4]Jain (2015).

[5]Carlsten et al. (2014).

[6]Bieber (2013).

which determine the appropriate use of medicine. Key goals of personalized medicine are avoiding trial and error phases through better and truly personalized medicine that will benefit both patients through better outcome of treatment and the healthcare systems in general.[7]

Second, the role of diagnostics is seeing the most drastic changes. The biggest turning point is giving preference for the so far poorly utilised prognostics over traditional diagnostics. Medicine is expected to be predictive, preventive, personalized and participatory.[8] The reason is the increasingly better understanding and exploring of DNA, genes and the complete human genome. The development of personalised medicine will depend critically on information and integration of different data sets to develop a comprehensive personal healthcare record.[9] The future of personalised medicine will probably bring about the possibility of altering the genome by finding the cause of a specific illness and adjusting the human genome thereby lowering the probability of the occurrence of diseases from harmful environment and lifestyle.

Third, it is the new role of prognostics that is helping to turn medicine's focus away from dealing with a person's current health condition to monitoring their health through the entire life span, including those periods of life characterised as illness. The goal of personalised medicine is no longer to only successfully and effectively treat a disease once identified, but to shape the human genome so as to facilitate—along with the appropriate living environment and lifestyle—a healthy, active and long life.

2   The Main Characteristics of Public Healthcare Systems

A basic component of public healthcare systems, which also distinguishes them from other healthcare systems, is solidarity between individuals with different health, income, age, gender, place of residence and employment status.[10]

Solidarity is a social value that can only be realised when the healthcare system is financed from national budget or compulsory health insurance as it requires income transfers between individuals in either the form of payment of the same healthcare contribution with different levels of healthcare goods being consumed or the payment of different healthcare contributions with the same level of healthcare goods being consumed. The state budget and compulsory health insurance fund(s) facilitate the healthcare system's collective financing, but only in the form of a limited basket of healthcare goods considering the amount of the funds available, although a person's needs for medical services are limitless. Co-ordinating the size of this

---

[7]Jakka and Rossbach (2013).

[8]Jakka and Rossbach (2013).

[9]Jain (2015).

[10]Meulen et al. (2001), Kornai and Eggleston (2001) and Saltman (2015).

basket of healthcare goods that is provided so that solidarity is assured, and the amount of funds for collectively financing the basket in public healthcare systems is implemented by the state or an organisation it appoints. In market systems, such co-ordination would be the task of each individual. The conduct of individuals upon entering a healthcare system can be managed by incentives on the demand side (co-payments, deductibles, gatekeeper system, pattern of supply through the network of suppliers etc.).[11] These incentives influence access to the healthcare system and thus partly regulate people's rational expression of their needs for healthcare goods.

The fact that, as an outcome of solidarity, a need has arisen in public healthcare systems to co-ordinate the limited amount of healthcare funds and the unlimited needs leads to the situation where it is impossible to fully meet the needs for healthcare goods by applying the solidarity principle. To avoid out-of-pocket payment for a large proportion of healthcare goods, public healthcare systems are making room for health insurance. Namely, availability of the latter may bridge the gap between access to healthcare goods with full solidarity and the market approach without any elements of solidarity whatsoever. Most health systems face fiscal constraints and voluntary health insurance is thus often seen as a way to address these pressures.[12]

The payer in a public healthcare system, i.e. the state or the compulsory health insurance fund(s), does not create a typical market price-elastic demand derived from the equilibrium of consumers. The payer is faced with income and price restrictions, but utility maximisation is the objective of users of healthcare goods who make decision under soft budget constraints.[13] Raising funds collectively also affects the supply side as providers of healthcare services do not operate on a profit-making basis. This implies that they do not create price-elastic supply that is typical of commercial providers. Therefore, in a public healthcare system the state or the organisation it authorises (usually the payer) must co-ordinate the relationship between the benefit basket, which is determined by means of funds collected on a solidarity basis, and service providers. It is about creating a public healthcare network. Co-ordination also encompasses the method for paying the providers (e.g. fee-for-service payment, case-based payment, capitation, lump sum) which must encourage providers to aim for efficiency, effectiveness and high quality.[14]

Providers of healthcare goods that are financed collectively and via solidarity can be public or private, but—because of collective financing—must operate on a non-profit basis and by clearly set output goals in order to supply quantities of goods included in the benefit basket. This makes them part of the public sector. As such a *modus operandi* does not always cater to the interests of private owners, the core network of providers is typically made up of public providers to guarantee a

---

[11]Phelps (2016) and McPake et al. (2013).

[12]Sagan and Thomson (2016).

[13]Kornai (1986).

[14]Jegers et al. (2002) and Phelps (2016).

stable network of providers for enabling access to healthcare goods at any time, and for all designated places.

This overview clearly demonstrates that the place and role of personalised medicine in public healthcare systems must be analysed from the perspectives of financing the healthcare system and co-ordinating healthcare activities and service providers. A possibility has opened up to integrate personalised medicine into a system funded by the state budget or the compulsory health insurance fund(s), a system in which health insurance companies are payers and organisers of healthcare activities, and into a market system where individuals act as buyers and companies as providers.

3 Co-dependence of Personalised Medicine and Public Healthcare Systems

The elements of public healthcare systems and the characteristics of personalised medicine are co-dependent in several ways. It is worth noting that personalised medicine shifts the focus away from illness towards an individual, gives priority to prognostics and the optional correction of processes leading to illness while dealing with an individual in terms of their entire life cycle and not only a state of illness.

Solidarity and Personalised Medicine In personalised medicine, expenditure can vary considerably in view of a person's genomic profile, environment and lifestyle. Is it reasonable to offer all individuals personalised medicine based on solidarity? As compulsory health insurance or the state budget funding are underpinned by solidarity, one could of course politically conclude that all individuals should be ensured personalised medicine according to the principle of equal access. However, this could mean—especially in poorer societies—that because of the high costs of a few individuals who need to use personalised medicine we could reduce the volume of healthcare goods funded based on solidarity for all other people who do not need personalised medicine. Therefore, at least in the period when personalised medicine is still emerging, it would be more reasonable and realistic to assume that only those healthcare goods whose consumption is not decided on by the individual's preferences but stems from an objectively established health condition should be included in solidarity-based financing. With this criterion, it would be reasonable to give an individual solidarily-funded access to the prognosis phase within personalised medicine. Given that the decision about acting upon prognostic information depends on a person's preferences, the financing of genetic modification or genetic engineering, tests for identifying health consequences based on an individual's genomic profile, preventive therapy, control over changes in a person's body and management of their health would have to be ensured by the individual using a method that does not enable full solidarity. That is the case with health insurance. Similar considerations can be applied for costs deriving from a person's lifestyle and living environment. This conclusion is largely based on the view that the use of genomic information is an individual's right that nobody can interfere with. Naturally, solidarity-based financing must include all those goods needed in disease treatment, including when the latter forms part of personalised medicine. The costs include the costs of treating the consequences of a person's genomic profile, environment and lifestyle along with the costs of new medicines and medical-technical devices related to personalised medicine.

The Individual Value of Personalised Medicine Is More Important Than the Social One Personalised medicine's focus on an individual does not lead to the conclusion that the goods in personalised medicine are public goods or that they yield more relevant externalities.[15] It is quite the opposite; whereas traditional medicine in many instances produces the effects of public or rather club goods and external effects, personalised medicine largely does away with these effects. The features of public goods can mostly be found in those capacities that are needed in personalised medicine and are currently an integral part of traditional medicine's capacities. It seems that personalised medicine profoundly influences an individual, but less society as a whole. This peculiarity, which in a public healthcare system proves to be much truer in the opposite direction, produces the conclusion that in terms of its application personalised medicine does not justify collective financing and the setting of clear output targets for providers in terms of the contracted quantity of goods and services. Therefore, one can justify the financing of personalised medicine through compulsory health insurance or the state budget with the need for enforcing solidarity and not use social effects (effects that exceed the benefits accruing to any individual person) as an argument of its implementation.

Out-of-Pocket Payments Are Limiting the Development of Personalised Medicine As personalised medicine's effects are private in nature, financing through out-of-pocket payments seems to be the most practical at first glance. Such financing may be understood as a type of higher standard that an individual pays for additional services designed specifically for them, bearing in mind that focussing on an individual is the very definition of personalised medicine. Yet this system of financing of personalised medicine has two weaknesses that might literally halt its development. First, the high costs of personalised medicine prevent it from becoming widespread among the population. Personalised medicine calls for a turnaround in technology, with certain therapies requiring the engagement of highly qualified staff. The inference that personalised medicine will only be available to the wealthiest if it continues to be paid out-of-pocket is not much of an exaggeration. Second, the out-of-pocket financing of personalised medicine entails a complete lack of solidarity and thus its use would not enhance the public healthcare system but, to a great extent, disintegrate it. Individuals with disease symptoms that are more prominent in terms of personalised medicine would have to bear substantially higher costs by themselves, whereas access to this medicine would be limited for low-income earners and the unemployed. Therefore, personalised medicine cannot become of

---

[15]Stiglitz and Rosengard (2015) and Carande-Kulis et al. (2007).

prime relevance until it is included, at least to some extent, in solidarity-based financing or the insurance system. From this perspective, public healthcare systems play a key role in the development and use of personalised medicine.

Lifelong Health Insurance The insurance business is based on the fact that individuals suffer losses randomly, not all of them or at least not all of them at the same time, and that an individual cannot control their occurrence (at least not fully). The occurrence of losses in personalised medicine is considerably less random than in traditional medicine. On the contrary, the goal of personalised medicine is to prognose the health condition and thus minimise the randomness of occurrence and reduce the losses incurred by an individual. Therefore, in insurance terms, there is a reduced need to create a pool of insured persons. In personalised medicine, insurance is limited to an individual and the aim is to facilitate the financial aspect of an individual's treatment when losses occur during their lifetime. Insurance companies may help an individual save money to cover the losses predicted for them by personalised medicine (treatment of the consequences of an individual's genomic characteristics), to settle debts in arrears for already incurred losses when personalised medicine has ensured their survival and losses that, through use of personalised medicine, prevent future losses from occurring (such as costs of genetic modification, examinations to determine health consequences based on genetic information, preventive therapies for preventing the occurrence of the outcomes because of specific genomic features and control of the changes in an individual's body). The absence of randomness, the focus on an individual person and particularly the very different individual specific medical prognoses would most likely lead to notable variability in the premiums set to finance personalised medicine. Basically, health insurance for personalised medicine would be similar to capital or advance-funded insurance systems,[16] such as pension endowment insurance, as payment of the premium would have to be tied to the entire life period (or the period from the time of taking out the insurance until the end of life), except that claims would not arise at the end of a person's life but primarily in the first part of it. As solidarity would to some degree still be provided in the public healthcare system independently of insurance, the above-mentioned health insurance or endowment insurance would probably be the most appropriate way of financing personalised medicine.

New Savings and New Costs It is reasonable to assume that personalised medicine will decrease costs to some extent. It will enable correct therapies at the right time and, particularly, without delay, do away with certain negative consequences of therapies as well as facilitate the more focused running of clinical practices and abolition of unnecessary, expensive and ineffective healthcare activities. It will thus make it possible to avoid trial-and-error phases of care.[17] However, such cost reduction will certainly coincide with a tendency to increase the costs of medical

---

[16]Henke and Borchardt (2003).

[17]Jakka and Rossbach (2013).

care. First, new activities will emerge in the healthcare system, calling for highly specialised experts—not only doctors—and expensive equipment. It is not possible to assume the strong effects of economies of scale in these activities as the focus on an individual will make them highly specific. Second, the costs of suppliers will grow—not those related to equipment but to pharmaceutical products. Pharmaceutical production is currently based on large-scale manufacturing and a wide range of effects of medicines. The technology has been adjusted accordingly. Personalised medicine will necessitate the adjustment of pharmaceutical products to each individual so it will have to be capable of producing a high number of variants of the same medicine in small quantities and 'a la carte'. The development of personalised medicine will surely force the pharmaceutical industry to redesign their manufacturing processes. Third, new costs will be incurred because of the development of new activities, along with new types of costs related exclusively to genomic medicine: (a) identification of human DNA and the genome; (b) gathering of information needed to define an individual's genomic profile; (c) procedures for genetic modification; (d) examinations for defining the consequences for health based on an individual's genomic features; (e) preventive therapies for preventing the occurrence of the consequences of the genomic features; (f) treatment of the consequences of the genomic features; (g) control of the changes in an individual's body; (h) costs of new medicines and medical-technical devices related to personalised medicine; and (i) management of an individual's health in relation to their lifestyle and place of living. It should be noted that personalised medicine does not exclude traditional medicine and its costs; it upgrades it very comprehensively and changes it in some respects. All of the above speaks in favour of the claim that public healthcare systems will require greater funds than today when personalised medicine is introduced.

Change in the Providers' Business Strategies Traditional medicine, especially if organised within the public healthcare system, mainly responds to a disease's occurrence in a person. Consequently, the providers still have passive business strategies although, as pointed out by Porter and Lee, "the transformation to value-based health care is well under way".[18] Unlike traditional medicine, personalised medicine does not only respond to a disease's occurrence. Especially at the time of its introduction and expansion, it is particularly important that personalised medicine offers medical services that are not initiated by users but encouraged by providers. Providers create demand, not only adjust to it. Instead of gaining business benefits from the occurrence of diseases in the population, they must trigger the need for their services among individuals so the latter can maintain their health throughout their life. Therefore, in the personalised medicine setting providers must develop active business strategies. This *modus operandi* is typical of private entrepreneurship and less of public providers, especially those with not-for-profit operations in the public healthcare network and focusing on set output targets that must be met to receive

---

[18]Porter and Lee (2013).

funding. To be able to include such providers in the range of personalised medicine products and services the stimulative role of payment models must be strengthened and the agent–principal issues need to be addressed more seriously.

Integration of Care An individual's lifelong treatment in personalised medicine requires the much stronger integration of medical treatments. This produces some relevant consequences. First, the establishment of personalised medicine would require a specific type of management throughout the entire life cycle as one cannot assume that all providers—in some cases also suppliers—would be integrated into a single one that could optimise, within itself, medical treatments in individual phases. It is reasonable to presume that an individual will mainly participate in decision-making on their treatment with the manager of their health condition than with the providers of healthcare services. Second, lifelong treatment will also stimulate special types of integration between insurance companies and providers that will involve more than just supervision over cost generation, as is typical of traditional patient treatments. In a specific phase, an (un)successful medical treatment should lead to a decrease (increase) in the costs of medical treatments in subsequent phases as well as those connected with the initial treatment. Therefore, special cost-sharing arrangements between the insured person, the insurance company and the providers will be reasonable as personalised medicine's success in an individual's life would also depend on a longer period of a healthy lifestyle and the payment of premiums, and thus the higher payment of claims by insurance companies and costs of healthcare services implemented by providers. Third, as personalised medicine will probably require a small number of highly specialised providers and it will not be reasonable to ensure them within the national networks, public healthcare networks will have to link up with each other. It is quite possible that several countries will establish a uniform network of public personalised medicine that will be connected with a uniform insurance and even a shared system of collective financing.

Reduced Importance of Medical Staff The large volume of information in the environment of highly developed personalised medicine will make it impossible for the human brain to process it and articulate the appropriate diagnosis. Without a machine (computer), reliable diagnoses will be unfeasible. This means that personalised medicine will notably change the role of physicians. The latter will still be needed for hospital treatments within personalised medicine as well, but their importance for diagnostics will decrease drastically. Radical changes will occur at least with some providers of personalised medicine, namely in their motivation and conflicts among staff members, only to deepen the problem of motivating staff for active business strategies, especially of public healthcare providers.

Changed Structure of Demand and Healthcare Capacities Traditional medicine strives to create value added with its activities (in terms of improving the health condition and life) in the following phases, stated according to life periods and the way people enter the healthcare system: prevention, emergency, primary healthcare, specialist healthcare, hospital healthcare, long-term treatment and palliative care. In personalised medicine, this chain of value-added generation is changing. The current healthcare value chain that starts with self-directed health care activities and triggers to advance to physician contact that leads to patient-physician interaction and eventually treatment will shift to the future healthcare value chain that starts with disease predisposition assessment and management of predisposed risks.[19] Personalised medicine is hence about the shift from the isolated processing of an individual phase to the comprehensive processing of all of the above-mentioned phases. Thus, personalised medicine no longer tries to maximise performance (in the sense of creating as good a health condition as possible) merely in an individual phase, separately from other phases, but to optimise (not maximise) the performance of healthcare in all phases. In terms of personalised medicine, the primary healthcare system will become less important as its 'gatekeeper' function will no longer be necessary; role of emergency will decrease because of better prognosis; the contents of prevention will change and will no longer be 'blind' as is the case currently, given that it is designed for the entire population and not for an individual; personalised medicine will focus on prevention for each individual; its therapies will still include hospital treatment and specialist examinations, whereas the problem of long-term treatment should be reduced. With personalised medicine, the structure of the demand for healthcare will change, along with the structure of healthcare suppliers and capacities.

Specialised and Monopolist Providers Personalised medicine will lead to the development of a number of specialist activities that, in most cases, will not have much in common with the present-day specialist activities. Personalised medicine is about radical innovative medicine that, by its very nature, limits the number of suppliers of goods, prevents the entry of new suppliers and thus turns selected suppliers into monopolists and sometimes also with earnings in the form of economic rents.[20] Regardless of the financing source for personalised medicine, the supervision of monopolies is of paramount importance. As providers and suppliers are closely connected with innovation, it cannot be expected that the state will establish state-owned companies to prevent monopolist consequences as innovation is nowadays in the domain of privately-owned profit-oriented companies. However, it is reasonable to plan the state's radical interference with providers' and suppliers' operations in personalised medicine in the form of supervision over monopolies and regulation of their business activity.

Private Ownership of the Information Needed in Personalised Medicine Personalised medicine is underpinned by the collection of a great volume of highly specialised information about the individual's genome, the developments in a person's body as well as the influences of their environment and lifestyle on their life. Personalised medicine cannot exist without this large pool of information. The information will also serve as a basis for creating a kind of virtual image of a

---

[19]Xinghua Hu et al. (2005).
[20]McPake et al. (2013).

person's body that will be available to that person online, at any stage of their life. As the information needed in personalised medicine can only be generated through the activities of a high number of providers and suppliers, it is understandable that this cannot be done at the place of occurrence because there are too many of such places. In these circumstances, the only 'natural' repository of the information is the individual involved. Health information will reallocate from the provider to the user. This would also ensure the privacy of information and a person's right to use it at his/her own discretion, to manage his/her own life and health condition. It is not possible to assume that all individuals will want to use personalised medicine. This implies that personalised medicine can reduce the importance of public prevention services if it is obligatory for a person to be part of public healthcare. Moreover, responsibility for health is mainly transferred from the public healthcare system to the individual.

4   Conclusions

This chapter confirms the initially presented hypothesis that the development of personalised medicine will radically alter the foundations of public healthcare systems. Today, we are probably incapable of creating a comprehensive definition of personalised medicine that will continue to be valid in the future. However, there is no doubt this medicine will be based on genomic medicine and will focus on an individual rather than disease, it will consider a person's entire life and be built on a large volume of information about them or a sort of virtual image of their body. We have thus arrived at a few substantial findings concerning the relationship between personalised medicine and public healthcare systems:

First, introducing personalised medicine will radically affect the healthcare value chain, namely in the form of lifelong care for a person's healthy life. This will call for several new providers and suppliers, the introduction of health managers for each person who will know how to guide that person through different phases, changing the contents of individual phases, and new prognosis phases. In the implemental phase, it will no longer be possible to exploit economies of scale, giving rise to a particular problem in terms of the costs and the technologies employed by providers and suppliers. Public healthcare networks will reflect all of the above changes and become increasingly international.

Second, in the current situation out-of-pocket payment is the most reasonable way of financing personalised medicine, seeing that the latter—the same as for out-of-pocket payment—is linked to an individual. The absence of randomness, the focus on the individual and especially the varying individual specific medical prognoses could give birth to a health insurance system that is limited to the inter-temporal financial management of personalised medicine. It will resemble the endowment type of pension insurance, as the payment of premium should be linked to the period from taking out the insurance to the end of life, with the sole difference that the claims would not arise only at the end of life. The collective financing of personalised medicine is linked to solidarity also in this case. Here it is probably sensible to consider the criterion that solidarity is acceptable for financing the basket of those healthcare goods whose consumption is not decided on by an individual according to their preferences.

Third, from the perspective of the collective financing of personalised medicine, one should consider the fact that this medicine brings strong individual effects to a few individuals and smaller social effects. Therefore, it is possible to ground collective financing only on solidarity and not on the differences between social and individual effects.

Fourth, because of innovative technologies being applied by providers and suppliers there is a big danger the latter will take on a monopolist position. Accordingly, personalised medicine requires a great deal of state regulation. Given the limited solidarity and weaker social effects, the main mechanism for co-ordinating the activity among the users, payers and providers in personalised medicine will be the market, not the state. Its role will be more effective if market conditions come closer to perfect competition.

Fifth, all of the above findings are overtaken in importance by the realisation that personalised medicine is based on a large volume of information which is only available to the person whose health is described by this information, that only a computer—and in no case solely a human—can articulate this information in the form of diagnoses that enable a person's health to be optimised throughout their entire life, and that only the individual will require assistance from the manager of their health and life if they wish to exploit the benefits of personalised medicine.

References

Bieber T (2013) Stratified medicine: a new challenge for academia, industry, regulators and patients. Future Medicine Ltd, London

Carande-Kulis VG, Getzen TE, Thacker SB (2007) Public goods and externalities: a research agenda for public health economics. J Public Health Man 13(2):227–232

Carlsten C, Brauer M, Brinkman F, Brook J, Daley D, McNagny K, Pui M, Royce D, Takaro T, Denburg J (2014) Genes, the environment and personalized medicine: we need to harness both environmental and genetic data to maximize personal and population health. EMBO Rep 15 (7):736–739

Council conclusions on personalised medicine for patients (2015) Official Journal of the European Union, 2015/C421/03

Henke KD, Borchardt K (2003) Reform proposals for health-care systems. Dice Report 3:3–8

Jain KK (2015) Textbook of personalized medicine. Humana Press, Basel

Jakka S, Rossbach M (2013) An economic perspective on personalized medicine. HUGO J 7(1)

Jegers M, Kesteloot K, De Graeve D, Gilles W (2002) A typology for provider payment systems in health care. Health Policy 60(3):255–273

Kornai J (1986) The soft budget constraint. Kyklos 39(1):3–30

Kornai J, Eggleston K (2001) Welfare, choice, and solidarity in transition. Cambridge University Press, Cambridge

McPake B, Normand C, Smith S (2013) Health economics: an international perspective. Routledge, Abingdon

Meulen R, Arts W, Muffels R (2001) Solidarity, health and social care in Europe: introduction to the volume. In: Meulen R, Arts W, Muffels R (eds) Solidarity in health and social care in Europe. Kluwer, Dordrecht, pp 1–11

Phelps CE (2016) Health economics, 5th edn. Routledge, New York

Porter ME, Lee TH (2013) The strategy that will fix health care. Harv Bus Rev 91(10)

Redekop WK, Mladsi D (2013) The faces of personalized medicine: a framework for understanding its meaning and scope. Value Health 16(6 Suppl):S4–S9

Sagan A, Thomson S (2016) Voluntary health insurance in Europe: role and regulation. World Health Organization, European Observatory on Health Systems and Policies, Copenhagen

Saltman RB (2015) Health sector solidarity: a core European value but with broadly varying content. Isr J Health Policy Res 4(5)

Stiglitz JE, Rosengard JK (2015) Economics of the public sector, 4th edn. W.W. Norton, cop., New York, London

Xinghua Hu S, Foster T, Kieffaber A (2005) Pharmacogenomics and personalized medicine: mapping of future value creation. BioTechniques 39(4)

Part IV
Clinical Aspects of Personalised Medicine

Targeted Breast Cancer Therapy

Ingrid Belac Lovasić and Franjo Lovasić

Abstract Despite great advances in treatment, breast cancer is still the most common cause of death in cancer-treated women. From the results of numerous clinical studies and meta-analyses, the development of chemotherapy in the treatment of breast cancer has brought significant clinical benefit to survival, whether the treatment is adjuvant or the one of metastatic disease. The development of core oncology, translational and clinical research has led to a better understanding of the biology and immunology of tumors, the generation of new immunotherapeutic possibilities and their implementation in everyday clinical practice. For now, mostly monoclonal antibodies, primarily trastuzumab, are used in clinical practice, which is the gold standard for the treatment of HER-2 positive patients. Besides lapatinib, further development of this area has resulted in introducing pertuzumab, a monoclonal antibody directed against the second binding site of the HER-2 receptor, and trastuzumab-DM1, a true pathway for further development of immunotherapy, a cytostatic and antibody conjugate. Phase III clinical trials have confirmed the efficacy of pertuzumab and trastuzumab-DM1. The other direction the development of tumor immune therapy was based on was focusing on the infrastructure of the host, especially the blood vessels. For this purpose, a monoclonal antibody directed against the vascular endothelial growth factor (VEGF), bevacizumab, has been developed.

1 Introduction

Nowadays, monoclonal antibodies are an unavoidable standard in the treatment of breast cancer patients. First of all, this pertains to trastuzumab, and more recently, pertuzumab. One step further is the development of trastuzumab-DM1, which is the antibody and cytostatic conjugate. All these medications are used in treatment of patients with HER-2-positive disease. Unlike targeted immunotherapy in the treatment of HER-2 positive disease, bevacizumab is used in treatment of HER-2

I. Belac Lovasić (✉) · F. Lovasić
Clinic for Radiotherapy and Oncology, University Hospital Center Rijeka, Rijeka, Croatia

© Springer Nature Switzerland AG 2019
N. Bodiroga-Vukobrat et al. (eds.), *Personalized Medicine in Healthcare Systems*,
Europeanization and Globalization 5, https://doi.org/10.1007/978-3-030-16465-2_23

negative metastatic disease, without affecting any particular biomarker. The basic mechanisms of antibody activity imply that, by binding to their receptors or ligands in plasma, the antibodies prevent signal transduction down the cascade pathway inside the cell and thus inhibit proliferation, growth, differentiation and neo-angiogenesis, while by binding to the cell they simultaneously promote lymphocyte activation or cytotoxicity mediated by antibodies. Likewise, monoclonal antibodies can serve as a carrier for some other drugs.

Trastuzumab is the first monoclonal antibody to be established as targeted immunotherapy acting on the HER-2 receptor in HER-2 positive patients when combined with chemotherapy. Already in the 1990s, Slamon et al. (2001) showed for the first time that trastuzumab, in combination with chemotherapy, leads in the first line treatment for metastatic breast cancer to a significant survival prolongation (25.1 versus 20.3 months, $p = 0.046$) and to a significantly higher response rate (50% vs. 32%, $p < 0.001$).[1] Today trastuzumab is the basis for treatment of HER-2 positive breast cancer and its efficacy has been demonstrated in numerous clinical studies.

2　Trastuzumab in Adjuvant Therapy for Breast Cancer

Major studies of trastuzumab in adjuvant therapy, listed in Table 1, have included more than 13,000 patients and all but two of them (PACS04 and FinHer) showed a significantly longer period of time without the onset of disease and reduction in the risk of death for at least one third.[2,3,4,5,6,7] The use of trastuzumab in combination

Table 1 Evaluation of clinical efficacy of trastuzumab in breast cancer treatment

Early stage breast cancer		Metastatic breast cancer	
Adjuvant therapy	Neo-adjuvant therapy	First line treatment	Second and further lines of treatment
BCIRG006	Gepar Quattro	M77001	BO17929
NSABP B31	NOAH	HO648g	GBG-26
NCCTGN9831		US Oncology	EGF104900
HERA		BCIRG 007	
FinHer		RHEA	
PACS04			

[1] Slamon et al. (2001).
[2] Slamon et al. (2009).
[3] Perez et al. (2007).
[4] Perez et al. (2009).
[5] Piccart-Gebhart et al. (2005).
[6] Joensuu et al. (2009).
[7] Spielmann et al. (2009).

with anthracycline and non-anthracycline based chemotherapy protocols has also been investigated. The BCIRG 006 study compared the treatment with the combination of docetaxel/carboplatin/trastuzumab (TCH) versus the standard AC-TH protocol versus AC-T (without trastuzumab. After a median follow-up of 65 months, the clinical benefit of adding trastuzumab to the therapy in HER-2 positive patients was confirmed again. Five-year disease-free survival time is 75% for AC-T, 84% for AC-TH and 81% for TCH. The total 5-year survival rate is 85% for AC-T, 92%, for AC-TH and 91% for TCH. The benefit was also achieved in patients with both positive and negative lymph nodes. Only AC-TH was superior in patients with negative lymph nodes. Patients treated with the TCH protocol had a lower rate of side effects and lower incidence of grade 3 side effects. Significant heart failure rates were the highest in the group receiving AC-TH although it was lower than 1%. Thus, trastuzumab has been shown to have a similar and significantly beneficial effect on total survival and disease-free survival, either in combination with chemotherapy based on anthracycline (AC-TH) or non-anthracycline (TCH) protocols in both high and low risk patients.[8] The next unresolved question was whether to administer trastuzumab together with chemotherapy or sequentially, upon completion of chemotherapy with anthracyclines and cyclophosphamide. The evaluation (median follow-up of 5.5 years) conducted by the Interagency Study (N9831) compared the sequential application of trastuzumab after chemotherapy (AC-T-H) with co-administration of trastuzumab with chemotherapy (AC-TH).[9] It was concluded that the concomitant application of trastuzumab and paclitaxel is a better solution with a five year disease-free survival of 84.2%, while the sequential application resulted in 80% survival rate (HR:0.77). The difference in the disease-free survival between the studies in which trastuzumab was administered exists and is in favor of simultaneous administration of trastuzumab with paclitaxel ($p = 0.019$).[10]

3   Trastuzumab in Treatment of Metastatic Breast Cancer

The use of trastuzumab in the treatment of metastatic disease has changed HER-2 positive status from poor prognosis indicators to one of the best overall recovery outcomes. Trastuzumab monotherapy has been shown to be effective in treating breast cancer with excessive HER-2 expression with response rates ranging from 12% to 26%.[11] In major studies listed in the table, the clinical benefit of trastuzumab

---

[8]Slamon et al. (2009).

[9]Perez et al. (2007).

[10]Perez et al. (2009).

[11]Cobleigh et al. (1999); Baselga and Swan (2009); Vogel et al. (2002).

in combination with various chemotherapy protocols in the treatment of metastatic breast cancer has been presented.[12,13,14,15,16,17,18,19]

4 Trastuzumab in Neo-Adjuvant Therapy for Breast Cancer

The addition of trastuzumab to neoadjuvant chemotherapy was studied in the NOAH phase III trial. Non-adjuvant chemotherapy in combination with trastuzumab was investigated, after which adjuvant trastuzumab was ordered instead of neo-adjuvant chemotherapy in patients with a HER-2 positive locally advanced breast cancer. Trastuzumab significantly prolonged survival without progression of disease (3-year survival without progression of the disease was 71% with trastuzumab and 56% without trastuzumab HR: 0.59 $p = 0.013$). Trastuzumab was well tolerated; 2 out of 235 patients had undesirable cardiotoxic effects.[20] In the second non-adjuvant phase III trial, GepardQuattro ($n = 1500$), non-adjuvant application of trastuzumab in combination with several types of chemotherapy in HER-2 positive and negative patients was examined. The application of trastuzumab in patients with HER-2 positive tumors resulted in a significantly higher rate of complete pathological response (31.7% versus 15.5% in the control group not treated with trastuzumab).[21]

5 Trastuzumab in Combination with Other Biological Agents

Although trastuzumab has become a standard in treatment, there are still many unresolved issues such as resistance, cardiotoxicity, and appearance of metastases in CNS as the first site. Isolated metastases in the CNS in HER-2 positive breast cancer patients are associated with improved peripheral disease control and prolongation of survival with trastuzumab, and, at the same time, the trastuzumab inability to penetrate into the CNS. Unfortunately, despite significant progress in the

---

[12]Piccart-Gebhart et al. (2005).

[13]Marty et al. (2005).

[14]Robert et al. (2006).

[15]Forbes et al. (2006).

[16]Láng et al. (2014).

[17]von Minckwitz et al. (2009).

[18]Baselga and Swan (2009).

[19]Blackwell et al. (2009).

[20]Untch et al. (2010).

[21]Gianni et al. (2010).

treatment of HER-2 positive tumors, a significant number of patients with HER-2 positive breast cancer do not respond to trastuzumab therapy while the other patients, after the initial response, develop resistance to it during further treatment. To improve the effect of this form of immunotherapy, numerous studies combine the action of trastuzumab and small molecules, primarily lapatinib, in metastatic disease. Lapatinib acts as an inhibitor of intracellular part of tyrosine kinase HER-2 and HER-1 receptors. The synergistic effects of lapatinib and trastuzumab have been established, as well as the importance of continuous HER-2 blockade even in very advanced disease. The intracellular and extracellular domain receptor blockade has shown clear clinical benefit.[22,23] The same was established in neo-adjuvant application of lapatinib and trastuzumab. Results of NeoALLTO randomized Phase III trial involving 455 patients showed a significantly higher rate of complete disappearance of tumors in patients receiving lapatinib and trastuzumab versus only trastuzumab or lapatinib (51.3% versus 29.5%, $p = 0.0001$).[24]

6 Pertuzumab

Further development of drugs acting on HER-2 receptors led to clinical application of pertuzumab. Pertuzumab is a humanized monoclonal antibody that binds to the II subunit of the extracellular HE-2 receptor domain, thereby blocking the dimerization process with other ligand-activated HER receptors, primarily HER-3. The fact is that trastuzumab and pertuzumab bind to different subunits, that they have complementary modes of action and that they have a synergistic effect when administered in combination. Based on the results of the pre-clinical and early clinical studies in which the strong anti-inflammatory effect of the aforementioned treatment was observed, the Cleopatra study was designed. This is a randomized double-blind phase III trial that compares the efficacy of two antibodies, pertuzumab and trastuzumab with docetaxel with a combination of docetaxel/trastuzumab in the first line treatment of metastatic HER-2 positive breast cancer. The study included 808 patients. The study showed a significantly longer survival without progression of disease (PFS) among those treated with docetaxel/pertuzumab/trastuzumab (HR: 0.62, $p < 0.001$), i.e., PFS median increased from 12.4 months to 18.5 months.[25] The addition of pertuzumab did not significantly reduce the quality of life nor did it contribute to increased cardiotoxicity.[26,27] After 30 months of median follow-up, it was concluded that adding pertuzumab to the therapy resulted in statistically

---

[22]Di Cosimo and Baselga (2008).

[23]Geyer et al. (2006).

[24]Baselga et al. (2012a).

[25]Baselga et al. (2012b).

[26]Cortes et al. (2013).

[27]Swain et al. (2013a).

significant prolongation of total survival and reduction of death risk by 34% (HR: 0, 66, $p = 0.0008$).[28] These results represent a significant statistical breakthrough and, more importantly, the clinical benefit in the first-line treatment of metastatic HER-2 positive breast cancer.

7 Trastuzumab-Emtansine (T-DM1)

The next step in developing immunotherapy is the development of drugs that consist of cytostatics and antibodies. It is known that antibodies, among other things, may serve as a carrier for various substances, which they then delivered to the cells and produce corresponding effects. An example of this is T-DM1 which is the conjugate of antibodies and cytostatics linked with a stable link. In this combination, the antibody is trastuzumab and the cytostatic emtansine, a maytansine derivative that blocks the microtubule polymerization. It is inactive and non-toxic in the conjugate (unlike the fact that it is extremely toxic if used as a classic cytostatic). Cytostatic is released from the conjugate only after entry into the tumor cell within the lysosomal system after antibody destruction. T-DM1 has a dual mechanism of action: anti-HER activity (antibody) and intracellular strong anti-tubular activity (cytostatic). The clinical value of this drug was established in EMILIA phase III trial.[29] It is the second line of treatment for metastatic HER-2 positive breast cancer in patients who have progressed to treatment with a combination of trastuzumab and taxan. 978 patients in 2 branches were randomized: a standard second line that included a combination of capecitabine/lapatinib versus T-DM1 study branch. Median PFS for T-DM1 was 9.6 months and for capecitabine/lapatinib 6.4 (HR: 0.65, $p < 0.0001$)). At the end of 2012, the results of total survival analysis after 20 months of monitoring median were presented. Total survival median for T-DM1 was 30.9 months versus 25.1 months for combination of lapatinib/capecitabine (HR 0.68, $p < 0.001$).[30] The tolerability profile of T-DM1 was significantly better than the one for the combination of capecitabine/lapatinib. Combination of capecitabine and lapatinib more commonly caused diarrhea, palmoplantar erythema, vomiting, rash and neutropenia. Clinical benefit and statistically significantly longer survival without progression of disease as well as total survival and lower toxicity compared to the gold standard of second line treatment of metastatic HER-2 positive breast cancer resulted in rapid approval of said drug in the aforementioned indication by the US Food and Drug Administration (FDA) in February 2013.

---

[28]Swain et al. (2013b).

[29]Kimberly et al. (2012).

[30]Dieras et al. (2017).

8 Bevacizumab

There is no predictive marker to define a subgroup of patients who would benefit from bevacizumab therapy. Therefore, it can be used in nearly every patient with HER-2 negative metastatic breast cancer. Bevacizumab is a monoclonal antibody that binds to VEGF in circulation, resulting in a bevacizumab-VEGF complex that cannot bind to the VEGF receptor on the endothelial cell surface so that signaling pathways cannot be activated. Drugs acting on VEGF will hypothetically reduce tumor vascularization and thus inhibit tumor growth and tumor transplantation process. They can reduce microvascular permeability, reduce tumor interstitial pressure and help normalize morphology and tumor vessel functions, thus enabling a better effect of chemotherapy. Three randomized phase III trials (E2100, AVADO and RIBBON-1), have shown that the addition of bevacizumab to chemotherapy in the first line of treatment for locally recurrent or metastatic breast cancer increases response rate and time to progression of the disease compared to chemotherapy alone without the benefit in total survival.[31,32,33] The results of RIBBON-2 trial have shown that the addition of bevacizumab to chemotherapy in the second line of treatment for metastatic breast cancer increases the overall response rate versus chemotherapy alone (from 29% to 39%, ($p = 0.019$) and increases the mean time to progression from 51 to 72 months ($p = 0.007$)).[34] A further step was the study of the efficacy of adding bevacizumab to the standard combination of first-line treatment of HER-2 positive metastatic breast cancer, docetaxel/trastuzumab (AVAREL study). The initial results showed a significantly better median survival rate without progression of disease when bevacizumab was administered (16.5 versus 13.7 months, HR: 0.82, $p = 0.08$), while the independent committee analysis reached a statistically significant difference (16.8 versus 13.9 months, HR: 0.72, $p = 0.02$).[35]

9 Conclusion

Progress in developing new targeted drugs such as trastuzumab, lapatinib, pertuzumab and T-DM1 brings a significant improvement to the treatment of breast cancer. It is necessary to set proper position of these drugs primarily in the treatment of metastatic disease, that is, to select the correct order of treatment line and treatment combination. It is also necessary to further investigate these drugs in combination with chemotherapy and their mutual combinations in adjuvant and non-adjuvant treatment to obtain optimal understanding of their value. In

---

[31] Schneider and Sledge (2011).

[32] Miles et al. (2010).

[33] Robert et al. (2011).

[34] Brufsky et al. (2011).

[35] Gianni et al. (2013).

conclusion, the combination of chemotherapy and targeted therapy is consistent with the results of major clinical studies and has dramatically improved breast cancer treatment outcome. It can be said that the combination of chemotherapy and targeted therapy is indeed a paradigm in treatment of breast cancer. All of these will provide an individualized approach to each patient. The goal of all is, of course, to have a better quality treatment to the benefit of patients.

References

Baselga J, Swan MS (2009) Novel anticancer targets: revisiting ERBB2 and discovering ERBB3. Nat Rev Canc 9(7):463–475. https://doi.org/10.1038/nrc2656

Baselga J, Bradbury I, Eidtmann H et al (2012a) Lapatinib with trastuzumab for HER2-positive early breast cancer (NeoALTTO): a randomized, open-label, multicentre, phase 3 trial. Lancet 379(9816):633–640. https://doi.org/10.1016/S0140-6736(11)61847-3

Baselga J, Cortes J, Kim SB et al (2012b) Pertuzumab plus trastuzumab docetaxel for metastatic breast cancer. N Engl J Med 366(2):109–119. https://doi.org/10.1056/NEJMoa1113216

Blackwell KL, Burstein HJ, Sledge GW (2009) Updated survival analysis of a randomized study of Lapatinib alone or in combination with trastuzumab in women with HER2-positive metastatic breast cancer progressing on trastuzumab therapy. Cancer Res 69(24 Suppl 3):Abstract 61. https://doi.org/10.1158/0008-5472.SABCS-09-61

Brufsky AM, Hurvitz S, Perez E et al (2011) RIBBON-2: a randomized, double-blind, placebo-controlled phase III trial evaluating the efficacy and safety of bevacizumab in combination with chemotherapy, for second-line treatment of human epidermal growth factor receptor 2-negative metastatic breast cancer. J Clin Oncol 29(32):4286–4293. https://doi.org/10.1200/JCO.2010.34.1255

Cobleigh MA, Vogel C, Tripathy D et al (1999) Multinational study of the efficacy and safety of humanized anti-HER2 monoclonal antibody in women who have HER2-overexpressing metastatic breast cancer that has progressed after chemotherapy for metastatic disease. J Clin Oncol 17(9):2639–2648. https://doi.org/10.1200/jco.1999.17.9.2639

Cortes J, Baselga J, Im YH et al (2013) Health-related quality-of-life assessment in CLEOPATRA, a phase III study combining pertuzumab with trastuzumab and docetaxel in metastatic breast cancer. Ann Oncol 24(10):2630–2635. https://doi.org/10.1093/annonc/mdt274

Di Cosimo S, Baselga J (2008) Targeted therapy in breast cancer: where are we now? Eur J Cancer 44(18):2781–2790. https://doi.org/10.1016/j.ejca.2008.09.026

Dieras V, Miles D, Verma S et al (2017) Trastuzumab emtansine versus capecitabine plus lapatinib in patients with previously treated HER2-positive advanced breast cancer (EMILIA): a descriptive analysis of final overall survival results from a randomised, open-label, phase 3 trial. Lancet Oncol 18(6):732–742. https://doi.org/10.1016/S1470-2045(17)30312-1

Forbes JF, Kennedy J, Pienkowski T et al (2006) BCIRG 007: randomized phase III trial of trastuzumab plus docetaxel with or without carboplatin first line in HER2 positive metastatic breast cancer(MBC): main time to progression (TTP) analysis J Clin Oncol 24(Suppl 18):A-LBA516, 7s

Geyer CE, Forster J, Lindquist D et al (2006) Lapatinib plus capecitabine for HER2-positive advanced breast cancer. N Engl J Med 355(26):2733–2743. https://doi.org/10.1056/NEJMoa064320

Gianni L, Eirmann W, Semiglazov V et al (2010) Neoadjuvant chemotherapy with trastuzumab followed by adjuvant trastuzumab versus neoadjuvant chemotherapy alone, in patients with HER2-positive locally advanced breast cancer (the NOAH trial). Lancet 375(9712):377–384

Gianni L, Romieu GH, Lichinitser M et al (2013) AVEREL: a randomized phase III trial evaluating Bevacizumab in combination with docetaxel and trastuzumab as first-line therapy for HER2-positive locally recurrent/metastatic breast cancer. J Clin Oncol 31(14):1719–1725. https://doi.org/10.1200/JCO.2012.44.7912

Joensuu H, Bono P, Kataja V et al (2009) Fluorouracil, epirubucun, and cyclophosphamide with either docetaxel or vinorelbine, with or without trastuzumab, as adjuvant treatments of breast cancer: final results of the FinHer Trial. J Clin Oncol 27(34):5685–5692

Kimberly L, Blackwell K, Miles D et al (2012) Primary results from EMILIA, a phase 3study of trastuzumab-emtansine (T-DM-1) vs capecitabine (X) and lapatinib (L) in HER2 positive locally advanced or metastatic breast cancer (MBC) previously treated with trastuzumab (T) and a taxane. J Clin Oncol 30:18_suppl,LBA-LBA1. https://doi.org/10.1200/jco.2012.30.18_suppl.lba1

Láng I, Bell R, Feng FY, Lopez RI et al (2014) Trastuzumab retreatment after relapse on adjuvant trastuzumab therapy for human epidermal growth factor receptor 2-positive breast cancer: final results of the retreatment after herceptin adjuvant trial. Clin Oncol (R Coll Radiol) 26(2):81–89. https://doi.org/10.1016/j.clon.2013.08.011

Marty M, Cognetti F, Maraninchi D et al (2005) Randomized phase II trial of the efficacy and safety of trastuzumab combined with docetaxel in patients with human epidermal growth factor receptor 2-positive breast cancer administreted as firstline treatment: the M77001 study group. J Clin Oncol 23(19):4265–4274

Miles DW, Chan A, Dirix LY et al (2010) Phase III study of bevacizumab plus docetaxel compared with placebo plus docetaxel for the first-line treatment of human epidermal growth factor receptor 2-negative metastatic breast cancer. J Clin Oncol 28(20):3239–3247. https://doi.org/10.1200/JCO.2008.21.6457

Perez E, Suman V, Davidson N et al (2009) Results of chemotherapy alone with sequential or concurrent addition of 52 weeks of trastuzumab in the NCCTG N9831 HER2 positive adjuvant breast cancer trial. In: Program and abstracts of the 32nd Annual San Antonio Breast Cancer Symposium; December 9–13, San Antonio, Texas, Abstract 80

Perez EA, Romond EH, Suman VJ et al (2007) Updated results of the combined analysis of NCCTG N9831 and NSABP B-31 adjuvant chemotherapy with/witouth trastuzumab in patients with HER-2 breast cancer (abstract). J Clin Oncol 25(18):Abstract 512. https://doi.org/10.1200/jco.2007.25.18_suppl.512

Piccart-Gebhart MJ, Procter M, Leyland-Jones B et al (2005) Trastuzumab after adjuvant chemotherapy in HER2-positive breast cancer. N Engl J Med 353(16):1659–1672

Robert N, Leyland-Jones B, Asmar L et al (2006) Randomised phase III study of trastuzumab, paclitaksel, and carboplatin compared with trastuzumab and palitaksel in women with HER-2 overexpressing metastatis breast cancer. J Clin Oncol 24(18):2786–2792

Robert NJ, Dieras V, Glaspy J et al (2011) RIBBON-1: randomized, double-blind, placebo-controlled, phase III trial of chemotherapy with or without bevacizumab for first-line treatment of human epidermal growth factor receptor 2-negative, locally recurrent or metastatic breast cancer. J Clin Oncol 29(10):1252–1260. https://doi.org/10.1200/JCO.2010.28.0982

Schneider BP, Sledge GW Jr (2011) Anti-vascular endothelial growth factor therapy for breast cancer: can we pick the winners? J Clin Oncol 29(18):2444–2447. https://doi.org/10.1200/JCO.2011.34.9266

Slamon D, Eiermann W, Robert N et al (2009) Phase III trial comparing AC→T with AC→TH and with TCH in the adjuvant treatment of HER2-amplified early breast cancer patients: BCIRG 006 study. In: Third Planned Efficacy Analysis. Program and abstracts of the 32nd Annual San Antonio Breast Cancer Symposium; December 9-13, San Antonio, Texas, Abstract 62

Slamon DJ, Leyland-Jones B, Shak S et al (2001) Use of chemotherapy plus monoclonal antibody against Her2 for metastatic breast cancer that overexpresses Her2. N Engl J Med 344(11):783–792

Spielmann M, Roche H, Delozier T et al (2009) Trastuzumab for patients with axillary-node-positive breast cancer: results of the FNCLCC-PACS 04 trial. J Clin Oncol 27(36):6129–6134

Swain SM, Ewer MS, Cortes J et al (2013a) Cardiac tolerability of pertuzumab plus trastuzumab plus docetaxel in patients with HER2-positive metastatic breast cancer in CLEOPATRA: a randomized, double-blind, placebo-controlled phase III study. Oncologist 18(3):257–264. https://doi.org/10.1634/theoncologist.2012-0448

Swain SM, Sung-Bae K, Cortes J et al (2013b) Overall survival benefit with pertuzumab, trastuzumab, and docetaxel for HER2-positive metastatic breast cancer in CLEOPATRA, a randomised Phase 3 study. Lancet Oncol 14(6):461–471. https://doi.org/10.1016/S1470-2045 (13)70130-X

Untch M, Rezai M, Loibl S et al (2010) Neoadjuvant treatment with trastuzumab in HER2-positive breast cancer: results from the GeparQUattro study. J Clin Oncol 28(12):2024–2031

Vogel CL, Cobleigh MA, Tripathy D et al (2002) Efficacy and safety of trastuzumag as a single agent in first-line treatment of HER2-overexpressing metastatic breast cancer. J Clin Oncol 20 (3):719–726. https://doi.org/10.1200/JCO.2002.20.3.719

von Minckwitz G, du Bois A, Schmidt M et al (2009) Trastuzumab beyond progression in human epidermal growth factor receptor 2-positive advanced breast cancer: A German Breast Group 26/Breast International Group 03-05 study. J Clin Oncol 27(12):1999–2006. https://doi.org/10. 1200/JCO.2008.19.6618

Personalized Medicine in Ophthalmology: Treatment of Total Limbal Stem Cell Deficiency with Autologous *Ex Vivo* Cultivated Limbal Epithelial Stem Cell Graft

Iva Dekaris, Mirna Tominac-Trcin, Nikica Gabrić, Budimir Mijović, and Adi Pašalić

Abstract Most of the blinding corneal diseases are treatable by corneal transplantation in which a corneal allograft is used. However, in severe corneal burns that often result in total limbal epithelial stem cell (LECS) deficiency, corneal transplantation alone is not feasible, as corneal graft in eyes without stem cells cannot survive. Total LESC deficiency is clinically characterized by growth of conjunctival tissue over the cornea, corneal neovascularization and opacification. It unfortunately affects mostly younger population. Two decades ago, it has been shown that a successful corneal graft in patients with corneal burns can only be performed as a second surgical act; namely only after transplantation of limbal stem cells cultivated *ex vivo* have restored a healthy anterior ocular surface. Cultivation of LESC *ex vivo* has been adopted as treatment of choice for such cases. Various carriers of LESC *in vitro* has been tested and clinically applied, such as fibrin, amniotic membrane and contact lens. LESC samples for cultivation *in vitro* can be autologous grafts harvested from the contralateral healthy eye (if only one eye has corneal burn), or allografts retrieved from a healthy relative or donor corneo-scleral rim. The most effective way of treatment is collection of healthy LESC from patient's healthy eye, their multiplication *ex vivo* on certain carrier and final grafting of cultivated epithelial sheet on the diseased eye of the same patient. Transplantation of such LESC becomes a personalized ocular treatment as epithelial sheet of cells must be cultivated for each particular patient. Other sources of LESC for *ex vivo* cultures, such as

I. Dekaris (✉) · N. Gabrić · A. Pašalić
Specialty Eye Hospital 'Svjetlost', Department of Ophthalmology, University of Rijeka, Zagreb, Croatia

M. Tominac-Trcin
Tissue Bank, University Department of Traumatology, University Hospital "Sestre Milosrdnice", Zagreb, Croatia

B. Mijović
Department of Basic Natural and Technical Sciences, Faculty of Textile Technology, University of Zagreb, Zagreb, Croatia

© Springer Nature Switzerland AG 2019
N. Bodiroga-Vukobrat et al. (eds.), *Personalized Medicine in Healthcare Systems*, Europeanization and Globalization 5, https://doi.org/10.1007/978-3-030-16465-2_24

allografts, are significantly less successful and has disadvantage that the patient must receive systemic immunosuppressive treatment with unwanted side-effects.

1 Introduction

According to the World Health Organization, corneal blindness is the fourth leading cause of blindness globally (5.1%). The impact of corneal blindness is huge because it tends to affect younger people. Corneal transplantation may restore vision in many corneal diseases, however in case of corneal burns in which limbal epithelial stem cells (LESC) are destroyed corneal transplantation is not feasible. For centuries, patients with total LESC deficiency caused by corneal burns were untreatable, until two decades ago when first results of successful cultivation of LESC ex vivo followed by their transplantation in human eye were reported.[1]

Since that time, different carriers for LESC cultivation have been tried in vitro, and their efficacy was tested in a clinical setting.[2] Most of the early-published papers on this subject addressed only dozens of cases and shorter follow-up, until the prominent works of Rama and Sangwan et al., when results of over 100 operated eyes with LESC deficiency with/without subsequent corneal graft were reported with a follow-up of over 10 years.[3] This novel treatment for severe corneal burns is nowadays performed in several ophthalmic centers using different LECS carriers such as fibrin, amniotic membrane or contact lens. It also became clear that the most successful approach is to cultivate LESC from patient contralateral uninjured eye (if feasible), as allografts induce strong immune response to foreign tissue and patients must receive strong systemic immunosuppressive treatment. Therefore, optimal way of treatment for corneal burns today fits into category of personalized medicine, where a small part of limbal tissue is obtained from patient's healthy eye, cultivated *in vitro* in a tissue/eye bank on a specific carrier, and finally grafted back to the same patient in approximately 10–14 days.

2 Cornea and Limbal Epithelial Stem Cells

The cornea is the transparent front surface of the eye acting as a window to the world; hence, corneal transparency is essential for vision. It also provides the majority of the refractive power of the eye because it refracts the light onto the retina at the back of the eye. The cornea is comprised of five layers, the most superficial one being the non-keratinised stratified epithelium. Dead squamous

---

[1]Pellegrini et al. (1997).

[2]Schwab et al. (2000), Rama et al. (2001) and Grueterich et al. (2003).

[3]Rama et al. (2010) and Sangwan et al. (2011).

cells are constantly sloughed from the corneal epithelium during blinking and repopulated with new epithelial cells. Limbal epithelial stem cells are responsible for constant epithelial renewal; they are situated at the corneo-scleral junction in an area known as the limbus. They share common features with other adult somatic stem cells including small size, high nuclear to cytoplasmic ratio, high proliferative potential, clonogenicity, multipotency, expression of stem cell markers, but lacking expression of differentiation markers such as cytokeratins 3 and 12. The transcription factor p63 is required for formation of epidermis and has been proposed as a putative positive LESC marker.[4]

In vitro, p63 was found to be expressed in limbal epithelial cell derived holoclones with little or no expression in meroclones and paraclones. *In vivo,* p63 is located in the limbal basal epithelium. Further work has since indicated that the ABCG2 may more specifically label LESC.[5] Later on, other markers such as ABCG2 and Notch signaling molecules were also found to be elevated in limbal cultures.[6] Limbal stem cells also prevent the conjunctivalepithelial cells from migrating onto the surface of the cornea. In case of LESC deficiency normal corneal epithelial homeostasis is disrupted and this may occur because of primary or acquired insults. Deficiency of the LESC may be partial or full.[7] The leading cause of total LESC deficiency are corneal burns with chemical or thermal substances and corneal diseases such as aniridia and Stevens Johnson syndrome. Because of LESC deficiency, conjunctivalization, neovascularisation, chronic inflammation, recurrent erosions, ulceration and stromal scarring can occur causing painful vision loss.[8] Typical clinical appearance of an eye with total LESC deficiency and conjunctivalization of the cornea is shown in Fig. 1. Conventional corneal transplantation has been unsuccessfully tried in such cases, as donor cornea cannot survive in a "milieu" where no LESC are present. Only renewal of the corneal epithelium, through replacement of the stem cell population may bring long term visual improvement. This was traditionally achieved by grafting limbal auto- or allografts.[9] In such cases, a larger amount of tissue had to be collected either from a contralateral healthy eye, thus carrying a risk of damage to healthy eye; or, if LESC graft was provided from allogenic tissue, a risk from side effects of long-term immunosuppression was present.[10] First successful attempt to grow ocular surface epithelial cells in a culture for consequent use as grafts was made in a mice model.[11] Twenty years ago, Pellegrini et al. have reported first successful epithelialization of a

---

[4]Pellegrini et al. (2001).

[5]Di Iorio et al. (2005) and Schlötzer-Schrehardt and Kruse (2005).

[6]Dhamodaran et al. (2015).

[7]Chen and Tseng (1991) and Dua et al. (2003).

[8]Kenyon and Tseng (1989) and Puangsricharern and Tseng (1995).

[9]Kenyon and Tseng (1989) and Tsai et al. (2000).

[10]Schwab (1999), Schwab et al. (2000) and James et al. (2001).

[11]Lindberg et al. (1993), Koizumi et al. (2000) and Meller et al. (2002).

Fig. 1 Appearance of the eye with total limbal epithelial stem cell deficiency caused by corneal burn

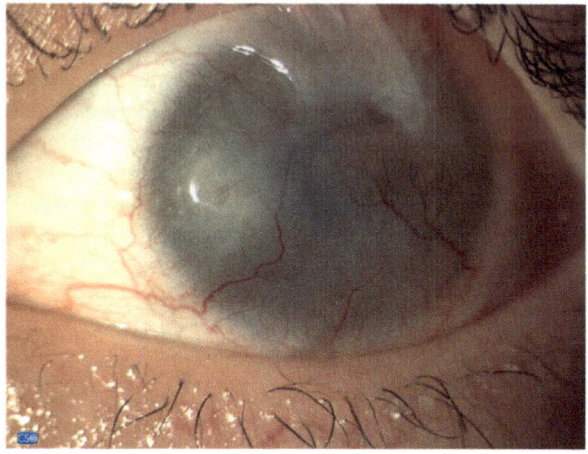

burned human cornea treated with a novel approach—transplantation of *in vitro* expanded LESC.

Cells were cultivated from a 1 mm^2 biopsy sample taken from the limbus of the healthy eye of two patients with severe alkali burn in another eye. Normal corneal differentiation *in vitro* was tested with a specific biochemical marker, and then the cells were grafted onto the burned eye. Successful re-epithelialization of the corneal surface was achieved in a 2-year follow-up.[12] These results provided a new perspective on the treatment of ocular disorders characterized by stem-cell deficiency. Cultured LESC therapy has been further developed by several investigators using different protocols and carriers—mostly amniotic membrane or fibrin, in the presence or absence of growth arrested 3T3 fibroblast feeder layers.[13] After those first findings many groups around the globe have continued to treat patients with LESC deficiency with *ex vivo* expanded limbal stem cells on different carriers such as amniotic membrane, fibrin or contact lens.[14] The most widely used ones in clinical work today are fibrin and amniotic membrane, although other potential carriers are also tested. Same methodology is theoretically applicable for patients with bilateral corneal burns, when LESC allografts obtained from a relative or unrelated donor are used; however with much lower success rate and a negative impact of aggressive systemic immunosuppressive treatment. The effort is also made to grow LSEC in a media completely free of any animal-derived products, and successful clinical results of such technique, using only autologous human serum as the only growth supplement are already reported.[15] Later on, oral mucosal epithelial cell grafts have been tried, which is of special interest in cases of bilateral corneal burns where autologous

---

[12]Pellegrini et al. (1997).

[13]Sidney et al. (2015) and López-Paniagua et al.(2016).

[14]Shimazaki et al. (2002), Zakaria et al. (2010), González et al. (2016) and Bobba et al. (2015).

[15]Pathak et al. (2013) and O'Callaghan et al. (2016).

grafts from other healthy eye cannot be obtained.[16] The transplantation of bioengineered oral mucosal epithelium is good strategy in bilateral LESC deficiency; however further studies are required to optimize the culture conditions and visual outcome.[17] Novel approach to graft bioengineered oral mucosal cells in bilateral disease again involves personalized approach, as the cells are retrieved from the same patient who is receiving the graft of *ex vivo* cultured cells.

It has been shown that also other stem cell populations like human embryonic stem cells, orbital fat cells and mesenchymal stem cells can be driven towards a corneal epithelial-like phenotype.[18] Future studies will tell whether such epithelial-like cells may be used clinically instead of LESC.

3   Cultivation of LESC in Croatian Tissue Bank

We are currently using amniotic membrane as a preferred carrier for LESC cultivation *in vitro*. All procedures regarding preparation of carriers and cell cultures are made in aseptic conditions of clean room facility for cell cultures (class A and B of air cleanness), which was licensed from Croatian Competent Authority for advance therapy medicinal products under hospital exemption rule. Amniotic membranes are prepared from human placenta obtained from healthy woman during caesarean section, under the established procedure.[19] Limbal stem cells isolation is carried out from a 1–2 mm^2 biopsy sample obtained from a contralateral healthy eye of a patient with total LESC deficiency. After disinfection with 5% ABAM solution and DPBS, sample is incubated in 0.05% enzyme trypsin/1 mM EDTA solution. Human limbal cells are counted and seeded in 2:1 ratio to previously prepared mice fibroblast nutrient layer. Media is changed every third day until 80% confluence, when cells are counted. Cell cultures are regularly monitored by optical microscopy for their viability (Fig. 2). Immunocytochemical method and confocal microscopy is used to test cells for the presence of stem-cells and differentiation markers (Fig. 3). In the experimental part of Tissue bank work, other potential carriers (scaffolds) completely free of animal-derived products are tested, like synthetic electrospun polyurethane and polycaprolactone nano-scaffolds fabricated by electrospinning.[20] Compared to natural carriers, electrospun scaffolds have the advantage of carrying no risk of disease transmission. Synthetic materials enable better control of mechanics, geometry, porosity, and rate of degradation. Carriers with porous structure and specified architecture allow by different size and distribution of pores spatially oriented cell proliferation and provide desired three-dimensional tissue-equivalent.

---

[16]Dobrowolski et al. (2015) and Utheim (2015).

[17]Priya et al. (2011).

[18]Ahmadet al. (2007), Ho et al. (2011), Holan et al. (2015) and Brzeszczynska et al. (2014).

[19]Dekaris and Gabrić (2009).

[20]Tominac Trcin et al. (2016).

Fig. 2 Cultivation of limbal epithelial stem cells on the amniotic membrane *in vitro*. Electronic microscopy image of limbal epithelial cells cultured on amnion

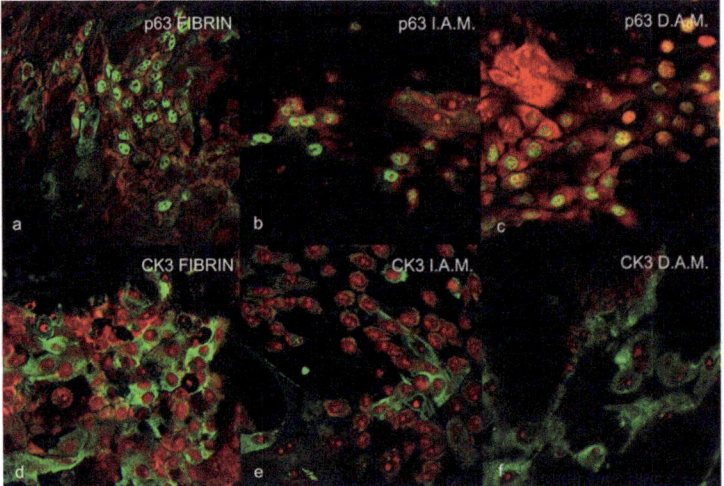

Fig. 3 Immunofluorescence analysis of p63 (**a, b, c**) and CK3 (**d, e, f**) markers of limbal epithelial stem cells and differentiated limbal cells, cultured on fibrin (**a, d**), intact amniotic membrane (I.A. M.) (**b, e**) and denuded amniotic membrane (D.A.M.) (**c, f**) respectively

Nano-scaffolds produced from nanofibers show advantages of high porosity and surface to volume ratio.

From the first results, electrospun scaffold show high percentage of p63 positive cells, indicating that great majority of cultured cells at high confluence were primitive ones with less differentiated phenotype (stem cells and young transient amplifying cells); namely those particularly useful in clinical sense (Fig. 4).[21]

---

[21]Tominac Trcin et al. (2016).

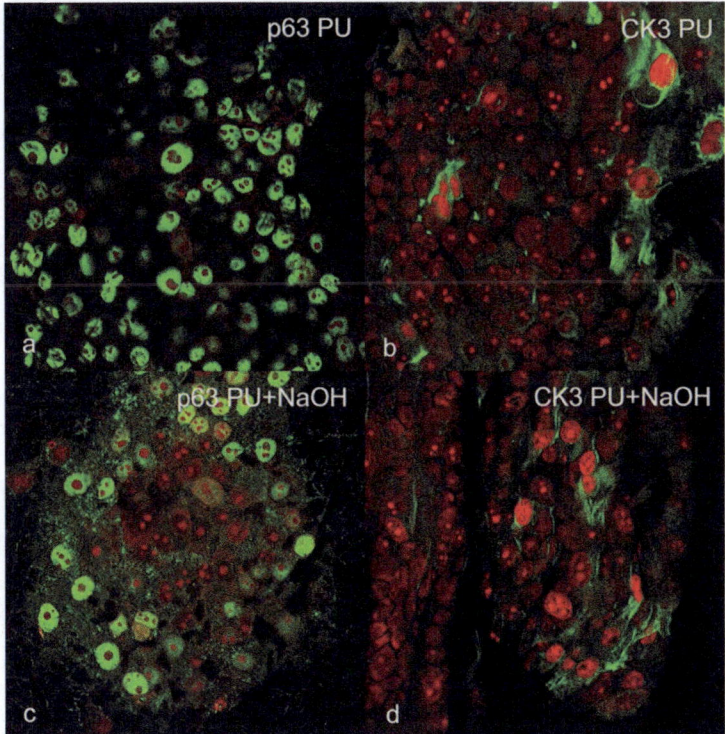

Fig. 4 Immunofluorescence analysis of p63 (**a,c**) and cytokeratin (CK) 3 (**b,d**) markers of limbal stem cells and differentiated limbal cells cultured on electrospun polyurethane (Pu) (**a,b**) and electrospun Pu/NaOH (**c,d**) respectively. Nuclei are counterstained with red stain propidium iodide (PI)

4 Clinical Application of *Ex Vivo* Expanded Epithelial Cells

Transplantation of *ex vivo* cultured LESC has become a method of choice in treating patients with unilateral corneal combustion. It is mostly applicable as a personalized type of ophthalmic treatment, as limbal cells are taken from the same individual whom they are going to be grafted after their multiplication *ex vivo*, and they cannot be successfully used for another patient. After LESC cultivation, and once the number or percentage of p63 positive cells is achieved *in vivo*, LESC on a specific carrier are transferred to corneal surgeon for clinical application. Surgery is done under local anesthesia. Limbal peritomy is performed and fibrovascular pannus is carefully dissected from the cornea in all 360°. The amniotic-membrane carrying cultivated LESC is then gently placed on the prepared corneal bed with LESC facing toward the cornea. Perilimbal region of 3–4 mm bare sclera is also covered with LESC sheet and the border of the amniotic membrane is sutured to the adjacent conjunctiva with resorptive 8.0 suture. The eyelids are kept closed for 1 week. Post-

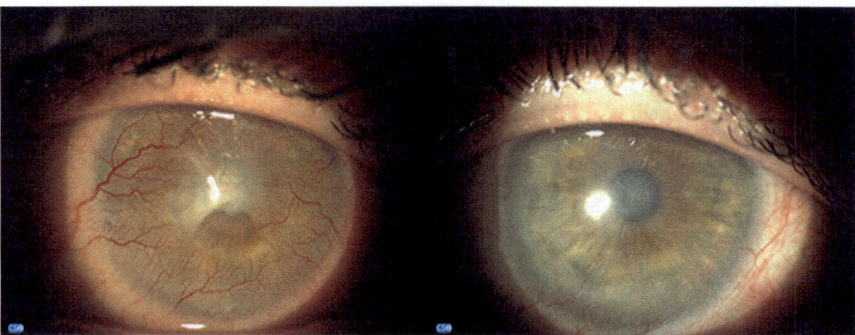

Fig. 5 Preoperative (limbal stem cell deficiency caused by tear gas burn) and 6-months postoperative appearance of the eye treated with *ex vivo* cultivated limbal epithelial stem cells. Visual acuity improved from preoperative value of light perception to 60% postoperatively

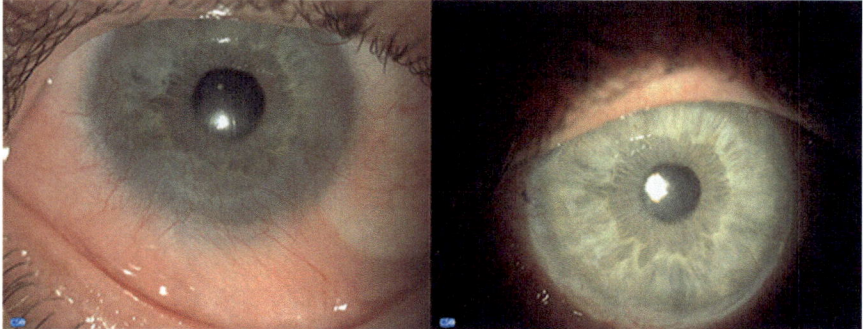

Fig. 6 Preoperative (limbal stem cell deficiency caused by alkali burn) and 1-month postoperative appearance of the eye treated with *ex vivo* cultivated limbal epithelial stem cells. Visual acuity improved from preoperative value of 15% to 55% postoperatively

operatively, patients receive 2-week systemic treatment with amoxicillin (500 mg tid) and 1-month systemic prednisone (24 mg) and ranitidine with gradual decrease of dosage. Topical steroid and antibiotic drops, and frequent artificial drops, are started at day 14 after surgery to prevent damage to the graft with lid manipulation. Throughout the postoperative follow-up, operated eye is controlled for the regular epithelialization, decrease of corneal neovascularization and improvement of vision. Once the ocular surface becomes regular, improvement of vision is tested to determine whether patient is cured by LESC alone or next surgery—corneal transplantation (CT) is needed. With the treatment of LESC deficiency vision may be adequately restored and patient completely cured like in cases shown in Figs. 5 and 6. If the cornea is still too opaque for good vision—conventional CT can be successfully performed as a second-step procedure.

5   Conclusion

Personalized medicine is finding its place in most medical subspecialties, ophthalmology alike. Example of such personalized approach is treatment of severe corneal burns with consequent epithelial stem cell deficiency and vision loss. In such cases, only stem cells from autologous source are able to restore vision; thus, the treatment must be done in personalized manner. Best source of stem cells is from the other uninjured eye with their multiplication by *ex vivo* cultivation. If the disease is bilateral it seems that other autologous stem cells, such as oral mucosal cells, orbital fat cells and mesenchymal stem cells, might also be an option. These exciting data may lead to alternative therapeutic strategies in the future.

References

Ahmad S, Stewart R, Yung S et al (2007) Differentiation of human embryonicstem cellsinto corneal epithelial-likecellsby in vitro replication of the corneal epithelialstemcell niche. Stem Cells 25 (5):1145–1155

Bobba S, Chow S, Watson S et al (2015) Clinical outcomes of xeno-free expansion and transplantation of autologous ocular surface epithelial stem cells via contact lens delivery: a prospective case series. Stem Cell Res Ther 6:23. https://doi.org/10.1186/s13287-015-0009-1

Brzeszczynska J, Samuel K, Greenhough S et al (2014) Differentiation and molecular profiling ofhumanembryonicstemcell-derived corneal epithelialcells. Int J Mol Med 33(6):1597–1606. https://doi.org/10.3892/ijmm.2014.1714

Chen JJ, Tseng SC (1991) Abnormal corneal epithelial wound healing in partial-thickness removal of limbal epithelium. Invest Ophthalmol Vis Sci 32(8):2219–2233

Dekaris I, Gabrić N (2009) Preparation and preservation of amniotic membrane. Dev Ophthalmol 43:97–104

Dhamodaran K, Subramani M, Jeyabalan N et al (2015) Characterization of ex vivo cultured limbal, conjunctival, and oral mucosal cells: a comparative study with implications in transplantation medicine. Mol Vis 21:828–845. eCollection 2015

Di Iorio E, Barbaro V, Ruzza A et al (2005) Isoforms of DeltaNp63 and the migration of ocularlimbalcellsin human corneal regeneration. Proc Natl Acad Sci U S A 102(27):9523–9528

Dobrowolski D, Orzechowska-Wylegala B, Wowra B et al (2015) Cultivated oral mucosa epithelium in ocular surface reconstruction in aniridia patients. Biomed Res Int 281870. https://doi.org/10.1155/2015/281870

Dua HS, Joseph A, Shanmuganathan VA et al (2003) Stem cell differentiation and the effects of deficiency. Eye (London) 17(8):877–885

González S, Mei H, Nakatsu MN et al (2016) A 3D culture system enhances the ability of human bone marrow stromal cells to support the growth of limbal stem/progenitor cells. Stem Cell Res 16(2):358–364. https://doi.org/10.1016/j.scr.2016.02.018

Grueterich M, Espana EM, Tseng SC (2003) Ex vivo expansion of limbal epithelial stem cells: amniotic membrane serving as a stem cell niche. Surv Ophthalmol 48(6):631–646

Ho JH, Ma WH, Tseng TC et al (2011) Isolation and characterization of multi-potent stem cells from human orbital fat tissues. Tissue Eng A 17(1–2):255–266. https://doi.org/10.1089/ten.TEA.2010.0106

Holan V, Trosan P, Cejka C et al (2015) A comparative study of the therapeutic potential of mesenchymalstem cellsandlimbalepithelialstem cellsfor ocular surface reconstruction. Stem Cells Transl Med 4(9):1052–1063. https://doi.org/10.5966/sctm.2015-0039

James SE, Rowe A, Ilari L et al (2001) The potential for eye bank limbal rings to generate cultured corneal epithelial allografts. Cornea 20(5):488–494

Kenyon KR, Tseng SC (1989) Limbalautograft transplantation for ocular surface disorders. Ophthalmology 96(5):709–722; discussion 722-3

Koizumi N, Inatomi T, Quantock AJ et al (2000) Amniotic membrane as a substrate for cultivating limbal corneal epithelial cells for autologous transplantation in rabbits. Cornea 19(1):65–71

Lindberg K, Brown ME, Chaves HV et al (1993) Towards therapeutic application of ocular stem cells. Invest Ophthalmol Vis Sci 34(9):2672–2679

López-Paniagua M, Nieto-Miguel T, de la Mata A et al (2016) Successful consecutive expansion oflimbalexplants using a biosafe culture medium under feeder layer-free conditions. Curr Eye Res 2:1–11

Meller D, Pires RT, Tseng SC (2002) Ex vivo preservation and expansion of human limbal epithelial stem cells on amniotic membrane cultures. J Ophthalmol 86(4):463–471

O'Callaghan AR, Morgan L, Daniels JT et al (2016) Human-derived feeder fibroblasts for the culture of epithelial cells for clinical use. J Tissue Eng Regen Med 11(6):529–543. https://doi.org/10.2217/rme-2016-0039

Pathak M, Cholidis S, Haug K et al (2013) Clinical transplantation of ex vivo expanded autologous limbal epithelial cells using a culture medium with human serum as single supplement: a retrospective case series. Acta Ophthalmol 91(8):769–775. https://doi.org/10.1111/j.1755-3768.2012.02521.x

Pellegrini G, Traverso CE, Franzi AT et al (1997) Long-term restoration of damaged corneal surfaces with autologous cultivated corneal epithelium. Lancet 349(9057):990–993

Pellegrini G, Dellambra E, Golisano O et al (2001) p63 identifies keratinocyte stem cells. Proc Natl Acad Sci U S A 98(6):3156–3161

Priya CG, Arpitha P, Vaishali S et al (2011) Adult human buccal epithelialstem cells: identification, ex-vivo expansion, and transplantation for corneal surface reconstruction. Eye (London) 25(12):1641–1649. https://doi.org/10.1038/eye.2011.230

Puangsricharern V, Tseng SC (1995) Cytologic evidence of corneal diseases withlimbalstem cell deficiency. Ophthalmology 102(10):1476–1485

Rama P, Bonini S, Lambiase A et al (2001) Autologous fibrin-cultured limbal stem cells permanently restore the corneal surface of patients with total limbal stem cell deficiency. Transplantation 72(9):1478–1485

Rama P, Matuska S, Paganoni G et al (2010) Limbal stem-cell therapy and long-term corneal regeneration. N Engl J Med 363(2):147–155. https://doi.org/10.1056/NEJMoa0905955

Sangwan VS, Basu S, Vemuganti GK et al (2011) Clinicaloutcomes of xeno-free autologous cultivatedlimbalepithelial transplantation: a 10-year study. J Ophthalmol 95(11):1525–1529. https://doi.org/10.1136/bjophthalmol-2011-300352

Schlötzer-Schrehardt U, Kruse FE (2005) Identification and characterization oflimbalstem cells. Exp Eye Res 81(3):247–264

Schwab IR (1999) Cultured corneal epithelia for ocular surface disease. Trans Am Ophthalmol Soc 97:891–986

Schwab IR, Reyes M, Isseroff RR (2000) Successful transplantation of bioengineered tissue replacements in patients with ocular surface disease. Cornea 19(4):421–426

Shimazaki J, Aiba M, Goto E et al (2002) Transplantation of human limbal epithelium cultivated on amniotic membrane for the treatment of severe ocular surface disorders. Ophthalmology 109(7):1285–1290

Sidney LE, Branch MJ, Dua HS et al (2015) Effect of culture medium on propagation and phenotype of corneal stroma-derived stem cells. Cytotherapy 17(12):1706–1722. https://doi.org/10.1016/j.jcyt.2015.08.003

Tominac Trcin M, Dekaris I, Mijović B, Bujić M, Zdraveva E, Dolenec T, Pauk-Gulić M, Primorac D, Crnjac J, Špoljarić B, Mršić G, Kuna K, Špoljarić D, Popović M (2016) Synthetic vs natural scaffolds for human limbal stem cells. Croat Med J 56(3):246–256

Tsai RJ, Li LM, Chen JK (2000) Reconstruction of damaged corneas by transplantation of autologous limbal epithelial cells. N Engl J Med 343(2):86–93

Utheim TP (2015) Concise review: transplantation of cultured oral mucosal epithelial cells for treating limbal stem cell deficiency-current status and future perspectives. Stem Cell 33 (6):1685–1695. https://doi.org/10.1002/stem.1999

Zakaria N, Koppen C, Van Tendeloo V et al (2010) Standardized limbal epithelial stem cell graft generation and transplantation. Tissue Eng C Methods 16(5):921–927. https://doi.org/10.1089/ten.TEC.2009.0634

Personalized Total Knee Arthroplasty: Better Fit for Better Function

Gordan Gulan, Hari Jurdana, and Leo Gulan

Abstract Total knee arthroplasty (TKA) is one of the most frequently performed and most effective surgeries in the field of orthopedics, and represents the gold standard for treating symptomatic late-stage knee osteoarthritis. The success of a TKA depends on multiple factors. Accurate alignment, proper bone cuts, good soft tissue balancing, proper component sizing and positioning are all key components that determine the short and long-term success of total knee arthroplasty. Despite great success of knee arthroplasty, there are according to some studies up to 25% of patients that are not satisfied with operation. One of the reasons could be inability to completely replicate the anatomy and kinematics of natural knee. The latest technological opportunities provide a way to achieve the desired goal.

1 Brief History of Total Knee Arthroplasty

The era of total knee arthroplasty (TKA) began in nineteenth century when Fergusson reported the first resection for knee osteoarthritis in 1860.[1] Interposition arthroplasties, using materials such as joint capsules, muscle, fascia and free fascial grafts, were used in the following years, but with no success.[2] The first reports of total joint replacement were made by German surgeon from Berlin, Themistocles Gluck, in the 1880s, who used an ivory hinged design fixed with a meance made from plaster of Paris, pumice and colophony.[3] The modern era of total knee replacement started in 1972 with John Insall who designed prosthesis for

---

[1] Gordon-Taylor (1961).
[2] Ranawat (2002).
[3] Amendola et al. (2012) and Williams et al. (2010).

G. Gulan (✉) · H. Jurdana
Clinic for Orthopaedic Surgery Lovran, Medical Faculty, University of Rijeka, Lovran, Croatia
e-mail: gordan.gulan@medri.uniri.hr

L. Gulan
Department of Anatomy, Medical Faculty, University of Rijeka, Rijeka, Croatia

© Springer Nature Switzerland AG 2019   307
N. Bodiroga-Vukobrat et al. (eds.), *Personalized Medicine in Healthcare Systems*,
Europeanization and Globalization 5, https://doi.org/10.1007/978-3-030-16465-2_25

replacement all three knee's compartments—total condylar prosthesis.[4] Since then, there has been a wide increase in the number of TKAs performed annually, even if the results of comparative studies among many of the designs have not demonstrated the marked improvements in outcomes that were expected.[5]

Nowadays, the most common types of conventional TKA designs are posterior cruciate ligament retaining and posterior stabilized implants that usually provide sufficient stability in the primary setting, through various level of built-in constrain or stability to megaprotheses for replacing all bone.

2 Anatomy of the Human Knee and Its Relationship to Total Knee Arthroplasty

Knee is the most complex joint in the human body. The convex surface is represented by the femoral condyles, and concave with the proximal part of the tibia. The integral part of the joint is patella, which is the largest sezamoid bone in the body. Patella and facies patellaris—joint surface on anterior part of the distal femur formed the patellofemoral joint, which is important in knee biomechanics and can be the source of many pathological problems.[6] Intraarticularly, knee contains the semilunar fibrocartilaginous structure—menisci and two intraarticular ligaments—anterior and posterior cruciate ligament. These structures play important role during load transmission as well as in stability and joint kinematics.

The main characteristics of the convex articular surface are that the curvature has different radii, increasing from posterior toward anterior part of femoral condyle. Besides that, the lateral femoral condyle has greater radius of curvature comparing to the medial condyle.[7] The counterpart joint surface on the tibia is not congruent. The medial tibial condyle is just slightly concave, whereas lateral tibial plateau is flat in anterior part and convex in posterior part. In sagittal plane the tibial joint surface is not perpendicular to anatomical axis of the tibia, but has posterior inclination on average 8 ± 3.3 degrees on lateral and 6.8 ± 3.3 degrees on medial compartment from line placed perpendicular on anatomical tibial axis.[8]

Moreover, the tibial condyle is not of equal dimension. Medial condyle has a slightly greater mediolateral as well as anterioposterior diameter than the lateral one.[9]

Lack of congruence between the bone surfaces permits 6 degrees of freedom of knee movements, three translational (anterior-posterior, medial-lateral, and

---

[4]Insall et al. (1983) and Insall and Kelly (1986).

[5]Vaienti et al. (2017).

[6]Kelly (2001) and Petersen et al. (2014).

[7]Vaienti et al. (2017), Grood and Suntay (1983), Hollister et al. (1993) and Kurosawa et al. (1985).

[8]Noble et al. (2005).

[9]Clary et al. (2014).

inferior-superior) and three rotational (flexion-extension, intra- external rotation, adduction-abduction).[10] The movements are determined by the articular surfaces geometry of the tibia and femur and the orientation of the extra articular and intraarticular ligaments of the knee. Flexion and extension are the broadest and most important with amplitude ranging from 0 to 120–140 degrees. Flexion is ensured by a combination of rotation ("roll-back") and sliding of the femur over the tibia and is coupled with internal and external rotation of the tibia respectively.[11] Another important factor in knee biomechanics and load transmission is the knee alignment, which is responsible for optimal mechanical and shear stresses placed on the bearing surfaces. Normal knee alignment implies the lateral angle between femur and tibia on average 174 degree with mechanical axis connecting center of the hip, and the foot passing through knee passing immediately medial to the center of the knee near the medial tibial spine.[12]

3 Conventional Knee Arthroplasty

Total knee arthroplasty is the gold standard for treating symptomatic, late-stage knee osteoarthritis. Optimal restoration of normal knee anatomy and alignment is the prerequisite for the successful total knee arthroplasty. The design of components in conventional knee arthroplasty is based on average knee anthropometry. However, the population group and sample size over which the average anatomic data is obtained varies between total knee replacement manufacturers. Total knee arthroplasty has evolved towards a reliable and long lasting surgical procedure, offering pain relief and improved function to many patients who suffer from degenerative arthritis of the knee. Improvements in surgical technique and prosthesis design continue to enhance long-term outcomes.[13] The ability to restore walking without pain and limping in more than 90% of cases has led surgeons to offer this operation to younger patients.[14] However, the functional demands and activity levels of these younger patients exceed current capacity to restore the damaged knee joint.

Pain, Instability and limited range of motion are listed as important limiting factors to normal function.[15] When looking at failed knee arthroplasties, instability and stiffness rank in second and third place amongst the causes of early failure, only preceded by infection.[16] Pain, range of motion and stability are three key factors in the success of total knee arthroplasty.

---

[10]Vaienti et al. (2017).

[11]Frankel et al. (1971) and Radermacher et al. (1998).

[12]Nigel et al. (1998).

[13]Robertson et al. (2001).

[14]Kurtz et al. (2005).

[15]Robertson et al. (2001).

[16]Lavernia et al. (2006) and Sharkey et al. (2002).

Although surgical techniques and implant designs have improved through the years, as evidenced by excellent survivorship and long-term results, patients' satisfaction after TKA is still no more than 70–75%.[17] This percentage is much lower than following total hip arthroplasty, representing the complexity of the knee joint and the difficulty in restoring the knee anatomy.[18] There is paucity of literature dealing with the effects of improperly sized and malpositioned implants on patient outcome. Medial or lateral overhang on the femur or tibia could result in soft tissue impingement and irritation affecting balancing.[19] Undersizing of the components could leave cancellous bone exposed, which could be a source of increased bleeding into the knee, and may permit increased osteolysis from wear debris with longer follow-up. Undersizing of the femoral component can also lead to altering the proper restoration of joint line, joint stiffness posterior soft tissue impingement, instability, notching with possibility of fracture early loosening and altered kinematics of the knee joint.[20] Overhanging can cause altered patellofemoral stresses and soft tissue irritation.[21]

Unique specifity of each knee and significant diversity among gender were recognized as some of the reasons responsible for bone-component mismatch. Many researchers have studied the bone morphometrics of the knee in different population and obtained the similar results. They have shown that the ratio between anterior-posterior diameter and medial-lateral diameter of the femur significantly differ between male and female.[22] Further, significantly different knee geometry was observed analyzing the Asian and Indian population. The race-specific morphologic characteristics were observed on distal femur as well as on proximal tibia.[23] With aim to restore some of anatomical specificities and improve the results of TKA, some of manufacturers have produced the components, which are more anatomical such as: asymmetric tibial base plate, gender specific knee component with different AP-LL ratio for male and female. Gender specific TKA have shown better fitting especially in female and forthcoming long-term follow-up study will show us the beneficial of this kind of gender specific approach. Malposition of the patella and patellar maltracking have multifactorial aethyology and were recognized as leading causes in anterior pain in knee arthroplasty, so great efforts are directed toward reproducing the natural patellar tracking by anatomical reconstruction of patellar

---

[17]Kurtz et al. (2005), Noble et al. (2005), Slamin and Parsley (2012) and Ritter et al. (2005).

[18]Vaienti et al. (2017) and Victor and Hoste (2004).

[19]Mahoney and Kinsey (2010).

[20]Banks et al. (2003), Bellemans et al. (2002), Gujarathi et al. (2009), Laskin and Beksac (2004), Lemaire et al. (1997), Lie et al. (2005), Meding et al. (2008) and Zalzal et al. (2006).

[21]Bong and Di Cesare (2004), Kawahara et al. (2012), Laskin and Beksac (2004) and Mahoney and Kinsey (2010).

[22]Chin et al. (2002), Hitt et al. (2003), Rosenstein et al. (2008), Yan et al. (2014) and Yue et al. (2011).

[23]Kim et al. (2017), Mahfouz et al. (2012) and Vaienti et al. (2017).

grove on femoral component.[24] Various techniques for reproducing original distal femoral rotation as well as patella positioning were evolved.

4 New Technology in Achieving Personalized Knee Arthroplasty

With the desire to improve patient satisfaction, new technologies have been investigated. In the beginning of the knee replacement era, there were only a few sizes of implants. The Total Condylar (Howmedica, Rutherford, NJ) when first introduced in 1974, was available in just 3 sizes. By the time the PFC (Johnson & Johnson, Raynham, MA) came along in 1986, it was available in 6 sizes, and had left and right components. Today, total knee replacement systems have as many as 8 to 10 femoral sizes in left and right components and a similar number of tibial base plate sizes. Gender specific implants and asymmetrical base plate were introduced in an attempt to better accommodate the variation in patient geometry that makes important progress toward customized approach. The great step toward production of personalized implants was done in 1998, when Rademacher introduced the techniques that allow manufacturing of personalized instrumentation based on computerized tomography (CT) scans for spine, hip and knee surgery.[25] The typical process used to manufacture the custom implants is described in detail by Slamin and it starts by providing the magnetic resonance imaging (MRI) or computer tomography (CT) scans of the patient whole leg, from hip to ankle.[26] Each of the imaging method has its own advantages and is better suited to a particular type of joint analysis. In both cases, MRI and CT, the scan data is provided to the implant manufacturer. This data is then converted into a special software system through a process referred to as segmentation.

The segmentation process relies on laying individual points along the outer surface of each individual scan slice. When the entire joint surface has been segmented, a point cloud has been created that is representative of the outer surface of the joint. The point cloud is then imported into a traditional computer assisted design (CAD) program. The point cloud that now resides within the CAD system is then converted into a solid model that can be used to design a product around. The MRI data is better suited for the analysis of soft tissues. This means that the segmentation process is typically performed on the surface of the articular cartilage. The CT scan is better suited for the imaging of bones. In the case of the CT scan, the segmentation process is performed on the subchondral surface creating an image of the bone. Based on this scans, patient specific instruments for bone cut, bone preparation and personalized implants are produced, which guarantee precise and

---

[24]Kelly (2001) and Petersen et al. (2014).

[25]Rosenstein et al. (2008).

[26]Slamin and Parsley (2012).

accurate positioning with restoration of knee alignment. The expectations of the introduction of personal specific instrumentation and personal specific implants were promising: smaller incision, shorter operative time, complete coverage of cancellous bone, reduction of blood loss, better economic cost and effectiveness, reduction of operative set-up time, tight conformity, shorter rehabilitation, reduction of cost and better functional outcome. Although short-term follow-up did not yield all expectations, long-term studies are needed to demonstrate implant survival rate and outcomes compared with conventional methods.

5 Conclusion

All the efforts in developing knee prostheses are aimed to produce implants that could reproduce the natural knee anatomy, individual knee alignment and can mimic a natural knee motion. Until the current date, it has not been possible to produce a prosthetic design that fulfills all requirements, however, a great progress have been made in personalized approach in knee arthroplasty.

References

Amendola L, Tigani D, Fosco M, Dallari D (2012) History of condylar total knee arthroplasty. In: Fokter S (ed) Recent advances in hip and knee arthroplasty. In-Tech, Rijeka

Banks S, Bellemans J, Nozaki H, Whiteside LA, Harman M, Hodge WA (2003) Knee motion during maximal flexion in fixed and mobile bearing arthroplasties. Clin Orthoop Res 410:131–138

Bellemans J, Banks S, Victor J, Vandenneucker H, Moemans A (2002) Fluoroscopic analysis of the kinematics of deep flexion in total knee arthroplasty. Influence of posterior condylar offset. J Bone Joint Surg Br 84(1):50–53

Bong MR, Di Cesare PE (2004) Stiffness after total knee arthroplasty. J Am Acad Orthop Surg 12 (3):164–171

Chin KR, Dalury DF, Zurakowski D, Scott RD (2002) Intraoperative measurements of male and female distal femurs during primary total knee arthroplasty. J Knee Surg 15(4):213–217

Clary C, Aram L, Deffenbaugh D, Heldreth M (2014) Tibial base design and patient morphology affecting tibial coverage and rotational alignment after total knee arthroplasty. Knee Surg Sports Traumatol Arthrosc 22(12):3012–3018

Frankel VH, Burstein AH, Brooks DB (1971) Biomechanics as determined by analysis of the instant centers of motion. J Bone Joint Surg 53:945–977

Gordon-Taylor G (1961) Sir William Fergusson 1808–1877. Med Hist 5:1–14

Grood ES, Suntay WJ (1983) A joint coordinate system for the clinical description of three-dimensional motions: application to the knee. J Biomech Eng 105:136–144

Gujarathi N, Putti AB, Abboud RJ, MacLean JG, Espley AJ, Kellett CF (2009) Risk of periprosthetic fracture after anterior femoral notching. Acta Orthop 80(5):553–556

Hitt K, Shurman JR 2nd, Greene K, McCarthy J, Moskal J, Hoeman T, Mont MA (2003) Anthropometric measurements of the human knee: correlation to the sizing of current knee arthroplasty systems. J Bone Joint Surg Am 85-A(Suppl 4):115–122

Hollister AM, Jatana SAK, Sullivan WW, Lupichuk A (1993) The axes of rotation of the knee. Clin Orthop Relat Res 290:259–268

Insall JN, Kelly M (1986) The total condylar prosthesis. Clin Orthop Relat Res 205:43–48

Insall JN, Hood RW, Flawn LB, Sullivan DJ (1983) The total condylar knee prosthesis in gonarthrosis. A five to nine-year follow-up of the first one hundred consecutive replacements. J Bone Joint Surg Am 65(5):619–628

Kawahara S, Matsuda S, Fukagawa S, Mitsuyasu H, Nakahara H, Higaki H, Shimoto T, Iwamoto Y (2012) Upsizing the femoral component increases patellofemoral contact force in total knee replacement. J Bone Joint Surg Br 94(1):56–61

Kelly MA (2001) Patellofemoral complications following total knee arthroplasty. Instr Course Lect 50:403–407

Kim TK, Phillips M, Bhandari M, Watson J, Malhotra R (2017) What differences in morphologic features of the nee exist among patients of various races? A systematic review. Clin Orthop Relat Res 475(1):170–182. https://doi.org/10.1007/s11999-016-5097

Kurosawa H, Walker PS, Abe S, Garg AT, Hunter T (1985) Geometry and motion of the knee for implant and orthotic design. J Biomech 18(7):487–491

Kurtz S, Mowat F, Ong K (2005) Prevalence of primary and revision total hip and knee arthroplasty in the United States (1990–2002). J Bone Joint Surg Am 87:1487–1497

Laskin RS, Beksac B (2004) Stiffness after total knee arthroplasty. J Arthroplasty 19(4 Suppl 1):41–46

Lavernia C, Lee DJ, Hernandez VH (2006) The increasing financial burden of knee revision surgery in the United States. Clin Orthop 446:221–226

Lemaire P, Pioletti DP, Meyer FM, Meuli R, Dorfl J, Leyvraz PF (1997) Tibial component positioning in total knee arthroplasty: bone coverage and extensor apparatus alignment. Knee Surg Sports Traumatol Arthrosc 5(4):251–257

Lie DT, Gloria N, Amis AA, Lee BP, Yeo SJ, Chou SM (2005) Patellar resection during total knee arthroplasty: effect on bone strain and fracture risk. Knee Surg Sports Traumatol Arthrosc 13 (3):203–208

Mahfouz M, Abdel Fatah EE, Bowers LS, Scuderi G (2012) Three-dimensional morphology of the knee reveals ethnic differences. Clin Orthop Relat Res 470(1):172–185. https://doi.org/10.1007/s11999-011-2089-2

Mahoney OM, Kinsey TJ (2010) Overhang of the femoral component in total knee arthroplasty: risk factors and clinical consequences. Bone Joint Surg Am 92(5):1115–1121. https://doi.org/10.2106/JBJS.H.00434

Meding JB, Fish MD, Berend ME, Ritter MA, Keating EM (2008) Predicting patellar failure after total knee arthroplasty. Clin Orthop Relat Res 466(11):2769–2774

Nigel P, Derek F, Roger S (1998) The hip joint. In: Anatomy and human movement - structure and function, 3rd edn. Butterworth-Heinemann, Oxford, pp 432–438

Noble PC, Gordon MJ, Weiss JM (2005) Does total knee replacement restore normal knee function? Clin Orthop 431:157–165

Petersen W, Rembitzki IV, Brüggemann GP, Ellermann A, Best R, Koppenburg AG, Liebau C (2014) Anterior knee pain after total knee arthroplasty: a narrative review. Int Orthop 38 (2):319–328. https://doi.org/10.1007/s00264-013-2081-4

Radermacher K, Portheine F, Anton M, Zimolong A, Kaspers G, Rau G, Staudte HW (1998) Computer assisted orthopaedic surgery with image based individual templates. Clin Orthop Relat Res 354:28–38

Ranawat CS (2002) History of total knee replacement. J South Orthop Assoc 11(4):218–226

Ritter MA, Thong AE, Keating EM, Faris PM, Meding JB, Berend ME, Pierson JL, Davis KE (2005) The effect of femoral notching during total knee arthroplasty on the prevalence of postoperative femoral fractures and on clinical outcome. J Bone Joint Surg Am 87 (11):2411–2414

Robertson O, Knutson K, Lewold S, Lidgren L (2001) The Swedish Arthroplasty Register 1975–1997. An update with special emphasis on 41.223 knees operated on in 1988–1997. Acta Orthop Scand 72(5):503–513

Rosenstein AD, Veazey B, Shephard D, Xu KT (2008) Gender differences in the distal femur dimensions and variation patterns in relation to TKA component sizing. Orthopedics 31(7):652

Sharkey PF, Hozack WJ, Rothman RH (2002) Why are TKA's failing today? Clin Orthop 404:7–13

Slamin J, Parsley B (2012) Evolution of customization design for total knee arthroplasty. Curr Rev Musculoskelet Med 5(4):290–295. https://doi.org/10.1007/s12178-012-9141-z

Vaienti E, Scita G, Ceccarelli F, Pogliacomi F (2017) Understanding the human knee and its relationship to total knee replacement. Acta Biomed 88(2-S):6–16. https://doi.org/10.23750/abm.v88i2-S.6507

Victor J, Hoste D (2004) Image-based computer-assisted total knee arthroplasty leads to lower variability in coronal alignment. Clin Orthop 428:131–139

Williams D, Garbuz D, Masri B (2010) Total knee arthroplasty: techniques and results. BC Med J 52(9):447–454

Yan M, Wang J, Wang Y, Zhang J, Yue B, Zeng Y (2014) Gender-based differences in the dimensions of the femoral trochlea and condyles in the Chinese population: correlation to the risk of femoral component overhang. Knee 21(1):252–256. https://doi.org/10.1016/j.knee.2012.11.005

Yue B, Varadarajan KM, Ai S, Tang T, Rubash HE, Li G (2011) Differences of knee anthropometry between Chinese and white men and women. J Arthroplasty 26(1):124–130. https://doi.org/10.1016/j.arth.2009.11.020

Zalzal P, Backstein D, Gross AE, Papini M (2006) Notching of the anterior femoral cortex during total knee arthroplasty characteristics that increase local stresses. J Arthroplasty 21(5):737–743

Comprehensive Approach to Personalized Medicine into Chronic Musculoskeletal Diseases

The "BaR" Concept

Dalibor Krpan

Abstract Chronic musculoskeletal diseases, well known as osteoporosis and osteoarthritis, are among the most common diseases. Despite various pharmacological treatments, the problem of osteoporosis is not yet solved nor decreased. Drug's adverse event and fractures after long termed pharmacotherapy indicate a need for new treatment modalities.

Regarding osteoarthritis, conventional clinical practice is based on symptomatic treatments with limited and temporary effect and in the severe cases surgically replacement of knee or hip with endo-prosthesis, are often left as the only option. There is no any prevention or treatment with the aim of improving the quality and functional ability of skeleton as a whole.

However, because of the intensive scientific research in the last two decades, significant advance in understanding of skeleton physiology, influence of metabolic and biomechanical factors on bone has been achieved. Those, as well as development of new technologies and treatment modalities, provide us with better possibilities for treatment and prevention of complications in chronic skeleton diseases. But, it also indicates a necessity of changing the clinical approach towards the principles of personalized and integrative medicine with the goal of improving bio-mechanical and metabolic balance, stimulating bone formation and cartilage regeneration, with consequent improvement of the functional capacity of the skeleton as a whole.

1 Introduction

Osteoarthritis and Osteoporosis are one of the most common medical problems and big public health issue. Complications associated with these diseases cause disabilities and significant deterioration of the quality of life, but they are also big financial burden not only for the patient and their family but for the whole society. Despite

D. Krpan (✉)
Polyclinic K-center, Zagreb, Croatia

© Springer Nature Switzerland AG 2019
N. Bodiroga-Vukobrat et al. (eds.), *Personalized Medicine in Healthcare Systems*,
Europeanization and Globalization 5, https://doi.org/10.1007/978-3-030-16465-2_26

this, osteoporosis has been ignored for many years and considered as consequence of natural aging, while the therapy of osteoarthritis was only partial and symptomatic. Unfortunately, even today the situation has not changed much and prevention is still neglected.

Since 1994, the benchmark for diagnosis of osteoporosis has been the assessment of bone mineral density (BMD). Significant decrease of BMD was considered because of increased bone reabsorption over bone formation with consequent increase risk of fracture. Following that hypothesis, pharmacotherapy has been introduced with the intention to reduce fracture risk by suppressing bone reabsorption or increasing bone formation. But, despite various pharmacological treatments the problem of osteoporosis is not yet solved nor decreased.[1] About the application of bone modifying drugs, the existing real life data do not support clear relevant anti-fracture effects.[2] On the contrary, new problems appeared such as drug's adverse event and fractures after long term of pharmacotherapy.[3] Additionally, there is still an absence of early prevention and education with an aim of increasing awareness of prevention.

Regarding osteoarthritis, the symptomatic treatment with limited and temporary effect is still the most common option and there isn't any kind of prevention. But, that cannot affect the cause of disease or restore the normal function. Gradual deterioration occurs and the surgical implementation of endo-prosthesis often left as the only solution. In many cases neither this resolves the problem. The function of treated joints could be improved, but in vast majority damage affects the whole skeleton, therefore the surgery cannot be the final solution, and cannot cure the patient.

Such clinical practice regarding bone and joint diseases is mostly from lack of basic education about the physiology of the skeleton and biological mechanisms that affect the skeleton. Until recently the skeleton was not even considered an organ, so it is not surprising that there is still no specialization in clinical medicine to deal with musculoskeletal disease. Orthopedics, physical medicine, rheumatology and endocrinology only deal with parts of this large and complex organ, so it is no wonder that the clinical approach is only partial.

Fortunately, the intensive scientific activities in last two decades provide significant advance in understanding of skeleton physiology, influence of metabolic and biomechanical factors on bone which indicates the necessity of changing clinical approach towards the principles of personalized and integrative medicine.

---

[1] Duque (2014) and Kanis et al. (2008).
[2] Erviti et al. (2013) and Crilly et al. (2014).
[3] Kamel (2007).

1.1   Why Do We Need a New Concept in Treatment of Chronic Skeleton Diseases?

1. Skeleton is a complex organ which must be consider as a whole. It consists of a number of bones and joints and at least three types of tissues: bone, cartilage and muscle-fibrotic tissue.
2. Skeleton is affected by many factors which can be grouped into genetic, bio-mechanical and metabolic. As the structure of the bone is constantly changing through a process of bone remodeling we can say that bone structure and quality is the result of all of these factors.
3. Function of the skeleton depends on the structure and quality of all of its parts. Therefore it is always necessary to implement integrated treatment for the skeleton as a whole.
4. There are no diagnostic methods able to measure the bone strength or quality neither of cartilage, nor to measure quality of skeleton in general. Therefore we need to make a plan of treatment based on the assessment of skeleton status and risks of complication. Because there are significant diversities among the people regarding the influence of those factors, personalized approach in diagnostic evaluation and treatment is necessary.
5. Because it is not possible for the same therapeutic agent or a drug to act on all parts of the skeleton, it is necessary to implement a combination of several methods when conducting the treatment.
6. Common clinical practice regarding the treatment of chronic bone and joint diseases does not yield satisfactory results and does not accept any of the above facts. Therefore it is necessary to change the approach and introduce a new concept.

2   "BaR": Holistic Concept Based on the Principles of Personalized and Integrative Medicine

"BaR" stands for: **"B"**—biomechanics and biochemical balance **"a"** and **"R"**—regeneration. It is an integrated, holistic approach to treatment using a combination of methods to improve "bio-mechanics", provide regular bio-mechanical stress to bone, as well as good metabolic balance, and to stimulate the regeneration of cartilage and bone formation.

2.1 Why Is It Important and How Does It Work in Clinical Practice?

Skeleton is a complex organ which is constantly adjusting to bio-mechanical and metabolic balance. Because of gravity, it absorbs significant load which is permanently changing during the daily activity. Skeleton is specifically designed to reduce the load by distributing it equally to all parts. In the case of skeleton deformities like hip dysplasia, spinal and foot deformities or any disproportion which causes overload (sport, sedentary life style, etc.), certain parts of the skeleton will be exposed to overload which will cause damage to cartilage. Under abnormal mechanical stimuli the balance of the chondrocyte metabolism (degradation and synthesis of matrix molecules) is disturbed leading to matrix loss and degeneration of cartilage. If the overload exceeds the regenerative capacity of chondrocytes, regeneration will be replaced by scarring process which will, by the time, cause a decrease of cartilage properties and its capacity to absorb the load. As there are no nerves in the cartilage, there is no pain or any signal until the overload has been extended to the ligaments, tendons and bone causing chronic inflammation of joints, which we recognize as osteoarthritis. Biomechanical imbalance is getting worst by the time, causing "domino effect" regarding other parts of skeleton. Therefore, in most cases, osteoarthritis is not limited on one joint. Additionally, because biomechanical stimuli significantly influence on bone turnover, biomechanical imbalance will cause deterioration of bone microarchitecture with consequent decreasing of bone strength and osteoporosis. Therefore, the correction of the biomechanics and regular biomechanical stimulation are crucial in the treatment and prevention of osteoarthritis and osteoporosis.

Because of significant diversity among people, correction of bio-mechanical balance needs to be done based on personalized assessment of muscular balance in which methods such as isokinetic dynamometry and digital pedometry could be helpful.

The most important part of biomechanical therapy is appropriate exercise. It is crucial, particularly in prevention and treatment of osteoporosis, and improving mobility, because biomechanical stress (= mechanical stimulation) provides signals to bone cells to improve bone microarchitecture (= mechanoresponses of cells!).

2.2 The Basic Principles Which Exercise Need to Meet

1. Exercises must cause the intermittent contraction of the muscles; thus achieving the alternating action of forces onto the bone, which is an important stimulus for bone remodeling. Muscles' contractions stimulate bone cells, giving the information where bone needs to be improved.
2. The more muscles are engaged by causing them to contract, the more bones will be stimulated in the right way.

3. The movements in the exercises must be strictly controlled to avoid any damage of the joints and to diminish influence of biomechanical imbalance.
4. Exercises must be linked together in a logical system which is easy to remember, which is motivating, interesting and simple so that the patient will enjoy performing it, as even the best thought-out exercise system is useless if those at whom it is aimed are not satisfied when they perform it.

The exercise program which meets all of the above is "Tae do".[4]

2.3   What Is "TAE-DO"?

"Tae-do" is a special program of exercise based on the principles of the Korean marshal art taekwondo. It consists of controlled movements with energy directed contractions of the muscles. The title "tae-do" comes from words in the Korean language. "Tae" means movement with the legs and "do" means the method, or way of doing. In a figurative sense tae-do means an active attitude towards something, for example towards disease.

2.4   What Are the Advantages of Tae-do Over Other Standard Exercises?

The basic principle, on which martial arts are based, is how to use the energy of the mind and body in the most rational manner while performing movements. Although the final aim of these skills is to prepare for battle with potential opponents, the techniques of the exercises based on these principles have a far wider significance because they basically offer a way of achieving the balance between the "spirit and the body", enabling the person exercising to move in the most efficient way. These exercises affect the entire system of movement, starting with the brain, where the "command" is created for a certain movement, via the nerve system by which that stimulus is carried to muscles, as the executing organs who perform the movement.

Using the techniques and principles of taekwondo, tae-do influences not only the muscles and, by means of muscle contractions, the bones, but more than standard exercises it also affects the balance and speed of reaction of the system of movement, which is important to reduce the risk of falls, which are particularly dangerous to those who suffer from osteoporosis, as even a minor fall may cause serious fractures.

Tae-do as a system of physical exercises is not only suitable for patients with osteoporosis, osteopenia and other metabolic bone diseases, but it is a universal system of exercises and may be undertaken by anyone regardless of their gender or

---

[4]Krpan (2003).

age. Therefore there is no limitation regarding when to start or when to do these exercises.

In providing the optimal biomechanical balance, the pain relief treatment is also important because pain limits the mobility and increases biomechanical imbalance. So, if a patient has a pain, it is important to reduce it by using various methods, such as acupuncture, magnetic resonance therapy-MBST, physical therapy, drugs, sometimes even surgery.

Because various metabolic and hormonal diseases have negative impact to the skeleton, it is also important to recognize and to treat such diseases.

Additionally to regular exercises, correction of biomechanics and metabolic balance, the important part in the treatment of chronic skeleton diseases is stimulation of regeneration of cartilage and stimulation of bone formation. So far we have not had methods or technologies that can regenerate cartilage, but in recent years such opportunities have appeared. One of these is Nuclear magnetic resonance therapy (MBST).

3   Nuclear Magnetic Resonance Therapy: MBST

Nuclear Magnetic Resonance (NMR), a well-known technology used in diagnostics has been developed for the treatment and patented under the brand MBST. The MBST equipment is using field strengths from 0.4 to 2.35 mT for 17 to 100 kHz in the magnetic resonance frequency. The field strength varies depending on the treatment system and regime. Numerous scientific studies on cell culture and animal model confirmed the regeneration of the cartilage and stimulation of bone formation, while clinical studies demonstrate long term therapeutic effects of NMR-Therapy (MBST) in osteoarthritis and osteoporosis.[5] Recent studies also showed that nuclear magnetic resonance (MBST) shifts the oscillation of the circadian clock light independently, alters the cellular redox environment and affects the circadian expression of Hif-1alfa. Both, the circadian clock and the hypoxic signaling pathway play central roles in the generation and progression of osteoarthritis.[6]

A therapeutic use of the nuclear magnetic resonance for osteoarthritis, sports and accident injuries, osteoporosis, and metabolic disorders of the bones is a reasonable alternative and supplement of today's existing therapeutic spectrums as there is a tremendous need for effective therapies for these medical problems. In particular because conventional therapies, which are commonly used, are only symptomatic

---

[5]Temiz-Artmann et al. (2005), Diegel et al. (2007), Jansen et al. (2006), Steinecker-Frohnwieser et al. (2014), Kullich et al. (2013a, b), Mařík et al. (2014), Kullich (2014), Steinecker-Frohnwieser et al. (2013), Krpan (2011), Steinecker-Frohnwieser et al. (2009), Kullich et al. (2006a, b), Auerbach et al. (2005), Kullich et al. (2005), Kullich and Ausserwinkler (2008), Fagerer (2007), Frobose et al. (2000), Krpan et al. (2015), Zhou et al. (2013), Jing et al. (2014), He et al. (2014), Handschuh and Melzer (2008) and Krpan and Kullich (2017).

[6]Oliva and Egg (2017).

and are not able to achieve the effect MBST can. Additional advantage of this method is that it has shown no side effects so far and is considered as painless. Because there are several different treatment programs, it is important to use MBST according to the personalized assessment, to achieve maximum effect.

As an illustration of "BAR" method of personalized and integrated approach, two typical cases from the real clinical practice are presented:

3.1   Case 1

Patient, mail of 71 suffered from chronic pain related with the severe osteoarthritis of hip, knees and lumbosacral spine, confirmed by X-ray and MRI. In spite of repeatedly conducted physical treatment, progression of the disease caused limited mobility and patient was scheduled to surgery, left hip replacement.

Following treatment based on the "BAR" concept was recommended:

1. MBST treatment, program for bone which stimulates osteoblasts to produce new osteoid and increase bone formation, before surgery. Thus, the bone will be better "prepared" for implementation of endo-prosthesis.
2. Isokinetic dynamometry and therapy, after surgery and standard rehabilitation to correct biomechanics and reduce deterioration of other joints.
3. MBST, treatment for the osteoarthritis of knees and spine, with the aim to stimulate chondrocytes and regeneration of the cartilage, one cycle of 7 days once per year.
4. "Tae do" exercise daily to stimulate bone formation and prevent deterioration of bone strength.

Following this recommendations patient was recovered very well and he didn't need another surgery. He is now 79 years old.

3.2   Case 2

Female, 70 years old with previous fractures and chronic back pain. Severe osteoarthritis of hip and spine has been confirmed by X-ray and MRI. Low BMD has been found on DXA. She was treated by bisphosphonate for five years. Treatment has been stopped because of adverse events and the fact that she experienced a fracture in spite therapy.

Following treatment based on the "BAR" concept was recommended:

1. MBST, program for osteoporosis and repeat it after six months, and then once per year.
2. MBST, program for the osteoarthritis, region of LS spine and both hip, once per year.

3. "Tae do" exercise 30 min per day.
4. Vitamin D supplementation.
5. Isokinetic dynamometry and therapy to correct biomechanics.

Patient was getting much better after three months. She is mobile without fractures and significant pain since "BAR" treatment was introduced. She had several falls during the period of follow up but no fractures. She is now 77 years old.

4 Conclusion

It is well known that the best therapy is to treat the origin of the disease. But for this to be done it is necessary to discover the cause of the disease, that is to establish a pathogenic mechanism leading to the disease. In majority of chronic diseases it is not easy. Additionally, the problem is that it is very common clinical practice to make the diagnosis based on one diagnostic parameter and then to treat all patients in similar way. But, because of the significant diversities among the patients, pathogenesis of the most chronic diseases is too complex to be reduced to one or few parameters. A good example is osteoporosis. Patients are being treated with similar drugs only based on bone mineral density measured by densitometry (BMD), regardless of differences in pathogenic mechanisms which cause osteoporosis. The advantage of measuring BMD is that densitometry is non-invasive method, but BMD is not reliable enough for assessing the risk of fractures, and particularly not for assessing therapeutic effect. Further, BMD does not reveal pathogenic mechanism of osteoporosis. Fracture risk depends on bone strength, which is mostly influenced by bone microarchitecture and quality of bone matrix, not so much on bone density. As we cannot measure bone strength, decision about the treatment modalities needs to be based on the assessment of the fracture risk which depends on the knowledge and experience of doctors, not on the measurement of some parameter.

Additionally, in the case of chronic skeleton diseases the problem is that skeleton is not just a collection of bones and joints, but a complex organ with multiple functions, metabolic and bio-mechanic, which are linked in a whole. Therefore, changes in one part of the skeleton are transmitted to the whole skeleton. For example, knee osteoarthritis is not only knee disease, because it affects bio-mechanics of the whole skeleton, and overloads other joints with consecutive osteoarthritis in these joints. Therefore, possible knee replacement cannot solve the problem as a whole. It will reduce pain in the operated knee, but won't correct complete bio-mechanics and cure the patient. Less known fact is that osteoarthritis of spine, hip and knees as well as foot causes bio-mechanical imbalance, which negatively affects bone strength and is likely to increase the risk of fracture. Because of the calcifications that follow osteoarthritis, in such cases low mineral density on the bone densitometry will often not be recognized meaning that the diagnose of osteoporosis is missed, although it is the case. That might explain a well-known fact that in almost 50% of minor trauma fractures, which is a sure sign of poor bone quality meaning osteoporosis, normal results of bone densitometry were found.

The holistic concept indicates that skeleton is very sensitive in relation to various factors: genetic ones like every other organ, biochemical and metabolic factors as well, but much more than other organs, on biomechanics. Because there are significant diversities among people regarding the influence of those factors, personalized approach in diagnostic evaluation and treatment is necessary. But, to introduce it in the routine clinical practice, the education of doctors and other medical professionals is mandatory, as well as of population in general, to increase awareness of prevention.

Certain problem in the case of the chronic skeleton diseases is that there are no diagnostic methods able to measure the bone strength or quality of cartilage, nor to measure the quality of skeleton in general. So, it is not possible to conduct clinical study which can objectively measure the effect of any therapy on the quality of the cartilage or the bone. In the case of osteoarthritis, most clinical studies are based on the follow up of subjective parameters such as pain and mobility. In the case of osteoporosis it is even more difficult, because there are no specific symptoms or reliable parameters for fracture risk. The best evidence for the successful treatment of osteoporosis would be the resistance of the bone on the strong force which happens amid severe trauma. However it is not possible to make a double blind, prospective, placebo controlled clinical study based on purposely exposing patients to accidents with potential fracture trauma. Still, well documented case reports could be important evidence despite the fact those aren't prospective double-blind, randomized studies, and there are a number of well documented clinical case reports showing that patients didn't suffer from a fracture after a severe trauma, even several years after starting the treatment based on the "BaR" concept.[7] Additionally, despite the fact that, at this moment, there aren't many clinical studies based on this concept, there is enough scientific data which explains importance of personalized approach considering chronic musculoskeletal diseases.

References

Auerbach B et al (2005) Prospective study over a period of 1 year in respect to the effectiveness of the MBST® - Nuclear Magnetic Resonance Therapy as used during the conservative therapy of Gonarthrosis; Orthopadische Praxis, Taucha. Lecture, Poster Presentation at the 1st Collective Congress Orthopedic - Accident Surgery, 19–22 October 2005, Berlin. Published in: Congress Catalogue, Abstract, Poster R2-446

Crilly RG et al (2014) Comparison of hip fracture and osteoporosis medication prescription rates across Canadian provinces. Osteoporos Int 25:205–210

Diegel I et al (2007) Decrease in extracellular collagen crosslinking after NMR magnetic field application in skin fibroblasts. J Int Fed Med Biol Eng 45(1):91–97

---

[7]Krpan and Kullich (2017).

Duque N (2014) Ostéoporose: traitement et soins pharmaceutiques [Osteoporosis: treatment and pharmaceutical care] (French Article). J Pharm Belg 2:14–24

Erviti J et al (2013) Oral bisphosphonates may not decrease hip fracture risk in elderly Spanish women: a nested case-control study. BMJ Open 3. pii: e002084. https://doi.org/10.1136/bmjopen-2012-002084

Fagerer N (2007) Use of magnetic resonance as new therapy options for Osteoarthritis. Arzt & Praxis 927:180–182

Frobose U et al (2000) Evaluation of the effectiveness three-dimensional pulsating electromagnetic fields of the MultiBioSignalTherapy (MBST®) on the regeneration of cartilage structures. Orthopadische Praxis 8:510–515

Handschuh T, Melzer C (2008) Behandlung der Osteoporose mit MBST® KernSpin. ORTHODOC 5(Sonderdruck):1–4

He J et al (2014) Effects of pulsed electromagnetic fields on the expression of NFATc1 and CAII in mouse osteoclast-like cells. Aging Clin Exp Res 29:PMID: 24869857

Jansen H et al (2006) Does have low-energy NMR an effect on gonarthrosis in rabbits. In: 52nd Annual Meeting Orthopedic Research Society. Chicago, March 2006. Scientific lecture

Jing D et al (2014) Pulsed electromagnetic fields partially preserve bone mass, microarchitecture, and strength by promoting bone formation in hindlimb-suspended rats. J Bone Miner Res 29 (10):2250–2261

Kamel HK (2007) Update on osteoporose management in long-term care: focus on bisphosphonates. J Am Med Dir Assoc 8:434–440

Kanis JA et al (2008) A reference standard for the description of osteoporosis. Bone 42:467–475

Krpan D (2003) Tae do, exercises for the prevention and treatment of osteoporosis. Repro-Color, Zagreb

Krpan D (2011) MBST – nuclear magnetic resonance therapy the new possibility of osteoarthritis and osteoporosis treatment. Balneoclimatologia, Dijagnostica I Lecenje Osteoporoze 35:61–66

Krpan D, Kullich W (2017) Nuclear magnetic resonance therapy (MBST) in the treatment of osteoporosis - case report study. Clin Cases Min Bone Metabol XIV(2):237–240

Krpan D et al (2015) Non-pharmaceutical treatment of osteoporosis with Nuclear Magnetic Resonance Therapy (NMR-Therapy). Periodicum biologorum, 117 (1): 160 -165

Kullich W (2014) New active principle: therapy with nuclear magnetic resonance. Scientific lecture at the "Special pain therapy" course, Pain diploma of the Austrian Medical Chamber, Leogang, Austria, 19th June 2014

Kullich W, Ausserwinkler M (2008) Functional improvement in osteoarthritis of finger joints with therapeutic use of nuclear magnetic resonance. Orthopädische Praxis 44(6):287–290

Kullich W et al (2005) MBST®-Nuclear Magnetic Resonance Therapy improves rehabilitation outcome in patients with low back pain; The EULAR Journal. Annals of the rheumatic diseases, Annual European Congress of Rheumatology, June 8–11, 2005, p 519

Kullich W et al (2006a) The effect of MBST®-Nuclear Magnetic Resonance Therapy with a complex 3-dimensional electromagnetic nuclear resonance field on patients with low back pain. J Back Musculoskelet Rehabil 19:79–87

Kullich W et al (2006b) Additional outcome improvement in the rehabilitation of chronic low back pain after nuclear resonance therapy. Rheumatologia 1:7–12

Kullich W et al (2013a) One year survey with multicenter data of more than 4500 patients with degenerative rheumatic disease treated with therapeutic nuclear magnetic resonance. J Back Musculoskelet Rehabil 26:93–104

Kullich W et al (2013b) Long-term efficacy of Nuclear Magnetic Resonance Therapy on Osteoarthritis provided by metacentric data of more than 4500 patients. LBG meeting for Health Sciences 2013, December 2, 2013, Vienna

Mařík I et al (2014) Application of Nuclear Magnetic Resonance Therapy as treatment of degenerative diseases of loco motor system. 19th Kubat's Podiatric day, 08. März 2014, Prag

Oliva R, Egg M (2017) Effect of nuclear magnetic resonance on the circadian clock and the hypoxia signaling pathway. Institute of Zoology, University of Innsbruck, Austria, poster on the scientific meeting

Steinecker-Frohnwieser B et al (2009) Influence of NMR therapy on metabolism of osteosarcoma and chondrosarcoma cell lines. Bone 44(2):295

Steinecker-Frohnwieser B et al (2013) Intracellular calcium is influenced by Nuclear Magnetic Resonance Therapy (NMRT) in Cal-78 chondrosarcoma cells. L. Journal für Mineralstoffwechsel 20(4):161–162

Steinecker-Frohnwieser B et al (2014) The influence of Nuclear Magnetic Resonance Therapy (NMRT) and Interleukin IL1-β stimulation on Cal 78 chondrosarcoma cells and C28/I2 chondrocytes. J Orthop Rheumatol 1(3):9

Temiz-Artmann A et al (2005) NMR in vitro effects on proliferation, apoptosis, and viability of human chondrocytes and osteoblasts. Methods Find Exp Clin Pharmacol 27(5):391–394

Zhou J et al (2013) Pulsed electromagnetic field stimulates osteoprotegerin and reduces RANKL expression in ovariectomized rats. Rheumatol Int 33(5):1135–1141

Circadian Rhythms and Personalized Melanoma Therapy

Elitza P. Markova-Car, Davor Jurišić, Nikolina Ružak,
and Sandra Kraljević Pavelić

Abstract Disruption of the body circadian rhythms has been described in the pathogenesis of many health conditions including cancer. Aberrant circadian rhythms indeed, result in deregulation of circadian clock genes and proteins, which may alter cell proliferation and promote oncogenesis and cancer, including melanoma. Moreover, circadian rhythms are often involved in outcomes of anticancer therapy as well. At the molecular level, the mammalian circadian clock is controlled by transcriptional and posttranslational feedback loops comprising a set of key elements, so-called 'clock genes' involved in regulation of a wide range of circadian rhythms in physiological processes and behavior. So far, experimental evidence suggests alteration in circadian clock genes' expression in human melanoma such as for example *PER1, PER2, CLOCK* and *CRY1*. However, no comprehensive data on the specific clock genes' genetic alterations in melanoma were published so far. The current targeted melanoma therapy is mainly directed towards well-established general targets such as for example mutated BRAF and its signaling or towards immunological targets, namely cytotoxic T-lymphocyte antigen 4 (CTLA-4) and programmed cell death protein 1 (PD-1). Still, chronobiological intervention and its potential in melanoma treatment remain an unexploited area. In particular, optimization of melanoma therapy regimens according to the circadian rhythms or circadian clock function activation in melanoma by a particular therapy might represent a new therapeutic approach for treatment of malignant melanoma.

E. P. Markova-Car (✉) · S. Kraljević Pavelić
Department of Biotechnology, Centre for High-Throughput Technologies, University of Rijeka, Rijeka, Croatia
e-mail: elitza@biotech.uniri.hr

D. Jurišić
University Hospital Centre Rijeka, Clinic for Surgery, Department for Plastic and Reconstructive Surgery, Rijeka, Croatia

N. Ružak
Pula General Hospital, Pula, Croatia

© Springer Nature Switzerland AG 2019
N. Bodiroga-Vukobrat et al. (eds.), *Personalized Medicine in Healthcare Systems*,
Europeanization and Globalization 5, https://doi.org/10.1007/978-3-030-16465-2_27

327

1 Circadian Disruption and Skin Cancers

Currently, 132,000 melanoma skin cancers occur globally each year. In fact, according to skin Cancer Foundation Statistic one in every three cancer diagnosed is a skin cancer.[1] Skin, the largest organ in the human body, provides the first line of defense against external environmental factors. These include the ultraviolet radiation (UVR), which is considered as the most important pathological environmental factor for inducing DNA damage and leading to skin melanocytes malignant transformation. The existing scientific evidence clearly correlates exposure rates to sun and/or indoor UVR tanning devices with melanoma, basal cell carcinoma (BCC) and squamous cell carcinoma (SCC) development.[2] Besides these actions, the UVR and its diurnal variations, may also contribute to the disruption of our circadian rhythms. By definition, the phenomenon of a circadian rhythm represents physical, mental and behavioral changes which follow an approximately 24 h cycle dependent on the organism's responds to light and dark changes in the environment. Circadian rhythms within the body are thought to be synchronized through the system located in the suprachiasmatic nucleus (SCN) of the anterior hypothalamus. The SCN generates circadian signals responsible for the peripheral physiological or behavioral events and are entrained by external signals, *e.g.* light. These endogenous, self-sustained and cell-autonomous oscillations are functional in most body cells present in liver, kidney, heart or skin. Circadian disruption plays a role in the pathogenesis of many health conditions and long-term diseases, including cancer. It can also modulate the outcomes of anticancer therapy.[3] Melatonin is the pineal hormone with an important role in circadian regulation. Its release is closely related to circadian rhythms and light exposure. Melatonin acts as an output factor that primarily translates the length of the photoperiod to the organism and is involved in protecting the skin from harmful effects originating from the UV.[4] The main protective mechanism of melatonin is a free radical scavenging, resulting in an antioxidant effect against UV-induced formation of reactive oxygen species (ROS). Accordingly, melatonin prevents the DNA damage and potential cancer development and retains anti-apoptotic and anti-tumor properties. On the other side, its indirect action is through up-regulation of genes coding for anti-oxidative enzymes activities. The melatonin related transcriptional activation triggers endogenous enzymatic protective system against oxidative stress. Melatonin oscillation depends on a light exposure and its peak expression is during the night. Considering its pleiotropic function aberrations in melatonin production can be important for developing potential therapies aimed to target circadian disorders.[5]

---

[1]Kosary et al. (2014) and Siegel et al. (2016).
[2]Desotelle et al. (2012) and Plikus et al. (2015).
[3]Dauchy et al. (2014) and Desotelle et al. (2012).
[4]Markova-Car et al. (2014).
[5]Yu and Reiter (1993), Slominski et al. (2005), Yi et al. (2014) and Kleszczyński et al. (2011).

Aberrant circadian rhythms cause deregulation of circadian clock genes and proteins, which, when combined, may alter cellular proliferation and subsequently lead to oncogenesis and cancer. For example, disruption of melatonin rhythms is related to carcinogenesis and may contribute to skin cancer development. Indeed, the human lifestyle has changed over the past few hundred years mainly because of technological advancements. Some of the consequences of this lifestyle changes directly relate to the disruption of circadian rhythms, such as night-shift work, exposure to artificial light, irregular diet, and electromagnetic (EM) waves.[6]

At the molecular level, the mammalian circadian clock is controlled by transcriptional and posttranslational feedback loops comprising a set of key elements, so-called 'clock genes' involved in regulation of a wide range of circadian rhythms which are relevant for physiological processes and behavior. The positive limb of the mammalian clock machinery involve some bHLH-PAS (basic helix-loop-helix-PAS) transcription factors, including BMAL1 (brain and muscle ARNT-like protein 1, referred in nomenclature as ARNTL), CLOCK (circadian locomotor output cycles kaput) and NPAS2 (neuronal PAS domain protein). The BMAL1 and CLOCK/NPAS2 heterodimerize and stimulate the expression of Period genes (*PER1*, *PER2* and *PER3*) and Cryptochrome (*CRY1* and *CRY2*) genes by binding to an E-box enhancer region of *PER* and *CRY* genes. Accumulated PER and CRY proteins in turn, translocate from the cytoplasm into the nucleus and inhibit BMAL1-CLOCK/NPAS2 transcriptional activity, thereby repressing their own expression. In the second loop, *BMAL1* gene expression is regulated. In particular, BMAL1-CLOCK/NPAS2 heterodimers bind E-boxes in the promoters of retinoic acid-related orphan nuclear receptors *RORα* and *REV-ERBα* genes and initiate their expression. Those two transcription factors actually compete for the ROR element in the *BMAL1* promoter region, whereas RORα up-regulates and REV-ERBα down-regulates *BMAL1* expression. A number of kinases and phosphatases are crucial for sustainment of circadian rhythmicity as they posttranslationally modify majority of the clock proteins. For more details on the clock molecular mechanism, please refer to Albrecht et al.[7] Further, chromatin remodeling appears to be an integral part of the clock function as well. For example, CLOCK has an intrinsic histone acetyl transferase (HAT) activity, which is important for clock controlled circadian gene expression. Furthermore, CLOCK acetylates non-histone proteins such as its own binding partner BMAL1, but also other cellular proteins, which are key regulators of different cellular events like the cell cycle, various metabolic pathways including sleep-wake cycle.[8] Moreover, it has been shown that SIRT1 (histone deacetylase sirtuin 1), the class III histone deacetylase (HDAC), regulates circadian rhythms by counteracting the HAT activity of CLOCK. Therefore, SIRT1 deacetylates BMAL1 and can also deacetylate and regulate proteins involved in metabolism and cell proliferation. With this in mind, it is worth to put more efforts in further

---

[6]Sahar and Sassone-Corsi (2009) and Li et al. (2013).

[7]Albrecht (2012).

[8]Bellet and Sassone-Corsi (2010).

understanding of the clock-controlled mechanisms of tumor suppression as this might provide novel insights into cancer pathogenies.

2 Circadian Rhythms and Melanoma

Multiple cell types and structures are present in the skin and circadian oscillators were found to be present in several skin cell types, including epidermal and hair follicle keratinocytes, dermal fibroblasts, and melanocytes. Melanomas are malignant tumors that arise from melanocytes, specialized pigment-producing cells residing in the skin to protect the body from damaging UVR. Indeed, the skin is a useful model to study autonomous circadian clock regulation mechanisms. For example, the expression of *CLOCK* and *PER1* genes has already been described in various types of human skin cells, including primary keratinocytes, melanocytes, and dermal fibroblasts.[9] Moreover, circadian clock genes *PER1*, *CRY1*, and *BMAL1* have been shown to oscillate in human skin biopsies.[10] Sandu and coworkers have demonstrated for the first time the presence of the molecular circadian machinery in primary human melanocytes, and showed that skin cells possess complex circadian organization. Moreover, these autonomous oscillators likely operate locally and interact with signals from the central pacemaker for driving rhythmic skin functions.[11]

It has been already accepted that circadian disruption caused by irregular work schedules, frequent travelling, as well as light pollution, which are all important features of modern society, can lead to various pathological conditions, particularly metabolic and cardiovascular syndromes and malignancies. Therefore, a lifestyle based on the following natural environmental signals and daily biological rhythms might be considered as a preventive factor in general, including cancer.[12] Several studies suggested higher risks of skin cancer among professions associated with shift work, including firefighters, nurses, and occupations in aviation like airline pilots and cabin crewmembers,[13] who are exposed to a higher levels of UVR and primary cosmic (ionizing) radiation. Accordingly, multiple studies have been consistent in showing a higher incidence of melanoma and other skin tumors in these professions.[14] In fact, the International Commission on Radiological Protection has already recognized the importance of controlling the exposure of these professionals, because their radiation doses are similar to those of healthcare employees exposed to radiation.[15] However, the exact cause for increasing incidence of skin cancer in

---

[9]Zanello et al. (2000).

[10]Bjarnason et al. (2001).

[11]Sandu et al. (2012).

[12]Salavaty (2015).

[13]Pukkala et al. (2014), Schernhammer et al. (2011) and Kvaskoff and Weinstein (2010).

[14]Pukkala et al. (2012) and Gutierrez and Arbesman (2016).

[15]International Commission on Radiological Protection (ICRP) (1997).

flight-based occupations is yet to be discovered. The effect of night shift work on skin carcinogenesis has been studied in population of nurses. Schernhammer et al. found lower risks of skin cancer (BBC, SCC and melanoma) in female nurses with longer durations of rotating night shift, with over 10 years of time working, compared to those who had worked nightly for a short period. Interestingly, the strongest association was shown for cutaneous melanoma where darker-haired women had the lowest risk.[16] So far, available epidemiologic data does not give a clear correlation between circadian disruption and skin carcinogenesis, particularly melanoma development. Because of a number of puzzling variables, evidence exist for association between shift work and skin cancer in some populations. Artificial light at night cannot only strongly suppress melatonin expression shifting circadian rhythm and promote malignancies such as melanoma, but can also disrupt clock gene regulation and induce a plethora of different biological outcomes. Such light alterations lead to clock genes deregulation as well as to epigenetic changes. Accordingly, chromatin remodeling can be affected by several environmental causes, such as light exposure, and it has been proposed that circadian behavior is a light reprogrammed by plastic DNA methylation.[17] Indeed, epigenetic modifications such as histone phosphorylation, methylation and acetylation are essential part of the circadian rhythm regulation of clock genes expression as clock driven dynamic epigenome contributes to the transcriptome rhythmicity.[18]

Epigenetic dysregulation has been shown as essential for cancer development, especially in hypermethylating or demethylating promoters of tumor suppressor genes and oncogenes, respectively. A common oncogenic B-Raf proto-oncogene (BRAF) variant BRAF (V600E) directed pathway was recently found to mediate methylation and epigenetic silencing in colorectal cancer and melanoma, through forming the protein complexes that contain the DNA methyltransferase DNMT3B.[19] Furthermore, it has been already shown that in some malignancies, i.e. hematological malignancies and lung a number of clock genes are transcriptionally silenced by promoter hypermethylation that might potentially be correlated with clinical stages of the disease.[20] However, further investigations are needed to clarify whether some circadian clock genes are epigenetically dysregulated in melanoma. As circadian rhythms regulate diverse physiologic processes, this area of exploration might be particularly interesting in the translational research of skin pathologies as conclusive investigations performed in this area are still lacking.

---

[16]Schernhammer et al. (2011).

[17]Azzi et al. (2014).

[18]Aguilar-Arnal and Sassone-Corsi (2013).

[19]Fang et al. (2016).

[20]Taniguchi et al. (2009), Yang et al. (2006) and Gery et al. (2007).

2.1 Genetic Alterations in Clock Genes Associated with Melanoma

The skin appears to be a highly suitable biological system for exploration of the interrelationships between circadian clock, cell cycle, and malignances as well as for studying of the clock's role in regulation of the immune functions.[21] Skin is under direct influence of the environmental stimuli and is particularly sensitive to light exposure. Consequently, it developed a unique protective pigment cells aimed for protection from sunlight, particularly from DNA-damaging UV light. However, melanoma prevalence remains high, and a high mortality rate still poses problems in melanoma management. Indeed, in melanoma pathogenesis skin retains a functional canonical clock mechanism. However, the exact importance of the each clock gene, specific circadian profiles or molecular clock functions remains unexplored so far. The first clinical evidence for a possible association between circadian clock genes expression status and melanoma came from the investigation of Lengyel et al.[22] The authors investigated expression of circadian clock genes in human melanoma biopsies and correlated them with histopathological characteristics of melanoma. The study revealed that *PER1*, *PER2*, *CLOCK* and *CRY1* expression levels and corresponding PER1 and CLOCK protein levels were significantly reduced in melanoma and nevus biopsies in comparison with adjacent non-tumorous specimens. Further, reciprocal correlation between the PER1 protein expression with the Breslow thickness and presence of ulceration was observed in melanoma biopsies. Consecutively, *CLOCK* gene was up-regulated in non-tumorous cells of melanoma biopsies, but not in melanoma cells or nevus cells. The *CLOCK* gene is involved in cellular metabolism, and its role in impaired regulation of metabolism in malignant tumors was suggested. In conclusion, according to the authors the observed clock genes deregulation seemed not to be a solitary characteristic of malignant cells themselves but a feature of surrounding non-malignant cells as well.[23]

Moreover, Hamilton et al. explored circadian clock molecular changes that occur in tumors using a zebrafish melanoma model which is recognized as an excellent model for investigation of melanoma.[24] The authors examined circadian clock genes expression profiles during several days. Downregulation of core clock genes *per1*, *bmal1a* and *clock* expression in melanoma tumors was observed in comparison with healthy skin, which was in agreement with previously discussed findings. Furthermore, the study revealed that disruption in central clock components was because of the impaired light input pathway. Specifically, reduction in expression of *per2* and *cry1a* genes, known to be involved in zebrafish clock entrainment, was observed.

---

[21]Geyfman et al. (2012).
[22]Lengyel et al. (2013a).
[23]Lengyel et al. (2013a, b).
[24]Hamilton et al. (2015).

This was accompanied by loss of light-dependent activation of DNA-repair genes, suggesting a compromised DNA repair mechanism and a concomitantly higher potential for accelerated melanoma development. Moreover, the circadian timing of mitosis in tumors was disrupted along with deregulation of some of the main cell cycle regulators, leading to arhythmical cell division.[25] For instance, in humans and mice, the nucleotide excision repair is the main system responsible for elimination of the UV-induced damaged nucleotides. Accordingly, individuals with mutations in excision repair genes suffer from xeroderma pigmentosum, a disorder with a typically high incidence of skin cancers from defective repair of the UV-induced DNA damage.[26] It is known from the mouse model that the xeroderma pigmentosum group A (XPA) protein represents a rate-limiting subunit of excision repair under circadian clock regulation. The circadian oscillation of XPA is transcriptionally and posttranscriptionally regulated by circadian core clock genes and the HERC2 ubiquitin ligase, respectively. Daily oscillations of XPA underlie a daily rhythm of excision repair activity as well.[27] Specifically, mice exposed to UVR while the excision repair activity was low and DNA replication was at its maximum, developed skin cancer faster and with a higher incidence than mice exposed to UVR in the evening, when excision repair activity was at its highest peak and the DNA replication was at its minimum. Accordingly, the time-window of the day determines the rate of damage which occurs upon the exposure to the UVR. For that reason, the specific time-window appears to be an essential factor for the level of carcinogenicity in mice and most likely in humans. Importantly, it provides a good rationale for development of chronopharmacotherapy approach for preventing and treating melanoma and other skin cancers.[28] Moreover, genetic variants (polymorphisms and/or mutations) may cause transcriptional alterations although there is no comprehensive data related to existence/importance of specific polymorphisms and/or mutations of clock genes in melanoma. Such information might be particularly helpful from a precision medicine perspective and may be useful in discovery of new melanoma biomarkers or melanoma predisposition assessment.

3   Melanoma Therapy and Targeted Approach

An important segment of the personalized paradigm in general is the stratified approach. The term "stratified" refers to grouping of patients based on the risk of disease or response to chosen therapy. For such grouping, physicians usually use diagnostic tests or different techniques and according to the test results, they adjust the treatment, specifically for each patient. This approach is helpful in optimizing

---

[25]Hamilton et al. (2015).

[26]Sancar et al. (2015).

[27]Kang et al. (2010).

[28]Gaddameedhi et al. (2011).

clinical outcomes and preventing side effects. Thus, the benefit resulting from targeted approach is significant. The major tools for such approach are molecular methods aimed for valid biomarker assessment. Advancements in the field may eventually lead to better prognosis, better overall survival or recurrence free survival, and fewer side effects. Current therapeutic options for patients suffering from melanoma might also include the targeted immunotherapy or "smart" therapy regimens which should complement the primary therapeutic approaches: surgery, chemotherapy or chemoradiotherapy. While surgery remains the first treatment choice for early melanoma stages, a specific combined therapeutic approach will depend on the tumor stage and its molecular properties. Immunotherapy of melanoma is very important for patients who have an increased risk for recurrence and metastases. It can also be useful for patients with advanced disease, as it may prolong the expected life span. Targeted therapy of melanoma includes several approved drugs, commonly called "magic bullets" as they can target only those cells that have expressed a specific (mutated) protein. The very first studies with this approach were performed on melanoma cell lines *in vitro*. One of identified targets was the mutated NRAS, a member of Ras family of G-protein oncogenes[29] and mutated proteins which constitute the MAP-kinase signaling pathway.[30] Mutations in NRAS are present in 20% of melanomas of different stages. Experimental data provides particular evidence on the NRAS role in melanomas that derive from giant congenital naevi.[31] Later, it was shown that NRAS downstream target BRAF (serine-threonine kinase) is also mutated in 50% of all melanoma tumors. Discovery of BRAF mutations was a decisive milestone for improved targeted melanoma treatment. The mutation hotspot for BRAF is at position V600 which accounts for 92% of all known BRAF mutations in melanoma.[32] Mutated BRAF, particularly BRAF V600E and V600K (a substitution of valine into glutamic acid and lysine, respectively) is currently acknowledged as a major known target for melanoma therapy, in particular for subsets of metastatic and/or unresectable tumors. For example, according to Bollag et al.[33] the BRAF inhibitor Vemurafenib causes rapid tumor regression in the vast majority of BRAF V600E-mutant melanoma patients. Targeted therapies obtained together with the genetic test for BRAF gene mutation are also recommended for those patients with late melanoma stages.[34] As mutated BRAF signaling is mediated via MEK and ERK, selective MEK inhibitors including cobimetinib, dabrafenib and trametinib may increase efficacy of BRAF inhibitors. The following combined BRAF targeted therapies are therefore, approved by the FDA for the treatment of BRAF mutation positive melanoma patients:

---

[29]Padua et al. (1984).

[30]Inamdar et al. (2010).

[31]Shakhova et al. (2012).

[32]Besaratinia and Pfeifer (2008).

[33]Bollag et al. (2012).

[34]Tsai et al. (2008) and Lee et al. (2010).

Zelboraf + Cotellic (Cobimetinib), Tafinlar + Mekinist, Tafinlar (dabrafenib), Mekinist (trametinib) and Zelboraf (Vemurafenib).[35] However, the occurrence of resistance to BRAF inhibitors after an average of 6 months BRAF inhibitor monotherapy and after 9–10 months of BRAF–MEK inhibitor combination therapy seems to hamper further advancements. More research in the resistance mechanisms is therefore required. Melanoma patients have often a history of chronic UV exposure that led to somatic BRAF mutations. Further, UVB rays were identified as responsible for more than 80% of all non-silent mutations in melanoma patients,[36] including mutations in RAC1 gene.[37] On the contrary, the presence of mutations in the receptor with tyrosine kinase activity c-KIT is seen in melanomas related to low-levels of ultraviolet exposure, *i.e.* mucosal and acral melanomas. This mutations account for less than 10% of described melanoma mutations. In the c-KIT mutation positive subgroup of patients, a targeted treatment by tyrosine kinase inhibitors, such as for example imatinib, nilotinib, sorafenib or dasatanib is highly plausible.[38]

At last, melanoma immunotherapy based on 'checkpoint inhibitors' should be also considered as a valuable targeted treatment approach. The checkpoint inhibitors acts on immune cells, *i.e.* T cells by blocking the so called 'check proteins' which would otherwise act as inhibitors of the immune response. For example, ipilimumab a monoclonal antibody, targets the T-cell surface molecule called cytotoxic T-lymphocyte antigen 4 (CTLA-4). Therefore, inhibition of CTLA-4 activity and negative regulation of the T cells function occurs. Therefore, a cellular response against melanoma cells occurs. Moreover, monoclonal antibodies nivolumab or pembrolizumab target programmed cell death protein 1 (PD-1) receptor on CD4+ and CD8+ T cells, B cells and natural killer cells. PD-1 abrogates the cytotoxic immune response by binding to its ligand PD-L1 which is highly expressed in many tumors.[39] These monoclonal antibodies make therefore, T cells permanently activated. Checkpoint inhibitors pembrolizumab (Keytruda), nivolumab (Opdivo), and ipilimumab (Yervoy), are approved by FDA for melanoma treatment and are good candidates for combined application with IL2 or interferon.[40] In conclusion, targeted melanoma immunotherapy based on genetic analysis of specific gene mutations present in melanoma, has drastically improved the melanoma treatment outcome in recent years. Still, the success remains confined to stratified fractions of patients that may benefit from targeted inhibitors treatment and more research into new genetic markers is encouraged to provide additional treatment opportunities.

---

[35]Melanoma Research Foundation. Melanoma Treatment. Accessed 25.02.2017; American Cancer Society. Treatment of Melanoma Skin Cancer by Stage. Accessed 25.02.2017.

[36]Hodis et al. (2012).

[37]Krauthammer et al. (2012).

[38]Ravnan and Matalka (2012) and Chapman et al. (2011).

[39]Johnson et al. (2015).

[40]Alexander (2016), Robert et al. (2015a, b) and Hodi et al. (2010).

3.1   Chronotherapy in Melanoma Patients

Chronotherapy emerged as a promising area of research and is based on administration of drugs in coordination with circadian rhythms to achieve maximum therapeutic effect with minimum side effects.[41] The rationale for using a chronotherapeutic approach is the knowledge on existence of daily rhythms governing physiological functions and pathological processes. Moreover, it has also been established that the treatment effectiveness, tolerability, and toxicity of anticancer drugs vary in relation to the timing of the drug application. These findings gave rise to the concept known as cancer chronotherapy based on a circadian clock in designing and optimizing the cancer treatment.[42] This therapeutic approach is particularly interesting in relation to circadian regulation control of both drug pharmacokinetics (PK) and pharmacodynamics (PD). Circadian drug delivery schedules should be carefully adjusted, keeping in mind that the molecular clocks rhythmically control Phase I, II and III drug metabolism, detoxification and elimination. A deeper knowledge on intimate connections between chronoPK and chronoPD may therefore help in optimization and personalization of drug delivery schedules. Chronotherapeutic delivery regimens of drugs have already shown benefits in metastatic colorectal cancer patients. Multicentric clinical trial revealed that the best tolerated chronotherapy schedule correlated with best antitumor effect and was accompanied by fewer side effects. Further studies revealed major differences between males and females in response to therapy. For instance, it has been found that in colorectal cancer, the benefit from chronotherapy was actually restricted to males while females had a better outcome based on a standard therapy approach.[43] It may be speculated that hormone differences may account for these observations. Lévi and Okyar reviewed the relevance of an optimal circadian schedule validated in randomized Phase III trial. Benefits were observed in patients with rheumatologic, respiratory and malignant diseases. However, some of the trials did not exhibit expected positive outcome and no inclusive reasons have been finally suggested. Nevertheless, the results based on large cohort cancer patients from multiple Phase I, II, and III trials have revealed notable benefits for the chronotherapeutic delivery in comparison with fixed chronotherapy schedules, although with some discrepancies according to sex and circadian function. In fact, the characteristics of human circadian timing system varied among individuals, in association with age, gender or chronotype, and these differences must be considered in the personalized chronotherapy drug delivery strategies, reviewed in Ortiz-Tudela et al.[44] Indeed, comprehensive analysis of different comparative methodological approaches for chemotherapy administration profiles within the 24 h day-period revealed significances related to the circadian time status within all stages of drug development. This

---

[41]Lévi and Okyar (2011).
[42]Ortiz-Tudela et al. (2013).
[43]Innominato et al. (2010).
[44]Ortiz-Tudela et al. (2013).

has therefore, a clear implication in optimization of therapeutic index of new cancer drugs in accordance to circadian rhythms. Additional factors including sex, clock gene polymorphisms, gene deregulation, and individual circadian biology differences of host and cancer, are important issues in optimization of individualized chronotherapy approach as well. For instance, it has been suggested that patients suffering from metastatic melanoma exhibit a dynamic immune response, governed by infradian biorhythms of immune cells as well as cytokines, and is highly individualized among patients. An infradian rhythm is a rhythm with a period longer than the period of a circadian rhythm and accordingly, chemotherapy administration of temozolomide (TMZ), a lymphodepliting cytotoxic drug, during the distinctive phase of this cycle appeared to correlate with better response, corroborating the benefits of individualized chemotherapy approach for improving clinical outcomes in metastatic melanoma by synchronizing the drug delivery with the specific patient biorhythm.[45] Indeed, a Phase II large validation clinical trial is ongoing, studying individualized TMZ administration in treating patients with stage IV melanoma. The drug is given at different, individually determined times, according to the immune system response phase against the tumor, feasible improving drug response and efficiency of killing tumor cells.[46] Nevertheless, chronotherapy remains insufficiently explored in skin cancer treatment. In that sense, the knowledge from zebrafish melanoma model study, showing asynchrony of circadian profile of cell cycle genes between melanoma tumors and healthy skin cells, points to a possibility of anticancer drug delivery at a time when it will be less harmful for healthy tissue. Moreover, another possible melanoma chronotherapy approach comes from an idea of Plikus et al. where the administration of drugs should be done in a time when their targets have the highest expression level and/or when pathways that metabolize them are at lowest level. In fact, a recent study by Kiessling et al. demonstrated how enhanced circadian clock function in cancer cells might actually inhibit tumor growth. In particular, authors found clock gene repression in B16 melanoma cells and tumors, and induction of circadian rhythmicity by use of dexamethasone, forskolin and heat shock. These treatments triggered clock rhythm and cell cycle gene expression, which reduced the number of cells in the S phase and increased the cell number in the G1 phase. Inhibition of B16 cell proliferation *in vitro* and tumor growth *in vivo* was consequently observed. Dexamethasone effects on the cell cycle and tumor growth was found to be mediated by the tumor-intrinsic circadian clock. This finding adds evidence on specific treatment-activation of circadian clock function in tumors, which might represent a new therapeutic approach for malignant melanoma therapy in humans as well as a novel strategy to control cancer

---

[45]Leontovich et al. (2012) and Dronca et al. (2012).

[46]Individualized Temozolomide in Treating Patients With Stage IV Melanoma That Cannot Be Removed By Surgery.

progression, therefore opening a space for new opportunities for chronobiological intervention in cancer treatment.[47,48]

References

Aguilar-Arnal L, Sassone-Corsi P (2013) The circadian epigenome: how metabolism talks to chromatin remodeling. Curr Opin Cell Biol 25(2):170–176

Albrecht U (2012) Timing to perfection: the biology of central and peripheral circadian clocks. Neuron 74(2):246–260

Alexander W (2016) The checkpoint immunotherapy revolution: what started as a trickle has become a flood, despite some daunting adverse effects; new drugs, indications, and combinations continue to emerge. P T 41(3):185–191

American Cancer Society. Treatment of Melanoma Skin Cancer by Stage. https://www.cancer.org/cancer/melanoma-skin-cancer/treating/by-stage.html. Accessed 25 Feb 2017

Azzi A, Dallmann R, Casserly A et al (2014) Circadian behavior is light-reprogrammed by plastic DNA methylation. Nat Neurosci 17(3):377–382

Bellet MM, Sassone-Corsi P (2010) Mammalian circadian clock and metabolism – the epigenetic link. J Cell Sci 123(Pt 22):3837–3848

Besaratinia A, Pfeifer GP (2008) Sunlight ultraviolet irradiation and BRAF V600 mutagenesis in human melanoma. Hum Mutat 29(8):983–991

Bjarnason GA, Jordan RC, Wood PA et al (2001) Circadian expression of clock genes in human oral mucosa and skin: association with specific cell-cycle phases. Am J Pathol 158(5):1793–1801

Bollag GE, Tsai J, Zhang J et al (2012) Vemurafenib: the first drug approved for BRAF-mutant cancer. Nat Rev Drug Discov 11(11):873–886

Chapman PB, Hauschild A, Robert C et al (2011) Improved survival with vemurafenib in melanoma with BRAF V600E mutation. N Engl J Med 364(26):2507–2516

Dauchy RT, Xiang S, Mao L et al (2014) Circadian and melatonin disruption by exposure to light at night drives intrinsic resistance to tamoxifen therapy in breast cancer. Cancer Res 74(15):4099–4110

Desotelle JA, Wilking MJ, Ahmad N (2012) The circadian control of skin and cutaneous photodamage. Photochem Photobiol 88(5):1037–1047

Dronca RS, Leontovich AA, Nevala WK et al (2012) Personalized therapy for metastatic melanoma: could timing be everything? Future Oncol 8(11):1401–1406

Fang M, Hutchinson L, Deng A et al (2016) Common BRAF (V600E)-directed pathway mediates widespread epigenetic silencing in colorectal cancer and melanoma. Proc Natl Acad Sci U S A 113(5):1250–1255

Gaddameedhi S, Selby CP, Kaufmann WK et al (2011) Control of skin cancer by the circadian rhythm. Proc Natl Acad Sci U S A 108(64):18790–18795

Gery S, Komatsu N, Kawamata N et al (2007) Epigenetic silencing of the candidate tumor suppressor gene Per1 in non-small cell lung cancer. Clin Cancer Res 13(5):1399–1404

Geyfman M, Kumar V, Liu Q et al (2012) Brain and muscle Arnt-like protein-1 (BMAL1) controls circadian cell proliferation and susceptibility to UVB-induced DNA damage in the epidermis. Proc Natl Acad Sci U S A 109(29):11758–11763

---

[47]Kiessling et al. (2017).

[48]We acknowledge the project "Research Infrastructure for Campus-based Laboratories at University of Rijeka", co-financed by European Regional Development Fund (ERDF).

Gutierrez D, Arbesman J (2016) Circadian dysrhythmias, physiological aberrations, and the link to skin cancer. Int J Mol Sci 17(5):621

Hamilton N, Diaz-de-Cerio N, Whitmore D (2015) Impaired light detection of the circadian clock in a zebrafish melanoma model. Cell Cycle 14(8):1232–1241

Hodi FS, O'Day SJ, McDermott DF et al (2010) Improved survival with ipilimumab in patients with metastatic melanoma. N Engl J Med 363(8):711–723

Hodis E, Watson IR, Kryukov GV et al (2012) A landscape of driver mutations in melanoma. Cell 150(2):251–263

Individualized Temozolomide in Treating Patients With Stage IV Melanoma That Cannot Be Removed By Surgery. https://clinicaltrials.gov/ct2/show/NCT01328535?term=melanoma +and+temozolomide+and+mayo&rank=1

Inamdar GS, Madhunapantula SV, Robertson GP (2010) Targeting the MAPK pathway in melanoma: why some approaches succeed and other fail. Biochem Pharmacol 80(5):624–637

Innominato PF, Lévi FA, Bjarnason GA (2010) Chronotherapy and the molecular clock: clinical implications in oncology. Adv Drug Deliv Rev 62(9–10):979–1001

International Commission on Radiological Protection (ICRP) (1997) General principles for the radiation protection of workers. Ann ICRP 27(1):1–60

Johnson DB, Peng C, Sosman JA (2015) Nivolumab in melanoma: latest evidence and clinical potential. Ther Adv Med Oncol 7(2):97–106

Kang T-H, Lindsey-Boltz LA, Reardon JT et al (2010) Circadian control of XPA and excision repair of cisplatin-DNA damage by cryptochrome and HERC2 ubiquitin ligase. Proc Natl Acad Sci U S A 107(11):4890–4895

Kiessling S, Beaulieu-Laroche L, Blum ID et al (2017) Enhancing circadian clock function in cancer cells inhibits tumor growth. BMC Biol 15(1):13

Kleszczyński K, Hardkop LH, Fischer TW (2011) Differential effects of melatonin as a broad range UV-damage preventive dermato-endocrine regulator. Dermatoendocrinol 3(1):27–31

Kosary CL, Altekruse SF, Ruhl J et al (2014) Clinical and prognostic factors for melanoma of the skin using SEER registries: collaborative stage data collection system, version 1 and version 2. Cancer 120(Suppl 23):3807–3814

Krauthammer M, Kong Y, Ha BH et al (2012) Exome sequencing identifies recurrent somatic RAC1 mutations in melanoma. Nat Genet 44(9):1006–1014

Kvaskoff M, Weinstein P (2010) Are some melanomas caused by artificial light? Med Hypotheses 75(3):305–311

Lee JT, Li L, Brafford PA et al (2010) PLX4032, a potent inhibitor of the B-Raf V600E oncogene, selectively inhibits V600E-positive melanomas. Pigment Cell Melanoma Res 23(6):820–827

Lengyel Z, Lovig C, Kommedal S et al (2013a) Altered expression patterns of clock gene mRNAs and clock proteins in human skin tumors. Tumor Biol 34(2):811–819

Lengyel Z, Battyáni Z, Szekeres G et al (2013b) Circadian clocks and tumor biology: what is to learn from human skin biopsies? Gen Comp Endocrinol 188:67–74

Leontovich AA, Dronca RS, Suman VJ et al (2012) Fluctuation of systemic immunity in melanoma and implications for timing of therapy. Front Biosci (Elite Ed) 4:958–975

Lévi F, Okyar A (2011) Circadian clocks and drug delivery systems: impact and opportunities in chronotherapeutics. Expert Opin Drug Deliv 8(12):1535–1541

Li S, Ao X, Wu H (2013) The role of circadian rhythm in breast cancer. Chin J Cancer Res 25 (4):442–450

Markova-Car EP, Jurišić D, Ilić N et al (2014) Running for time: circadian rhythms and melanoma. Tumour Biol 35(9):8359–8368

Melanoma Research Foundation. Melanoma Treatment. https://www.melanoma.org/understand-melanoma/melanoma-treatment. Accessed 25 Feb 2017

Ortiz-Tudela E, Mteyrek A, Ballesta A et al (2013) Cancer chronotherapeutics: experimental, theoretical, and clinical aspects. Handb Exp Pharmacol 2017:261–288

Padua RA, Barrass N, Currie GA (1984) A novel transforming gene in a human malignant melanoma cell line. Nature 311(5987):671–673

Plikus MV, Van Spyk EN, Pham K et al (2015) The circadian clock in skin: implications for adult stem cells, tissue regeneration, cancer, aging, and immunity. J Biol Rhythms 30(3):163–182

Pukkala E, Helminen M, Haldorsen T et al (2012) Cancer incidence among Nordic airline cabin crew. Int J Cancer 131(12):2886–2897

Pukkala E, Martinsen JI, Weiderpass E et al (2014) Cancer incidence among firefighters: 45 years of follow-up in five Nordic countries. Occup Environ Med 71(6):398–404

Ravnan MC, Matalka MS (2012) Vemurafenib in patients with BRAF V600E mutation-positive advanced melanoma. Clin Ther 34(7):1474–1486

Robert C, Schachter J, Long GV et al (2015a) Pembrolizumab versus Ipilimumab in advanced melanoma. N Engl J Med 372(26):2521–2532

Robert C, Long GV, Brady B et al (2015b) Nivolumab in previously untreated melanoma without BRAF mutation. N Engl J Med 372(4):320–330

Sahar S, Sassone-Corsi P (2009) Metabolism and cancer: the circadian clock connection. Nat Rev Cancer 9(12):886–896

Salavaty A (2015) Carcinogenic effects of circadian disruption: an epigenetic viewpoint. Chin J Cancer 34(9):375–383

Sancar A, Lindsey-Boltz LA, Gaddameedhi S et al (2015) Circadian clock, cancer, and chemotherapy. Biochemistry 54(2):110–123

Sandu C, Dumas M, Malan A et al (2012) Human skin keratinocytes, melanocytes, and fibroblasts contain distinct circadian clock machineries. Cell Mol Life Sci 69(19):3329–3339

Schernhammer ES, Razavi P, Li TY et al (2011) Rotating night shifts and risk of skin cancer in the nurses' health study. J Natl Cancer Inst 103(7):602–606

Shakhova O, Zingg D, Schaefer SM et al (2012) Sox10 promotes the formation and maintenance of giant congenital naevi and melanoma. Nat Cell Biol 14(8):882–890

Siegel RL, Miller KD, Jemal A (2016) Cancer statistics, 2016. CA Cancer J Clin 66(1):7–30

Slominski A, Fischer TW, Zmijewski MA et al (2005) On the role of melatonin in skin physiology and pathology. Endocrine 27(2):137–148

Taniguchi H, Fernández AF, Setién F et al (2009) Epigenetic inactivation of the circadian clock gene BMAL1 in hematologic malignancies. Cancer Res 69(21):8447–8454

Tsai J, Lee JT, Wang W et al (2008) Discovery of a selective inhibitor of oncogenic B-Raf kinase with potent antimelanoma activity. Proc Natl Acad Sci U S A 105(8):3041–3046

Yang MY, Chang JG, Lin PM et al (2006) Downregulation of circadian clock genes in chronic myeloid leukemia: alternative methylation pattern of hPER3. Cancer Sci 97(12):1298–1307

Yi C, Zhang Y, Yu Z et al (2014) Melatonin enhances the anti-tumor effect of fisetin by inhibiting COX-2/iNOS and NF-κB/p300 signaling pathways. PLoS One 9(7):e99943

Yu HS, Reiter RJ (eds) (1993) Melatonin biosynthesis, physiological effects, and clinical applications. CRC Press, Boca Raton

Zanello SB, Jackson DM, Holick MF (2000) Expression of the circadian clock genes clock and period1 in human skin. J Invest Dermatol 115(4):757–760

Genetic and Epigenetic Profiling in Personalized Medicine: Advances in Treatment of Acute Myeloid Leukemia

Sonja Pavlović and Natasa Tosic

Abstract Medicine was always aspired to be personalized, directed to each patient as a unique case. In our time, advancement of biomedical sciences and computational and other technologies has provided solid foundation for personalized medicine. Personalized medicine, also called genome-based medicine and precision medicine, uses the knowledge of genomic and epigenomic basis of the disease to individualize treatment for each patient. Hematological malignancies and especially acute myeloid leukemia are the best examples of implementation of personalized medicine in clinical practice. Acute myeloid leukemia (AML) is a heterogeneous group of malignant diseases of hematopoietic progenitor cells, characterized by different molecular genetic and epigenetic abnormalities. It is the most common type of acute leukemia in adults, and the second most common in children. Until recently, the treatment of AML was based on standard cytotoxic chemotherapy, having resulted in the overall survival of only 30–40% in the majority of patients. Application of new high-throughput technologies has enabled better insight into genetic and epigenetic landscape of AML. The most important achievement of genome-based medicine is more precise classification of AML patients based on newly discovered molecular markers, and molecular–targeted therapy, tailored to genetic and epigenetic profile of a disease, leading to improved survival of the AML patients. Additionally, development of pharmacogenomic platforms, immunotherapies and cellular therapies has open new possibilities for personalized treatment of AML patients. There is no doubt that we are getting closer to full implementation of personalized medicine in hematological clinical practice.

The aim of personalized medicine is the tailoring of medical treatment to the individual characteristics of each patient. The concept of personalized medicine dates back many hundreds of years. It was Hippocrates (IV century BC) who sent a message to the future generations of physicians: "It's far more important to know what sort of person has a disease, than what sort of disease a person has".

S. Pavlović (✉) · N. Tosic
Laboratory for Molecular Biomedicine, Institute of Molecular Genetics and Genetic Engineering University of Belgrade, Belgrade, Serbia
e-mail: sonya@sezampro.rs

© Springer Nature Switzerland AG 2019
N. Bodiroga-Vukobrat et al. (eds.), *Personalized Medicine in Healthcare Systems*, Europeanization and Globalization 5, https://doi.org/10.1007/978-3-030-16465-2_28

1 Introduction

Clinicians have long observed that patients with similar symptoms may suffer from diseases that have different causes, and also, that the treatment can be effective for some patients but not for others, although they are suffering of, apparently, the same disease. Today, we are witnessing the advances in a wide range of fields from genomics to medical imaging and regenerative medicine, along with increased computational and other technologies, enabling patients to have individualized treatment. Personalized medicine has a strong scientific basis in genomics. Genetic variation influences every aspect of human physiology, development and adaptation. Consequently, understanding of human genetic variation plays an important role in promoting health and combating disease. Personalized medicine, known also as genome-based medicine or precision medicine, uses the knowledge about genetic basis of the disease to individualize treatment of each patient.

The modifiers of gene expression, independent of DNA sequence (genome), constitute the epigenome. The epigenome comprises the complex dynamic modifications of DNA and its associated structures, such as DNA methylation, histone modification and RNA-associated silencing. The epigenome integrates the information encoded in the genome with all the molecular and chemical signals of cellular, extracellular, and environmental origin. Actually, through epigenetic processes genome meets its environment. Many diseases are shown to be associated with epigenetic modifications. Both genomics and epigenomics are already integrated in medical practice. Individual genomic and epigenomic profiling represents the basis of personalized medicine.

Identification of disease related genes and disease causing genetic and epigenetic variants enables accurate diagnosis, prognosis and follow—up of the disease. It is also a basis for designing the strategies that should minimize the risk for developing the disease (predictive genetics and preventive medicine) and for the establishing the guidelines for using therapeutics according to a person's genomic and epigenomic profile (pharmacogenomics). The final achievement of the study of molecular genetic markers is the implementation of therapeutic approaches that "repair" the affected genes (gene therapy) and the design of molecular therapeutics which target the biological mechanism that causes the disease (molecular targeted therapy). Cell therapy, using patient's own cells in the treatment of the disease, has been recognized as an important field in personalized medicine. Furthermore, stem cell therapy represents one of the most promising approaches in medicine of today and tomorrow.

When it comes to cancer, each patient's cancer is unique, driven by distinct genetic and epigenetic alterations. Advances in basic science, technology, therapeutics, and the understanding of the genetic and epigenetic causes of cancer have led to introduction of personalized medicine in cancer care. Today, many patients have treatment options based on the particular markers in their tumors. These patients get specific treatments, which also have fewer harmful side effects.

Hematological malignancies represented the ideal context for the implementation of personalized medicine programs. Several steps from bench to bedside for personalized treatment in hematology have been successfully climbed, with many complex problems to be solved at future steps.

2 Genetic Landscape of Acute Myeloid Leukemia

Acute myeloid leukemia (AML) is a clonal hematopoietic disorder characterized by the presence of differentiation blockage and accumulation of leukemic blasts in blood and bone marrow. It is the most common type of acute leukemia in adults, and the second most common in children. The main feature of AML is its vast clinical and genetic heterogeneity.

In the treatment of leukemia, today's medicine mostly relies on proper stratification of patients and established treatment protocols. All of the patients belonging to one risk group are treated in the uniform way, using the same protocol. Consequently, the overall survival of adult and pediatric patients is only 30% and 60%, respectively.[1]

For many decades, pretreatment karyotype analysis is the main leukemic feature used for risk-stratification. Nevertheless, only the post-remission treatment is risk-adapted, while the initial treatment remains largely unchanged for all patients. Clonal chromosome aberrations can be found in about 55% of AML patents and, based on that, patients are divided into favorable, intermediate and adverse risk group.[2] The disadvantage of this approach to risk-classification is that nearly half of the patients do not have any detectable cytogenetic changes. This group of patients is referred to as AML with normal karyotype (AML-NK) and it is categorized into intermediate risk group. Over the years, a need for more precise risk stratification led to the discovery of new molecular markers. Some of these markers, such as mutations in fms-related tyrosine kinase-3 (*FLT3*), nucleophosmin (*NPM1*) and CCAAT/ enhancer binding protein alpha (*CEBPA*) gene, have already been included in the World Health Organization (WHO) classification of leukemias. In the revised WHO classification from 2016, even more molecular markers have been incorporated. Thus, a new provisional entity has been defined by the presence of mutations in *RUNX1* gene—AML with mutated *RUNX1* gene.[3] The additional data on mutational status of these genes contributed remarkably to refining the AML patients into appropriate risk groups (Table 1). The discovery of new molecular markers for AML leads to better stratification of patients and opens new perspectives on using these markers as a target for designing efficient therapy.[4]

---

[1]Perry and Attar (2014).

[2]Byrd et al. (2002).

[3]Arber et al. (2016).

[4]Dohner et al. (2017).

Table 1 Current stratification of patients with acute myeloid leukemia based on cytogenetic and molecular analyses

Risk group	Cytogenetic abnormality	Molecular abnormalities
Favorable	t(15;17)(q22;q21)	$NPM1^+$ and $FLT3/$ ITD$^-$ (normal karyotype)
	t(8;21)(q22;q22)	
	inv(16)/t(16;16)(p13;q22)	Mutated $CEBP$A-bialelic (normal karyotype)
		c-KIT$^+$ and t(8;21)(q22;q22) c-KIT$^+$ and inv(16)/t(16;16)(p13; q22)
Intermediate	Normal karyotype	$NPM1^+$ and $FLT3/$ITD$^+$ (normal karyotype), $NPM1^-$ and $FLT3/$ ITD$^+$ (normal karyotype), $NPM1^-$ and $FLT3/$ ITD$^-$ (normal karyotype)
Adverse	+8, t(9;11)(p22;q23) Cytogenetic abnormalities not classified as favorable or adverse	
	inv(3)/t(3;3)(q21;q26) add(5q), del(5q), -5, -7, add(7q)/del(7q) 11q23 other than t(9;11) Complex karyotype t(9;22)(q34;q11)	$NPM1^-$ and $FLT3/$ ITD$^+$ (normal karyotype) $RUNX1^+$(only if not associated with favorable karyotype) $ASXL1^+$(only if not associated with favorable karyotype) $TP53^+$

The application of next generation sequencing (NGS) for the detection of new somatic mutations has contributed to a better understanding of the biology of cancer in general, and especially of AML, like no other technical innovation before. NGS technology has been applied in several studies enabling better understanding of mutational profiling that underlines AML pathology. The first sequencing of primary AML genome was reported by Ley TJ and coworkers in 2008.[5] Subsequently, a number of studies of additional AML genomes have been reported,[6,7,8] reveling new somatic mutations that are very frequent in AML, such as *DNMT3a*, *IDH1*, *IDH2* and *TET2* genes. For instance, *IDH* mutations (*IDH1* and *IDH2*) have been found to occur in approximately 20% of AML patients, placing them among the most common molecular aberrations in AML-NK.[9]

Modern concept of leukemogenesis is based on the existence of "Leukemic Stem Cell" (LSC). Namely, the development of the disease is associated with gradual accumulation of genetic and epigenetic alterations in hematopoietic stem cell (HSC),

---

[5]Ley et al. (2008).

[6]Ley et al. (2010).

[7]Mardis et al. (2009).

[8]Welch et al. (2011).

[9]Marcucci et al. (2010).

which convert normal progenitor cell into a LSC.[10] Genetic changes can occur at the level of LSC, but can also occur at the level of more differentiated progenitor. In this way, leukemia is represented as a mixture of the subclones, characterized by a special combination of the mutations. Some of the mutations are so called "driver" mutations, essential for the process of leukemogenesis, and others are "passenger" mutations. Subclones of leukemic cells are hierarchically organized, and this hierarchy is susceptible to changes during the course of the disease.[11] During the course of the disease, some subclones are eradicated by the therapy applied, while the others become dominant because of their resistance to therapy. Some subclones can continue to evolve by acquiring more mutations, forming new clones appearing for the first time in a patient. Technology like NGS becomes indispensable because of its ability to detect even the rarest subclones, because of its enormous sensitivity and specificity. It enables insight into the presence or absence of certain mutations/ subclones at any time during the treatment. It also enables the physician to apply treatment targeting a particular molecular marker, making therapy more effective and more "tailored" to the measure of each patient. Another feature of the AML, discovered by the application of the NGS technology, is that AML has one of the lowest number of mutations per case of any adult cancer studied to date, on average only 3–5 mutations per patient.[12,13] Moreover, only mutations in ten genes appear to have frequency higher than 5% in AML, such as *FLT3*, *NPM1*, *DNMT3a*, *IDH1*, *IDH2*, *TET2*, *RUNX1*, *p53*, *NRAS*, *CEBP*A, and *WT1*. Therefore, they tend to be called leukemia specific genes.

A great number of data has been accumulated leading to elucidation of the complexity of AML. The next step is to recognize and point out genetic mutations that are suitable for the targeted therapy. Classical chemotherapy (based on cytarabine and anthracycline) has been the backbone of AML treatment for many decades now, but the situation has started to change with the introduction of new drugs that are highly specific and therefore less toxic.

3   Pharmacogenomics and Drug Response

Pharmacogenomic research is being developed in two main directions: first, identification of genes and gene allelic variants that might influence response to a drug that has already been used in therapy, and second, identification of specific genes and gene products that are correlated with different diseases, and therefore could represent targets for new therapeutics (molecular targeted therapy).[14]

---

[10]Warner et al. (2004).

[11]Traulsen et al. (2010).

[12]Cancer Genome Atlas Research Network (2013).

[13]Marjanovic et al. (2016).

[14]Wolf et al. (2000).

As previously mentioned, the combinations of various doses and schedules of cytarabine and different anthracyclines have been the backbone of treatment for AML. AML pharmacogenomics deals with the impact of genetic and epigenetic variation on cytarabine and anthracycline pharmacokinetics (absorption, distribution, metabolism and excretion) and pharmacodynamics (efficacy and toxicity of drugs).

Variants in the genes for cytarabine and anthracycline drug-metabolizing enzymes and drug transporters have been considered as pharmcogenetic markers for AML.

3.1 Cytarabine Pharmacogenomics

Cytarabine (ara-C) was synthesized in 1959, and since then it has been the most effective and universally used chemotherapeutic agent in the treatment of AML.[15] Mechanisms of action of ara-C include induction of miscoding after incorporation into DNA and RNA, and inhibition of DNA dependent DNA polymerase.[16,17] After entering the cells via transporter, human equilibrative nucleoside transporter (hENT1, SLC29A1), ara-C is phosphorylated to the active metabolite, ara-CTP. Intracellular concentration of ara-CTP is directly correlated with the therapeutic effect of ara-C. Inactivation of ara-C can occur through dephosphorilation and deamination. The most important parameters in sensitivity or resistance to ara-C include: inefficient cellular uptake of ara-C because of low levels and/or activity of the transporter hENT1; reduced level of activating enzymes, primarily kinases (deoxycytidine kinase, DCK, CMPK1 and NDPK); increased levels of enzymes for ara-C inactivation via dephosphorylation (5′ nucleotidases, NTPC2) and deamination by deaminases (CDA); half-life duration of active form ara-CTP, and the magnitude of its incorporation into DNA.[18,19]

Significant differences in the mRNA expression levels of Ara-C transporter (hENT1, SLC29A1), have been noted in patients with AML. Namely, AML patients with hENT1 deficiency at diagnosis had significantly shorter disease-free survival (DFS) and overall survival (OS).[20] It has been noted that both variants in *hENT1* gene as well as variability in *hENT1* expression mediated by transcriptional regulation, could be used as pharmacogenomic markers for AML.[21,22]

---

[15]Cohen (1966).
[16]Borun et al. (1969).
[17]Creasey et al. (1968).
[18]Emadi and Karp (2012).
[19]Lamba (2009).
[20]Kim et al. (2016).
[21]Wan et al. (2014).
[22]Montero et al. (2012).

Deoxycytidine kinase (DCK) is an enzyme that catalyzes the first step in the activation of nucleoside analogs such as ara-C, gemcitabine, cladribine, fludarabine and clofarabine. Several studies provide evidence for the involvement of DCK in the activation of ara-C and other nucleosides, thereby making it a key candidate for pharmacogenetic studies.[23] Numerous *DCK* SNPs with potential functional or clinical implications have been identified.[24]

Multiple reports have suggested involvement of cytosolic nucleotidases in drug resistance to ara-C.[25] So, for example, cytosolic 5′-nucleotidase II (NT5C2) is involved in the development of ara-C resistance and has been associated with clinical outcome in patients receiving ara-C-based chemotherapy. Some reports suggest that genetic variations in *NT5C2* influence its expression and, potentially, cellular responses to ara-C.[26]

Cytidine deaminase (CDA) is the predominant inactivating enzyme in the ara-C metabolic pathway. *CDA* overexpression results in Ara-C resistance, while decreased expression is associated with toxicity.[27] The presence of several genetic variants of *CDA* gene could explain the variation in its RNA expression, and therefore, they can be suitable candidates for Ara-C therapy individualization.[28]

Genome-wide studies using lymphoblast cell lines derived from subjects with different ancestries have identified previously unknown candidate genes of relevance to ara-C sensitivity, such as *RR, ABCC10, ABCC11, FKBP5, NT5C3, ES2, GCAT, MYBBP1A, TLE4, ZNF278,* and *GIT1*.[29,30,31] Also, comparative analysis of genome-wide gene-expression profiles of ara-C sensitive versus ara-C resistant cell lines, have identified candidate genes of pharmacodynamic significance. A number of coding and regulatory polymorphisms of functional and clinical significance have been identified in these candidate genes.[32,33]

3.2 Anthracyclines Pharmacogenomics

Anthracycline antibiotics (daunorubicin. idarubicin, doxorubicin, epirubicin) are another most important class of chemotherapeutic agents used in AML treatment.

---

[23]Galmarini et al. (2002).

[24]Lamba et al. (2007).

[25]Galmarini et al. (2005).

[26]Mitra et al. (2011).

[27]Maring et al. (2005).

[28]Abraham et al. (2012).

[29]Abraham et al. (2012).

[30]Li et al. (2008).

[31]Hartford et al. (2009).

[32]Takagaki et al. (2003).

[33]Yin et al. (2007).

The mechanisms of action of anthracyclines include DNA intercalation, prevention of DNA replication and production of reactive oxygen species.

Variations in drug transporters, the ATP-binding cassettes (ABCs) membrane proteins, represent most clinically relevant pharmacogenomic markers for anthracyclines.

Three ABC proteins (P-gp/ABCB1/MDR1, MRP1/ABCC1 and BCRP/ABCG2/ABCP/MXR) are primarily responsible for multidrug resistance (MDR) related to antracyclines.[34] Polymorphisms in the genes for ABC drug transporters have been investigated extensively to better understand the significant variability in response to anthracycline chemotherapy in AML patients.[35]

Another pharmacogenomically relevant mechanism is associated with glutathione S-transferase (GST) enzymes, cellular detoxifiers that are also involved in metabolism of anthracyclines.[36] GST genotypes have been correlated with response to AML therapeutic protocols that include anthracyclines.[37] It is worth noting that multi-gene panel pharmacogenomic platforms for precision medicine, based on high-throughput technology, are available and used for optimization of treatment of AML patients.[38]

4 Molecular Targeted Therapies and Current Drugs

4.1 Targeted Therapy in AML with Recurrent Translocations

The first AML subtype treated with an agent targeted to a specific molecular genetic aberration was acute promyelocytic leukemia (APL). More than 98% of APL cases are characterized by the presence of *PML/RARA* fusion. The oncogenic fusion protein PML/RARA acts as a dominant-negative inhibitor of RARA. It binds to RARA target genes as a homodimer or a heterodimer with retionoid X receptor. In that way PML/RARA inhibits expression of target genes necessary for granulocytic differentiation (see footnote 38). This repression of RARA target genes is associated with the recruitment of DNA-modifying and histone-modifying enzymes. Consequently, highly repressive chromatin environment is formed, which in turn affects multiple pathways.[39,40] Moreover, PML/RARA fusion protein may also act in a

---

[34]Sharom (2008).

[35]Megías et al. (2015).

[36]L'Ecuyer et al. (2004).

[37]Voso et al. (2008).

[38]Iacobucci et al. (2013).

[39]Wang and Chen (2008).

[40]Carbone et al. (2006).

dominant negative manner against PML tumor supressor protein.[41] All of the above leads to cells being blocked at the promyelocytic stage of differentiation.

PML/RARA oncogenic fusion protein that blocks the promyelocytic stage of differentiation was the target for designing specific therapeutic agent—*all-trans* retinoic acid (ATRA). ATRA leads to a conformational change of the multifunctional molecule complex around PML/RARA. In that way corepressors are released, normal regulation of RARA- responsive genes is restored and the terminal differentiation of APL cells is induced.[42] The application of ATRA therapy has become the standard in the treatment of newly diagnosed patients with APL. This resulted in high clinical remission rates of APL patients.[43] However, a number of patients relapsed after developing resistance to ATRA. New therapeutic agent, arsenic trioxide (ATO) emerged as an option for overcoming ATRA resistance.[44] ATO shows a dual mode of action; at low concentrations, ATO induces a partial morphologic differentiation in APL cells, whereas at high concentrations, the emphasis is on apoptosis induction. Both effects are associated with degradation of PML/RARA.[45,46]

The application of both ATRA and ATO in the treatment of APL is, to date, the most successful example of differentiation therapy, which serves as a model for development of similar therapeutic agents for treatment of other leukemias and cancers.

More than 12 different translocations, accounting for about 25% of all AML cases, cause disruption in the core-binding factor (CBF) complex. The two most common are t(8;21), present in 12–15% of AML cases and inv(16), associated with 8–10% of AML cases.[47] The CBF complex is a heterodimer consisting of AML1 (RUNX1) and CBFB protein. In the case of t(8;21) and inv(16), the resulting fusion proteins, AML1/ETO and CBFB/MYH11, act as dominant-negative inhibitors of CBF transcriptional regulation and repressors of AML1 target genes.[48]

Frequent deregulation of transcriptional factors such as CBF (associated with the presence of *AML1/ETO* and *CBFB/MYH11* fusion transcripts) and C/EBPA, appears to be a central theme in AML. Therefore, they represent an obvious target for the development of specific therapeutic agents. Dominant-negative action of the aberrant transcriptional factors causes aberrant recruitment of the nuclear corepressor complex, and may result both in modification of chromatin structure in key hematopoietic promoters, as well as in aberrant acetylation of proteins that regulate cell-

---

[41]Villa et al. (2007).

[42]Scaglioni and Pandolfi (2007).

[43]Grignani et al. (1998).

[44]Tallman et al. (2002).

[45]Estey et al. (2006).

[46]Chen et al. (1997).

[47]Speck and Gililand (2002).

[48]Meyers et al. (1995).

cycle progression and other functions.[49,50] The block in the differentiation process of AML cells can be reversed by abrogation of epigenetic silencing using epigenetically targeted therapy.[51]

4.2   FLT3 Mutations and FLT3 Inhibitors

FLT3, FMS-like tyrosine kinase 3 gene, encodes a membrane-bound receptor tyrosine kinase. It is normally expressed in myeloid progenitor cells, and its expression is downregulated during differentiation process. It plays an important role in proliferation, differentiation and survival of hematopoietic stem cells, and is overexpressed in AML.[52] Mutations in *FLT3* gene are one of the most frequent molecular markers in AML, found in 25–45% of patients. The most common *FLT3* mutation is internal tandem duplication (*FLT3/ITD*) affecting the juxtamembrane protein domain, seen in up to 25% of adult AML.[53,54,55] The length of the duplicated region varies from 3 to 400 nucleotides but despite this heterogeneity, the resultant transcripts are always in-frame (see footnote 53). The second type of *FLT3* mutation is a missense point mutation in the activation loop domain (*FLT3/TKD*), found in 5–10% of AML patients. The most frequent mutations involve codons D835Y and/or I836L+D, and less frequently N841I or Y842C.[56] *FLT3* mutations and overexpression of wild type *FLT3* lead to constitutive phosphorylation of the receptor in the absence of FLT3-ligand, which in turn activates downstream signaling pathways and eventually enhances cell proliferation.[57]

FLT3 inhibitors are tyrosine kinase inhibitors (TKI). Mutated FLT3 protein is in constitutively activated form. TKI works by competing for the adenosine triphosphate (ATP) binding site, preventing the phosphorylation of the kinase and diminishing its activity.

For the first-generation FLT3 inhibitors like midostaurin, sunitinib and sorafenib, it can be said that they are quite nonspecific for FLT3, because they have affinity for other targets like KIT, PDGFR (platelet-derived growth factor receptor), VEGFR (vascular endothelial growth factor receptor) and JAK2 (Janus kinase 2). They are used in clinical practice mostly in *FLT3/ITD* positive AML patients, as their use in the *FLT3/TKD* leukemia is not so efficient. There are studies that support the fact that

---

[49]Lutterbach et al. (1999).

[50]Strahl and Allis (2000).

[51]Figueroa et al. (2008).

[52]Carow et al. (1996).

[53]Schnittger et al. (2002).

[54]Colovic et al. (2007).

[55]Krstovski et al. (2010).

[56]Yamamoto et al. (2001).

[57]Dicker et al. (2007).

this type of mutation develops in a patient treated with FLT3 inhibitors as a defense mechanism i.e. as a mechanism of resistance.[58,59] FLT3 inhibitors are used alone or in combination with conventional chemotherapy.

Midostaurin is a small-molecule inhibitor of KIT, VEGFR, PDGFR and FLT3. Its effectiveness as monotherapeutic was disappointing, but its application in all phases of therapy accompanied by standard chemotherapy is continuously studied and currently is in the stage III clinical trial.[60] Sorafenib is a small-molecule inhibitor of RAF kinase. Sorafenib inhibits growth and proliferation of *FLT3/ITD* mutated AML cells. Also, it induces apoptosis by dephosphorylating MEK1/2 and ERK.[61,62] It has been observed that the best effects in the treatment with sorafenib are achieved in combination with conventional therapy based on cytarabine and anthracyclines, because of the existence of a synergistic effect.[63,64]

In recent years, the second-generation inhibitors, like quizartinib and crenolanib, have been developed. Their main advantage lies in the fact that they are more specific, therefore more potent, and less toxic compared to first generation inhibitors. Quizartinib (AC-220) is a high-potency bis-aryl urea FLT3 inhibitor. In AML patients, quizartinib shows prolonged inhibition effect on FLT3, and does that as a single agent, which makes it the most clinically effective FLT3 inhibitor.[65] Quizartinib is often used in the treatment of relapsed and refractory AML. Another second-generation inhibitor, crenolanib, has been found to be very efficient in the treatment of drug-resistant *FLT3/ITD* positive AML, and, more importantly, crenolanib is very active against *FLT3*/TKD mutations.[66] The development of next-generation inhibitors is ongoing, and the latest study of a phase I/II trial of ASP-2215, a novel inhibitor of FLT3, showed exquisite overall response rate of the patients treated.[67]

4.3 RAS Mutations and Targeted Therapy

RAS oncogenes encode a family of proteins that function as GDP/GTP molecular switches and control diverse signaling pathways involved in regulation of cell proliferation, survival, differentiation and gene expression. Their constitutive

---

[58]Moore et al. (2012).

[59]Smith et al. (2015).

[60]Stone et al. (2015).

[61]Zhang et al. (2008a).

[62]Zhang et al. (2008b).

[63]Ravandi et al. (2013).

[64]Macdonald et al. (2013).

[65]Zarrinkar et al. (2009).

[66]Randhawa et al. (2014).

[67]Levis et al. (2015).

activation, resulting from the presence of point mutations, disrupts these important cell processes, like differentiation and apoptosis.[68] The most common mutations are point mutations in codons 12, 13 or 61 of *N-RAS* and *K-RAS*. They are found in approximately 5–15% of all AML patients. The subgroup of AML with inv (16) shows the highest frequency of *RAS* mutations, reaching up to 35%.[69]

RAS proteins deliver signals from receptor tyrosine kinases across to the downstream signaling networks. One of the downstream signaling pathways that is deregulated by the presence of *RAS* mutations is through mitogen activated protein kinase (MAPK), which can serve as therapeutic target. Inhibition of this pathway using MEK-inhibitor, trametinib, is in the phase II clinical trial, and new oral administered inhibitors are being investigated.[70,71]

Interestingly, proteomics analyses have shown that mutated RAS, apart from the activation of RAS-MAPK signaling pathway, simultaneously activates phosphatidylinositol 3-kinase-protein kinase B (PI3K/AKT) signaling pathway. This finding pointed to the potential advantage of dual inhibitor administration. Currently, phase II clinical study on trametinib and AKT Inhibitor GSK2141795 in treating patients with AML is in progress (NCT01907815).

One subgroup of AML patients characterized with abnormalities affecting *EVI1* gene, like inv(3) and t(3;3), may specially benefit from RAS-targeted therapy. It was found that in 98% of the cases, these AML patients have mutations leading to activated RAS or receptor tyrosine-kinase signaling.[72] Application of combined therapy, consisting of several inhibitors, for this group of patients with very poor prognosis, could result in significantly better outcome.

4.4 NPM1 Mutations and Targeted Therapy

Nucleophosmin (NPM) is ubiquitously expressed nucleolar protein that continuously shuttles between nucleus and cytoplasm. NPM regulates the assembly and transport of preribosomal particles; it is involved in cell-cycle progression, response to stress and regulation of the alternate reading frame protein (ARF)/p53 tumor suppressor pathway.[73,74] It is also involved in DNA repair through its interaction with DNA polymerase-eta.[75]

[68]Mesa and Kaufmann (2007).
[69]Bacher et al. (2006).
[70]Borthakur et al. (2016).
[71]Badar et al. (2015).
[72]Groschel et al. (2015).
[73]Bertwistle et al. (2004).
[74]Colombo et al. (2002).
[75]Ziv et al. (2014).

Mutations in *NPM1* gene cause aberrant localization of the NPM protein, abrogating its normal shuttle function and, thus, inhibiting ARF/p53 tumor suppressor pathway.[76] Mutations in exon 12 of *NPM1* gene are the most frequent mutations found in AML, occurring in 30% of adult AML and up to 50% in the AML-NC patients.[77,78] About 40 different mutations have been identified up to date. The majority of them represent a heterozygous 4-bp insertion at position 960 that causes frame shifts in C-terminal region of the NPM protein, creating a novel nuclear export signal. Considering the high frequency of these mutations in AML, it is thought that aberrant cytoplasmic localization of mutated NPM protein is critical for its role in leukemogenesis.

NPM1 mutations are considered to be driver genetic mutations, primarily for the reason that they are AML-specific, highly stable during the course of the disease. Additionally, they are mutually exclusive with typical recurrent AML genetic abnormalities; they exhibit unique gene expression profile and unique microRNA signature.[79] Therefore, therapy designed against *NPM1* mutations would have great impact on eradication of leukemia cells. The first approach of targeted therapy is to influence the unmutated, wild type, NPM protein. As *NPM1* mutations are always heterozygous, a small amount of functional NPM is found in nucleolus, contrary to the large amount of mutated protein dislocated in the cytoplasm.[80] Mutated NPM protein binds to a non-mutated one, disrupting the residual wild type function. Therefore, targeting the nucleolus with wild-type NPM might be efficient way for more selectively killing AML cells positive for *NPM1* mutations than AML with wild-type NPM. Accumulation of wild-type NPM in nucleolus is dependent on the process of oligomerization, so prevention of oligomerization could have effect of targeted therapy. Balusu et al. showed that a compound called NSC348884 interferes with oligomerization of NPM, particularly in *NPM1*-mutated AML cells, inducing differentiation and apoptosis.[81]

NPM protein as a dimer can interact with histones and in that way it participates in chromatin remodeling. Consequently, it is of no surprise that therapy designed to act on epigenetic mechanism can have an effect on *NPM1*-mutated AML patients.[82] Epigenetic targeted therapy is discussed later in the text. Recent studies have showed that ATRA (therapeutic designed to act against PML/RARA oncoprotein) induces proteasome-degradation of mutated NPM *in vitro* by unknown mechanism. The

---

[76]Falini et al. (2007).

[77]Falini et al. (2009).

[78]Kuzmanovic et al. (2012).

[79]Falini et al. (2011).

[80]Falini and Martelli (2011).

[81]Balusu et al. (2011).

[82]Wei et al. (2015).

same researchers also showed the influence of ATO on decreasing mutant NPM levels and inducing apoptosis.[83,84]

4.5 Mutations in Epigenetic Regulator Genes and Epigenetically Targeted Therapy

Epigenetic changes play an important role in the process of leukemogenesis and the development of AML. This is supported by a number of mutations that were detected in the epigenetic modifying genes such as *IDH1*, *IDH2*, *TET2* and *DNMT3A* genes (Table 2).

The two most common mechanisms of epigenetic silencing found in AML have led to the development of clinically applicable drugs. First mechanism of the epigenetic silencing is aberrant DNA methylation. This mechanism relies on excessive methylation of cytidine-phosphate-guanosine (CpG) dinucleotides, which are accumulated in "CpG islands" of the promoter regions of genes. Cytidine analogs, such as 5-azacytidine (azacitidine) or 5-aza-2-deoxycytidine (decitabine), integrate into DNA as alternative nucleotides and trap DNA methyltransferases resulting in the formation of demethylated DNA.[85] Because of this mechanism, hypermethylation of DNA in malignant cells is reversed in the course of several cell divisions. These drugs are administered in smaller doses over a long period to induce differentiation and inhibit proliferation of the malignant cells.[86] Currently, phase III trial of low dose decitabine and azacitidine for the treatment of AML is in the final stage.[87] The results are very satisfactory, and the group of patients above 65 years of age can benefit the most from this kind of therapy because these drugs represent an effective alternative to cytotoxic chemotherapy.

Second mechanism of epigenetic silencing is deacetylation of histones. Deacetylation of histones results in their stronger binding to DNA and ultimately to a transcriptional repression. Newly developed histonedeacetylase (HDAC) inhibitors manipulate cell growth and differentiation by inhibiting deacetylation of histones, reversing transcriptional repression of tumor suppressors or factors responsible for normal differentiation.[88] HDAC inhibitors generally display low toxicity and some of them can be administered orally. Furthermore, it has been shown that some of them work synergistically with ATRA, like valporic acid (VPA), causing hyperacetylation of histones and myelomonocytic differentiation of

[83]Martelli et al. (2015).

[84]El Hajj et al. (2015).

[85]Egger et al. (2004).

[86]Issa et al. (2004).

[87]Kantarjian et al. (2012).

[88]Bolden et al. (2006).

Table 2 Selected molecular targets in AML, potential targeted therapy and mechanism of action

Target	Potential therapy	Mechanism of action
PML/ RARA	All-trans retinoic acid (ATRA), Arsenic trioxide (ATO)	Restores terminal differentiation of APL cells Induces differentiation in APL cells and induces apoptosis
AML1/ ETO	Histonedeacetylase (HDAC) inhibitors	
CBF/ MYH11	Histonedeacetylase (HDAC) inhibitors	
FLT3	I class FLT3 inhibitors: Midostaurin and sunitinib Sorafenib II class FLT3 inhibitors: Quizartinib (AC-220), Crenolanib	Inhibitors of KIT, VEGFR, PDGFR and FLT3 Inhibitor of RAF kinase; inhibits growth and proliferation of *FLT3*/ITD mutated AML cells High-potency bis-aryl urea FLT3 inhibitor Very active against *FLT3*/TKD mutations
RAS	Trametinib (MEK-inhibitor) GSK2141795 (AKT Inhibitor)	Inhibition of mitogen activated protein kinase (MAPK) with MEK-inhibitor Inhibition of phosphatidylinositol 3-kinase-protein kinase B (PI3K/AKT) signaling pathway
NPM1	NSC348884 Histonedeacetylase (HDAC) inhibitors	Interferes with oligomerisation of NPM, particularly in NPM1-mutated AML cells inducing differentiation and apoptosis
MLL (11q23)	BET (bromodomen) inhibitors DOT1L (DOT1-Like Histone H3K79 Methyltransferase) inhibitors	Inhibition of BET proteins attached to the acetylated hystones inactivates gene expression Inhibition of DOT1L restores normal histone lysine methylation activity and inhibits gene expression
IDH1 and IDH2	HMS-101 inhibitor of the IDH1 AG-120 inhibitor of the IDH1 AGI-6780 inhibitor of the IDH2-R140Q AG-221 inhibitor of the IDH2	Inhibition of 2-HG production and induction of differentiation Changes in the DNA and histone methylation status Decrease in 2-HG production
TET2	Hypomethylating agents	
DNMT3A	Hypomethylating agents	

circulating blasts.[89] Recently published study showed significant clinical efficacy of this joined treatment protocol.[90]

However, the process opposite to deacetylation, histone acetylation, is catalyzed by the histone lysine acetyltransferase and results in open chromatin conformation. Acetylated histones are recognized by proteins that contain bromodomains. These proteins are so called "reader" proteins that can add, remove and read posttranslational modifications (acetylation or methylation).[91]

---

[89]Cimino et al. (2006).
[90]Fredly et al. (2013).
[91]Lindsley and Ebert (2013).

BET proteins (bromodomain and extra terminal), BRD2, BRD3 and BRD4, are attached to acetylated histones, present at some gene promoters and enhancers. Inhibition of BET proteins results in a very large changes in expression level of those genes. Important oncogenes, such as *MYC* oncogene, are regulated by BET proteins. Inhibition of BRD4 protein that activates *MYC* transcription, is an attractive therapeutic target. A small molecule JQ1, an inhibitor of BRD4, blocks the transcription of *MYC* and has strong antileukemic activity.[92] Currently, multiple clinical trials on BET bromodomen inhibitors are ongoing.[93,94]

Histone modification can occur through a process of histone lysine methylation. Histone lysine methylation alters the affinity of the reader proteins in histones, and can result in activation or repression depending on the context of the gene. Some of these histone methylation proteins are altered by the presence of recurrent translocation that involves the gene that encodes them. Such is the case of gene encoding the MLL (mixed-lineage leukemia) protein and components of polycomb repressor complexes (PRCs). The function of wild type protein is to enable transcriptional activation.

The *MLL* gene (11q23) is frequently involved in translocations (5–10%), and also 5–7% partial tandem duplications of *MLL* genes are found in AML patients.[95,96] Aberrant protein encoded by the *MLL*-translocations lacks some wild type domains that are replaced by the genes encoding super elongation complex nucleolar proteins like AF9 and AF10. Aberrant MLL fusion protein retains its DNA-binding property but it loses its normal histone lysine methylation activity. Actually it acquires the ability to recruit DOT1L (DOT1-Like Histone H3K79 Methyltransferase) and that leads to uncontrolled expression of targeted genes.[97] Inhibition of DOT1L would have a huge antileukemic effect. In fact, small-molecule inhibitors of DOT1L are showing promising results in preclinical models and in clinical trials in AML.[98]

Several other genes are frequently involved in AML pathogenesis. EZH2 (enhancer of zeste homolog 2) is a methyltrasferase whose action results in transcriptional repression. Mutations affecting *EZH2* gene have loss-of function effect, resulting in increased expression of target genes. The same consequences arise in the presence of the mutations in other genes that are members of PRC2 complex (polycomb repressor complex 2), such as *ASXL1* (additional sex combs like transcriptional regulator 1) and *JARID2* (jumonji AT-rich interactive domain 2).[99] All of

---

[92]Valent and Zuber (2014).

[93]Dawson et al. (2011).

[94]Dombret et al. (2014).

[95]Krivtsov and Armstrong (2007).

[96]Basecke et al. (2006).

[97]Daigle et al. (2013).

[98]Stein and Tallman (2015).

[99]Puda et al. (2012).

these mutated genes represent a potential target in the development of new therapies.[100]

4.5.1 *IDH* Mutations in AML and IDH-Targeted Therapy

Isocitrate dehydrogenases 1 and 2 (IDH1 and IDH2) isoenzymes catalyze an essential step in the Krebs cycle that catalyzes conversion of isocitrate to α-ketoglutarate (a-KG). IDH1 enzyme is localized in the cytoplasm, while the IHD2 enzyme performs its function in the mitochondria.[101] Both of the enzymes are involved in the metabolism of glucose and fatty acids, and in the regulation of the cellular redox system. Heterozygous point mutations in *IDH1* and *IDH2* genes frequently affect the evolutionary conserved arginine in position R132 in exon 4 of *IDH1* (*IDH1R^{132}*), and either the homologous positions R172 (*IDH2R^{172}*), or the second arginine R140 (*IDH2R^{140}*) in *IDH2* gene.[102]

The presence of *IDH1/2* mutations changes substrate affinity, leading to disruption in the function of both enzymes, which is reflected in inhibiting the activity of wild type enzymes, coupled with a gain-of-function to catalyze the NADPH dependent reduction of a-KG to 2-hydroxyglutarate (2-HG) which is suspected to play a role in carcinogenesis. Namely, 2-HG in leukemic cells acts as some kind of oncometabolite, interfering with the function of epigenetic modifiers in the leukemic cells.[103] Aberrant production of 2-HG inhibits enzymes involved in epigenetic function, like TET family of dioxygenases that are involved in demethylation of cytosine residues in DNA and Jumonji-C domain containing (JMJC) family of enzymes that demethylase lysine residues in histone proteins.[104,105]

Mutations in the *IDH1* and *IDH2* genes have been described as frequent recurrent molecular lesions in AML, occurring in up to 20% of patients in AML-NK group.[106,107] The prognostic significance of these mutations remains controversial. A number of studies showed that the presence of these mutations have no effect in response to therapy and survival, while there are others that suggest a negative prognostic effect.[108,109,110]

---

[100]Knutson et al. (2012).

[101]Ward et al. (2010).

[102]Abbas et al. (2010).

[103]Dang et al. (2009).

[104]Xu et al. (2011).

[105]Chowdhury et al. (2011).

[106]Thol et al. (2010).

[107]Wagner et al. (2010).

[108]Schnittger et al. (2010).

[109]Virijevic et al. (2016).

[110]Nomdedeu et al. (2011).

Therapeutically, the consequences of the presence of mutations in the *IDH1* and *IDH2* genes can be dealt in two ways: first, by direct blocking of mutant enzymatic activity using specific inhibitors and second, indirectly, by interfering altered IDH signaling pathways.

HMS-101 is a specific inhibitor of the IDH1 mutated protein currently being tested in preclinical trials. In *in vitro* tests, it has been shown that HMS-101 selectively blocks colony formation of primary IDH1-mutated cells.[111] In the newest study conducted on *IDH1* mutant leukemic mice, the same group of researchers has demonstrated specific inhibition of 2-HG production and induction of differentiation in leukemic cells.[112] Another IDH1 inhibitor, AG-120, is currently in a phase I clinical study on relapsed and refractory *IDH1* mutated AML patients, and the results are promising.[113]

Regarding IDH2 inhibitors, AGI-6780 selective IDH2-R140Q inhibitor, is in the preclinical study and it demonstrated changes in the DNA and histone methylation status in primary human AML cells.[114] Another specific IDH2 inhibitor, AG-221, can be orally administered. In phase I clinical trial AG-221 has demonstrated a decrease in 2-HG production.[115]

ABT-199, BCL2 (B-cell lymphoma 2) inhibitor, has been studied for treatment of *IDH*-mutated AML patients. Recently, it was shown that there is a correlation between *IDH* mutations and BCL2 expression in AML. If the study shows satisfactory results, there might be another type of dual therapy for *IDH* -mutated patients, combining BCL2 inhibitors and IDH inhibitors.[116]

4.5.2 *TET2* Mutations and Targeted Therapy

As already mentioned, the enzymes of the TET family are a part of the IDH signaling pathway. TET2 (Tet methylcytosine dioxygenase 2) enzyme catalyzes the oxidation of 5-methyl cytosine to 5-hydroxymethylcytosine. The presence of mutations in *TET2* gene (point-mutations or indels) results in a loss-of-function of the protein, leading to increase of DNA methylation.[117]

TET2 mutations occur in about 6% in AML patients.[118,119] It is interesting to note that mutations in the *TET2* gene and *IDH* gene are mutually exclusive, presumably

---

[111]Chaturvedi et al. (2013).

[112]Chaturvedi et al. (2014).

[113]Davis et al. (2014).

[114]Wang et al. (2013).

[115]Stein (2015).

[116]Chan et al. (2015).

[117]Itzykson et al. (2011).

[118]Damm et al. (2014).

[119]Gaidzik et al. (2012).

because they both interfere with the same signaling pathway. Another indication that these two types of mutations are functionally similar is the finding that patients carrying these mutations exhibit similar DNA methylation patterns.[120]

TET2 targeted therapy is only staring to develop and includes only a few studies with hypomethylating agents with limited results (see footnote 117).

4.5.3 *DNMT3A* Mutations and Targeted Therapy

The DNA methyltranferase (DNMT) 3 enzyme is involved in catalyzing the addition of a methyl group to cytosine at CpG dinucleotides, leading to DNA methylation.[121] Mutations in *DNMT3A* gene are among the most frequent mutations in *de novo* AML, and can be present in up to 35% in AML-NK patients.[122] They are heterozygous and usually involve changes in residue R882 (in around 60%). The presence of *DNMT3A* mutations seem to have negative impact on the disease outcome, but the true mechanism underling the impact of these mutations in the leukemogenic process is still unknown. It has been shown that R882H mutation inhibits the wild type DNMT3A thus preventing its structural change needed for full methylation activity.[123] Further, wild type DNMT3A functions as a silencer of self-renewal genes, enabling proper differentiation in hematopoietic cells. The presence of loss-of-function mutations in *DNMT3A* gene decreases the differentiation capability of hematopoietic stem cells.[124]

Mutations in *DNMT3A* gene are very stable during the course of the disease. Moreover, they are detected in pre-leukemic stem cells.[125] These findings suggest that *DNMT3A* mutations represent driver mutations in the process of leukemogenesis, but additional studies have shown that it is not so. These mutations are detected in healthy individuals, especially in individuals older than 70 years.[126] Moreover, *DNMT3A* mutations are in some cases persistently present in long-term remission patients.[127] Therefore, *DNMT3A* mutations are not good target for monitoring of minimal residual disease and for therapy treatment in remission patients.

In a very small study, it has been shown that a low dose of decitabine may improve complete remission rate among the treated patients. It is supposed that decitabine blocks the DNMT3A separation from DNA, initiating their proteosomal degradation. In that way, *DNMT3A*-mutated patients become more susceptible to the hypomethylatig agent therapy.[128]

---

[120]Figueroa et al. (2010).

[121]Bestor (2000).

[122]Marcucci et al. (2012).

[123]Russler-Germain et al. (2014).

[124]Challen et al. (2011).

[125]Shlush et al. (2014).

[126]Xie et al. (2014).

[127]Ploen et al. (2014).

[128]Metzeler et al. (2012).

5 Immunotherapy and Cell Therapy

The prominent feature of AML is immune evasion. It is an attribute that character-izes all cancer cells in addition to uncontrolled growth, differentiation blockage and impaired apoptosis.[129] Myeloid cells like macrophages, granulocytes, dendritic cells and also platelets play important roles in immunity, ether by activating or suppressing it. Immunotherapy in AML actually exploits this direct connection between myeloid cells (mature or immature) and immune process, modifying these processes in a way that they are capable of recognizing and targeting leukemic cells. Immunotherapy of AML is still in its initial phase, but with promising new findings that gives us hope of foreseeable appreciable clinical use.

5.1 Antibody-Based AML Therapy

CD33 molecule, frequently expressed on the surface of leukemic cells, represents potential target for the antibody-based therapy. Gemtuzumab ozogamicin (GO), a humanized anti-CD33 monoclonal antibody, has long been applied in the AML patients with refractory disease.[130] Recent studies on both adult and childhood patients have shown conflicting results about the benefit of GO therapy application during induction and post-consolidation/re-induction therapy.[131,132] Application of GO in the AML therapy is also associated with the issues related to the toxicity and drug resistance. These facts led to the development of new antibody-drug conjugate, SGN-CD33A, where the cysteines in CD33 are conjugated with synthetic DNA cross-linking pyrrolobenzodiazepine dimer.[133] This antibody-drug conjugate is showing better results than GO, increasing induced apoptosis, and it has been evaluated in Phase I clinical trial.[134]

The next step in improving the anti-CD33 therapy was the discovery of engineered immuno-conjugates that, on the one hand recognize CD33 on the leukemic cells, and on the other hand are linked to the T cell receptor (TCR). In that way these bi-specific antibodies redirect the cytotoxic activity of effector T cells against leukemic cells. The first of such synthetized bi-specific antibody was CD33/CD3-directed bi-specific T-cell engager (BiTE) antibody (AMG330).[135] Following the example of this antibody other antibodies have been created like CD33/CD16 bi-specific killer cell engagers (BiKE) that bridge CD33 leukemia-specific antigen

---

[129]Hanahan and Weinberg (2011).
[130]Bross et al. (2001).
[131]Petersdorf et al. (2013).
[132]Pollard et al. (2016).
[133]Kung Sutherland et al. (2013).
[134]Stein et al. (2015).
[135]Krupka et al. (2014).

and CD16 on natural killer (NK) cells. The fact that the CD123 is almost exclusively expressed only on leukemic stem cells has recommended it as a highly specific target for antibody-based therapy.[136] Therefore, bi-specific (CD16/CD123) and even tri-specific antibodies like CD16/CD33/CD123 have been designed to enhance the specificity towards malignantly transformed cells.[137,138]

5.2   Therapy Using Vaccination

This is another type of leukemia-antigen based therapy, in which patient's own immune system is stimulated to attack leukemic cells. Vaccines are made using peptides, modified leukemic cells or monocyte-derived dendritic cells (DCs). Still, regardless of the type, in all of the vaccines an epitope from the leukemia-antigen has been presented to the patient's immune system, in combination with adjuvant. This is the way by which researchers aim to induce long lasting immune response in the patients, helping them to fight minimal residual disease (MRD) and to prevent relapse of the disease. It is important to emphasize that vaccines are individual drugs, designed according to molecular markers characteristic for patient's leukemic cell. Further, in the vaccination, patient's own immune cells are used. Each leukemia is unique and therefore vaccines are the best example of individualized therapy.

Vaccines based on peptides, using characteristic leukemia-specific antigens like WT1 and Proteinase-3, have not been very effective because of a short-lived immune response. Therefore, the tendency today is to use this type of treatment only in consolidation therapy in combination with chemotherapy.[139,140,141]

To induce immune response directed against multiple leukemia antigens, immortalized leukemic cells have been used and presented to patient's immune system. The advantage of this approach lies in the fact that there is no need to detect and characterize leukemia specific antigens, but the drawback is in the fact that leukemic cells are by themselves immunosuppressive. Because of this, before treatment, leukemic cells must be processed *in vitro* to increase antigen-presenting capacity and the secretion of proinflamatory cytokines. Despite the efforts, only a few clinical studies have been conducted, with discouraging results.[142,143]

Vaccination with the help of patient's dendritic cells (DCs) relies on the ability of these cells to present an antigen and to induce a strong and persistent immune

---

[136]Jordan et al. (2000).

[137]Kugler et al. (2010).

[138]Gleason et al. (2014).

[139]Kuball et al. (2011).

[140]Keilholz et al. (2009).

[141]Uttenthal et al. (2014).

[142]Borrello et al. (2009).

[143]Hardwick et al. (2010).

response. DCs are usually generated from patient's monocytes through diverse differentiation processes. There are some reports that they can even be obtained from the peripheral blood stem cells collected for hematopoietic stem cell transplantation—HSCT.[144,145] After the maturation process, patient's DCs are loaded with leukemia-antigens using patient's leukemia-specific peptides or leukemia-specific antigen encoding RNA. Antigen-loading can be performed even with apoptotic remains of leukemic cells. In that way DCs are loaded with broad spectrum of antigens.[146]

Today, most clinical studies use monocyte-derived DCs and RNA electroporation as a way of antigen-loading. The first study of DCs vaccination in AML patients has been done in 2004,[147] followed by phase I/II clinical trial using *WT1* mRNA elecrtrophoreted DCs vaccination of AML patients in remission.[148,149] The latest studies showed encouraging results of WT1 targeted DCs vaccination applied as a post-remission therapy in AML patients.[150]

5.3   Therapy Using Chimeric Antigen Receptor (CAR)-Engineered T Cells (CAR-T Cells)

Chimeric Antigen Receptors (CARs) are cell surface molecules consisting of two fused components; (1) variable region of an antibody capable of recognizing and binding tumor-surface molecules and (2) intracellular domain (usually, signaling domains of TCR) that is capable of activating T cells. Activation of this chimeric CAR molecule results in combined activity of monoclonal antibody and of cytotoxic T cell.[151] From the first generation CAR-T cells containing only TCR, modern studies revealed that CAR-T cells containing different co-stimulatory and co-receptor signals in addition to TCR, could induce more sustained stimulation of immune response. Today, a number of second and the third generation of CAR-T cells have been synthetized and tested.[152,153,154]

---

[144]Skalova et al. (2010).

[145]Serrano-López et al. (2011).

[146]Ruben et al. (2014).

[147]Lee et al. (2004).

[148]Van Driessche et al. (2009).

[149]Van Tendeloo et al. (2010).

[150]Berneman et al. (2012).

[151]Eshhar et al. (1993).

[152]Jena et al. (2010).

[153]Uttenthal et al. (2012).

[154]Sadelain et al. (2013).

The most successful application of CAR-T cell therapies has been made in B-cell malignancies, using anti-CD19 CAR-T based therapy.[155,156] Still, the application of CAR-T cell therapy in AML is more complex, primarily because of the inability to select an appropriate leukemia-specific surface antigen in AML. Namely, AML is a very heterogeneous disease expressing many antigens like CD33, CD44v6, CD123, LeY, TIM-3 etc.[157]

Majority of the research have been focused on anti-CD33 CAR-T therapy, because this antigen is over expressed on leukemic AML cells, with little to no expression on normal cells.[158] The clinical experience of anti-CD33 CAR-T therapy is very limited, but with encouraging results.[159,160] Lately, there has been an attempt to simultaneously attack another abundantly expressed AML specific antigen, CD123.[161,162]

The usage of CAR-T cell therapy in AML is still at the beginning, especially regarding its testing in clinical settings. One of the biggest obstacles standing in the way of wider application of this type of therapy in AML is the heterogeneity of the disease itself, as well as the "on-target/off-leukemia" effect that this kind of therapy can have on normal, untransformed, cells.

5.4 Adoptive NK Cell Therapy in AML

Natural killer (NK) cells play an important role in the innate immunity by surveillance and elimination of malignant cells. Their anti-tumor activity is characterized by strong cytotoxicity without the need for previous sensitization (antigen priming). They also produce a number of cytokines, ultimately causing the activation of adoptive immune system.

The activity of NK cell is under control of the signals coming from the killer immunoglobulin receptors (KIR) complex that are expressed on the surface of NK cells. Interaction of KIRs with major histocompatibility complex (MHC) class I molecules results in activation or inhibition of NK cells. Under normal homeostatic conditions, NK cells remain under inhibition signals when encountering "self" MHC class I molecules, because they are "licensed" to distinguish "self" from "non-self".[163] On the other hand, malignant cells tend to avoid immune response through

---

[155]Gill and June (2015).

[156]Brentjens et al. (2013).

[157]Rotiroti et al. (2017).

[158]Dutour et al. (2012).

[159]O'Hear et al. (2015).

[160]Kenderian et al. (2015).

[161]Pizzitola et al. (2014).

[162]Mardiros et al. (2015).

[163]Kim et al. (2005).

the loss of expression of tumor-associated antigens and/or MHC molecules. In that way they can become susceptible to NK cell lysis by the mechanism called "missing self-recognition". This mechanism is also noted in the AML patients who underwent haploidentical transplantation process. Those patients had lower relapse rate because donor KIR/patient MHC class I mismatched.[164] Haploidentical, KIR/MHC class I mismatched NC cell therapy has been applied to treat AML outside of the transplantation settings. A number of clinical studies have proven the efficiency and safety of this approach both in childhood and adult patients.[165,166]

The advantage of NK cell therapy over vaccine therapy and antigen-specific adoptive T cell therapy is in the fact that NK cell do not need to identify target tumor antigen. Therefore this therapy can be more universally used even in the cases where leukemic cells lack tumor antigens or in the cases of diminished "self" MHC I expression.

6   Conclusions

Progress in the genetic and epigenetic profiling of acute myeloid leukemia has been huge in the last few years. Uncovering AML complexity on genetic and epigenetic level has been rather successful thanks to the application of high-throughput technology. The knowledge gained in numerous molecular studies resulted in the recognition of multiple AML entities characterized by distinct prognosis, outcome of the disease and specific therapeutic targets.

The basic science achievements are being translated into the clinical practice, leading to better therapeutic response and improved survival of the patients. The results are promising so far. For many AML subsets characterized by distinct molecular markers specific molecular targeted therapeutics are designed and clinically tested. Even for the classical therapy protocols, the dose and combination of pharmaceutics can be adjusted according to individual pharmacogenomic profile of the patient. Furthermore, major efforts are made on developing immunotherapies and cellular therapies for each leukemia patient.

From better understanding of molecular mechanism of occurrence and development of leukemia, therapy protocols individualized for every single AML patient can be designed. There is no doubt that we are getting closer to the full implementation of personalized medicine in AML.

Acknowledgments This work funded by the Ministry of Education, Science and Technological Development, Republic of Serbia (grant no. III 41004).

---

[164]Ruggeri et al. (2002).
[165]Rubnitz et al. (2010).
[166]Curti et al. (2011).

References

Abbas S, Lugthart S, Kavelaars FG et al (2010) Acquired mutations in the genes encoding IDH1 and IDH2 both are recurrent aberrations in acute myeloid leukemia: prevalence and prognostic value. Blood 116(12):2122–2126. https://doi.org/10.1182/blood-2009-11-250878

Abraham A, Varatharajan S, Abbas S et al (2012) Cytidine deaminase genetic variants influence RNA expression and cytarabine cytotoxicity in acute myeloid leukemia. Pharmacogenomics 13 (3):269–282. https://doi.org/10.2217/pgs.11.149

Arber DA, Orazi A, Hasserjian R et al (2016) The 2016 revision to the World Health Organization classification of myeloid neoplasms and acute leukemia. Blood 127(20):2391–2405. https://doi.org/10.1182/blood-2016-03-643544

Bacher U, Haferlach T, Schoch C et al (2006) Implications of NRAS mutations in AML: a study of 2502 patients. Blood 107(10):3847–3853. https://doi.org/10.1182/blood-2005-08-3522

Badar T, Cortes JE, Ravandi F et al (2015) Phase I study of S-trans, trans-farnesylthiosalicylic acid (salirasib), a novel oral RAS inhibitor in patients with refractory hematologic malignancies. Clin Lymphoma Myeloma Leuk 15(7):433–438. https://doi.org/10.1016/j.clml.2015.02.018

Balusu R, Fiskus W, Rao R et al (2011) Targeting levels or oligomerization of nucleophosmin 1 induces differentiation and loss of survival of human AML cells with mutant NPM1. Blood 118(11):3096–3106. https://doi.org/10.1182/blood-2010-09-309674

Basecke J, Whelan JT, Griesinger F, Bertrand FE (2006) The MLL partial tandem duplication in acute myeloid leukaemia. Br J Haematol 135(4):438–449. https://doi.org/10.1111/j.1365-2141.2006.06301.x

Berneman ZN, Van de Velde A, Anguille S et al (2012) WT1-targeted dendritic cell vaccination as a postremission treatment to prevent or delay relapse in acute myeloid leukemia. 2012 ASCO Annual Meeting, 1-5 June 2012, Chicago IL, USA. J Clin Oncol 30:2506

Bertwistle D, Sugimoto M, Sherr CJ (2004) Physical and functional interactions of the Arf tumor suppressor protein with nucleophosmin/B23. Mol Cell Biol 24(3):985–996. https://doi.org/10.1128/MCB.24.3.985-996.2004

Bestor TH (2000) The DNA methyltransferases of mammals. Hum Mol Genet 9(16):2395–2402. https://doi.org/10.1093/hmg/9.16.2395

Bolden JE, Peart MJ, Johnstone RW (2006) Anticancer activities of histone deacetylase inhibitors. Nat Rev Drug Discov 5(9):769–784. https://doi.org/10.1038/nrd2133

Borrello IM, Levitsky HI, Stock W et al (2009) Granulocyte-macrophage colony-stimulating factor (GM-CSF)-secreting cellular immunotherapy in combination with autologous stem cell transplantation (ASCT) as postremission therapy for acute myeloid leukemia (AML). Blood 114 (9):1736–1745. https://doi.org/10.1182/blood-2009-02-205278

Borthakur G, Popplewell L, Boyiadzis M et al (2016) Activity of the oral mitogen-activated protein kinase kinase inhibitor trametinib in RAS-mutant relapsed or refractory myeloid malignancies. Cancer 122(12):1871–1879. https://doi.org/10.1002/cncr.29986

Borun TW, Scharff MD, Robbins E (1969) Rapidly labeled, polyribosome-associated RNA having the properties of histone messenger. Proc Natl Acad Sci USA 58(5):1977–1983

Brentjens RJ, Davila ML, Riviere I et al (2013) CD19-targeted T cells rapidly induce molecular remissions in adults with chemotherapy-refractory acute lymphoblastic leukemia. Sci Transl Med 5(177):177ra38. https://doi.org/10.1126/scitranslmed.3005930

Bross PF, Beitz J, Chen G et al (2001) Approval summary: gemtuzumab ozogamicin in relapsed acute myeloid leukemia. Clin Cancer Res 7(6):1490–1496

Byrd JC, Mrozek K, Dodge RK et al (2002) Pretreatment cytogenetic abnormalities are predictive of induction success, cumulative incidence of relapse, and overall survival in adult patients with de novo acute myeloid leukemia: results from Cancer and Leukemia Group B (CALGB 8461). Blood 100(13):4325–4336. https://doi.org/10.1182/blood-2002-03-0772

Cancer Genome Atlas Research Network (2013) Genomic and epigenomic landscapes of adult de novo acute myeloid leukemia. N Engl J Med 368(22):2059–2074. https://doi.org/10.1056/NEJMoa1301689

Carbone R, Botrugno OA, Ronzoni S et al (2006) Recruitment of the histone methyltransferase SUV39H1 and its role in the oncogenic properties of the leukemia-associated PML-retinoic acid receptor fusion protein. Mol Cell Biol 26(4):1288–1296. https://doi.org/10.1128/MCB.26.4.1288-1296.2006

Carow CE, Levenstein M, Kaufmann SH et al (1996) Expression of the hematopoietic growth factor receptor FLT3 (STK-1/Flk2) in human leukemias. Blood 87(3):1089–1096

Challen GA, Sun D, Jeong M et al (2011) DNMT3A is essential for hematopoietic stem cell differentiation. Nat Genet 44(1):23–31. https://doi.org/10.1038/ng.1009

Chan SM, Thomas D, Corces-Zimmerman MR et al (2015) Isocitrate dehydrogenase 1 and 2 mutations induce BCL-2 dependence in acute myeloid leukemia. Nat Med 21(2):178–184. https://doi.org/10.1038/nm.3788

Chaturvedi A, Araujo Cruz MM, Jyotsana N et al (2013) Mutant IDH1 promotes leukemogenesis in vivo and can be specifically targeted in human AML. Blood 122(16):2877–2887. https://doi.org/10.1182/blood-2013-03-491571

Chaturvedi A, Araujo Cruz M, Goparaju R et al (2014) A novel inhibitor of mutant IDH1 induces differentiation in vivo and prolongs survival in a mouse model of leukemia. 56th ASH Annual meeting and exhibition. 6–9 December 2014, San Francisco CA, USA. Blood 124(21):3598

Chen GQ, Shi XG, Tang W et al (1997) Use of arsenic trioxide (As2O3) in the treatment of acute promyelocytic leukemia (APL): I, As2O3 exerts dosedependent dual effects on APL cells. Blood 89(9):3345–3353

Chowdhury R, Yeoh KK, Tian YM et al (2011) The oncometabolite 2-hydroxyglutarate inhibits histone lysine demethylases. EMBO Rep 12(5):463–469. https://doi.org/10.1038/embor.2011.43

Cimino G, Lo-Coco F, Fenu S et al (2006) Sequential valproic acid/all-trans retinoic acid treatment reprograms differentiation in refractory and highrisk acute myeloid leukemia. Cancer Res 66(17):8903–8911. https://doi.org/10.1158/0008-5472.CAN-05-2726

Cohen SS (1966) Introduction to the biochemistry of d-arabinosyl nucleosides. Prog Nucleic Acid Res Mol Biol 5:1–88

Colombo E, Marine JC, Danovi D et al (2002) Nucleophosmin regulates the stability and transcriptional activity of p53. Nat Cell Biol 4(7):529–533. https://doi.org/10.1038/ncb814

Colovic N, Tosic N, Aveic S et al (2007) Importance of early detection and follow-up of FLT3 mutations in patients with acute myeloid leukemia. Ann Hematol 86(10):741–747. https://doi.org/10.1007/s00277-007-0325-3

Creasey WA, Deconti RC, Kaplan SR (1968) Biochemical studies with 1-β-d-arabinofuranosylcytosine in human leukemic leukocytes and normal bone marrow cells. Cancer Res 28(6):1074–1081

Curti A, Ruggeri L, D'Addio A et al (2011) Successful transfer of alloreactive haploidentical KIR ligand-mismatched natural killer cells after infusion in elderly high risk acute myeloid leukemia patients. Blood 118(12):3273–3279. https://doi.org/10.1182/blood-2011-01-329508

Daigle SR, Olhava EJ, Therkelsen CA et al (2013) Potent inhibition of DOT1L as treatment of MLL-fusion leukemia. Blood 122(6):1017–1025. https://doi.org/10.1182/blood-2013-04-497644

Damm F, Markus B, Thol F et al (2014) TET2 mutations in cytogenetically normal acute myeloid leukemia: clinical implications and evolutionary patterns. Genes Chromosomes Cancer 53(10):824–832. https://doi.org/10.1002/gcc.22191

Dang L, White DW, Gross S et al (2009) Cancer associated IDH1 mutations produce 2-hydroxyglutarate. Nature 462(7274):739–744. https://doi.org/10.1038/nature08617

Davis MI, Gross S, Shen M et al (2014) Biochemical, cellular, and biophysical characterization of a potent inhibitor of mutant isocitrate dehydrogenase IDH1. J Biol Chem 289(20):13717–13725. https://doi.org/10.1074/jbc.M113.511030

Dawson MA, Prinjha RK, Dittmann A et al (2011) Inhibition of BET recruitment to chromatin as an effective treatment for MLL-fusion leukaemia. Nature 478(7370):529–533. https://doi.org/10.1038/nature10509

Dicker F, Haferlach C, Kern W et al (2007) Trisomy 13 is strongly associated with AML1/RUNX1 mutations and increased FLT3 expression in acute myeloid leukemia. Blood 110(4):1308–1316. https://doi.org/10.1182/blood-2007-02-072595

Dohner H, Estey E, Grimwade D et al (2017) Diagnosis and management of AML in adults: 2017 ELN recommendations from an international expert panel. Blood 129(4):424–447. https://doi.org/10.1182/blood-2016-08-733196

Dombret H, Preudhomme C, Berthon C et al (2014) A phase 1 study of the BET-Bromodomain inhibitor OTX015 in patients with advanced acute leukemia. 56th ASH Annual Meeting and http://www.bloodjournal.org/content/124/21/117 Exposition. 6–9 December 2014, San Francisco CA, USA. Blood 124(21):117

Dutour A, Marin V, Pizzitola I et al (2012) In vitro and in vivo antitumor effect of anti-CD33 chimeric receptor-expressing EBV-CTL against CD33 acute myeloid leukemia. Adv Hematol 2012:683065. https://doi.org/10.1155/2012/683065

Egger G, Liang G, Aparicio A, Jones PA (2004) Epigenetics in human disease and prospects for epigenetic therapy. Nature 429(6990):457–463. https://doi.org/10.1038/nature02625

El Hajj H, Dassouki Z, Berthier C et al (2015) Retinoic acid and arsenic trioxide trigger degradation of mutated NPM-1 resulting in apoptosis of AML cells. Blood 125(22):3447–3454. https://doi.org/10.1182/blood-2014-11-612416

Emadi A, Karp JE (2012) The clinically relevant pharmacogenomic changes in acute myelogenous leukemia. Pharmacogenomics 13(11):1257–1269. https://doi.org/10.2217/pgs.12.102

Eshhar Z, Waks T, Gross G, Schindler DG (1993) Specific activation and targeting of cytotoxic lymphocytes through chimeric single chains consisting of antibody-binding domains and the gamma or zeta subunits of the immunoglobulin and T-cell receptors. Proc Natl Acad Sci USA 90(2):720–724

Estey E, Garcia-Manero G, Ferrajoli A et al (2006) Use of all-trans retinoic acid plus arsenic trioxide as an alternative to chemotherapy in untreated acute promyelocytic leukemia. Blood 107(9):3469–3473. https://doi.org/10.1182/blood-2005-10-4006

Falini B, Martelli MP (2011) NPM1-mutated AML: targeting by disassembling. Blood 118 (11):2936–2938. https://doi.org/10.1182/blood-2011-07-366146

Falini B, Albiero E, Bolli N et al (2007) Aberrant cytoplasmic expression of C-terminal-truncated NPM leukaemic mutant is dictated by tryptophans loss and a new NES motif. Leukemia 21 (9):2052–2054. https://doi.org/10.1038/sj.leu.2404839

Falini B, Sportoletti P, Martelli MP (2009) Acute myeloid leukemia with mutated NPM1: diagnosis, prognosis and therapeutic perspectives. Curr Opin Oncol 21(6):573–581. https://doi.org/10.1097/CCO.0b013e3283313dfa

Falini B, Martelli MP, Bolli N et al (2011) Acute myeloid leukemia with mutated nucleophosmin (NPM1): is it a distinct entity? Blood 117(4):1109–1120. https://doi.org/10.1182/blood-2010-08-299990

Figueroa ME, Reimers M, Thompson RF et al (2008) An integrative genomic and epigenomic approach for the study of transcriptional regulation. PloS ONE 3(3):e1882. https://doi.org/10.1371/journal.pone.0001882

Figueroa ME, Abdel-Wahab O, Lu C (2010) Leukemic IDH1 and IDH2 mutations result in a hypermethylation phenotype, disrupt TET2 function, and impair hematopoietic differentiation. Cancer Cell 18(6):553–567. https://doi.org/10.1016/j.ccr.2010.11.015

Fredly H, Gjertsen BT, Bruserud O (2013) Histone deacetylase inhibition in the treatment of acute myeloid leukemia: the effects of valproic acid on leukemic cells, and the clinical and experimental evidence for combining valproic acid with other antileukemic agents. Clin Epigenetics 5 (1):12. https://doi.org/10.1186/1868-7083-5-12

Gaidzik VI, Paschka P, Späth D et al (2012) TET2 mutations in acute myeloid leukemia (AML): results from a comprehensive genetic and clinical analysis of the AML study group. J Clin Oncol 30(12):1350–1357. https://doi.org/10.1200/JCO.2011.39.2886

Galmarini CM, Thomas X, Calvo F et al (2002) Potential mechanisms of resistance to cytarabine in AML patients. Leuk Res 26:621–629. https://doi.org/10.1016/S0145-2126(01)00184-9

Galmarini CM, Cros E, Thomas X et al (2005) The prognostic value of cN-II and cN-III enzymes in adult acute myeloid leukemia. Haematologica 90(12):1699–1701

Gill S, June CH (2015) Going viral: chimeric antigen receptor T-cell therapy for hematological malignancies. Immunol Rev 263(1):68–89. https://doi.org/10.1111/imr.12243

Gleason MK, Ross JA, Warlick ED et al (2014) CD16xCD33 bispecific killer cell engager (BiKE) activates NK cells against primary MDS and MDSC CD33+ targets. Blood 123(19):3016–3026. https://doi.org/10.1182/blood-2013-10-533398

Grignani F, De Matteis S, Nervi C et al (1998) Fusion proteins of the retinoic acid receptor-alpha recruit histone deacetylase in promyelocytic leukaemia. Nature 391(6669):815–818. https://doi.org/10.1038/35901

Groschel S, Sanders MA, Hoogenboezem R et al (2015) Mutational spectrum of myeloid malignancies with inv(3)/t(3,3) reveals a predominant involvement of RAS/RTK signaling pathways. Blood 125(1):133–139. https://doi.org/10.1182/blood-2014-07-591461

Hanahan D, Weinberg RA (2011) Hallmarks of cancer: the next generation. Cell 144(5):646–674. https://doi.org/10.1016/j.cell.2011.02.013

Hardwick N, Chan L, Ingram W et al (2010) Lytic activity against primary AML cells is stimulated in vitro by an autologous whole cell vaccine expressing IL 2 and CD80. Cancer Immunol Immunother 59(3):379–388. https://doi.org/10.1007/s00262-009-0756-x

Hartford CM, Duan S, Delaney SM et al (2009) Population-specific genetic variants important in susceptibility to cytarabine arabinoside cytotoxicity. Blood 113(10):2145–2153. https://doi.org/10.1182/blood-2008-05-154302

Iacobucci I, Lonetti A, Candoni A et al (2013) Profiling of drug-metabolizing enzymes/transporters in CD33+ acute myeloid leukemia patients treated with Gemtuzumab-Ozogamicin and Fludarabine, Cytarabine and Idarubicin. Pharmacogenomics J 13(4):335–341. https://doi.org/10.1038/tpj.2012.13

Issa JP, Garcia-Manero G, Giles FJ et al (2004) Phase 1 study of low-dose prolonged exposure schedules of the hypomethylating agent 5-aza-2-deoxycytidine (decitabine) in hematopoietic malignancies. Blood 103(5):1635–1640. https://doi.org/10.1182/blood-2003-03-0687

Itzykson R, Kosmider O, Cluzeau T et al (2011) Impact of TET2 mutations on response rate to azacitidine inmyelodysplastic syndromes and low blast count acute myeloid leukemias. Leukemia 25(7):1147–1152. https://doi.org/10.1038/leu.2011.71

Jena B, Dotti G, Cooper LJ (2010) Redirecting T cell specificity by introducing a tumor-specific chimeric antigen receptor. Blood 116(7):1035–1044. https://doi.org/10.1182/blood-2010-01-043737

Jordan CT, Upchurch D, Szilvassy SJ et al (2000) The interleukin-3 receptor alpha chain is a unique marker for humanacute myelogenous leukemia stem cells. Leukemia 14:1777–1784

Kantarjian HM, Thomas XG, Dmoszynska A et al (2012) Multicenter, randomized, open-label, phase III trial of decitabine versus patient choice, with physician advice, of either supportive care or low-dose cytarabine for the treatment of older patients with newly diagnosed acute myeloid leukemia. J Clin Oncol 30(21):2670–2677. https://doi.org/10.1200/JCO.2011.38.9429

Keilholz U, Letsch A, Busse A et al (2009) A clinical and immunologic phase 2 trial of Wilms tumor gene product 1 (WT1) peptide vaccination in patients with AML and MDS. Blood 113 (26):6541–6548. https://doi.org/10.1182/blood-2009-02-202598

Kenderian SS, Ruella M, Shestova O et al (2015) CD33 specific chimeric antigen receptor T cells exhibit potent preclinical activity against human acute myeloid leukemia. Leukemia 29 (8):1637–1647. https://doi.org/10.1038/leu.2015.52

Kim JH, Lee C, Cheong HS et al (2016) SLC29A1 (ENT1) polymorphisms and outcome of complete remission in acute myeloid leukemia. Cancer Chemother Pharmacol 78(3):533–540. https://doi.org/10.1007/s00280-016-3103-x

Kim S, Poursine-Laurent J, Truscott SM et al (2005) Licensing of natural killer cells by host major histocompatibility complex class I molecules. Nature 436(7051):709–713. https://doi.org/10.1038/nature03847

Knutson SK, Wigle TJ, Warholic NM et al (2012) A selective inhibitor of EZH2 blocks H3K27 methylation and kills mutant lymphoma cells. Nat Chem Biol 8(11):890–896. https://doi.org/10.1038/nchembio.1084

Krivtsov AV, Armstrong SA (2007) MLL translocations, histone modifications and leukaemia stem-cell development. Nat Rev Cancer 7(11):823–833. https://doi.org/10.1038/nrc2253

Krstovski N, Tosic N, Janic D et al (2010) Incidence of FLT3 and nucleophosmin gene mutations in childhood acute myeloid leukemia: Serbian experience and the review of the literature. Med Oncol 27:640–645. https://doi.org/10.1007/s12032-009-9261-5

Krupka C, Kufer P, Kischel R et al (2014) CD33 target validation and sustained depletion of AML blasts in long-term cultures by the bispecific T-cell-engaging antibody AMG 330. Blood 123 (3):356–365. https://doi.org/10.1182/blood-2013-08-523548

Kuball J, de Boer K, Wagner E et al (2011) Pitfalls of vaccinations with WT1, Proteinase3 and MUC1 derived peptides in combination with MontanidISA51 and CpG7909. Cancer Immunol Immunother 60(2):161–171. https://doi.org/10.1007/s00262-010-0929-7

Kugler M, Stein C, Kellner C et al (2010) A recombinant trispecific single-chain Fv derivative directed against CD123 and CD33 mediates effective elimination of acute myeloid leukaemia cells by dual targeting. Br J Haematol 150(5):574–586. https://doi.org/10.1111/j.1365-2141.2010.08300.x

Kung Sutherland MS, Walter RB, Jeffrey SC et al (2013) SGN-CD33A: a novel CD33-targeting antibody-drug conjugate using a pyrrolobenzodiazepine dimer is active in models of drug-resistant AML. Blood 122(8):1455–1463. https://doi.org/10.1182/blood-2013-03-491506

Kuzmanovic M, Tosic N, Colovic N et al (2012) Prognostic impact of NPM1 mutations in Serbian adult patients with acute myeloid leukemia. Acta Haematol 128:203–212. https://doi.org/10.1159/000339506

L'Ecuyer T, Allebban Z, Thomas R, Vander Heide R (2004) Glutathione S-transferase overexpression protects against anthracycline-induced H9C2 cell death. Am J Physiol Heart Circ Physiol 286(6):H2057–H2064. https://doi.org/10.1152/ajpheart.00778.2003

Lamba JK (2009) Genetic factors influencing cytarabine therapy. Pharmacogenomics 10 (10):1657–1674. https://doi.org/10.2217/pgs.09.118

Lamba JK, Crews K, Pounds S et al (2007) Pharmacogenetics of deoxycytidine kinase: identification and characterization of novel genetic variants. J Pharmacol Exp Ther 323:935–945. https://doi.org/10.1124/jpet.107.128595

Lee JJ, Kook H, Park MS et al (2004) Immunotherapy using autologous monocyte-derived dendritic cells pulsed with leukemic cell lysates for acute myeloid leukemia relapse after autologous peripheral blood stem cell transplantation. J Clin Apher 19(2):66–70. https://doi.org/10.1002/jca.10080

Levis MJ, Perl AE, Altman JK et al (2015) Results of a first-in-human, phase I/II trial of ASP2215, a selective, potent inhibitor of FLT3/Axl in patients with relapsed or refractory (R/R) acute myeloid leukemia (AML). 51th ASCO Annual Meeting; May 29 - June 2,Chicago, IL, USA. J Clin Oncol 33(15)suppl:7003. https://doi.org/10.1200/jco.2015.33.15_suppl.7003

Ley TJ, Mardis ER, Ding L et al (2008) DNA sequencing of a cytogenetically normal acute myeloid leukaemia genome. Nature 456(7218):66–72. https://doi.org/10.1038/nature07485

Ley TJ, Ding L, Walter MJ et al (2010) DNMT3A mutations in acute myeloid leukemia. N Engl J Med 363(25):2424–2433. https://doi.org/10.1056/NEJMoa1005143

Li L, Fridley B, Kalari K et al (2008) Gemcitabine and cytosine arabinoside cytotoxicity: association with lymphoblastoid cell expression. Cancer Res 68(17):7050–7058. https://doi.org/10.1158/0008-5472.CAN-08-0405

Lindsley RC, Ebert BL (2013) The biology and clinical impact of genetic lesions in myeloid malignancies. Blood 122(23):3741–3748. https://doi.org/10.1182/blood-2013-06-460295

Lutterbach B, Hou Y, Durst KL, Heibert SW (1999) The inv(16) encodes an acute myeloid leukemia 1 transcriptional corepressor. Proc Natl Acad Sci USA 96(22):12822–12827

Macdonald DA, Assouline SE, Brandwein J et al (2013) A phase I/II study of sorafenib in combination with low dose cytarabine in elderly patients with acute myeloid leukemia or high-risk myelodysplastic syndrome from the National Cancer Institute of Canada Clinical Trials Group: trial IND.186. Leuk Lymphoma 54(4):760–766. https://doi.org/10.3109/10428194.2012.737917

Marcucci G, Maharry K, Wu YZ et al (2010) IDH1 and IDH2 gene mutations identify novel molecular subsets within de novo cytogenetically normal acute myeloid leukemia: a Cancer and Leukemia Group B study. J Clin Oncol 28(14):2348–2355. https://doi.org/10.1200/JCO.2009.27.3730

Marcucci G, Metzeler KH, Schwind S et al (2012) Age-related prognostic impact of different types of DNMT3A mutations in adults with primary cytogenetically normal acute myeloid leukemia. J Clin Oncol 30(7):742–750. https://doi.org/10.1200/JCO.2011.39.2092

Mardiros A, Forman SJ, Budde LE (2015) T cells expressing CD123 chimeric antigen receptors for treatment of acute myeloid leukemia. Curr Opin Hematol 22(6):484–488. https://doi.org/10.1097/MOH.0000000000000190

Mardis ER, Ding L, Dooling DJ et al (2009) Recurring mutations found by sequencing an acute myeloid leukemia genome. N Engl J Med 361(11):1058–1066. https://doi.org/10.1056/NEJMoa0903840

Maring JG, Groen HJ, Wachters FM et al (2005) Genetic factors influencing pyrimidine antagonist chemotherapy. Pharmacogenomics J 5(4):226–243. https://doi.org/10.1038/sj.tpj.6500320

Marjanovic I, Kostic J, Stanic B et al (2016) Parallel targeted next generation sequencing of childhood and adult acute myeloid leukemia patients reveals uniform genomic profile of the disease. Tumour Biol 37(10):13391–13401. https://doi.org/10.1007/s13277-016-5142-7

Martelli MP, Gionfriddo I, Mezzasoma F et al (2015) Arsenic trioxide and all-trans-retinoic acid target NPM1 mutant oncoprotein levels and induce apoptosis in NPM1-mutated AML cells. Blood 125(22):3455–3465. https://doi.org/10.1182/blood-2014-11-611459

Megías JE, Montesinos P, Herrero MJ et al (2015) Impact of transporter genes polymorphisms in standard induction of acute myeloid leukemia. Blood 126(23):4842. http://www.bloodjournal.org/content/126/23/4842

Mesa RA, Kaufmann SH (2007) Altered apoptosis in AML: potential implications for pathogenesis and therapeutic response. In: Karp JE (ed) Acute myeloid leukemia. Springer, Berlin, pp 133–161. https://doi.org/10.1007/978-1-59745-322-6_6

Metzeler KH, Walker A, Geyer S et al (2012) DNMT3A mutations and response to the hypomethylating agent decitabine in acute myeloid leukemia. Leukemia 26(5):1106–1107. https://doi.org/10.1038/leu.2011.342

Meyers S, Lenny N, Hiebert SW (1995) The t(8;21) fusion protein interferes with AML-1B-dependent transcriptional activation. Mol Cell Biol 15(4):1974–1982

Mitra AK, Crews KR, Pounds S et al (2011) Genetic variants in cytosolic 5′-nucleotidase II are associated with its expression and cytarabine sensitivity in HapMap cell lines and in patients with acute myeloid leukemia. J Pharmacol Exp Ther 339(1):9–23. https://doi.org/10.1124/jpet.111.182873

Montero TD, Racordon D, Bravo L et al (2012) PPARα and PPARγ regulate the nucleoside transporter hENT1. Biochem Biophys Res Commun 419(2):405–411. https://doi.org/10.1016/j.bbrc.2012.02.035

Moore AS, Faisal A, Gonzalez de Castro D et al (2012) Selective FLT3 inhibition of FLT3-ITD+ acute myeloid leukaemia resulting in secondary D835Y mutation: a model for emerging clinical resistance patterns. Leukemia 26(7):1462–1470. https://doi.org/10.1038/leu.2012.52

Nomdedeu J, Bussaglia E, Villamor N et al (2011) Adverse impact of IDH1 and IDH2 mutations in primary AML: experience of the Spanish CETLAM group. Leuk Res 35(2):163–168. https://doi.org/10.1016/j.leukres.2010.05.015

O'Hear C, Heiber JF, Schubert I et al (2015) Anti-CD33 chimeric antigen receptor targeting of acute myeloid leukemia. Haematologica 100(3):336–344. https://doi.org/10.3324/haematol.2014.112748

Perry AM, Attar EC (2014) New insights in AML biology from genomic analysis. Semin Hematol 51(4):282–297. https://doi.org/10.1053/j.seminhematol.2014.08.005

Petersdorf SH, Kopecky KJ, Slovak M et al (2013) A phase 3 study of gemtuzumab ozogamicin during induction and postconsolidation therapy in younger patients with acute myeloid leukemia. Blood 121(24):4854–4860. https://doi.org/10.1182/blood-2013-01-466706

Pizzitola I, Anjos-Afonso F, Rouault-Pierre K et al (2014) Chimeric antigen receptors against CD33/CD123 antigens efficiently target primary acute myeloid leukemia cells in vivo. Leukemia 28(8):1596–1605. https://doi.org/10.1038/leu.2014.62

Ploen GG, Nederby L, Guldberg P et al (2014) Persistence of DNMT3A mutations at long-term remission in adult patients with AML. Br J Haematol 167(4):478–486. https://doi.org/10.1111/bjh.13062

Pollard JA, Loken M, Gerbing RB et al (2016) CD33 Expression andiIts association with gemtuzumab ozogamicin response: Results from the randomized Phase III Children's Oncology Group Trial AAML0531. J Clin Oncol 34(7):747–755. https://doi.org/10.1200/JCO.2015.62.6846

Puda A, Milosevic JD, Berg T et al (2012) Frequent deletions of JARID2 in leukemic transformation of chronic myeloid malignancies. Am J Hematol 87(3):245–250. https://doi.org/10.1002/ajh.22257

Randhawa JK, Kantarjian HM, Borthakur G et al (2014) Results of a phase II study of crenolanib in relapsed/refractory acutemyeloid leukemia patients (pts) with activating FLT3 mutations. 56th ASH Annual Meeting and Exposition. 6–9 December 2014, San Francisco CA, USA. Blood 124(21):389. https://ash.confex.com/ash/2014/webprogram/Paper74499.html

Ravandi F, Alattar ML, Grunwald MR et al (2013) Phase 2 study of azacytidine plus sorafenib in patients with acute myeloid leukemia and FLT-3 internal tandem duplication mutation. Blood 121(23):4655–4662. https://doi.org/10.1182/blood-2013-01-480228

Rotiroti MC, Arcangeli S, Casucci M et al (2017) Acute myeloid leukemia targeting by chimeric antigen receptor T cells: bridging the gap from preclinical modeling to human studies. Hum Gene Ther 28(3):231–241. https://doi.org/10.1089/hum.2016.092

Ruben JM, van den Ancker W, Bontkes HJ et al (2014) Apoptotic blebs from leukemic cells as a preferred source of tumor-associated antigen for dendritic cell-based vaccines. Cancer Immunol Immunother 63(4):335–345. https://doi.org/10.1007/s00262-013-1515-6

Rubnitz JE, Inaba H, Ribeiro RC et al (2010) NKAML: a pilot study to determine the safety and feasibility of haploidentical natural killer cell transplantation in childhood acute myeloid leukemia. J Clin Oncol 28(6):955–959. https://doi.org/10.1200/JCO.2009.24.4590

Ruggeri L, Capanni M, Urbani E et al (2002) Effectiveness of donor natural killer cell alloreactivity in mismatched hematopoietic transplants. Science 295(5562):2097–2100. https://doi.org/10.1126/science.1068440

Russler-Germain DA, Spencer DH, Young MA et al (2014) The R882H DNMT3A mutation associated with AML dominantly inhibits wild-type DNMT3A by blocking its ability to form active tetramers. Cancer Cell 25(4):442–454. https://doi.org/10.1016/j.ccr.2014.02.010

Sadelain M, Brentjens R, Riviere I (2013) The basic principles of chimeric antigen receptor design. Cancer Discov 3(4):388–398. https://doi.org/10.1158/2159-8290.CD-12-0548

Scaglioni PP, Pandolfi PP (2007) The theory of APL revisited. Curr Top Microbiol Immunol 313:85–100

Schnittger S, Schoch C, Dugas M et al (2002) Analysis of FLT3 length mutations in 1003 patients with acute myeloid leukemia: correlation to cytogenetics, FAB subtype, and prognosis in the AMLCG study and usefulness as a marker for the detection of minimal residual disease. Blood 100(1):59–66. https://doi.org/10.1182/blood.V100.1.59

Schnittger S, Haferlach C, Ulke M et al (2010) IDH1 mutations are detected in 6.6% of 1414 AML patients and are associated with intermediate risk karyotype and unfavorable prognosis in adults younger than 60 years and unmutated NPM1 status. Blood 116(25):5486–5196. https://doi.org/10.1182/blood-2010-02-267955

Serrano-López J, Sanchez-Garcia J, Serrano J et al (2011) Nonleukemic myeloid dendritic cells obtained from autologous stem cell products elicit antileukemia responses in patients with acute myeloid leukemia. Transfusion 51(7):1546–1555. https://doi.org/10.1111/j.1537-2995.2010. 03042.x

Sharom FJ (2008) ABC multidrug transporters: structure, function and role in chemoresistance. Pharmacogenomics 9(1):105–127. https://doi.org/10.2217/14622416.9.1.105

Shlush LI, Zandi S, Mitchell A et al (2014) Identification of pre-leukaemic haematopoietic stem cells in acute leukaemia. Nature 506(7488):328–333. https://doi.org/10.1038/nature13038

Skalova K, Mollova K, Michalek J (2010) Human myeloid dendritic cells for cancer therapy: does maturation matter? Vaccine 28(32):5153–5160. https://doi.org/10.1016/j.vaccine.2010.05.042

Smith CC, Lin K, Stecula A et al (2015) FLT3-D835 mutations confer differential resistance to type II FLT3 inhibitors. Leukemia 29(12):2390–2392. https://doi.org/10.1038/leu.2015.165

Speck NA, Gilliland DG (2002) Core-binding factors in haematopoiesis and leukaemia. Nat Rev Cancer 2(7):502–513. https://doi.org/10.1038/nrc840

Stein AS, Walter RB, Erba HP et al (2015) A phase I trial of SGN-CD33A as immunonotherapy in patients with CD33-positive acute myeloid leukemia (AML). 57th ASH Annual meeting and exhibition. 5-8 December 2015, Orlando FL, USA. Blood 126(23):324. https://ash.confex.com/ ash/2015/webprogramscheduler/Paper83162.html

Stein EM (2015) IDH2 inhibition in AML: finally progress? Best Pract Res Clin Haematol 28 (2-3):112–115. https://doi.org/10.1016/j.beha.2015.10.016

Stein EM, Tallman MS (2015) Mixed lineage rearranged leukaemia: pathogenesis and targeting DOT1L. Curr Opin Hematol 22(2):92–96. https://doi.org/10.1097/MOH.0000000000000123

Stone RM, Mandrekar S, Sanford BL et al (2015) The multi-kinase inhibitor midostaurin (M) prolongs survival compared with placebo (P) in combination with daunorubicin (D)/ cytarabine (C) induction (ind), high-dose C consolidation (consol), and as maintenance (maint) therapy in newly diagnosed acute myeloid leukemia (AML) patients (pts) age 18–60 with FLT3 mutations (muts): an international prospective randomized (rand) P-controlled double-blind trial (CALGB 10603/RATIFY). 57th ASH Annual Meeting & Exposition; 5–8 December 2015, Orlando, FL, USA. Blood 126(23):6. https://ash.confex.com/ash/2015/ webprogram/Paper80269.html

Strahl B, Allis C (2000) The language of covalent histone modifications. Nature 403(6765):41–45. https://doi.org/10.1038/47412

Takagaki K, Katsuma S, Horio T et al (2003) cDNA microarray analysis of altered gene expression in Ara-C-treated leukemia cells. Biochem Biophys Res Commun 309(2):351–358. https://doi. org/10.1016/j.bbrc.2003.08.009

Tallman MS, Andersen JW, Schiffer CA et al (2002) All-trans retinoic acid in acute promyelocytic leukemia: long-term outcome and prognostic factor analysis from the North American Intergroup Protocol. Blood 100(13):4298–4302. https://doi.org/10.1182/blood-2002-02-0632

Thol F, Damm F, Wagner K et al (2010) Prognostic impact of IDH2 mutations in cytogenetically normal acute myeloid leukemia. Blood 116(4):614–616. https://doi.org/10.1182/blood-2010-03-272146

Traulsen A, Pacheco JM, Luzzatto L, Dingli D (2010) Somatic mutations and the hierarchy of hematopoiesis. Bioessays 32(11):1003–1008. https://doi.org/10.1002/bies.201000025

Uttenthal B, Martinez-Davila I, Ivey A et al (2014) Wilms' Tumour 1 (WT1) peptide vaccination in patients with acute myeloid leukaemia induces short-lived WT1-specific immune responses. Br J Haematol 164(3):366–375. https://doi.org/10.1111/bjh.12637

Uttenthal BJ, Chua I, Morris EC, Stauss HJ (2012) Challenges in T cell receptor gene therapy. J Gene Med 14(6):386–399. https://doi.org/10.1002/jgm.2637

Valent P, Zuber J (2014) BRD4: a BET (ter) target for the treatment of AML? Cell Cycle 13 (5):689–690. https://doi.org/10.4161/cc.27859

Van Driessche A, Van de Velde AL, Nijs G et al (2009) Clinical-grade manufacturing of autologous mature mRNA-electroporated dendritic cells and safety testing in acute myeloid leukemia patients in a Phase I dose-escalation clinical trial. Cytotherapy 11(5):653–668. https://doi.org/10.1080/14653240902960411

Van Tendeloo VF, Van de Velde A, Van Driessche A et al (2010) Induction of complete and molecular remissions in acute myeloid leukemia by Wilms' tumor 1 antigen-targeted dendritic cell vaccination. Proc Natl Acad Sci USA 107(31):13824–13829. https://doi.org/10.1073/pnas.1008051107

Villa R, Pasini D, Gutierrez A et al (2007) Role of the polycomb repressive complex 2 in acute promyelocytic leukemia. Cancer Cell 11(6):513–525. https://doi.org/10.1016/j.ccr.2007.04.009

Virijevic M, Karan-Djurasevic T, Marjanovic I et al (2016) Somatic mutations of isocitrate dehydrogenases 1 and 2 are prognostic and follow-up markers in patients with acute myeloid leukaemia with normal karyotype. Radiol Oncol 50(4):385–393. https://doi.org/10.1515/raon-2016-0044

Voso MT, Hohaus S, Guidi F et al (2008) Prognostic role of glutathione S-transferase polymorphisms in acute myeloid leukemia. Leukemia 22(9):1685–1691. https://doi.org/10.1038/leu.2008.169

Wagner K, Damm F, Göhring G et al (2010) Impact of IDH1 R132 mutations and an IDH1 single nucleotide polymorphism in cytogenetically normal acute myeloid leukemia: SNP rs11554137 is an Adverse Prognostic Factor. J Clin Oncol 28(14):2356–2364. https://doi.org/10.1200/JCO.2009.27.6899

Wan H, Zhu J, Chen F et al (2014) SLC29A1 single nucleotide polymorphisms as independent prognostic predictors for survival of patients with acute myeloid leukemia: an in vitro study. J Exp Clin Cancer Res 33(1):90. https://doi.org/10.1186/s13046-014-0090-9

Wang F, Travins J, De La Barre B et al (2013) Targeted inhibition of mutant IDH2 in leukemia cells induces cellular differentiation. Science 340(6132):622–626. https://doi.org/10.1126/science.1234769

Wang ZY, Chen Z (2008) Acute promyelocytic leukemia: from highly fatal to highly curable. Blood 111(5):2505–2515. https://doi.org/10.1182/blood-2007-07-102798

Ward PS, Patel J, Wise DR et al (2010) The common feature of leukemia-associated IDH1 and IDH2 mutations is a neomorphic enzyme activity converting a-ketoglutarate to 2-hydrozyglutarate. Cancer Cell 17(3):225–234. https://doi.org/10.1016/j.ccr.2010.01.020

Warner JK, Wang JCY, Hope KJ et al (2004) Concepts of human leukemic developement. Oncogene 23(43):7164–7177. https://doi.org/10.1038/sj.onc.1207933

Wei A, Tan P, Perruzza S et al (2015) Maintenance lenalidomide in combination with 5-azacytidine as post remission therapy for acute myeloid leukemia. Br J Haematol 169(2):199–210. https://doi.org/10.1111/bjh.13281

Welch JS, Westervelt P, Ding L et al (2011) Use of whole-genome sequencing to diagnose a cryptic fusion oncogene. JAMA 305(15):1577–1584. https://doi.org/10.1001/jama.2011.497

Wolf CR, Smith G, Smith RL (2000) Science, medicine, and the future: Pharmacogenetics. BMJ 320(7240):987–990

Xie M, Lu C, Wang J et al (2014) Age related mutations associated with clonal hematopoietic expansion and malignancies. Nat Med 20(12):1472–1478. https://doi.org/10.1038/nm.3733

Xu W, Yang H, Liu Y et al (2011) Oncometabolite 2-hydroxyglutarate is a competitive inhibitor of alpha-ketoglutarate dependent dioxygenases. Cancer Cell 19(1):17–30. https://doi.org/10.1016/j.ccr.2010.12.014

Yamamoto Y, Kiyoi H, Nakano Y et al (2001) Activating mutation of D835 within the activation loop of FLT3 in human hematologic malignancies. Blood 97(8):2434–2439. https://doi.org/10.1182/blood.V97.8.2434

Yin B, Tsai ML, Hasz DE et al (2007) A microarray study of altered gene expression after cytarabine resistance in acute myeloid leukemia. Leukemia 21(5):1093–1097. https://doi.org/10.1038/sj.leu.2404595

Zarrinkar PP, Gunawardane RN, Cramer MD et al (2009) AC220 is a uniquely potent and selective inhibitor of FLT3 for the treatment of acute myeloid leukemia (AML). Blood 114(14):2984–2992. https://doi.org/10.1182/blood-2009-05-222034

Zhang W, Konopleva M, Shi YX et al (2008a) Mutant FLT3: a direct target of sorafenib in acute myelogenous leukemia. J Natl Cancer Inst 100(3):184–198. https://doi.org/10.1093/jnci/djm328

Zhang W, Konopleva M, Shi YX et al (2008b) Sorafenib induces apoptosis of AML cells via Bim-mediated activation of the intrinsic apoptotic pathway. Leukemia 22(4):808–818. https://doi.org/10.1038/sj.leu.2405098

Ziv O, Zeisel A, Mirlas-Neisberg N et al (2014) Identification of novel DNA-damage tolerance genes reveals regulation of translesion DNA synthesis by nucleophosmin. Nat Commun 5:5437. https://doi.org/10.1038/ncomms6437

The Future of Cartilage Repair

Damir Hudetz, Željko Jeleč, Eduard Rod, Igor Borić, Mihovil Plečko,
and Dragan Primorac

Abstract Articular cartilage is a hyaline cartilage 2–4 mm thick. It is composed of
95% of dense extracellular matrix (ECM) and 5% of highly specialized cells called
chondrocytes. Because of its avascular, aneural and alymphatic state, it has a limited
repair potential. Articular cartilages' main function is to provide smooth, lubricated
surface for low friction articulation while minimizing the stress and strains on the
matrix. Articular cartilage could be damaged by normal wear and tear or injury and it

D. Hudetz
St. Catherine Specialty Hospital, Zagreb, Croatia

Clinical Hospital "Sveti Duh", Zagreb, Croatia

School of Medicine, JJ Strossmayer University of Osijek, Osijek, Croatia

Ž. Jeleč · E. Rod
St. Catherine Specialty Hospital, Zagreb, Croatia

School of Medicine, JJ Strossmayer University of Osijek, Osijek, Croatia

I. Borić
St. Catherine Specialty Hospital, Zagreb, Croatia

School of Medicine, University of Split, Split, Croatia

School of Medicine, University of Rijeka, Rijeka, Croatia

M. Plečko
St. Catherine Specialty Hospital, Zagreb, Croatia

D. Primorac (✉)
St. Catherine Specialty Hospital, Zagreb, Croatia

School of Medicine, JJ Strossmayer University of Osijek, Osijek, Croatia

School of Medicine, University of Split, Split, Croatia

Gen-Info, Zagreb, Croatia

Children's Hospital Srebrnjak, Zagreb, Croatia

Eberly College of Science, The Pennsylvania State University, University Park, State College,
PA, USA

The Henry C. Lee College of Criminal Justice and Forensic Sciences, University of New Haven,
West Haven, CT, USA

© Springer Nature Switzerland AG 2019   375
N. Bodiroga-Vukobrat et al. (eds.), *Personalized Medicine in Healthcare Systems*,
Europeanization and Globalization 5, https://doi.org/10.1007/978-3-030-16465-2_29

can cause severe pain, inflammation and some degree of disability. Its management consist of pharmacological (acetaminophen, NSAID, salicylate, selective COX-2 inhibitors or opioids) and non-pharmacological therapies. Non-pharmacological treatment includes physical therapy and decreasing the load in the joint by modifying patient's habits. A new class of agents (symptomatic or disease modifying osteoarthritic drugs (S/DMOADs) including glucosamine and chondroitin sulfate is receiving wide publicity. At the same time, numerous published reports advising the use of hyaluronic acid injections: viscosupplementation in patients with symptomatic osteoarthritis. Operative treatment includes different surgical debridement and microfracture techniques, osteochondral autograft transfers, osteochondral allograft transplantation, etc. New techniques and concepts are being developed not only to treat damaged or diseased joint cartilage but also to find ways of achieving regeneration to normal cartilage that will give long-lasting improvements and allow patients to return to a fully active lifestyle. Nevertheless, as two stage procedures involving cell culture are expensive and cumbersome, there is an increasing push towards a single stage stem cell treatment. Currently, there are a number of new methods with cartilage repair aim, including autologous chondrocyte implantation (ACI), matrix-induced autologous chondrocyte implantation (MACI), intra-articular administration of autologous microfragmented fat tissue with Ad-MSCs, etc. In this chapter, we discuss some current treatments and the emerging strategies/techniques employed by researchers and physicians thriving to repair articular cartilage through biological means.

1   Introduction

Articular cartilage is a tissue that has a unique role in providing mechanical support to the joint. Its role is to resist physical loads and to lower the friction between two articular surfaces thus enabling movements in joints. Because of specific microporous architecture, biochemical composition of the matrix and directed composition of collagen fibers, cartilage has elastic characteristics and the ability to sustain a wide range of mechanical loads. Articular cartilage has no blood vessels, lymph vessels or nerves, obtaining most of its nutrients by diffusion from synovial fluid inside of the joint capsule and through capilares in the surrounding connective tissue (perichondrium).[1] Cartilage consists of chondrocytes, which are localized in lacunas, small areas surrounded by extra-cellular matrix. Chondrocytes make up to 5% of total cartilage tissue, while extra-cellular matrix makes 95% thus being responsible for biomechanical properties of the cartilage.[2]

Chondrocytes produce and maintain cartilaginous extra-cellular matrix, which consists mainly of collagen, water, hyaluronic acid and proteoglycans combined with a smaller amount of calcium salts and other glycoproteins. Firmness of the

---

[1]Fanghänel et al. (2009).
[2]Bhosale and Richardson (2008).

cartilage depends on electrostatic bonds between collagen fibers and glycosamino-glycan side-chains and on bondage of water to negatively charged glycosaminogly-can side-chains. Glycosaminoglycans are long unbranched polysaccharides made of repeating disaccharide units consisting of an amino sugar (glucosamine or galactos-amine) and a uronic sugar (glucuronic acid or iduronic acid). With the exception of hyaluronic acid, glycosaminoglycan chains are bonded with covalent bonds for one centrally located protein called aggrecan, forming a molecule called proteoglycan. The importance of aggrecan in limb formation in the vertebrae has been studied extensively. Primorac et al.[3] have shown that the premature termination codon in exon 10 (codon 1513) in the eighth repeat of the chondroitin sulfate 2 domain of the aggrecan gene is responsible for nanomelia, a recessively inherited connective tissue disorder of chicken affecting cartilage development. In cartilage, proteoglycans bond with a chain of hyaluronic acid forming structures called proteoglycan aggregates. Proteoglycans are made mostly of carbohydrates that make up to 90% of the total weight of the molecule. Because of these features proteoglycans can bind a large number of cations (mostly Na^+) through ionic bonds, which makes them extremely hydratized with a layer of water around them, fulfilling a wider area in that manner. Because of different needs within the body, we distinguish three types of cartilage tissue—hyaline, elastic and fibrous cartilage, all with a different composition of extra-cellular matrix.

The most common type in the body is hyaline cartilage, located on articular surfaces of movable joints, as a part of structures in large airways (nose, larynx, trachea, bronchi) and on ventral ends of ribs. Hyaline cartilage consists of collagen type II molecules and proteoglycans of which chondroitin-4-sulfate, chondroitin-6-sulfate and keratan sulfate are of utmost importance. Proteoglycans, forming earlier mentioned proteoglycan aggregates, bind with collagen fibers. A study[4] showed that the primary failure in aggrecan production by nanomelic chondrocytes has an unexpected secondary effect on type II collagen. The decrease in type II collagen mRNA suggests a possible coordination of transcription between genes that code for interacting extracellular matrix proteins. Another important molecule is chondronectin, glycoprotein that mediates binding of chondrocytes to collagen type II. Function of chondrocytes depends on the hormonal homeostatis in the body. Growth hormone, thyroxine and testosterone stimulate while cortisol, hydro-cortisone and estradiol decelerate formation of glycosaminoglycans. Growth of the cartilage is mostly correlated with effects of somatotropin, which indirectly stimu-lates chondrocytes through somatomedin C, hormone whose production in liver is stimulated by somatotropin. There are two mechanisms of damaging of the carti-lage—trauma and degeneration. Cartilage lesions can be described as full-thickness or partial. Further, cartilage lesions can be focal or generalized. Regeneration of the cartilage starts from the perichondrium, a layer of extra-articular connective tissue surrounding the hyaline cartilage that contains undifferentiated cells with the

---

[3]Primorac et al. (1994).
[4]Primorac (1995).

capability of differentiation into chondrocytes.[5] Parallel to chondrocyte's synthetic activity, proteolytic enzymes moderate processes of degeneration of the extra-cellular matrix. In physiological conditions this two processes are in balance. When chondrocytes fail to maintain homeostasis between this two processes, a disease called osteoarthritis (OA) starts to develop.[6]

Osteoarthritis, also known as degenerative joint disease or osteoarthrosis, is the most common form of arthritis and the leading cause of physical disability in the modern world. OA is a heterogeneous condition and most likely many different causes exist that initiate or at least promote the disease process. There are some risk factors for the development of OA. The majority of them are obesity, previous trauma, overuse, occupational habit, impact sports activity and genetics. The pres-ence of other risk factors such as age, skeletal shape abnormalities or joint overload may have a synergistic effect for OA initiation.[7]

According to Peyron and Altman,[8] two main mechanisms are thought to initiate osteoarthritis. In most patients, the initiating mechanism is damage to normal articular cartilage by physical forces, which can be either a single event of macrotrauma or repeated microtrauma. Less commonly, fundamentally defective cartilage initially fails under normal joint loading, i.e. a type II collagen gene defect.

According to Aigner and Schmitz,[9] the destruction of articular cartilage and the loss of its biomechanical function is largely because of the destruction and loss of the (inter)territorial cartilage matrix. So far, our knowledge focuses on degradation processes of the two major components of the interterritorial cartilage matrix, the collagen network and the interwoven proteoglycan aggregates. The most likely candidate enzymes responsible for the increased matrix degradation in OA cartilage are metalloproteinases including matrix metalloproteinases (MMPs), as well as adamalysins such as ADAMs (a disintegrin and metalloproteinase) and ADAMTSs (a disintegrin and metalloproteinase with thrombospondin type-1 motifs).[10] Some of other possible factors that could have a role in OA development are inflammatory cytokines,[11,12,13] nitrous oxide,[14,15] leptins,[16,17] angiogenesis[18] and T-cells.[19]

---

[5]Junqueira and Carneiro (2005).

[6]Heijink et al. (2012).

[7]Roman-Blas and Herrero-Beaumont (2014).

[8]Peyron and Altman (1992).

[9]Aigner and Schmitz (2011).

[10]Burrage and Brinckerhoff (2007).

[11]Fan et al. (2004).

[12]Stannus et al. (2010).

[13]van de Loo et al. (1995).

[14]Abramson (2008).

[15]Clancy (1999).

[16]Dumond et al. (2003).

[17]Loeser (2003).

[18]Bonnet and Walsh (2005).

[19]Sakkas and Platsoucas (2007).

One of the newest theories about pathogenesis of OA suggests that the early damage to the cartilage is caused by the bone underneath it. The changes in subchondral bone cause formation of surplus bone which stretches the cartilage above and speeds its deterioration. Zhen et al.[20] showed that transforming growth factor β1 (TGF-β1) is activated in subchondral bone in response to altered mechanical loading in an anterior cruciate ligament transection (ACLT) mouse model of osteoarthritis. High concentrations of TGF-β1 induced formation of nestin-positive mesenchymal stem cell (MSC) clusters, leading to formation of marrow osteoid islets accompanied by high levels of angiogenesis. They found that transgenic expression of active TGF-β1 in osteoblastic cells induced osteoarthritis, whereas inhibition of TGF-β activity in subchondral bone attenuated the degeneration of articular cartilage. Authors concluded that high concentrations of active TGF-β1 in subchondral bone could initiate the pathological changes of osteoarthritis, and inhibition of this process could be a potential therapeutic approach to treating osteoarthritis.

The importance of subchondral bone in pathogenesis of OA was emphasized by Uygur et al. in their review article.[21] They adopted the "joint as an organ" approach in understanding, diagnosing and treating of OA and showed the need for further examination of subchondral bone to characterize its involvement and importance in OA pathogenesis. The principle of OA as a disease of the whole joint is also recognized by other authors.[22] Many authors showed that bone marrow lesions (BML) and subchondral bone attrition have an effect on the overlying cartilage. BML presence, incidence and progression have been associated with development and worsening of cartilage loss, including in locations adjacent to the BML[23,24,25,26] and subchondral bone attrition also increases the risk for cartilage loss to occur in the same subregion.[27] Osteoarthritis affects the articular cartilage, the bone and the capsule of the joint. This results in osteophyte formation, subchondral sclerosis, and capsular thickening (Fig. 1). In 2003, the International Cartilage Repair Society (ICRS) published the ICRS Hyaline Cartilage Lesion Classification System, which is currently used as the international standard.[28] International Cartilage Repair Society (ICRS) Grading (reproduced from the ICRS Cartilage Injury Evaluation Package [www.cartilage.org]):

---

[20]Zhen et al. (2013).

[21]Uygur et al. (2015).

[22]Dieppe (2011).

[23]Davies-Tuck et al. (2010).

[24]Felson et al. (2003).

[25]Hunter et al. (2006).

[26]Wluka et al. (2009).

[27]Neogi et al. (2009).

[28]Brittberg and Winalski (2003).

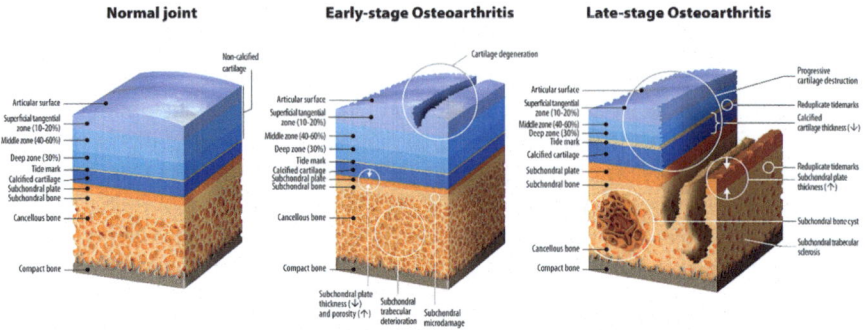

Fig. 1 Normal joint architecture and microarchitecture changes in Osteoarthritis

Grade 0: Normal
Grade 1: Nearly Normal (soft indentation and/or superficial fissures and cracks)
Grade 2: Abnormal (lesions extending down to <50% of cartilage depth)
Grade 3: Severely Abnormal (cartilage defects >50% of cartilage depth)

- Cartilage defects extending down >50% of cartilage depth (A) as well as down to calcified layer (B) and down to but not through the subchondral bone (C). Blisters are included in this grade (D)

Grade 4: Severely abnormal (through the subchondral bone)

2 Therapy

2.1 Pharmacologic Management

2.1.1 Non-Steroidal Anti-Inflammatory Drugs and Opioid Analgesics

The main goals of pharmacological treatment of OA are to reduce pain, improve function and slow down progress of the disease. Unfortunately, the final achievement of most standard OA drugs is decrease of symptoms, but not reparation of cartilage damage. Because of high incidence of adverse effects, benefits and potential damage should be considered.

In most cases, the first analgesic for OA treatment is acetaminophen or paracetamol. According to Richmond et al., acetaminophen has a statistically significant effect on pain relief without risk of toxicity.[29] Osteoarthritis Research Society International (OARSI) recommend up to 4 g per day as an effective therapy for patients with mild to moderate pain.[30] European League Against Rheumatism

---

[29]Richmond et al. (2009).

[30]Zhang et al. (2008a, b).

(EULAR) recommendations are very similar and in addition, EULAR recommends that acetaminophen should be used as the preferred long-term oral analgesic (see footnote 37). Higher doses of acetaminophen can result with hepatotoxicity in some patients.

Salicylates are well known drugs with the most important role in prevention of cardiac incidents. They are also capable of controlling joint inflammation and pain. Like acetaminophen, they also have potential side effects such as gastrointestinal irritation, but if used in small doses in generally healthy people, they can be very helpful in controlling the pain and inflammation of osteoarthritis.

Non-steroidal anti-inflammatory drugs (NSAIDs) are very commonly used drugs that provide anti-inflammatory and analgesic effects. Under the OARSI guidelines, NSAIDs should be used at the lowest effective dose but their long-term use should be avoided if possible (see footnote 37). The efficacy of NSAIDs is well documented, especially in comparison with acetaminophen.[31,32] NSAIDs are associated with more adverse effects, i.e. more frequent gastrointestinal (GI) side-effects in range between discomfort to formation of peptic ulcers, perforation and bleeding (see footnotes 36, 37). Other possible adverse events are cardiovascular problems and renal toxicity.

Selective inhibitors of cyclooxygenase-2 (COX-2) are a type of NSAIDs. They are recommended in patients with greater GI risk, as well as a combination of NSAIDs and proton pump inhibitors (see footnote 37). Selective COX-2 inhibitors pretend to be safer than standard NSAIDs but there are a few papers that show the potential risk of cardiovascular adverse events (celecoxib).[33] Because of that reason, some of selective COX-2 inhibitors (rofecoxib, valdecoxib) were withdrawn from the market.[34,35] Under the OARSI guidelines, the cardiovascular risk with COX-2 inhibitors is not significantly higher than with NSAID (see footnote 37).

Opioid analgesics (i.e. tramadol, morphine, oxycodone) are used in patients whose pain management is insufficient with the use of NSAIDs and acetaminophen or in patients where weaker analgesics are contraindicated (see footnote 37). They are a good choice in patients who do not want joint replacement or who are not candidates for joint replacement because of other reasons. They have a positive effect in pain control but also many side-effects like: nausea, constipation, dizziness, somnolence and vomiting (see footnote 37). Under the AAOS guidelines, opioid analgesics are strongly recommended for symptomatic knee osteoarthritis.[36] OARSI recommends opioid analgesics for the treatment of refractory pain in patients with hip or knee OA (see footnote 37).

---

[31]Zhang et al. (2004).

[32]Towheed et al. (2006).

[33]FDA (2005).

[34]FDA (2004).

[35]FDA (2005).

[36]AAOS (2013).

2.1.2   Structure/Disease Modifying Osteoarthritic Drugs (S/DMOADs)

Glycosaminoglycans such as chondroitin sulfate (CS) and glucosamine are two natural compounds from the group of structure/disease modifying osteoarthritic drugs (S/DMOAD). They have been recognized by clinical trials to potentially influence the course of OA beneficially.

CS has been shown to improve the anabolic/catabolic balance of the extra-cellular cartilage matrix, to modify the chondrocyte apoptosis process, to reduce some pro-inflammatory and catabolic factors and to reduce the resorptive capacity of subchondral bone osteoblasts.[37,38,39,40,41] Meta-analyses of randomized placebo-controlled trials in patients with knee OA have demonstrated the efficacy of CS to relieve joint pain.[42,43] CS taken orally once per day at a dose of 800 mg has shown to significantly slow down the rate of joint space narrowing over a period of 2 years in patients with symptomatic radiographic knee OA.[44] In their randomized, double-blinded, placebo-controlled pilot study, Wildi et al.[45] showed using quantitative MRI measurements that CS treatment significantly reduces the cartilage volume loss in patients with knee OA after 6 months of treatment, and BML after 12 months.

Use of glucosamine is based on studies conducted on animal models and in vitro studies which showed normalization of the joint metabolism during the healing process of chondral lesions, along with slight anti-inflammatory activity.[46,47] There are three types of glucosamine available on the market: glucosamine hydro-chloride (taken from crab shells), glucosamine sulfate (taken from shrimp shells) and synthetic glucosamine (sulfate). Some studies showed that glucosamine is more efficient than placebo in improving symptoms and diminishing the speed of pro-gression of joint narrowing in OA.[48]

The potential synergic effects of parallel application of glucosamine and chon-droitin are still being studied. Some recent studies did not find any strong evidence that associating the medications promotes improvement of the symptoms in com-parison with placebo for treating patients with OA.[49,50] However, the study of

---

[37]Ronca et al. (1998).

[38]Chan et al. (2006).

[39]Tat et al. (2007).

[40]Martel-Pelletier et al. (2010).

[41]du Souich et al. (2009).

[42]Leeb et al. (2000).

[43]Richy et al. (2003).

[44]Hochberg et al. (2008).

[45]Wildi et al. (2011).

[46]McCarty (1994).

[47]Bassleer et al. (1998).

[48]Reginster et al. (2001).

[49]Clegg et al. (2006).

[50]Lopes Junior and Inacio (2013).

Zeng et al.[51] provided evidence that combination of glucosamine and chondroitin resulted with improvement of symptoms in patients with knee OA.

According to OARSI recommendations, treatment with glucosamine and/or chondroitin sulfate has a positive effect in patients with knee OA.[52] AAOS does not recommend using chondroitin sulfate and glucosamine in patients with symptomatic knee OA (see footnote 43). According to available literature, recommended daily dose for chondroitine sulfate (see footnotes 50, 51)[53] is 800 mg and for glucosamine sulfate (see footnotes 54, 59) 1500 mg.

2.2 Growth Factors Treatment

Regenerative and anti-inflammatory potential of platelet-rich plasma (PRP) is widely used as a treatment for a variety of musculoskeletal problems, including osteoarthritis.[54] The idea of the therapy is to use platelets, growth factors and cytokines found in blood with a known potential to induce and promote regeneration when used in different tissues. Some of the most important growth factors and cytokines are platelet-derived growth factor, transforming growth factor beta, fibroblast growth factor, insulin-like growth factor, vascular endothelial growth factor, epidermal growth factor, interleukin 8 etc.[55] Preparation includes collection of patient's whole blood and centrifugation to divide platelet-rich plasma from platelet-poor plasma and erythrocytes. Several types of preparation lead to a product with different content. In general, there are four main groups: leukocyte-rich PRP, leukocyte-poor PRP, leukocyte-rich platelet-rich fibrin and pure platelet-rich fibrin.[56] Product mostly used in treatment of cartilage defects is leukocyte-poor PRP, injected into the affected joint. Results of the study were well to excellent in 80% of patients.[57] Further, the study outlined worse outcomes related to older age of patients. Furthermore, a decrease of clinical improvement was noticed 6 months after the end of the treatment. The most commonly reported side effects were pain at the site of injection, lasting a couple of minutes, swelling and post injective pain in the affected joint that usually subsided in a few days.[58] Failure of non-operative management may be an indication for surgical procedures ranging from palliative therapy to more advanced restorative techniques.

---

[51]Zeng et al. (2015).

[52]Zhang et al. (2008a, b).

[53]Lee et al. (2010).

[54]Marmotti et al. (2015).

[55]Borrione et al. (2010).

[56]Ehrenfest et al. (2014).

[57]Kon et al. (2010).

[58]Filardo et al. (2012).

2.3   Joint Injections

2.3.1   Use of Corticosteroids

When conventional therapy fails to control symptoms or prevent disability, local steroid therapy may be an option.[59] Corticosteroids are generally known for their anti-inflammatory, immunosuppressive, anti-proliferative and vasoconstrictive effects[60]. Some studies reported that injections of corticosteroids resulted in short-term improvement of symptoms in patients with OA (i.e. OA of the knee[61]) while others reported there was no clinical benefit (i.e. OA of the carpometacarpal joint of the thumb[62]). Furthermore, there were some reports of steroid-induced (Charcot-like) arthropathy developing after multiple injections.[63] Although the role of intra-articular corticosteroid injections is still controversial, it is commonly used. Relative contraindications include infection, anti-coagulant therapy, uncontrolled diabetes mellitus, severe joint destruction or deformity, such as an unstable knee and obesity. Complications of intra-articular corticosteroid therapy are rare but include systemic effects, joint infection, post injection flare, localized subcutaneous or cutaneous atrophy and capsular (periarticular) calcifications.[64]

2.3.2   Use of Hyaluronic Acid Injections

Viscosupplementation is the procedure of intra-articular injection of exogenous hyaluronic acid (HA) to restore the normal rheologic environment in a joint affected by OA. HA is a molecule which is found in every joint and it provides viscoelasticity to synovial fluid.[65] It has a positive effect on subchondral bone, proteoglycan and glycosaminoglycan synthesis and has anti-inflammatory, mechanical and analgesic effects.

Most frequently reported mechanism of beneficial effect of HA is chondroprotection. It is a result of HA binding to cluster of differentiation 44 (CD44) receptors. By binding to CD44 HA inhibits interleukin-1 (IL-1) beta expression. The direct result is a decrease of matrix metalloproteinase (MMP) 1,2,3,9 and 13 production.[66]

---

[59]Bellamy et al. (2006).

[60]Liu et al. (2013).

[61]Arroll and Goodyear-Smith (2004).

[62]Meenagh et al. (2004).

[63]McDonough (1982).

[64]Jüni et al. (2015).

[65]Elmorsy et al. (2014).

[66]Julovi et al. (2004).

During the progress of OA, the concentration of intrinsic proteoglycans and glycosaminoglycans within the cartilage declines. It is shown that intra-articular— HA injections could suppress degradation and enhance synthesis of aggrecan, the primary proteoglycan.[67]

Anti-inflammatory effect of HA is shown through the suppression of IL-1 beta which results with down-regulation of MMP[68] as well as suppression of pro-inflammatory mediators IL-6 and prostaglandin E2 (PGE2).[69]

HA provides lubrication of the joint capsule and protects it by absorbing shocks.[70] Also, by absorbing pressure and vibration in the joint, HA protects chondrocytes from degradation.[71]

Moreover, HA has a positive effect on subchondral bone by inhibiting MMP-13 and IL-6, which leads to suppression of abnormal osseous metabolism.[72] The same author suggested that suppression of MMP-13 is one of the most important factors in the effect of HA on OA subchondral bone.

In conclusion, we can say that HA injections have a positive effect through few mechanisms, and it is yet to be determined which of them is the most important one. It should be noticed that the majority of exogenous HA remains in the joint for a very short period of time (only a few days) and that the beneficial effect of the treatment could be seen for a much longer period. From that, we can conclude that HA has disease modifying properties, and not only the effect that improves viscoelasticity.[73]

Contrary to some previous reviews, current papers suggest that high molecular weight HA (HMW HA) ensures better effect on the joint than low molecular weight HA (LMW HA).[74]

HA injections are recommended by OARSI as a treatment option in patients with knee and/or hip OA (see footnote 37). However, in 2013, AAOS changed the recommendation on HA from an inconclusive level to a non-affirming level (see footnote 43).

2.4 Arthroscopic Lavage and Debridement

The simplest surgical option is palliative arthroscopic lavage and debridement.[75] The goal is to debride loose flaps of cartilage. Removal of loose chondral fragments may

---

[67]Kobayashi et al. (2004).

[68]Sasaki et al. (2004).

[69]Lajeunesse et al. (2003).

[70]Forsey et al. (2006).

[71]Lu et al. (2013).

[72]Hiraoka et al. (2009).

[73]Dougados (2000).

[74]Altman et al. (2015).

[75]Tetteh et al. (2012).

relieve mechanical symptoms. Treatment is convenient for low physical demanding individuals and can improve pain and mechanical symptoms in the short term but does not address the potential to improve symptoms of progressive joint degeneration in the long term. Short-term benefits can be noticed in 50–70% of patients. Advantages of this type of treatment include fast and simple arthroscopic procedure and fast rehabilitation. Disadvantages include problems with exposed subchondral bone or layers of injured cartilage and unknown natural course of progression after treatment.

Patients with higher physical demands may be better suited for reparative or a restorative strategy. The aim of any cartilage repair procedure is to restore the defect with a mechanically stable and optimally repaired tissue.

2.5 Marrow Stimulation Techniques: Microfractures and Augmentation

Without any intervention, articular cartilage injuries have a limited ability to heal. Before any intervention, cartilage defect must be assessed with respect to the size (cm^2), location, thickness of the defect (ICRS or similar classification), chronicity, underlying bone status and axis alignment. All these parameters are referred to as cartilage lesion personality. Depending on the size of the defect, there are several treatment options like microfracturing or autologous cartilage implantation (Fig. 2).

One option for treating articular cartilage lesions is a microfracture procedure. Microfracture treatment is a single-stage arthroscopic articular cartilage repair procedure.[76] The surgery was developed in the late 1980s and early 1990s by Dr. Richard Steadman. Procedure harnesses the body's inherent healing capacity. In this procedure, narrow fractures are created through the subchondral bone in a repetitive manner throughout the defect with a specific instrument (microfracture awl) to allow access to marrow based progenitor cells and growth factors. Disruption of the subchondral bone gives a pathway for blood and fat droplets to flow into the lesion and induce fibrin clot formation in the area of the chondral defect. Matured mesenchymal clot forms fibrocartilage with varying amounts of type I, II, and III collagen content.[77] There are two key steps during the surgical procedure: removal of calcified cartilage and preservation of adequate height of the cartilage on the rim of the lesion. Removal of calcified cartilage while maintaining the underlying bone plate provides an optimal attachment and amount of repair tissue.[78] When mesenchymal clot is formed, optimal results necessitates adequate height of cartilage on the rim of the lesion to hold the clot in place (see footnote 84).

---

[76]Harnly (2007).

[77]Kreuz et al. (2006a, b).

[78]Steadman et al. (2001).

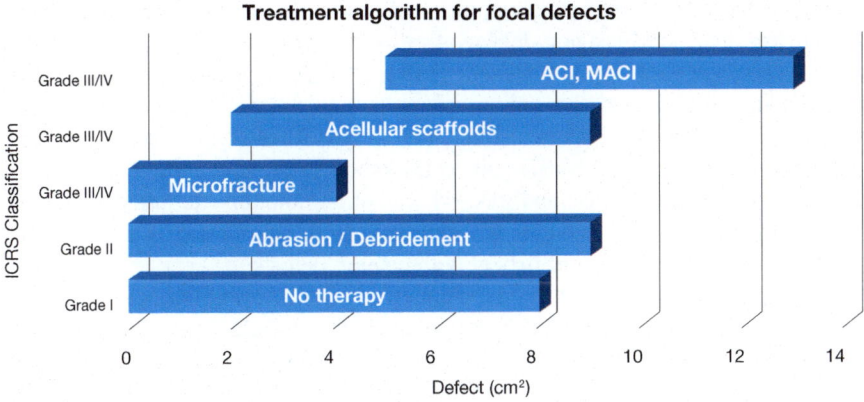

Fig. 2 Treatment algorithm for focal defects of cartilage

General indications for microfractures include full-thickness defects and unstable cartilage that overlies the subchondral bone. Contraindications include malalignment, global degenerative osteoarthrosis, systemic immune-mediated disease, disease induced arthritis or cartilage disease.[79] Relative contraindications are patients' age and lesions bigger than 4 cm^2 (see footnote 84).

There is a paucity of literature regarding long-term clinical outcomes following the microfracture procedure.[80,81]

A successful outcome and the time of recovery is dependent on the patient's age, patient's body mass, lesion size, chronicity of pain, presence of arthritis, previous surgeries and post-operative rehabilitation program (see footnote 84).

The postoperative protocol is designed to promote the ideal physical environment for clot maturation. The specific protocol that is recommended depends on anatomic location and the size of defects. The duration of rehabilitation depends on patient's activity and body mass index (BMI). Maximum improvement is expected 6 to 12 months after microfrature procedure (see footnote 85).

Microfracture procedure has gained popularity because of its minimally invasive approach, technical simplicity, limited surgical morbidity and low costs.

2.6   *Osteochondral Grafts*

The goal of osteochondral autograft transplantation surgery is to replace cartilage defect in a high weight-bearing area with normal autologous cartilage and bone plug (s) from a lower weight-bearing area. Osteochondral autograft transplantation

---

[79]Steadman et al. (2010).

[80]Miller et al. (2004).

[81]Steadman et al. (2003).

surgery is indicated in symptomatic, unipolar lesions of the distal femoral condyle that are less than 2 cm^2 in a non-degenerative joint of patients with an upper age limit of 50 years (see footnote 81). Benefits include usage of autologous tissue, cost-effectiveness and arthroscopically performed single-stage surgery. Limitations include donor site size constraints and morbidity, difficulty in matching the size and radius of curvature of cartilage defect, fixation strength of graft that decreases with initial healing response and long rehabilitation duration. Reported results are well to excellent with osteochondral autograft in 92% of patients with femoral condyle defects and in 74% of patient with patellar defects.[82]

Osteochondral allograft transplantation uses fresh, cold-preserved cadaveric donor tissue (mature articular cartilage) to repair lesions larger than 2 cm^2 without the risk of donor site morbidity. Benefits include ability to address larger defects, possibility to correct significant bone loss and the procedure is useful in revision of other techniques. Disadvantages of this procedure include graft availability, cost, cell viability and risk of immune response and disease transmission. Osteochondral allograft transplantation can be done arthroscopically but more often requires an arthrotomy. This technique has demonstrated 10-year Kaplan-Meier survival rate of 85% for femoral condyle lesions and 80% 10-year survival rates for tibial plateau grafts.[83] Chondral defects that involve subchondral bone formation require osteochondral autograft or allograft transplantation.

2.7   Cell-Based Products

2.7.1   Autologous Chondrocyte Implantation and Matrix-Associated Chondrocyte Implantation

Autologous chondrocyte implantation (ACI) is hyaline-like cartilage restorative cell therapy. It has become an option to treat medium to large full-thickness cartilage lesions in the knee since Brittberg et al.[84] presented early results of a new cartilage repair method in 1994. Initially, ACI was performed as a two-stage surgical procedure that consisted firstly of harvesting procedure on the index knee. Small biopsy of autologous articular cartilage is harvested from a minimal weight-bearing area or from the damaged tissue of cartilage defect itself. The cartilage is enzymatically digested in the laboratory to release the chondrocytes. Chondrocytes are cultured, and returned to the surgeon for implantation into the defect at a second surgical procedure on the same knee where chondrocyte suspension was implanted under a sutured and sealed periosteum. The technique described by Brittberg et al. is referred to as first generation of ACI. ACI is indicated for young patients (15 to 50 years of

---

[82]Hangody et al. (2008).

[83]Camp et al. (2014).

[84]Brittberg et al. (1994).

age) with moderate symptoms and well-contained full-thickness femoral chondral lesions measuring between 2 and 10 cm^2 with an intact bone bed (see footnote 81). Furthermore, ACI has the advantage of using the patient's own cells, so there is no possibility of immune-induced tissue rejection. It has the disadvantage of being a two-stage procedure, hence it lasts for several weeks, and requires an open incision and full-thickness cartilage margins around the defect.

First generation of ACI surgery includes the usage of autologous periosteum as a patch, which is harvested from the proximal tibia and microsutured to the surrounding cartilage to create a watertight space that is then injected with the chondrocyte suspension at a density of greater than one million cells per square centimeter. Periosteum is prone to hypertrophy, calcification and delamination.[85] Furthermore, periosteum is often hard to suture thus leading to significant possibility of cell leakage.[86] Nevertheless, ACI demonstrates good long term outcomes with over 70% of success.[87] The next and second generation of ACI included improvement that eliminated the necessity of harvesting periosteal flaps, namely it introduced collagen membrane as an of the shelf product to cover and seal chondrocytes in the defects. The defect is covered and sutured with collagen membrane and then injected with chondrocyte suspension. Issues negatively affecting clinical outcomes, such as periosteal patch hypertrophy associated with first generation of ACI and extensive suturing along with cell leakage in second generation ACI have led to the development of the third generation of ACI. Third generation introduced matrices or 3D scaffolds that were precultured with chondrocytes in static condition and implanted in the defect of the affected knee. The biocompatible scaffolds are used to secure the delivery of chondrocytes to the location of the lesion. Therefore this technique was termed as matrix assisted autologous chondrocyte implantation (MACI). Materials used as matrix are collagen hydrogels or membranes, copolymer of polyglycolic/polylactic acid, polydioxanone and hyaluronic acid, where chondrocytes are seeded into a collagen matrix and then fixed to the chondral defect with fibrin glue.[88] Chondrocytes can primarily be cultured or can be directly embedded into the matrix. Benefits of MACI include the ability to perform the surgery without suturing of the periosteum and avoiding all the complications associated with it.

One of the most promising representatives of MACI is a three dimensional hydrogel called Cartilage Regeneration System (CaReS), system based on collagen type I which has been prepared from rat tail tendons. Autologous chondrocytes are derived from a cartilage biopsy specimen and embedded into the matrix without any additional processing. Furthermore, CaRes implants are manufactured custom made in height and size thus providing an exact fit into the cartilage defect. Recent study (see footnote 92) showed that CaReS is clinically effective and leads to significant functional improvement and reduction of pain level.

---

[85]Bartlett et al. (2005).

[86]Sohn et al. (2002).

[87]Zaslav et al. (2009).

[88]Schneider et al. (2011).

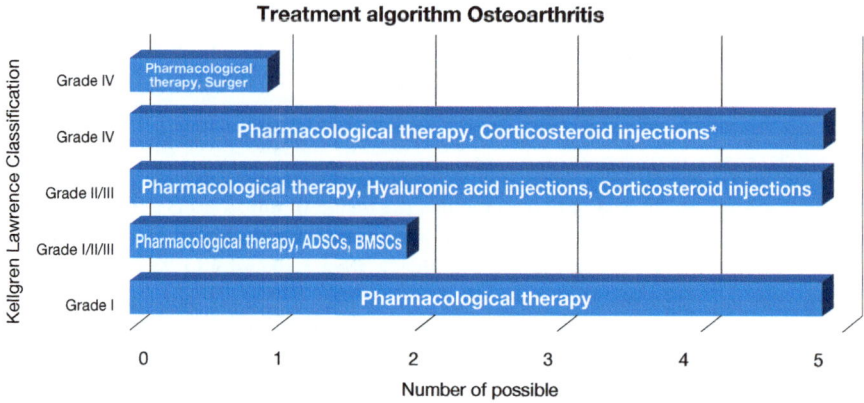

Fig. 3 Treatment algorithm for Osteoarthritis (∗treatment used only as a palliative option)

Literature reports various outcomes after ACI and MACI treatment. Patients undergoing ACI/MACI treatment have favorable mid to long-term results. A significantly higher treatment rate was found in the tibiofemoral joint compared with the patellofemoral joint.

2.7.2 Bone Marrow Mesenchymal Stem Cells

The lack of successful treatments for osteoarthritis often leads to arthroplasty in end stage. In recent years, there are numerous attempts to reveal less invasive treatment. Hence, different grades of OA require different therapeutical approach/es (Fig. 3).

The human body has a remarkable capacity to repair itself. Regenerative medicine has to support, stimulate, and enhance the body's natural repair mechanisms to help them heal defects that they could not normally heal on their own. Simultaneous action of cells, scaffolds, and growth factors play a crucial role in regenerative medicine and tissue engineering. In this regard various cell types have been investigated for their suitability in regenerative medicine, including adult mesenchymal stem cells (MSCs).[89] MSCs are undifferentiated biological cells that have a capacity for self-renewal and capability of proliferation and differentiation to various cell lineages.

Mesenchymal stem cells were first isolated from the bone marrow.[90] Bone marrow mesenchymal stem cells (BMSCs) have several unique features and can be used for both autologuos and allogenic therapy. Furthermore, studies showed the potential of BMSCs to differentiate into a variety of cells, including chondrocytes.[91]

---

[89]Wei et al. (2013).

[90]Friedenstein et al. (1976).

[91]Pittenger et al. (1999).

Preclinical studies showed that intra-articular injection of BMSCs resulted with regeneration of cartilage tissue in goats with surgically induced OA.[92] Moreover, BMSCs embedded into hyaluronan-based scaffold provided promising results in rabbits OA models.[93] A clinical study was conducted to compare outcomes of the first generation of ACI therapy with autologous BMSCs therapy. It showed that using BMSCs in cartilage repair is as effective as using chondrocytes for articular cartilage repairment. Moreover, it required 1 less knee surgery, reduced costs and minimized donor-site morbidity in comparison to first generation of ACI.[94] Several clinical trials are being conducted considering BMSCs and treatment of OA. One clinical trial showed in its early phase that patients with OA who underwent intra-articular administration of allogenic BMSCs have significantly lower level of pain than the placebo group. Furthermore, this effect is present both in the group that got a low dose of BMSCs administered (50×10^6 cells) aswell as in the group with a high dose of BMSCs administered (150×10^6 cells).[95] Another study[96] was conducted on 30 patients with chronic knee pain unresponsive to conservative treatments and showing radiological evidence of OA. Patients were randomized and divided into two groups. The test group was treated with allogenic BMSCs by intra-articular injection of 40×10^6 cells, while the control group received intra-articular injections of hyaluronic acid. Results showed significant improvement in pain and function levels over a period of 1 year aswell as a significant decrease in poor cartilage areas with cartilage quality improvements measured by MRI T2 relaxation. Although the mechanism of how BMSCs induce or promote cartilage regeneration is yet to be determined and studies are still in early phases without long-term follow-ups, currently published results are promising and endorse further research.[97]

2.7.3 Autologous Microfragmented Fat Tissue with Adipose Tissue-Derived Mesenchymal Stem Cells

In recent years, there has been plenty of evidence that suggests MSCs reside in perivascular niche,[98] hence these cells can be isolated from most of the tissues inside the body. Furthermore, perivascular cells, named pericytes posses stem cell-like qualities and could be precursors of MSCs.[99] Stem cells become highly clinically attractive because of their ability to differentiate into a variety of different cell

---

[92]Murphy et al. (2003).

[93]Grigolo et al. (2009).

[94]Nejadnik et al. (2010).

[95]Osiris Therapeutics Announces Positive One Year Data from Chondrogen Trial for Knee Repair (2007).

[96]Vega et al. (2015).

[97]Paschos and Sennett (2017).

[98]Lin and Lue (2013).

[99]Caplan (2008).

lineages and their capacity of paracrine secretion. They secrete many bioactive molecules and we can consider them as "mini- drugstores".[100] Paracrine secretion of a broad selection of cytokines, chemokines, and growth factors trigger trophic, anti-apoptotic, anti-inflammatory, proangiogenic, immunomodulatory, antimicrobial and anti-scarring effects (Fig. 4).

Because of its abundance, human adipose tissue has been introduced as a new source of multipotent stem cells.[101] Adipose tissue-derived stem cells (ADSCs) are considered to be ideal for application in regenerative therapy. Their main advantage is that they can be easily and repeatedly harvested using minimally invasive techniques. Further, their proliferation and differentiation potential stays on the same level with patient ageing.[102] ADSCs are routinely obtained enzymatically from fat lipoaspirate as stromal vascular fraction and/or may undergo prolonged ex vivo expansion. Unfortunately, such procedures lead to significant senescence and a decline in multipotency.[103] Furthermore, enzymatic treatment and/or cell expansion have complex regulatory issues. The clinical use of cell-based therapies in regenerative medicine should be effective and safe for the patients. Stem cell therapy is being regulated by different regulatory agencies worldwide (see footnote 106). The availability of a new minimally manipulated autologous adipose tissue harvesting technique as a therapeutic option has remarkable clinical relevance. Throughout the procedure, processed fat is subjected to only slight mechanical forces. Such product preserves the adipose structural niches and allows post-transplant availability of patient's own ADSCs. Further, because of the optimal size of clusters such products could be easily injected in joints. Current results suggest that the use of autologous and micro-fragmented adipose tissue in patients with knee OA significantly reduces the pain, improves cartilage GAG content and slows expected GAG decrease in the natural course of the disease.[104,105] The procedure is simple, economic, quick, minimally invasive, one-step and with low percentage of complications.

An important question is whether these cells could promote possible residual tumor cells to proliferate, differentiate, metastasize or even induce de novo carcinogenesis. No malignant behavior of human ADSCs has been reported in clinical studies so far.[106]

---

[100]Caplan and Correa (2011).

[101]Zuk et al. (2002).

[102]Stolzing et al. (2008).

[103]Tremolada et al. (2016).

[104]Koh et al. (2015).

[105]Hudetz et al. (2017).

[106]Centeno et al. (2010).

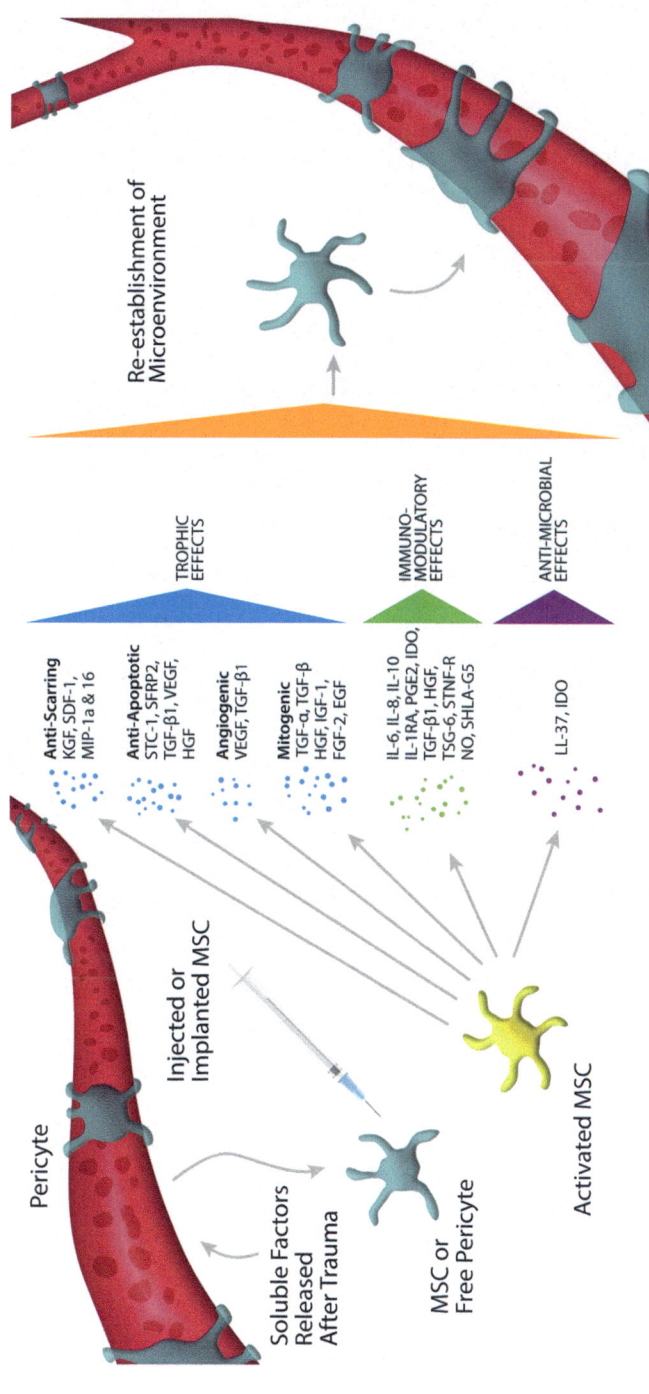

Fig. 4 The trophic, immunomodulatory and antimicrobial effect of mesenchymal stem sells or medicinal signalling cells (MSCs). Pericytes are stimulated by soluble growth factors and chemokines to become activated MSCs, which respond to the microenvironment by secreting trophic (mitogenic, angiogenic, anti-apoptotic or scar reduction), immunomodulatory or antimicrobial factors. After the microenvironment is re-established, MSCs return to their native pericyte state attached to blood vessels. Murphy BM, Moncivais K, Caplan IA. Experimental & Molecular Medicine (2013) 45, e54; https://doi.org/10.1038/emm.2013. 94 (Used with permission of Prof. Arnold I Caplan)

3   Imaging of the Articular Cartilage Repair

Postoperative imaging is necessary for assessing the technical success of the procedure and the state of cartilage healing, as well as for identifying potential complications. Radiography is limited by insensitivity to cartilage imaging. Ultrasonography
is unable to show the entire articular cartilage because of limited penetration through
the bone. Computed tomography is useful only after intra-articular contrast media
injection (arthrography), offers only evaluation of the cartilage surface but with the
harmful influence of ionizing radiation. Magnetic resonance (MR) imaging provides
non-invasive assessment of the cartilage changes and lesions as well as assessment
of the repair site and all other joint tissues. MR imaging is a less invasive method
than arthroscopy, and it allows a more comprehensive evaluation of repair tissue,
from the articular surface of the joint to the bone-cartilage interface. MR observation
of cartilage repair tissue is a well-established semi-quantitative scoring system for
repair tissue that has primarily been used in clinical research studies. MR imaging
techniques also can be used to depict the components of the extracellular matrix and
help assess the biochemical status of the reparative cartilage.[107,108,109]

MR imaging techniques used for evaluation of articular cartilage and cartilage
repair tissue can be divided into two main categories according to their possibilities
for morphologic or compositional evaluation. As for all cartilage imaging, 1.5-T,
3.0-T, and, for research, 7.0-T magnet systems with extremity coils are
recommended. To assess the structure of cartilage the same morphological MRI
technique are used for repair tissue and native cartilage: combination of cartilage-
sensitive sequences such as fat-suppressed 3D gradient-echo (GRE) and fluid-
sensitive sequences such as fat-suppressed proton-density–weighted, T2-weighted,
or intermediate-weighted fast spin-echo techniques, as recommended by the International Cartilage Repair Society[110,111] (Fig. 5).

The 3D GRE sequences with fat suppression or water excitation allow the
accurate depiction of the thickness and surface of cartilage, whereas the aforementioned fast spin-echo sequences outline the internal structure of cartilage and enable
detection of focal cartilage defects at higher sensitivity compared with GRE
sequences (Fig. 6). These techniques allow the detection of morphologic defects in
the articular cartilage and cartilage repair tissue and are commonly used for semi-
quantitative and quantitative assessments. Morphologic characteristics of joint cartilage are assessed in conjunction with those of other structures around the knee:
menisci, subchondral bone, osteophytes, and synovia. The parameters that can be
evaluated with MR imaging in assessment of cartilage repair include the degree of
defect filling, the extent of integration of repair tissue with adjacent tissues, the

---

[107]Potter and Foo (2006).

[108]Guermazi et al. (2015).

[109]Link et al. (2017).

[110]Bobic (2000).

[111]Schreiner et al. (2017).

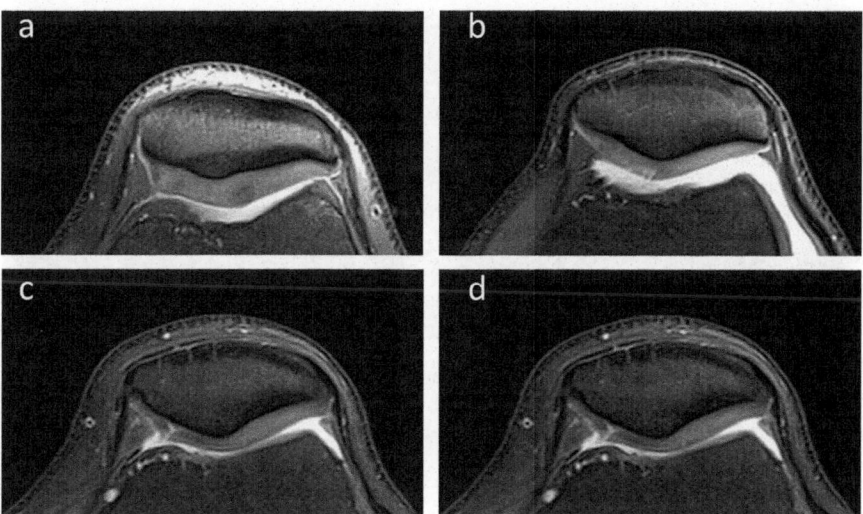

Fig. 5 (**a–d**) Axial PD fat saturated MR images shows different stages of cartilage damage according to International Cartilage Repair Society classification: (**a**) stage 1; (**b**) stage 2; (**c**) stage 3, (**d**) stage 4

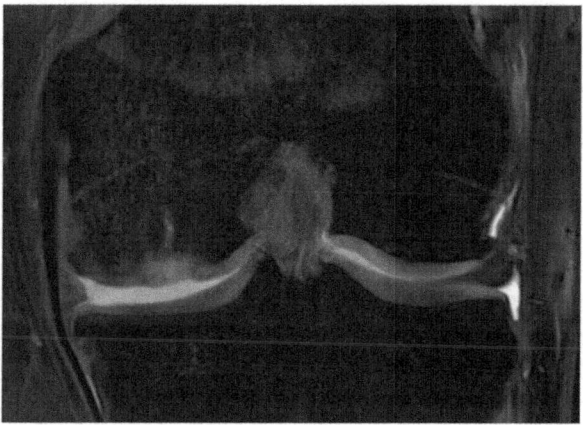

Fig. 6 Coronal 3D GRE MR image after medial femoral condyle microfracture shows that new fibrocartilaginous tissue completely filled with earlier defect, the surface of the "new" cartilage is wavy but is aligned with the surrounding cartilage

presence or absence of proud subchondral bone formation (extension of repair tissue beyond the adjacent subchondral plate to include new bone formation), the characteristics of the graft substance and surface (its structure and signal intensity), and the appearance of the underlying subchondral bone.

Ideally, the repair tissue should have the same thickness as the adjacent native cartilage, the articular surface should be smooth, should completely fill the defect

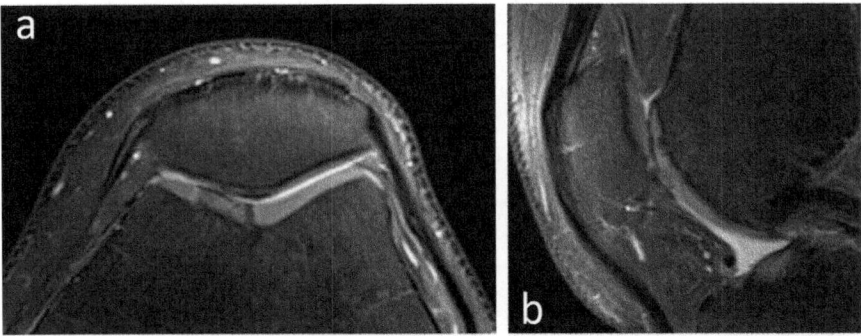

Fig. 7 Morphological appearance of the cartilage repair: (**a**) axial and (**b**) sagittal PD fat saturated MR images after femoral trochlea microfractures shows good result: new fibrocartilaginous tissue completely filled with earlier defect and is aligned with the surrounding cartilage without subchondral bone edema

and the margins of the repair tissue should be continuous with the adjacent native articular cartilage without gaps between the repair tissue and adjacent cartilage or between the repair tissue and adjacent bone.

The MOCART (MR observations of cartilage repair tissue) system has excellent interobserver reproducibility for scoring of the defined variables, and it is an effective method for standardized reporting of the imaging features of autologous chondrocyte implants. MOCART scores may be helpful in long-term follow-up of cartilage repair.[112]

The morphologic appearance of cartilage repair sites evolves over time. Complete filling of the defect can take several months to years (Fig. 7). The newly formed fibrocartilage is initially poorly organized and highly water permeable. In the early postoperative period, the repair tissue appears hyperintense to native cartilage on T2-weighted images, and, initially, the repair tissue may be difficult to differentiate from fluid or appear very thin. As the repair tissue matures, its signal intensity decreases and becomes hypointense to native cartilage. After 1 or 2 years, the repair tissue should have grown to fill the defect with a smooth and well-defined surface.[113]

Bone marrow edema in subchondral bone after micro/nanofractures or within the grafts and the surrounding bone is seen during the first 12 months and may persist for 3 years, but decrease in size and signal intensity during the time. With bone incorporation, the edema in the osteochondral plugs and surrounding bone resolves and the plugs are no longer different from the recipient bone.

Poorly filled defects and incomplete peripheral integration after 2 years are associated with poor functional outcomes. Persistent edema-like marrow signal intensity within subchondral bone beyond 18 months and subchondral cyst

---

[112]Marlovits et al. (2006).

[113]Choi et al. (2008).

formation are concerning and may be signs of poor tissue integration (see footnotes 112, 117).

Hyaline articular cartilage is composed of a fluid-filled macromolecular network that supports mechanical loads. This macromolecular network consists mainly of collagen and proteoglycans. Because collagen and proteoglycan-associated glycosaminoglycan are important to preserve the functional and structural integrity of cartilage, compositional MR imaging assessment of cartilage is focused on its molecular status, specifically on its collagen and glycosaminoglycan content.

To evaluate the collagen network and proteoglycan content in the knee cartilage matrix, compositional assessment techniques such as T2 mapping, delayed gadolinium-enhanced MR imaging of cartilage (or dGEMRIC), T1ρ imaging, sodium imaging, and diffusion-weighted imaging are available. These techniques may be used in various combinations and at various magnetic field strengths in clinical and research settings to improve the characterization of changes in cartilage (see footnote 115).

3.1 Delayed Gadolinium-Enhanced MR Imaging of Cartilage (dGEMRIC)

dGEMRIC is a molecular imaging technique that has been used to study GAG loss in the articular cartilage of patients with primary OA and after cartilage repair procedure. With dGEMRIC, T1-maps of hyaline cartilage are created following the intravenous (IV) administration of an anionic gadolinium-based contrast agent [Gd (DTPA)2-]. As cartilage matrix is largely composed of GAG molecules with negatively-charged carboxyl and sulfate groups, it repels the negatively charged contrast ions. Consequently, the gadolinium concentrations are higher in cartilage regions with low GAG concentrations, and the cartilage T1-relaxation time (T1gd) is reduced. The Gd-DTPA2- concentration per voxel is described by means of the dGEMRIC index (T1gd) which is calculated from the five different inversion times using a curve fitting method. In areas with low GAG the calculated T1gd will be low, and vice versa. The resulting dGEMRIC index (the average T1gd in a region of interest) is related to both the GAG concentration and the time between gadolinium administration and image acquisition (Fig. 8). Therefore, healthy cartilage containing an abundance of GAGs will have low concentrations of Gd(DTPA)2- whereas degraded cartilage will have high concentrations of the contrast agent in areas where GAGs have been lost. T1 relaxation times are inversely proportional to the concentration of Gd(DTPA)2-, and thus provide a quantitative metric of cartilage integrity (see footnote 115).[114]

For dGEMRIC study patient receive 0.2 mmol/Kg paramagnetic contrast media (Gd(DTPA)2), administered by slow IV infusion through a catheter placed in the

---

[114]Gray et al. (2008).

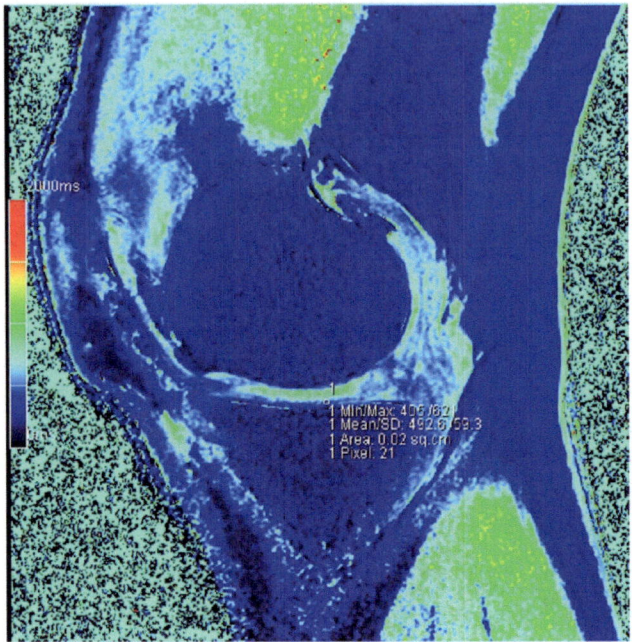

Fig. 8 Sagittal dGEMRIC image of the knee shows numbers that represents proteoglycans content of the femoral and tibial cartilage

antecubital vein. The contrast agent injection time must be less than 5 min followed by exercising by (walking up and down stairs) for approximately 10 min, starting 5 min after injection to promote delivery of the contrast agent to the joint. Post-contrast imaging of the cartilage must be performed with a delay of at least 90 min after contrast injection; delay is needed for penetration of the contrast agent into the cartilage. Although the 90-min delay is still required, this might increase the clinical applicability of the dGEMRIC technique. Drawbacks of dGEMRIC study are: the use of i. v. contrast agent administration in double dose of contrast agent, and time consuming because of at least 90 min delay of examination after contrast agent injection.[115,116,117]

In a dGEMRIC study in which microfracture and matrix-assisted autologous transplantation are compared, a significantly higher relative DR1 was found in microfracture repair tissue than in matrix-assisted autologous transplantation, which suggests that the GAG content is lower in the microfracture repair tissue, most probably fibrocartilage.[118]

---

[115]Young et al. (2005).

[116]Williams et al. (2004).

[117]Burstein et al. (2001).

[118]Trattnig et al. (2008).

Another dGEMRIC study found that the dGEMRIC index in matrix-assisted chondrocyte transplantation repair tissue was higher than that in microfracture repair tissue, presumably from higher extracellular matrix proteoglycan content.[119]

Maturation of autologous chondrocyte implantation repair tissue has also been demonstrated with the dGEMRIC, with a lower index in early postoperative tissue that increased to values similar to that of native cartilage after 1 year. The authors concluded that the time dependent changes indicate increasing extracellular matrix proteoglycans as the repair tissue matures.[120]

3.2 T2 Mapping

Value of T2 in hyaline articular cartilage reflects interactions between water molecules and surrounding macromolecules and is highly sensitive to alterations of the cartilage matrix.

In normal cartilage, differences in density and organization of the collagen matrix appear as variations in T2 values. A multiecho-SE technique is currently used to measure T2 values—quantitative T2 mapping provides objective data by generating either a color or a gray-scale map representing the variations in relaxation time within cartilage.[121] There is good evidence that T2 mapping is useful for identifying sites of early-stage degeneration (early disruption of the collagen matrix) in cartilage, which appear as areas with T2 higher than that of normal cartilage. Compared with the T2 values mapped in normal hyaline cartilage, those found in osteoarthritic cartilage are more heterogeneous.[122] Increased T2 is most commonly associated with cartilage damage; however, low-signal-intensity lesions that may be because of increased water interaction with molecular fragments in cartilage are seen in some cases. Although T2 maps can be used to differentiate normal areas of cartilage from areas of degeneration, there does not appear to be any linear relationship between T2 and osteoarthritis grade that could aid differentiation between mild and more severe disease.[123] T2 maps may be used to monitor the effectiveness of cartilage repair over time, with eventual success signaled by the emergence of a collagen network that has a shape and overall and zonal organization similar to those seen in normal cartilage.[124] In several studies laminar analysis with T2 mapping has shown differences between healthy cartilage and cartilage repair tissue in subjects after matrix-associated autologous chondrocyte transplantation. While healthy cartilage showed

---

[119]Trattnig et al. (2007).

[120]Kurkijärvi et al. (2007).

[121]Hesper et al. (2014).

[122]Dunn et al. (2004).

[123]Koff et al. (2007).

[124]Welsch et al. (2008a).

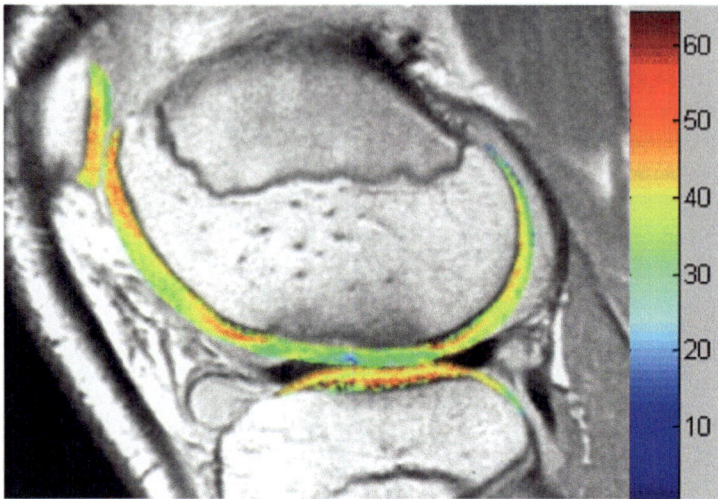

Fig. 9 T2 mapping image of the knee in sagittal plane after microfractures of the left femoral condyle shows increased water content in fibrocartilage tissue at the place of microfractures (green coloured area) than in surrounding cartilage as a sign of collagen matrix loss

a significant increase from deep to superficial cartilage zones, cartilage repair tissue did not show a significant stratification of T2 values.[125]

T2 measurements have also been shown to detect differences in cartilage repair tissue following different repair procedures. It is expected that after repair procedure, cartilage repair tissue develops a collagen network with a zonal organisation similar to normal hyaline cartilage over time. Welsch et al. compared cartilage T2 values after microfracture therapy and matrix-associated autologous chondrocyte transplantation (Fig. 9). The global mean T2 in the cartilage repair area was significantly lower in patients after microfracture, compared to matrix-associated autologous chondrocyte transplantation. Repair tissue after matrix-associated autologous chondrocyte transplantation showed a significant increase in T2 values from deep to superficial zones, however no such zonal variation was seen in repair tissue after microfracture. These findings correlated with histologic evaluation of repair tissue after microfracture and matrix-associated autologous chondrocyte transplantation, which have described a disorganized fibrocartilage after microfracture, while repair tissue after matrix-associated autologous chondrocyte transplantation being normal zonal collagen organisation.

Studies have suggested that zonal T2 mapping may be able to visualize the maturation process of cartilage repair tissue. T2 mapping showed promise for longitudinal monitoring of changes in cartilage (see footnote 128).

---

[125]Welsch et al. (2008b).

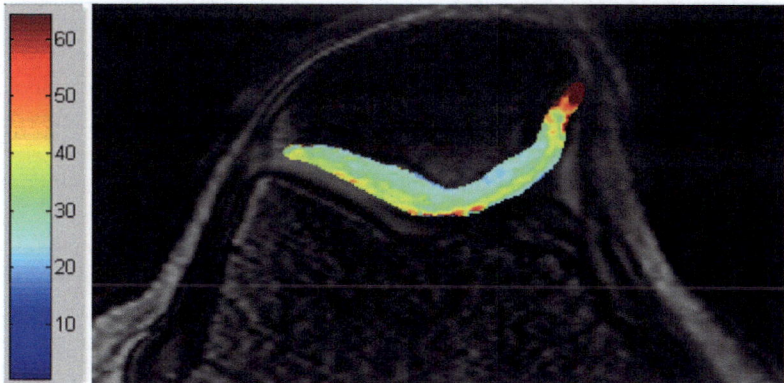

Fig. 10 Axial MR image of the patella in T1ρ technique shows alteration of normal T1ρ value in medial patellar facet cartilage (red coloured area) as a sign of proteoglycan reduction in cartilage lesion

3.3 T1ρ Imaging

The interactions between motion-restricted water molecules and their local macro-molecular environment can be monitored by measuring T1ρ values. Changes to the extracellular matrix, such as proteoglycan reduction, may alter T1ρ values measured in cartilage. In the osteoarthritic knee, damaged hyaline cartilage demonstrates higher T1ρ values than normal cartilage, and T1ρ imaging has higher sensitivity than T2-weighted imaging for differentiating between normal cartilage and early-stage osteoarthritis (Fig. 10). Some other factors other than proteoglycan reduction may contribute to variations in T1ρ values; these factors include collagen fiber orientation and concentration and the concentration of other macromolecules.[126,127]

T1ρ has been studied for longitudinal evaluation of microfracture repair tissue. T1ρ and T2 values in repair tissue were longer than those in native cartilage, 3–6 months after surgery. After 1 year, however, the difference between native cartilage and repair tissue decreased and remained significant only for the T1ρ measurements. A zonal distribution with higher T1ρ and T2 values in the superficial layers of repair tissue was demonstrated in this study, with the difference maintained after 1 year only with T1ρ measurements. The authors concluded that T1ρ might complement T2 relaxation time in the assessment of repair tissue maturation (see footnote 112).[128,129]

---

[126]Duvvuri et al. (2001).

[127]Mlynarik et al. (1999).

[128]Amano et al. (2017).

[129]Holtzman et al. (2010).

3.4 Sodium (23Na) Imaging

Normal hyaline cartilage that is glycosaminoglycan-rich has high concentrations of sodium, and areas of cartilage with glycosaminoglycan depletion have lower concentrations. Because sodium possesses a nuclear spin momentum, it has a specific resonance frequency that is measurable at MR imaging without intravenous contrast administration.

Sodium MR imaging has shown promising results in the compositional assessment of articular cartilage. The advantages of the technique are that sodium occurs naturally in the cartilage matrix, that the signal intensity of cartilage is high in comparison with that of the background, and that sodium MR imaging can depict regions of proteoglycan depletion, which exhibit lower signal intensity than do areas of normal cartilage. Therefore, sodium imaging may be useful for differentiating between early-stage degenerated cartilage and normal cartilage.

Sodium MRI has limited clinical applicability because it requires dedicated coils, and, because of limited signal-to-noise ratio, requires 3T or higher MR field strength. While sodium MRI has shown great promise, further technical improvements are necessary to incorporation sodium MRI into a clinical feasible method.[130]

A study involving long-term follow-up (7.9 years) of autologous osteochondral transplantation showed that sodium imaging with 7.0-T MR imaging could help differentiate between repair tissue and the native cartilage. However, results of sodium imaging with 7.0-T MR imaging did not correlate with clinical outcomes determined with Lysholm and Visual Analogue Scale scores.[131]

In a study following matrix-assisted chondrocyte transplantation, sodium imaging showed differences between normal articular cartilage and matrix-assisted chondrocyte transplantation repair tissue and good correlation with dGEMRIC, which indicates that both methods are similarly GAG specific.[132]

A pilot study that evaluated microfracture and matrix-assisted chondrocyte transplantation with sodium imaging found higher GAG content after matrix-assisted chondrocyte transplantation, which is suggestive of better-quality repair tissue.[133]

3.5 Diffusion-Weighted Imaging

Diffusion-weighted imaging (DWI) provides the ability to map diffusion of water and therefore enables analysis of cartilage extracellular matrix microarchitecture. Increased mobility of water is seen in degenerated cartilage and repair cartilage tissue.

---

[130]Wang et al. (2009).

[131]Krusche-Mandl et al. (2012).

[132]Trattnig et al. (2010).

[133]Zbýň et al. (2012).

Diffusion tensor imaging (DTI) is a DWI-based technique that evaluates the direction of water mobility in the extracellular matrix. The microarchitecture of normal cartilage causes anisotropic (directionally dependent) water diffusion. A change in anisotropy can indicate changes in collagen architecture, seen in degenerated and repair cartilage tissue. DTI has been shown to be able to detect and grade early cartilage damage, too. Measurement of diffusion anisotropy also provides information on mechanical function of articular cartilage and on the transport of nutrients to the chondrocytes and for the removal of their metabolic waste product. A limitation of DTI is that it is time-consuming to acquire and process data.[134,135,136]

A study which compare DWI of the ankle in patients after matrix-associated autologous chondrocyte transplantation and microfracturing of the talar dome found that DWI showed revealed significant differences between both study groups that indicate that these two repair procedures resulted in different cartilage repair tissue quality, as described previously in histological studies, although the morphological scoring and the clinical scoring was nearly identical between those two groups of patients.[137]

3.6   Glycosaminoglycan CEST

Chemical exchange dependent saturation transfer (CEST) imaging is the newest compositional cartilage imaging technique. The glycosaminoglycan (GAG) chemical exchange saturation transfer (CEST) imaging method (gagCEST) makes it possible to assess and quantify the GAG concentration in human cartilage. This biochemical imaging technique facilitates detection of the loss of GAG in the course of osteoarthritis. The gagCEST technique was used to analyse the peri-lesional zone (PLZ) adjacent to repair tissue after cartilage repair surgery, to determine whether there are biochemical changes present in the sense of degeneration.

Some publications suggested that gagCEST does not lead to accurate quantification of glycosaminoglycan content in healthy or degenerated cartilage at 3T. This may limit the clinical applicability of this technology to 7T MRI, which is a research tool and not clinically feasible.[138,139] Long-term results 8 years after autologous osteochondral transplantation (see footnote 135) show that GagCEST imaging indicated reduced GAG content in repair sites compared to native cartilage, which is confirmed by a correlation between the results from other imaging methods.

---

[134]Raya et al. (2013).

[135]Raya (2015).

[136]Binks et al. (2013).

[137]Apprich et al. (2012).

[138]Singh et al. (2012).

[139]Koller et al. (2017).

References

Abramson SB (2008) Osteoarthritis and nitric oxide. Osteoarthr Cartil 16(Suppl 2):S15–S20. https://doi.org/10.1016/s1063-4584(08)60008-4

Aigner T, Schmitz N (2011) Pathogenesis and pathology of osteoarthritis. In: Hochberg M, Silman A, Smolen J, Weinblatt M, Weisman M (eds) Rheumatology, 5th edn. Mosby Elsevier, Philadelphia, pp 1741–1759

Altman R, Manjoo A, Fierlinger A, Niazi F, Nicholls M (2015) The mechanism of action for hyaluronic acid treatment in the osteoarthritic knee: a systematic review. BMC Musculoskelet Disord 16:321

Amano K, Li AK, Pedoia V, Koff MF, Krych AJ, Link TM et al (2017) Effects of surgical factors on cartilage can be detected using quantitative magnetic resonance imaging after anterior cruciate ligament reconstruction. Am J Sports Med 45(5):1075–1084

American Academy of Orthopaedic Surgeons (2013) Treatment of osteoarthritis of the knee, 2nd edn. American Academy of Orthopaedic Surgeons, Rosemont

Apprich S, Trattnig S, Welsch GH, Noebauer-Huhmann IM, Sokolwski M, Hirschfeld C et al (2012) Assessment of articular cartilage repair tissue after matrix-associated autologous chondrocyte transplantation or the microfracture technique in the ankle joint using diffusion-weighted imaging at 3 Tesla. Osteoarthr Cartil 20(7):703–711

Arroll B, Goodyear-Smith F (2004) Corticosteroid injections for osteoarthritis of the knee: meta-analysis. BMJ 328(7444):869

Bartlett W, Skinner JA, Gooding CR, Carrington RWJ, Flanagan AM, Briggs TWR, Bentley G (2005) Autologous chondrocyte implantation versus matrix-induced autologous chondrocyte implantation for osteochondral defects of the knee: a prospective, randomised study. Bone Joint J 87(5):640–645

Bassleer C, Rovati L, Franchimont P (1998) Stimulation of proteglycan production by glucosamine sulfate in chondrocite isolated from human osteoarthritic cartilage in vitro. Osteoarthr Cartil 6 (6):427–434

Bellamy N, Campbell J, Welch V, Gee TL, Bourne R, Wells GA (2006) Viscosupplementation for the treatment of osteoarthritis of the knee. Cochrane Database Syst Rev (2): CD005321. https://doi.org/10.1002/14651858.CD005321.pub2

Bhosale AM, Richardson JB (2008) Articular cartilage: structure, injuries and review of management. Br Med Bull 87(1):77–95

Binks DA, Hodgson RJ, Ries ME, Foster RJ, Smye SW, McGonagle D, Radjenovic A (2013) Quantitative parametric MRI of articular cartilage: a review of progress and open challenges. Br J Radiol 86(1023):20120163

Bobic V (2000) ICRS articular cartilage imaging committee. ICRS MR imaging protocol for knee articular cartilage. International Cartilage Repair Society, Wetzikon, Switzerland, p 12

Bonnet CS, Walsh DA (2005) Osteoarthritis, angiogenesis and inflammation. Rheumatology (Oxford) 44(1):7–16. https://doi.org/10.1093/rheumatology/keh344

Borrione P, Di Gianfrancesco A, Pereira MT, Pigozzi F (2010) Platelet-rich plasma in muscle healing. Am J Phys Med Rehabil 89(10):854–861

Brittberg M, Winalski CS (2003) Evaluation of cartilage injuries and repair. J Bone Joint Surg Am 85(suppl 2):58–69

Brittberg M, Lindahl A, Nilsson A, Ohlsson C, Isaksson O, Peterson L (1994) Treatment of deep cartilage defects in the knee with autologous chondrocyte transplantation. N Engl J Med 331 (14):889–895

Burrage PS, Brinckerhoff CE (2007) Molecular targets in osteoarthritis: metalloproteinases and their inhibitors. Curr Drug Targets 8(2):293–303

Burstein D, Velyvis J, Scott KT, Stock KW, Kim YJ, Jaramillo D et al (2001) Protocol issues for delayed Gd (DTPA) 2–-enhanced MRI (dGEMRIC) for clinical evaluation of articular cartilage. Magn Reson Med 45(1):36–41

Camp CL, Stuart MJ, Krych AJ (2014) Current concepts of articular cartilage restoration techniques in the knee. Sports Health 6(3):265–273

Caplan AI (2008) All MSCs are pericytes? Cell Stem Cell 3(3):229–230

Caplan AI, Correa D (2011) The MSC: an injury drugstore. Cell Stem Cell 9(1):11–15

Centeno CJ, Schultz JR, Cheever M, Robinson B, Freeman M, Marasco W (2010) Safety and complications reporting on the re-implantation of culture-expanded mesenchymal stem cells using autologous platelet lysate technique. Curr Stem Cell Res Ther 5(1):81–93

Chan PS, Caron JP, Orth MW (2006) Short-term gene expression changes in cartilage explants stimulated with interleukin beta plus glucosamine and chondroitin sulfate. J Rheumatol 33:1329–1340

Choi YS, Potter HG, Chun TJ (2008) MR imaging of cartilage repair in the knee and ankle. Radiographics 28(4):1043–1059

Clancy R (1999) Nitric oxide alters chondrocyte function by disrupting cytoskeletal signaling complexes. Osteoarthr Cartil 7(4):399–400. https://doi.org/10.1053/joca.1998.0223

Clegg DO, Reda DJ, Harris CL, Klein MA, O'Dell JR, Hooper MM et al (2006) Glucosamine, chondroitin sulfate, and the two in combination for painful knee osteoarthritis. N Engl J Med 354(8):795–808

Davies-Tuck ML, Wluka AE, Forbes A, Wang Y, English DR, Giles GG et al (2010) Development of bone marrow lesions is associated with adverse effects on knee cartilage while resolution is associated with improvement-a potential target for prevention of knee osteoarthritis: a longitudinal study. Arthritis Res Ther 12(1):1

Dieppe P (2011) Developments in osteoarthritis. Rheumatology 50(2):245–247

Dougados M (2000) Sodium hyaluronate therapy in osteoarthritis: arguments for a potential beneficial structural effect. Semin Arthritis Rheum 30(2 Suppl 1):19–25

du Souich P, García AG, Vergés J, Montell E (2009) Immunomodulatory and anti-inflammatory effects of chondroitin sulphate. J Cell Mol Med 13(8a):1451–1463

Dumond H, Presle N, Terlain B, Mainard D, Loeuille D, Netter P, Pottie P (2003) Evidence for a key role of leptin in osteoarthritis. Arthritis Rheum 48(11):3118–3129. https://doi.org/10.1002/art.11303

Dunn TC, Lu Y, Jin H, Ries MD, Majumdar S (2004) T2 relaxation time of cartilage at MR imaging: comparison with severity of knee osteoarthritis. Radiology 232(2):592–598

Duvvuri U, Charagundla SR, Kudchodkar SB, Kaufman JH, Kneeland JB, Rizi R et al (2001) Human knee: in vivo T1ρ-weighted MR imaging at 1.5 T—preliminary experience. Radiology 220(3):822–826

Ehrenfest DMD, Andia I, Zumstein MA, Zhang CQ, Pinto NR, Bielecki T (2014) Classification of platelet concentrates (Platelet-Rich Plasma-PRP, Platelet-Rich Fibrin-PRF) for topical and infiltrative use in orthopedic and sports medicine: current consensus, clinical implications and perspectives. Muscles Ligaments Tendons J 4(1):3

Elmorsy S, Funakoshi T, Sasazawa F, Todoh M, Tadano S, Iwasaki N (2014) Chondroprotective effects of high-molecular-weight cross-linked hyaluronic acid in a rabbit knee osteoarthritis model. Osteoarthr Cartil 22(1):121–127

Fan Z, Bau B, Yang H, Aigner T (2004) IL-1beta induction of IL-6 and LIF in normal articular human chondrocytes involves the ERK, p38 and NFKappaB signaling pathways. Cytokine 28 (1):17–24. https://doi.org/10.1016/j.cyto.2004.06.003

Fanghänel J, Pera F, Anderhuber F, Nitsch R (2009) Waldeyerova anatomija čovjeka. Golden marketing - Tehnička knjiga, Zagreb

Felson DT, McLaughlin S, Goggins J, LaValley MP, Gale ME, Totterman S et al (2003) Bone marrow edema and its relation to progression of knee osteoarthritis. Ann Intern Med 139 (5_Part_1):330–336

Filardo G, Kon E, Di Martino A, Di Matteo B, Merli ML, Cenacchi A et al (2012) Platelet-rich plasma vs hyaluronic acid to treat knee degenerative pathology: study design and preliminary results of a randomized controlled trial. BMC Musculoskelet Disord 13(1):229

Forsey R, Fisher J, Thompson J, Stone M, Bell C, Ingham E (2006) The effect of hyaluronic acid and phospholipid based lubricants on friction within a human cartilage damage model. Biomaterials 27(26):4581–4590

Friedenstein AJ, Gorskaja JF, Kulagina NN (1976) Fibroblast precursors in normal and irradiated mouse hematopoietic organs. Exp Hematol 4(5):267–274

Gray ML, Burstein D, Kim YJ, Maroudas A (2008) 2007 Elizabeth Winston Lanier Award Winner. Magnetic resonance imaging of cartilage glycosaminoglycan: basic principles, imaging technique, and clinical applications. J Orthop Res 26(3):281–291

Grigolo B, Lisignoli G, Desando G, Cavallo C, Marconi E, Tschon M et al (2009) Osteoarthritis treated with mesenchymal stem cells on hyaluronan-based scaffold in rabbit. Tissue Eng Part C Methods 15(4):647–658

Guermazi A, Roemer FW, Alizai H, Winalski CS, Welsch G, Brittberg M, Trattnig S (2015) State of the art: MR imaging after knee cartilage repair surgery. Radiology 277(1):23–43

Hangody L, Vásárhelyi G, Hangody LR, Sükösd Z, Tibay G, Bartha L, Bodó G (2008) Autologous osteochondral grafting—technique and long-term results. Injury 39(1):32–39

Harnly HW (2007) Microfracture: indications, technique, and results. Instr Course Lect 56:419–428

Heijink A, Gomoll AH, Madry H, Drobnič M, Filardo G, Espregueira-Mendes J, Van Dijk CN (2012) Biomechanical considerations in the pathogenesis of osteoarthritis of the knee. Knee Surg Sports Traumatol Arthrosc 20(3):423–435

Hesper T, Hosalkar HS, Bittersohl D, Welsch GH, Krauspe R, Zilkens C, Bittersohl B (2014) T2* mapping for articular cartilage assessment: principles, current applications, and future prospects. Skelet Radiol 43(10):1429–1445

Hiraoka N, Takahashi Y, Arai K, Honjo S, Nakawaga S, Tsuchida S et al (2009) Hyaluronan and intermittent hydrostatic pressure synergistically suppressed MMP-13 and Il-6 expressions in osteoblasts from OA subchondral bone. Osteoarthr Cartil 17(1):S97

Hochberg MC, Zhan M, Langenberg P (2008) The rate of decline of joint space width in patients with osteoarthritis of the knee: a systematic review and meta-analysis of randomized placebo-controlled trials of chondroitin sulfate. Curr Med Res Opin 24:3029–3035

Holtzman DJ, Theologis AA, Carballido-Gamio J, Majumdar S, Li X, Benjamin C (2010) T1ρ and T2 quantitative magnetic resonance imaging analysis of cartilage regeneration following microfracture and mosaicplasty cartilage resurfacing procedures. J Magn Reson Imaging 32 (4):914–923

Hudetz D, Borić I, Rod E, Jeleč Ž, Radić A, Vrdoljak T et al (2017) The effect of intra-articular injection of autologous microfragmented fat tissue on proteoglycan synthesis in patients with knee osteoarthritis. Genes 8(10):270

Hunter DJ, Zhang Y, Niu J, Goggins J, Amin S, LaValley MP et al (2006) Increase in bone marrow lesions associated with cartilage loss: a longitudinal magnetic resonance imaging study of knee osteoarthritis. Arthritis Rheum 54(5):1529–1535

Julovi SM, Yasuda T, Shimizu M, Hiramitsu T, Nakamura T (2004) Inhibition of interleukin-1beta-stimulated production of matrix metalloproteinases by hyaluronan via CD44 in human articular cartilage. Arthritis Rheum 50(2):516–525

Jüni P, Hari R, Rutjes AWS, Fischer R, Silletta MG, Reichenbach S, da Costa BR (2015) Intra-articular corticosteroid for knee osteoarthritis. Cochrane Database Syst Rev 22(10):CD005328. https://doi.org/10.1002/14651858.CD005328.pub3

Junqueira LC, Carneiro J (2005) Osnove histologije. Školska knjiga, Zagreb

Kobayashi K, Matsuzaka S, Yoshida Y, Miyauchi S, Wada Y, Moriya H (2004) The effects of intraarticularly injected sodium hyaluronate on levels of intact aggrecan and nitric oxide in the joint fluid of patients with knee osteoarthritis. Osteoarthr Cartil 12(7):536–542

Koff MF, Amrami KK, Kaufman KR (2007) Clinical evaluation of T2 values of patellar cartilage in patients with osteoarthritis. Osteoarthr Cartil 15(2):198–204

Koh YG, Choi YJ, Kwon SK, Kim YS, Yeo JE (2015) Clinical results and second-look arthroscopic findings after treatment with adipose-derived stem cells for knee osteoarthritis. Knee Surg Sports Traumatol Arthrosc 23(5):1308–1316

Koller U, Apprich S, Schmitt B, Windhager R, Trattnig S (2017) Evaluating the cartilage adjacent to the site of repair surgery with glycosaminoglycan-specific magnetic resonance imaging. Int Orthop 41(5):969–974

Kon E, Buda R, Filardo G, Di Martino A, Timoncini A, Cenacchi A et al (2010) Platelet-rich plasma: intra-articular knee injections produced favorable results on degenerative cartilage lesions. Knee Surg Sports Traumatol Arthrosc 18(4):472–479. https://doi.org/10.1007/s00167-009-0940-8

Kreuz PC, Erggelet C, Steinwachs MR, Krause SJ, Lahm A, Niemeyer P et al (2006a) Is microfracture of chondral defects in the knee associated with different results in patients aged 40 years or younger? Arthroscopy 22(11):1180–1186

Kreuz PC, Steinwachs MR, Erggelet C, Krause SJ, Konrad G, Uhl M, Südkamp N (2006b) Results after microfracture of full-thickness chondral defects in different compartments in the knee. Osteoarthr Cartil 14(11):1119–1125

Krusche-Mandl I, Schmitt B, Zak L, Apprich S, Aldrian S, Juras V et al (2012) Long-term results 8 years after autologous osteochondral transplantation: 7 T gagCEST and sodium magnetic resonance imaging with morphological and clinical correlation. Osteoarthr Cartil 20(5):357–363

Kurkijärvi JE, Mattila L, Ojala RO, Vasara AI, Jurvelin JS, Kiviranta I, Nieminen MT (2007) Evaluation of cartilage repair in the distal femur after autologous chondrocyte transplantation using T2 relaxation time and dGEMRIC. Osteoarthr Cartil 15(4):372–378

Lajeunesse D, Delalandre A, Martel-Pelletier J, Pelletier J-P (2003) Hyaluronic acid reverses the abnormal synthetic activity of human osteoarthritic subchondral bone osteoblasts. Bone 33 (4):703–710

Lee YH, Woo JH, Choi SJ, Ji JD, Song GG (2010) Effect of glucosamine or chondroitin sulfate on the osteoarthritis progression: a meta-analysis. Rheumatol Int 30:357–363

Leeb BF, Schweitzer H, Montag K, Smolen JS (2000) A metaanalysis of chondroitin sulfate in the treatment of osteoarthritis. J Rheumatol 27:205–211

Lin CS, Lue TF (2013) Defining vascular stem cells. Stem Cells Dev 22(7):1018–1026

Link TM, Neumann J, Li X (2017) Prestructural cartilage assessment using MRI. J Magn Reson Imaging 45(4):949–965

Liu D, Ahmet A, Ward L, Krishnamoorthy P, Mandelcorn ED, Leigh R et al (2013) A practical guide to the monitoring and management of the complications of systemic corticosteroid therapy. Allergy Asthma Clin Immunol 9(1):30

Loeser RF (2003) Systemic and local regulation of articular cartilage metabolism: where does leptin fit in the puzzle? Arthritis Rheum 48(11):3009–3012. https://doi.org/10.1002/art.11315

Lopes Junior OV, Inacio AM (2013) Use of glucosamine and chondroitin to treat osteoarthritis: a review of the literature. Rev Bras Ortop 48(4):300–306

Lu HT, Sheu MT, Lin YF, Lan J, Chin YP, Hsieh MS et al (2013) Injectable hyaluronic-acid-doxycycline hydrogel therapy in experimental rabbit osteoarthritis. BMC Vet Res 9:68

Marlovits S, Singer P, Zeller P, Mandl I, Haller J, Trattnig S (2006) Magnetic resonance observation of cartilage repair tissue (MOCART) for the evaluation of autologous chondrocyte transplantation: determination of interobserver variability and correlation to clinical outcome after 2 years. Eur J Radiol 57(1):16–23

Marmotti A, Rossi R, Castoldi F, Roveda E, Michielon G, Peretti GM (2015) PRP and articular cartilage: a clinical update. Biomed Res Int 2015:542502

Martel-Pelletier J, Kwan Tat S, Pelletier JP (2010) Effects of chondroitin sulfate in the pathophysiology of the osteoarthritic joint: a narrative review. Osteoarthr Cartil 18(Suppl 1):S7–S11

McCarty M (1994) The neglect of glucosamine as treatment for osteoarthritis. A personal perspective. Med Hypotheses 42(5):323–327

McDonough AL (1982) Effects of corticosteroids on articular cartilage: a review of the literature. Phys Ther 62(6):835–839

Meenagh GK, Patton J, Kynes C, Wright GD (2004) A randomised controlled trial of intra-articular corticosteroid injection of the carpometacarpal joint of the thumb in osteoarthritis. Ann Rheum Dis 63(10):1260–1263

Miller BS, Steadman JR, Briggs KK, Rodrigo JJ, Rodkey WG (2004) Patient satisfaction and outcome after microfracture of the degenerative knee. J Knee Surg 17(01):13–17

Mlynarik V, Trattnig S, Huber M, Zembsch A, Imhof H (1999) The role of relaxation times in monitoring proteoglycan depletion in articular cartilage. J Magn Reson Imaging 10(4):497–502

Murphy JM, Fink DJ, Hunziker EB, Barry FP (2003) Stem cell therapy in a caprine model of osteoarthritis. Arthritis Rheum 48(12):3464–3474

Nejadnik H, Hui JH, Feng Choong EP, Tai BC, Lee EH (2010) Autologous bone marrow–derived mesenchymal stem cells versus autologous chondrocyte implantation: an observational cohort study. Am J Sports Med 38(6):1110–1116

Neogi T, Felson D, Niu J, Lynch J, Nevitt M, Guermazi A et al (2009) Cartilage loss occurs in the same subregions as subchondral bone attrition: a within-knee subregion-matched approach from the multicenter osteoarthritis study. Arthritis Care Res 61(11):1539–1544

Osiris Therapeutics Announces Positive One Year (2007) Data from Chondrogen Trial for Knee Repair, Osiris Therapeutics. Inc., Ref. Type: Internet Communication

Paschos NK, Sennett ML (2017) Update on mesenchymal stem cell therapies for cartilage disorders. World J Orthop 8(12):853

Peyron JG, Altman R (1992) Osteoarthritis: diagnosis and management. In: Howell DS, Moskowitz RW, Goldberg VM, Mankin HJ (eds) The epidemiology of osteoarthritis, vol 2. Saunders, Philadelphia, p 15

Pittenger MF, Mackay AM, Beck SC, Jaiswal RK, Douglas R, Mosca JD et al (1999) Multilineage potential of adult human mesenchymal stem cells. Science 284(5411):143–147

Potter HG, Foo LF (2006) Magnetic resonance imaging of articular cartilage: trauma, degeneration, and repair. Am J Sports Med 34(4):661–677

Primorac D (1995) Reduced type II collagen mRNA in nanomelic cultured chondrocytes: an example of extracellular matrix/collagen feedback regulation? Croat Med J 36:85–92

Primorac D, Stover ML, Clark SH, Rowe DW (1994) Molecular basis of nanomelia, a heritable chondrodystrophy of chicken. Matrix Biol 14(4):297–305

Raya JG (2015) Techniques and applications of in vivo diffusion imaging of articular cartilage. J Magn Reson Imaging 41(6):1487–1504

Raya JG, Melkus G, Adam-Neumair S, Dietrich O, Mützel E, Reiser MF et al (2013) Diffusion-tensor imaging of human articular cartilage specimens with early signs of cartilage damage. Radiology 266(3):831–841

Reginster JY, Deroisy R, Rovati LC, Lee RL, Lejeune E, Bruyere O et al (2001) Long term effects of glucosamine sulphate on osteoarthritis progression: a randomised, placebo controlled clinical trial. Lancet 357(9252):251–256

Richmond J, Hunter D, Irrgang J et al (2009) Treatment of osteoarthritis of the knee (nonarthroplasty). J Am Acad Orthop Surg 17:591–600

Richy F, Bruyere O, Ethgen O, Cucherat M, Henrotin Y, Reginster JY (2003) Structural and symptomatic efficacy of glucosamine and chondroitin in knee osteoarthritis: a comprehensive meta-analysis. Arch Intern Med 163(13):1514–1522

Roman-Blas JA, Herrero-Beaumont G (2014) Targeting subchondral bone in osteoporotic osteo-arthritis. Arthritis Res Ther 16(6):494. https://doi.org/10.1186/s13075-014-0494-0

Ronca F, Palmieri L, Panicucci P, Ronca G (1998) Anti-inflammatory activity of chondroitin sulfate. Osteoarthr Cartil 6(Suppl A):14–21

Sakkas LI, Platsoucas CD (2007) The role of T cells in the pathogenesis of osteoarthritis. Arthritis Rheum 56(2):409–424. https://doi.org/10.1002/art.22369

Sasaki A, Sasaki K, Konttinen YT, Santavirta S, Takahara M, Takei H et al (2004) Hyaluronate inhibits the interleukin-1beta-induced expression of matrix metalloproteinase (MMP)-1 and MMP-3 in human synovial cells. Tohoku J Exp Med 204(2):99–107

Schneider U, Rackwitz L, Andereya S, Siebenlist S, Fensky F, Reichert J et al (2011) A prospective multicenter study on the outcome of type I collagen hydrogel–based autologous chondrocyte implantation (CaReS) for the repair of articular cartilage defects in the knee. Am J Sports Med 39(12):2558–2565

Schreiner MM, Mlynarik V, Zbýň Š, Szomolanyi P, Apprich S, Windhager R, Trattnig S (2017) New technology in imaging cartilage of the ankle. Cartilage 8(1):31–41

Singh A, Haris M, Cai K, Kassey VB, Kogan F, Reddy D et al (2012) Chemical exchange saturation transfer magnetic resonance imaging of human knee cartilage at 3 T and 7 T. Magn Reson Med 68(2):588–594

Sohn DH, Lottman LM, Lum LY, Kim SG, Pedowitz RA, Coutts RD, Sah RL (2002) Effect of gravity on localization of chondrocytes implanted in cartilage defects. Clin Orthop Relat Res 394:254–262

Stannus O, Jones G, Cicuttini F, Parameswaran V, Quinn S, Burgess J, Ding C (2010) Circulating levels of IL-6 and TNF-alpha are associated with knee radiographic osteoarthritis and knee cartilage loss in older adults. Osteoarthr Cartil 18(11):1441–1447. https://doi.org/10.1016/j.joca.2010.08.016

Steadman JR, Rodkey WG, Rodrigo JJ (2001) Microfracture: surgical technique and rehabilitation to treat chondral defects. Clin Orthop Relat Res 391:S362–S369

Steadman JR, Briggs KK, Rodrigo JJ, Kocher MS, Gill TJ, Rodkey WG (2003) Outcomes of microfracture for traumatic chondral defects of the knee: average 11-year follow-up. Arthroscopy 19(5):477–484

Steadman JR, Rodkey WG, Briggs KK (2010) Microfracture: its history and experience of the developing surgeon. Cartilage 1(2):78–86

Stolzing A, Jones E, McGonagle D, Scutt A (2008) Age-related changes in human bone marrow-derived mesenchymal stem cells: consequences for cell therapies. Mech Ageing Dev 129 (3):163–173

Tat SK, Pelletier JP, Vergés J, Lajeunesse D, Montell E, Fahmi H et al (2007) Chondroitin and glucosamine sulfate in combination decrease the pro-resorptive properties of human osteoarthritis subchondral bone osteoblasts: a basic science study. Arthritis Res Ther 9:R117

Tetteh ES, Bajaj S, Ghodadra NS, Cole BJ (2012) The basic science and surgical treatment options for articular cartilage injuries of the knee. J Orthop Sports Phys Ther 42(3):243–253

Towheed TE, Maxwell L, Judd MG et al (2006) Acetaminophen for osteoarthritis. Cochrane Database Syst Rev:D4257

Trattnig S, Marlovits S, Gebetsroither S, Szomolanyi P, Welsch GH, Salomonowitz E et al (2007) Three-dimensional delayed gadolinium-enhanced MRI of cartilage (dGEMRIC) for in vivo evaluation of reparative cartilage after matrix-associated autologous chondrocyte transplantation at 3.0 T: preliminary results. J Magn Reson Imaging 26(4):974–982

Trattnig S, Mamisch TC, Pinker K, Domayer S, Szomolanyi P, Marlovits S et al (2008) Differentiating normal hyaline cartilage from post-surgical repair tissue using fast gradient echo imaging in delayed gadolinium-enhanced MRI (dGEMRIC) at 3 Tesla. Eur Radiol 18(6):1251–1259

Trattnig S, Welsch GH, Juras V, Szomolanyi P, Mayerhoefer ME, Stelzeneder D et al (2010) 23Na MR imaging at 7 T after knee matrix–associated autologous chondrocyte transplantation preliminary results. Radiology 257(1):175–184

Tremolada C, Colombo V, Ventura C (2016) Adipose tissue and mesenchymal stem cells: state of the art and Lipogems® technology development. Curr Stem Cell Rep 2(3):304–312

US Food and Drug Administration (2004) FDA Public Health Advisory: Safety of Vioxx. FDA, Silver Spring. Available at http://www.fdagov/drugs/drugsafety/postmarketdrugsafetyinformationforpatientsandproviders/ucm106274htm. 25 September 2015

US Food and Drug Administration (2005) Information for Healthcare Professionals: Valdecoxib (marketed as Bextra). FDA, Silver Spring. Available at http://www.fda.gov/Drugs/DrugSafety/

PostmarketDrugSafetyInformationforPatientsandProviders/ucm124649.htm.   25   September
    2015
US Food and Drug Administration Information for Healthcare Professionals: Celecoxib (Marketed
    as Celebrex) (2005) FDA, Silver Spring. Available at http://www.fda.gov/Drugs/DrugSafety/
    Postmarket   DrugSafetyInformationforPatientsandProviders/ucm124655.htm.   25   September
    2015
Uygur E, Kilic B, Demiroglu M, Ozkan K, Cift HT (2015) Subchondral bone and its role in
    osteoarthritis. Open J Orthopedics 5(11):355–360
van de Loo FA, Joosten LA, van Lent PL, Arntz OJ, van den Berg WB (1995) Role of interleukin-1,
    tumor necrosis factor alpha, and interleukin-6 in cartilage proteoglycan metabolism and destruc-
    tion. Effect of in situ blocking in murine antigen- and zymosan-induced arthritis. Arthritis
    Rheum 38(2):164–172
Vega A, Martín-Ferrero MA, Del Canto F, Alberca M, García V, Munar A et al (2015) Treatment of
    knee osteoarthritis with allogeneic bone marrow mesenchymal stem cells: a randomized con-
    trolled trial. Transplantation 99(8):1681–1690
Wang L, Wu Y, Chang G, Oesingmann N, Schweitzer ME, Jerschow A, Regatte RR (2009) Rapid
    isotropic 3D-sodium MRI of the knee joint in vivo at 7T. J Magn Reson Imaging 30(3):606–614
Wei X, Yang X, Han ZP, Qu FF, Shao L, Shi YF (2013) Mesenchymal stem cells: a new trend for
    cell therapy. Acta Pharmacol Sin 34(6):747
Welsch GH, Mamisch TC, Domayer SE, Dorotka R, Kutscha-Lissberg F, Marlovits S et al (2008a)
    Cartilage T2 assessment at 3-T MR imaging: in vivo differentiation of normal hyaline cartilage
    from reparative tissue after two cartilage repair procedures—initial experience. Radiology 247
    (1):154–161
Welsch GH, Mamisch TC, Hughes T, Zilkens C, Quirbach S, Scheffler K et al (2008b) In vivo
    biochemical 7.0 Tesla magnetic resonance: preliminary results of dGEMRIC, zonal T2, and T2∗
    mapping of articular cartilage. Investig Radiol 43(9):619–626
Wildi L, Raynauld J, Martel-Pelletier J, Beaulieu A, Bessette L (2011) Chondroitin sulphate
    reduces both cartilage volume loss and bone marrow lesions in knee osteoarthritis patients
    starting as early as 6 months after initiation of therapy: a randomized, double-blind, placebo-
    controlled pilot study using MRI. Ann Rheum Dis 70:982–989
Williams A, Gillis A, McKenzie C, Po B, Sharma L, Micheli L et al (2004) Glycosaminoglycan
    distribution in cartilage as determined by delayed gadolinium-enhanced MRI of cartilage
    (dGEMRIC): potential clinical applications. Am J Roentgenol 182(1):167–172
Wluka AE, Hanna F, Davies-Tuck M, Wang Y, Bell RJ, Davis SR et al (2009) Bone marrow lesions
    predict increase in knee cartilage defects and loss of cartilage volume in middle-aged women
    without knee pain over 2 years. Ann Rheum Dis 68(6):850–855
Young AA, Stanwell P, Williams A, Rohrsheim JA, Parker DA, Giuffre B, Ellis AM (2005)
    Glycosaminoglycan content of knee cartilage following posterior cruciate ligament rupture
    demonstrated by delayed gadolinium-enhanced magnetic resonance imaging of cartilage
    (dGEMRIC): a case report. J Bone Joint Surg Am 87(12):2763–2767
Zaslav K, Cole B, Brewster R, DeBerardino T, Farr J, Fowler P, Nissen C (2009) A prospective
    study of autologous chondrocyte implantation in patients with failed prior treatment for articular
    cartilage defect of the knee results of the study of the treatment of articular repair (STAR)
    clinical trial. Am J Sports Med 37(1):42–55
Zbyň Š, Stelzeneder D, Welsch GH, Negrin LL, Juras V, Mayerhoefer ME et al (2012) Evaluation
    of native hyaline cartilage and repair tissue after two cartilage repair surgery techniques with
    23Na MR imaging at 7 T: initial experience. Osteoarthr Cartil 20(8):837–845
Zeng C, Wei J, Li H, Wang Y, Xie D, Yang T et al (2015) Effectiveness and safety of glucosamine,
    chondroitin, the two in combination, or celecoxib in the treatment of osteoarthritis of the knee.
    Sci Rep 5:16827
Zhang W, Jones A, Doherty M (2004) Does paracetamol (acetaminophen) reduce the pain of
    osteoarthritis? A meta-analysis of randomised controlled trials. Ann Rheum Dis 63:901–907

Zhang W, Moskowitz RW, Nuki G et al (2008a) OARSI recommendations for the management of hip and knee osteoarthritis, part I: OARSI evidence-based, expert consensus guidelines. Osteoarthr Cartil 16:137–162

Zhang W, Moskowitz RW, Nuki G et al (2008b) OARSI recommendations for the management of hip and knee osteoarthritis, part II: OARSI evidence-based, expert consensus guidelines. Osteoarthr Cartil 16:137–162

Zhen G, Wen C, Jia X, Li Y, Crane JL, Mears SC et al (2013) Inhibition of TGF-beta signaling in mesenchymal stem cells of subchondral bone attenuates osteoarthritis. Nat Med 19(6):704–712. https://doi.org/10.1038/nm.3143

Zuk PA, Zhu M, Ashjian P, De Ugarte DA, Huang JI, Mizuno H et al (2002) Human adipose tissue is a source of multipotent stem cells. Mol Biol Cell 13(12):4279–4295

Printed by Printforce, the Netherlands